# C++ User's Guide

VERSION 5.0

# Borland® C++

Borland International, Inc., 100 Borland Way
P.O. Box 660001, Scotts Valley, CA 95067-0001

1E0R0196    WBC1350WW21770
  97 98 99 00-9 8 7 6 5
D2
ISBN 0-672-30922-X

# Contents

## Chapter 4
## Building Applications with
## AppExpert      **127**

## Chapter 7
## Using the integrated debugger   159

Part II
# Resource Workshop user's guide   217

Chapter 9
# Getting started with Resource Workshop   219

Chapter 8
# Compiling and linking from the command line   197

## Chapter 26
# Profiling strategies 433

# Introduction

Borland C++ is a powerful, professional programming tool for creating and maintaining DOS, Win16, and Win32 applications. Borland C++ supports both the C and C++ languages with its integrated development environment and command-line tools.

## How this book is organized

This book is divided into the following parts:

**Part I, "The integrated development environment,"** introduces you to the integrated development environment (commonly known as the IDE).

**Part II, "Resource Workshop user's guide,"** teaches you how to use Resource Workshop to build resources for your Windows applications.

**Part III, "Borland C++ tools and utilities,"** describes additional tools you can use to build and debug your applications.

**Part IV, "Turbo Profiler user's guide,"** explains how to use Turbo Profiler to analyze the performance of your program as well as to monitor critical computer resources.

**Appendix A, "Borland C++ error messages and warnings,"** lists and describes the error messages that can be generated by the Borland C++ programming tools.

## Typefaces and icons used in this book

This book uses the following special fonts:

| | |
|---|---|
| Monospace | This type represents text that you type or text as it appears onscreen. |
| *Italics* | These are used to emphasize and introduce words, and to indicate variable names (identifiers), function names, class names, and structure names. |
| **Bold** | This type indicates reserved keywords words, format specifiers, and command-line options. |
| *Keycap* | This type represents a particular key you should press on your keyboard. For example, "Press *Del* to erase the character." |

| | |
|---|---|
| *Key1+Key2* | This indicates a command that requires you to press *Key1* with *Key2*. For example, *Shift+a* (although not a command) indicates the uppercase letter "A." |
| ALL CAPS | This type represents disk directories, file names, and application names. (However, header file names are presented in lowercase to be consistent with how these files are usually written in source code.) |
| Menu ǀ Choice | This represents menu commands. Rather than use the phrase "choose the Save command from the File menu," Borland manuals use the convention "choose File ǀ Save." |

**Note**    This icon indicates material that you should take special notice of.

Part

# I

# Using the integrated development environment

Part I of this manual describes how to use the components of the Borland C++ integrated development environment (IDE).

The IDE integrates development of DOS, Win16, and Win32 applications. Using the Project Manager, you can easily build several application types from a single project file. AppExpert and ClassExpert let you take advantage of ObjectWindows 5.0. The integrated debugger and browser let you debug your source code and browse class objects and hierarchies without leaving the IDE.

The following chapters cover the tools available through the IDE:

- **Chapter 1, "Getting started,"** introduces you to the Borland C++ IDE and takes you through the creation of simple DOS, Windows, and 32-bit Windows programs.

- **Chapter 2, "Managing projects,"** describes the Project Manager and shows you how to use the TargetExpert and Source Pools to create the projects for your applications.

- **Chapter 3, "Specifying project options and compiling,"** shows you how to use Style Sheets and local overrides to set your project options and how to compile from the IDE. It also contains a complete reference to the options available for both the IDE and the command-line tools.

- **Chapter 4, "Building applications with AppExpert,"** describes AppExpert and shows you how to create the source-code foundation for your ObjectWindows applications.

- **Chapter 5, "Modifying applications with ClassExpert,"** describes how to use ClassExpert to modify the applications you create.

- **Chapter 6, "Browsing classes and objects,"** shows you how to use the browser to examine your C++ classes.

- **Chapter 7, "Using the integrated debugger,"** describes the integrated debugger and how to use it to step and trace through your program code.

- **Chapter 8, "Using the command-line tools,"** provides an overview of using command-line tools rather than the IDE as you program.

# Getting started

Borland C++ is a development package that contains the compilers, tools, and utilities you need for developing Win16, Win32, and DOS applications. While the tools included with Borland C++ can be run from either Windows or the DOS command-line, you'll find that you can accomplish most of your application development using the Integrated Development Environment (IDE).

To help you get familiar with the IDE, this chapter offers an overview of the following IDE features:

• Starting the Borland C++ IDE
• Using SpeedMenus in the IDE
• Using the Edit window
• Working with simple projects
• Customizing the IDE
• Running other programs from the IDE

## Starting the Borland C++ IDE

After installing Borland C++, the Program Manager contains a program group titled Borland C++ 5.0. Open this group to reveal the icons for the C++ IDE (labeled Borland C++) and the other programming tools that ship with Borland C++.

When you double-click the Borland C++ icon, the IDE opens. Inside the IDE, you'll find all the tools you'll need to create C++ programs. Along with windows for the editor, browser, and debugger, the IDE contains windows for project files and compiler and programming tool messages. Figure 1.1 shows how the IDE might look after compiling a simple Windows project.

**Figure 1.1**    The Borland C++ IDE

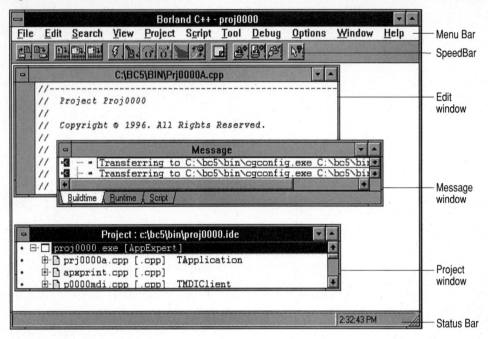

## The IDE menu system

Table 1.1 describes the menus on the IDE menu bar.

**Table 1.1**    The IDE menus

| Menu item | Command descriptions |
|---|---|
| File | Commands to open, save, and print files. Also includes the IDE exit command. |
| Edit | Clipboard commands and commands for undoing and redoing program edits. |
| Search | Commands for searching and replacing strings, browsing symbols, locating functions, and reviewing error messages generated by the programming tools. |
| View | Commands to open the ClassExpert, Project Manager, Message window, and Browser. Also contains commands to open the various integrated debugger windows. |
| Project | Commands to open, close, and compile projects. Also contains the AppExpert command. |
| Script | Provides commands to run and compile scripts to automate IDE functionality. |
| Tool | Commands to launch programming tools from the IDE, including Turbo Debugger. |
| Debug | Commands to run your project under control of the integrated debugger. |
| Options | IDE customization and project configuration commands. |
| Window | IDE window management commands. |
| Help | Commands to access the Borland C++ online Help system. |

## The IDE SpeedBar

The SpeedBar (located under the main menu) has buttons that give quick access to menu commands which relate to the area of the IDE you're working in. For example, if you're editing code, the SpeedBar contains cut and paste commands, file save commands, and so on. When the Project window has focus, the SpeedBar has buttons that pertain to projects, such as commands for adding project nodes and browsing option settings.

The Status Bar at the bottom of the IDE contains "flyby" help hints; when the cursor is over a button, the Status Bar describes the button command. You can configure the flyby hints and other SpeedBar options as described in "Customizing the SpeedBars" on page 14.

# Using SpeedMenus in the IDE

*Right-clicking* (clicking the right mouse button) accesses the Borland C++ *SpeedMenus*. SpeedMenus contain commands that are context-sensitive to the area of the program you're working in. For example, the SpeedMenu for the Edit window contains commands that are related to the editor. In the Project Manager, the SpeedMenus contain commands to help you with managing your projects.

To get a feeling for SpeedMenus, try the following:

1 From the IDE, choose Project I Open, then open the project file MULTITRG.IDE in the \BC5\EXAMPLES\IDE\MULTITRG directory.

2 Double-click the MULTITRG [.CPP] node to open the file in an Edit window.

3 Move the cursor to the **string.h** header file reference by clicking on the file name in the source code.

4 Right click to open the Edit window SpeedMenu, then choose Open Source to open an Edit window that contains this header file.

Note    In addition to right-clicking, the IDE speedmenus can be accessed at any time by pressing *Alt+F10*.

# Using the Edit window

Edit windows contain the Borland C++ editor, which you can use to create and edit your program code. When you're editing a file, the IDE status bar displays the following information about the file you're editing:

• The line number and character position of the cursor. For example, if the cursor is on the first line and first character of an Edit window, you'll see 1:1 in the status bar; if the cursor is on line 68 and character 23, you'll see 68:23.

• The edit mode: insert or overwrite. Press *Insert* to toggle whether your text additions overwrite existing characters or insert new ones into the file.

- The file's save status. The word Modified appears if you've made changes to the file in the active Edit window, and you have not yet saved your edits or changes.

Note The Borland C++ editor contains many powerful features to help you enter and modify your program code. For example, you can undo multiple edits by choosing Edit | Undo or pressing *Alt+Backspace*. You can also open multiple Edit windows; tile the windows as you wish; subdivide the window into different Edit panes; and cut, copy, and paste text between any open files.

Although this chapter provides a brief introduction to the editor, complete details on how to use and customize the editor can be found in the online Help that accompanies the IDE. Choose Help | Contents, then click Integrated Development Environment for a list of topics that relate to the IDE. From here, view the Editor topic, and the Menu Commands topics Edit Menu and Search Menu.

## Creating a new file

To introduce you to the editor, step through the following instructions to create a DOS program that's used as an example later in this chapter.

1 Create the directory \MYSOURCE using the File Manager or DOS (you'll use this directory to hold the project files you create later in this chapter).

2 From the IDE, choose File | New to open a new Edit window with an empty file.

By default, Borland C++ names new files NONAME*xx*.CPP, where *xx* is a number that's incremented with each new file opened.

3 In the Edit window, type the following C++ code to create a DOS program:

```
#include <iostream.h>

int main (void)
{
    cout << "Welcome to the World of DOS!\n";      //print text
    return(0);
}
```

4 Choose File | Save As, and save your new file in the \MYSOURCE directory with the file name DOS_TEST.CPP (this file is used later in this chapter).

# Working with simple projects

After you first install Borland C++, you'll want to make sure the program is correctly set up; the details of the compiler and the IDE can wait until later. The best way to test your setup is to compile a few sample programs.

In this section, you'll learn how to create and run several simple programs. The first program is a DOS program. After creating the DOS program, you'll be taken through the steps to create a 16-bit Windows program. Then, using the TargetExpert, you'll be shown how to change the 16-bit program into a 32-bit program.

# Creating a DOS program using EasyWin

You can become familiar with the Project Manager and the C++ compiler by following these steps to create a simple DOS program:

1 From the IDE, choose Project | New Project, then set the following options in the New Target dialog box:

1 Type the path and name for your new project in the Project Path And Name input box. In this case, type:

    \mysource\dos_test.ide

**Note**    If the directory doesn't exist, the IDE creates the directory for you.

2 In the Target Type list box, click EasyWin [.EXE]. This selection creates a Windows program from a program that uses character-mode input and output.

The New Target dialog box should now resemble the one shown in Figure 1.2.

**Figure 1.2**    The New Target dialog box

2 Choose OK to close the New Target dialog box. The Project window opens and displays the target and dependencies of the project you just created.

Notice that one of the nodes in the project points to the file DOS_TEST.CPP, the file you created earlier in the chapter (if you haven't already done so, create this file by following the instructions listed in the previous section, "Creating a new file").

3 Because the .DEF and .RD files are unnecessary for this project, you must delete the .DEF and .RC nodes created by the Project Manager:

1 Select the DOS_TEST [.DEF], then press *Ctrl* and select DOS_TEST [.RC].

**2** From the Project Manager SpeedMenu (press the right mouse button), choose Delete Node, then choose *Yes* to confirm your request to delete 2 project nodes.

**4** Compile and run the program by double-clicking the DOS_TEST [.EXE] project node.

If you correctly followed all the steps in this section, the program builds without errors and then runs in a window. If the compiler reports errors or warnings during the compile, retrace the steps in this section to ensure you correctly followed the steps. When the program compiles without errors, the Project Manager creates an executable program called DOS_TEST.EXE and places it in the \MYSOURCE directory.

**Note** You can also create DOS programs that run from the DOS command line, and not in a window as the EasyWin program does. To do so, make the following selections in the New Target dialog box instead of the ones listed in the previous steps:

**1** Under Target Type, choose Application [.EXE] (this is the default Target Type).

**2** In the Platform combo box, choose DOS (Standard) as the target platform (to reveal the full range of platform options, click the arrow on the right side of the combo box).

**3** Choose OK to confirm your settings.

Note that when you make these selections, the Project Manager doesn't create the .DEF and .RC nodes, as it does for Windows target programs.

## Creating a Windows program

This section demonstrates how to compile a simple Windows program. First you'll create a 16-bit Windows program, then you'll use the TargetExpert to modify the output to create a 32-bit Windows program.

If you followed the steps in the preceding section to create a DOS program, you'll find that most of the steps for creating this Windows program are identical to those listed for the DOS program. When you're finished with this example, the tasks involved with creating and compiling simple programs with the IDE should be familiar:

**1** Create a new project.

**2** Set the target options using the New Target dialog box.

**3** Add code to the appropriate nodes in the project.

**4** Compile and run the project.

Indeed, most projects will require more involved steps, but the basic steps for creating and compiling projects remains the same. With this in mind, follow these steps to create a simple Windows program:

**1** Choose Project | New Project to open the New Target dialog box, then make the following settings:

    **1** Type the following path and name for your new project in the Project Path And Name input box:

```
\mysource\win_test.ide
```

**Note** If the directory doesn't exist, the IDE creates the directory for you.

    **2** In the Target Type list box, click Application [.EXE] to set the type of program you plan to create (this is the default setting).

    **3** In the Platform combo box, set the Target Type to Windows 3.*x* (16).

**2** Click the Advanced button, then uncheck both the .RC and .DEF options in the dialog box that appears. Unchecking these settings tells the Project Manager that this project doesn't use definition and resource files, as most Windows programs do.

**3** Choose OK to accept the settings, then choose OK again to close the New Target dialog box. The Project window opens with your new project.

**4** In the Project window, double-click the win_test [.cpp] node to open an empty file in the Edit window.

**5** In the Edit window, type the following code to create a Windows program, then save the program by choosing File | Save:

```
#include <windows.h>
int PASCAL WinMain(HINSTANCE hCurInstance, HINSTANCE hPrevInstance,
    LPSTR lpCmdLine, int nCmdShow)
{
    MessageBox(NULL, "Welcome to the World of Windows!", "A Windows Program",
               MB_OK | MB_ICONEXCLAMATION );
    return(0);
}
```

**6** Choose Project | Build All to compile this program, then choose OK after the compilation is finished. If you followed the steps correctly, you can arrange the windows so the IDE resembles the screen shown in Figure 1.1 on page 6.

When you build this project, the compiler produces several warnings, but it still creates an .EXE file in the \MYSOURCE directory. Even though a program that compiles with warnings can still be executed, it's not a good idea to ignore the warnings without first understanding why the compiler complained.

The first warnings that appear indicate that the parameters in *WinMain* are never used in the program. In this small program, it is safe to ignore these warnings. The last warning indicates that the default module-definition settings are being used; this is expected since we didn't create a module-definition (.DEF) file.

**7** To run the program from the IDE, choose Debug | Run.

When you run this program, a small dialog box with the text "Welcome to the World of Windows!" appears. To terminate the program and return to the IDE, choose OK.

## Modifying the program target

The last exercise in this chapter modifies the previous Windows example so that it creates a 32-bit Windows program that can take advantage of a Win32 operating system, such as Win32s or Windows NT. Before you can complete this exercise, you must be running a 32-bit operating system (such as Windows NT) or you must have Win32s installed on your system (you can choose to install Win32s when you install Borland C++).

**1** If it is not already open, open the WIN_TEST.IDE project file through the Project | Open menu command.

**2** In the Project window, right-click the target node (WIN_TEST [.EXE]) to display the SpeedMenu, then choose TargetExpert.

**3** Change the platform to Win32 in the Platform combo box, then choose OK to close the TargetExpert.

**4** Recompile the program by choosing Project | Build All, then choose OK when the compilation finishes.

**Note**　It is important to choose Build All (and not Make) whenever you change the target type in your project. This ensures that the new target is rebuilt correctly.

**5** Run the program by double-clicking the WIN_TEST [.EXE] node in the Project Manager.

## Single file programs

Usually when you begin to write a new program, you start by creating a new project for that program. Although it's possible to compile a single-source file program without using a project, it's usually easier to maintain the program settings through a project file. However, if you want to set target options for a single-source file program without creating a project,

**1** Choose Project | Close Project to make sure you don't have a project file open.

**2** Choose File | Open, then open the source file containing your program.

**3** Open the TargetExpert by right-clicking in the Edit window and choosing TargetExpert from the SpeedMenu.

**4** Adjust the target settings for your single-source file program using the TargetExpert dialog box, as described in "Editing target attributes using TargetExpert" on page 27.

**5** Choose Options | Project from the menu, and set the project options, as described in Chapter 3, "Specifying project options and compiling."

**6** Choose Project | Compile (this command compiles the code in the current Edit window if no project is loaded).

# Customizing the IDE

You can configure the IDE in many ways to create a customized environment that meets your programming needs. For example, you can have the IDE do tasks automatically (such as saving backups of your files in the Editor windows) or handle special events.

The Environment Options dialog box (accessed with the Options | Environment command) lets you configure the different elements and windows of the IDE. Once you've customized the IDE to your liking, choose Options | Save, check the options you want to save, then choose OK; the IDE saves your environment settings to a file called BCCONFIG.BCW. By default, the file is saved to the BIN directory in your Borland C++ directory tree. This default directory is specified by the DefaultDesktopDir field of your BCW5.INI file, which is located in your Windows directory.

The Environment Options dialog box displays a list of customizable topics on the left and each topic's configurable options on the right. Some topics contain subtopics, indicated by a + next to the topic. For example, the Editor topic has subtopics called Options, File, and Display. To view a topic's subtopics, click the + sign next to the topic; its subtopics appear under it and the + turns to a – (you can then click the – to collapse the list of subtopics). Topics without subtopics appear with a dot next to their name.

**Figure 1.3**    The Environment Options dialog box

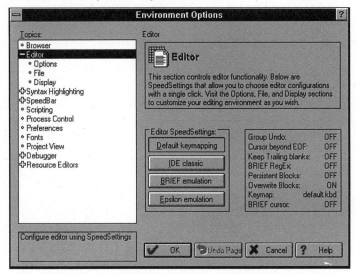

This chapter discusses the following Environment Options topics:

- Configuring the IDE editor
- Syntax highlighting
- Customizing the SpeedBars
- Setting IDE preferences
- Saving your IDE settings

**Note**    Although this chapter doesn't offer a complete reference to the Environment Options dialog box, a complete reference is available by clicking the Help button in the Environment Options dialog box.

## Configuring the IDE editor

You can configure the editor so that it looks and behaves like other editors such as Brief and Epsilon. The IDE editor uses keyboard mapping files (.KBD files) that set the keyboard shortcuts for the editor and the other windows in the IDE. You can modify this behavior using ObjectScripting. For more information see the online Help.

# Syntax highlighting

Syntax highlighting lets you define a color and font attribute (such as bold) for certain elements of code. For example, you could display comments in blue and strings in red. Syntax highlighting is on by default.

Syntax highlighting works on files whose extensions are listed in the Syntax Extensions list (by default, these files are .CPP, .C, .H, .HPP, .RH and .RC). You can add or delete any extension from this list, but be sure to separate extensions with semicolons.

The Syntax Highlighting section displays the default color scheme and four predefined color settings. To use a predefined color scheme,

1 Choose Options | Environment | Syntax Highlighting.

2 Choose one of the four color predefined schemes (Defaults, Classic, Twilight, or Ocean) by choosing the Color SpeedSetting; the sample code changes to the color scheme you select.

To customize the syntax highlighting colors,

1 Choose Options | Environment, then select the Syntax Highlighting topic.

2 Select a predefined color scheme to use as a base for your customized colors.

3 Choose the Customize topic listed under the Syntax Highlighting topic. Elements and sample code appear on the right of the Environment Options dialog box.

4 Select an element you want to modify from the list of elements (for example, choose Comment), or click the element in the sample code (this selects the name in the Element list). You might need to scroll the sample code to view more elements.

5 Select a color for the element. The element color in the sample code reflects your selection. Use the left mouse button to select a foreground color for the element (FG appears in the color). Use the right mouse button to select a background color (BG appears in the color). If FB appears in the color, the color is used as both a background and a foreground color.

6 If you want, choose an Attribute (for example, bold).

7 You can check Default FG (foreground) or BG (background) to use the Windows default colors for an element.

8 Repeat steps 2–4 for the elements you want to modify.

To *turn off* syntax highlighting, Choose Options | Environment | Syntax Highlighting, then uncheck Use Syntax Highlighting.

# Customizing the SpeedBars

The IDE has context-sensitive SpeedBars for all its windows, including the Edit, Browser, Debugger, Project Manager, Message, Desktop, and ClassExpert windows. When a window has focus, the corresponding SpeedBar appears. Using the Environment Options dialog box, you can customize each of the SpeedBars so that they include only the buttons you want.

To add or delete buttons from the SpeedBars,

**1** Choose Options | Environment from the IDE's main menu.

**2** Choose the SpeedBar topic on the left. The right side of the dialog box displays general options for all SpeedBars.

The options here let you specify if you want to hide or view the SpeedBar, where you want the SpeedBar to appear (on the top or bottom of the IDE), and if you want to use the Flyby Help Hints. If you check Use Flyby Help Hints, the IDE displays descriptions of the SpeedButtons on the status line when you pass the mouse pointer over a button. If you leave this box unchecked, the hints show on the status line only when you click a SpeedButton.

**3** Choose the Customize topic listed under the SpeedBar topic to customize the SpeedBar for a particular window.

**4** In the Window combo box, choose the specific window (Editor, Browser, Debugger, Project, Message, IDE Desktop, or ClassExpert) whose SpeedBar you want to customize.

The Available Buttons list box displays all the available (unused) buttons that you can add to a particular window's SpeedBar. (Each button has a name next to it that describes the button's function.) The Active Buttons list box displays the buttons that are currently contained in the selected window's SpeedBar.

- To *add a button* to a SpeedBar, double-click the button icon in the Available Buttons list, or select it and click the right-pointing arrow. The IDE places the button in front of the selected button in the Active Buttons list.

- To *remove a button* from a SpeedBar, double-click the button icon in the Active Buttons list, or select it and click the left-pointing arrow. The button moves to the Available Buttons list.

- To *reorder the button positions* for a SpeedBar, select a button in the Active Buttons list, and use the up and down arrows to move the button within the list (the top button in the list appears on the left side of the SpeedBar; the last button in the list appears on the right side of the SpeedBar).

- To *put separator spaces between buttons* on the SpeedBar, select a button from the Active Buttons list, then click the Separator button. The separator is added *before* the selected button.

You can also make all SpeedBars identical by selecting a SpeedBar in the Window list, then pressing the Copy Layout button. A dialog box appears in which you check all the SpeedBars you want to make identical to the selected SpeedBar. For example, if you first choose the Editor SpeedBar and then click Copy Layout, the dialog box appears with Editor dimmed. If you then check Project and Message, those SpeedBars will be exactly the same as the Editor SpeedBar.

You can restore any SpeedBar to its original defaults by selecting the SpeedBar in the Window list, then clicking the Restore Layout button.

## Setting IDE preferences

The Preferences command lets you customize what IDE settings you want automatically saved and how you want some IDE windows to work.

To set preferences,

1  Choose Options | Environment | Preferences.

2  Check and uncheck the options you want, then choose OK. For an explanation of each option, see the online Help (press the Help button).

## Saving your IDE settings

The IDE automatically saves information when you exit the IDE, use a transfer tool, build or make a project, run the integrated debugger, or close or open a project. You can control which areas of the IDE get saved from the Preferences topic in the Environment Options dialog box (choose Options | Environment from the main menu).

If you want to save your settings manually, you can do so as follows:

1  Choose Options | Save.

2  Check **Environment** to save the settings from the Editor, Syntax Highlighting, SpeedBar, Browser, and Preferences sections of the Environment Options dialog box. These settings are saved in a file called BCCONFIG.BCW.

3  Check **Desktop** to save information about open windows and their positions. This information is saved to a file called <prjname>.DSW. If you don't have a project open, the information is saved to a file called BCWDEF.DSW.

4  Check **Project** to save changes to your project (.IDE) file, including build options and node attributes.

# Running other programs from the IDE

By default, the IDE lists Turbo Debugger, Resource Workshop, GREP, WinSight, WinSpector, and Key Map Compiler on the Tool menu. To run any of these tools from the IDE, choose Tool | *ProgramName*, where *ProgramName* is the name of the program you want to run (for example, Tool | GREP runs the GREP utility).

You can run any executable program or utility without leaving the IDE by adding it to the Tool menu. For a complete discussion on adding items to the Tool menu, see "Adding translators, viewers, and tools to the IDE" on page 32.

# Using online Help in Borland C++

Borland C++ provides complete online documentation through the Help system. Using Help is a convenient way to get information about extensive language features, compiler options, and any tasks you need to perform while developing applications in Borland C++.

# Online Help Organization

The Help system is organized into Help files that reflect the structure of the documentation set as follows:

**Table 1.2**     Borland C++ Help files

| Help file | Description |
| --- | --- |
| How to Use Help (OPENHELP.HLP) | Features of Borland C++ Help |
| Borland C++ Programmer's Reference (BCPP.HLP) | Programming tips, language details, and library reference |
| Borland C++ User's Guide (BCW.HLP) | IDE tasks, projects, tools |
| Borland Windows Customer Controls Reference (BWCC.HLP) | BWCC reference |
| Class Libraries Guide (CLASSLIB.HLP) | Programming and reference material |
| DOS Reference (BCDOC.HLP) | Reference material for DOS |
| Error Messages and Warnings (BCERRMSG.HLP) | Error message descriptions |
| ObjectComponents Programmer's Reference (OCF.HLP) | OCF programming and reference |
| ObjectScripting Programmer's Guide (SCRIPT.HLP) | Script programming and reference |
| ObjectWindows 5.0 Programmer's Reference (OWL.HLP) | OWL programming and reference |
| Resource Script Language Reference (RSL.HLP) | Resource scripting language reference |
| Resource Workshop User's Guide (WORKSHOP.HLP) | Resource Workshop user's guide and reference |
| Standard C++ Library Programmer's Reference (STL.HLP) | Rogue Wave STL user's guide and reference |
| Tools and Utilities (BCTOOLS.HLP) | Command-line tools |
| Visual Database Tools Programmer's Reference (BCVDTREF.HLP) | Database reference and developer's guide |
| Windows System Classes Guide (WINSYS.HLP) | WinSys classes reference |
| WinSight User's Guide (WINSIGHT.HLP) | WinSight debugging tool |
| WinSpector User's Guide (WINSPECTR.HLP) | WinSpector post mortem debugging |

These Help files are all located in the ..\BC5\HELP directory. If you want to display one of the specific Help files shown in Table 1.1, you can click on its name whether or not you have opened BC5.

# Getting Help in Borland C++

In Borland C++, you can get Help in the following ways:

- Context-Sensitive Help (*F1*)
- Contents Screens
- Index
- Keyword Search (*F1* or *Ctrl+F1* in the Edit Window)

- SpeedMenus (in the Help window)
- Help files

## Getting context-sensitive Help

You can get context-sensitive Help for items in the Borland C++ Integrated Development Environment (IDE). To access context-sensitive Help:

1  Select the element you want help on (menu, menu command, an item in a dialog box.

2  Press *F1* or *Ctrl+F1*.

Help buttons are available on many dialog boxes and for most error messages.

Click Help to view information about:

- The entire dialog box
- An error message
- The current group of topics in an Options settings dialog box

## Accessing and using contents screens

Each Help Contents offers an entry into a Help system installed with Borland C++. From the Contents, select the category of information that best suits your needs, then click on it.

- To display the Master Contents, choose **Contents** on the **Help** menu in the Borland C++ IDE. From the Master Contents, you can access all of the Help files.
- To access the Help Contents from within a topic in the active Help file, click the **Contents** tab.
- To access the Help Contents of a different Help file installed with Borland C++, right-click and select the name of the Help file you want to view.

To return to a previous topic or Help file, click the **Back** button.

You can expand books that appear on the Contents, or jump directly to a topic. To view a topic, click on it.

## Using the index

In Help, click the Index tab to view a list of index entries. Either type the word you're looking for or scroll through the list.

## Searching for keywords

Keyword Search gives you direct access to Help about a term in your program. To get help on a term:

1  In the Edit window, place the insertion point on the term you want help on.

2   Use one of the following methods:

  • Press *F1* or *Ctrl+F1*.

  • Choose **Keyword Search** on the Help menu.

  • Choose **Go To Help Topic** on the Edit Window SpeedMenu.

3   One of these events occurs:

  • The topic associated with the term you selected is displayed.

  • If more than one topic is available on the term for which you requested Help, the Topics Found dialog box is displayed listing topics associated with the term. Double-click the topic you want to view.

  • If no Help is available for the term nearest the insertion point, the index is displayed. You can then select a different searching method to locate a topic associated with that term. The term for which you requested Help appears highlighted in the top box. Click the **Display** button or double-click the term to view the list of topics associated with the term.

To return to a previous topic or Help file, click the **Back** button.

## Help SpeedMenus

All the Borland C++ Help files have SpeedMenus that you access by right-clicking on the mouse. These menus provide quick access to commands for copying or printing a Help topic, or exiting Windows Help.

The SpeedMenu also lists additional Help files containing information related to the current Help file. Right-click and select a Help file from the SpeedMenu. The Contents screen for that Help file is displayed.

# Using Windows Help

More information about using standard Windows Help features is available if you need it. To learn more about the features of Help in Windows 95 and Windows NT, see the following instructions.

If you're already in a Help topic, press *F1* to display Windows Help.

Otherwise, for details about using Help in **Windows 95**,

1   Choose Start in the lower left corner of the Windows Desktop, then choose Help.

  Windows Help is displayed.

2   In the Help Contents, open the How To book, then open Use Help.

3   To choose a book in the Help Contents, double-click it or move to it with the arrow keys and press Enter.

For details about using Help in **Windows NT**, choose Help | How To Use Help in the Program Manager.

2

# Managing projects

The Borland C++ IDE contains a Project Manager that gives you a visual representation of the files contained in your project. With the Project Manager, you can see exactly what files you're building, the files you're using in the builds, and the options that you've set for the builds.

This chapter covers the following topics, which describe how to use the Project Manager to organize the files in your project:

- Project management
- Using the Project Manager
- Grouping sets of files with Source Pools
- Translators, viewers, and tools

## What is project management?

As your applications grow in size and complexity, you'll discover that your programs become more and more dependent on different intermediate files. In addition, you'll find that some of the modules in your project must be compiled with different compilers or different compiler options. A Windows program, for example, can be composed of resource scripts, import libraries, and source code, with each different file type requiring a different compiler and compiler settings.

As the complexity of your projects increase, the need increases for a way to manage the different components of your projects. By studying the files that make up a project, you can see how a project combines different *source files* to produce different *target files*. Target files, for example, can be .DLL or .EXE files. The source files that these targets are dependent upon can consist of files like .C, .CPP, and .H files. *Project management* is the organization and management of the sources and targets that make up your project.

# Using the Project Manager

The Project Manager visually organizes all the files in your project using a *Project Tree*. The Project Tree displays files in a hierarchy diagram. Each level of the hierarchy contains a single target and all the target's dependencies. To show their relationship to the target, dependencies are indented below the target listing. Figure 2.1 shows how the Project window displays a Project Tree. To expand and collapse the hierarchy tree, click nodes containing the + and – symbols.

**Figure 2.1**    The Project window displaying a Project Tree

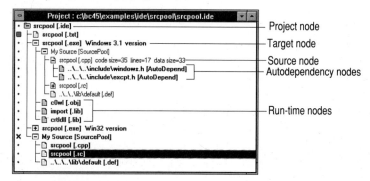

The Project Manager uses the following types of *nodes* to distinguish the different types of files in your project:

- The *project node*, located at the top of the Project Tree, represents the entire project. All the files used to build that project appear under the project node (a project node is similar to a symbolic target in a makefile). By default, the project node is not displayed in the Project Tree. To display the project node, choose Options | Environment and select Project View from the list of Topics, then check Show Project Node.

- A *target node* represents a file that is created when its dependent nodes are built (a target is usually an .EXE, .DLL, or .LIB file that you're creating from source code). A project can contain many target nodes. For example, in a single project, you might build an executable file and two separate DLL files, making three targets in all.

- *Source nodes* refer to the files that are used to build a target. Files such as .C, .CPP, and .RC are typical source nodes.

- A *run-time node* refers to files that the Project Manager uses during the linking stage of your project, such as startup code and .LIB files. The Project Manager adds different run-time nodes, depending on the options you specify in TargetExpert. By default, run-time nodes are not displayed by the Project Manager. To view run-time nodes, choose Options | Environment | Project View, then check Show Runtime Nodes.

- *Autodependency nodes* are the files that your program automatically references, such as included header files. By viewing autodependency nodes, you can see the files that source nodes are dependent upon, and you can easily navigate to these files from the Project Manager. By default, autodependency nodes are not displayed in the Project

Manager. To view autodependency nodes, choose Options | Project | Make, then check Autodependencies: Cache & Display. Note that you must build the project before the Project Manager can display autodependency information.

The Project Manager uses the following color scheme for its nodes:

- Blue nodes are those that were added by the programmer.

- White nodes indicate project targets.

- Yellow nodes are those that were added programmatically by the compiler (when it posts dependencies and Autodependencies), by AppExpert or ClassExpert (when they add .CPP nodes), or by TargetExpert (when it adds nodes based on the target type).

The Project Manager uses special *glyphs* in the left margin to indicate the build attributes of project nodes. To apply build attributes to a node (and for a reference on the different Project Manager glyphs), choose Edit Local Options from the Project Manager SpeedMenu, then select the Build Attributes topic.

In addition to helping you organize your project files, you can use the Project Manager to access source files and build targets.

- To bring a source file into an Edit window, double-click the node in the Project Tree, or highlight the node and either press *Enter* or choose View | Text Edit from the Project Manager SpeedMenu.

- Using the Project Manager to *make* a project is very effective because you can use the Project Manager to *translate* only the files that have changed since the last project build; computer resources are not wasted on unnecessary file updates. (The term "translate" refers to using one file type to create another. For example, the C++ compiler is a translator because it generates .OBJ files from .CPP files.)

There are several ways to customize the build options of the nodes in your project. Maintaining project options and compiling project targets is described in detail in the following chapter.

## Project Manager reference

The project tree can be traversed with the mouse or the keyboard.

**Note**    You can also select a node by typing the node name.

| Task | Keyboard | Mouse |
| --- | --- | --- |
| Add Node | Insert | |
| Collapse Hierarchy | - (hyphen) | |
| Collapse node | Minus | Left Click |
| Collapse/Expand node | Spacebar | |
| Copy Node | | Ctrl+Left Click Drag |
| Default action for node | Enter | Double Click |

| Task | Keyboard | Mouse |
|------|----------|-------|
| Delete Node | Delete | |
| Demote a node | Alt+RightArrow | Left Click Drag |
| End node search | Esc | |
| Expand Hierarchy | * (asterisk) | |
| Expand node | Plus | Left Click |
| Find a node | Incremental search (start typing) | |
| Move down in project | DownArrow | Scroll Bar |
| Move node down | Alt+DownArrow | Left Click Drag |
| Move node up | Alt+UpArrow | Left Click Drag |
| Move to bottom of hierarchy | End | Scroll Bar |
| Move to top of hierarchy | Home | Scroll Bar |
| Move up in project | UpArrow | Scroll Bar |
| Open SpeedMenu | Alt+F10 | Right Click |
| Page down | PgDn | Scroll Bar |
| Page up | PgUp | Scroll Bar |
| Promote a node | Alt+LeftArrow | |
| Reference Copy Node | | Alt+Left Click Drag |
| Scroll left | LeftArrow | Scroll Bar |
| Scroll right | RightArrow | Scroll Bar |
| Select a node | Up/DownArrow | Left Click |
| Select Contiguous nodes | Shift+UpArrow | Shift+Left Click |
| Select Non-Contiguous nodes | | Ctrl+Left Click |

# Creating a project

When you begin to write a new application, the first step is to create a new project to organize your application's files. The command Project | New Project opens the New Target dialog box.

## Setting target options with the New Target dialog box

When you create a new project, the IDE automatically assigns default file names to the nodes in your project. The following steps show how to change these default settings and how to complete the initial project setup.

1 Type the path and name for the new project into the Project Path And Name input box (the project name must contain eight characters or less). Note that you don't have to type a file extension because the IDE automatically assigns the extension .IDE to all project files.

**2** In the Target Name input box, type the name for the first target in your project. This is usually the name of the .EXE or .DLL file that you want to create.

**Note** The remaining fields in the New Target dialog box set the options for the first target in the project. These fields are commonly referred to as the *TargetExpert*, since these are the fields contained in the TargetExpert dialog box.

**3** Choose the type of target you want to build using the Target Type list. For information on the target types, see the online Help for the IDE. Information on using the Help compiler can be found in the online Help file CWH.HLP.

**4** Choose a platform for your target using the Platform drop-down list. Information for the individual platform types can be found in online Help.

**5** Select the memory model of the target from the Target Model options:

- **Tiny**, available for only 16-bit DOS applications, sets four segment registers (CS, DS, SS, and ES) to the same starting address, giving you a total of 64K for all your code, data, and stack.
- **Small** uses different code and data segments, giving you near code and near data.
- **Medium** gives you near data and far code.
- **Compact** is the inverse of the Medium model, giving you near code and far data.
- **Large** gives you far code and far data.
- **Huge**, used with only 16-bit DOS applications, is the same as Large model, but allows more than 64K of static data.
- **GUI** is used with Win32 GUI applications.
- **Console** is used with Win32 console applications.

**Note** Windows and DOS programs have different uses for the DS and SS segments. In Windows, they're always the same; however, in DOS these segments are different for Compact, Large, and Huge memory models.

The entries in the Target Model list adjust according to the Platform type you've selected.

**6** Using the Frameworks group, choose the framework to use with your application (the available choices depend on your Platform and Target choices). Frameworks are the class libraries upon which you build your application. Choose any combination of the following libraries for your application:

- **Class library** is a template-based container class library that uses encapsulation so you can maximize container storage with a minimal amount of reprogramming. When you select this option, TargetExpert links the appropriate BIDS*xxx*.LIB or BIDS*xxx*.DLL libraries to your program.
- **OWL** (*ObjectWindows Library*) is an object-oriented class library that encapsulates the behaviors (application-level and window-level) that Windows applications commonly perform.
- **OCF** consists of Borland ObjectComponents classes for simplifying the creation of OLE applications in C++. ObjectComponents implements a set of high-level interfaces on top of OLE.
- **MFC** supports Microsoft Foundation Class libraries. Choose 3.0 or 4.0 depending on the version of MFC you are using.

**7** Using the Controls options, choose what type of controls your application uses. Borland C++ supports the following types of controls:

- **BWCC** (Borland Windows Custom Control Library) is a collection of classes, functions, and bitmap buttons that you can link into your program for an alternative graphical look to standard Windows controls.

- **VBX** allows you to use Visual Basic controls in your applications. This option is available for both 16- and 32-bit Windows applications.

- **CTL3D** lets you use the standard Windows 3-dimensional controls contained in CTL3DV32.DLL.

**8** TargetExpert displays different library options, depending upon the Target Type and Platform you select. Choose which libraries to add to your project or which standard definitions to use if you are building a static library.

- **OLE** is an operating system extension that lets applications achieve a high degree of integration. OLE provides a set of standard interfaces so that one OLE program can interact fully with another OLE program.

- **No exceptions** specifies which RTL to link with 16-bit applications. Enable this option if you are building a 16-bit target that you plan to use in a non-C++ environment (such as a .DLL target that will be linked to a Paradox application).

- **BGI** (DOS only) uses the BGI graphics library file for BGI graphics.

**9** Compile your program using the following different types of framework libraries:

- **Dynamic** links the dynamic (.DLL) form of the selected libraries. This option allows your application to bind to the standard libraries at run time. The functions in the standard libraries are located in .DLL files rather than directly attached to your application. This greatly reduces the size of an application, but the target is then dependent on the presence of the .DLL libraries at run time. This option forces the large model for 16-bit targets.

- **Static** links the static (.LIB) form of the selected libraries. This option causes the standard library functions to be bound directly to your executable file, creating a larger, standalone executable. If you're building many .DLLs with statically bound RTLs, each .DLL gets its own copy of the routines it uses.

- **Diagnostic** links the diagnostic ObjectWindows or Class Libraries. Diagnostic libraries add debug information to the files. A diagnostic version of these libraries is supplied on the CD version of Borland C++. If you are using the disk version of the product and you select Diagnostic, you must build these libraries. Both OWL and Class Library sources are provided.

  To build a diagnostic version of the libraries, use the following make line:

  ```
  MAKE -DDIAGS
  ```

**Note** See the makefile for other options.

- **Multithreaded** links the 32-bit, multithreaded, flat model run-time library. Multithread is available only if your platform is Win32.

- **Alternate Startup** (DOS applications only) links the alternate startup library module COF*x*.OBJ, which makes SS=DS for all memory models.

**10** If needed, click the Advanced button to specify the types of source nodes created with your new target (this procedure is described in the following section).

**11** Click OK to accept the settings and close the New Target dialog box. The Project Manager creates the project file, which is denoted with an .IDE extension.

When you close the New Target dialog box, the Project Manager draws a graphical representation of your project in the Project window. The Project Manager creates a target node with one or more source nodes below with the project node. After creating the initial target for a project, you can add, delete, or modify the nodes in your project, as described in the following sections.

## Specifying the source node types

The Advanced button in the New Target dialog box opens the Advanced Options dialog box. Use this dialog box to set the types of source nodes that the IDE creates with a new target node.

- **.CPP Node** creates a C+ source node.

- **.C Node** creates a C language source node.

- **No Source Node** creates a target node that doesn't use a source node. Use this option when you do not want to create a source node that uses the same file name as the name of the project. When you create a new target with this option, you must specifically add the source node.

If your program is a Windows program, check the following boxes according to the files your target uses:

- **.RC** creates a source node that is associated with a resource script.

- **.DEF** creates a source node that's associated with a Windows definition file.

## Opening existing projects

To open an existing project, choose Project | Open Project, then use the file browser to select an existing .IDE or .PRJ project file (.PRJ files are converted to .IDE files when you save the project). If the project opens, but the Project window is not visible, choose View | Project to access the Project window.

# Adding source nodes to your project

To add a source node to a project:

**1** Select any node in the Project Tree under which you want the new node to appear. For example, if you want the new node to appear under the target, select the target node.

**2** Press *Ins*, click the button on the SpeedBar, or right-click the node to open the Project window SpeedMenu, then choose Add Node.

**3** Using the file browser, choose the file or files you want associated with the new node. Alternatively, you can type the name of the file you want to add.

**4** Choose OK to confirm your settings.

You can use the Windows File Manager to add one or more source nodes.

**1** Open the File Manager and arrange the windows so you can still view the Project window in the IDE.

**2** In the File Manager, press *Ctrl* and select the files you want to add as source nodes.

**3** Drag the files from the File Manager and drop them on a node in the Project window. The Project Manager automatically adds the source files under the selected node.

### Deleting source nodes

To delete a node in a project, select the node and press *Del*, or choose Delete Node from the SpeedMenu. To delete many nodes, select the ones you want to delete (press *Ctrl* or *Shift* and click the left mouse button to select multiple nodes), then press *Del*. The Project Manager asks if you want to delete the nodes before it proceeds.

## Adding files without relative path information

Because the project tree supports drag and drop, you can copy files right from a desktop file manager. Relative path information is included when files are copied. If you move sources or the IDE, the relative path information will be incorrect. Here is how to add files to your project without the presence of relative path information:

- Make sure that Absolute (Options | Project | Make | New Node Path) is turned off (this is the default setting).

- Right click on the node under which the added files will become children once they are dropped.

- Choose Add Node from the Project Tree SpeedMenu.

- Browse and highlight the file(s) you want to add. (Hold down the *Ctrl* key to select non-contiguous files.)

- After highlighting the desired files, shift focus to the input box and capture to the Clipboard (*Ctrl+C*).

- Browse back to the project file location.

- Shift focus to the input box, paste from the Clipboard (*Ctrl+V* or *Shift +Insert*) and choose OK.

Files added to the project by this method do not have relative path information.

## Editing source node attributes

*Node attributes* describe the node and define the tool that translates it (if applicable). To edit the attributes of a source node:

**1** Right-click the source node (or select the node and press *Alt+F10*), then choose Edit Node Attributes from the SpeedMenu. The Node Attributes dialog box appears.

**2** Update the node attributes, then choose OK to confirm your settings.

Node attributes are defined as follows:

- **Name** is the file name of the node, without a file extension.
- **Description** is an optional text description of the node.
- **Style Sheet** is the name of the Style Sheet the Project Manager uses when it translates that node. If <<None>> is specified, the Project Manager uses the option settings in the parent's Style Sheet.
- **Translator** names the translator used on that node. The IDE assigns a default translator for the node type (for example, CppCompile for a .CPP node), which can be overridden using this field.
- **Node type** defines the node extension, which in turn defines the available translators for that node.

## Adding target nodes to your project

To add a target to a project with the New Target dialog box:

**1** Choose Project | New Target, or click the button on the SpeedBar.

**2** Type the name for the new target, then choose one of the following target types:

- **Standard** (default) can be an executable, DLL, or other file.
- **AppExpert** is an automatically generated ObjectWindows-based application.
- **Source Pool** is a collection of files that can be referenced in other targets.

**3** Choose OK. If the target type is Standard, the TargetExpert dialog box appears so you can further define your target. If the target type is SourcePool, the target is added to the project and you can add nodes to it immediately. If you choose AppExpert as the target, AppExpert appears.

When you add a new target, it is always appended to the end of the Project Tree.

To view a sample project with two targets, open the MULTITRG.IDE project in the \BC5\EXAMPLES\IDE\MULTITRG directory. This project file builds a 16-bit and a 32-bit version of the WHELLO program. The project file contains a text file that describes how to use two or more targets in a project.

With more than one target in a project, you can choose to build a single target, multiple targets, or the whole project.

### Deleting target nodes

To delete a target node:

**1** Right-click the target node you want to delete (or highlight it and press *Alt+F10*).

**2** Choose Delete Node from the SpeedMenu.

**3** The Project Manager asks if you're sure you want to delete the target. Choose OK to delete the target and all its dependencies from the project.

You can also delete several nodes by pressing *Ctrl* and clicking the nodes you want to delete, then press *Del*.

**Warning!**   Use care when deleting target nodes—you cannot undo the deletion.

## Editing target attributes using TargetExpert

*Target attributes* describe the target. For example, target attributes can describe either a 32-bit Windows DLL or a 16-bit DOS executable. Using TargetExpert, you can modify the attributes for Standard and AppExpert target types. However, you can't change target attributes for Source Pools.

To change a target's attributes:

1   In the Project window, right-click the target node (or select it and press *Alt+F10*), then choose TargetExpert from the SpeedMenu to open the TargetExpert dialog box.

**Note**   The TargetExpert fields are a subset of the fields in the New Target dialog box.

2   Update the target attributes, then choose OK to confirm your new settings.

## Moving nodes within a project

You can move nodes within a project in the following ways:

- By dragging the node to its new location.
- By selecting the node and press *Alt* and the arrow keys. This moves the selected node up or down through the *visible* nodes. You can also use *Alt* and the right and left arrow keys to promote and demote nodes through levels of dependencies. For example, if you have a .CPP file dependent that's on a header file (the .H file appears under and right of the .CPP in the project window), you can move the header file to the same level as the .CPP file by selecting the header file and pressing *Alt* ←.

## Copying nodes in a project

You can copy nodes in your project file either by value or by reference. When you copy a node by value, the Project Manager places an identical, but *separate*, copy of the node in the location you specify. The nodes you copy inherit all the attributes from the original node and you have the ability to modify any of the copied node's attributes.

When you copy by reference, you simply point to one node from a different location in the project; a reference copy isn't distinct from the original node. If you modify the structure of the original node, the reference copy is also modified. However, a reference copy does not inherit the options of the original node; you're free to attach Style Sheets and override options in the copied node without affecting the original node.

To copy a node by value:

1   Select the node or nodes you want to copy (press *Shift* or *Ctrl* and click to select multiple nodes). You don't need to select the node's dependents because they are copied automatically.

2   Hold down the *Ctrl* key and drag the selected nodes to where you want to place the complete copies.

**3** When you release the mouse button, the copied nodes appear. At this point, you can edit either the original or the copied nodes without changing other nodes in the project.

To copy a node by reference:

**1** Select the node you want to copy by reference. You don't need to select the node's dependents because they are automatically copied by reference.

**2** Hold down the *Alt* key and drag the selected node to where you want to place the reference copy.

**3** When you release the mouse button, the reference-copied node appears and is displayed in a *lighter* font. This helps you remember that the node is copied by reference rather than by value. If you edit the original node (such as adding or deleting dependents), *all* referenced copies are updated.

**Warning!** You cannot add to, delete, or modify nodes that have been copied by reference; to modify nodes copied by reference, you must edit the master copy. If you delete an original node, *all* reference copies to that node are also deleted. You cannot undo this deletion.

## Converting project files into makefiles

Using the IDE, you can convert project files (.IDE files) into makefiles (.MAK files). To convert a project file to a makefile:

**1** Open the project file you want to convert.

**2** Choose Project | Generate Makefile. The IDE generates a makefile with the same name as the project file, but with the extension .MAK, and places it in the edit buffer. The IDE displays the new makefile in an Edit window.

**3** Choose File | Save to save your new makefile.

## Customizing the Project window

By default, the Project window displays target nodes and source nodes. To control the display of nodes and options:

**1** Choose Options | Environment to open the Environment Options dialog box, then choose Project View. The right side of the dialog box displays the Project View options.

**2** Check or uncheck the options you want. A sample node called WHELLO changes as you select or deselect options. This sample shows you how all nodes appear in the Project window.

- **Build translator** displays the translator used on the node.
- **Code size** displays the total size of code segments in bytes. This information appears only after the node has been compiled.
- **Data size** displays the size of the data segment in bytes. This information appears only after the node has been compiled.

- **Description** displays an optional description of the node in the Project Tree. Type the description using the Edit Node Attributes dialog box available from the Project Manager SpeedMenu.
- **Location** lists the path to the source file associated with the node.
- **Name** displays the name of the node.
- **Number of lines** displays the number of lines of code in the file associated with the node (note that this appears only after you compile the code).
- **Node type** describes the type of node (for example, .cpp or .c).
- **Style Sheet** names the Style Sheet attached with the node.
- **Output** names the path and file name that's created when the node is translated. For example, a .CPP node creates an .OBJ file.
- **Show runtime nodes** displays the nodes the Project Manager uses when the project is built. For example, it lists startup code and libraries.
- **Show project node** displays the project node, of which all targets are dependents.

**3** Click OK to close the Environment Options dialog box.

**4** To save your project customizations, choose Options | Save, then check Project. Note that you can save different option sets with the different projects you work on.

## Grouping sets of files with Source Pools

A *Source Pool* is a collection of source nodes that can be referenced by multiple target nodes. When a Source Pool is referenced by a target node, the nodes in the Source Pool take on the options and target attributes of the target. Because Source Pools let you create different targets using a common set of source nodes, it's easy to maintain the files that the targets use. For example, with Source Pools, you can create both 16-bit and 32-bit applications using a single set of source nodes. Then, when you add or delete a file from the Source Pool, you don't have to worry about updating all your target nodes; they're updated automatically through the reference to the Source Pool.

You can also use Source Pools when you have several header files that you need to include throughout your project. If you place the header files in a Source Pool, you can reference them wherever you need them in your project. Then, you only have to update the original Source Pool when you need to make changes to the group of header files; if you add a new header file to the Source Pool, all the referenced copies are automatically updated.

Source Pools are also useful when you want to assign a single Style Sheet to multiple nodes. For example, if three targets in a project need to use the same Style Sheet, you can reference a Source Pool that contains the Style Sheet instead of attaching the same Style Sheet to each individual node. Then, if you need to update the Style Sheet (for example, if you want change from compiling with debug information to compiling without it), you can update all the targets by modifying the single Style Sheet. You can also use Source Pools to apply custom tools to project nodes. For more information, see the example project \BC5\EXAMPLES\IDE\DELIVER.

## Creating a Source Pool

When you create a Source Pool, you create a target node with a group of nodes under it. However, the target node of the Source Pool cannot be compiled—to compile the nodes in a Source Pool, you must copy the Source Pool to another target node. Source Pools work to your best advantage when you copy them by reference.

1 In your project, create a new target node by choosing Project | New Target.

2 Type the name of the Source Pool in Target Name.

3 Select SourcePool from the Type list, then press OK to create a Source Pool target node in your project.

4 Select the Source Pool node in the Project Tree, and press *Ins* to open the Add To Project List dialog box.

5 Select the source files you want, then press OK to add them to the Source Pool.

6 Copy the Source Pool by reference by holding down *Alt* and dragging the Source Pool to the target nodes you want.

**Note** To see a working example of Source Pools, open the sample project called SRCPOOL.IDE in the \BC5\EXAMPLES\IDE\SRCPOOL directory. The project file includes a text file that describes how the Source Pool is used in the example.

# Translators, viewers, and tools

Translators, viewers, and tools are internal and external programs that are available to you through the IDE.

- *Translators* are programs that create one file type from another. For example, the C++ compiler is a translator that creates .OBJ files from .CPP files; the linker is a translator that creates .EXE files from .OBJ, .LIB, .DEF, and .RES files.

- *Viewers* are programs that let you examine the contents of a selected node. For example, an editor is a viewer that lets you examine the source code of a .CPP file. Resource Workshop is a viewer for Windows resource files.

- *Tools* are programs that help you create and test your applications. Turbo Debugger and GREP are examples of programming tools.

The IDE associates each node in a project with different translators or viewers, depending on the file extension of the node. Although each node can be associated with several different translators or viewers, each node is associated with a *single* default translator or viewer. This is how the IDE knows to open the Edit window when you double-click a .CPP node (double-clicking a node invokes the default viewer on the node). To see the default node type (determined by file extension) for a specific translator or viewer:

1 Choose Options | Tools to open the Tools dialog box.

2 Select the item you want to inspect from the Tools list.

**3** Choose Edit to access the Tools Options dialog box.

**4** Choose Advanced to access the Tool Advanced Options dialog box, then inspect the Default For text box.

When you right-click a node, you'll find that some source nodes have a Special command on the SpeedMenu. This command lists the alternative translators that are available for the node type selected. For example, the commands C To Assembler, C++ To Assembler, and Preprocess appear on the Special menu of a .CPP node. The command Implib appears if you selected a .DLL node. Using the Special command, you can invoke any translator that is available for a selected node type. Also, by selecting a source node in the Project Tree and choosing Edit Node Attributes from the SpeedMenu, you can reassign the default translator for the selected node.

## Adding translators, viewers, and tools to the IDE

The Tools dialog box displays the default set of translators, tools, and viewers. The following steps show how to add an item to this list of programs:

**1** Choose Options | Tools to access the Tools dialog box. This dialog box displays the default list of translators, tools, and viewers.

**2** Choose New to add a new program to the Tools list (to modify a program that's already listed, select the tool, then choose Edit).

**3** Set the following options in the Tools Options dialog box:

  - **Name** is a description of the item you're adding. This is placed on the Tools list.

  - **Path** is the path and executable program name. You can use the Browse button to complete this selection.

  - **Command-line** holds any command-line options, transfer macros, and IDE filters you want to pass to the program. For information on transfer macros, refer to online Help. (Try using **$prompt** if you want to experiment with transfer macros.) IDE filters are .DLL files that let tools interface with the IDE (for example, the GrepFile tool uses a filter to output text to the Message window). See the FILTER.IDE project in \BC5\EXAMPLES\IDE\FILTER for more information on filters. To see transfer macros and filters in use, choose Options | Tools, then select GrepFiles and choose Edit.

  - **Menu Text** appears on SpeedMenus and on the Tools menu. If you want to assign a shortcut key to your menu text, precede the shortcut letter with an ampersand— this letter appears underlined in the menu. For example, &File assigns F as the shortcut key for File. If you want an ampersand to appear in your menu text, use two ampersands (&&Up&date appears as &Update in the menu).

**Note**    You *must* supply Menu Text if you want the program item to appear on the SpeedMenu or Tools menu.

  - **Help Hint** is descriptive text that appears in the status line of the Tools dialog box when you select the program item.

**4** Open the Advanced Options dialog box (choose Advanced) to set the options for your new program. Depending on the Tool Type you choose (Simple Transfer,

Translator, or Viewer), different fields become available. If you create a Translator, the program becomes available for make and build processes.

- **Place On Tools Menu** adds the item to the Tools menu.
- **Place On SpeedMenu** adds a viewer or translator to the associated SpeedMenu.
- **Target Translator**, available for translators and viewers. For translators, this field specifies whether the program produces a final target (such as an .EXE file) or an intermediate file (such as an .OBJ or .I file). If you check this box, the translator produces a final target that's saved to the directory you specify in the Final text box (choose Project | Options | Directories). If you don't check Target Translator, the translated file is saved in the directory you specify in the Intermediate text box.

  For viewers, Target Translator specifies that the viewer works only on nodes that have been translated (such as .OBJ or .EXE files); the node has to be translated before you can view it.

- **Translate From** defines the node types (determined by file extension) that a translator can translate. To specify multiple node types, use a semicolon to separate file extensions.

  When you enter a file extension in this field, the Project Manager adds the translator to the Special menu of the project nodes that have that file extension. When you choose Special from the Project Manager SpeedMenu, the Project Manager displays all the available translators for that node type. However, it's important that each node type can have only a single, default translator (see the description for Default For).

  To see how this works, look at the tool CppCompile (choose Options | Tools, double-click CppCompile, then click Advanced). The Tool Advanced Options dialog box shows that the C++ compiler is a translator for .CPP, .C, .CAS, and .H files. If you have a source node with a .C extension, CppCompile appears on the Special menu when you right-click the node and choose Special.

- **Translate To** defines the extension of the file that the translator generates. For example, HC31.EXE converts .HPJ files to .HLP, so HC31.EXE holds `.hlp` in this field.

- **Applies To** is similar to the Translate From field, except that it's used for viewers instead of translators.

- **Default For** changes the IDE's default translator or viewer for the file types you specify. Type the file extensions (separating each with a semicolon) for the file types whose default you want to override.

**5** Choose OK twice to confirm your settings, then close the Tools dialog box.

Your new tool has now been added to the Tools list of the associated project, and to the Tools menu or SpeedMenu, depending on where you chose to add the item. If you added the item to the Tools menu, you can check the addition by choosing Tools from the main menu; the new program name appears on the Tools list.

**Note** Although the Project Manager lets you define your own Tools items, these items apply only to the project that you add them to; they aren't added as permanent parts of the IDE. However, translators, viewers, and tools can be *passed* to new and existing projects.

# 3

# Specifying project options and compiling

After you create a project file and write the code for the source nodes in your project, you need to set the options for the different project nodes before you can compile the project. This chapter describes how to set options in a project, how to view the options you set, how to compile a project, and how to use the Message window to view and fix compile-time errors. In addition, this chapter contains a complete reference to the compiler and linker options that can be set from the IDE.

## Setting project options

This section explains how to set, view, and manage project options.

Project options tell the IDE how to compile and link the nodes in your project to form the targets you need. The settings of the project options can indicate whether or not to generate debugging information, where to look for source code, what types of compiler optimizations you want to use, and so on.

The Project Manager lets you set project options in two different ways:

• You can attach Style Sheets to your project nodes.

• You can override the settings in a Style Sheet using local overrides.

Style Sheets group a collection of option settings into a single unit. Once a Style Sheet is created, you can attach it to a node, a group of nodes, or an entire project. Local overrides are settings that take precedence over Style Sheet settings at the node level.

# Using Style Sheets

Often, different project nodes require different option settings. For example, you might want to compile .C files with one set of options and .CPP files with another, or you might want to build one target with debugging information, and another one without it. By applying different Style Sheets to different nodes in your projects, you can easily control how the different nodes get built. In addition, Style Sheets make it easy to view and maintain the settings of your project options.

To view the options that can be incorporated into a Style Sheet, open the Project Options dialog box by choosing Options | Project. This dialog box contains a hierarchical list of topics on the left, with the options that relate to each topic listed on the right. To expand and collapse the Topic list, click the + and – icons to the left of the topic listings.

To see an example of how Style Sheets are used in a project, open the STYLESHT.IDE project file located in the EXAMPLES\IDE\STYLESHT directory of your Borland C++ directory tree. This file uses a different Style Sheet for each of its two versions of WHELLO. The project also contains a text file that explains the use of Style Sheets.

## Predefined Style Sheets

The Project Manager contains several predefined Style Sheets that you can attach to any node in your project. You can also customize a predefined Style Sheet to meet the special needs of your projects.

To inspect the predefined Style Sheets, choose Options | Style Sheets. This opens the Style Sheets dialog box, which lists the predefined Style Sheets on the left and a description of the selected Style Sheet on the right.

## The default project options

When you initially create a project, the project inherits the Style Sheet known as the Default Project Options. If you can build all the components in your project with the same options, you can edit this Style Sheet using the Project Options dialog box. However, if different nodes in your project require different option settings, you should override the default option settings by attaching different Style Sheets to the nodes in your project.

**Warning!** Be careful when you use the Options | Project command to modify option settings; if your project contains more than a single target node, the changes you make always modify the project's Default Project Options (regardless of the node you have selected when you choose the command). Because of this, all targets in your project inherit the changes you make when you use the Options | Project command. In addition, if you modify project options when you don't have a project loaded, your modifications update the Default Project Options Style Sheet; the projects you later create will inherit these new default settings. If you need to revert to the IDE's factory default settings, delete the file BCWDEF.BCW (located in the \BC5\BIN directory), then open and close the IDE to create a new file.

## Managing Style Sheets

The buttons at the bottom of the Style Sheets dialog box let you create, compose, copy, edit, rename, and delete user-defined Style Sheets.

- Create lets you design a new Style Sheet for the currently loaded project. To create a Style Sheet:

  1 Choose the Create button, then enter a name for your new Style Sheet into the Create Style Sheet dialog box. Choose OK to add the new Style Sheet to the Available Style Sheets list.

  2 Select the new Style Sheet from the Available Style Sheets list, then use the Compose, Copy, or Edit buttons to create your custom Style Sheet.

- Compose lets you create a Style Sheet that contains the combined options from one or more Style Sheets. To compose a Style Sheet:

  1 Create a new Style Sheet using the Create button.

  2 Select the new Style Sheet in the Available Style Sheets list, then click Compose.

  3 Select the Style Sheet you want included in your new Style Sheet from the Available Style Sheets list, then move the Style Sheet to the Composite Style Sheets list by double-clicking it or by clicking the → button. (You can also remove Style Sheets from the Composite Style Sheet list by selecting a Style Sheet there and clicking ←.)

  4 Continue modifying the composed Style Sheet, then choose OK when you're finished.

**Note**   You cannot edit the option settings in a composed Style Sheet. However, you can edit the option settings in the Style Sheets contained in the composed Style Sheet, which affects the settings in the composed Style Sheet.

- Copy lets you create a new Style Sheet from an existing one. When you choose Copy, you're prompted for the new Style Sheet's name. Enter the new name, then choose OK to make an exact copy of the selected Style Sheet. Copying is a fast way to create a Style Sheet that closely resembles another—you only have to change the options you want.

- Edit lets you modify the option settings of an existing Style Sheet, including any predefined Style Sheet.

- Rename lets you rename a selected Style Sheet.

- Delete lets you remove an unwanted Style Sheet. (This action cannot be reversed.)

## Attaching Style Sheets to a node

To attach a Style Sheet to a project node:

1 Right-click the node in the Project Tree (or select it and press *Alt+F10*).

2 Choose Edit Node Attributes from the SpeedMenu. The Node Attributes dialog box appears.

3 Select a Style Sheet from the drop-down box, then choose OK.

When you attach a Style Sheet to a node, all the child nodes of that node inherit the settings of the selected Style Sheet. To change the settings of a child node, attach a different Style Sheet, or override an option setting using a local override.

**Note** Although you can attach only a single Style Sheet to a project node, one Style Sheet can be composed of several different Style Sheets.

## Sharing Style Sheets between projects

When you create a custom Style Sheet, that Style Sheet remains with the project for which it was created; it doesn't get added to the list of predefined Style Sheets. However, if you want a new project to use one of your custom Style Sheets or user-defined tools, you can do so by letting a project inherit the settings of another project.

Before a project can inherit the settings of another project, you must modify the BCW.INI file that resides in your Windows directory. If the file doesn't contain an inherit setting, then you must add the settings to the file as follows:

```
[Project]
;To have new projects inherit settings from the Default Project Settings
(default):
inherit=0

;To have new projects inherit settings from currently open project:
inherit=1

;To have new projects inherit factory default settings:
inherit=2
```

To pass Style Sheets or user-defined tools from one project to a new project:

**1** Modify BCW.INI so that inherit=1.

**2** Open the project that contains the Style Sheet or tools you want to share.

**3** Choose Project I New Project.

When the new project is created, it inherits the Style Sheets and user-defined tools of the project that was open when you choose Project I New Project.

## Project Description Language files

You can also use Project Description Language (.PDL) files to share Style Sheets and tools between projects. When you save a project, you can instruct the IDE to create a .PDL file that has the same file name as the project's .IDE file. Likewise, when you open a project, you can instruct the IDE to read the project's .PDL file. Because a .PDL file contains information about the Style Sheets and tools used in a project, you can edit a project's .PDL file so that it uses the Style Sheets and tools of your choosing. However, care must be taken whenever you edit a .PDL file—it's easy to corrupt the file to the point where the Project Manager can't read it.

If you plan to use .PDL files to share Style Sheets and tools, you must first ensure that the IDE creates and reads the files. To do so, open the BCW.INI file (found in your Windows directory) and add the following settings to the [Project] section of the .INI file:

```
[Project]
saveastext=1
readastext=1
```

The `saveastext` setting tells the IDE to save a .PDL file whenever a project is saved. The readastext setting tells the IDE to update an .IDE file if its associated .PDL file is newer than the .IDE file.

To share Style Sheets or user-defined tools between projects:

1 Modify your BCW.INI file as just described.

2 Open the project that you need to transfer Style Sheets or tools to, then close the project (choose Project | Close Project). This creates a .PDL file for the project.

3 Open the project that contains the Style Sheets or tools you want to share, then close the project to save the current settings in the .PDL file.

4 Using a text editor, open the .PDL file containing the Style Sheet or tools you want to share (the .PDL file name matches the file name of the .IDE file).

5 Search for the Style Sheet's name. For example, if you created a Style Sheet called MYSTYLE, you'll see a section in the .PDL file that starts { StyleSheet = "MYSTYLE".

6 Copy all the text from the beginning brace to the ending brace. If needed, you can copy more than a single Style Sheet.

**Note**     To share a user-defined tool, copy the section that reads Subsystem=<tool>.

7 Open the .PDL file that is to receive the Style Sheet.

8 Find the section for Style Sheets, then paste the copied text to the end of the existing Style Sheet list.

9 Save the .PDL file that received the copied Style Sheet.

10 Open the project that received the copied Style Sheet to update the project's Style Sheets and tools from the .PDL file.

After transferring Style Sheets, it's a good idea to reset the saveastext and the readastext flags in the BCW.INI file to 0. This tells the IDE to not save to or update from .PDL files.

## Setting local overrides

Option settings can be overridden at the node level using local overrides. Local overrides are useful when a node's option settings must differ from its associated Style Sheet by one or two settings.

**Note**     Although local overrides make it easy to set options for individual nodes, they have the disadvantage of being difficult to track. While the Options Hierarchy dialog box displays the Style Sheet and local override settings for a selected node, you must examine each individual node to see which ones have been overridden. Because of this, it's recommended that you use separate Style Sheets for nodes that require different option settings, and use local overrides only in special cases.

To override an option setting:

1 Choose the node whose settings you want to override.

2 Right-click the node (or press *Alt+F10*) and choose Edit Local Options from the SpeedMenu. The Options dialog box (which is similar to the Project Options dialog box) appears and displays the settings for that node.

**3** Select the option you want to override. The IDE automatically checks the Local Override box whenever you modify a Style Sheet setting.

**4** Choose OK to confirm your new settings.

**Warning!** The Local Override check box is enabled only when an option within a topic is selected; otherwise, the check box is grayed. When you select an option (using Tab, or by clicking and dragging the mouse off the option), the Local Override check box shows the status of the selected option. Because of this, you must individually select each option in a topic to see which ones have been overridden locally. If you choose an option (by clicking it, or by selecting it and pressing *Enter*), you change its setting, which always causes the Local Override check box to be checked.

To undo an override:

**1** Right-click the node whose setting you want to modify, then choose Edit Local Options from the SpeedMenu.

**2** In the Options dialog box, select the topic that contains the overridden setting.

When you select a topic page that has a locally overridden option, the Project Manager enables the Undo Page button.

**3** Select the option (using Tab, or by clicking and dragging the mouse off the option) whose local override you want to undo; the Local Override check box will be checked.

**4** Click the Local Override check box to undo the override; the option will revert to its default Style Sheet setting. To revert the entire topic to the settings contained in the associated Style Sheet, choose the Undo Page button.

**5** Choose OK to confirm your modifications.

## Viewing project options

Because each node can have its own Style Sheet *and* you can override the options in the Style Sheet, you need a quick way to view the option settings for each node.

To view option settings for the nodes in your project:

**1** Right-click any node in the Project window and choose View Options Hierarchy, or click the button on the SpeedBar.

The Options Hierarchy dialog box appears, listing the nodes in the project on the left and the options that each node uses on the right. You can expand and collapse the list of nodes in the dialog box just like you can in the Project window, however, Autodependency nodes don't appear.

An option that's surrounded by double-asterisks (**) in the Options listing indicates that the option is overridden (by either a Style Sheet or local override) by a dependent node located farther down in the Options listing. (The asterisks display only when you select the node where the option is overridden.)

**2** When you select a node in the Project Options At list, its settings appear to the right in the Options list.

The Options list displays components of the project in square brackets. At the top of the list, you'll see the name of the project followed by its Default Project Options. Below this is the name of the target associated with the node you've selected. If the node has a Style Sheet associated with it, it's displayed beneath the node (also in brackets), along with the settings of the Style Sheet. If you've overridden any settings, these are displayed beneath the [Node overrides] listing. The Options list displays the settings for all the ancestors of the node selected in the Project Tree.

3 If you want to edit an option, double-click the option in the Option list, or select it and click Edit.Whenever you edit options in this manner, the modifications become local overrides.

4 When you finish viewing your project's option settings, choose Close.

# Compiling projects

There are two basic ways to compile projects: build and make. Build compiles and links all the nodes in a project, regardless of file dates. Make compares the time stamp of the target with the time stamps of all the files used to build the target. Make then compiles and links only those nodes necessary to bring the target up to date.

To compile a project, open the project using the Project | Open command, then choose one Compile, Make All, or Build All from the Project menu (note that the SpeedBar has three similar looking buttons that correspond to these Project Menu commands).

- Compile (*Alt+F9*) builds the code in the currently active Edit window. If a Project window is selected, all the selected nodes in the project are translated; child nodes aren't translated unless they're selected.

- Make All (*F9*) translates all the out-of-date nodes in a project. If a project is not open, the file contained in the active Edit window buffer is built.

  When you choose Make All, the Project Manager moves down the Project Tree until it finds a node with no dependents. The Project Manager then compares that node's date and time against the date and time of the node's parent. The Project Manager translates the node only if the child node is newer than the parent node. The Project Manager then moves up the Project Tree and checks the next node's date and time. In this way, the Project Manager recurses through the Project Tree, translating only those nodes that have been updated since the last compile.

- Build All translates all nodes in a project—even if they are up-to-date. Build All always starts at the project node and builds each successive target down the project. Choose Cancel to stop a build.

  When you choose Build All, the Project Manager starts at the first target and works down the Project Tree until it comes to a node with no dependents. The Project Manager compiles that node first (and other nodes on the same level), then works back up the Project Tree, compiling and linking all the nodes needed to create the target. This process is then repeated down the Project Tree, until all the targets have been updated.

  For example, if you have a project with an .EXE target that is dependent on two separate .OBJ files, the Project Manager creates the first .OBJ file by compiling all its dependents. It then creates the next .OBJ file. Once a target node's dependents are created, it can compile or link the target node. In this case, the Project Manager will link the two .OBJ files (and any run-time nodes) to create the final .EXE.

## Compiling part of a project

There are several ways to compile specific parts of a project. You can

- Translate an individual node
- Build a node and its dependents
- Make a node and its dependents
- Select several nodes and compile

To translate an individual node:

**1** Select the node you want to translate.

**2** Choose Project | Compile from the main menu or choose the default translation command from the SpeedMenu. For example, if you've selected a .CPP file, the node SpeedMenu contains the command C++ Compile, which compiles only the selected node.

To build a node and its dependents:

**1** Select the node you want to build.

**2** Right-click the node (or press *Alt+F10*) and choose Build Node from the SpeedMenu. All the dependent nodes are built regardless of whether they're out-of-date.

To make a node and its dependents:

**1** Select the node you want to build.

**2** Right-click the node (or press *Alt+F10*) and choose Make Node from the SpeedMenu. This command compiles only the dependent nodes whose source files are newer than their associated target files.

To compile several selected nodes:

**1** Select the project nodes you want to compile by pressing *Ctrl* and clicking the desired project nodes. (The nodes must be of the same file type, such as .CPP).

**2** Choose Make Node or Build Node from the Project Manager SpeedMenu to compile the selected nodes.

# Fixing compile-time errors

Compile-time errors, or *syntax* errors, occur when your code violates a syntax rule of the language you're programming in; the C++ compiler cannot compile your program unless it contains valid language statements. If the compiler encounters a syntax error while compiling your code, the Message window opens and displays the type of error or warning it encountered. By choosing Options | Environment | Preferences, you can specify if old messages should be preserved or deleted between calls to different programming tools (such as a compiler, GREP, or the resource compiler). Check Save Old Messages if you want the Message window to retain its current listing of messages when you run a tool.

To clear the Message window, choose Remove All Messages from the Message window SpeedMenu.

## Viewing errors

To view the code that caused a compiler error or warning, select the message in the Message window; the IDE updates the Edit window so that it displays the location in your code where the error or warning occurred (this is called Automatic Error Tracking). If the file containing the error isn't loaded in an Edit window, press Spacebar to load the file (you can also load the file by pressing *Alt+F10*, then choosing View Source from the SpeedMenu). When you view errors in this manner, the Message window remains selected so you can navigate from message to message.To open or view the Message window, click the button on the SpeedMenu, or choose View | Message.

## Fixing errors

To edit the code associated with an error or warning, do one of the following:

- Double-click the message in the Message window.
- Select the message in the Message window and press *Enter*.
- Press *Alt+F10* and choose Edit Source from the SpeedMenu.

The Edit window gains focus with the insertion point placed on the line and column in your source code where the compiler detected the error. From here, edit your code to fix the error. After fixing the error, press *Alt+F7* to move to the next error message in the list or press *Alt+F8* to go back to the previous message.

# Project options reference

You set compiler, linker, librarian, and make options from two different places in the IDE: the Project Options multiple-page dialog box and TargetExpert. The remainder of this chapter describes the options available in the Project Options dialog box. They are described in alphabetical order.

# 16-bit compiler options

The 16-bit Compiler options affect the compilation of all 16-bit source modules. It is usually best to keep the default setting for most options in this section.

## Calling Conventions

Calling Convention options tell the compiler which calling sequences to generate for function calls. The C, Pascal, and Register calling conventions differ in the way each handles stack cleanup, order of parameters, case, and prefix of global identifiers.

You can use the _ _cdecl, _ _pascal, or _ _fastcall keywords to override the default calling convention on specific functions.

**Note** These options should be used by experts only.

## C
Command-line equivalent: **-pc, -p-**

This option tells the compiler to generate a C calling sequence for function calls (generate underbars, case sensitive, push parameters right to left). This is the same as declaring all subroutines and functions with the _ _cdecl keyword. Functions declared using the C calling convention can take a variable parameter list (the number of parameters does not need to be fixed).

## Pascal
Command-line equivalent: **-p**

This option tells the compiler to generate a Pascal calling sequence for function calls (do not generate underbars, all uppercase, calling function cleans stack, pushes parameters left to right). This is the same as declaring all subroutines and functions with the _ _pascal keyword. The resulting function calls are usually smaller and faster than those made with the C (**-pc**) calling convention. Functions must pass the correct number and type of arguments.

## Register
Command-line equivalent: **-pr**

This option forces the compiler to generate all subroutines and all functions using the **Register** parameter-passing convention, which is equivalent to declaring all subroutines and functions with the _ _fastcall keyword. With this option enabled, functions or routines expect parameters to be passed in registers.

Default = C (**-pc**)

# Entry/Exit code

These options specify which type of prolog and epilog code the compiler generates for each module's functions.

**Note** Although these options are listed in the 16-bit compiler section, they also apply to 32-bit programs.

## Windows all functions exportable
Command-line equivalent: **-tW**

This option creates a Windows object function prolog/epilog for all _ _far functions, then sets up those functions to be called from another module. This option assumes that all functions can be called by the Windows kernel or by other modules and generates the necessary overhead information for every _ _**far** function (whether the function needs it or not).

To export the function address from the .EXE to a .DLL, the code includes a call to *MakeProcInstance()*, passing the resulting pointer to the .DLL that requested the address of the function. For the function to be exportable, the function must be declared as _**export** or the function name must be included in the .DEF file of the executable.

This option creates the most general Windows executable, but not necessarily the most efficient.

**Note** The **-W** command-line option is supported for backward compatibility, and is equivalent to **-tW**.

Default = ON

## Windows explicit functions exported

Command-line equivalent: **-tWE**

This option creates a Windows object module in which only _ _**far** functions declared as _**export** functions are exportable. Use this option if you have functions that will not be called by the Windows kernel. Windows Explicit Functions Exported operates the same as Windows All Functions Exportable except that only those functions marked with the _**export** keyword (and methods of classes marked as _**export**) are given the extra prolog/epilog.

This option is far more efficient than Windows All Functions Exportable, since only those functions called from outside the module get the prolog overhead. This option requires that you determine in advance which functions or classes need to be exported. *MakeProcInstance()* is still used, but no .DEF file manipulation is needed (if you use this option along with _**export**, you don't need to define exports in your .DEF files).

**Note** The **-WE** command-line option is supported for backward compatibility, and is equivalent to **-tWE**.

Default = OFF

## Windows smart callbacks, all functions exportable

Command-line equivalent: **-tWS**

This option creates an object module with smart callbacks for all _ _**far** functions exported. Use this option only if the compiler can assume that DS == SS for all functions in the module (which is true for the vast majority of Windows programs and the default for Borland tools).

This option creates a Windows .EXE function prolog/epilog for all _ _**far** functions and sets them up to be called from another module. *MakeProcInstance()* does not need to be called and you do not need to edit the .DEF file.

**Note** The **-WS** command-line option is supported for backward compatibility, and is equivalent to **-tWS**.

Default = OFF

### Windows smart callbacks, explicit functions exportable

Command-line equivalent: **-tWSE**

This option is the same as Windows Smart Callbacks except that only those functions marked with the **_export** keyword (and methods of classes marked as **_export**) are given the extra prolog/epilog. This is efficient since only those functions called from outside the module get the prolog overhead. This option requires determining in advance which functions/classes need to be exported.

**Note**　The **-WSE** command-line option is supported for backward compatibility, and is equivalent to **-tWSE**.

Default = OFF

### Windows DLL, all functions exportable

Command-line equivalent: **-tWD**

This option creates a Windows .DLL function prolog/epilog for all _ _**far** functions, then sets up those functions to be called from another module. To actually export function addresses from the .DLL, the functions must be marked with the **_export** keyword or the function names need to be included in the .DEF file of the executable.

**Note**　The **-WD** command-line option is supported for backward compatibility, and is equivalent to **-tWD**.

Default = OFF

### Windows DLL, explicit functions exported

Command-line equivalent: **-tWDE**

This option is the same as Windows DLL, All Functions Exportable except that only _ _**far** functions marked with the **_export** keyword (and methods of classes marked as **_export**) are given the extra prolog/epilog. This is far more efficient than the Windows DLL, All Functions Exportable option since only those functions called from outside the module get the prolog overhead. This option requires determining which functions or classes need to be exported in advance. No .DEF file manipulation is needed.

**Note**　The **-WDE** command-line option is supported for backward compatibility, and is equivalent to **-tWDE**.

Default = OFF

## Memory model

The Memory Model section lets you specify the organization of segments for code and data in your 16-bit programs. (32-bit programs always use the flat memory model.) Large is the most common memory model used for Windows programs. All .OBJ and .LIB files in your program should be compiled in the same memory model.

## Assume SS equals DS

The Assume SS Equals DS options specify how the compiler considers the stack segment (SS) and the data segment (DS).

### Always (DOS only)

Command-line equivalent: **-Fs**

The compiler always assumes that SS is equal to DS in all memory models. This option causes the compiler to use the alternate C0F*x*.OBJ startup module (which places the stack in the data segment) instead of C0*x*.OBJ. You can use this option when porting code originally written for an implementation that makes the stack part of the data segment.

Default = Default for Memory Model

### Default for memory model

The memory model you use determines whether the stack segment (SS) is equal to the data segment (DS). Usually, the compiler assumes that SS is equal to DS in the small and medium memory models (except for DLLs).

### Never

Command-line equivalent: **-Fs-**

The compiler assumes that the SS is never equal to DS. This is always the case in the compact and large memory models and when building a Windows DLL.

## Automatic far data

Command-line equivalent: **-Ff**

When the Automatic Far Data option is enabled, the compiler automatically places data objects larger than or equal to the threshold size into far data segments. The threshold size defaults to 32,767. This option is useful for code that doesn't use the huge memory model, but declares enough large global variables that their total size is close to or exceeds 64K. This option has no effect for programs that use tiny, small, and medium memory models.

When this option is disabled, the size value is ignored

This option and the Far Data Threshold input box work together. The Far Data Threshold specifies the minimum size above which data objects will be automatically made far.

If you use this option with the Generate COMDEFs option (**-Fc**), the COMDEFs become far in the compact, large, and huge models.

Default = OFF

The command-line option **-Fm** enables all the other -F options (**-Fc**, **-Ff**, and **-Fs**). You can use **-Fm** as a handy shortcut when porting code from other compilers. To do this in the IDE, check the Automatic Far Data and Always options on this Project Options page, and the Generate COMDEFs option on the Compiler | Floating Point page.

## Far data threshold

Command-line equivalent: **-Ff=***size*, where *size* = threshold size

Use Far Data Threshold to specify the size portion needed to complete the Automatic Far Data option.

Default = 32767 (if Automatic Far Data is disabled, this option value is ignored)

## Far virtual tables

Command-line equivalent: **-Vf**

When you turn this option on, the compiler creates virtual tables in the code segment instead of the data segment, unless you override this option using the Far Virtual Tables Segment (**-zV**) or Far Virtual Tables Class (**-zW**) options. Virtual table pointers are made into full 32-bit pointers (which is done automatically if you are using the huge memory model).

You can use Far Virtual Tables to remove the virtual tables from the data segment (which might be getting full). You might also use this option to share objects (of classes with virtual functions) between modules that use different data segments (for example, a DLL and an executable that uses that DLL).

You must compile all modules that might share objects entirely with or entirely without this option. Note that you can get the same effect by using the **huge** or **_export** modifiers on a class-by-class basis.

This option changes the mangled names of C++ objects.

Default = OFF

## Fast huge pointers

Command-line equivalent: **-h**

This option offers an alternative method of calculating huge pointer expressions. This option behaves differently for DOS and Windows programs.

For Windows programs, huge pointers are normalized by the value of the variable _ALTINCR, which is initialized by Windows at the startup time of the application.

For DOS programs, this option offers a faster method of "normalizing" than the standard method. (*Normalizing* is resolving a memory address so that the offset is always less than 16.) When you use this option, huge pointers are normalized only when a segment wraparound occurs in the offset part, which causes problems with huge arrays if an array element crosses a segment boundary.

Usually, Borland C++ normalizes a huge pointer whenever adding or subtracting from it. This ensures, for example, that if you have an array of **struct**s that's larger than 64K, indexing into the array and selecting a **struct** field always works with **struct**s of any size. Borland C++ accomplishes this by always normalizing the results of huge pointer operations—the address offset contains a number that is no higher than 15 and a segment wraparound never occurs with huge pointers. The disadvantage of this approach is that it tends to be quite expensive in terms of execution speed.

Default = OFF

## Model

The Model options specify the memory model you want to use. The memory model you choose determines the default method of memory addressing.

### Compact

Command-line equivalent: **-mc**

Use the compact model if your code is small but you need to address a lot of data. The Compact model is the opposite of the medium model: far pointers are used for data but not for code; code is limited to 64K; pointers can point almost anywhere. All functions are near by default and all data pointers are far by default.

### Huge

Command-line equivalent: **-mh**, DOS only

Use the huge model for very large applications only. Far pointers are used for both code and data. Borland C++ normally limits the size of all static data to 64K; the huge memory model sets aside that limit, allowing data to occupy more than 64K.

Default = Large in IDE; Small in BCC.EXE

### Large

Command-line equivalent: **-ml**

Use the large model for very large applications only. Far pointers are used for both code and data. Data is limited to 1MB. Far pointers can point almost anywhere. All functions and data pointers are far by default.

### Medium

Command-line equivalent: **-mm**

Use the medium model for large programs that do not keep much data in memory. Far pointers are used for code but not for data. Data and stack together are limited to 64K, but code can occupy up to 1MB.

The **-mm!** command-line option compiles using the medium model and assumes DS != SS. To achieve this in the IDE, you need to check both the **Medium** and **Never** options.

**Note**  The net effect of the **-ms!** and **-mm!** options is actually very small. If you take the address of a stack variable (parameter or auto), the default (DS == SS) is to make the resulting pointer a near (DS relative) pointer. This way, you can assign the address to a default-sized pointer in those models without problems. When DS != SS, the pointer type created when you take the address of a stack variable is an **_ss** pointer. This means that the pointer can be freely assigned or passed to a far pointer or to an **_ss** pointer. But for the memory models affected, assigning the address to a near or default-sized pointer produces a "Suspicious pointer conversion" warning. Such warnings are usually errors.

### Small
Command-line equivalent: **-ms**

Use the small model for average size applications. The code and data segments are different and don't overlap, so you have 64K of code and 64K of data and stack. Near pointers are always used.

The **-ms!** command-line option compiles using the small model and assumes DS != SS. To achieve this in the IDE, you need to check both the **Small** and **Never** options.

### Tiny
Command-line equivalent: **-mt** ,DOS only

This is the smallest of the memory models. Use this model when memory is at an absolute premium. All four segment registers (CS, DS, SS, ES) are set to the same address. You have a total of 64K for all of your code, data, and stack. Near pointers are always used. Tiny model programs can be converted to .COM format by linking with the **/t** option.

## Put constant strings in code segments
Command-line equivalent: **-dc**

This option moves all string literals from the data segment to the code segment of the generated object file, making the data type **const**.

Note  Use this option only with compact or large memory models. In addition, this option does not work with overlays.

Using this option saves data segment space. In large programs, especially those with a large number of literal strings, this option shifts the burden from the data segment to the code segment.

Default = OFF

# Processor

The Processor options let you specify the minimum CPU type compatible with your program. These options introduce instructions specific to the CPU type you select to increase performance.

## 16-bit instruction set
The Instruction Set options specify for which CPU instruction set the compiler should generate code.

### 80186
Command-line equivalent: **-1**

Choose the 80186 option if you want the compiler to generate extended 16-bit code for the 80186 instruction set. Also supports the 80286 running in Real mode.

### 80286

Command-line equivalent: **-2**

Choose the 80286 option if you want the compiler to generate 16-bit code for the 80286 protected-mode–compatible instruction set.

### 80386

Command-line equivalent: **-3**

Choose the 80386 option if you want the compiler to generate 16-bit code for the 80386 protected-mode–compatible instruction set.

### 8086

Command-line equivalent: **-1-**

Choose the 8086 option if you want the compiler to generate 16-bit code for the 8086-compatible instruction set. (To generate 8086 code, you must not turn on the options **-2**, **-3**, **-4**, or **-5**.)

### i486

Command-line equivalent: **-4**

Choose the i486 option if you want the compiler to generate 80386/i486 instructions running in enhanced-mode Windows.

Default = 8086 (**-1-**)

## Data alignment

The Data Alignment options let you choose how the compiler aligns data in stored memory. Word, double-word, and quad-word alignment force integer-size and larger items to be aligned on memory addresses that are a multiple of the type chosen. Extra bytes are inserted in structures to ensure that members align correctly.

### Byte alignment

Command-line equivalent: **-a1** or **-a-**

When Byte Alignment is turned on, the compiler does not force alignment of variables or data fields to any specific memory boundaries; the compiler aligns data at either even or odd addresses, depending on which is the next available address.

While byte-wise alignment produces more compact programs, the programs tend to run a bit slower. The other data alignment options increase the speed that 80x86 processors fetch and store data.

### Double word (4-byte)

Command-line equivalent: **-a4**, 32-bit only

Double Word alignment aligns non-character data at 32-bit word (4-byte) boundaries.

**Quad word (8-byte)**
Command-line equivalent: **-a8**, 32-bit only

Quad Word alignment aligns non-character data at 64-bit word (8-byte) boundaries.

Default = Byte Alignment (**-a-**)

**Word alignment (2-byte)**
Command-line equivalent: **-a2**

When Word Alignment is on, the compiler aligns non-character data at even addresses. Automatic and global variables are aligned properly. **char** and **unsigned char** variables and fields can be placed at any address; all others are placed at an even-numbered address.

## Segment names code

Segment Names Code options let you specify a new code segment name and reassign the group and class.

### Code

Use Code to change the name of the code segment as well as the code group and class.

In all options, use an asterisk (*) for *name* to select the default segment names.

**Note**   Do not change the settings in this dialog box unless you are an expert.

#### Code class
Command-line equivalent = **-zA***name*

Changes the name of the code segment class to *name*. By default, the code segment is assigned to class CODE.

Default = * (default segment name) for all options

#### Code group
Command-line equivalent = **-zP***name*

Causes any output files to be generated with a code group for the code segment named *name*.

#### Code segment
Command-line equivalent = **-zC***name*

Sets the name of the code segment to *name*. By default, the code segment is named _CODE for near code and *modulename*_TEXT for far code, except for the medium and large models where the name is *filename*_CODE (*filename* is the source file name).

# Segment names data

Use Segment Names Data to change the default segment, group, and class names for initialized and uninitialized data.

**Note**  Do not change the settings in this dialog box unless you have a good understanding of segmentation on the 80x86 processor. Under normal circumstances, you do not need to specify segment names.

## Initialized Data

Use Initialized Data to change the default segment, group, and class names for initialized data.

In all options, use an asterisk (*) for *name* to select the default segment names.

**Note**  Do not change the settings in this dialog box unless you have a good understanding of segmentation on the 80x86 processor. Under normal circumstances, you do not need to specify segment names.

### Initialized data class

Command-line equivalent = **-zT***name*

Sets the name of the initialized data segment to *name*. By default, the initialized data segment class is named DATA.

Default = * (default segment namc) for all options

### Initialized data group

Command-line equivalent = **-zS***name*

Sets the name of the initialized data segment group to *name*. By default, the data group is named DGROUP.

### Initialized data segment

Command-line equivalent = **-zR***name*

Sets the name of the initialized data segment to *name*. By default, the initialized data segment is named _DATA for **near** data and *modulename*_DATA for **far** data.

## Uninitialized data

Use Uninitialized Data to change the default segment, group, and class names for code uninitialized data.

In all options, use an asterisk (*) for *name* to select the default segment names.

**Note**  Do not change the settings in this dialog box unless you have a good understanding of segmentation on the 80x86 processor. Under normal circumstances, you do not need to specify segment names.

### Uninitialized data (BSS class)
Command-line equivalent = **-zB**_name_

Sets the name of the uninitialized data segment class to _name_. By default, the uninitialized data segments are assigned to class _BSS_.

Default = * (default segment name) for all options

### Uninitialized data (BSS group)
Command-line equivalent = **-zG**_name_

Sets the name of the uninitialized data segment group to _name_. By default, the data group is named DGROUP.

### Uninitialized data (BSS segment)
Command-line equivalent = **-zD**_name_

Sets the name of the uninitialized data segment. By default, the uninitialized data segment is named _BSS for **near** uninitialized data and _modulename_\_BSS for **far** uninitialized data.

## Segment names far data

16-bit Compiler | Segment Names Far Data options set the far data segment name, group, class name, and the far virtual tables segment name and class.

### Far data
Use Far Data to change the default segment, group, and class names for far data.

In all options, use an asterisk (*) for **name** to select the default segment names.

**Note**  Do not change the settings in this dialog box unless you have a good understanding of segmentation on the 80*x*86 processor. Under normal circumstances, you do not need to specify segment names.

### Far data class
Command-line equivalent = **-zF**_name_

Sets the name of the class for _ _**far** objects to _name_. By default, the name is FAR_DATA.

Default = * (default segment name) for all options

### Far data group
Command-line equivalent = **-zH**_name_

Causes _ _**far** objects to be placed into the group _name_. By default, far objects are not placed into a group.

### Far data segment
Command-line equivalent = **-zE**_name_

Sets the name of the segment where _ _**far** objects are placed to *name*. By default, the segment name is the name of the far object followed by _DATA.

### Far virtual tables

Use Far Virtual Tables to change the default segment and class names virtual tables.

In all options, use an asterisk (*) for *name* to select the default segment names.

**Note** Do not change the settings in this dialog box unless you have a good understanding of segmentation on the 80x86 processor. Under normal circumstances, you do not need to specify segment names.

#### Virtual table class
Command-line equivalent = **-zW***name*

Sets the name of the far virtual table class segment to *name*. By default, far virtual table classes are generated in the CODE segment.

Default = * (default segment name) for all options

#### Virtual table segment
Command-line equivalent = **-zV***name*

Sets the name of the _ _**far** virtual table segment to *name*. By default, far virtual tables are generated in the CODE segment.

# 32-bit compiler options

The 32-bit Compiler page contains two radio buttons that allow you to select which 32-bit compiler you want to use when compiling 32-bit applications.

## Use Borland optimizing compiler

The Borland optimizing compiler is a faster compiler than the Intel compiler and it produces smaller executable files.

## Use Intel optimizing compiler

The Intel optimizing compiler produces faster executable files than does the Borland compiler at the expense of slower compilation times and slightly larger executable file sizes.

## 32-bit compiler options

32-bit Compiler options listed on the Processor and Calling Convention pages affect the compilation of all 32-bit Windows applications for Windows NT and Windows 95.

Because 32-bit programs use a flat memory model (they are not segmented), there are fewer options to configure than for 16-bit programs.

## Calling conventions

Calling Convention options tell the compiler which calling sequences to generate for function calls. The C, Pascal, and Register calling conventions differ in the way each handles stack cleanup, order of parameters, case, and prefix of global identifiers.

You can use the _ _cdecl, _ _pascal, _ _fastcall, or _ _stdcall keywords to override the default calling convention on specific functions.

**Note**    These options should be used by experts only.

### C
Command-line equivalent: **-pc, -p-**

This option tells the compiler to generate a C calling sequence for function calls (generate underbars, case sensitive, push parameters right to left). This is the same as declaring all subroutines and functions with the _ _cdecl keyword. Functions declared using the C calling convention can take a variable parameter list (the number of parameters does not need to be fixed).

You can use the _ _pascal, _ _fastcall, or _ _stdcall keywords to specifically declare a function or subroutine using another calling convention.

### Pascal
Command-line equivalent: **-p**

This option tells the compiler to generate a Pascal calling sequence for function calls (do not generate underbars, all uppercase, calling function cleans stack, pushes parameters left to right). This is the same as declaring all subroutines and functions with the _ _pascal keyword. The resulting function calls are usually smaller and faster than those made with the C (**-pc**) calling convention. Functions must pass the correct number and type of arguments.

You can use the _ _cdecl, _ _fastcall, or _ _stdcall keywords to specifically declare a function or subroutine using another calling convention.

### Register
Command-line equivalent: **-pr**

This option forces the compiler to generate all subroutines and all functions using the **Register** parameter-passing convention, which is equivalent to declaring all subroutines and functions with the _ _fastcall keyword. With this option enabled, functions or routines expect parameters to be passed in registers.

You can use the _ _pascal, _ _cdecl, or _ _stdcall keywords to specifically declare a function or subroutine using another calling convention.

### Standard Call (32-bit compiler only)
Command-line equivalent: **-ps**

This option tells the compiler to generate a Stdcall calling sequence for function calls (does not generate underscores, preserve case, called function pops the stack, and pushes parameters right to left). This is the same as declaring all subroutines and functions with the _ _stdcall keyword. Functions must pass the correct number and type of arguments.

You can use the _ _cdecl, _ _pascal, _ _fastcall keywords to specifically declare a function or subroutine using another calling convention.

Default = C (-pc)

## Processor

32-bit Compiler Processor options specify which CPU instruction set to use and how to handle floating-point code for 32-bit programs.

### 32-bit instruction set

The Instruction Set options specify for which CPU instruction set the compiler should generate code.

**80386**
Command-line equivalent: -3

Choose the 80386 option if you want the compiler to generate 80386 protected-mode–compatible instructions running on Windows 95 or Windows NT.

**i486**
Command-line equivalent: -4

Choose the i486 option if you want the compiler to generate i486 protected-mode–compatible instructions running on Windows 95 or Windows NT.

**Pentium**
Command-line equivalent: -5

Choose the Pentium option if you want the compiler to generate Pentium instructions on Windows 95 or Windows NT.

While this option increases the speed at which the application runs on Pentium machines, expect the program to be a bit larger than when compiled with the **80386** or **i486** options. In addition, **Pentium**-compiled code will sustain a performance hit on non-Pentium systems.

**Pentium Pro**
Command-line equivalent: -6

Choose the Pentium Pro option if you want the compiler to generate Pentium Pro instructions running on Windows 95 or Windows NT.

**Note** This option is valid only if you are using the 32-bit Intel compiler (choose 32-bit Compiler | Intel Optimizing Compiler in the Project Options dialog box or use the BCC32i.EXE command-line compiler).

Default = 80386 (**-3**)

# Build Attributes options

Build attributes affect whether or not a node is built during compilation. The icons associated with each of these options are displayed next to the nodes in the Project hierarchy diagram.

**Note** This set of options is not available for an AppExpert project.

## Always build

Check Always Build and the node is always built, even if it has not changed.

## Build when out of date

Check Build When Out of Date and the node is built only if it has changed.

## Can't build

Check Can't Build to be notified when a node cannot be built.

## Exclude from parent

Check Exclude from Parent and the system indicates when a node should be excluded from parent (such as with source pools).

## Never build

Check Never Build and the node is not built.

# C++ options

C++ Options affect compilation of all C and C++ programs. For most options in this section, you usually want to keep the default settings.

# C++ compatibility

Use the C++ Compatibility options to handle C++ compatibility issues, such as handling 'char' types, specifying options about hidden pointers, passing class arguments, adding hidden members and code to a derived class, passing the 'this' pointer to 'Pascal' member functions, changing the layout of classes, or insuring compatibility when class instances are shared with non-C++ code or code compiled with previous versions of Borland C++.

## 'deep' virtual bases
Command-line equivalent: **-Vv**

When a derived class overrides a virtual function which it inherits from a virtual base class, and a constructor or destructor for the derived class calls that virtual function using a pointer to the virtual base class, the compiler can sometimes add hidden members to the derived class. These "hidden members" add code to the constructors and destructors.

This option directs the compiler *not* to add the hidden members and code so that the class instance layout is the same as with previous version of Borland C++; the compiler does not change the layout of any classes to relax the restrictions on pointers.

Default = OFF

## Calling convention mangling compatibility
Command-line equivalent: **-VC**

When this option is enabled, the compiler disables the distinction of function names where the only possible difference is incompatible code generation options. For example, with this option enabled, the linker will not detect if a call is made to a **_ _fastcall** member function with the **cdecl** calling convention.

This option is provided for backward compatibility only; it lets you link old library files that you cannot recompile.

Default = OFF

## Disable constructor displacements
Command-line equivalent: **-Vc**

When the Disable Constructor Displacements option is enabled, the compiler does not add hidden members and code to a derived class (the default).

This option insures compatibility with previous versions of the compiler.

Default = OFF

## Do not treat 'char' as distinct type
Command-line equivalent: **-K2**, 16-bit

Allow only signed and unsigned char types. The Borland C++ compiler allows for signed char, unsigned char, and char data types. This option treats **char** as signed.

This option is provided for compatibility with previous versions of Borland C++ (3.1 and earlier) and supports only 16-bit programs.

Default = OFF

## Don't restrict scope of 'for' loop expression variables

Command-line equivalent: **-Vd**

This option lets you specify the scope of variables declared in **for** loop expressions. The output of the following code segment changes, depending on the setting of this option.

```
int main(void)

{

  for(int i=0; i<10; i++)
  {
        cout << "Inside for loop, i = " << i << endl;
  }     //end of for-loop block

  cout << "Outside for loop, i = " << i << endl;  //error without -Vd


}       //end of block containing for loop
```

If this option is disabled (the default), the variable *i* goes out of scope when processing reaches the end of the **for** loop. Because of this, you'll get an Undefined Symbol compilation error if you compile this code with this option disabled.

If this option is enabled (**-Vd**), the variable *i* goes out of scope when processing reaches the end of the block containing the **for** loop. In this case, the code output would be:

```
Inside for loop, i = 0
...
Outside for loop, i = 10
```

Default = OFF

## Pass class values via reference to temporary

Command-line equivalent: **-Va**

When this option is enabled, the compiler passes class arguments using the "reference to temporary" approach. When an argument of type class with constructors is passed by value to a function, this option instructs the compiler to create a temporary variable at the calling site, initialize this temporary variable with the argument value, and pass a reference from this temporary to the function.

This option insures compatibility with previous versions of the compiler.

Default = OFF

## Push 'this' first for Pascal member functions

Command-line equivalent: **-Vp**

When this option is enabled, the compiler passes the **this** pointer to Pascal member functions as the first parameter on the stack.

By default, the compiler passes the **this** parameter as the last parameter on the stack, which permits smaller and faster member function calls.

Default = OFF

## Treat 'far' classes as 'huge'

Command-line equivalent **-Vh**

When this option is enabled, the compiler treats all classes declared _ _**far** as if they were declared as _ _**huge**. For example, the following code normally fails to compile. Checking this option allows the following code fragment to compile:

```
struct __huge A
{
virtual void f();  // A vtable is required to see the error.
};
struct __far B  :  public A
{
};
// Error: Attempting to derive a far class from the huge base 'A'.
```

Default = OFF

## Virtual base pointers

When a class inherits virtually from a base class, the compiler stores a hidden pointer in the class object to access the virtual base class subobject.

The Virtual Base Pointers options specify options about the hidden pointer.

### Always near

Command-line equivalent: **-Vb-**

When the Always Near option is on, the hidden pointer will always be a near pointer. (When a class inherits virtually from a base class, the compiler stores a *hidden pointer* in the class object to access the virtual base class subobject.)

This option allows for the smallest and most efficient code.

### Same size as 'this' pointer

Command-line equivalent: **-Vb**

When the Same Size as 'this' Pointer option is on, the compiler matches the size of the hidden pointer to the size of the **this** pointer in the instance class.

This allows for compatibility with previous versions of the compiler.

Default = Always Near (**-Vb-**)

## Vtable pointer follows data members

Command-line equivalent -**Vt**

When this option is enabled, the compiler places the virtual table pointer after any nonstatic data members of the specified class.

This option insures compatibility when class instances are shared with non-C++ code and when sharing classes with code compiled with previous versions of Borland C++.

Default = OFF

# Exception handling / RTTI

Use the Exceptions Handling options to enable or disable exception handling and to tell the compiler how to handle the generation of run-time type information.

If you use exception handling constructs in your code and compile with exceptions disabled, you'll get an error.

## Enable exceptions

Command-line equivalent: -**x**

When this option is enabled, C++ exception handling is enabled. If this option is disabled (-**x**-) and you attempt to use exception handling routines in your code, the compiler generates error messages during compilation.

Disabling this option makes it easier for you to remove exception handling information from programs; this might be useful if you are porting your code to other platforms or compilers.

**Note**   Disabling this option turns off only the compilation of exception handling code; your application can still include exception code if you link .OBJ and library files that were built with exceptions enabled (such as the Borland standard libraries).

Default = ON

## Enable run-time type information

Command-line equivalent: -**RT**

This option causes the compiler to generate code that allows run-time type identification.

In general, if you set Enable Destructor Cleanup (-**xd**), you will need to set this option as well.

Default = ON

### Enable compatible exceptions
Command-line equivalent: -**xc**, 16-bit only

This option allows .EXEs and .DLLs built with Borland C++ to be compatible with executables built with other products. When Enable Compatible Exceptions is disabled, some exception handling information is included in the .EXE, which could cause compatibility issues.

**Note**  Libraries that can be linked into .DLLs need to be built with this option enabled.

Default = OFF

### Enable destructor cleanup
Command-line equivalent: **-xd**

When this option is enabled and an exception is thrown, destructors are called for all automatically declared objects between the scope of the catch and throw statements.

In general, when you enable this option, you should also set Enable Runtime Type Information (**-RT**) as well.

**Note**  Destructors are not automatically called for dynamic objects allocated with **new**, and dynamic objects are not automatically freed.

Default = ON

### Enable exception location information
Command-line equivalent: **-xp**

When this option is enabled, run-time identification of exceptions is available because the compiler provides the file name and source-code line number where the exception occurred. This enables the program to query file and line number from where a C++ exception was thrown.

Default = OFF

### Enable fast exception prologs
Command-line equivalent: **-xf**

When this option is enabled, inline code is expanded for every exception handling function. This option improves performance at the cost of larger executable file sizes.

**Note**  If you select both Fast Exception Prologs and Enable Compatible Exceptions (**-xc**), fast prologs will be generated but Enable Compatible Exceptions will be disabled (the two options are not compatible).

Default = OFF

## General

### Zero-length empty base classes
Command-line equivalent: **-Ve**

Usually the size of a class is at least one byte, even if the class does not define any data members. When this option is enabled, the compiler ignores this unused byte for the memory layout and the total size of any derived classes.

Default = OFF

# Member pointers

Use C++ Member Pointers options to direct member pointers and affect how the compiler treats explicit casts.

## Honor precision of member pointers

Command-line equivalent: **-Vmp**

When this option is enabled, the compiler uses the declared precision for member pointer types. Use this option when a pointer to a derived class is explicitly cast as a pointer-to-member of a simpler base class (when the pointer is actually pointing to a derived class member).

Default = OFF

## Member pointer representation

The C++ Member Pointers options specify what member pointers can point to.

### Smallest for class

Command-line equivalent: **-Vmd**

When this option is enabled, member pointers use the smallest possible representation that allows member pointers to point to all members of their particular class. If the class is not fully defined at the point where the member pointer type is declared, the most general representation is chosen by the compiler and a warning is issued.

Default = OFF

### Support all cases

Command-line equivalent: **-Vmv**

When this option is enabled, the compiler places no restrictions on where member pointers can point. Member pointers use the most general (but not always the most efficient) representation.

Default = ON

### Support multiple inheritance

Command-line equivalent: **-Vmm**

When this option is enabled, member pointers can point to members of multiple inheritance classes (with the exception of virtual base classes).

Default = OFF

### Support single inheritance

Command-line equivalent: **-Vms**

When this option is enabled, member pointers can point only to members of base classes that use single inheritance.

Default = OFF

# Templates

Use the options under C++ Options | Templates to tell the compiler how to generate template instances in C++.

## Templates instance generation

The Template Instance Generation options specify how the compiler generates template instances in C++.

### External
Command-line equivalent: **-Jgx**

When the External option is on, the compiler generates external references to all template instances.

When you use this option, all template instances in your code must be publicly defined in another module with the external option (**-Jgd**) so that external references are properly resolved.

Default = OFF

### Global
Command-line equivalent: **-Jgd**

When the Global option is on, the compiler generates public (global) definitions for all template instances.

The Global option does not merge duplicates. If the same template instance is generated more than once, the linker reports public symbol re-definition errors.

Default = OFF

### Smart
Command-line equivalent: **-Jg**

When the Smart option is enabled, the compiler generates public (global) definitions for all template instances. If more than one module generates the same template instance, the linker automatically merges duplicates to produce a single copy of the instance.

To generate the instances, the compiler must have available the function body (in the case of a template function) or the bodies of member functions and definitions for static data members (in the case of a template class), typically in a header file.

This is a convenient way of generating template instances.

Default = ON

# Virtual Tables

C++ Options | Virtual Tables options control C++ virtual tables and the expansion of inline functions when debugging.

## Virtual tables linkage

The C++ Virtual Tables options control C++ virtual tables and the expansion of inline functions when debugging.

### External

Command-line equivalent: **-V0**

You use the External option to generate external references to virtual tables. If you don't want to use the Smart or Local options, use the External and Public options to produce and reference global virtual tables.

**Note**   When you use this option, one or more of the modules comprising the program must be compiled with the Public option to supply the definitions for the virtual tables.

Default = OFF

### Local

Command-line equivalent: **-Vs**

You use the Local option to generate local virtual tables (and out-of-line inline functions) so that each module gets its own private copy of each virtual table or inline function it uses.

The Local option uses only standard .OBJ and .ASM constructs, but produces larger executables.

Default = OFF

### Public

Command-line equivalent: **-V1**

Public produces public definitions for virtual tables. When using the External option (**-V0**), at least one of the modules in the program must be compiled with the Public option to supply the definitions for the virtual tables. All other modules should be compiled with the External option to refer to that Public copy of the virtual tables.

Default = OFF

### Smart

Command-line equivalent: **-V**

This option generates common C++ virtual tables and out-of-line inline functions across the modules in your application. As a result, only one instance of a given virtual table or out-of-line inline function is included in the program.

The Smart option generates the smallest and most efficient executables, but produces .OBJ and .ASM files compatible only with TLINK and TASM.

Default = ON

# Compiler options

Compiler options are common to all C and C++ programs. They directly affect how the compiler generates code.

## Defines

Command-line equivalent: **–D*name*** and **–D*name*=*string***

The macro definition capability of Borland C++ lets you define and undefine macros (also called *manifest* or *symbolic* constants) in the IDE or on the command line. The macros you define override those defined in your source files.

### Defining macros from the IDE

Preprocessor definitions (such as those used in **#if** statements and macro definitions) can be entered on the Compiler Defines page. The following rules apply when using the Defines input box:

Separate multiple definitions with semicolons (;), and assign values with an equal sign (=). For example:

```
Switch1;Switch2;Switch3=OFF
```

- Leading and trailing spaces are stripped, but embedded spaces are left intact.
- If you want to include a semicolon in a macro, precede the semicolon with a backslash (\).

### Defining macros on the command line

On the command line, the **-D*name*** option defines the identifier *name* to the null string. **-D*name*=*string*** defines *name* to *string*. In this assignment, *string* cannot contain spaces or tabs. You can also define multiple **#define** options on the command line using either of the following methods:

Include multiple definitions after a single **-D** option by separating each define with a semicolon (;) and assigning values with an equal sign (=). For example:

```
BCC.EXE -Dxxx;yyy=1;zzz=NO MYFILE.C
```

Include multiple **-D** options, separating each with a space. For example:

```
BCC.EXE -Dxxx -Dyyy=1 -Dzzz=NO MYFILE.C
```

## Code generation

Compiler Code Generation options affect how code is generated.

## Allocate enums as ints

Command-line equivalent: **-b**

When the Allocate Enums As Ints option is on, the compiler always allocates a whole word (a two-byte **int** for 16-bits or a four-byte **int** for 32-bits) for enumeration types (variables of type **enum**).

When this option is off (**-b-**), the compiler allocates the smallest integer that can hold the enumeration values: the compiler allocates an **unsigned** or **signed char** if the values of the enumeration are within the range of 0 to 255 (minimum) or -128 to 127 (maximum), or an **unsigned** or **signed short** if the values of the enumeration are within the following ranges:

   0 to 65,535 (minimum) or -32,768 to 32,767 (maximum) (16-bit)

The compiler allocates a a two-byte **int** (16-bit) or a four-byte **int** (32-bit) to represent the enumeration values if any value is out of range.

Default = ON

## Duplicate strings merged

Command-line equivalent: **-d**

When you check the Duplicate Strings Merged option, the compiler merges two literal strings when one matches another. This produces smaller programs (at the expense of a slightly longer compile time), but can introduce errors if you modify one string.

Default = OFF (**-d-**)

## fastthis

Command-line equivalent: **-po**, 16-bit only

This option causes the compiler to use the _ _**fastthis** calling convention when passing the **this** pointer to member functions. The **this** pointer is passed in a register (or a register pair in 16-bit large data models). Likewise, calls to member functions load the register (or register pair) with **this**. Note that you can use _ _**fastthis** to compile specific functions in this manner.

When **this** is a 'near' (16-bit) pointer, it is supplied in the SI register; for 'far' **this** pointers, DS:SI is used. If necessary, the compiler saves and restores DS. All references in the member function to member data are done via the SI register.

The names of member functions compiled with _ _**fastthis** are mangled differently from non-fastthis member functions, to prevent mixing the two. It is easiest to compile all classes with _ _**fastthis**, but you can compile some classes with _ _**fastthis** and some without, as in the following example:

```
// no -po on the command-line
class X;
#pragma option -po
class Y      //Y will use fastthis
{
...
```

```
    };
    class X        //X will not use fastthis,
    {              //since its class declaration
                   //appeared before fastthis was turned on
    ...
    };
    #pragma option -po-
```

**Note**    If you use a makefile to build a version of the class library that has _ _**fastthis** enabled, you must define _CLASSLIB_ALLOW_po and use the **-po** option. The _CLASSLIB_ALLOW_po macro can be defined in BORLANDC\INCLUDE\ SERVICES\borlandc.h.

If you use a makefile to build a _ _fastthis version of the runtime library, you must define _RTL_ALLOW_po and use the **-po** option.

If you rebuild the libraries and use **-po** without defining the appropriate macro, the linker emits undefined symbol errors.

```
    Default = OFF
```

## Register variables

These options suppress or enable the use of register variables.

### Automatic
Command-line equivalent: **-r**

Choose Automatic to tell the compiler to automatically assign register variables if possible, even when you do not specify a register variable by using the register type specifier.

Generally, you can keep this option set to Automatic unless you are interfacing with preexisting assembly code that does not support register variables.

Default = Automatic (**-r**)

### None
Command-line equivalent: **-r-**

Choose None to tell the compiler not to use register variables even if you have used the **register** keyword.

### Register keyword
Command-line equivalent: **-rd**

Choose Register Keyword to tell the compiler to use register variables only if you use the **register** keyword and a register is available. Use this option or the Automatic option (**-r**) to optimize the use of registers.

**Note**    You can use **-rd** in **#pragma** options.

## Unsigned characters

Command-line equivalent: **-K**

When the Unsigned Characters option is on, the compiler treats all **char** declarations as if they were **unsigned char** type, which provides compatibility with other compilers.

Default = OFF (**char** declarations default to **signed**; **-K-**)

# Floating point

The Floating Point options specify how the compiler handles floating-point numbers in your code.

## Correct Pentium FDIV flaw

Command-line equivalent: **-fp**

Some early Pentium chips do not perform specific floating-point division calculations with full precision. Although your chances of encountering this problem are slim, this switch inserts code that emulates floating-point division so that you are assured of the correct result. This option decreases your program's FDIV instruction performance.

**Note**     Use of this option only corrects FDIV instructions in modules that you compile. The run-time library also contains FDIV instructions which are not modified by the use of this switch. To correct the run-time libraries, you must recompile them using this switch.

The following functions use FDIV instructions in assembly language which are not corrected if you use this option

| | | |
|---|---|---|
| acos | cosh | pow101 |
| acos | coshi | owl |
| asin | cosi | sin |
| asini | exp | sinh |
| atan | expl | sinhl |
| atan2 | fmod | sinl |
| atan21 | [pow | tahn |
| cos | pow10 | tanh |
| tanl | | |

In addition, this switch does not correct functions that convert a floating-point number to or from a string (such as printf or scanf).

Default = OFF

## Fast floating point

Command-line equivalent: **-ff**

When Fast Floating Point is on, floating-point operations are optimized without regard to explicit or implicit type conversions. Calculations can be faster than under ANSI operating mode.

When this option is unchecked (**-ff-**), the compiler follows strict ANSI rules regarding floating-point conversions.

Default = OFF

## No floating point

Command-line equivalent: **-f-**

Choose No Floating Point if you are not using floating point. No floating-point libraries are linked when this option is enabled (**-f-**). If you enable this option and use floating-point calculations in your program, you will get link errors. When unchecked (**-f**), the compiler emulates 80x87 calls at runtime.

Default = OFF (**-f**)

# Compiler output

Set control of object file contents on the Compiler Output page.

## Autodependency information

Command-line equivalent: **-X-**

When the Autodependency option is checked (**-X-**), the compiler generates autodependency information for all project files with a .C or .CPP extension.

The Project Manager can use autodependency information to speed up compilation times. The Project Manager opens the .OBJ file and looks for information about files included in the source code. This information is always placed in the .OBJ file when the source module is compiled. After that, the time and date of every file that was used to build the .OBJ file is checked against the time and date information in the .OBJ file. The source file is recompiled if the dates are different. This is called an autodependency check.

If the project file contains valid dependency information, the Project Manager does the autodependency check using that information. This is much faster than reading each .OBJ file.

When this option is unchecked (**-X**), the compiler does not generate the autodependency information.

Modules compiled with autodependency information can use Make's autodependency feature.

Default = ON (**-X-**)

## Generate COMDEFs

Command-line equivalent: **-Fc**, 16-bit only

Generate COMDEFs generates communal variables (COMDEFs) for global C variables that are not initialized and not declared as **static** or **extern**. Use this option when header files included in several source files contain global variables.

For example, a definition such as

```
int SomeArray[256];
```

could appear in a header file that is then included in many modules. When this option is on, the compiler generates *SomeArray* as a communal variable rather than a public definition (a COMDEF record rather than a PUBDEF record). You can use this option when porting code that uses a similar feature with another implementation.

The linker generates only one instance of the variable, so it will not be a duplicate definition linker error. As long as a given variable does not need to be initialized to a nonzero value, you do not need to include a definition for it in any of the source files.

Default = OFF

## Generate underscores

Command-line equivalent: **-u**

When the Generate Underscores option is on, the compiler automatically adds an underscore character (_) in front of every global identifier (functions and global variables) before saving them in the object module. Pascal identifiers (those modified by the _ _**pascal** keyword) are converted to uppercase and are not prefixed with an underscore.

Underscores for C and C++ are optional, but you should turn this option on to avoid errors if you are linking with the standard Borland C++ libraries.

Default = ON

# Source

Compiler | Source options set source code interpretation.

## Identifier length

Command-line equivalent: **-i*n***, where *n* = significant characters

Use the Identifier Length input box to specify the number of significant characters (those which will be recognized by the compiler) in an identifier.

Except in C++, which recognizes identifiers of unlimited length, all identifiers are treated as distinct only if their significant characters are distinct. This includes variables, preprocessor macro names, and structure member names.

Valid numbers for *n* are 0, and 8 to 250, where 0 means use the maximum identifier length of 250.

By default, Borland C++ uses 250 characters per identifier. Other systems (including some UNIX compilers) ignore characters beyond the first eight. If you are porting to other environments, you might want to compile your code with a smaller number of significant characters, which helps you locate name conflicts in long identifiers that have been truncated.

Default = 250

## Language compliance

The Language Compliance options tell the compiler how to recognize keywords in your programs.

### ANSI

Command-line equivalent: **-A**

The ANSI option compiles C and C++ ANSI-compatible code, allowing for maximum portability. Non-ANSI keywords are ignored as keywords.

### Borland extensions

Command-line equivalents: **-A-, -AT**

The Borland Extensions option tells the compiler to recognize Borland's extensions to the C language keywords, including **near**, **far**, **huge**, **asm**, **cdecl**, **pascal**, **interrupt**, **_export**, **_ds**, **_cs**, **_ss**, **_es**, and the register pseudovariables (**_AX**, **_BX**, and so on). For a complete list of keywords, see the keyword index.

### Kernighan and Ritchie

Command-line equivalent: -AK

The Kernighan and Ritchie option tells the compiler to recognize only the K&R extension keywords and treat any of Borland's C++ extension keywords as normal identifiers.

If you get declaration syntax errors from your source code, check that this option is set to Borland Extensions.

Default = Borland Extensions (**-A-**)

### UNIX V

Command-line equivalent: **-AU**

The UNIX V option tells the compiler to recognize only UNIX V keywords and treat any of Borland's C++ extension keywords as normal identifiers.

## MFC compatibility

Command-line equivalents: **-VF**

Turn this option on to compile code that is compatible with the Microsoft Foundation Classes (MFC). Among other things, the compiler makes the following adjustments to be compatible with MFC:

- Accepts spurious semicolons in a class scope.

- Allows anonymous structs.

- Uses the old-style scoping resolution in **for** loops.

- Allows methods to be declared with a calling convention, but leaves off the calling convention in the definition.

- Tries the operator **new** if it cannot resolve a call to the operator **new[ ]**.

- Lets you omit the operator & on member functions.

- Allows a const class that is passed by value to be treated as a trivial conversion, not as a user conversion.

- Allows you to use a cast to a member pointer as a selector for overload resolution, even if the qualifying type of the member pointer is not derived from the class in which the member function is declared.

- Accepts declarations with duplicate storage in a class, as in

  ```
  extern "C" typedef
  ```

- Accepts and ignores *#pragma comment(linker, "...")* directives.

Default = OFF

### Nested comments
Command-line equivalent: **-C**

When the Nested Comments option is on, you can nest comments in your C and C++ source files.

Nested comments are not allowed in standard C implementations, and they are not portable.

Default = OFF

## Debugging

Compiler Debugging options affect the generation of debug information during compilation. When linking larger .OBJ files, you may need to turn these options off to increase the available system resources.

### Browser reference information in OBJs
Command-line equivalent: **-R**

When the Browser Reference Info In OBJs option is on, the compiler generates additional browser-specific information such as location and reference information. This information is then included in your .OBJ files. In addition to this option, you need debugging information (**-v**) to use the Browser.

When this option is off, you can link and create larger object files. While this option does not affect execution speed, it does affect compilation time and program size.

Default = ON

## Debug information in OBJs

Command-line equivalent: **-v**

When the Debug Info In OBJs option is on, debugging information is included in your .OBJ files. The compiler passes this option to the linker so it can include the debugging information in the .EXE file. For debugging, this option treats C++ inline functions as normal functions.

You need debugging information to use either the integrated debugger or the standalone Turbo Debugger.

When this option is off (**-v-**), you can link and create larger object files. While this option does not affect execution speed, it does affect compilation and link time.

**Note**    When Line Numbers is on, make sure you turn off Jump Optimization in the 16-bit specific optimizations and Pentium scheduling in the 32-bit Compiler options. When these options are enabled, the source code will not exactly match the generated machine instructions, which can make stepping through code confusing.

Default = ON

## Line numbers

Command-line equivalent: **-y**

When the Line Numbers option is on, the compiler automatically includes line numbers in the object and object map files. Line numbers are used by both the integrated debugger and Turbo Debugger.

Although the Debug Info in OBJs option (**-v**) automatically generates line number information, you can turn that option off (**-v-**) and turn on Line Numbers (**-y**) to reduce the size of the debug information generated. With this setup, you can still step and trace, but you will not be able to watch or inspect data items.

Including line numbers increases the size of the object and map files but does not affect the speed of the executable program.

**Note**    When Line Numbers is on, make sure you turn off Jump Optimization in the 16-bit specific optimizations and Pentium scheduling in the 32-bit Compiler options. When these options are enabled, the source code will not exactly match the generated machine instructions, which can make stepping through code confusing.

Default = OFF

## Out-of-line inline functions

Command-line equivalent: **-vi**

When the Out-of-Line Inline Functions option is on, the compiler expands C++ inline functions inline.

To control the expansion of inline functions, the Debug Information In OBJs option (**-v**) acts slightly differently for C++ code: when inline function expansion is disabled, inline functions are generated and called like any other function.

Because debugging with inline expansion can be difficult, the command-line compilers provide the following options:

- **-v** turns debugging on and inline expansion off
- **-v-** turns debugging off and inline expansion on
- **-vi** turns inline expansion off (no inline substitution will occur)
- **-vi-** turns inline expansion on

For example, if you want to turn both debugging and inline expansion on, use the **-v** and **-vi-** options.

Default = OFF

## Standard stack frame

Command-line equivalent: **-k**

When the Standard Stack Frame option is on, the compiler generates a standard stack frame (standard function entry and exit code). This is helpful when debugging, since it simplifies the process of tracing through the stack of called subroutines.

When this option is off, any function that does not use local variables and has no parameters is compiled with abbreviated entry and return code. This makes the code smaller and faster.

The Standard Stack Frame option should always be on when you compile a source file for debugging.

Default = ON

## Test Stack Overflow

Command-line equivalent: **-N**, 16-bit only

When the this option is on, the compiler generates stack overflow logic at the entry of each function.

Even though this is costly in terms of both program size and speed, it can be a real help when trying to track down difficult stack overflow bugs. If an overflow is detected, the run-time error message `Stack overflow!` is generated, and the program exits with an exit code of 1.

**Note** Stack overflow testing is always enabled in the 32-bit compilers (this adds a minimal overhead to 32-bit programs).

Default = OFF

## Precompiled headers

Using precompiled header files can dramatically increase compilation speed by storing an image of the symbol table on disk in a file, then later reloading that file from disk instead of parsing all the header files again. Directly loading the symbol table from disk is much faster than parsing the text of header files, especially if several source files include the same header file.

## Cache precompiled header

Command-line equivalent: **-Hc**

When you enable this option, the compiler caches the precompiled headers it generates. This is useful when you are precompiling more than one header file.

**Note**    To use this option, you must also enable the Generate and Use (**-H**) precompiled header option.

Default = OFF

## Precompiled header name

Command-line equivalent: **-H=***filename*

This option lets you specify the name of your precompiled header file. The compilers set the name of the precompiled header to *filename*.

When this option is enabled, the compilers generate and use the precompiled header file that you specify.

## Precompiled headers

Using precompiled headers can dramatically increase compilation speeds, though they require a considerable amount of disk space.

### Do not generate or use

Command-line equivalent: **-H-**

When the Do Not Generate Or Use option is on, the compilers do not generate or use precompiled headers.

Default = Do not generate or use (**-H-**)

### Generate and use

Command-line equivalent: **-H**

When this option is enabled, the IDE generates and uses precompiled headers. The default file name is *<projectname>*.CSM for IDE projects and BCDEF.CSM (16-bit) or BC32DEF.CSM (32-bit) for the command-line compilers.

### Use but do not generate

Command-line equivalent: **-Hu**

When the Use But Do Not Generate option is on, the compilers use preexisting precompiled header files; new precompiled header files are not generated.

### Stop precompiling after header file

Command-line equivalent: **-H"*xxx* "**; for example **-H"owl/owlpch.h"**

This option terminates compiling the precompiled header after the compiler compiles the file specified as *xxx*. You can use this option to reduce the amount of disk space used by precompiled headers.

When you use this option, the file you specify must be included from a source file for the compiler to generate a .CSM file.

**Note**  You cannot specify a header file that is included from another header file. For example, you cannot list a header included by windows.h because this would cause the precompiled header file to be closed before the compilation of windows.h was competed.

# Directories options

The Directories options tell the Borland C++ compiler where to find or where to put header files, library files, source code, output files, and other program elements.

## Source directories

The Source Directories options let you specify the directories that contain your standard include files, library and .OBJ files, and program source files.

### Include

Command-line equivalent: **-I*path*,** where *path* = directory path

Use the Include list box to specify the drive and/or directories that contain program include files. Standard include files are those given in angle brackets (<>) in an **#include** statement (for example, **#include <myfile>**).

**Note**  The Borland compilers and linkers use specific file search algorithms to locate the files needed to complete the compilation and link cycles.

### Library

Command-line equivalent: **-L*path*,** where *path* = directory path

Use the Library list box to specify the directories that contain the Borland C++ IDE startup object files (C0*x*.OBJ), run-time library files (.LIB files), and all other .LIB files. By default, the linker looks for them in the directory containing the project file (or in the current directory if you're using the command-line compiler).

**Note**  You can also use the linker option **/L*path*** to specify the library search directories when you link files from the command line.

### Source

The Source list box specifies the directories where the compiler and the integrated debugger should look for your project source files.

## Specifying multiple directories

Multiple directory names are allowed in each of the list boxes; use a semicolon (;) to separate the specified drives and directories. To display a history list of previously entered directory names, click the down-arrow icon or press Alt+Down arrow.

From the command line, you can enter multiple include and library directories in the following ways:

- You can stack multiple entries with a single **-L** or **-I** option by separating directories with a semicolon:

  ```
  BCC.EXE -Ldirname1;dirname2;dirname3 -Iinc1;inc2;inc3 myfile.c
  ```

- You can place more than one of each option on the command line, like this:

  ```
  BCC.EXE -Ldirname1 -Ldirname2 -Iinc1 -Iinc2 -Iinc3 myfile.c
  ```

- You can mix listings:

  ```
  BCC.EXE -Ldirname1;dirname2 -Iinc1 -Ld:dirname3 -Iinc2;inc3 myfile.c
  ```

If you list multiple **-L** or **-I** options on the command line, the result is cumulative; the compiler searches all the directories listed in order from left to right.

# File search algorithms

## #include-file search algorithms

Borland C++ searches for files included in your source code with the **#include** directive in the following ways:

If you specify a path and/or directory with your include statement, Borland C++ searches only the location specified. For example, if you have the following statement in your code:

```
#include "c:\bc\include\owl\owl.h"
```

the header file owl.h must reside in the directory C:\BC\INCLUDE\OWL. In addition, if you use the statement:

```
#include <owl\owl.h>
```

and you set the Include option (**-I**) to specify the path c:\bc\include, the file owl.h must reside in C:\BC\INCLUDE\OWL, and not in C:\BC\INCLUDE or C:\OWL.

- If you put an **#include <somefile>** statement in your source code, Borland C++ searches for "somefile" only in the directories specified with the Include (**-I**) option.

- If you put an **#include "somefile"** statement in your code, Borland C++ first searches for "somefile" in the current directory; if it does not find the file there, it then searches in the directories specified with the Include (**-I**) option.

## Library file search algorithms

- The library file search algorithms are similar to those for include files:

- Implicit libraries: Borland C++ searches for implicit libraries only in the specified library directories; this is similar to the search algorithm for `#include <somefile>`.

  Implicit library files are the ones Borland C++ automatically links in and the start-up object file (C0x.OBJ). To see these files in the Project Manager, turn on run-time nodes (choose Options | Environment | Project View, then check Show Runtime Nodes).

- Explicit libraries: Where Borland C++ searches for explicit (user-specified) libraries depends in part on how you list the library file name. Explicit library files are ones you list on the command line or in a project file; these are file names with a .LIB extension.

  - If you list an explicit library file name with no drive or directory (like this: mylib.lib), Borland C++ first searches for that library in the current directory. If the first search is unsuccessful, Borland C++ looks in the directories specified with the Library (**-L**) option. This is similar to the search algorithm for `#include "somefile"`.

  - If you list a user-specified library with drive and/or directory information (like this: c:\mystuff\mylib1.lib), Borland C++ searches only in the location you explicitly listed as part of the library path name and not in any specified library directories.

## Output Directories

The Output Directories options specify the directories where your .OBJ, .EXE, .DLL, and .MAP files are placed. The Borland C++ IDE looks for those directories when performing a make or run and to check dates and times of .OBJs, .EXEs, and .DLLs. If the entry is blank, the files are stored in the current directory.

Click the down-arrow icon or press *Alt+Down* arrow to display the history list of previously entered directory names.

### Intermediate

Use the Intermediate list box to specify where Borland C++ places object (.OBJ) and map (.MAP) files when it builds your project. This is also the directory where a tool (such as Resource Workshop) places any temporary files that it might create.

### Final

Command-line equivalent: **-n*path***, where *path* = directory path

The Final list box specifies the location where the IDE places the generated target files (for example, .EXE and .DLL files).

### Guidelines for entering directory names

Use the following guidelines when entering directories in the Directories options pages.

- You must separate multiple directory path names (if allowed) with a semicolon (;).

- You can use up to a maximum of 127 characters (including white space).

- White space before and after the semicolon is allowed but not required.

- Relative and absolute path names are allowed, including path names relative to the logged position in drives other than the current one.

For example:

```
C:\;C:..\BORLAND\BC;D:\myprog\source
```

# Librarian options

Librarian options affect the behavior of the built-in librarian. The built-in librarian combines the .OBJ files in your project into .LIB files. Options in this section control that process. In addition, you can cause the librarian to generate a list (.LST) file containing the .OBJs in a generated .LIB and the functions those .OBJs contain.

TLIB.EXE is the command-line librarian.

## Case-sensitive library

Command-line equivalent = /C

When the Case-Sensitive Library option is on, the librarian treats case as significant in all symbols in the library. For example, if Case-Sensitive Library is checked, "CASE", "Case", and "case" are all treated as different symbols.

## Create extended dictionary

Command-line equivalent = /E

When the Create Extended Dictionary option is on, the librarian includes, in compact form, additional information that helps the linker process library files faster.

## Generate list file

When the Generate List File option is on, the librarian automatically produces a list file (.LST) that lists the contents of your library when it is created.

## Library page size

Command-line equivalent = /Psize, where size is number of pages

The Library Page Size input box is where you set the number of bytes in each library "page" (dictionary entry).

The page size determines the maximum size of the library. Page size must be a power of 2 between 16 and 32,768 inclusive. The default page size of 16 allows a library of about 1 MB in size.

To create a larger library, change the page size to the next higher value (32).

## Purge comment records

Command-line equivalent = /0

When the Purge Comment Records option is on, the librarian removes all comment records from modules added to the library.

# Linker options

Linker options affect how an application is linked.

Linker options let you control how intermediate files (.OBJ, .LIB, and .RES) are combined into executables (.EXE) and dynamic-link libraries (.DLL). For most options in this section, you will usually want to keep the default settings.

## 16-bit linker

16-bit Linker options tell the linker how to link 16-bit programs.

### Discard nonresident name table
Command-line equivalent = **/Gn**, 16-bit only

When the Discard Nonresident Name Table option is enabled, the linker does not emit the nonresident name table. The resultant image will contain only the module description in the nonresident names table.

See Transfer resident names to nonresident names table for usage details.

Default = OFF

### Enable 32-bit processing
Command-line equivalent = **/3**, 16-bit only

The Enable 32-bit processing option lets you link 32-bit DOS object modules produced by TASM or a compatible assembler. This option increases the memory requirements for TLINK and slows down linking.

Default = OFF

### Inhibit optimizing far call to near
Command-line equivalent = **/f**, 16-bit only

When the linker patches two code segments together, and far calls are made from one to the other, the linker will optimize the code by converting the far calls to near calls. When Inhibit Optimizing Far Call To Near is enabled, this optimization does not occur.

You might want to enable this option when you experience run-time crashes that appear to be related to corrupt virtual tables. Because virtual tables reside in the code segment, their contents can sometimes be interpreted by the linker as one of these far calls.

Default = OFF

## Initialize segments

Command-line equivalent = **/i**, 16-bit only

When the Initialize Segments option is on, the linker initializes uninitialized trailing segments to be output into the executable file even if the segments do not contain data records. This is normally not needed and will increase the size of your .EXE files.

Default = OFF

## Linker goodies

- Discard nonresident name table
- Transfer resident names to nonresident names table

## Segment alignment

Command-line equivalent = **/A:dd**, 16-bit only

Use the Segment Alignment input box to change the current byte value on which to align segments. The operating system seeks pages for loading based on this alignment value. You can enter numbers in the range of 2 to 65,535.

**Note**   The alignment factor is automatically rounded up to the nearest power of two. For example, if you enter 650, it is rounded up to 1,024 (this is different from the 32-bit Segment Alignment option).

For efficiency, you should use the smallest value that still allows for correct segment offsets in the segment table.

Default = 512

## Transfer resident names to nonresident names table

Command-line equivalent = **/Gr**, 16-bit only

This option causes the linker to copy all names in the resident names table which have not been specified as RESIDENTNAME in the .DEF file to the nonresident names table. The resultant image contains only the module name and the symbol names of the exported symbols that were specified as RESIDENTNAME in the .DEF file.

When you use this option, you must also specify the WEP entry point as a RESIDENTNAME in the EXPORTS section of the .DEF file (Windows obtains the WEP entry point for this symbol by looking it up in the resident names table).

**Note**   When building .DLLs that contain many exports, it's possible to exceed the 64K header file limitation. Because the .DLL contains the resident names table in its header, moving the exports out of the header using the **/Gr** option usually remedies this problem. The **/Gr** option causes the linker to transfer the names in the resident names table to the nonresident names table. Names in the nonresident names table are then assigned ordinal numbers, which your .EXE file uses when referencing the entry points in the .DLL.

There are two ways to create input files for the linker:

- Run IMPLIB on the .DLL to create an import library for linking purposes.
- Run IMPDEF in the .DLL to create a .DEF file for linking purposes.

Once the import library or .DEF file has been created, there is no need to keep the names in either the resident or the nonresident names tables. Relinking the .DLL and specifying both the Transfer Resident Names to Nonresident Names Table (**/Gr**) and Discard Nonresident Name Table (**/Gn**) options causes the linker to build a .DLL with an "empty" names table. Not only does this post-processing avoid the problem of exceeding the header limitation, but it also creates a .DLL that loads faster (because it's smaller) and runs faster (because references to entry points are by ordinal number instead of by name).

To summarize this process, you must

1  Enable the **/Gr** switch to transfer the names in the resident names table to the nonresident names table. This also assigns ordinal numbers to the names. However, before doing so, make sure you have included a .DEF file with the following export definition in the EXPORTS section:

```
EXPORTS
    WEP @1 RESIDENTNAME
```

2  Build the .DLL.

3  Run IMPLIB or IMPDEF on the new .DLL file.

4  Enable the **/Gn** switch (along with the already enabled **/Gr** switch).

5  Relink the .DLL.

To see an example of this process, refer to the makefile that builds the ObjectWindows example programs.

Default = OFF

# 16-bit optimizations

The 16-bit Optimizations control how the linker optimizes 16-bit .EXE programs. In most cases the final executable file size is reduced, which results in a faster load time.

Whenever you use one or more of these options, the linker reorders the .EXE segments as follows:

- PRELOAD segments
- PRELOAD resources
- LOAD ON CALL segments
- LOAD ON CALL resources

**Note**  These options work only with 16-bit Windows and DPMI programs.

## Chain fixups
Command-line equivalent = **/Oc**, 16-bit only

Chain fixups removes duplicate and/or unnecessary fixup data from the .EXE file. This is done by emitting only one fixup record for each unique internal fixup and "remembering" the duplicate fixups by creating a linked list of the internal fixup locations within the .EXE data segment. When the loader loads the .EXE, it applies the fixup specified in the fixup record to each of the locations specified in the linked list. Specifying this optimization also causes trailing zeros in data segments to be eliminated. This usually results in a significantly smaller .EXE file, which loads faster.

Default = OFF

### Iterate data

Command-line equivalent = **/Oi**, 16-bit only

This option scans data segments for patterns of data (for example, a block with 128 bytes filled with "0"). Instead of emitting the data, TLINK emits a "description" of the block of data which matches the pattern (for example, a 5-byte descriptor specifying a 128 bytes of 0). Specifying this optimization also causes trailing zeros in data segments to be eliminated. This usually results in a significantly smaller .EXE file, which loads faster.

Default = OFF

### Minimize resource alignment

Command-line equivalent = **/Or**, 16-bit only

This optimization switch is the same as the Minimize segment alignment switch (**/Oa**), except that it applies to resource alignment values instead of segment alignment values.

Default = OFF

### Minimize segment alignment

Command-line equivalent = **/Oa**, 16-bit only

This optimization switch determines the minimum segment alignment value by examining the size of the .EXE file. An .EXE that has a size of 1 byte to 64K bytes results in an alignment value of 1; if the .EXE file size is 64K+1 bytes to 128K bytes, the alignment value is 2; and so on.

While this optimization results in a smaller .EXE file, the .EXE might load slower because the newly calculated alignment value may cause the segments to cross physical disk sector boundaries more often. Unless you have also specified the Segment Alignment (**/A**) linker option, the linker initially generates an .EXE using the default alignment value of 512. Note that this option overrides whatever alignment value the linker might have used to initially generate the .EXE file.

Default = OFF

# 32-bit linker

32-bit Linker options tell the linker how to link 32-bit programs.

## Allow import by ordinal

Command-line equivalent = /o, 32-bit only

This option lets you import by ordinal value instead of by the import name. When you specify this option, the linker emits only the ordinal numbers (and not the import names) to the resident or nonresident name table for those imports that have an ordinal number specified. If you do not specify this option, the linker ignores all ordinal numbers contained in import libraries or the .DEF file, and emits the import names to the resident and nonresident tables.

**Note**    This option is different than the 16-bit /o (overlays) option.

## Committed stack size (in hexadecimal)

Command-line equivalent = /Sc:xxxx, 32-bit only

Specifies the size of the committed stack in hexadecimal. The minimum allowable value for this field is 4K (0x1000) and any value specified must be equal to or less than the Reserved Stack Size setting (/S).

**Note**    Specifying the committed stack size here overrides any STACKSIZE setting in a module definition file.

The command-line version of this option (/Sc:xxxx) accepts hexadecimal numbers as the stack reserve value.

Default = 8K (0x2000)

## Committed stack size (in hexadecimal)

Command-line equivalent = /Hc:xxxx, 32-bit only

Specifies the size of the committed heap in hexadecimal. The minimum allowable value for this field is 0 and any value specified must be equal to or less than the Reserved Heap Size setting (/H).

**Note**    Specifying the committed heap size here overrides any HEAPSIZE setting in a module definition file.

The command-line version of this option (/Hc:xxxx) accepts hexadecimal numbers as the stack reserve value.

Default = 4K (0x1000)

## File alignment (in hexadecimal)

Command-line equivalent = /Af:xxxx, 32-bit only

The File Alignment option specifies page alignment for code and data within the executable file. The linker uses the file alignment value when it writes the various objects and sections (such as code and data) to the file. For example, if you use the default value of 0x200, the linker stores the section of the image on 512-byte boundaries within the executable file.

When using this option, you must specify a file alignment value that is a power of 2, with the smallest value being 16.

**Note** The old style of this option (**/A:dd**) is still supported for backward compatibility. With this option, the decimal number dd is multiplied by the power of 2 to calculate the file alignment value.

The command-line version of this option (**/Af:xxxx**) accepts either decimal or hexadecimal numbers as the file alignment value.

Default = 512 (0x200)

## Image base address (in hexadecimal)

Command-line equivalent = **/B:xxxx**, 32-bit only

The Image Base Address option specifies an image base address for an application, and is used in conjunction with the Image is Based option. If this setting is turned on, internal fixups are removed from the image and the requested load address of the first object in the application is set to the hexadecimal number specified. All successive objects are aligned on 64K linear address boundaries. This option makes applications smaller on disk and improves both load-time and run-time performance (the operating system no longer has to apply internal fixups).

The command-line version of this option (**/B:xxxx**) accepts either decimal or hexadecimal numbers as the image base address.

**Note** It is not recommended that you enable this option when producing a DLL. In addition, do not use the default setting of 0x400000 if you intend to run your application on Win32s systems.

Default = 0x400000 (recommended for true Win32 system applications)

## Image is based

The Image is Based option affects whether an application has an image base address. If this setting is turned on, internal fixups are removed from the image and the requested load address of the first object in the application is set to the number specified in the Image Base Address input box. Using this option can greatly reduce the size of your final application module; however, it is not recommended for use when producing a DLL.

Default = OFF

## Maximum linker errors

Command-line equivalent = **/Enn**

Specifies maximum errors the linker reports before terminating. **/E0** (default) reports an infinite number of errors (that is, as many as possible).

## Object alignment (in hexadecimal)

Command-line equivalent = **/Ao:xxxx**, 32-bit only

The linker uses the object alignment value to determine the virtual addresses of the various objects and sections (such as code and data) in your application. For example, if you specify an object alignment value of 8192, the linker aligns the virtual addresses of the sections in the image on 8192-byte (0x2000) boundaries.

When using this option, you must specify an object alignment value that is a power of 2, with the smallest value being 4096 (the default).

The command-line version of this option (**/Ao:xxxx**) accepts either decimal or hexadecimal numbers as the object alignment value.

Default = 4096 (0x1000)

### Reserved heap size (in hexadecimal)
Command-line equivalent = **/H:xxxx**, 32-bit only

Specifies the size of the reserved heap in hexadecimal. The minimum allowable value for this field is 0.

**Note**   Specifying the reserved heap size here overrides any HEAPSIZE setting in a module definition file.

The command-line version of this option (**/H:xxxx**) accepts hexadecimal numbers as the stack reserve value.

Default = 1Mb (0x1000000)

### Reserved stack size (in hexadecimal)
Command-line equivalent = **/S:xxxx**, 32-bit only

Specifies the size of the reserved stack in hexadecimal. The minimum allowable value for this field is 4K (0x1000).

**Note**   Specifying the reserved stack size here overrides any STACKSIZE setting in a module definition file.

The command-line version of this option (**/S:xxxx**) accepts hexadecimal numbers as the stack reserve value.

Default = 1Mb (0x1000000)

### Verbose
Command-line equivalent = **/r**, 32-bit only

This option causes the linker to emit messages that indicate what part of the link cycle is currently being executed by the linker. With this option turned on, the linker emits some or all of the following messages:

- Starting pass 1
- Generating map file
- Starting pass 2
- Reading resource files
- Linking resources

# General

Use the Linker | General options to include or exclude debugging information from your .EXE or .DLL. Debug information must be included in your program if you want to use the debugger (you can turn it off for production versions).

## Case-sensitive exports and imports

Command-line equivalent = /C, 16-bit only

When the Case-Sensitive Exports option is on, the linker is case sensitive when it processes the names in the IMPORTS and EXPORTS sections of the module definition file.

Use this option when you are trying to export non-callback functions from DLLs, as in exported C++ member functions or dynamic versions of ObjectWindows Library and BIDS.

Do not use this option for normal Windows callback functions (declared FAR PASCAL).

Default = OFF

## Case-sensitive link

Command-line equivalent = /c

When the Case-Sensitive Link option is enabled, the linker differentiates between upper and lower-case characters in public and external symbols. Normally, this option should be checked, since C and C++ are both case-sensitive languages.

Default = ON

### Code pack size

Command-line equivalent = /P=n, 16-bit only

Use Code Pack Size to change the default code-packing size to any value between 1 and 65,536. (On the command line, set n to a value between 1 and 65,536.)

You would probably want the limit to be a multiple of 4K under 386 enhanced mode because of the paging granularity of the system. Although the optimum segment size in 386 enhanced mode is 4K, the default code segment packing size is 8K because typical code segments are from 4K to 8K in size, and the default of 8K might pack more efficiently.

Code segment packing typically increases performance because each maintained segment requires system overhead. On the command-line, /P- turns code segment packing off, which can be useful if you've turned it on in the configuration file, but want to turn it off for a particular link.

Default = 8192 bytes (8K)

## Default libraries

Command-line equivalent = /n

When you are linking with modules created by a compiler other than the Borland C++ compiler, the other compiler might have placed a list of default libraries in the object file.

When the Default Libraries option is unchecked (off), the linker tries to find any undefined routines in these libraries and in the default libraries supplied by the C++ IDE.

When this option is checked (on), the linker searches only the default libraries supplied by the C++ IDE and ignores any defaults in .OBJ files. You might want to check this option when linking modules written in another language.

Default = ON

## Include debug information

Command-line equivalent = /v

When the Include Debug Information option is on, the linker includes information in the output file needed to debug your application with the Borland C++ Integrated Debugger or Turbo Debugger.

On the command line, this option causes the linker to include debugging information in the executable file for all object modules that contain debugging information. You can use the /v+ and /v- options to selectively enable or disable debugging information on a module-by-module basis (but not on the same command-line where you use /v). For example, the following command includes debugging information for modules mod2 and mod3, but not for mod1 and mod4:

```
TLINK mod1 /v+ mod2 mod3 /v- mod4
```

Default = ON in IDE; OFF on the command line

## Pack code segments

Command-line equivalent = /P

Pack Code Segments has different meanings for 16-bit and 32-bit applications. In addition, Code Segment Packing applies only to Windows applications and DLLs.

For 16-bit links, Code Segment Packing causes the linker to minimize the number of code segments by packing as many code segments as possible into one physical segment up to (and never greater than) the code-segment packing limit, which is set to 8,192 (8K) by default. TLINK starts a new segment if needed.

Because there is a certain amount of system overhead for every segment maintained, code segment packing typically increases performance by reducing the number of segments.

For 32-bit links, Code Packing Segments means the linker packs all code into one "segment." On the command line, /P- turns this option off.

Default = ON

## Subsystem version (major.minor)

Command-line equivalent = /Vd.d

This option lets you specify the Windows version ID on which you expect your application will be run. The linker sets the Subsystem version field in the .EXE header to number you specify in the input box.

You can also set the Windows version ID in the SUBSYSTEM portion of the module definition file (.DEF file). However, any version setting you specify in the IDE or on the command line overrides the setting in the .DEF file.

### Command-line usage

When you use the **/Vd.d** command-line option, the linker sets the Windows version ID to the number specified by d.d. For example, if you specify **/V4.0**, the linker sets the Subsystem version field in the .EXE header to 4.0.

Default = 4.0

## Map file

Linker I Map File options tell what type of map file to produce. You can configure your map file output using the Map File options, which gives you information on segment ordering, segment sizes, and public symbols.

### Include source line numbers

Command-line equivalent: **/l**, 16-bit only

When the Include Source Line Numbers option is on, the linker includes source line numbers in the object map files.

For this option to work, linked .OBJ files must be compiled with debug information using **-v**.

When Include Source Line Numbers is on, make sure you turn Jump Optimizations off in the Optimization I 16 bit Specific options page, otherwise the compiler might group together common code from multiple lines of source text during jump optimization, or it might reorder lines (which makes line-number tracking difficult).

Default = OFF

### Map file

You use the Map File options to choose the type of map file to be produced at link time.

For settings other than Off, the map file is placed in the output directory defined in the Directories I Output page.

### Off

Command-line equivalent = **/x**

The Off option tells the linker not to create a map file.

Default = OFF

## Publics

Command-line equivalent = /m

This option causes the linker to produce a map file that contains an overview of the application segments and two listings of the public symbols. The segments listing has a line for each segment, showing the segment starting address, segment length, segment name, and the segment class. The public symbols are broken down into two lists, the first showing the symbols in sorted alphabetically, and the second showing the symbols in increasing address order. Symbols with absolute addresses are tagged Abs.

A list of public symbols is useful when debugging: many debuggers use public symbols, which lets you refer to symbolic addresses while debugging.

## Segments

Command-line equivalent = /s

The Segments option adds a "Detailed map of segments" to the map file created with the Publics option (/m). The detailed list of segments contains the segment class, the segment name, the segment group, the segment module, and the segment ACBP information. If the same segment appears in more than one module, each module appears as a separate line.

The ACBP field encodes the A (alignment), C (combination), and B (big) attributes into a set of four bit fields, as defined by Intel. TLINK uses only three of the fields: A, C, and B. The ACBP value in the map is printed in hexadecimal. The following field values must be ORed together to arrive at the ACBP value printed.

| Field | Value | Description |
|---|---|---|
| A (alignment) | 00 | An absolute segment |
| | 20 | A byte-aligned segment |
| | 40 | C (combination)00Cannot be combined |
| | 60 | A paragraph-aligned segment |
| | 80 | A page-aligned segmentr |
| | A0 | An unnamed absolute portion of storage |
| C(combination) | 00 | Cannot be combined |
| | 08 | A public combining segment |
| B(big) | 00 | Segment less than 64K |
| | 02 | Segment exactly 64K |

With the Segments options enabled, public symbols with no references are flagged idle. An idle symbol is a publicly defined symbol in a module that was not referenced by an EXTDEF record or by any other module included in the link. For example, this fragment from the public symbol section of a map file indicates that symbols Symbol1 and Symbol3 are not referenced by the image being linked:

```
0002:00000874    Idle        Symbol1
0002:00000CE4                Symbol2
0002:000000E7    Idle        Symbol3
```

### Print mangled names in map file

Command-line equivalent = /M

Prints the mangled C++ identifiers in the map file, not the full name. This can help you identify how names are mangled (mangled names are needed as input by some utilities).

Default = OFF

# Warnings

Warnings options enable or disable the display of Linker warnings.

### "No stack" warning

Command-line equivalent = /k 16-bit, /wstk 32-bit

This option lets you control whether or not the linker emits the "No stack" warning. The warning is generated if no stack segment is defined in any of the object files or in any of the libraries included in the link. Except for .DLLs, this indicates an error. If a Borland C++ program produces this error, make sure you are using the correct COx startup object file.

Use the TLINK32 command-line option /w-stk to turn this warning off.

Default = OFF

### 32-bit warnings

- No entry point
- Duplicate symbol
- No def file
- Import does not match previous definition
- Extern not qualified with _import
- Using based linking in DLL
- Self-relative fixup overflowed
- .EXE module built with a .DLL extension

### Warn duplicate symbol in .LIB

Command-line equivalent = /d 16-bit, /wdpl 32-bit

When the Warn Duplicate Symbols option is on, the linker warns you if a symbol appears in more than one object or library files.

If the symbol must be included in the program, the linker uses the symbol definition from the first file it encounters with the symbol definition.

Use the TLINK32 command-line option /w-dpl to turn this warning off.

Default = OFF

# Make options

Make options control the conditions under which the building of a project stops and how the project manager uses autodependency information.

## Autodependencies

When the Make | Autodependencies option is selected, the Project Manager automatically checks dependencies for every target that has a corresponding source file in the project list.

### Cache

When Cache is selected, autodependency information is stored in memory to make dependency checking faster. This option speeds up compilation, but autodependency information will not display in the project tree.

### Cache and display

When Cache and Display is selected, the Project Manager stores the autodependency information in the project file. Once the autodependency information is generated (after a compile) the information is displayed in the project tree. This makes dependency checking faster, but makes project files larger.

### None

When None is selected, no autodependency checking is performed.

### Use

When Use is selected, autodependency checking is performed by reading the autodependency information out of the .OBJ files.

## Break make on

The Make | Break Make On options specify the error condition that stops the making of a project.

### Errors

This option stops a make when the compiler encounters errors.

### Fatal errors

This option tells the Project Manager to generate a list of errors and warnings for all files and all targets in the project. The Project Manager will go on to link if no errors occur.

Default = Errors

## Warnings

Command-line equivalent = **-w!**

This option stops a make if the compiler encounters warnings.

When this compiler option is enabled, the compiler terminates the compile and returns a non-zero error code if a warning is encountered; an .OBJ file is not created.

## New node path

Turn on the Absolute option if you want new nodes to have an absolute, instead of a relative, path.

# Messages options

Messages options let you control the messages generated by the compiler. Compiler messages are indicators of potential trouble spots in your program. These messages can warn you of many kinds of problems that may be waiting to happen, such as variables and parameters that are declared but never used, type mismatches, and many others.

Setting a message option causes the compiler to generate the associated message or warning the specific condition arises. Note that some of the messages are on by default.

## ANSI Violations

Compiler Messages | ANSI Violations options enable or disable individual warning messages about statements that violate the ANSI standard for the C language.

The options are:

- Void functions may not return a value
  Command-line equivalent: **-wvoi**, Default = ON
- Both return and return of a value used
  Command-line equivalent: **-wret**, Default = ON
- Suspicious pointer conversion
  Command-line equivalent: **-wsus**, Default = ON
- Undefined structure 'ident'
  Command-line equivalent: **-wstu**, Default = ON
- Redefinition of 'ident' is not identical
  Command-line equivalent: **-wdup**, Default = ON
- Hexadecimal value more than three digits
  Command-line equivalent: **-wbig**, Default = ON
- Bit fields must be signed or unsigned int
  Command-line equivalent: **-wbbf**, Default = OFF
- 'ident' declared as both external and static
  Command-line equivalent: **-wext**, Default = ON
- Declare 'ident' prior to use in prototype
  Command-line equivalent: **-wdpu**, Default = ON
- Division by zero
  Command-line equivalent: **-wzdi**, Default = ON

- Initializing 'ident' with 'ident'
  Command-line equivalent: **-wbei**, Default = ON
- Initialization is only partially bracketed
  Command-line equivalent: **-wpin**, Default = OFF
- Non-ANSI keyword used
  Command-line equivalent: **-wnak**, Default = OFF

## Display warnings

Use the Display Warnings options to choose which warnings are displayed.

### All

Command-line equivalent: **-w**

Display all warning and error messages.

Default = OFF

### None

Suppresses the display of warning messages. Errors are still displayed.

Default = OFF

### Selected

Command-line equivalent: **-w*aaa***

Choose which warnings are displayed. Using pragma warn in your source code overrides messages options set either at the command line or in the IDE.

To disable a message from the command line, use the command-line option **-w-*aaa***, where *aaa* is the 3-letter message identifier used by the command-line option.

Default = ON

## General

Compiler Messages | General options enable or disable a few general warning messages.

The options are

- Unknown assembler instruction
  Command-line equivalent: **-wasm**, Default = OFF
- Ill-formed pragma
  Command-line equivalent: **-will**, Default = ON
- Array variable 'ident' is near
  Command-line equivalent: **-wias**, Default = ON
- Superfluous & with function
  Command-line equivalent: **-wamp**, Default = OFF
- 'ident' is obsolete
  Command-line equivalent: **-wobs**, Default = OFF

- Cannot create precompiled header
  Command-line equivalent: **-wpch**, Default = OFF
- User-defined warnings
  Command-line equivalent: **-wmsg**, Default = ON

### User-defined warnings

Command-line equivalent: **-wmsg**

The User-defined warnings option allows user-defined messages to appear in the IDE's Message window. User-defined messages are introduced with the **#pragma** message compiler syntax.

**Note**   In addition to messages that you introduce with the **#pragma** message compiler syntax, user-defined warnings allows warnings introduced by third-party libraries to be displayed. Remember, if you need help on a third-party warning, please contact the vendor of the header file that issued the warning.

Default = ON

## Inefficient C++ coding

Compiler Messages | Inefficient C++ Coding options enable or disable individual warning messages about inefficient C++ coding.

The options are:

- Functions containing 'ident' not expanded inline
  Command-line equivalent: **-winl**, Default = ON
- Temporary used to initialize 'ident'
  Command-line equivalent: **-wlin**, Default = ON
- Temporary used for parameter 'ident'
  Command-line equivalent: **-wlvc**, Default = ON

## Inefficient coding

Compiler Messages | Inefficient Coding options are used to enable or disable individual warning messages about inefficient coding.

The options are:

- 'ident' assigned a value which is never used
  Command-line equivalent: **-waus**, Default = ON
- Parameter 'ident' is never used
  Command-line equivalent: **-wpar**, Default = ON
- 'ident' declared but never used
  Command-line equivalent: **-wuse**, Default = OFF
- Structure passed by value
  Command-line equivalent: **-wstv**, Default = OFF
- Unreachable code
  Command-line equivalent: **-wrch**, Default = ON
- Code has no effect
  Command-line equivalent: **-weff**, Default = ON

**Note** The warnings Unreachable Code and Code Has No Effect can be indicators of serious coding problems. If the compiler generates these warnings, be sure to examine the lines of code which cause the errors to be generated.

## Obsolete C++

Compiler Messages | Obsolete C++ options choose which specific obsolete items or incorrect syntax C++ warnings to display.

The options are:

- Base initialization without class name is obsolete
  Command-line equivalent: **-wobi**, Default = ON
- This style of function definition is obsolete
  Command-line equivalent: **-wofp**, Default = ON
- Overloaded prefix operator used as a postfix operator
  Command-line equivalent: **-wpre**, Default = OFF

## Portability

Compiler Messages | Portability options enable or disable individual warning messages about statements that might not operate correctly in all computer environments.

The options are:

- Non-portable pointer conversion
  Command-line equivalent: **-wrpt**, Default = ON
- Non-portable pointer comparison
  Command-line equivalent: **-wcpt**, Default = ON
- Constant out of range in comparison
  Command-line equivalent: **-wrng**, Default = ON
- Constant is long
  Command-line equivalent: **-wcln**, Default = OFF
- Conversion may lose significant digits
  Command-line equivalent: **-wsig**, Default = OFF
- Mixing pointers to signed and unsigned char
  Command-line equivalent: **-wucp**, Default = OFF

## Potential C++ Errors

Compiler Messages | Potential C++ Errors options enable or disable individual warning messages about statements that violate C++ language implementation.

The options are:

- Constant member 'ident' is not initialized
  Command-line equivalent: **-wnci**, Default = ON
- Assigning 'type' to 'enumeration'
  Command-line equivalent: **-weas**, Default = OFF
- 'function' hides virtual function 'function2'
  Command-line equivalent: **-whid**, Default = ON

- Non-const function 'ident' called for const object
  Command-line equivalent: **-wncf**, Default = ON
- Base class 'ident' inaccessible because also in 'ident'
  Command-line equivalent: **-wibc**, Default = OFF
- Array size for 'delete' ignored
  Command-line equivalent: **-wdsz**, Default = OFF
- Use qualified name to access nested type 'ident'
  Command-line equivalent: **-wnst**, Default = OFF
- Handler for '<type1>' Hidden by Previous Handler for '<type2>'
  Command-line equivalent: **-whch**, Default = ON
- Conversion to 'type' will fail for virtual base members
  Command-line equivalent: **-wmpc**, Default = ON
- Maximum precision used for member pointer type
  Command-line equivalent: **-wmpd**, Default = ON
- Use '> >' for nested templates instead of '>>'
  Command-line equivalent: **-wntd**, Default = ON
- Non-volatile function called for volatile object
  Command-line equivalent: **-wncf**, Default = ON

## Potential errors

Compiler Messages | Potential Errors options enable or disable individual warning messages about potential coding errors.

The options are:

- Possibly incorrect assignment
  Command-line equivalent: **-wpia**, Default = ON
- Possible use of 'ident' before definition
  Command-line equivalent: **-wdef**, Default = ON
- No declaration for function 'ident'
  Command-line equivalent: **-wnod**, Default = OFF
- Call to function with no prototype
  Command-line equivalent: **-wpro**, Default = ON
- Function should return a value
  Command-line equivalent: **-wrvl**, Default = ON
- Ambiguous operators need parentheses
  Command-line equivalent: **-wamb**, Default = OFF
- Condition is always (true/false)
  Command-line equivalent: **-wccc**, Default = OFF

## Stop after ... errors

Command-line equivalent: **-j***n*

Errors: Stop After causes compilation to stop after the specified number of errors has been detected. You can enter any number from 0 to 255.

Entering 0 causes compilation to continue until the end of the file.

Default = 25

## Stop after ... warnings

Command-line equivalent: **-g***n*

Warnings: Stop After causes compilation to stop after the specified number of warnings has been detected. You can enter any number from 0 to 255.

Entering 0 causes compilation to continue until either the end of the file or the error limit set in Errors: Stop After has been reached, whichever comes first.

Default = 100

# Optimization options

Optimization options are the software equivalent of performance tuning. There are two general types of compiler optimizations:

- Those that make your code smaller
- Those that make your code faster

Although you can compile with optimizations at any point in your product development cycle, be aware when debugging that some assembly instructions might be "optimized away" by certain compiler optimizations.

## General settings

The main Optimizations page in the Project Options dialog box contains four radio buttons that let you select the overall type of optimizations you want to use. Because of the complexities of setting compiler optimizations, it is recommended that you use either the Optimize for Size or the Optimize for Speed radio buttons.

The general optimization settings are:

- Disable all optimizations
- Use selected optimizations
- Optimize for size
- Optimize for speed

## 16 and 32-bit

The 16- and 32-bit compiler options specify optimization settings for all compilations.

### Common subexpression

The Common Subexpressions options tell the compiler how to find and eliminate duplicate expressions in your code.

### No optimization

When the No Optimization option is on, the compiler does not eliminate common subexpressions. This is the default behavior of the command-line compilers.

### Optimize Globally
Command-line equivalent: **-Og**

When you set this option, the compiler eliminates common subexpressions within an entire function. This option globally eliminates duplicate expressions within the target scope and stores the calculated value of those expressions once (instead of recalculating the expression).

Although this optimization could theoretically reduce code size, it optimizes for speed and rarely results in size reductions. Use this option if you prefer to reuse expressions rather than create explicit stack locations for them.

### Optimize locally
Command-line equivalent: **-Oc**

When the Optimize Locally option is on, the compiler eliminates common subexpressions within groups of statements unbroken by jumps (basic blocks).

## Induction variables
Command-line equivalent: **-Ov**

When this option is enabled, the compiler creates induction variables and it performs strength reduction, which optimizes for loops speed.

Use this option when you're compiling for speed and your code contains loops. The optimizer uses induction to create new variables (induction variables) from expressions used in loops. The optimizer assures that the operations performed on these new variables are computationally less expensive (reduced in strength) than those used by the original variables.

Optimizations are common if you use array indexing inside loops, because a multiplication operation is required to calculate the position in the array that is indicated by the index. For example, the optimizer creates an induction variable out of the operation v[i] in the following code because the v[i] operation requires multiplication. This optimization also eliminates the need to preserve the value of i:

```
int v[10];
void f(int x, int y, int z)
{
  int i;
  for (i = 0; i < 10; i++)
    v[i] = x * y * z;
}
```

With Induction variables enabled, the code changes:

```
int v[10];
void f(int x, int y, int z)
{
  int i, *p;
  for (p = v; p < &v[10]; p++)
    *p = x * y * z;
}
```

## Inline intrinsic functions

Command-line equivalent: **-Oi**

When the Inline Intrinsic Functions option is on, the compiler generates the code for common memory functions like *strcpy()* within your function's scope. This eliminates the need for a function call. The resulting code executes faster, but it is larger.

The following functions are inlined with this option:

| | | | |
|---|---|---|---|
| alloca | fabs | memchr | memcmp |
| memcpy | memset | rotl | rotr |
| stpcpy | strcat | strchr | strcmp |
| strcpy | strlen | strncat | strncmp |
| strncpy | strnset | strrchr | |

You can control the inlining of these functions with the pragma **intrinsic**. For example, **#pragma intrinsic strcpy** causes the compiler to generate inline code for all subsequent calls to **strcpy** in your function, and #pragma intrinsic -strcpy prevents the compiler from inlining **strcpy**. Using these pragmas in a file overrides any compiler option settings.

When inlining any intrinsic function, you must include a prototype for that function before you use it; the compiler creates a macro that renames the inlined function to a function that the compiler recognizes internally. In the previous example, the compiler would create a macro **#define strcpy _ _strcpy_ _**.

The compiler recognizes calls to functions with two leading and two trailing underscores and tries to match the prototype of that function against its own internally stored prototype. If you don't supply a prototype, or if the prototype you supply doesn't match the compiler's prototype, the compiler rejects the attempt to inline that function and generates an error.

# 16-bit

The Optimizations I 16-bit options pertain to 16-bit applications only.

## Assume no pointer aliasing

Command-line equivalent: **-Oa**

When the Assume No Pointer Aliasing option is on, the compiler assumes that pointer expressions are not aliased in common subexpression evaluation.

Assume No Pointer Aliasing affects the way the optimizer performs common subexpression elimination and copy propagation by letting the optimizer maintain copy propagation information across function calls and by letting the optimizer maintain common subexpression information across some stores. Without this option the optimizer must discard information about copies and subexpressions. Pointer aliasing might create bugs that are hard to spot, so it is only applied when you enable this option.

Assume No Pointer Aliasing controls how the optimizer treats expressions that contain pointers. When compiling with global or local common subexpressions and Assume No

Pointer Aliasing is enabled, the optimizer recognizes *p * x as a common subexpression in function *func1*.

```
int g, y;
int func1(int *p)
{
  int x=5;
  y = *p * x;
  g = 3;
  return (*p * x);
}
void func2(void)
{
  g=2;
  func1(&g);  // This is incorrect--the assignment g = 3
              // invalidates the expression *p * x
}
```

## Copy propagation

Command-line equivalent: **-Op**

When this option is enabled, copies of constants, variables, and expressions are propagated whenever possible.

Copy propagation is primarily speed optimization, but it never increases the size of your code. Like loop-invariant code motion, copy propagation relies on the analysis performed during common subexpression elimination. Copy propagation means that the optimizer remembers the values assigned to expressions and uses those values instead of loading the value of the assigned expressions. With this, copies of constants, expressions, and variables can be propagated.

## Dead code elimination

Command-line equivalent: **-Ob**

When the Dead Code Elimination option is on, the compiler reveals variables that might not be needed. Because the optimizer must determine where variables are no longer used (live range analysis), you might also want to set Global Register Allocation (**-Oe**) when you use this option.

## Global register allocation

Command-line equivalent: **-Oe**

When this option is enabled, global register allocation and variable live range analysis are enabled. This option should always be used when optimizing code because it increases the speed and decreases the size of your application.

## Invariant code motion

Command-line equivalent: **-Om**

When this option is enabled, invariant code is moved out of loops and your code is optimized for speed. The optimizer uses information about all the expressions in the function (gathered during common subexpression elimination) to find expressions whose values do not change inside a loop.

To prevent the calculation from being done many times inside the loop, the optimizer moves the code outside the loop so that it is calculated only once. The optimizer then reuses the calculated value inside the loop.

You should use loop-invariant code motion whenever you are compiling for speed and have used global common subexpressions, because moving code out of loops can result in enormous speed gains. For example, in the following code, x * y * z is evaluated in every iteration of the loop:

```
int v[10];
void f(int x, int y, int z)

{
  int i;
  for (i = 0; i < 10; i++)
    v[i] = x * y * z;
}
```

The optimizer rewrites the code:

```
int v[10];
void f(int x, int y, int z)
{
  int i,t1;
  t1 = x * y * z;
  for (i = 0; i < 10; i++)
    v[i] = t1;
}
```

## Jump optimization
Command-line equivalent: **-O**

When Jump Optimization option is on, the compiler reduces the code size by eliminating redundant jumps and reorganizing loops and switch statements.

When this option is enabled, the sequences of tracing and stepping in the debugger can be confusing because of the reordering and elimination of instructions. If you are debugging at the assembly level, you might want to disable this option.

Default = ON

## Loop optimization
Command-line equivalent: **-Ol**

When this option is enabled, loops are compacted into REP/STOSx instructions.

Loop optimization takes advantage of the string move instructions on the 80x86 processors by replacing the code for a loop with a string move instruction, making the code faster.

Depending on the complexity of the operands, the compacted loop code can also be smaller than the corresponding non-compacted loop.

## Suppress redundant loads

Command-line equivalent: **-Z**

When this option is enabled, the compiler suppresses the reloading of registers by remembering the contents of registers and reusing them as often as possible.

Exercise caution when using this option; the compiler cannot detect if a value has been modified indirectly by a pointer.

## Windows prolog/epilog

Command-line equivalent: **-OW**

Use the Windows Prolog/Epilog option to suppress the **inc bp** / **dec bp** of an exported Windows far function prolog and epilog code.

If Debug Information in .OBJ Files (**-v**) is enabled, this option is disabled because some debugging tools (such as WinSpector and Turbo Debugger) need the **inc bp** / **dec bp** instructions to display stack-frame information.

# 32-bit

Use the Optimizations | 32-bit options to specify options specific to the Pentium processor and the Intel optimizing compiler. The options are:

## Cache hit optimizations (Intel compiler only)

Command-line equivalent: **-OM**

Specifies a set of memory accessing optimizations that improves cache hits and reduces the number of memory accesses. These optimizations include:

- Loop interchange
- Loop distribution
- Strip mining and preloading
- Loop blocking
- Alternate loops
- Loop unrolling

## Optimize across function boundaries (Intel compiler only)

Command-line equivalent: **-OI**

Specifies a set of interprocedural optimizations. These optimizations eliminate call overhead and can create opportunities for further optimizations. They are applied across procedure boundaries but are restricted to routines within the same file, including routines in files combined by the **#include** preprocessor directive. These optimizations include:

- Monitoring module-level static variables
- Inline function expansion
- Cloning
- Passing arguments in registers
- Constant argument propagation

**Note**   Currently, these optimizations are disabled if your source code contains embedded assembly code.

## Pentium instruction scheduling

Command-line equivalent: **-OS**

When enabled, this switch rearranges instructions to minimize delays that can be caused by Address Generation Interlocks (AGI) that occur on the i486 and Pentium processors. This option also optimizes the code so that it takes advantage of the Pentium parallel pipelines. Best results for Pentium systems are obtained when you use this switch in conjunction with the 32-bit Compiler | Pentium option in the Project Options dialog box (**-5**).

Note that scheduled code is more difficult to debug at the source level because instructions from a particular source line may be mixed with instructions from other source lines. Stepping through the source code is still possible, although the execution point might make unexpected jumps between source lines as you step. Also, setting a breakpoint on a source line may result in several breakpoints being set in the code. This is especially important to note when inspecting variables, since a variable may be undefined even though the execution point is positioned after the variable assignment.

Stepping through the following function when this switch is enabled demonstrates the stepping behavior:

```
int v[10];
void f(int i, int j)
{
  int a,b;

  a = v[i+j];
  b = v[i-j];
  v[i] = a + b;
  v[j] = a - b;
}
```

Execution starts by computing the index i-j in the assignment to b (note that a is still undefined although the execution point is positioned after the assignment to a). The index i+j is computed, v[i-j] is assigned to b, and v[i+j] is assigned to a. If a breakpoint is set on the assignment to b, execution will stop twice: once when computing the index and again when performing the assignment.

Default = OFF (**-O-S**)

# General optimization settings

## Disable all optimizations

Command-line equivalent: **-Od**

Disables all optimization settings, including ones which you may have specifically set and those which would normally be performed as part of the speed/size tradeoff.

Because this disables code compaction (tail merging) and cross-jump optimizations, using this option can keep the debugger from jumping around or returning from a function without warning, which makes stepping through code easier to follow.

**Note**  You can override this setting using the predefined Style Sheets in the Project Manager.

## Optimize for size

Command-line equivalents: **-O1**

This radio button sets an aggregate of optimization options that tells the compiler to optimize your code for size. For example, the compiler scans the generated code for duplicate sequences. When such sequences warrant, the optimizer replaces one sequence of code with a jump to the other and eliminates the first piece of code. This occurs most often with **switch** statements. The compiler optimizes for size by choosing the smallest code sequence possible.

This option (**-O1**) sets the following optimizations:

- Jump optimizations (**-O**)
- Dead code elimination (**-Ob**)
- Duplicate expressions (**-Oc**)
- Register allocation and live range analysis (**-Oe**)
- Loop optimizations (**-Ol**)
- Instruction scheduling (**-OS**)
- Register load suppression (**-Z**)

**Note**  The compiler options **-Ot** and **-G** are supported for backward compatibility only, and are equivalent to the **-O1** compiler option.

## Optimize for speed

Command-line equivalent: **-O2**

This radio button sets an aggregate of optimization options that tells the compiler to optimize your code for speed. This switch (**-O2**) sets the following optimizations:

- Dead code elimination (**-Ob**)
- Register allocation and live range analysis (**-Oe**)
- Duplicate expression within functions (**-Og**)
- Intrinsic functions (**-Oi**)
- Loop optimizations (**-Ol**)
- Code motion (**-Om**)
- Copy propagation (**-Op**)
- Instruction scheduling (**-OS**)
- Induction variables (**-Ov**)

- Register load suppression (**-Z**)

If you are creating Windows applications, you'll probably want to optimize for speed.

**Note**　The compiler options **-Os** and **-G-** are supported for backward compatibility only, and are equivalent to the **-O2** compiler option. The **-Ox** option is also supported for backward compatibility and for compatibility with Microsoft make files.

### Use selected optimizations

Does not set any optimization by default, but lets you set the specific optimization options you need through the settings contained in the Optimization subtopics. The subtopic pages are:

- 16 and 32-bit
- 16-bit specific
- 32-bit specific

**Note**　Configuring your own optimization settings should be reserved for expert users only.

# Resources options

The Resources options let you set several options for how resources are compiled and bound to your application by the integrated resource compiler and resource linker.

## 16-bit Resources

The 16-bit Resource options let you choose options for resources targeted for 16-bit applications.

### Target Windows version

Use the Target Windows Version options to choose the Windows version with which you are working. These options specify which version of Windows your resources are marked with when you create 16-bit resources.

You cannot mix 16-bit and 32-bit files in a resource project. To add resources from existing 32-bit .RES or .EXE files to a 16-bit resource project, save the files as .RC files and add the .RC files to your project; .RC files are not version specific.

**Windows 3.1**
Command-line equivalent: (Rlink.EXE) **-V31**

Creates 16-bit resources for a Windows 3.1 application.

**Windows 95**
Command-line equivalent: (Rlink.EXE) **-V40**

Creates 16-bit resources for a Windows 95 application.

## Pack fastload area

The Pack Fastload Area option optimizes the executable file by packing all PRELOAD segments and resources in a contiguous area in the.EXE file.

When Pack Fastload Area is enabled, the resource linker writes all data segments, all nondiscardable code segments, and the entry-point code segment to a contiguous area in the executable file. This makes your executable files load faster at runtime.

If you uncheck Pack Fastload Area, no such optimizations will be done.

Default = OFF

# Librarian

Librarian options affect the behavior of the built-in librarian. The built-in librarian combines the .OBJ files in your project into .LIB files. Options in this section control that process. In addition, you can cause the librarian to generate a list (.LST) file containing the .OBJs in a generated .LIB and the functions those .OBJs contain.

TLIB.EXE is the command-line librarian.

## Case-sensitive library

Command-line equivalent = /C

When the Case-Sensitive Library option is on, the librarian treats case as significant in all symbols in the library. For example, if Case-Sensitive Library is checked, "CASE", "Case", and "case" are all treated as different symbols.

## Create extended dictionary

Command-line equivalent = /E

When the Create Extended Dictionary option is on, the librarian includes, in compact form, additional information that helps the linker process library files faster.

## Generate list file

When the Generate List File option is on, the librarian automatically produces a list file (.LST) that lists the contents of your library when it is created.

## Library page size

Command-line equivalent = /P*size*, where *size* is number of pages

The Library Page Size input box is where you set the number of bytes in each library "page" (dictionary entry).

The page size determines the maximum size of the library. Page size must be a power of 2 between 16 and 32,768 inclusive. The default page size of 16 allows a library of about 1 Mb in size.

To create a larger library, change the page size to the next higher value (32).

### Purge comment records
Command-line equivalent = /0

When the Purge Comment Records option is on, the librarian removes all comment records from modules added to the library.

## 32-bit Resources

The 32-bit resource options let you choose options for resources targeted for 32-bit applications.

### Language
Use the Language list boxes to select the base and sub-languages to be used for the resources in the your project.

Multiple resources with the same ID may be bound to a single .EXE or .DLL if they each have different major and/or minor languages specified. The language currently specified by Windows will determine which resource identified by the ID will actually be loaded.

The language you choose must match the language that Windows NT systems are set to. If not, your resources might not be correctly displayed (this is especially true for menu resources).

#### Major
Use the Major list box to select the base (or primary) language to be used for the resources.

#### Minor
Use the Minor list box to select the sub-language (or dialect) to be used for the resources.

For example, you might define your resource to have English as the base language and U.S. as the sub-language.

Note    These options set the default languages for the Resource compiler. You can override these default settings by embedding language statements in your .RC file.

Default = Neutral

#### Target Windows version
Use the Target Windows Version options to choose the Windows version with which you are working. These options specify which version of Windows your resources are marked with when you create 32-bit resources.

You cannot mix 16-bit and 32-bit files in a resource project. To add resources from existing 16-bit .RES or .EXE files to a 32-bit resource project, save the files as .RC files and add the .RC files to your project; .RC files are not version specific.

**Win32s/Windows NT 3.1**

This options links your resources so that your 32-bit applications can be run on Win32s, Windows NT 3.1, and Windows NT 3.5 systems (this is not compatible with Windows NT 3.51 systems).

**Windows 95/Windows NT 3.51**

This options links your resources so that your 32-bit applications can be run on Windows 95 and Windows NT 3.51 systems.

# Command-line only options

The options are available only from the command line.

## Object search paths

Command-line equivalent = **/j**

This option lets you specify the directories the linker will search if there is no explicit path given for an .OBJ module in the compile/link statement. This option works with both TLINK and TLINK32.

The Specify Object Search Path uses the following command-line syntax:

```
/j<PathSpec>[;<PathSpec>][...]
```

The linker uses the specified object search path(s) if there is no explicit path given for the .OBJ file and the linker cannot find the object file in the current directory. For example, the command

```
TLINK32 /jc:\myobjs;.\objs splash .\common\logo,,,utils logolib
```

directs the linker to first search the current directory for SPLASH.OBJ. If it is not found in the current directory, the linker then searches for the file in the C:\MYOBJS directory, and then in the .\OBJS directory. However, notice that the linker does not use the object search paths to find the file LOGO.OBJ because an explicit path was given for this file.

## 16 and 32-bit command-line switches

The following command-line switches are supported by the command-line compilers BCC.EXE, BCC32.EXE, and BCC32i.EXE.

### C++ compile
Command-line equivalent = **-P**

The **-P** command-line option causes the compiler to compile all source files as C++ files, regardless of their extension. Use **-P-** to compile all .CPP files as C++ source files and all other files as C source files.

The command-line option **-P***ext* causes the compiler to compile all source files as C++ files and it changes the default extension to whatever you specify with *ext*. This option is provided because some programmers use different extensions as their default extension for C++ code.

The option **-P-*ext*** compiles files based on their extension (.CPP compiles to C++, all other extensions compile to C) and sets the default extension (other than .CPP).

### Compile .OBJ to filename
Command-line equivalent = **-o*filename***

Use this option to compile the specified source file to *filename*.OBJ.

### Compile to .ASM, then assemble
Command-line equivalent = **-B**

This command-line option causes the compiler to first generate an .ASM file from your C++ (or C) source code (same as the **-S** command-line option). The compiler then calls TASM (or the assembler specified with the **-E** option) to create an .OBJ file from the .ASM file. The .ASM file is then deleted. To use this 32-bit compiler option, you must install a 32-bit assembler, such as TASM32.EXE, and then specify this assembler with the **-E** option. In the IDE, right-click the source node in the Project Manager, then choose Special | C++ to Assembler.

### Compile to .OBJ, no link
Command-line equivalent = **-c**

Compiles and assembles the names .C, .CPP, and .ASM files, but does not execute a link on the resulting .OBJ files. In the IDE, choose Project | Compile.

### Compile to assembler
Command-line equivalent = **-S**

This option causes the compiler to generate an .ASM file from your C++ (or C) source code. The generated .ASM file includes the original C or C++ source lines as comments in the file.

### Create a map file
Command-line equivalent = **-M**

Use this command-line option tells the linker to create a map file.

### Pass option to linker
Command-line equivalent = **-l*x***

Use this command-line option to pass option(s) *x* to the linker from a compile command. Use the command-line option **-l-*x*** to disable a specific linker option.

### Specify assembler
Command-line equivalent = **-E*filename***

Assemble instructions using *filename* as the assembler. The 16-bit compiler uses TASM as the default assembler. In the IDE, you can configure a different assembler using the Tool menu.

## Specify assembler option

Command-line equivalent = **-T***x*

Use this command-line option to pass the option(s) *x* to the assembler you specify with the **-E** option. To disable all previously enabled assembler options, use the **-T-** command-line option.

## Specify executable file name

Command-line equivalent = **-e***filename*

Link file using *filename* as the name of the executable file. If you do not specify an executable name with this option, the linker creates an executable file based on the name of the first source file or object file listed in the command.

## Undefine symbol

Command-line equivalent = **-U***name*

This command-line option undefine the previous definition of the identifier *name*.

# 16-bit command-line switches

The following switches are supported by the 16-bit command-line compiler (BCC.EXE) and linker (TLINK.EXE).

## Compile to DOS .COM

Command-line equivalent = **-tDc**

The compiler creates a DOS tiny-model .COM file. DOS .COM applications cannot exceed 64K in size, have segment-relative fixups, or define a stack segment. In addition, .COM files must have a starting address of 0:100H. If you change the file extension (to .BIN, for example), the starting address can be either 0:0 or 0:100H. The linker can't generate debugging information for .COM files, so you'll need to debug it as an .EXE file, then recompile and link the application as a .COM file.

## Compile to DOS .EXE

Command-line equivalent = **-tD**

The compiler creates a DOS .EXE file (same as **-tDe**).

## Compile to DPMI .EXE

Command-line equivalent = **-WX**

The compiler creates a DOS Protected Mode Interface (DPMI) .EXE file.

## Enable backward compatibility options

Command-line equivalent = **-Vo**

This compiler option enables the following 16-bit backward compatibility options: **-Va**, **-Vb**, **-Vc**, **-Vp**, **-Vt**, **-Vv**. Use this option as a handy shortcut when linking libraries built with older versions of Borland C++.

### Expanded memory swapping

Command-line equivalent = **/ye**

This 16-bit linker option controls how TLINK uses expanded memory for I/O buffering. If the linker needs more memory for active data structures (while reading object files or writing the executable file), it either clears buffers or swaps them to expanded memory.

When reading files, the linker clears the input buffer so that its space can be used for other data structures. When creating an executable, it writes the buffer to its correct place in the executable file. In both cases, you can substantially increase the link speed by swapping to expanded memory. By default, swapping to expanded memory is enabled and swapping to extended memory is disabled. If swapping is enabled and no appropriate memory exists in which to swap, then swapping doesn't occur.

Default = ON

### Extended memory swapping

Command-line equivalent = **/yx**

This TLINK option controls the linker's use of extended memory for I/O buffering. By default, the linker can use up to 8Mb of extended memory. You can control the linker's use of extended memory with one of the following forms of this switch:

- **/yx** or **/yx+** uses all available extended memory, up to 8Mb
- **/yx**$n$ uses only up to $n$ Kb of extended memory

Default = OFF

### Generate 8087 instructions

Command-line equivalent = **-f87**

Use this 16-bit compiler option to create DOS 8087 floating point code.

### Generate overlay code

Command-line equivalent = **-Y**

The compiler generates the DOS code needed to create overlay files.

### Link DOS .COM

Command-line equivalent = **/Tdc**

TLINK generates a real-mode DOS .COM file. (The command-line option **/t** is supported for backward compatibility only; it has the same functionality as **/Tdc**.)

### Link DOS .EXE

Command-line equivalent = **/Tde**

TLINK generates a real-mode DOS .EXE file.

### Link DPMI .EXE

Command-line equivalent = **/Txe**

TLINK generates a DOS Protected Mode Interface (DPMI) .EXE file.

### Link Windows .DLL

Command-line equivalent = **/Twd**

TLINK generates a Windows .DLL file.

### Link Windows .EXE

Command-line equivalent = **/Twe**

TLINK generates a Windows .EXE file.

### Overlay the compiled files

Command-line equivalent = **-Yo**

The compiler overlays the compiled overlay files which you've specified with the **-Y** option.

### Overlay the compiled files

Command-line equivalent = **/o**

This DOS -only option causes TLINK to overlay all the modules or libraries that follow the option on the command line. Use **/o-** on the command line to turn of overlays. If you list a class name after this option, TLINK overlays all the segments in that class (this also works for multiple classes). If you don't list any name after this option, TLINK overlays all segments of classes ending with CODE. This option uses the default overlay interrupt number 3FH. To specify a different interrupt number, use **/o**$xx$, whrere $xx$ is a two-digit hexademimal number.

### Specify option to RLINK

Command-line equivalent = **/R**$x$

TLINK passes the option $x$ to RLINK.EXE ($x$ can be either **e**, **k**, **m**, **p**, or **v**).

## 32-bit command-line switches

The following switches are supported by the 32-bit command-line compilers (BCC32.EXE and BCC32i.EXE) and linker (TLINK32.EXE).

**Note** The following 32-bit command-line options are not needed if you include a module definition file in your compile and link commands which specifies the type of 32-bit application you intend to build.

### Link 32-bit .DLL file

Command-line equivalent = **/Tpd**

TLINK32 generates a 32-bit protected-mode Windows .DLL file.

### Link 32-bit .EXE file

Command-line equivalent = **/Tpe**

TLINK32 generates a 32-bit protected-mode Windows .EXE file.

### Link for 32-bit console application

Command-line equivalent = **/ap**

TLINK32 generates a protected-mode executable file that runs in console mode.

### Link using 32-bit Windows API

Command-line equivalent = **/aa**

TLINK32 generates a protected-mode executible that runs using the 32-bit Windows API.

# Command-line options quick reference

This section presents two quick reference tables for command-line options. The first table lists command-line options available from the Options | Project menus and dialog boxes, and they're organized function. The second table lists options that are available only from the command line.

**Table 3.1**    Command-line options by function

| Option | Description |
|---|---|
| **16-bit Compiler | Calling Convention** | |
| **-p** | Use Pascal calling convention. |
| **-pc** | Use C calling convention. (Default: -pc, -p-.) |
| **-po** | Use fastthis calling convention for passing this parameter in registers. |
| **-pr** | Use fastcall calling convention for passing parameters in registers. |
| **16-bit Compiler | Entry/Exit Code** | |
| **-tW** | Make the target a Windows .EXE with all functions exportable. (Default) |
| **-tWD** | Make the target a Windows .DLL with all functions exportable. |
| **-tWDE** | Make the target a Windows .DLL with explicit functions exportable. |
| **-tWE** | Make the target a Windows .EXE with explicit functions exportable. |
| **-tWS** | Make the target a Windows .EXE that uses smart callbacks (16-bit compiler only). |
| **-tWSE** | Make the target a Windows .EXE that uses smart callbacks, with explicit functions exportable (16-bit compiler only). |
| **-W** | Make the target a Windows .EXE with all functions exportable. (Default) (Note there is no space between the -W and the !.) |
| **-WD** | Make the target a Windows .DLL with all functions exportable. |
| **-WDE** | Make the target a Windows .DLL with explicit functions exportable. |

**Table 3.1**    Command-line options by function

| Option | Description |
|---|---|
| **-WE** | Make the target a Windows .EXE with explicit functions exportable. |
| **-WS** | Make the target a Windows .EXE that uses smart callbacks (16-bit compiler only). |
| **-WSE** | Make the target a Windows .EXE that uses smart callbacks, with explicit functions exportable (16-bit compiler only). |
| **16-bit Compiler | Memory Model** | |
| **-dc** | Move string literals from data segment to code segment (16-bit compiler only). |
| **-F** | Uses fast huge pointers. |
| **-Ff** | Create far variables automatically. |
| **-Ff=size** | Create far variables automatically; set the threshold to "size" (16-bit compiler only). |
| **-Fs** | Assume DS=SS in all memory models (16-bit compiler only). |
| **-mc** | Compile using compact memory model (16-bit compiler only). |
| **-mh** | Compile using huge memory model. |
| **-ml** | Compile using large memory model (16-bit compiler only). |
| **-mm** | Compile using medium memory model (16-bit compiler only). |
| **-mm!** | Compile using medium memory model; assume DS!=SS (16-bit compiler only). (Note: there is no space between the -mm and the !.) |
| **-ms** | Compile using small memory model (16-bit compiler only). (Default) |
| **-ms!** | Compile using small memory model; assume DS! = SS (16-bit compiler only). (Note: there is no space between the -ms and the !.) |
| **-Vf** | Far C++ virtual tables (16-bit compiler only). |
| **16-bit Compiler | Processor** | |
| **-1-** | Generate 8086 compatible instructions. |
| **-1** | Generate the 80186/286 compatible instructions (16-bit only). |
| **-2** | Generate 80286 protected-mode compatible instructions (16-bit compiler only). (Default for 16- bit) |
| **-3** | Generate 80386 protected-mode compatible instructions. (Default for 32-bit) |
| **-4** | Generate 80386/80486 protected-mode compatible instructions. |
| **-a** | Align byte. (Default: -a- use byte-aligning.) |
| **-an** | Align to "n". 1=byte, 2=word (16-bit = 2 bytes), 4=Double word (32-bit compiler only, 4 bytes) |
| **16-bit Compiler | Segment Names Code** | |
| **-zAname** | Code class set to "name". |
| **-zCname** | Code segment class set to "name". |
| **-zPname** | Code group set to "name". |
| **16-bit Compiler | Segment Names Data** | |
| **-zBname** | BSS class set to "name". |
| **-zDname** | BSS segment set to "name". |
| **-zGname** | BSS group set to "name". |
| **-zRname** | Data segment set to "name". |
| **-zSname** | Data group set to "name". |
| **-zTname** | Data class set to "name". |
| **16-bit Compiler | Segment Names Far Data** | |

**Table 3.1**    Command-line options by function

| Option | Description |
| --- | --- |
| **-zE***name* | Far segment set to "name". |
| **-zF***name* | Far class set to "name". |
| **-zH***name* | Far group set to "name". |
| **-zV***name* | Far virtual segment set to "name" (16-bit compiler only). |
| **-zW***name* | Far virtual class set to "name" (16-bit compiler only). |
| **32-bit Compiler I Calling Convention** | |
| **-p** | Use Pascal calling convention. |
| **-pc** | Use C calling convention. (Default: -pc, -p-.) |
| **-pr** | Use fastcall calling convention for passing parameters in registers. |
| **-ps** | Use stdcall calling convention (32-bit compiler only). |
| **32-bit Compiler I Processor** | |
| **-3** | Generate 80386 protected-mode compatible instructions. (Default for 32-bit) |
| **-4** | Generate 80386/80486 protected-mode compatible instructions. |
| **-5** | Generate Pentium protected-mode compatible instructions. |
| **C++ Options I C++ Compatibility** | |
| **-K2** | Allow only two character types (signed and unsigned). Char is treated as signed. Compatibility with Borland C++ 3.1 and earlier. |
| **-Va** | Pass class arguments by reference to a temporary variable (16-bit compiler only). |
| **-Vb** | Make virtual base class pointer same size as 'this' pointer of the class (16-bit compiler only). (Default) |
| **-Vc** | Do not add the hidden members and code to classes with pointers to virtual base class members (16-bit compiler only). |
| **-Vp** | Pass the 'this' parameter to 'pascal' member functions as the first. |
| **-Vt** | Place the virtual table pointer after nonstatic data members (16-bit compiler only). |
| **C++ Options I Exception Handling** | |
| **-RT** | Enable runtime type information. (Default) |
| **-x** | Enable exception handling. (Default) |
| **-xc** | Enable compatible exception handling. |
| **-xd** | Enable destructor cleanup. (Default) |
| **-xf** | Enable fast exception prologs. |
| **-xp** | Enable exception location information. |
| **C++ Options I Member Pointer** | |
| **-Vmd** | Use the smallest representation for member pointers. |
| **-Vmm** | Member pointers support multiple inheritance. |
| **-Vmp** | Honor the declared precision for all member pointer types. |
| **-Vms** | Member pointers support single inheritance. |
| **-Vmv** | Member pointers have no restrictions (most general representation). (Default) |
| **C++ Options I Templates** | |
| **-Jg** | Generate definitions for all template instances and merge duplicates. (Default) |
| **-Jgd** | Generate public definitions for all template instances; duplicates result in redefinition errors. |
| **-Jgx** | Generate external references for all template instances. |

**Table 3.1**     Command-line options by function

| Option | Description |
|---|---|
| **C++ Options | Virtual Tables** | |
| **-V** | Use smart C++ virtual tables. (Default) |
| **-V0** | External C++ virtual tables. |
| **-V1** | Public C++ virtual tables. |
| **-Vs** | Local C++ virtual tables. |
| **Compiler | Code Generation** | |
| **-b** | Make enums always integer-sized. (Default: -b- make enums byte-sized when possible.) |
| **-d** | Merge duplicate strings. (Default) |
| **-K** | Default character type unsigned. (Default: -K- default character type signed.) |
| **-po** | Use fastthis calling convention for passing this parameter in registers (16-bit compiler only). |
| **-r** | Use register variables. (Default) |
| **-rd** | Allow only declared register variables to be kept in registers. |
| **-Y** | Generate overlay-compatible code. |
| **-Yo** | Overlay compiled files. |
| **Compiler | Compiler Output** | |
| **-Fc** | Generate COMDEFs (16-bit compiler only). |
| **-u** | Generate underscores. (Default) |
| **-X** | Disable compiler autodependency output. (Default: **-X-** use compiler autodependency output.) |
| **Compiler | Debugging** | |
| **-k** | Turn on standard stack frame. (Default) |
| **-N** | Check for stack overflow. |
| **-R** | Include browser information in generated .OBJ files. |
| **-v** | Turn on source debugging. |
| **-vi** | Control expansion of inline functions. |
| **-y** | Line numbers on. |
| **Compiler | Defines** | |
| **-D**_name_ | Define "name" to the null "string". |
| **-D**_name=string_ | Define"name" to "string". |
| **-U**_name_ | Undefine any previous definitions of "name". |
| **Compiler | Floating Point** | |
| **-f** | Emulate floating point. (Default) |
| **-ff** | Fast floating point. (Default) |
| **Compiler | Precompiled Headers** | |
| **-H** | Generate and use precompiled headers. (Default) |
| **-H**_filename_ | Sets the name of the file for precompiled headers. |
| **-H=filename** | Set the name of the file for precompiled headers. |
| **-Hu** | Use but do not generate precompiled headers. |
| **Compiler | Source** | |
| **-A** | Use only ANSI keywords. |
| **-AK** | Use only Kernigham and Ritchie keywords. |

**Table 3.1**   Command-line options by function

| Option | Description |
|--------|-------------|
| -AT | Use Borland C++ keywords (also **-A-**). |
| -AU | Use only UNIX V keywords. |
| -C | Turn nested comments on. (Default: -C- turn nested comments off.) |
| -in | Make significant identifier length to be "n". (Default) |

**Configuration Files**

| | |
|--------|-------------|
| @filename | Read compiler options from the response file "filename" |

**Messages**

| | |
|--------|-------------|
| -gn | Warnings: stop after "n" messages. (Default: 255.) |
| -jn | Errors: stop after "n" messages. (Default) |
| -w | Display warnings on. |
| -wxxx | Enable "xxx" warning message. (Default) |

**Messages | ANSI Violations**

| | |
|--------|-------------|
| -wbbf | Bit fields must be signed or unsigned int. |
| -wbig | Hexadecimal value contains more than three digits. (Default) |
| -wdpu | Declare type 'type' prior to use in prototype (Default) |
| -wdup | Redefinition of 'macro' is not identical. (Default) |
| -wext | 'identifier' is declared as both external and static (Default) |
| -wnak | Non-ANSI Keyword Used: '<keyword>' (Note: Use of this option is a requirement for ANSI conformance.) |
| -wpin | Initialization is only partially bracketed. |
| -wret | Both return and return of a value used. (Default) |
| -wstu | Undefined structure 'structure' |
| -wsus | Suspicious pointer conversion. (Default) |
| -wvoi | Void functions may not return a value. (Default) |
| -wzdi | Division by zero (Default) |

**Messages | General**

| | |
|--------|-------------|
| -Ff=1 | Array variable 'identifier' is near. (Default) |
| -wamp | Superfluous & with function. |
| -wasm | Unknown assembler instruction. |
| -will | Ill-formed pragma. (Default) |
| -wpch | Cannot create precompiled header: header. (Default) |

**Messages | Inefficient C++ Coding**

| | |
|--------|-------------|
| -winl | Functions containing reserved words are not expanded inline. (Default) |
| -wlin | Temporary used to initialize 'identifier'. (Default) |
| -wlvc | Temporary used for parameter 'parameter' in call to 'function' (Default) |

**Messages | Inefficient Coding**

| | |
|--------|-------------|
| -waus | 'identifier' is assigned a value that is never used. (Default) |
| -weff | Code has no effect. (Default) |
| -wpar | Parameter 'parameter' is never used. (Default) |

**Table 3.1**    Command-line options by function

| Option | Description |
| --- | --- |
| -wrch | Unreachable code. (Default) |
| -wstv | Structure passed by value. |
| -wuse | 'identifier' declared but never used. |

**Messages | Obsolete C++**

| Option | Description |
| --- | --- |
| -wobi | Base initialization without a class name is now obsolete. (Default) |
| -wofp | Style of function definition is now obsolete. (Default) |
| -wovl | Overload is now unnecessary and obsolete. (Default) |
| -wpre | Overloaded prefix operator 'operator' used as a postfix operator. |

**Messages | Portability**

| Option | Description |
| --- | --- |
| -wcln | Constant is long. |
| -wcpt | Nonportable pointer comparison. (Default) |
| -wrng | Constant out of range in comparison. (Default) |
| -wrpt | Nonportable pointer conversion. (Default) |
| -wsig | Conversion may lose significant digits. |
| -wucp | Mixing pointers to different 'char' types. |

**Messages | Potential C++ Errors**

| Option | Description |
| --- | --- |
| -wbei | Initializing 'identifier' with 'identifier'. (Default) |
| -wdsz | Array size for 'delete' ignored. (Default) |
| -whch | Handler for '<type1>' hidden by Previous Handler for '<type2>'. |
| -whid | 'function1' hides virtual function 'function2'. (Default) |
| -wibc | Base class 'base1' is inaccessible because also in 'base2'. (Default) |
| -wmpc | Conversion to type fails for members of virtual base class base. (Default) |
| -wmpd | Maximum precision used for member pointer type type. (Default) |
| -wncf | Non-const function 'function' called for const object. (Default) |
| -wnci | The constant member 'identifier' is not initialized. (Default) |
| -wnst | Use qualified name to access nested type 'type'. (Default) |
| -wntd | Use '> >' for nested templates instead of '>>'. (Default) |
| -wnvf | Non-volatile function function called for volatile object. (Default) |

**Messages | Potential Errors**

| Option | Description |
| --- | --- |
| -wamb | Ambiguous operators need parentheses. |
| -wccc | Condition is always true OR Condition is always false. (Default) |
| -wdef | Possible use of 'identifier' before definition. |
| -wnod | No declaration for function 'function'. |
| -wpia | Possibly incorrect assignment. (Default) |
| -wpro | Call to function with no prototype. (Default) |
| -wrvl | Function should return a value. (Default) |

**Optimizations**

| Option | Description |
| --- | --- |
| -Od | Disable all optimizations. |

**Optimizations | Size**

| Option | Description |
| --- | --- |
| -O | Optimize jumps. |

**Table 3.1**    Command-line options by function

| Option | Description |
|---|---|
| **-Ob** | Eliminate dead code. |
| **-Oe** | Allocate global registers and analyze variable live ranges. |
| **-Ol** | Compact loops. |
| **-OW** | Suppress the inc bp/dec bp on windows far functions (16-bit compiler only). |
| **-Z** | Enable register load suppression optimization. |
| **Optimizations \| Specific** | |
| **-O1** | Generate smallest possible code (same as using **-O, -Ob, -Oe, -Og, -Oi, -Ol, -Om, -Op, -Ot, -Ov, -k-, -Oc,** and **-Z**) |
| **-O2** | Generate fastest possible code. |
| **-Oa** | Optimize assuming pointer expressions are not aliased on common subexpression evaluation. |
| **-Oc** | Eliminate duplicate expressions within basic blocks. |
| **-Og** | Eliminate duplicate expressions within functions. |
| **-Ox** | Generate fastest code; Microsoft compatible. |
| **Optimizations \| Speed** | |
| **-Oi** | Expand common intrinsic functions. |
| **-Om** | Move invariant code out of loops. |
| **-Op** | Propagate copies. |
| **-Ov** | Enable loop induction variable and strength reduction. |
| **Response Files** | |
| **+filename** | Use alternate configuration file "filename" |

# Command-line options

The following table lists all options that are available only from the command-line.

**Table 3.2**    Command-line options only

| Option | Description |
|---|---|
| -B | Compiles assembly and calls TASM or TASM32. If TASM isn't in your path, checking this option generates an error. Also, old versions of TASM might have problems with 32-bit code. |
| -c | Compiles and assembles the named .C, .CPP, and .ASM files, but does not execute a link command. |
| *-efilename* | Derives the executable program's name from filename by adding the file extension .EXE (the program name is then filename.EXE). filename must immediately follow the -e, with no intervening whitespace. Without this option, the linker derives the .EXE file's name from the name of the first source or object file in the file name list. |
| *-Efilename* | Use "filename" as the name of the assembler to use. By default, TASM is used. |
| -Fm | Enables all the other -F options (**-Fc, -Ff,** and **-Fs**). You can use it as a handy shortcut when porting code from other compilers. |
| -h | This option offers an alternative method of calculating huge pointer expressions; this method is much faster than the standard method, but must be used with caution. When you use this option, huge pointers are normalized only when a segment wraparound occurs in the offset part. This causes problems with huge arrays if any array elements cross a segment boundary. |

**Table 3.2**    Command-line options only

| Option | Description |
| --- | --- |
| -B | Compiles assembly and calls TASM or TASM32. If TASM isn't in your path, checking this option generates an error. Also, old versions of TASM might have problems with 32-bit code. |
| -Hc | Cache precompiled headers. Use with **-H, -Hxxx, -Hu,** or **-Hfilename**. This option is useful when compiling more than one precompiled header. (32-bit compiler only) |
| -lx | Pass option "x" to the linker (TLINK for BCC and TLINK32 for BCC32). More than one option can appear after the -l (which is a lowercase L). |
| -o*filename* | Compile source file to "filename".OBJ. |
| -P | Perform a C++ compile regardless of source file extension. (Default) |
| -P*ext* | Perform a C++ compile regardless of source file extension and set the default extension to "ext". This option is available because some programmers use .C or another extension as their default extension for C++ code. |
| -S | Generate assembler source compiles the named source files and produces assembly language output files (.ASM), but does not assemble. When you use this option, Borland C++ includes the C or C++ source lines as comments in the produced .ASM file. |
| -T- | Remove all previous assembler options. |
| -T*string* | Pass "string" as an option to TASM, TASM32, or assembler specified with -E. |
| -tWM | Make a multithreaded application or DLL. |
| -U*name* | Undefines any previous definitions of the named identifier "name". |
| -Vo | This option is a "master switch" that sets on all of the backward-compatibility options listed in this section. It can be used as a handy shortcut when linking with libraries built with older versions of Borland C++. |
| -Vv | This option directs the compiler not to change the layout of any classes (which it needs to do to allow pointers to virtual base class members, which were not supported in previous versions of Borland C++). If this option is used, the compiler will not be able to create a pointer to a member of a base class that can be reached only from the derived class through two or more levels of virtual inheritance (16-bit compiler only). |
| -W | Creates a Windows GUI application. |
| -WC | Creates a 32-bit console mode application. |
| -WCD | Creates a 32-bit console mode DLL with all functions exportable and exported. |
| --WD | Creates a GUI DLL with all functions exportable. |
| -WDE | Creates a GUI DLL with explicit functions exportable and exported. |
| -weas | 'type' assigned to 'enumeration'. (Default) |
| -WM | Make a multithreaded application or DLL. |
| -zX* | Use default name for X. For example, **-zA** assigns the default class name CODE to the code segment class. |

4

# Building Applications with AppExpert

AppExpert lets you create ObjectWindows-based Windows applications with features such as a tool bar, a status bar, a menu structure, online Help, and MDI windows. You can also select options to support printing, print preview, and document/view. AppExpert works with Resource Workshop, ObjectWindows classes, and the IDE's project manager to form a visual approach to application generation.

Creating applications with AppExpert consists of four steps:

1 Use AppExpert to define the user interface and application features and to generate the code.

2 Use ClassExpert to add classes and event handlers, to implement virtual functions, to navigate to existing class source code, and automate classes. ClassExpert can also associate Resource Workshop objects (such as menus and dialog boxes) with classes or handlers.

3 Use Resource Workshop to edit or add resources.

4 Use the project tree to build your application.

AppExpert always creates the following files for each application:

- A database file for the AppExpert source (.APX) that ClassExpert uses
- A main header file (.H)
- A main source file (.CPP)
- A project file (.IDE)
- A resource header file (.RH)
- A resource script file (.RC)

Depending on which options you choose, AppExpert can create the following files:

- Help source files (.RTF)
- A Help project file (.HPJ)
- Icon and bitmap files (.ICO and .BMP)

## Steps for Creating an Application with AppExpert

To create an AppExpert application:

1 Start the IDE and choose File | New | AppExpert. A dialog box appears.

2 Type a name for your project file. By default, most generated files (including the .EXE) are derived from the target name (for example, `<targetname>.CPP`). Select a path where you want the AppExpert project and source files to be stored. AppExpert will create the directory if it does not already exist. Click OK. The AppExpert Application Generation Options dialog box appears.

3 The Application Generation Options dialog box contains a list of topics on the left and a brief description of the topic on the right. You can change options in the dialog box to customize the type of application you want generated.

4 Click the Generate button at the bottom of the Options dialog box.

5 The Generate dialog box appears, asking you to confirm that you want the code generation for your application to begin. Click Yes to generate the code for your application. While AppExpert is generating your application, a message box displays the current status.

6 The project window appears, listing some of the files required for your application (files for bitmaps, icons, and help text are not displayed). You can use ClassExpert to modify your application or you can build it first. To build your application, choose either Project | Make All or Project | Build All.

**Hint** The application generates and builds faster, if you uncheck unneeded options.

**Note** With AppExpert, you choose your application options once, then generate the code. After you generate the code and resources, you can edit and add to them, but you cannot go back to AppExpert and change options. For example, if you use AppExpert to generate an application that does not contain a status line and then decide to add one. You will need to write code to add that functionality.

## Application options

- Use the AppExpert | Application options to define the specific characteristics of the application you want to generate.

- Use the Customize Application button to open the group (if necessary) and go to the first option in the first subtopic available for the Application section of the AppExpert options.

- If you simply want to use the default options, you can generate your application now by pressing the Generate button.

# Application | Window Model

The Application I Window Model options determine which model to use for your application and how application objects will be handled.

## MDI (Multiple Document Interface)

The MDI option sets the style of your application to follow the Multiple Document Interface (MDI) model. This model causes child windows to be constrained within the boundaries of the application window.

## SDI (Single Document Interface)

The SDI option sets the style of your application to follow the Single Document Interface (SDI) model. This model supports child windows that can exist outside of the constraints of the application window without being clipped.

## Dialog Client

The Dialog Client option sets the style of your application so that the main (and only) window of your application is a dialog window, making the client area of the application a dialog box.

## Document/View

The Document/View option determines whether your application supports the Document/View model for handling application objects. The Document/View model breaks data handling into two discrete parts: data storage and control, in the document class (derived from TDocument), and data display and manipulation, in the view class (derived from TView).

You can use the Document/View option with either SDI, MDI, or Dialog Client applications.

# Application | Basic Options

The Application I Basic Options options define the general characteristics of the application you are going to generate, such as the initial state of the application's main window, and the generation of help files, as well as the directories where files will be stored.

If you simply want to use the default options, you can generate your application now by pressing the Generate button.

## Target Name

Use Application I Basic Options I Target Name to name the AppExpert target that will be used to build your application. This name is the basis for the default names of other elements in your project (e.g., header files, class database, application class, and source files).

The default name is the same as the IDE project. You can use this name or enter your own.

## Base Directory

Use Application | Basic Options | Base Directory to define the main project directory. All other directories associated with the project are placed relatively to this directory.

You can enter a directory by entering it yourself or press the Browse button to select one from the Select Directory dialog box.

The default base directory is the one you choose in the New AppExpert Project dialog box. The name of this directory is passed to the Project Manager for the new AppExpert target.

# Application | Basic Options | Features to Include

Use the Application | Basic Options | Features to Include options to specify which additional user interface elements your application supports.

### Dockable Toolbar

Turn on the Dockable Toolbar option to include a dockable toolbar in your application.

### Status Line

Turn on the Status Line option to place a status line at the bottom of your application's main window. The code generated will display help hints in the status line when menu items are highlighted.

### Recently Used Files List

Turn on the Recently Used Files List option to include a list of the four most recently accessed files under the File menu of your application.

### Registry Support

Turn on the Registry Support option to register your application's icons and document types with the system registry when the application is run.

### Drag/Drop

Turn on the Drag/Drop option to have code generated so that your application will support drag-and-drop actions from File Manager and Explorer.

### Printing

Turn on the Printing option if you want your application to support printing-related activities. The code generated will handle the Print Setup, Print Preview, and Print commands.

### Mail Support

Turn on the Mail Support option to include support for Common Message Call (CMC) mail in your application.

## Help File Support

If you select the Application | Basic Options | Include Help File Support option, AppExpert will generate RTF source files and a Help project file when it generates your application. The Help project file will be added to the Project Manager project and automatically built with the target application.

This Help file contains placeholder text for the menus and menu options present in the generated application.

## Help File Name

Use Application | Basic Options | Help File Name to specify the name of the help file associated with your application. This file name identifies the source and Help project files.

The default value for the file name is the same as the application project. You can also enter your own file name.

# Application | Advanced Options

The Application | Advanced Options options define some specific characteristics of the application you are going to generate, such as the initial state of the application's main window, and the type of controls the application will use.

## Application Startup State

Use the Application Startup State options to set the initial state of the application's main window.

## Control Style

Use the Control Style options to determine which type of controls the application will use.

# Application | Advanced Options | Application Startup State

Use the Application | Advanced Options | Application Startup State options to set the initial state of the application's main window.

## Normal (sizeable)

Turn on the Normal option to set the application window to start in a default size. This is the default setting.

## Minimized (iconic)

Turn on the Minimized option to set the application window to start in a minimized state (as an icon on the Windows desktop).

## Maximized (entire screen)

Turn on the Maximized option to set the application window to fill the entire Windows desktop when it starts running.

# Application | Advanced Options | Control Style

Use the Application | Advanced Options | Control Style options to determine which type of controls the application will use.

## Standard Windows

Turn on the Standard Windows option to specify that the application will use standard Windows controls. This is the default setting.

## Borland BWCC

Turn on the Borland BWCC option to specify that the application will use the Borland custom control style.

## MS Control 3D

Turn on the MS Control 3D option to specify that the application will use the three-dimensional Windows controls provided by CTL3DV2.DLL and CTL3D32.DLL.

# Application | OLE 2 Options

Use the Application | OLE 2 Options options to set the behavior of your OLE 2 application.

## OLE 2 Container Options

Choose whether or not you want your application to be an OLE 2 and OCX container application. AppExpert only allows MDI and SDI applications which use the DocView model to be containers.

## OLE 2 Server Options

Choose whether you want your application to be an OLE 2 Server EXE, DLL, or not a server at all. AppExpert only allows MDI and SDI applications which use the DocView model to be servers.

## Enable Automation in the Application

Select the Enable Automation in the Application option if you want your application to be an OLE 2 automation server.

## Server ID

If you set your application to be an OLE 2 Server, use the Server ID field to specify the identifier for your application.

# Application | Code Generation Control

Use the Application | Code Generation Control options to control various aspects of the code generation process.

## Target Name

Displays the name of the project as defined in Basic Options | Target Name.

## Base Directory

Displays the base directory for the project as defined in Basic Options | Base Directory.

## Source Directory

Use Application | Code Generation Control | Source Directory to specify the directory where the source files for the application will be placed during code generation. This path is relative to the directory specified as the Base Directory. If an absolute path is specifed, it is converted to a path relative to the Base Directory.

You can enter a directory or press the Browse button to select one from the Select Directory dialog box. The default value for the Source Path is the current directory, which is the directory specified in Base Directory.

## Header Directory

Use Application | Code Generation Control | Header Directory to specify the directory where the header files for the application will be placed during code generation. This path is relative to the directory specified as the Base Directory. If an absolute path is specifed, it is converted to a path relative to the Base Directory.

You can enter a directory or press the Browse button to select one from the Select Directory dialog box. The default value for the Header Path is " . \ ", whjch causes source files to be placed in the current directory.

## Main Source File

Use Main Source File to name the main application source file. The default filename is the name of the project: `<TargetName>App.CPP`. AppExpert will parse and shorten the project name if it is longer than eight characters, unless the Use Long File Names option is enabled.

## Main Header File

Use Main Header File to name the main application header file. The default filename is the name of the project: `<TargetName>App.H`. AppExpert will parse and shorten the project name if it is longer than eight characters, unless the Use Long File Names option is enabled.

## Application Class

Use Application Class to name the class that AppExpert will derive from *TApplication*. The default class name is `T<TargetName>App`.

### About Dialog Class

Use About Dialog Class to name the class that AppExpert will derive from *TDialog*. The default class name is T<TargetName>AboutDlg.

### Use Long File Names

The Use Long File Names option determines whether or not the source files of your application are generated using long file names.

**Note**    Some installations of Novell Netware do not support long file names.

### Comments

Use the Comments options to specify how the generated code is documented.

### Terse

Turn on the Terse option to sparsely comment the generated code.

### Verbose

Turn on the Verbose option to heavily comment the generated code.

## Application | Administrative Options

Use the Application | Administrative Options to specify identifying information that will be placed in a comment block at the beginning of all of the generated project files. Some of the information is also displayed in the About... dialog box of the application.

### Version Number

Use Version Number to provide the version number for the project. This value will be displayed in the application's "About …" dialog box. The default version number is "1.0."

### Copyright

Use Copyright to provide the copyright information for your application. This value will be displayed in the application's "About …" dialog box and will be placed in all of the comment blocks generated by AppExpert.

### Description

Use Description to provide a description of your application. This value will be displayed in the application's "About …" dialog box. The default value is the name of the project.

### Author

Use Author to provide the name of the programmer who generated the source code. This will be placed in all of the comment blocks generated by AppExpert.

### Company

Use Company to provide the name of the programmer's company. This will be placed in all of the comment blocks generated by AppExpert.

# Main Window options

- Use the AppExpert | Main Window options to control the appearance and operation of the main window of the generated application.

- Use the Customize Main Window button to open the group (if necessary) and go to the first option in the first subtopic available for the Main Window section of the AppExpert options.

- If you want to simply use the default options, you can generate your application now by pressing the Generate button.

## Window Title

Use Window Title to specify the name that will be displayed as the caption for the application's main window.

## Main Window | Background Color

The Main Window | Background Color options determine the background color of the application's main window.

### Use Default Color

The Use Default Color options causes no code to be generated to set the main window background color. In this way, the color used will be the current default for the system.

### Use System Color Constant

The Use System Color Constant option sets the background color of the main window to a specified constant. Choose the constant from the list box provided.

### Use Specified Color

The Use Specified Color option sets the background color of the main window to a specified color. Choose the color from the Color dialog.

## Main Window | Basic Options

Use the Main Window | Basic Options to control the general appearance of the main window of your application.

## Window Styles

Use the Window Styles options to control the appearance of the application's main window, specifying its border style and whether it contains system and control menus.

### Caption

Turn on the Caption radio button to create a single, thin border and a title bar where a caption can be displayed.

### Border

Turn on the Border option to get a single, thin border without a caption for the application's main window.

### Max Box

Turn on the Max Box option to add a maximize button to the right side of the application's main window caption.

### Min Box

Turn on the Min Box option to add a minimize button to the right side of the application's main window caption.

### Vertical Scroll

Turn on the Vertical Scroll option to add a vertical scroll bar to the right side of the application's main window.

### Horizontal Scroll

Turn on the Horizontal Scroll option to add a horizontal scroll bar to the bottom of the application's main window.

### System Menu

Turn on the System Menu option to add a system menu button on the left side of the application's main window caption.

### Visible

Turn on the Visible option to make the application's main window visible. This is the default setting. When this option is off, the WS_VISIBLE style is changed to NOT WS_VISIBLE.

### Disabled

Turn on the Disabled option to disable the application's main window.

### Thick Frame

Turn on the Thick Frame option to place a double border around the application's main window. If this option if off, users cannot resize the main window.

### Clip Siblings

Turn on the Clip Siblings option to protect the siblings of the application's main window. Painting is restricted to that window.

### Clip Children

Turn on the Clip Children option to protect child windows from being repainted by the application's main window.

## Main Window | SDI Client Window

Use the Main Window | SDI Client Window options to define the class that represents the client area of the Single Document Interface main window. These options are only applicable if you select the Single Document Interface option from Application | Window Model options.

### Client/View Class

Use Client/View Class to name the class of the SDI client area window or view.

### Document Class

Use Document Class to name the class of the default document. If the Doc/View option in the Application | Window Model options is selected, the default value is TFileDocument; otherwise, Document Class is blank.

### Description

Use Description to describe the class of files associated with the Files of Type List in Windows common file dialog boxes. The default value is All Files (*.*). This value serves as the description for the value entered in Filters.

### Filters

Use Filters to list wildcard file specifications (separated by semicolons) for the file names you want the application to recognize. This value is passed to Windows common file dialog boxes to filter files displayed in the list box of those dialog boxes. The default value is *.*. The values entered in Description serves as the explanation of this value.

### Default Extension

Use Default Extension to specify the default filename extension. This value is passed to Windows common file dialog boxes and added to filenames without extensions. The default value is TXT.

### Class Name

Use Class Name to specify the name AppExpert uses for the class derived from Client/ View Class that represents the client area of the SDI frame window. The default value is T<ProjectName><Client/ViewClass> (without the leading "T").

### Source File

Use Source File to name the source file that will store the implementation of the class named in Client/View Class. The default value is `<ClassName>.CPP`. AppExpert will parse and shorten the class name if it is larger than eight characters, unless the Use Long File Names option is enabled.

### Header File

Use Header File to name the header file that will store the definition of the class named in Client/View Class. The default value is `<ClassName>.H`. AppExpert will parse and shorten the class name if it is larger than eight characters, unless the Use Long File Names option is enabled.

## Client/View Class

Use Main Window | SDI Client | Client/View Class to name the class of the SDI client area or view. The interpretation of this value depends on whether you select the Doc/View option in the Application | Window Model options.

If the Doc/View option is not selected, Client/View Class selects the class of the client window; otherwise, Client/View Class selects the class of the view of the default document/view.

| Doc/View On | Doc/View Off |
| --- | --- |
| TEditView (default) | TEditFile (default) |
| TListView | TListBox |
| TWindowView | TWindow |

This value is automatically mapped to the Doc/View options. For example, if you turn off the Doc/View option, TListView is switched to TListBox. Conversely, if you select the Doc/View option, TListBox changes to TListView.

## Main Window | MDI Client Window

Use the Main Window | MDI Client Window options to describe the class that defines the client window of the Multiple Document Interface main window. These options are only applicable if you select the Multiple Document Interface option from Application | Window Model options.

### Client Class

Use Client Class to specify the name AppExpert uses for the class derived from TMDIClient that represents the client area of the MDI frame window. The default value is `T<TargetName><ClientClass>`.

### Source File

Use Source File to name the source file that will store the implementation of the class named in Client Class. The default value is `<ClientClass>.CPP`. AppExpert will parse and shorten the client class name if it is larger than eight characters, unless the Use Long File Names option is enabled.

### Header File

Use Header File to name the header file that will store the definition of the class named in Client Class. The default value is `<ClientClass>.H`. AppExpert will parse and shorten the client class name if it is larger than eight characters, unless the Use Long File Names option is enabled.

## Main Window | Dialog Client Window

Use the Main Window I Dialog Client Window options to describe the characteristics of an application where the main window is a dialog window.

### Client Class

Use Client Class to specify the name AppExpert uses for the class derived from TDialog that represents the main window of the application. The default value is `T<TargetName><ClientClass>`.

### Source File

Use Source File to name the source file that will store the implementation of the class named in Client Class. The default value is `<ClientClass>.CPP`. AppExpert will parse and shorten the project name if it is larger than eight characters, unless the Use Long File Names option is enabled.

### Header File

Use Header File to name the header file that will store the definition of the class named in Client Class. The default value is `<ClientClass>.H`. AppExpert will parse and shorten the class name if it is larger than eight characters, unless the Use Long File Names option is enabled.

### Dialog ID

Use Dialog ID to specify the identifier associated with the dialog that functions as the main window of your application.

### Include a Menu Bar

Select Include a Menu Bar if you want a menu bar on your main window.

# MDI Child/View Options

Use the AppExpert I MDI Child/View options to define the class that will define a default child window or document/view of the Multiple Document Interface application. These options are only applicable if you select the Multiple Document Interface option from Application I Window Model options.

## MDI Child Class

Use MDI Child Class to name the class derived from TMDIChild that represents the frame of the default MDI child windows. The default value is T<TargetName>MDIChild.

## Source File

Use Source File to name the source file that will store the implementation of the class named in MDI Child. The default value is <MDIChildClass>.CPP. AppExpert will parse and shorten the child class name if it is larger than eight characters, unless the Use Long File Names option is enabled.

## Header File

Use Header File to name the header file that will store the definition of the class named in Client Class. The default value is <MDIChildClass>.H. AppExpert will parse and shorten the child class name if it is larger than eight characters, unless the Use Long File Names option is enabled.

## MDI Child/View | Basic Options

Use the MDI Child/View | Basic Options to define the default child window of an MDI application.

### MDI Client/View Class

Use MDI Child/View | Basic Options | MDI Client/View Class to name the class of the MDI client area or view. The interpretation of this value depends on whether you selected the Doc/View option in the Application | Window Model options.

If the Doc/View option is not selected, MDI Client/View Class selects the class of the client window; otherwise, MDI Client/View Class selects the class of the view of the default document/view.

| Doc/View On | Doc/View Off |
|---|---|
| TEditView (default) | TEditFile (default) |
| TListView | TListBox |
| TWindowView | TWindow |

This value is automatically mapped to the Doc/View options. For example, if you turn off the Doc/View option, TListView is switched to TListBox. Conversely, if you select the Doc/View option, TListBox changes to TListView.

### Document Class

Use Document Class to name the class of the default document. If the Doc/View option in the Application | Window Model options is selected, the default value is *TFileDocument*; otherwise, Document Class is blank.

## Description

Use Description to describe the class of files associated with the Files of Type List in Windows common file dialog boxes. The default value is `All Files (*.*)`. This value serves as the description for the value entered in Filters.

## Filters

Use Filters to list wildcard file specifications (separated by semicolons) for the file names you want the application to recognize. This value is passed to Windows common file dialog boxes to filter files displayed in the list box of those dialog boxes. The default value is `*.*`. The values entered in Description serves as the explanation of this value.

## Default Extension

Use Default Extension to specify the default filename extension. This value is passed to Windows common file dialog boxes and added to filenames without extensions. The default value is TXT.

## Class Name

Use Class Name to specify the name AppExpert uses for the class derived from the MDI Client/View Class that represents the client area of the MDI frame window. The default value is `<ProjectName><ClientViewClass>` (without the leading "T").

## Source File

Use Source File to name the source file that will store the implementation of the class entered in Class Name. The default value is `<ClassName>.CPP`. AppExpert will parse and shorten the project name if it is larger than eight characters, unless the Use Long File Names option is enabled.

## Header File

Use Header File to name of the header file that will store the definition of the class entered in Class Name. The default value is `<ClassName>.H`. AppExpert will parse and shorten the class name if it is larger than eight characters, unless the Use Long File Names option is enabled.

# 5

# Managing your classes with ClassExpert

ClassExpert lets you create new classes, edit and refine the implementation of classes, and navigate through the source code for existing classes in your AppExpert applications. You can use ClassExpert with Resource Workshop to associate classes to resources (for example, associating a *TDialog* class to a dialog resource). ClassExpert displays virtual functions and events for existing classes and checks the ones implemented in your application. You can also use ClassExpert to instantiate and automate classes in your AppExpert project.

## Starting ClassExpert

To start ClassExpert:

1 Open an AppExpert_IDE project file by choosing File | Open.

2 Double-click the AppExpert target node (ClassExpert is the default viewer for AppExpert targets), or choose View | ClassExpert. ClassExpert appears, listing the classes and their implementation for your application.

The ClassExpert window contains three panes, each with a specific function:

• **Classes** displays the classes used in the application.

• **Events** displays the events handled by the selected class.

• **Edit** lets you view and edit the source associated with the selected class.

# ClassExpert Classes pane

The Classes pane lists the set of classes known to ClassExpert that are used in the current project. This includes all classes created during code generation and any classes you might have added afterward using ClassExpert.

Selecting a class from this list changes the contents displayed in the Events and Edit panes to show the events and source file associated with the selected class.

## Classes pane SpeedMenu

Use the Classes pane SpeedMenu to access frequently used Edit commands.

### Add New Class

Use the Add New Class command from the Classes pane SpeedMenu to create a new class in your application. Choosing this option displays the Add New Class dialog box which you can use to define the new class you are creating.

### Automate Class

Use the Automate Class command from the Classes pane SpeedMenu to expose existing classes in your application to OLE 2 automation. This will cause additional code to be added to your source files to support the automation of the class currently selected in the Classes pane. If the *TApplication* class is not already exposed, automating a class will automatically automate it.

### Delete Automation

Use the Delete Automation command from the Classes pane SpeedMenu to remove the OLE 2 automation code from the class currently selected in the Classes pane.

Choosing this command displays a dialog box warning you that the class will be removed from automation. Click Yes to remove the automation code, or No to cancel the operation.

**Note**   This command is only available if the class has already been automated.

### View Document Templates

Use the View Document Templates command from the Classes pane SpeedMenu to create, delete, and view document and view pairings. Choosing this option displays the Document Templates dialog box in which you can define the document templates.

This option is only applicable if you selected the Document/View option from the Application | Window Model settings in AppExpert when you set the options for your application.

### View Class Info

Use the View Class Info command from the Classes pane SpeedMenu to view a summary of the properties of the class currently selected in the Classes pane. Choosing this command displays the Class Info dialog box.

If the selected class is derived from *TFrameWindow,* you can also use this option to change the client class.

### Edit Source

Use the Edit Source command from the Classes pane SpeedMenu to edit the source file associated with the class currently selected in the Classes pane.

Choosing this option opens the source file in an IDE editor window (not in the ClassExpert Edit pane) and positions the cursor on the class constructor.

### Edit Header

Use the Edit Header command from the Classes pane SpeedMenu to edit the header file associated with the class currently selected in the Classes pane.

Choosing this option opens the header file in an IDE editor window (not in the ClassExpert Edit pane) and positions the cursor on the class definition.

### Edit Dialog

Use the Edit Dialog command to edit the dialog template associated with the class currently selected in the Classes pane. Choosing this command starts Resource Workshop and loads the associated dialog resource into the Dialog Editor.

**Note**    This option is only applicable if the currently selected class is derived from *TDialog.*

### Edit Menu

Use the Edit Menu command to edit the menu resource associated with the class currently selected in the Classes pane. Choosing this command starts Resource Workshop and loads the associated menu resource into the Menu Editor. Typically, an application has only one menu.

## ClassExpert Events pane

The Events pane contains an outliner list with several categories. The available categories depend on the derivation of the class currently selected in the Classes pane.

These are the categories that can be displayed:

- Automation (automated classes only)
- Command Notifications
- Control Notifications (dialog classes only)
- Virtual Functions
- Windows Messages

### Events pane SpeedMenu

Use the Events pane SpeedMenu to access frequently used ClassExpert commands.

## Add Handler

Use the Add Handler option from the Events pane SpeedMenu to create a default member function skeleton in the source file for the class currently selected in the Classes pane. The source file will appear in the Edit pane.

- If you add a handler for a Windows message, ClassExpert adds an entry to the response table whose name is defined by default. The function associated with the handler appears in the edit window with the appropriate default handling.

- If you add a handler for a Virtual Function, the function associated with the handler appears in the edit window with the appropriate default handling.

- If you add a handler for either Commands or Control Notifications, ClassExpert will prompt you for the function name before adding the entry to the response table.

This option is only applicable if the event currently selected in the Events pane is not already handled by a member function of the selected class. Unhandled events and non-overriden virtual functions will not have a check mark next to them.

## Delete Handler

Use the Delete Handler option from the Events pane SpeedMenu to delete a member function from the event currently selected in the Edit pane.

**Note**    The member function is removed, but the code that implements the function is not deleted. You will be warned of this and will need to remove the code. For events, commands, and control notifications, the response table entries are removed.

This option is only applicable if the currently selected event has a member function associated with it; the handled event will have a check mark next to it.

For dialog classes (those derived from *TDialog*), you will get these additional commands:

## Add Instance Variable

Use the Add Instance Variable option from the Events pane SpeedMenu to add an *instance variable* for the item currently selected in the Events pane.

Choosing this option prompts you for the name of the variable. The type of the variable is fixed and determined by the associated control. ClassExpert then adds the following to your application code:

- In the header file, a structure declaration is added with an entry for the instance variable.

- In the source file,

  1 The instance variable is allocated in the class constructor (this associates the ObjectWindows class with the resource object).

  2 A static instance of the transfer structure is declared.

**Note**    This command is only available if the class currently selected in the Classes pane is derived from *TDialog*.

### Delete Instance Variable

Use the Delete Instance Variable option from the Events pane SpeedMenu to delete the *instance variable* associated with the item currently selected in the Events pane.

ClassExpert deletes the following from your code:

- The entry from the structure

- The pointer variable in the class declaration

- The allocation of the class variable associated with the resource control in the constructor

If you delete all instance variables from your code, you will have an empty structure and the set transfer buffer call. This information does not affect the rest of your code, so you do not need to delete it manually.

**Note**  This command is only available if the class currently selected in the Classes pane is derived from *TDialog*.

For Automation events, you will get these additional commands:

### Add Data

Use the Add Data command to add automation data to the class currently selected in the Classes pane. Choosing this command displays the Automate Data dialog box where you can enter information about the automation data.

**Note**  This command is only available for classes that you have exposed to OLE 2 automation using the Automate Class command.

### Delete Data

Use the Delete Data command to remove automation data from the class currently selected in the Classes pane.

**Note**  The automation data is removed from the OLE 2 automation symbol table, but the code that implements the data is not deleted. You will be warned of this and will need to remove the code.

This option is only applicable if the currently selected class has automation data associated with it and you have selected a data member in the Events pane.

### View Data

Use the View Data command to view the automation data for the class currently selected in the Classes pane. Choosing this command displays the Automate Data dialog box where you can view (but not change) the information about the selected automation data.

This option is only applicable if the currently selected class has automation data associated with it and you have selected a data variable in the Events pane.

### Add Method

Use the Add Method command to expose an automation method to OLE 2 automation in the class currently selected in the Classes pane. Choosing this command displays the

Automate Method dialog box where you can enter information about the automation method.

**Note** This command is only available for classes that you have exposed to OLE 2 automation using the Automate Class command.

### Delete Method

Use the Delete Method command to remove an exposed method selected in the Classes pane from the OLE 2 automation symbol table.

**Note** The automation method is removed from the OLE 2 automation symbol table, but the code that implements the method is not deleted. You will be warned of this and will need to remove the code.

This option is only applicable if the currently selected class has an automation method associated with it and you have selected a method in the Events pane.

### View Method

Use the View Method command to view the automation method for the class currently selected in the Classes pane. Choosing this command displays the Automate Method dialog box where you can view the information (but not change it) about the selected automation method.

This option is only applicable if the currently selected class has an automation method associated with it and you have selected a method in the Events pane.

### Add Property

Use the Add Property command to expose a property to OLE 2 automation of the class currently selected in the Classes pane. Choosing this command displays the Automate Property dialog box where you can enter information about the automation property.

### Delete Property

Use the Delete Property command to remove an exposed automation property from the class currently selected in the Classes pane.

**Note** The automation property is removed from the OLE 2 automation symbol table, but the code that implements the property is not deleted. You will be warned of this and will need to remove the code.

This option is only applicable if the currently selected class has an automation property associated with it and you have selected a property in the Events pane.

### View Property

Use the View Property command to view the automation property for the class currently selected in the Classes pane. Choosing this command displays the Automate Property dialog box where you can view information about the selected automation property.

This option is only applicable if the currently selected class has an automation property associated with it and you have selected a property in the Events pane.

## Events | Automation

The Events | Automation category lists all of the automation data, methods, and properties for the automated class currently selected in the Classes pane.

## Events | Command Notifications

The Events | Command Notifications category lists all of the commands inherited from the base class of the class currently selected in the Classes pane, as well as command events that can be generated by other objects in the application, such as menus. This list is dynamically updated to reflect any changes you might make to objects that generate commands in your application.

Each item in the Command Notifications category expands to two items: Command and Command Enabled. The Command handler causes the associated class to handle the command event, while the Command Enabled handler allows the associated class to control whether the command event is enabled or disabled (grayed).

A check mark next to an event indicates that it is handled by the class currently selected in the Classes pane.

## Events | Control Notifications

The Events | Control Notifications category appears only for classes derived from *TDialog*. This category lists the identifiers for all of the controls in the dialog associated with the class. Each control identifier expands to a list of messages it can send to or receive from the dialog class.

A check mark next to an event indicates that it is handled by the class currently selected in the Classes pane. A light gray check mark indicates that one or more of the child events are handled.

## Events | Virtual Functions

The Events | Virtual Functions category lists all of the virtual functions inherited from the base class of the class currently selected in the Classes pane. The contents of this list is fixed for a given class.

A check mark next to an event indicates that it is handled by the class currently selected in the Classes pane.

## Events | Windows Messages

The Events | Windows Messages category lists the set of Windows messages. This set includes:

- Basic Messages

- Other Messages

- Win32 Messages

- OLE 2 Messages

A check mark next to a message indicates that it is handled by the event currently selected in the Events pane.

## ClassExpert Edit pane

The Edit pane is an Edit window that supports most of the features of the editor in the IDE. It contains the C++ source file associated with the class currently selected in the Classes pane.

You can freely edit the file displayed in the Edit pane, adding, deleting, and modifying code as needed.

### Edit pane SpeedMenu

Use the Edit pane SpeedMenu to access frequently used ClassExpert commands.

### Use Class

Use the Use Class command to generate the code to instantiate a class in your application. Choosing this commands displays the Use Class dialog box that allows you to choose which class you want to instantiate.

# Using Rescan

Rescan is a special project tool that examines all the source code listed in your AppExpert project (.IDE file) and updates or rebuilds the project's database (the .APX file) according to what it finds in the source code. Rescan looks for special markers in the source code to reconstruct the AppExpert database file and then starts Resource Workshop to reconstruct information about project resources. If Rescan is successful, the original project database file is renamed to *.~AP and a new database file is created; otherwise, the original database is left as *.APX.

You can use Rescan to:

- Delete a class
- Move a class from one source file to another
- Rename a class, handler, instance variable, or dialog ID
- Import a class from another AppExpert project
- Rebuild a lost or damaged project database (*.APX) file

## Deleting a class

To delete a class:

1 Remove the class source file from the IDE project by selecting the source node, right-clicking the node, and choosing Delete Node. If the class shares a source file with other classes, delete the code related to the class from the source file and delete references to the class from other source files; otherwise, you will get errors during compilation.

2 Select the AppExpert target in the project, right-click it, then choose Special | Rescan. Rescan scans the source files listed as dependencies for the AppExpert target.

Resource Workshop scans and updates the resource files. When Rescan is complete, you will return to the updated project file where you can either build your application or use ClassExpert.

You can add the deleted class back to the project by adding the class source file (and its associated header file as a dependent node under the class source file ) as a dependent of the AppExpert target (use Add Node from the SpeedMenu), then rescanning.

3 Look at the Classes pane in ClassExpert to see that the class is now omitted from the list.

## Moving a class

To move a class from one source file to another:

1 Move (cut and paste) the code or definition of the class to the new source or header file. Be certain to also copy the comments generated by AppExpert or else ClassExpert will be unable to locate the correct location in the new source or header files where the class is referenced or defined.

2 Add the new source file if it is not in the project (and its associated header file as a dependent node under the class source file) as a dependent node of the AppExpert target (use Add Node from the SpeedMenu). If the moved class was in its own source file, you can delete the now-empty source file from the project.

3 Select the AppExpert target in the project, right-click it to view the SpeedMenu, then select Special I Rescan. When Rescan is finished, it returns you to the project window in the IDE.

## Renaming an AppExpert element

To rename a class, event handler function, instance variable, or dialog ID:

1 Use the IDE editor to search and replace all occurrences of the original name with the new name. Be sure to check all source files associated with the project (.CPP, .H, .RC, and .RH files).

2 In the project window, select the AppExpert target, right-click it, then choose Special I Rescan. When Rescan is finished, it returns you to the project window in the IDE.

**Note** After following this procedure, check your #include statements, as well as the #ifdef and #define statements that AppExpert created. Verify that none of these have changed as a result of searching and replacing the name of your class within the source files.

## Importing a class

To import a class from one AppExpert project to another:

1 Move or copy the source and header file that defines the class to the source and header directory of the other project. All source files for a project must be in the

project's source directory (.CPP files) or header directory (.H files). These directories were created when you first generated the AppExpert project. (Unless you specified a different source or header directory, your source and header files will be in the same directory as your project [.IDE] file.)

2 Add the class source file as a dependent node under the AppExpert target in the IDE project (use Add Node from the SpeedMenu).

3 Add the header file that contains the class definition as a dependent node under class source file in the AppExpert project (use Add Node from the SpeedMenu).

4 In the project window, select the AppExpert target, right-click, then choose Special | Rescan.

## Rebuilding the .APX database file

To rebuild a lost or damaged database file (the .APX file):

1 Open the project (.IDE) file that contains the AppExpert target and dependent nodes.

2 Select the AppExpert target, right-click it, then choose Special | Rescan from the SpeedMenu. Rescan automatically creates a new database file using markers and the source code from the AppExpert application.

Chapter

# 6

# Browsing through your code

The Browser lets you search through your object hierarchies, classes, functions, variables, types, constants, and labels that your program uses. The Browser also lets you:

- Graphically view the hierarchies in your application, then select the object of your choice and view the functions and symbols it contains.

- List the variables your program uses, then select one and view its declaration, list all references to it in your program, or go to where it is declared in your source code.

- List all the classes your program uses, then select one and list all the symbols in its interface part. From this list, you can select a symbol and browse as you would with any other symbol in your program.

## Using the Browser

If the program in the current Edit window or the first file in your project has not yet been compiled, the IDE must first compile your program before invoking the Browser.

If you try to browse a variable or class definition (or any symbol that does not have symbolic debug information), the IDE displays an error message.

If you changed the following default settings on the Project Options dialog box, before you use the Browser, be sure to:

1 Choose Options | Project.

2 Choose Compiler | Debugging and check
  - Debug information in OBJs.
  - Browser reference information in OBJs.

3 Choose Linker | General and check Include Debug Information.

4 Compile your application.

## Starting the Browser

You can start browsing through your code the following ways:

- Place your cursor on a symbol in your code and choose Browse Symbol from the Edit window SpeedMenu.
- From the main menu or the SpeedBar, and choose one of the following commands:
  - Search | Browse Symbol
  - View | Classes
  - View | Globals

### Browser views

The Browser provides the following types of views:

- Global Symbols
- Objects (Class Overview)
- Symbol Declaration
- Class Inspection
- References

# Browsing objects (class overview)

Choose View | Classes to see an overall view of the object hierarchies in your application, as well as the small details.

The Browser draws your objects and shows their ancestor-descendant relationships in a horizontal tree. The red lines in the hierarchy help you see the immediate ancestor-descendant relationships of the currently selected object more clearly.

To see more detail about a particular object, double-click it. The Browser lists the symbols (the procedures, functions, variables, and so on) used in the object.

One or more letters appear to the left of each symbol in the object that describe what kind of symbol it is. See "Browser filters and letter symbols."

## Browsing global symbols

Choose View | Globals to open a window that lists every global symbol in your application in alphabetical order.

To see the declaration of a particular symbol listed in the Browser, use one of the following methods:

- Double-click the symbol.
- Select the symbol and press Enter.

- Select the symbol and choose Browse Symbol from the SpeedMenu.

## Search

The Search input box at the bottom of the window lets you quickly search through the list of global symbols by typing the first few letters of the symbol name. As you type, the highlight bar in the list box moves to a symbol that matches the typed characters.

## Browser SpeedMenu

Once you select the global symbol you are interested in, you can use the following commands on the Browser SpeedMenu:

- Edit Source
- Browse Symbol
- Browse References
- Return to Previous View
- Toggle Window Mode
- Set Options

# Browsing symbols in your code

You can browse any symbol in your code without viewing object hierarchies or lists of symbols first.

To do so, highlight or place your cursor on the symbol in your code and choose either

- Search | Browse Symbol from the main menu
- Browse Symbol from the Edit window SpeedMenu

If the symbol you select to browse is a structured type, the Browser shows you all the symbols in the scope of that type. You can then choose to inspect any of these further. For example, if you choose an object type, you will see all the symbols listed that are within the scope of the object.

## Symbol declaration window

This Browser window shows the declaration of the selected symbol.

You can use the following commands on the Browser SpeedMenu:

- Edit Source
- Browse References
- Browse Class Hierarchy
- Return to Previous View
- Toggle Window Mode

### Browsing references

This Browser window shows the references to the selected symbol.

You can use the following commands on the Browser SpeedMenu:

- Edit Source
- Browse Class Hierarchy
- Return to Previous View
- Toggle Window Mode
- Set Options

### Class inspection window

This Browser window shows the symbols (functions and variables) used in the selected class.

Once you select the symbol you are interested in, you can use the following commands on the Browser SpeedMenu:

- Edit Source
- Browse Symbol
- Browse References
- Browse Class Hierarchy
- Return to Previous View
- Toggle Window Mode
- Set Options

# Browser filters and letter symbols

When you browse a particular symbol, the same letters that appear on the left that identify the symbol appear in a Filters matrix at the bottom of the Browser window. The Filters matrix has a column for each letter which can appear in the top or bottom row of the column.

Use the filters to select the type of symbols you want to see listed. (You can also use the Browser Options settings to specify the types of symbols you want to see listed.)

| Letter | Symbol |
|--------|--------|
| F | Function |
| T | Type |
| V | Variable |
| C | Integral constants |
| ? | Debuggable |

| Letter | Symbol |
|--------|--------|
| I | Inherited from an ancestor |
| v | Virtual method |

**Note**    In some cases, more than one letter appears next to a symbol. Additional letters appear to the right of the letter identifying the type of symbol and further describe the symbol:

## To view all instances of a particular type of symbol

Click the top cell of the column.

For example, to view all the variables in the currently selected object, click the top cell in the V column. All the variables used in the object appear.

## To hide all instances of a particular type of symbol

Click the bottom cell of the letter column.

For example, to view only the functions and procedures in an object, you need to hide all the variables. Click the bottom cell in the V column, and click the top cells in the F and P columns.

## To change several filter settings at once

Drag your mouse over the cells you want to select in the Filters matrix.

# Customizing the Browser

Use the Environment Options dialog box to select the Browser options you want to use.

1   Choose Options | Environment.

2   Choose Browser.

3   Specify the types of symbols you want to have visible in the Browser using the Visible Symbols option.

4   Specify how many Browser views you can have open at one time. See single or multiple Browser window mode in the Browser Window Behavior option.

# Using the integrated debugger

No matter how careful you are when you write code, a newly completed program is likely to contain errors, or *bugs*, that prevent it from running the way you intended it to. *Debugging* is the process of locating and fixing the errors in your programs.

The Borland C++ IDE contains an *integrated debugger* that lets you debug 32-bit Windows programs from within the IDE. Among other things, the integrated debugger lets you control the execution of your program, inspect the values of variables and items in data structures, modify the values of data items while debugging. You can access the functionality of the integrated debugger through two menus: Debug and View along with local menus and keystrokes. This chapter introduces you to the functionality of the integrated debugger and gives a brief overview of the debugging process.

Note     The integrated debugger does not support 16-bit Windows or DOS debugging. This functionality is supported by Turbo Debugger.

## Types of bugs

The integrated debugger can help find two basic types of programming errors: run-time errors and logic errors.

### Run-time errors

If your program successfully compiles, but fails when you run it, you've encountered a *run-time error*. Your program contains valid statements, but the statements cause errors when they're executed. For example, your program might be trying to open a nonexistent file, or it might be trying to divide a number by zero. The operating system detects run-time errors and stops your program execution if such an error is encountered.

Without a debugger, run-time errors can be difficult to locate because the compiler doesn't tell you where the error is located in your source code. Often, the only clue you have to work with is where your program failed and the error message generated by the run-time error.

Although you can find run-time errors by searching through your program source code, the integrated debugger can help you quickly track down these types of errors. Using the integrated debugger, you can run to a specific program location. From there, you can begin executing your program one statement at a time, watching the behavior of your program with each step. When you execute the statement that causes your program to fail, you have pinpointed the error. From there, you can fix the source code, recompile the program, and resume testing your program.

## Logic errors

*Logic errors* are errors in design and implementation of your program. Your program statements are valid (they do *something*), but the actions they perform are not the actions you had in mind when you wrote the code. For instance, logic errors can occur when variables contain incorrect values, when graphic images don't look right, or when the output of your program is incorrect.

Logic errors are often the most difficult type of errors to find because they can show up in places you might not expect. To be sure your program works as designed, you must thoroughly test all of its aspects. Only by scrutinizing each portion of the user interface and output of your program can you be sure that its behavior corresponds to its design. As with run-time errors, the integrated debugger helps you locate logic errors by letting you monitor the values of your program variables and data objects as your program executes.

# Planning a debugging strategy

After program design, program development consists of a continuous cycle of program coding and debugging. Only after you thoroughly test your program should you distribute it to your end users. To ensure that you test all aspects of your program, it's best to have a thorough plan for your debugging cycles.

One good debugging method involves breaking your program down into different sections that you can systematically debug. By closely monitoring the statements in each program section, you can verify that each area is performing as designed. If you do find a programming error, you can correct the problem in your source code, recompile the program, and then resume testing.

# Starting a debugging session

To start a debugging session:

1 Build your program with debug information.
2 Run your program from within the IDE.

When debugging, you have complete control of your program's execution. You can pause the program at any point to examine the values of program variables and data structures, to view the sequence of function calls, and to modify the values of program variables to see how different values affect the behavior of your program.

## Compiling with debug information

Before you can begin a debugging session, you must compile your project with *symbolic debug information*. Symbolic debug information, contained in a *symbol table*, enables the debugger to make connections between your program's source code and the machine code that's generated by the compiler. This lets you view the actual source code of your program while running the program through the debugger.

To generate symbolic debug information for your project:

1 In the Project window, select the project node.

2 Choose Options | Project to open the Project Options dialog box.

3 From the Compiler | Debugging topic, check Debug Information In OBJs to include debug information in your project .OBJ files. (This option is checked by default.)

4 From the Linker | General topic, check Include Debug Information. This option transfers the symbolic debug information contained in your .OBJ files to the final .EXE file (this option is checked by default).

Adding debug information to your files increases their file size. Because of this, you'll want to include debug information in your files only during the development stage of your project. Once your program is fully debugged, compile your program without debug information to reduce the final .EXE file size. Or you can also use TDSTRIP.

**Note**    Not all of the .OBJ files in your project need symbolic debug information—only those modules you need to debug must contain a symbol table. However, since you can't statement step into a module that doesn't contain debug information, it's best to compile all your modules with a minimum of line number debug information during the development stages of your project.

## Running your program in the IDE

Once you've compiled your program with debug information, you can begin a debugging session by running your program in the IDE. By running your program in the IDE, you have control of when the program runs and when it pauses. Whenever the program is paused in the IDE, the debugger takes control.

When your program is running under the IDE, it behaves as it normally would: your program creates windows, accepts user input, calculates values, and displays output. During the time that your program is not running, the debugger has control, and you can use its features to examine the current state of the program. By viewing the values of variables, the functions on the call stack, and the program output, you can ensure that the area of code you're examining is performing as it was designed.

As you run your program through the debugger, you can watch the behavior of your application in the windows it creates. For best results during your debugging sessions, arrange your screen so you can see both the IDE Edit window and your application window as you debug. To keep windows from flickering as the focus alternates between the debugger windows and those of your application, arrange the windows so they don't overlap (tile the windows). With this setup, your program's execution will be quicker and smoother during the debugging session.

### Specifying program arguments

If the program you want to debug uses command-line arguments, you can specify those arguments in the IDE in two ways:

First:

**1** Choose Options | Environment, then select the Debugger topic.

**2** In the Arguments text box, type the arguments you want to use when you run your program under the control of the integrated debugger.

Second:

**1** Choose Debug | Load.

**2** Type your program name and arguments in the Load dialog box.

# Controlling program execution

An important advantage of a debugger is that it lets you control the execution of your program; you can control whether your program will execute a single machine instruction, a single line of code, an entire function, or an entire program block. By dictating when the program should run and when it should pause, you can quickly move over the sections that you know work correctly and concentrate on the sections that are causing problems.

The integrated debugger lets you control the execution of your program in the following ways:

- Running to the cursor location
- Stepping through code
- Running to a breakpoint
- Pausing your program

When running code through the debugger, program execution can be based on lines of source code or on machine instructions. When debugging at the source level, the integrated debugger lets you control the rate of debugging to the level of a single line of code. However, the debugger considers multiple program statements on one line of text to be a single line of code; you cannot individually debug multiple statements contained on a single line of text. In addition, the debugger regards a single statement that's spread over several lines of text as a single line of code.

## Running to the cursor location

Often when you start a debugging session, you'll want to run your program to a spot just before the suspected location of the problem. At that point, use the debugger to ensure that all data values are as they should be. If everything is OK, you can run your program to another location, and again check to ensure that your program is behaving as it should.

To run to a specific source line:

1  In the Edit window, position the cursor on the line of code where you want to begin (or resume) debugging.

2  Run to the cursor location in one of the following ways:
   • Click the Run To Here button on the SpeedBar.
   • Choose Run To Current from the Edit window SpeedMenu.

To run to a specific machine instruction:

1  After your process is loaded, open a CPU view and position the disassembly pane so that the highlight is on the address to which you want to run.

2  Choose Run To Current from the disassembly pane SpeedMenu.

   or

   Click the Run To Here button on the SpeedMenu.

When you run to the cursor, your program executes at full speed until the execution reaches the location marked by the cursor in the Edit window, or highlight in the CPU window. When the execution encounters the code marked by the text cursor or highlighted, the debugger regains control and places the execution point on that line of code.

## The execution point

The *execution point* marks the next line of source code to be executed by the debugger. Whenever you pause your program execution within the debugger (for example, whenever you run to the cursor or step to a program location), the debugger highlights a line of code using a green arrow and colored background (depending on your color setup), marking the location of the execution point.

The execution point always shows the next line of code to be executed, whether you are going to step through, step into, or run your program at full speed. If there is no source associated with the code at the current execution point, a CPU window is opened showing the instruction with the instruction at the current execution point.

### Finding the execution point

While debugging, you're free to open, close, and navigate through any file in an Edit window. Because of this, it's easy to lose track of the next program statement to execute, or the location of the current program scope. To quickly return to the execution point, choose Debug | Source At Execution Point or click the SpeedBar button. Even if you've closed the Edit window containing the execution point, Find Execution Point opens an Edit window, and highlights the source code containing the execution point.

If there is no source associated with the code at the current execution point, you will get an error stating that no line corresponds to the address. If this happens, you can see the current execution point by opening the CPU window.

## Stepping through code

Stepping is a simple way to move through your code a little bit at a time. Stepping lets you run your program one line at a time; the next line will not execute until you tell the debugger to continue. You can step until you reach the line in your code that contains the error and then examine the state of the program and its data, view the program output and the value of its variables, or modify or evaluate expressions in your program before you tell the debugger to execute the next line.

Using the Statement Step Over and Statement Step Into commands available on the Speedmenu in the Edit window (and the corresponding commands for instruction skipping in the CPU window) or using *F7* and *F8* offer the simplest ways of moving through your program code. While the two commands are very similar, they offer different ways to *step* through code. When you step, you watch your program execute statements or instructions one at a time. After stepping, the program execution pauses and you can use the debugger to investigate different aspects of your program.

The integrated debugger allows you to step through both statements and machine instructions. Most programming errors can be identified by stepping through source, although there will be times when you need the greater granularity provided by stepping through machine instructions. Your program need not be compiled with debugging information to step through modules which do not have debugging information. Although statement stepping is usually done in an edit window, you can statement step while in the CPU window. Likewise, it is also possible to instruction step while in an edit window.

### Statement Step Into

The Statement Step Into commands execute a single program statement or instruction at a time. If the execution point is located on a call to a function that was compiled with debugging information, Statement Step Into causes the debugger to step into that function by placing the execution point on the function's first statement or instruction. However, if the execution point is located on a function call that doesn't contain debugging information (a library function, for example), then Statement Step Into runs that function at full speed, (however, Instruction Step Into will actually step into the function) after which the execution point is positioned on the statement following the function call.

If the execution point is located on the last statement of a function, Statement Step Into (or a ret instruction) causes the debugger to return from the function, placing the execution point on the line of code that follows the function call.

The term *single stepping* refers to using Statement Step Into to successively run though the statements or instructions in your program code.

To choose Statement Step Into, you can:

- Click the Step Into SpeedBar button.
- Choose Statement Step Into on the Speedbar in the Edit window.
- Press *F7* under default keyboard mapping.

The following example helps explain how single stepping through statements works. Suppose you want to follow the sequence of events through the following two functions contained in a bubble sort program:

```
void bubble( int *ptr, int n)
{
   int i, j;

   for (i=0; i<n-1; i++)
      for (j=i+1; j<n; j++)
         order (ptr+i, ptr+j);
}

void order (int *n1, int *n2)
{
   if (*n1 > *n2)
   {
      int temp = *n1;
      *n1 = *n2;
      *n2 = temp;
   }
}
```

If you load the program into the Edit window and place the cursor on the first **for** statement in the *bubble* function, pressing *F4* runs the program to that location. Right-clicking and choosing Statement Step Into executes that line of code, and moves the execution point to the next line of code in the program (the second **for** statement). Choosing Statement Step Into again causes the debugger to execute the second **for** statement, this time placing the execution point on the line containing the call to the function *order*:

```
order (ptr+i, ptr+j);
```

Choosing Statement Step Into a third time calls the function *order*, causing the debugger to step through that function by placing the execution point on the first line of the function definition:

```
void order (int *n1, int *n2)
```

From here, successive Statement Step Into commands execute the lines of code in that function one at a time. When the execution point is located on the last line in the function, stepping (with either the Step Into or Step Over commands) causes the function to return, which places the execution point on the statement following the function call. In this case, the debugger returns the execution point to the call to order *bubble*.

## Statement Step Over

The Statement Step Over command, like Statement Step Into, lets you execute program statements or instructions one at a time. However, if you issue the Statement Step Over command when the execution point is located on a function call, the debugger runs that function at full speed (instead of stepping into it), then positions the execution point on the statement following the function call.

You can choose Statement Step Over:

- Click the Step Over button on the SpeedBar.
- Choose Statement Step Into on the Speedbar in the Edit window.

For example, in the previous bubble sort code, choosing Statement Step Over while the execution point highlights the function call *order* causes the debugger run *order* at full speed. The debugger then places the execution point on the statement following the function call, which in this case is the call to order *bubble*.

As you debug, you can choose to step through some functions and step over others. If you know a function performs as it was designed, you can step over calls to that function with confidence that the function call will not cause an error. If, on the other hand, you aren't sure that a function is well behaved, you can choose to step through the function to verify that it works as designed.

### Debugging member functions and external code

If you implement classes in your C++ programs, you can still use the integrated debugger to step through code. The debugger handles member functions the same way it would step through functions in a program that is not object-oriented.

You can also step through or step over external code written in any language (including C and C++) as long as the code meets all the requirements for external linking and the linked object file contains full Borland symbol debugging contains full Borland symbolic debugging information.

## Running to a breakpoint

You set *breakpoints* on lines of source code where you want the program execution to pause during a run. Running to a breakpoint is similar to running to a cursor position, in that the program runs at full speed until it reaches a certain source-code location. However, unlike Run To Cursor, you can have multiple breakpoints in your code and you can customize each one so it pauses the program's execution only when a specified condition is met. For more information on breakpoints, see "Examining program data values" on page 181.

## Pausing the program

In addition to stepping over or through code, you can also pause your program while it's running. Choosing Debug | Pause Process causes the debugger to pause your program. You can then use the debugger to examine the state of your program with respect to this program location. When you're done examining the program, continue debugging by running as usual.

## Terminating the program

Sometimes while debugging, you'll find it necessary to restart or reset the program from the beginning. For example, you might need to restart the program if you step past the location of a bug, or if variables or data structures become corrupted with unwanted values.

Choose Debug | Terminate Process (or press *Ctrl+F2*) to end the current program run. Terminating a program closes all open program files, releases all memory allocated by the program, and clears all variable settings. However, terminating a program does not delete any breakpoints or watches that you might have set. This makes it easy to resume a debugging session.

# Using breakpoints

You use *breakpoints* to pause your program execution at designated source code locations during a debugging session or to perform other actions. By setting breakpoints in potential problem areas of your source code, you can run your program at full speed, knowing that its execution will pause at a location you want to debug.

When your program execution encounters a breakpoint, the program pauses (before executing the line containing the breakpoint) and the debugger displays the breakpoint line in the Edit window. You can then use the debugger to view the state of your program.

Breakpoint behavior falls into two categories:

- Unconditional (or simple). The breakpoint is activated whenever the debugger reaches the line in your source or the machine instruction where you set the breakpoint.

- Conditional. The breakpoint is activated only when it satisfies the conditions specified on the Breakpoint Conditions/Action Options dialog box and saved in a breakpoint options set.

A source breakpoint has to be set on a line or program location that contains executable code. For example, you cannot set a breakpoint on a blank line, comment, or declaration.

The IDE keeps track of all your breakpoints during a debugging session and associates them with your current project. You can maintain all your breakpoints from a single Breakpoints window and not have to search through your source code files to look for them.

## Debugging with breakpoints

When you run your program from the IDE, it will stop whenever the debugger reaches the location in your program where the breakpoint is set, but before it executes the line or instruction. The line that contains the breakpoint (or the line that most closely corresponds to the program location where the breakpoint is set) appears in the Edit window highlighted by the execution point. At this point, you can perform any other debugging actions.

# Setting breakpoints

You can set a breakpoint the following ways:

To set an unconditional breakpoint on a line in your source code, use one of the following methods:

- Place the insertion point on a line in an Edit window and choose Toggle | Breakpoint from the Edit window SpeedMenu or press *F5* (default keyboard setting).

- Click the gutter in an Edit window next to the line where you want to set a breakpoint.

## Setting an unconditional breakpoint

To set an unconditional breakpoint on a machine instruction:

1 Highlight a machine instruction in the Disassembly pane in the CPU window.

2 Choose Toggle Breakpoint on the SpeedMenu or press *F5* (default keyboard setting).

## Setting a conditional breakpoint

To set a conditional breakpoint on a line or machine instruction:

1 Place the insertion point on a line in an Edit window or highlight a line in the Disassembly pane of the CPU window.

2 Choose Debug | Add breakpoint or choose Add Breakpoint from the SpeedMenu.

3 Complete the information on the Add Breakpoint dialog box.

4 Do one of the following:
- Click the Advanced button to display the Breakpoint Conditions/Action Options dialog box.
- Supply the conditions and action settings you want. See "Creating conditional breakpoints."
- Specify option set in the Options input box.

## Setting other breakpoints

To set other types of breakpoints:

1 Choose Debug | Add breakpoint from anywhere in the IDE or choose Add Breakpoint from the SpeedMenu in an active Edit or Breakpoint window, or the Disassembly pane of the CPU window.

2 Select a breakpoint type on the Add Breakpoint dialog box and supply any additional information associated with the type of breakpoint selected.

3 Either
- Click OK to set an unconditional breakpoint.
- Click the Advanced button to display the Breakpoint Conditions/Action Options dialog box. See "Creating conditional breakpoints."

## Setting breakpoints after program execution begins

While your program is running, you can switch to the debugger (just like you switch to any Windows application) and set a breakpoint. When you return to your application, the new breakpoint is set, and your application will pause or perform a specified action when it reaches the breakpoint.

# Creating conditional breakpoints

Use a *conditional breakpoint* when you want the debugger to activate a breakpoint only under certain conditions. For example, you may not want a breakpoint to activate every time it is encountered, especially if the line containing the breakpoint is executed many times before the actual occurrence in which you are interested. Likewise, you may not always want a breakpoint to pause program execution. In these cases, use a conditional breakpoint.

To set a conditional breakpoint:

1  Choose Debug | Add breakpoint to open the Add Breakpoint dialog box (Figure 7.1).

**Figure 7.1**     Add Breakpoint dialog box

2  Select a breakpoint type and supply the applicable information.

3  Click Advanced to display the Breakpoint Conditions/Action Options dialog box.

4  Click Expr. True and enter an expression that tells the debugger when to trigger the breakpoint. If the condition is not met, the debugger ignores the breakpoint along with any of its actions.

5  If you want the breakpoint to activate only while a specific thread is in process, click Thread ID and enter a Thread ID. Otherwise leave Thread ID unchecked.

6  If you want the debugger to activate a breakpoint only after it has been reached a certain number of times, click Pass count and enter the number of passes. Otherwise, your program will pause every time the breakpoint is activated.

7  If you want program execution to pause when the breakpoint is activated, click Break (the default). Otherwise, your program will not pause when the debugger activates the breakpoint.

8  If you want the debugger to perform various actions when the breakpoint activates, use the Actions. settings. Otherwise, click OK.

**Figure 7.2**    Breakpoint Conditions/Actions Options dialog box

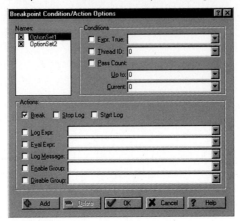

# Removing breakpoints

You can remove a breakpoint in the following ways:

- From an Edit window
- From an Edit window or the Disassembly pane of the CPU window
- From the Breakpoints window

## From an Edit window

To remove a breakpoint from an Edit window:

- Click the gutter in an Edit window next to the line that contains the breakpoint you want to remove.

## From an Edit window or the Disassembly pane of the CPU window

To remove a breakpoint from an Edit window or the Disassembly pane of the CPU window:

1  Place the insertion point on the line or highlight the instruction where the breakpoint is set.

2  Choose Toggle Breakpoint from the SpeedMenu.

## From the Breakpoints window

To remove a breakpoint from the Breakpoints window:

1  Choose View | Breakpoint to display the Breakpoints window.

2  Select one or more breakpoints.

3  Choose Remove Breakpoint(s) from the SpeedMenu.

To select multiple breakpoints in the Breakpoints window, hold down the *Shift* or *Ctrl* key as you select each breakpoint.

# Disabling and enabling breakpoints

Disable a breakpoint when you prefer not to activate it the next time you run your program, but want to save it for later use. The breakpoint remains listed in the Breakpoints window and available for you to enable when you want.

To enable or disable a breakpoint:

1 Choose View | Breakpoint to open the Breakpoints window.

2 Click the checkbox next to the breakpoint to enable it or clear the checkbox to disable it.

To disable or enable selected breakpoints:

1 In the Breakpoints window, hold down the *Shift* or *Ctrl* key as you select each breakpoint.

2 Choose Enable/Disable Breakpoints from the SpeedMenu.

To use a breakpoint to disable or enable a group of breakpoints:

1 Choose Debug | Add Breakpoint to open the Add Breakpoint dialog box.

2 Click Options to open the Breakpoint Conditions/Action Options dialog box.

3 Click Enable Group or Disable Group and enter a group name.

# Viewing and editing code at a breakpoint

Even if a breakpoint is not in your current Edit window, you can quickly locate it in your source code.

## Viewing code at a breakpoint

To view the code where a breakpoint is set:

1 Choose View | Breakpoint to display the Breakpoints window.

2 Select a breakpoint.

3 Choose View Source on the Breakpoints window SpeedMenu.

The source code displays in an Edit window at the breakpoint line and the Breakpoints window remains active. If the source code is not currently open in an Edit window, the IDE opens a new Edit window.

## Editing code at a breakpoint

To edit the code where a breakpoint is set:

1 Choose View | Breakpoint to display the Breakpoints window.

2 Select a breakpoint.

3 Choose Edit Source from the Breakpoints window SpeedMenu.

The source code displays in an active Edit window with your cursor positioned on the breakpoint line, ready for you to edit. If the source code is not currently open in an Edit window, the IDE opens a new Edit window.

## Resetting invalid breakpoints

A breakpoint must be set on executable code, otherwise it is invalid. For example, a breakpoint set on a comment, a blank line, or a declaration is invalid. A common error is to set a breakpoint on code that is conditionalized out using **#if** or **#ifdef**.

If you set an invalid breakpoint and run your program, the debugger displays an Invalid Breakpoint dialog box.

To reset an invalid breakpoint:

1  Close the Invalid Breakpoint dialog box.

2  Find the invalid breakpoint in the Breakpoints window and delete it.

3  Set the breakpoint in a proper location and continue to run your program.

If you ignore the Invalid Breakpoint (by dismissing the dialog box) and then choose Run, the IDE executes your program, but does not enable the invalid breakpoint.

## Using breakpoint groups

The integrated debugger lets you group breakpoints together so you can enable or disable several breakpoints with a single action.

### Creating a breakpoint group

To create a breakpoint group:

1  Choose Debug | Add Breakpoint to open the Add Breakpoint dialog box.

2  Enter a name in the Group input box.

### Disabling or enabling a breakpoint group

To disable or enable a group of breakpoints by using another breakpoint's option:

1  Choose Debug | Add Breakpoint to open the Add Breakpoint dialog box.

2  Click Options to open the Breakpoint Conditions/Action Options dialog box.

3  Click Enable Group or Disable Group and enter a group name.

To remove a breakpoint from a group, select the group name and press Delete.

## Using breakpoint option sets

To quickly specify the behavior of one more breakpoints as you create or modify them, store breakpoint settings in an *option set*.

## Creating a breakpoint option set

To create an option set:

1  Choose Debug | Breakpoint options to open the Breakpoint Conditions/Action Options dialog box.

2  Enter the conditions and actions. See "Creating conditional breakpoints."

3  Click Add.

4  Enter a name the dialog box that displays and click OK.

You can also create an option set when you create or edit a breakpoint.

## Associating a breakpoint with an option set

To associate a breakpoint with an option set:

• Enter the Option name in the Add or Edit Breakpoints dialog box.

# Changing breakpoint options

To change the conditions and actions of a breakpoint:

1  Choose View | Breakpoint to open the Breakpoints window.

2  Double-click on a breakpoint or choose Edit Breakpoint from the SpeedMenu.

3  Change the option set in the Options input box on the Edit Breakpoint dialog box.

   or

   Supply new information as described in "Creating conditional breakpoints."

# Changing the color of breakpoint lines

To use colors to indicate if a breakpoint is enabled, disabled, or invalid:

1  Choose Options | Environment.

2  Select Syntax Highlighting and choose Customize.

3  From the Element list, select the following breakpoint options you want to change:
   • Enabled Break
   • Disabled Break
   • Invalid Break

4  Select the background (BG) and foreground (FG) colors you want.

5  If you want highlighting, choose Default Color.

# Using the Breakpoints window

The Breakpoints window lists all breakpoints currently set in the loaded project (or the file in the active Edit window if a project is not loaded) and contains a tab for each of the following types of breakpoints:

- To display the Breakpoints window, choose View I Breakpoint (Figure 7.3).

**Figure 7.3**   Breakpoints window

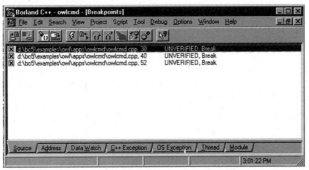

The Breakpoints window lets you perform the following actions:

- Click the checkbox beside a breakpoint to enable it or clear the checkbox to disable the breakpoint.
- Double-click or press *Enter* on a breakpoint to open the Edit Breakpoint dialog box to change breakpoint settings.
- Choose a command from the Breakpoint Window SpeedMenu.

## About the Breakpoints window

The Breakpoints window provides the following information about each breakpoint:

- Name of the source code file in which the breakpoint is set (for source breakpoints).
- Location (such as line number, file name, module, thread ID, or address number) where the breakpoint is set.
- Current state of the breakpoint:

| | |
|---|---|
| Verified | The breakpoint is legal and validated when the process was loaded. |
| Unverified | The process has not been loaded since you added the breakpoint. |
| Invalid | The breakpoint is illegal. The line on which you set the breakpoint does not contain executable code (such as a blank line, comment, or declaration) and the debugger will ignore it. |

- Number of times the debugger must reach the breakpoint before activating the breakpoint. This information appears after a breakpoint has been activated.

- Associated option set and group name as well as the conditions/action options specified. See "Creating conditional breakpoints."
- Last Event Hit shows the last breakpoint that was encountered.

## Integrated debugger features

### Add breakpoint
Use the Add Breakpoint dialog box to create a breakpoint. The options that appear in the middle of the dialog box change according to the breakpoint type selected:

- Source
- Address
- Data Watch
- C++ Exception
- OS Exception
- Thread
- Module

The following options always display on the right side of the dialog box:

- Qualifiers
- Other

If you want to set conditions and actions that control breakpoint behavior, click Advanced to open the Breakpoint Conditions/Action Options dialog box.

### Qualifiers
Contains the following options:.

| | |
|---|---|
| Program | Causes a breakpoint to activate only in a specific executable (.EXE) program. Leave it blank if you want a breakpoint to activate in all loaded processes. |
| Module | Causes a breakpoint to activate only when conditions are satisfied within a specific dynamic-link library (DLL). Leave this setting blank if you clicked Module under Breakpoint type. |

### Other
Contains the following options:

| | |
|---|---|
| Options | Indicates the name of the option set that defines breakpoint behavior. |
| Group | Indicates the name of group to which the breakpoint belongs. |

### Source breakpoint
Sets a breakpoint on a line in your source code.

### File
Indicates the file that contains the source code where the breakpoint is set.

## Line #

Indicates the line in the source file on which the breakpoint is set.

If you select a line of code in an Edit window and choose Add Breakpoint from the SpeedMenu, the debugger completes these settings for you.

## Address breakpoint

Sets a breakpoint on a a machine instruction.

## Offset

Indicates the address of the machine instruction on which the breakpoint is set.

## Data watch breakpoint

Use a Data Watch breakpoint to pause your program when a specific location in memory changes value. Data Watch breakpoints (also called watchpoints or changed memory breakpoints) let you monitor expressions that evaluate to a specific data object or memory location. Data watch breakpoints are monitored continuously during your program's execution.

Because the debugger checks the breakpoint conditions after the execution of every machine instruction, data watch breakpoints are excellent tools for pinpointing code that is corrupting data.

## Address

Enter a specific starting address or any symbol (such as a variable or a class data member) that evaluates to an address.

## Length

When entering an expression symbol, you can also enter a count of the number of bytes you want monitored.

For example, coding in C, suppose you have declared the following array:

```
int string[81];
```

You can watch for a change in the first ten elements of this array by entering the following item into the Condition Expression input box:

```
&string[0], 40
```

The area monitored is 40 bytes long which equals ten elements in the array (an **int** is 4 bytes).

## C++ exception breakpoint

Sets a breakpoint that pauses you program when it throws or catches a C++ exception.

## Type

Specifies the data type (such as **int**, **long**, **char**, or a class name) used with the exception.

## Stop on Throw

Pauses program execution when an exception is thrown.

## Stop on Catch

Pauses program execution when an exception is caught.

## OS exception breakpoint

Sets a breakpoint that pauses you program when it throws or catches an operating system defined exception.

## Exception #

Specifies the integer value assigned to the exception. Pick from the list that provides the most common OS exceptions or enter one defined in your application.

## Thread breakpoint

Sets a breakpoint on a specified thread. Programs will pause on thread creation and thread destruction.

## Thread

Specifies the thread ID on which the breakpoint is set. Program execution pauses whenever the thread is created.

- To obtain a thread ID, choose View | Process.

## Module breakpoint

Sets a breakpoint in a specified DLL.

## Module Name

Specifies the name of a DLL in which the breakpoint is set. The debugger activates the breakpoint each time the DLL startup code (as defined in **DllEntryPoint**) is executed. For example, if the Break action is on (the default), program execution will pause whenever your program attaches or detaches the DLL.

## Breakpoint Conditions/Action Options

Use this dialog box to

- Specify settings that control the behavior of one or more breakpoints, such as the conditions under which a breakpoint is activated and the type of actions that take place when it does.

- Enable and disable breakpoint groups

To display this dialog box, use any of the following methods:

- Choose Debug | Breakpoint Options.
- Choose Debug | Add Breakpoint and click the Advanced button on the Add Breakpoint window.
- Choose View | Breakpoint and double-click a breakpoint listed in the Breakpoints window. Then click the Advanced button on the Edit Breakpoint window.

The Breakpoint Conditions/Action Options dialog box contains the following options:

| | |
|---|---|
| Names | Lists the names of Option Sets that have been created. |
| Conditions | Provides settings that determine when and where a breakpoint is activated. |
| Actions | Provides settings that determine what actions take place when a breakpoint is activated. |

## Names (Breakpoint Conditions/Action Options)

Lists the names of existing option sets. Use the checkbox next to each option set to enable or disable it.

For example, if you clear the checkbox next to an option set called MyOptionSet, the debugger ignores its settings and all breakpoints that use this option set behave like unconditional breakpoints. To reactivate the breakpoint settings in MyOptionSet so that they will used by the debugger, click its checkbox.

## Conditions (Breakpoint Conditions/Action Options)

This group of settings determines when and where a breakpoint. is activated:

| | |
|---|---|
| Expr. True | Each time the debugger encounters the breakpoint, it evaluates an expression to determine if the breakpoint should activate. |
| Thread ID | Activates a breakpoint only while a specific thread is in progress. |
| Pass Count | Indicates the number of times the debugger encounters the breakpoint line before it activates. |

- Click Add or Delete to create or remove an option set.

## Expr. True (Breakpoint Conditions/Action Options)

Enter the expression you want to evaluate each time the debugger reaches the breakpoint. If the expression becomes true (nonzero) when the breakpoint is encountered, the debugger activates the breakpoint and carries out any actions specified for it. You can enter a Boolean expression that, for instance, tests if a value falls within a certain range or if a flag has been set.

For example:

If you enter the expression

```
x == 1
```

the debugger activates the breakpoint only if $x$ has been assigned the value 1 at the time the breakpoint is encountered.

If you enter the expression

```
x > 3
```

and select Break, when the debugger reaches the breakpoint, your program pauses if the current value of $x$ is greater than 3. Otherwise, the breakpoint is ignored.

## Thread ID (Breakpoint Conditions/Action Options)

Programs written for 32-bit operating systems consist of one or more executable threads. You can set a breakpoint on a specific thread, even though the code at the breakpoint location is shared by multiple threads. Unless specified, a breakpoint is set for all program threads.

Use this option to prevent a breakpoint from activating unless a specified thread is running. When the debugger reaches the breakpoint, it will not be activated unless the thread is in progress. If you leave this option blank, the breakpoint may activate while any thread is in progress.

## Pass Count (Breakpoint Conditions/Action Options)

This option includes the following settings:

| | |
|---|---|
| Up to | Specifies the number of times you want debugger to reach the breakpoint before it is activated. |
| Current | Shows the actual number of times the debugger has reached the breakpoint so far. You can change this setting if you want to. |

### Conditional breakpoint example

If Break is checked and you enter the expression $x>3$ and you enter 2 in the Pass Count box, your program will not stop until the second time the debugger reaches the breakpoint (that is, when the value of $x$ is greater than 3).

## Actions (Breakpoint Conditions/Action Options)

This group of options lets you specify the actions you want carried out each time the breakpoint is activated:

| | |
|---|---|
| Break | Pauses program execution |
| Stop Log | Stops posting debugger generated messages |
| Start Log | Starts posting debugger generated messages |
| Log Expr | Displays the value of an expression in the message window |
| Eval Expr | Evaluates an expression |
| Log Message | Displays a message in the message window |
| Enable Group | Reactivates a group of breakpoints |
| Disable Group | Disables a group of breakpoints |

### Break (Breakpoint Conditions/Action Options)

Click Break (the default) to pause program execution when the debugger activates the breakpoint. Clear this checkbox if you do not want your program to pause at the breakpoint.

### Stop Log (Breakpoint Conditions/Action Options)

Stops displaying debugger messages in the Runtime Tab of the Message window when the breakpoint is activated.

### Start Log (Breakpoint Conditions/Action Options)

Starts displaying debugger messages in the Runtime Tab of the Message window when the breakpoint is activated.

### Log Expr (Breakpoint Conditions/Action Options)

Click Log Expr if you want to display the value of an expression in the Runtime tab of the Message window. Then, enter the expression in the input box next to it. The debugger logs the value each time the breakpoint activates. Use this option when you want to output a value each time you reach a specific place in your program— this technique is known as instrumentation.

For example, you can place a breakpoint at the beginning of a routine and set it to log the values of the routine arguments. Then, after running the program, you can determine from where the routine was called, and if it was called with erroneous arguments. This will give you no idea where it was called from, but will tell you what the arguments are.

When you log expressions, be careful of expressions that unexpectedly change the values of variables or data objects (side effects).

### Eval Expr (Breakpoint Conditions/Action Options)

Click Eval Expr if you want the breakpoint to evaluate an expression. Then, enter an expression in the input box next to it. Use an expression that changes the value of a variable or data object (side effects), or this is a waste of time.

By "splicing in" a piece of code before a given source line, you can effectively test a simple bug fix; you do not have to go through the trouble of compiling and linking your program just to test a minor change to a routine.

You cannot use this technique to directly modify your compiled program.

### Log Message (Breakpoint Conditions/Action Options)

Click Log Message if you want the breakpoint to display a message in the Runtime tab of the Message window when the breakpoint is activated. Then, enter the text of the message in the input box next to it.

### Disable Group (Breakpoint Conditions/Action Options)

Click Disable Group if you want the breakpoint to disable a group of breakpoints. Then, enter a group name in the input box next to it.

When a group of breakpoints is disabled, the breakpoints are not erased, they are simply hidden from the debugger until you enable them.

### Enable Group (Breakpoint Conditions/Action Options)

Click Enable Group if you want the breakpoint to reactivate a group of breakpoints that have been previously disabled. Then, enter a group name in the input box next to it.

### Add Breakpoint Conditions/Action Option Set...

Enter a name for the option set and click OK to create a new set of options based on the current settings in the Breakpoint Conditions/Action Options dialog box.

### Edit Breakpoint dialog box

Use this dialog box to modify an existing breakpoint. The options that appear on left side of the dialog box change according to the breakpoint type selected.

The integrated debugger provides the following types of breakpoints:

- Source
- Address
- Data Watch
- C++ Exception
- OS Exception
- Thread
- Module

The following options always display on the right side of the dialog box:

- Qualifiers
- Other

If you want to set conditions and actions that control breakpoint behavior, click Advanced to open the Breakpoint Conditions/Action Options dialog box.

# Examining program data values

Even though you can discover many interesting things about your program by running and stepping through it, you'll usually need to examine the values of program variables to uncover bugs. For example, it's helpful to know the value of the index variable as you step though a **for** loop, or the values of the parameters passed to a function call.

After you have paused your application within the integrated debugger, you can examine the different symbols and data structures with regard to the location of the current execution point.

You can view the state of your program by:

- Watching program values
- Inspecting data elements
- Evaluating expressions
- Viewing the low-level state of your program
- Viewing the functions in the Call Stack window

You can also use the Browser to view the global variables and classes contained in your program.

## Modifying program data values

Sometimes you will find that a programming error is caused by an incorrect data value. Using the integrated debugger, you can test a "fix" by modifying the data value while your program is running. You can modify program data values using:

- The Evaluate dialog box
- The Inspector window's Change SpeedMenu command
- A breakpoint's Evaluate action
- The CPU window's Dump pane
- The Register & Stack window

## Understanding watch expressions

You use *watches* to monitor the changing values of variables or expressions during your program run. After you enter a watch expression, the Watch window displays the current value of the expression. Each time your program pauses (such as when it encounters a breakpoint), the value of the watch changes to reflect the current value of the expression according to the values of the variables in your program.

### Using the Watches window

To display the Watches window, choose View | Watch.

**Figure 7.4**    Watches window

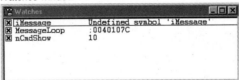

The Watches window lists the watches you are currently monitoring. Check the checkbox beside a watch to enable it. Clear the checkbox beside a watch to disable it.

**Note** The Watches window will be blank if you have not added any watches.

The left side of the Watches window lists the expressions you enter as watches and their corresponding data types and values appear on the right. The values of compound data objects (such as arrays and structures) appear between braces ({ }).

**Note** If the execution point steps out of the scope of a watch expression, the watch expression is undefined. When the execution point re-enters the scope of the expression, the Watches window again displays the current value of the expression.

## Formatting watch expressions

You can format the display of a watch expression using the Watch Properties dialog box. By default, the debugger displays integer values in decimal form. However, by checking the Hexadecimal button in the Watch Properties dialog box, you can specify that an integer watch be displayed as hexadecimal. You can also vary the display of the watches using the Display As buttons in the Watch Properties dialog box. For more on these buttons, refer to the online Help.

To format a floating-point expression, click the Floating Point button, then indicate the number of significant digits you want displayed in the Watch window by typing this number in the Significant Digits text box.

If you're setting up a watch on an element in a data structure (such as an array), you can display the values of consecutive data elements. For example, suppose you have an array of five integers named *xarray*. Type the number 5 in the Repeat Count text box of the Watch Properties dialog box to see all five values of the array.

You can also format watch expressions using the expression format specifiers shown in Table 7.1 on page 186. Format specifier settings override any settings specified in the Watch Properties dialog box. Format specifiers use the following syntax:

```
expression [,format_specifier]
```

## Adding a watch

You can add a watch using either of the following methods:

- Place the insertion point on a word in an Edit window and choose Watch from the Edit window SpeedMenu. The debugger adds a watch on the expression at the insertion point and opens the Watches window.

- Use the Add Watch dialog box to create a watch expression on any variable or expression available to the program you are debugging.

### Add Watch dialog box

The Add Watch dialog box lets you monitor the value of both simple variables (such as integers) and compound data objects (such as arrays). In addition, you can watch the values of calculated expressions that do not refer directly to memory locations. For example, you could watch the expression $x * y + 4$.

To create a watch expression using the Add watch dialog box:

**1** Choose Debug | Add watch or choose Add watch from the Watches window SpeedMenu.

**Figure 7.5**     Add watch dialog box

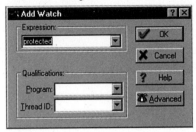

**2** Enter an expression into the Expression input box.

**3** Click OK to add the watch or choose any of the following optional settings:

- Program
- Thread ID
- Advanced

**Note**     After you add the watch expression, the IDE automatically opens the Watches window if it is not already open.

## Changing watch properties

To change the properties of a watch:

**1** Choose View | Watch, to open the Watches window.

**2** Double-click a watch to open the Edit Watch dialog box.

**Figure 7.6**     Edit Watch dialog box

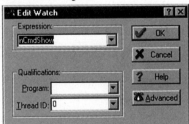

### Edit Watch dialog box

Use this dialog box to change the settings for a watch expression:

1 Either accept or change the information in either of the following options:
   - Program
   - Thread ID

2 Either
   - Choose OK to save your changes and close the dialog box.
   - Click Advanced to open the Watch Properties if you want to change how a watch expression displays in the Watches window.

## Disabling and enabling watches

Evaluating many watch expressions can slow down the process of debugging. Disable a watch expression when you prefer not to view it in the Watches window, but want to save it for later use.

To enable or disable a watch:

1 Choose View | Watch to open the Watch window.

2 Either
   - Click the checkbox next to a watch to enable it.
   - Clear the checkbox next to a watch to disable it.

To disable or enable selected watches:

1 Hold down the *Shift* or *Ctrl* key and click on one or more watches in the Watch window.

2 Choose Enable or Disable watches from the Watch window SpeedMenu.

## Deleting a watch

You can delete a watch the following ways:

1 Choose View | Watch to display the Watches window.

2 Select one or more watch expressions. (To make multiple selections, hold down the *Shift* or *Ctrl* key and click.)

3 Choose Remove Watch(es) on the SpeedMenu.

## Evaluating and modifying expressions

You can evaluate expressions using the Expression Evaluator dialog box. The Expression Evaluator dialog box has the advantage that it lets you change the values of variables and items in data structures during the course of your debugging session. This can be useful if you think you've found the solution to a bug, and you want to try it out before exiting the debugger, changing the source code, and recompiling the program.

## Evaluating expressions

Choose Debug | Evaluate to open the Expression Evaluator dialog box. By default, the token at the cursor position in the current Edit window is placed in the Expression text box. You can accept or modify this expression, enter another one, or choose an expression from the history list of expressions you've previously evaluated.

**Figure 7.7**    Evaluator dialog box

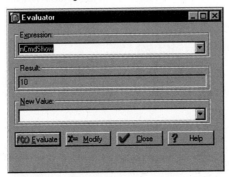

To evaluate the expression, click the Evaluate button. Using this dialog box, you can evaluate any valid language expression, except ones that contain

- Local or static variables that are not accessible from the current execution point
- Symbols or macros defined with **#define**

When you evaluate an expression, the current value of the expression is displayed in the Result field of the dialog box. If you need to, you can format the result by adding a comma and one or more format specifiers to the end of the expression entered in the Expression text box. Table 7.1 details the legal format specifiers.

**Table 7.1**    Expression format specifiers

| Character | Types affected | Function |
|-----------|----------------|----------|
| H or X | Integers | **Hexadecimal.** Shows integer values in hexadecimal with the **0x** prefix, including those in data structures. |
| C | Char, strings | **Character.** Shows special display characters for ASCII 0–31. By default, such characters are shown using the appropriate C escape sequences (**/n**, **/t**, and so on). |
| D | Integers | **Decimal.** Shows integer values in decimal form, including those in data structures. |
| F$n$ | Floating point | **Floating point.** Shows $n$ significant digits (where $n$ is in the range of 2–18, and 7 is the default). |
| $n$M | All | **Memory dump.** Shows $n$ bytes starting at the address of the indicated expression. If $n$ is not specified, it defaults to the size in bytes of the type of the variable.<br><br>By default, each byte shows as two hex digits. The C, D, H, S, and X specifiers can be used with M to change the byte formatting. |

**Table 7.1**    Expression format specifiers (continued)

| Character | Types affected | Function |
|---|---|---|
| P | Pointers | **Pointer.** Shows pointers as *seg:ofs* instead of the default *Ptr(seg:ofs)*. It tells you the region of memory in which the segment is located, and the name of the variable at the offset address, if appropriate. |
| R | Structures, unions | **Structure/Union.** Shows both field names and values such as (*X*:1;*Y*:10;*Z*:5) instead of (1,10,5). |
| S | Char, strings | **String.** Shows ASCII 0–31 as C escape sequences. Use only to modify memory dumps (see *n*M above). |

For example, to display a result in hexadecimal, type , H after the expression. To see a floating-point number to 3 decimal places, type , F3 after the expression.

You can also use a *repeat count* to reference a specific number of data items in arrays and structures. To specify a repeat count, follow the expression with a comma and the number of data items you want to reference. For example, suppose you declared the following array in your program:

```
int my_array[10];
```

The following expression evaluates the first 5 elements of this array and displays the result in hexadecimal:

```
my_array,5h
```

## Modifying the values of variables

Once you've evaluated a variable or data structure item, you can modify its value. Modifying the value of data items during a debugging session lets you test different bug hypotheses and see how a section of code behaves under different circumstances.

To modify the value of a data item:

1 Open the Expression Evaluator dialog box and enter the name of the variable you want to modify into the Expression input box.

2 Click Evaluate to evaluate the data item.

3 Type a value into the New Value text box (or choose a value from the drop down list), then click Modify to update the data item.

**Note**    When you modify the value of a data item through the debugger, the modification is effective for that specific program run only; the changes you make through the Expression Evaluator dialog box do not affect your program source code or the compiled program. To make your change permanent, you must modify your program source code in the Edit window, then recompile your program.

Keep these points in mind when you modify program data values:

• You can change individual variables or elements of arrays and data structures, but you cannot change the entire contents of an array or data structure.

• The expression in the New Value text box must evaluate to a result that is assignment-compatible with the variable to which you want to assign it. A good guideline is that if the assignment would cause a compile-time error, it's not a legal modification value.

**Warning!** Modifying values (especially pointer values and array indexes), can have undesirable effects because you can overwrite other variables and data structures. Use caution whenever you modify program values from the debugger.

## Inspecting data elements

You can use inspect windows to examine and modify data values. Inspect windows are extremely useful because they format the data according to the type of data being viewed; there are different types of Inspect windows for scalars, arrays, structures, functions, and classes with and without member functions.

The easiest way to inspect a data item is to highlight the expression you want to inspect (or just position the text cursor on the token) in the Edit window, and choose Inspect Object from the SpeedMenu (or press *Alt+F5*). If you inspect expressions using this method, the expression is always evaluated within the scope of the line on which the expression appears.

You can also inspect data expressions using the following method,

1  Choose Debug | Inspect to display the Inspect Expression window.

2  Type in the expression you want to inspect, or choose a previously entered expression from the drop down list.

3  Choose OK to display an Inspector window.

If the execution point is in the scope of the expression you're inspecting, the value appears in the Inspect window. If the execution point is outside the scope of the expression, the value is undefined.

If you're inspecting a compound data item, such as an array or a structure, you can view the details of the data item by opening another Inspect window on the element you want to inspect.

To inspect an element of a compound data item:

1  In the Inspect window, select the item you want to inspect.

2  Choose Inspect on the Inspect window SpeedMenu, or press *Enter*.

You can also use Inspector windows to change the value of a single data item:

1  Select the data item whose value you want to modify.

2  Choose Change on the Inspect window SpeedMenu.

3  Type the new value into the Change Value dialog box and click OK.

If you're inspecting a data structure, it's possible the number of items displayed might be so great that you'll have to scroll in the Inspector window to see data in which you're interested. For easier viewing, you can narrow the display to a range of data items:

1  Left-click in the Inspect window and choose Set Range from the SpeedMenu.

2  In the Starting Index text box, enter the index of the first item you want to view.

3  In the Count text box, enter the number of items you want to see in the Inspect window.

# Displaying low-level information about a running program

The CPU window consists of five separate panes. Each pane gives you a view into a specific low-level aspect of your running application:

- The Disassembly pane displays the assembly instructions that have been disassembled from your application's machine code. In addition, the Disassembly pane displays the original program source code above the associated assembly instructions.

- The Dump pane displays a memory dump of any memory accessible to the currently loaded executable module. By default, memory is displayed as hexadecimal bytes.

- The Stack pane displays the current contents of the program stack. By default, the stack is displayed as hexadecimal bytes.

- The Registers pane displays the current values of the CPU registers.

- The Flags pane displays the current values of the CPU flags.

Each pane has an individual SpeedMenu that provides commands specific to the contents of that pane.

**Figure 7.8**    CPU window

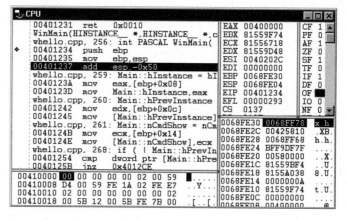

## Resizing the CPU window panes

You can customize the layout of the CPU window by resizing the panes within the window. Drag the pane borders within the window enlarge or shrink the windows to your liking.

## Listing addresses of disassembled instructions

The left side of the Disassembly pane lists the address of each disassembled instruction. An arrow to the right of the memory address indicates the location of the current execution point. To the right of the memory addresses, the Disassembly pane displays the assembly instructions that have been disassembled from the machine code produced by the compiler. If you are viewing code that has been linked with a symbol table, the debugger displays the source code that is associated with the disassembled instructions.

## The Disassembly pane SpeedMenu

The Disassembly pane has the following SpeedMenu commands:

- Run To
- Toggle Breakpoint
- Goto Address
- Goto Current PC
- Goto source
- Change Thread

## Run to

The Run To command lets you run your program at full speed to the instruction that you have selected in the Disassembly pane. This is a quick way to continue debugging at a specific program location.

## Toggle Breakpoint

When you choose Toggle Breakpoint, the debugger sets an unconditional breakpoint at the instruction which you have selected in the Disassembly pane. A unconditional breakpoint has no conditions, and the only action is that it will pause the program's execution.

If is a simple breakpoint exists on the selected instruction, then Toggle Breakpoint will delete the breakpoint at that code location.

## Goto address

The Goto Address command prompts you for a new area of memory to display in the Code, Dump, and Stack panes of the CPU window. Enter any expression that evaluates to a memory location that your program can access such as main. Be sure to precede hexadecimal values with 0x.

The debugger displays dashes if you try to access an address that is not within the scope of the application you are debugging.

## Goto current PC

Goto Current PC places positions the Disassembly pane at the location of the current program counter (the location indicated by the EIP register). This location indicates the next instruction to be executed by your program.

This command is useful when you have navigated through the Disassembly pane, and you want to return to the next instruction to be executed.

## Goto source

The Goto Source command activates the Edit window and positions the insertion point at the source code that corresponds to the disassembled instruction selected in the Disassembly pane. If there is no corresponding source code (for example, if you're examining Windows kernel code), this command has no effect.

## Change thread

Opens the Change Thread dialog box. Select the thread you want to debug from the thread listed on the process hierarchy.

If you choose a new thread from the CPU window, all panes in the window reflect the state of the CPU for that thread. Open multiple instances of the CPU window for low-level debugging of different threads.

# Displaying raw values in addressable areas of your program

The Dump pane displays the raw values contained in addressable areas of your program. The display is broken down into three sections: the memory addresses, the current values in memory, and an ASCII representation of the values in memory.

By default, the Dump pane displays the memory values in hexadecimal notation. The leftmost part of each line shows the starting address of the line. Following the address listing is an 8-byte hexadecimal listing of the values contained at that location in memory. Each byte in memory is represented by two hexadecimal digits. Following the hexadecimal display is an ASCII display of the memory. Non-printable values are represented with a period.

The format of the memory display depends on the format selected with the Display As SpeedMenu command. If you choose one of the floating-point display formats (Floats or Doubles), a single floating-point number is displayed on each line. The Bytes format displays 8 bytes per line, Words displays 4 words per line, and Longs displays 2 long words per line.

## The Dump pane SpeedMenu

The Dump pane has the following SpeedMenu commands:

- Goto Address
- Display As
- Change Thread

**Note** You can change the values of memory displayed in the Dump pane by pressing the *Ins* key and typing into the display (when you press *Ins*, the insertion point in the pane shrinks to highlight a single nibble in memory). Be extremely careful when changing program memory values; even small changes in program values can have disastrous effects on your running program.

## Display as

Use the Display As command to format the data that's listed in the Dump or Stack pane of the CPU window. You can choose any of the data formats listed in the following table:

**Table 7.2**      Data formats

| Data type | Display format |
|---|---|
| Bytes | Displays data in hexadecimal bytes |
| Words | Displays data in 2-byte hexadecimal numbers |
| Longs | Displays data in 4-byte hexadecimal numbers |
| Floats | Displays data in 4-byte floating-point numbers using scientific notation |
| Doubles | Displays data in 8-byte floating-point numbers using scientific notation |

# Displaying raw values in your program stack

The Stack pane displays the raw values contained in the your program stack. The display is divided into three sections:

- Memory addresses
- Current values on the stack
- ASCII representation of the stack values

By default, the Stack pane displays the memory values in hexadecimal notation. The leftmost part of each line shows the starting address of the line. Following the address listing is a 4-byte listing of the values contained at that memory location. Each byte is represented by two hexadecimal digits. Following the hexadecimal display is an ASCII display of the memory; non-printable values are represented with a period.

The format of the memory display depends on the format selected with the Display As SpeedMenu command. If you choose one of the floating-point display formats (Floats or Doubles), a single floating-point number is displayed on each line. The Bytes format displays 4 bytes per line, Words displays 2 words per line, and Longs displays 1 long word per line.

## The Stack pane SpeedMenu

The Stack pane has the following SpeedMenu commands:

- Goto Address
- Goto Top Frame
- Goto Top of Stack
- Display As
- Change Thread

**Note**    You can change the values of memory displayed in the Stack pane by pressing the Ins key and typing into the display (when you press Ins, the insertion point in the pane shrinks to highlight a single nibble in memory). Be extremely careful when changing program memory values; even small changes in program values can have disastrous effects on your running program.

### Goto top frame

Positions the insertion point in the Stack pane at the address of the frame pointer (the address held in the EBP register).

### Goto top of stack

Positions the insertion point in the Stack pane at the address of the stack pointer (the address held in the ESP register).

## Displaying CPU registers

The Registers pane displays the contents of the CPU registers of the 80386 and greater processors. These registers consist of eight 32-bit general purpose registers, six 16-bit segment registers, the 32-bit program counter (EIP), and the 32-bit flags register (EFL).

### The Registers pane SpeedMenu

The Registers pane has the following SpeedMenu commands:

- Increment Register
- Decrement Register
- Zero Register
- Change Register
- Show Old Registers/Show Current Registers

### Change Thread

**Note**  You can change the values of memory displayed in the Registers pane by pressing the Ins key and typing into the display (when you press Ins, the insertion point in the pane shrinks to highlight a single nibble in memory). Be extremely careful when changing register values; even small changes can have disastrous effects on your running program.

### Increment register

Increment Register adds 1 to the value in the currently highlighted register. This lets you test "off-by-one" bugs by making small adjustments to the register values.

### Decrement register

Decrement Register subtracts 1 from the value in the currently highlighted register. This lets you test "off-by-one" bugs by making small adjustments to the register values.

### Zero register

The Zero Register command sets the value of the currently highlighted register to 0.

## Change register

Change Register lets you change the value of the currently highlighted register. When you chose this command, the Change Register dialog box prompts you for a new value. You can make full use of the expression evaluator to enter new values. Be sure to precede hexadecimal values with 0x.

## Show old registers/Show current registers

This command toggles between Show Old Registers and Show Current Registers. When you select Show Old Registers, the Registers pane displays the values which the registers had the last time the program was paused. The menu command then changes to Show Current Registers, which changes the display back to the current register values.

# Displaying flags and current information

The Flags pane shows the current state of the flags and information bits contained in the 32-bit register EFL. The processor uses the following 14 bits in this register to control certain operations and indicate the state of the processor after it executes certain instructions:

**Table 7.3**     Flags pane indicators

| Letters in pane | Flag/bit name |
|---|---|
| CF | Carry flag |
| PF | Parity flag |
| AF | Auxiliary carry |
| ZF | Zero flag |
| SF | Sign flag |
| TF | Trap flag |
| IF | Interrupt flag |
| DF | Direction flag |
| OF | Overflow flag |
| IO | I/O privilege level |
| NF | Nested task flag |
| RF | Resume flag |
| VM | Virtual mode |
| AC | Alignment check |

## The Flags pane SpeedMenu

The Flags pane has the following SpeedMenu commands:

- Toggle Flag
- Change Thread

**Note**   You can change the values of memory displayed in the Flags pane by pressing the *Ins* key and typing into the display (when you press *Ins*, the insertion point in the pane shrinks to highlight a single binary value in memory). Be extremely careful when changing flag values; changes here can have disastrous effects on your running program.

### Toggle flag

The flag and information bits in the Flags pane can each hold a binary value of 0 or 1. This command toggles the selected flag or bit between these two binary values.

# Viewing function calls

While debugging, it can be useful to know the order of function calls that brought you to your current program location. Using the Call Stack window, you can view the current sequence of function calls. The Call Stack window is also helpful when you want to view the arguments passed to a function call; each function listing in the window is followed by a listing that details the arguments with which the call was made. Use View I Call Stack to display the Call Stack window.

**Figure 7.9**    Call Stack window

In the Call Stack window, the function that's currently executing is listed on top, with all previously called functions listed in sequence below. The bottom of the list always shows the first function in the calling sequence.

The Call Stack window is particularly useful if you accidentally step through code you wanted to step over. Using the Call Stack window, you can return to the point where the current function was called from, and then resume debugging from there:

1  In the Call Stack window, double-click the function that called the function you accidently stepped into (it will be the second function listed in the Call Stack window). The Edit window becomes active with the cursor positioned at the location of the function call.

2  In the Edit window, move the cursor to the statement following the function call.

3  Choose Run to Cursor on the Edit window SpeedMenu (or press *F4*).

## Navigating to function calls

Using the Call Stack window, you can view or edit the source code located at a particular function call. Right-clicking a function in the Call Stack window displays the SpeedMenu, from where you can choose either View Source or Edit Source. Each of these commands cause the Edit window to display the selected function; however, Edit

Source gives focus to the Edit window so you can modify the source code at that function location.

If you select the top function in the Call Stack window, these commands cause the Edit window to display the location of the execution point in the current function. Selecting any other function call causes the debugger to display the actual function call in the Edit window.

# Debugging dynamic-link libraries

When a DLL is loaded by the program you are debugging, its symbol table is automatically loaded by the debugger. (The DLL must have been compiled with Borland symbolic debug information for you to be able to statement step through it.)

# 8

# Compiling and linking from the command line

If you prefer to develop your applications outside of the Borland C++ IDE, you can compile and link your programs from the DOS command line using the Borland command-line tools. When you develop applications using this method, you must first write your program source code using a text editor, then compile the code into an object (.OBJ) file using the appropriate command-line compiler. After the .OBJ file is generated, you must link all the necessary files to create the final executable program.

## Using the command-line compilers

Borland C++ includes the following command-line compilers that generate either 16-bit or 32-bit object files:

- BCC.EXE is the 16-bit compiler.
- BCC32.EXE is the 32-bit compiler.
- BCC32i.EXE is a highly optimized 32-bit compiler.

When optimizations are turned on, BCC32i.EXE often produces faster executables than does BCC32.EXE. Notable speed increases can be found with programs that perform floating point calculations. However, the cost is slightly larger executable file sizes and slower compilation times than you will get with BCC32.EXE.

In general, these compilers all work the same, but have different defaults and generate different code.

# Command-line compiler syntax

The general syntax for Borland C++ command-line compilers is:

```
BCC | BCC32 | BCC32I [option [option...]] filename [filename...]
```

Items enclosed in brackets are optional. The *option* items refer to command-line options provided in "Command-Line Options" in online Help and in the *Quick Tour and Quick Reference,* and *filename* is one or more source-code files you want to compile.

To list the commonly used compiler options, type BCC, BCC32, or BCC32i at the command line (without any options or file names), then press *Enter.* This list shows the options that are enabled by default.

The command-line compiler name and each option and file name must be separated by at least one space. Precede each option with either a hyphen (-) or a forward slash (/); for example:

```
BCC -Ic:\code\hfiles
```

Options and file names entered on the command line override settings in configuration files.

You can use BCC to send files to TLINK (.OBJ files) or TASM (.ASM files if you have TASM installed on your machine). BCC32 and BCC32i send .OBJ files to TLINK32.

## Default settings

BCC.EXE, BCC32.EXE, and BCC32i each have options that are on by default. To turn off a default option or to override options in a configuration file, follow the option with a minus (-) sign.

Files without extensions and files with the .CPP extension compile as C++ files. Files with a .C extension or with extensions other than .CPP, .OBJ, .LIB, or .ASM compile as C files.

The compilers try to link with a module-definition file with the same name as the executable. To link with a module-definition file with a different name, specify the name on the compiler command line. You must include the .DEF extension and you cannot link with more than one module-definition file.

# Command-line options

You use *command-line options* to control the behavior of the command-line compilers. For example, you can specify where the compiler searches for source files, what type of object files the compiler should produce, what types of optimizations you want the compiler to use, and so on.

A complete, alphabetical list of the command-line options is included in the *Quick Tour and Quick Reference* provided with your Borland C++ package. For a list of the commonly used compiler options, type BCC or BCC32 (without any options or file names) on the command line, then press *Enter.* You can also refer to "Command-Line Options" in online Help for details on all of the options.

When entering command-line options, you must precede each option by either a dash
(–) or a forward slash (/). For example, you might specify an include path for BCC.EXE
with the following command:

```
BCC -Ic:\code\hfiles
```

Each of the compilers uses a different set of default options. To turn off a default option,
follow the option setting with a dash (–). For example, type BCC -w- to turn off warning
messages when compiling with BCC.EXE (note that warning messages are on by default
in all command-line compilers).

When linking Windows programs, Borland compilers, by default, try to link with a
module-definition file that has the same name as the object file. Use TLINK (or
TLINK32) to link with a module-definition file that has a different name. You can't link
with more than one module-definition file.

### Option precedence rules

The command-line compilers evaluate options from left to right, and follows these rules:

- If you duplicate any option except **-D, -U, -I,** or **-L,** the last option typed overrides any
  earlier one. (**-D, -U, -I,** and **-L** are cumulative.)

- Options typed at the command line override configuration and response file options.

## Using compiler configuration files

If you repeatedly use a certain set of options, you can list them in a configuration file
instead of continually typing them on the command line. A *configuration file* is a
standard ASCII text file that contains one or more command-line options. Each option
must be separated by one or more spaces or a new line.

Whenever you issue a compile command, BCC.EXE searches for a configuration file
called TURBOC.CFG and BCC32.EXE and BCC32i.EXE search for the file BCC32.CFG.
The compilers look for the .CFG files first in the directory where you issue the compile
command, then in the directory where the compilers are located.

You can create and use multiple configuration files in addition to using the default .CFG
file. To use a configuration file, use the following syntax where you would place the
compiler options:

```
+[path] filename
```

For example, you could use the following command line to use a configuration file
called MYCONFIG.CFG:

```
BCC +C:\MYPROJ\MYCONFIG.CFG mycode.cpp
```

Options typed on the command line override settings stored in configuration files.

## Using response files

*Response files* let you list both compiler options and file names in a single file (unlike
configuration files, which accept only compiler options). A response file is a standard

ASCII text file that contains one or more command-line options and/or file names, with each entry in the file separated by a space or a new line. In addition to simplifying your compile commands, response files let you issue a longer command line than most operating systems allow.

The syntax for using a single response file is:

```
BCC @[path]respfile.txt
```

The syntax for using multiple response files is:

```
BCC @[path]respfile.txt @[path]otheresp.txt
```

Response files shipped with Borland C++ have an .RSP extension.

Options typed at the command line override any option or file name in a response file.

## Entering directories for command-line options

Borland C++ can search multiple directories for include and library files. This means that the syntax for the library directories (-L) and include directories (-I) command-line options, like that of the **#define** option (-D), allows multiple listings of a given option. Here is the syntax for these options:

```
-Ldirname[;dirname;...]

-Idirname[;dirname;...]
```

The parameter *dirname* used with **-L** and **-I** can be any directory or directory path. You can enter these multiple directories on the command line in the following ways:

- You can stack multiple entries with a single **-L** or **-I** option by using a semicolon:

```
BCC.EXE -Ldirname1;dirname2;dirname3 -Iinc1;inc2;inc3 myfile.c
```

- You can place more than one of each option on the command line, like this:

```
BCC.EXE -Ldirname1;dirname2;dirname3 -Iinc1;inc2;inc3 myfile.c
```

- You can mix listings:

```
BCC.EXE -Ldirname1;dirname2;dirname3 -Iinc1;inc2 -Iinc3 myfile.c
```

If you list multiple **-L** or **-I** options on the command line, the result is cumulative: The compiler searches all the directories listed, in order from left to right.

Note    The IDE also supports multiple library directories.

TLINK uses a configuration file called TLINK.CFG (TLINK32 uses TLINK32.CFG), a response file (optional), and command-line options to link object modules, libraries, and resources into an executable file (.EXE or .DLL).

# Using TLINK and TLINK32

TLINK and TLINK32 are command-line tools that combine object modules (.OBJ files), library modules (.LIB files), and resources to produce executable (.EXE and .DLL) files. Because the compiler automatically calls TLINK, you don't need to use TLINK unless you suppress the linking stage of compiling (see the **-c** compiler option).

**Note**     In the following discussions, instructions and options for TLINK also apply to TLINK32 (unless otherwise specified).

TLINK is invoked from the command line to link a configuration file called TLINK.CFG (TLINK32 uses TLINK32.CFG), an optional response file, and command-line options to link object modules, libraries, and resources into an executable file.

TLINK links 16-bit (Windows) code and uses RLINK.EXE. TLINK32 links 32-bit Windows code and uses RLINK32.DLL.

## TLINK command-line syntax

The linker syntax controls how the linkers work. Linker command-line options are case-sensitive. Unless specified, instructions and options for TLINK also apply to TLINK32.

The linkers can also use a configuration file called TLINK.CFGTLINKCFG (or TLINK32.CFG) for options that you'd normally type at the command-line.

### Syntax

```
TLINK |TLINK32 [@respfile][options] startup myobjs, [exe], [mapfile],
    [libraries], [deffile], [resfile]
```

Where items enclosed in brackets are optional.

- *@respfile* is an ASCII file that lists linker options and file names that you would normally type at the command line (see "Linker response files" later in this chapter). By placing options and files names in a response file, you can save the amount of keystrokes you need to type to link your application.

- *options* are options that control how the linker works. For example, options specify whether to produce an .EXE or a DLL file. Linker options must be preceded by either a slash (/) or a hyphen (-).

    A complete, alphabetical list of the TLINK and TLINK32 options is included in the *Quick Tour and Quick Reference* provided with your Borland C++ package.

- startup is a Borland initialization module for executables or DLLs that arranges the order of the various segments of the program. Failure to link in the correct initialization module usually results in a long list of error messages telling you that certain identifiers are unresolved, or that no stack has been created.

- *myobjs* are the .OBJ files you want linked. Specify the path if the files are not in the current directory. (The linker appends an .OBJ extension if no extension is present.)

- *exe* is the name you want given to the executable file (.COM, .EXE, or .DLL). If you don't specify an executable file name, TLINK derives the name by appending .EXE or

.DLL to the first object file name listed. (The linker assumes or appends .EXE extensions for executable files if no extension is present. It also assumes or appends .DLL extensions for dynamic link libraries if no extension is present.)

- *mapfile* is the name you want given to the map file. If you don't specify a name, the map file name is given the same as the *exe* file (but with the .MAP extension). (The linker appends a .MAP extension if no extension is present.)

- *libraries* specify the library files you want included at link time. Do not use commas to separate the libraries listed. If a file is not in the current directory or the search path (see the /L option) then you must include the path in the link statement. (The linker appends a .LIB extension if no extension is present.)

The order in which you list the libraries is very important; be sure to use the order defined in this list:

- CodeGuard libraries (if needed)

- List any of your own user libraries, noting that if a function is defined more than once, the linker uses the first definition encountered

- If you're creating a DOS overlay, link the DOS overlay module OVERLAY.LIB

- DPMI libraries (DOS DPMI applications only)

- IMPORT.LIB (if you're creating an executable that uses the Windows API)

- Math libraries (if needed)

- Runtime libraries associated with your memory model and platform

[*deffile*]
The module definition file for a Windows executable. If you don't specify a module definition (.DEF) file and you have used the **/Twe** or **/Twd** option, the linker creates an application based on default settings. (The linker appends a .DEF extension if no extension is present.)

[*resfile*]
A list of .RES files (compiled resource files) to bind to the executable. (The linker appends an .RES extension if no extension is present.)

## File name extensions

TLINK assumes or appends these extensions to file names that have none:

- .OBJ for object files
- .EXE for executable files
- .DLL for dynamic-link libraries
- .MAP for map files
- .LIB for library files
- .DEF for module definition files
- .RES for resource files

## Linker configuration files

TLINK uses a configuration file called TLINK.CFG (or TLINK32.CFG for TLINK32) for options that you would normally type at the command line (note that configuration files can contain only options, not file names). Configuration files let you save options you use frequently, so you do not have to continually retype them. TLINK looks for TLINK.CFG in the current directory, then in the directory from which it was loaded.

The following configuration files tell the linkers to

- Look for libraries first in the directory C:\BORLANDC\LIB then in C:\WINAPPS\LIB

- Include debug information in the executables it creates

- Create a detailed segment map

- Produce a Windows executable (.EXE not .DLL)

| TLINK.CFG | TLINK32.CFG |
|---|---|
| /Lc:\bc45\lib;c\:winapps\lib | /Lc:\bc45\lib;c:\winapps\lib |
| /v /s | /v /s |
| /Twe | /Tpe |

**Note**     If you specify command-line options in addition to those recorded in a configuration file, the command-line options override any conflicting configuration options. For example, if you type **/v** in the .CFG file, but you use **/v–** at the command line, TLINK uses the command-line option **/v–**.

## Linker response files

You can use *response files* with the command-line linkers to specify linker options.

Response files are ASCII files that list linker options and file names that you would normally type at the command line. Response files allow you longer command lines than most operating systems support, plus you don't have to continually type the same information. Response files can include the same information as configuration files, but they also support the inclusion of file names.

Unlike the command line, a response file can be several lines long. To specify an added line, end a line with a plus character (+) and continue the command on the next line. Note that if a line ends with an option that uses the plus to turn it on (such as /v+), the + is not treated as a line continuation character (to continue the line, use /v+ +).

If you separate command-line components (such as .OBJ files from .LIB files) by lines in a response file, you must leave out the comma used to separate them on the command line. For example,

```
/c c0ws+
myprog,myexe +
mymap +
mylib cws
```

leaves out the commas you'd have to type if you put the information all on a command line:

```
TLINK /c c0ws myprog,myexe,mymap,mylib cws
```

To use linker response files,

1 Type the command-line options and file names into an ASCII text file and save the file. Response files shipped with Borland C++ have the .RSP extension.

2 Type

```
TLINK @[path]RESFILE.RSP
```

where RESFILE.RSP is the name of your response file.

You can specify more than one response file as follows:

```
tlink /c @listobjs.rsp,myexe,mymap,@listlibs.rsp
```

**Note** You can add comments to response files using semicolons; the linker ignores any text on a line that follows a semicolon.

## Using the linkers with the command-line compilers

You can pass options and files to the linkers through the command-line compilers by typing file names on the command line with explicit .OBJ and .LIB extensions. For example,

```
BCC mainfile.obj sub1.obj mylib.lib
```

links MAINFILE.OBJ, SUB1.OBJ, and MYLIB.LIB to produce the executable MAINFILE.EXE.

**Note** By default, BCC starts TLINK with the files C0WS.OBJ, CWS.LIB, and IMPORT.LIB (initialization module, run-time library, and Windows import library). BCC32 starts TLINK32 with the files C0W32.OBJ, CW32.LIB, and IMPORT32.LIB. In addition, the compilers always pass the linkers the **/c** (case-sensitive link) option.

## Linking libraries

You must always link the Borland C++ run-time library that contains the standard C and C++ library functions for the type of application you are linking. The following tables show the different .OBJ and .LIB files you need to use when linking 16-bit .EXEs and .DLLs. In addition to the files listed, you'll also need to link:

• IMPORT.LIB for all applications that use the Windows API.

• FP87.LIB or EMU.LIB for DOS applications that use floating-point math.

**Table 8.1**    Library and startup files for DOS applications

| Model | Regular startup module | Compatibility startup module | Math library | Run-time library |
|-------|------------------------|------------------------------|--------------|------------------|
| Tiny  | C0T.OBJ                | C0FT.OBJ                     | MATHS.LIB    | CS.LIB           |
| Small | C0S.OBJ                | C0FS.OBJ                     | MATHS.LIB    | CS.LIB           |

**Table 8.1**  Library and startup files for DOS applications (continued)

| Model | Regular startup module | Compatibility startup module | Math library | Run-time library |
|-------|------------------------|------------------------------|--------------|------------------|
| Compact | C0C.OBJ | C0FC.OBJ | MATHC.LIB | CC.LIB |
| Medium | C0M.OBJ | C0FM.OBJ | MATHM.OBJ | CM.LIB |
| Large | C0L.OBJ | C0FL.OBJ | MATHL.LIB | CL.LIB |
| Huge | C0H.OBJ | C0FH.OBJ | MATHH.LIB | CH.LIB |

**Table 8.2**  Library and startup files for statically linked 16-bit Windows .EXEs

| Model | Startup for .EXE | Math library | Run-time library |
|-------|------------------|--------------|------------------|
| Small | C0WS.OBJ | MATHWS.LIB | CWS.LIB |
| Compact | C0WC.OBJ | MATHWC.LIB | CWC.LIB |
| Medium | C0WM.OBJ | MATHWM.LIB | CWM.LIB |
| Large | C0WL.OBJ | MATHWL.LIB | CWL.LIB |

**Table 8.3**  Library and startup files for statically linked 16-bit Windows .DLLs

| Model | Startup for .DLL | Math library | Run-time library |
|-------|------------------|--------------|------------------|
| Small | C0DS.OBJ | MATHWS.LIB | CWC.LIB |
| Compact | C0DC.OBJ | MATHWC.LIB | CWC.LIB |
| Medium | C0DM.OBJ | MATHWM.LIB | CWL.LIB |
| Large | C0DL.OBJ | MATHWL.LIB | CWL.LIB |

**Table 8.4**  Library and startup files for dynamically linked 16-bit Windows .EXEs and .DLLs

| Model | Startup for .EXE or .DLL | Run-time library |
|-------|--------------------------|------------------|
| Large | C0DL.OBJ | CRTLDLL.LIB |

# Module definition file reference

A *module definition file* is an ASCII text file that provides information to TLINK about the contents and system requirements of a Windows application. More specifically, a module definition file

- Names the .EXE or .DLL

- Identifies the application type

- Lists imported and exported functions

- Describes the code and data segment attributes, and lets you specify attributes for additional code and data segments

- Specifies the size of the stack

- Provides for the inclusion of a stub program

You can create a module definition file using IMPDEFIMPDEF, and you can create import libraries from module definition files using IMPLIBIMPLIB.

This section describes module definition files and the statements that appear in them. An example module definition file is provided at the end of the chapter.

## Module definition file defaults

If no module definition file is specified, the following defaults are assumed:

```
CODE PRELOAD MOVEABLE DISCARDABLE
DATAPRELOAD MOVEABLE MULTIPLE        ; (for applications)
PRELOAD MOVEABLE SINGLE              ; (for DLLs)
HEAPSIZE 4096
STACKSIZE 5120                       ; (1048576 for TLINK32)
```

To change an application's attributes from these defaults, you need to create a module definition file.

To replace the EXETYPE statement, the Borland C++ linker can discover what kind of executable you want to produce by checking settings in the IDE or options on the command line.

You can include an import library to substitute for the IMPORTS section of the module definition.

You can use the **_export** keyword in the definitions of export functions in your C and C++ source code to remove the need for an EXPORTS section.

**Note**   If **_export** is used to export a function, that function is exported by name rather than by ordinal (ordinal is usually more efficient).

## CODE statement

CODE defines the default attributes of code segments. Code segments can have any name, but must belong to segment classes whose name ends in CODE (such as CODE or MYCODE). The 32-bit syntax is:

```
CODE [PRELOAD | LOADONCALL]
     [EXECUTEONLY | EXECUTEREAD]
```

The 16-bit syntax is:

```
CODE [FIXED | MOVEABLE]
     [DISCARDABLE | NONDISCARDABLE]
     [PRELOAD | LOADONCALL]
```

- PRELOAD means code is loaded when the calling program is loaded.

- LOADONCALL (the default) means the code is loaded when called by the program.

- EXECUTEONLY means a code segment can only be executed.

- EXECUTEREAD (the default) means the code segment can be read and executed.

- FIXED (the default) means the segment remains at a fixed memory location.

- MOVEABLE means the segment can be moved.

- DISCARDABLE means the segment can be discarded if it is no longer needed (this implies MOVEABLE).
- NONDISCARDABLE (the default) means the segment can not be discarded.

## DATA statement

DATA defines attributes of data segments. The syntax is:

```
DATA [NONE | SINGLE | MULTIPLE]
     [READONLY | READWRITE]
     [PRELOAD | LOADONCALL]
     [SHARED | NONSHARED]
```

- NONE means that there is no data segment created. This option is available only for libraries.
- SINGLE (the default for .DLLs) means a single data segment is created and shared by all processes.
- MULTIPLE (the default for .EXEs) means that a data segment is created for each process.
- READONLY means the data segment can be read only.
- READWRITE (the default) means the data segment can be read and written to.
- PRELOAD means the data segment is loaded when a module that uses it is first loaded.
- LOADONCALL (the default) means the data segment is loaded when it is first accessed (this is ignored for 32-bit applications).
- SHARED (the default for 16-bit .DLLs) means one copy of the data segment is shared among all processes.
- NONSHARED (the default for programs and 32-bit .DLLs) means a copy of the data segment is loaded for each process needing to use the data segment.

## DESCRIPTION statement

DESCRIPTION (optional) inserts text into the application module and is typically used to embed author, date, or copyright information. The syntax is:

```
DESCRIPTION 'Text'
```

*Text* is an ASCII string delimited with single quotes.

## EXETYPE statement

EXETYPE defines the default executable file (.EXE) header type for 16-bit applications. You can leave this section in for 32-bit applications for backward compatibility, but if you need to change the EXETYPE, see the NAME statement. The syntax for EXETYPE is:

```
EXETYPE  [WINDOWAPI]  |  [WINDOWCOMPAT]  |  [NOTWINDOWCOMPAT]
```

- WINDOWAPI is a Windows executable, and is equivalent to the TLINK option **/aa**.

- WINDOWCOMPAT is a Windows-compatible character-mode executable, and is equivalent to the TLINK option **/ap**.

- NOTWINDOWCOMPAT is a character-mode application which won't run under Windows. It is equivalent to the TLINK option **/ai**.

## EXPORTS statement

EXPORTS defines the names and attributes of functions to be exported. The EXPORTS keyword marks the beginning of the definitions. It can be followed by any number of export definitions, each on a separate line. The syntax is:

```
EXPORTS
     ExportName  [Ordinal]
     [RESIDENTNAME]  [Parameter]
```

- *ExportName* specifies an ASCII string that defines the symbol to be exported as follows:

  ```
  EntryName  [=InternalName]
  ```

  *InternalName* is the name used within the application to refer to this entry.

  *EntryName* is the name listed in the executable file's entry table and is externally visible.

- *Ordinal* defines the function's ordinal value as follows:

  ```
  @ordinal
  ```

  where *ordinal* is an integer value that specifies the function's ordinal value.

  When an application or DLL module calls a function exported from a DLL, the calling module can refer to the function by name or by ordinal value. It's faster to refer to the function by ordinal because string comparisons aren't required to locate the function. To use less memory, export a function by ordinal (from the point of view of that function's DLL) and import/call a function by ordinal (from the point of view of the calling module).

  When a function is exported by ordinal, the name resides in the nonresident name table. When a function is exported by name, the name resides in the resident name table. The resident name table for a module is in memory whenever the module is loaded; the nonresident name table isn't.

- RESIDENTNAME specifies that the function's name must be resident at all times. This is useful only when exporting by ordinal (when the name wouldn't be resident by default).

- *Parameter* is an optional integer value that specifies the number of words the function expects to be passed as parameters.

# HEAPSIZE statement

HEAPSIZE defines the number of bytes the application needs for its local heap. An application uses the local heap whenever it allocates local memory. The support for HEAPSIZE is slightly different for 16-bit or 32-bit applications.

The 16-bit syntax for HEAPSIZE is:

```
HEAPSIZE Allocate
```

- *Allocate* is an integer value which specifies the amount of heap allocated at program startup. For 16-bit applications, this size cannot exceed the physical segment size of 65,535 bytes (64K).

The 32-bit syntax for HEAPSIZE is:

```
HEAPSIZE Reserve[, Commit]
```

- *Reserve* can be a decimal or hex value, the default of which is 1MB. To help with backward (16-bit) compatibility, the linker uses the default value of 1MB if you specify in the .DEF file a reserve value less than 64K.

- *Commit* is a decimal or hex value. The commit size is optional, and if not specified defaults to 4K. The minimum commit size you can specify is 0. In addition, the specified or default commit size must always be smaller or equal to the reserve size.

*Reserved memory* refers to the maximum amount of memory that can be allocated either in physical memory or in the paging file. In other words, reserved memory specifies the maximum possible heap size. The operating system guarantees that the specified amount of memory will be reserved and, if necessary, allocated.

The meaning of *committed memory* varies among operating systems. In Windows NT, committed memory refers to the amount of physical memory allocated for the heap at application load or initialization time. Committed memory causes space to be allocated either in physical memory or in the paging file. A higher commit value saves time when the application needs more heap space, but increases memory requirements and possible startup time.

You can override any heap reserve or commit size specified in the .DEF file with the **/H** or **/Hc** command-line options. **/H** lets you specify a heap reserve size less than the 64K minimum allowed in the .DEF file.

# IMPORTS statement

IMPORTS defines the names and attributes of functions to be imported from DLLs. Instead of listing imported DLL functions in the IMPORTS statement, you can do either of the following:

- Specify an import library for the DLL in the TLINK command line

- Include the import library for the DLL in the project manager in the IDE

If you are programming for 32 bits, you must use _ _**import** to import any function, class, or data you want imported. For 16 bits, you must use _ _**import** with the classes you want imported.

The IMPORTS keyword marks the beginning of the definitions followed by any number of import definitions, each on a separate line. The syntax is:

```
IMPORTS
[InternalName=]ModuleName.Entry
```

- *InternalName* is an ASCII string that specifies the unique name the application uses to call the function.

- *ModuleName* specifies one or more uppercase ASCII characters that define the name of the executable module containing the function. The module name must match the name of the executable file. For example, the file SAMPLE.DLL has the module name SAMPLE.

- *Entry* specifies the function to be imported—either an ASCII string that names the function or an integer that gives the function's ordinal value.

## LIBRARY statement

LIBRARY defines the name of a DLL module. A module definition file can contain either a LIBRARY statement to indicate a .DLL or a NAME statement to indicate an .EXE.

A library's module name must match the name of the executable file. For example, the library MYLIB.DLL has the module name MYLIB. The syntax is:

```
LIBRARY LibraryName [INITGLOBAL | INITINSTANCE]
```

- *LibraryName* (optional) is an ASCII string that defines the name of the library module. If you don't include a *LibraryName*, TLINK uses the file name with the extension removed. If the module definition file includes neither a NAME nor a LIBRARY statement, TLINK assumes a NAME statement without a *ModuleName* parameter.

- INITGLOBAL means the library-initialization routine is called only when the library module is first loaded into memory.

- INITINSTANCE means the library-initialization routine is called each time a new process uses the library.

## NAME statement

NAME is the name of the application's executable module. The module name identifies the module when exporting functions. For 32-bit applications, NAME must appear before EXETYPE. If NAME and EXETYPE don't specify the same target type, the linker uses the type listed with NAME. The syntax is:

```
NAME ModuleName [WINDOWSAPI] | [WINDOWCOMPAT]
```

- *ModuleName* (optional) specifies one or more uppercase ASCII characters that name the executable module. The name must match the name of the executable file. For example, an application with the executable file SAMPLE.EXE has the module name SAMPLE.

If *ModuleName* is missing, TLINK assumes that the module name matches the file name of the executable file. For example, if you do not specify a module name and the executable file is named MYAPP.EXE, TLINK assumes that the module name is MYAPP.

If the module definition file includes neither a NAME nor a LIBRARY statement, TLINK assumes a NAME statement without a *ModuleName* parameter.

- WINDOWSAPI specifies a Windows executable, and is equivalent to the TLINK32 option **/aa**.

- WINDOWCOMPAT specifies a Windows-compatible character-mode executable, and is equivalent to the tlink32 option **/ap**.

## SECTIONS statement

The SECTIONS statement lets you set attributes for one or more section in the image file. You can use this statement to override the default attributes for each different type of section. The syntax for SECTIONS is:

```
SECTIONS
section_name (CLASS 'classname'] attributes
```

- SECTIONS marks the beginning of a list of section definitions.

- After the SECTIONS keyword, each section definition must be listed on a separate line. Note that the SECTIONS keyword can be on the same line as the first definition or on a preceding line. In addition, the .DEF file can contain one or more SECTIONS statements. The SEGMENTS keyword is supported as a synonym for SECTIONS. The syntax for the individual section listings is as follows:

  - In this syntax, *section_name* is case sensitive.
  - The CLASS keyword is supported for compatibility but is ignored.
  - The *attributes* argument can be one or more of the following: EXECUTE, READ, SHARED, and WRITE.

## SEGMENTS statement

SEGMENTS defines the segment attributes of additional code and data segments. The syntax is:

```
SEGMENTS
    SegmentName [CLASS 'ClassName']
    [MinAlloc]
    [SHARED | NONSHARED]
    [PRELOAD | LOADONCALL]
    [MIXED1632]
```

- *SegmentName* is a character string that names the new segment. It can be any name, including the standard segment names _TEXT and _DATA, which represent the standard code and data segments.

- *ClassName* (optional) is the class name of the specified segment. If no class name is specified, TLINK uses the class name CODE.

- *MinAlloc* (optional) is an integer that specifies the minimum allocation size for the segment. TLINK and TLINK32 ignore this value.

- SHARED (the default for 16-bit .DLLs) means one copy of the segment is shared among all processes.

- NONSHARED (the default for .EXEs and 32-bit .DLLs) means a copy of the segment is loaded for each process needing to use the data segment.

- PRELOAD means that the segment is loaded immediately.

- LOADONCALL means that the segment is loaded when it is accessed or called (this is ignored by TLINK32). The Resource Compiler may override the LOADONCALL option and preload segments instead.

- MIXED1632 (optional) is supported by the 16-bit linker only, and lets you link 32-bit modules with your 16-bit Windows 95 applications. The Windows 95 16-bit loader supports 32-bit segments when the 2000H bit is set in the segment table of the application.

## STACKSIZE statement

STACKSIZE defines the number of bytes the application needs for its local stack. An application uses the local stack whenever it makes function calls. The support for STACKSIZE is slightly different for 16-bit or 32-bit applications.

The 16-bit syntax for STACKSIZE is:

```
STACKSIZE Allocate
```

- *Allocate* is an integer value which specifies the amount of stack allocated at program startup. For 16-bit applications, this size cannot exceed the physical segment size of 65,535 bytes (64K).

The 32-bit syntax for STACKSIZE is:

```
STACKSIZE Reserve[, Commit]
```

- *Reserve* can be a decimal or hex value, the default of which is 1MB. To help with backward (16-bit) compatibility, the linker uses the default value of 1MB if you specify in the .DEF file a reserve value less than 64K.

- *Commit* is a decimal or hex value. The commit size is optional, and if not specified defaults to 8K. The minimum commit size you can specify is 4K. In addition, the specified or default commit size must always be smaller or equal to the reserve size.

*Reserved memory* refers to the maximum amount of memory that can be allocated either in physical memory or in the paging file. In other words, reserved memory specifies the maximum possible stack size. The operating system guarantees that the specified amount of memory will be reserved and, if necessary, allocated.

The meaning of *committed memory* varies among operating systems. In Windows NT, committed memory refers to the amount of physical memory allocated for the stack at application load or initialization time. Committed memory causes space to be allocated either in physical memory or in the paging file. A higher commit value saves time when the application needs more stack space, but increases memory requirements and possible startup time.

You can override any stack reserve or commit size specified in the .DEF file with the **/S** or **/Sc** command-line options. **/S** lets you specify a stack reserve size less than the 64K minimum allowed in the .DEF file.

**Note** Do not use the STACKSIZE statement when compiling .DLLs.

## STUB statement

STUB appends a DOS executable file specified by *FileName* to the beginning of the module. The executable stub displays a warning message and terminates if the user attempts to run the executable stub in the wrong environment (running a Windows application under DOS, for example).

Borland C++ adds a built-in stub to the beginning of a Windows application unless a different stub is specified with the STUB statement. You should not use the STUB statement to include WINSTUB.EXE because the linker does this automatically.

The syntax is:

```
STUB "FileName"
```

*FileName* is the name of the DOS executable file to be appended to the module. The name must have the DOS file name format.

If the file named by *FileName* is not in the current directory, TLINK searches for the file in the directories specified by the PATH environment variable.

## SUBSYSTEM statement

SUBSYSTEM lets you specify the Windows subsystem and subsystem version number for the application being linked. The syntax for SUBSYSTEM is:

```
SUBSYSTEM [subsystem,]subsystemID
```

• The optional parameter *subsystem* can be any one of the following values: WINDOWS, WINDOWAPI, WINDOWCOMPAT, NOTWINDOWCOMPAT. If you do not specify a subsystem, the linker defaults to a WINDOWS subsystem.

• You must specify the *subsystemID* parameter using the format *d.d* where *d* is a decimal number. For example, if you want to specify Windows 4.0, you could use either of the following SUBSYSTEM statements:

```
SUBSYSTEM 4.0
SUBSYSTEM WINDOWS,4.0
```

You can override any SUBSYSTEM statement in a .DEF file using the **/a** and **/V** command-line options.

# Example module definition file

Following is an example module definition file.

```
NAME          WHELLO
DESCRIPTION   'C++ Windows Hello World'
EXETYPE       WINDOWS
CODE          MOVEABLE
DATA          MOVEABLE MULTIPLE
HEAPSIZE      1024
STACKSIZE     5120
EXPORTS       MainWindowProc
```

Let's describe this file statement by statement:

- NAME specifies a name for an application. If you want to build a .DLL instead of an application, you would use LIBRARY instead of NAME. Every module definition file should have either a NAME or a LIBRARY statement, but never both. The name specified must be the same name as the executable file.

- DESCRIPTION lets you specify a string that describes your application or library.

- EXETYPE can be either WINDOWS or OS2. Only WINDOWS is supported in this version of Borland C++.

- CODE defines the default attributes of code segments. The MOVEABLE option means that the code segment can be moved in memory at run time.

- DATA defines the default attributes of data segments. MOVEABLE means that it can be moved in memory at run time. Windows lets you run more than one instance of an application at the same time. In support of that, the MULTIPLE options ensures that each instance of the application has its own data segment.

- HEAPSIZE specifies the size of the application's local heap.

- STACKSIZE specifies the size of the application's local stack. You can't use the STACKSIZE statement to create a stack for a .DLL.

- EXPORTS lists those functions in the WHELLO application that can be called by other applications or by Windows. Functions that are intended to be called by other modules are called callbacks, callback functions, or export functions.

- To help you avoid the necessity of creating and maintaining long EXPORTS sections, Borland C++ provides the **_export** keyword. Functions flagged with **_export** are identified by the linker and entered into an export table for the module.

    If the Smart Callbacks option is used at compile time (**/WS** on the BCC command-line, or Options | Compiler | Entry/Exit Code | Windows Smart Callbacks), then callback functions do not need to be listed either in the EXPORTS statement or flagged with the **_export** keyword. Borland C++ compiles them in such a way so that they can be callback functions.

- This application doesn't have an IMPORTS statement, because the only functions it calls from other modules are those from the Windows API; those functions are imported via the automatic inclusion of the IMPORT.LIB import library. When an application needs to call other external functions, these functions must be listed in the IMPORTS statement, or included via an import library.

- This application doesn't include a STUB statement. Borland C++ uses a built-in stub for Windows applications. The built-in stub simply checks to see if the application was loaded under Windows, and, if not, terminates the application with a message that Windows is required. If you want to write and include a custom stub, specify the name of that stub with the STUB statement.

# Resource Workshop user's guide

Part II explains how to create, compile, and link resources to applications running under Microsoft Windows 3.1 and higher. You will learn to:

- Work with resources in either text or binary format.
- Manage hundreds of resources stored in dozens of files.
- Use multilevel Undo and Redo to step back through changes you've made.
- Compile your resources only when you need to.
- Change a program's resources even if you don't have access to the source code.
- Automatically check for errors, such as incorrect syntax and duplicate resource IDs.

This part is organized into the following chapters:

- **Chapter 9, "Getting started,"** defines what resources are and explains the basic concepts involved in working with them.

- **Chapter 10, "Working with resource projects,"** explains how to create a new resource project. You use the Resource Project window to open a project, save it, embed a resource in it, and link a resource to it.

- **Chapter 11, "Working with bitmaps, cursors, and icons,"** explains how to use graphics images in your programs in forms of bitmaps, cursors, and icons.

- **Chapter 12, "Using the Graphics editor,"** explains how to create and edit any bitmapped resource, including bitmaps, cursors, and icons, using the Graphics editor.

- **Chapter 13, "Working with resources,"** shows how to create, load, edit, and manage resources by working with resource script, binary, and graphics files.

- **Chapter 14, "Working with dialog boxes,"** explains how to build, edit, and program dialog boxes for your programs.

- **Chapter 15, "Using the Dialog editor,"** explains how to use the Dialog editor and its Control palette, Tool palette, and Property Inspector.

- **Chapter 16, "Working with menus,"** explains how to use the Menu editor to create and edit menus.

- **Chapter 17, "Working with identifiers,"** explains how to create, edit, and manage resource identifiers that uniquely refer to specific resources.

- **Chapter 18, "Using the Text editor,"** explains how to use the Text editor to edit the text version of any resource.

- **Chapter 19, "Working with user-defined resources,"** explains how to define your own resource types when the standard types do not meet your needs.

Chapter

# 9

# Getting started with Resource Workshop

This chapter answers the following questions:

- What is a resource?

- Why you should link resources to your applications

- What is a resource script (.RC) file?

- What is a binary resource (.RES) file?

- What file types does Resource Workshop generate?

## What is a resource?

A resource is binary data that is linked to an application executable (.EXE), dynamic-link library (.DLL), or other binary file. Usually a resource defines one or more of the following user interface components:

- A dialog box, which is a pop-up window that uses labels, text boxes, buttons, check boxes, scroll bars and other controls to give information to and receive information from a user.

- A menu, which is a list of commands from which a user can choose. Types of menus include menus that appear on a application's menu bar, pop-up menus, which can appear anywhere on the workspace, and cascading menus, which can appear when you choose a menu command.

- An accelerator table, which is one or more key combinations that a user can press to perform an action.

- A string table, which is one or more text strings that can contain descriptions, prompts, and error messages.

- A bitmap, which is a graphic image, such as a picture, logo, or other drawing.

- A cursor, which is a graphic image that shows the position of the mouse on the screen and indicates the types of actions a user can perform.

- An icon, which is a graphic image that represents a minimized window.

A resource can also define:

- Version information, which is a block of data that can be used in several Windows API functions. The version information resource specifies the version number, file type, and operating system of a application.

- A custom data type, which is any data that you want to link to an application.

You create or edit resources using Resource Workshop, then you compile the resource, creating a binary (.RES) file that is linked into your application.

# Why you should link resources to your applications

By linking resources to an application, you can keep data separate from code. This separation lets you easily:

- Find and change parts of the application.

- Change an application without changing source files.

- Share data among your applications.

- Create and edit resources in a graphical environment.

Using Resource Workshop, you can extract, modify, and save resources directly into a binary file.

You can include the same resources in any application. You do not need to recreate a resource each time you want to use it.

As you create or edit a resource, you can see just how the resource will appear in your application. You do not have to compile and run your application to see user interface changes.

# What is a resource script (.RC) file?

A resource script (.RC) file contains one or more sets of ASCII data, called resource scripts, from which binary resources can be generated.

When you create and edit resources with Resource Workshop editors, you are creating and editing a resource script automatically. Each resource type has a different resource script format, but you do not need to know these formats unless you plan to edit a resource script in a text editor.

The resource script file for a resource project appears in the Resource Project window. Valid resource projects are .RC, RES, .ICO, .CUR, and .BMP files.

When a resource script file is compiled, it becomes a binary resource (.RES) file.

# What is a binary resource (.RES) file?

A binary resource file is a compiled resource script file. You can compile a resource script file into one or more binary resource files, then link the resources to an application.

Usually when creating a Windows program, you compile all resources for an application into a single .RES file, and then you bind the .RES file to the executable file as part of the linking process.

Once the resources are linked, the application's source code can refer to the resources using the identifiers used in resource script file.

If you want to change the resources in a compiled binary file, Resource Workshop decompiles the file and let you make the changes, then save the resources back to the original file.

# Setting preferences

When you first use Resource Workshop, you may want to set preferences for how it works.

Choose Options | Project | Resources or Options | Environment | Resource Editors to bring up the Options dialog box where you set configuration options.

You can:

- Choose the target for your resources
- Create backup files each time you save a project
- Choose how identifiers are generated and the identifier prefix
- Set the number of changes you want to trace when you undo or redo actions
- Add or remove control libraries
- Choose options for the Dialog, Menu, and Graphics editors

# Undoing mistakes

Resource Workshop lets you undo or redo any action with the Edit | Undo or the Edit | Redo commands. Edit | Undo "undoes" your most recent action. Edit | Redo reverses the effect of the most recent Undo command.

## Edit | Undo

The Edit | Undo command inserts any characters you deleted, deletes any characters you inserted, replaces any characters you overwrote, and moves your cursor back to its prior position. It also undoes operations in the Dialog, Menu, and the Graphics editors.

If you undo a block operation on a resource, the resource will appear as it was before you executed the block operation. The Undo command will not change an option setting that affects more than one window.

If you continue to press Undo, it continues to undo changes until it reaches the number specified in the Undo Levels box (one of the Options | Environment | Resource Editors SpeedSettings.) Depending on the amount of memory in your computer, you can undo or redo up to 99 actions. The default number is 10.

## Edit | Redo

The Edit | Redo command is effective only immediately after you use Edit | Undo or Edit | Redo. A series of Redo commands reverses the effects of a series of Undo commands.

# Starting Resource WorkShop

To start Resource Workshop, do one of the following

- Double-click an existing .RC node in the IDE Project Window
- Choose File | Open and open an existing .RC file
- Choose File | New | Resource Project
- Right-click an .EXE or .DLL node and select Edit Resources

**Note**    Clicking on a .RES, .BMP, .ICO, or .CUR node also invokes the editor on that project.

Chapter

# 10

# Working with resource projects

A resource project is a collection of one or more resources. A resource project is stored in a file that contains one or more resources, or refers to files containing resources, or both. This file is usually a resource script (.RC) file.

When you first use Resource Workshop, you need to create a new resource project or open an existing one. Once the resource project is open, it is displayed in the Resource Project window.

You need to save the resource project when you exit. If you try to exit or close the Resource Project window without saving, Resource Workshop will ask you if you want to save it.

## Creating a new resource project

To create a new resource project,

1 Choose File | New | Resource Project. The New Resource Project dialog box is displayed.

2 Select the type of resource on which you want to base your project.

Usually this will be a resource script file (.RC).

If the Options button is available, choose it to select resource options.

3 When you are done, click OK; then OK again to close the New Resource Project dialog box.

Resource Workshop displays your new project in the Resource Project window. You name your project when you save it.

# Opening an existing resource project

An existing resource project is usually one that you created with Resource Workshop. It can also be an .RC file you created with other resource development software.

You can also work with the resources in any application developed for Windows 3.1 or higher, even if you do not have access to the source code. If you have access only to an executable file, Resource Workshop can decompile the file to let you make changes to the resources.

To open an existing project,

1  Choose File | Open (or double-click the .RC node in an open project in the IDE).

2  In the Open a File dialog box, select the file containing the resource project you want to open.

**Note**    If you want to open a binary file (.EXE or .DLL), select Edit Resources in the Viewer field.

What Resource Workshop does next depends on whether the resource project is a binary file or a file containing resource data.

- If the resource project is a binary file (an executable file, a .RES file, or a dynamic-link library file), Resource Workshop decompiles the resources and shows you its progress on the status line.

- If the resource project consists of a main .RC file and other files containing resource data, Resource Workshop reads the resource project file and then compiles each resource, showing you its progress.

- If Resource Workshop cannot compile the resource project file, an error is displayed that shows you the error and where it occurred. Double-click the error message in a message window to view the script as text.

**Note**    If a compiler error occurs in an .RC file, you can open the .RC file in text edit mode by viewing the message window and double-clicking the error message.

Once the resource project is compiled or decompiled, Resource Workshop displays the Resource Project window with the resources listed in it.

When the resource project is open, you can add resources to it. You can also modify or remove resources. Save the resource project when you finish.

# Saving a resource project

It is a good idea to save your work often. Resource Workshop provides you with a variety of save commands so you can choose exactly what you want to save and how to save it.

Choose the File menu and select one of these options:

- File | Save saves everything in your current resource project. This is the option you usually choose. When you save a new resource project that has not been named yet,

Resource Workshop displays the Save File As dialog box, where you can specify a name and directory.

Resource Workshop always saves the resource project file and any files it refers to. Resource Workshop can also save to a .RES file or bind the resources to an executable or dynamic-link library file.

- File | Save File As lets you rename the current resource project when you save it. Resource Workshop displays the Save File As dialog box, where you can enter the new file name.

# Embedding a resource in a resource project

To embed a resource in your project (to create a new resource in script form), open the resource project you want to work with and follow these steps:

1 Choose Resource | New to display the New Resource dialog box.

2 Choose the type of resource you want to create.

3 Click the Options button to set options for the resource type and to select the header files you want the resource and its identifier to appear in.

You can only select from header files currently attached to your project. (Use Add To Project on the local menu to add a new header file to your project.)

The next steps depend on the type of resource you are creating:

- If you are creating an accelerator, menu, dialog box, string table, RCDATA, or VERSIONINFO resource, Resource Workshop puts an entry for the resource in the Resource Project window and opens the appropriate resource editor.

- If you are creating an image resource (an icon, cursor, or bitmap), Resource Workshop click Options to display the New Resource Options dialog box. To embed the image, check the Source Form box. (If Source Form is clear, enter a file name.)

# Linking a resource to a resource project

You can link a resource stored in an external file to the current resource project by using the Add to Project command on the SpeedMenu. You use this command to add an existing resource file or to create a new file for a new resource.

To link a resource in a separate file to your project,

1 Open the resource project.

The Resource Project window is displayed.

2 Right-click and choose Add to Project. Resource Workshop displays the Add to Project dialog box.

3 Specify the name of the file containing the resource.

If the resource you specify is not an existing resource, Resource Workshop asks you if you want to create a new resource file. If you choose OK, Resource Workshop creates a file of the appropriate type based on the file extension, and inserts a reference to the file in the resource project window.

**4** In the RCINCLUDE Will Be Placed In box you see the current project file listed, which is most likely where you will put the reference to the new file. If your project contains more than one .RC file and you want to put the reference elsewhere, scroll down the list to find the name of the file in which you want to place the reference.

**5** Choose OK to add the file to the resource project.

Resource Workshop puts an entry that points to this file in the Resource Project window.

If you choose Show | List By File on the SpeedMenu you see the file name and the resource name. Any changes you make in the resource project to this resource are reflected in the original resource file.

# Using the Resource Project window

The Resource Project window lists the resources in your project. It acts as an effective file management tool, making it easy to look at an overall view of a resource project. Even if your project contains a large number of resources, you can quickly scan the resource project by scrolling through the Resource Project window.

Once you open a new or existing resource project, Resource Workshop displays the Resource Project window. For a new project, the window is empty. You have to put resources into it by creating them or adding them as files.

For an existing project, you can see these items:

- A complete list of files in the resource project
- The types of resources contained in each file
- The identifiers associated with resources

## Embedded and linked resources

The resources in your project file can be embedded in the file or linked to it.

- An embedded resource is stored in resource script form in the resource project file. It exists only as part of the resource project in which it is stored, and it cannot be used in other projects.

- A linked resource is a separate file that is referred to in the resource project file. Linked resources can be used in other projects.

Use the Resource menu and SpeedMenu to determine how the resource project window displays information. You can group resources by file or type; display the identifiers in the resource project; list the names of resources; display items in resources; and display all possible types of resources.

## Status line

The status line at the bottom of the Resource Workshop displays information about commands and tools.

The status line displays information about the currently highlighted menu command. For example, if you choose the Resource | New command, the status line displays "Create new resource."

When you are in a resource editor such as the Dialog editor or the Graphics editor, the status line displays details about the editor and tool you are working with.

# 11

# Creating bitmaps, cursors, and icons

This chapter explains how to do the following:

- Work with bitmaps
- Work with cursors
- Work with icons

## Working with bitmaps

Bitmap resources display graphic images in your Windows program. Windows programs use bitmaps to represent scroll bar arrows, the Minimize and Maximize buttons, and so on.

To create bitmaps, you use the Resource Workshop Graphics editor.

Working with bitmaps involves four basic tasks:

1 Start the Bitmap editor.

2 Create or edit a bitmap.

3 Test the bitmap.

4 Save the bitmap.

## Creating a new bitmap

You can add a new bitmap to a new or existing resource project file, or create the bitmap in a standalone file. To add a new bitmap to a new or existing .RC file:

1 Open the resource project you want to add the bitmap to, or create a new one by choosing File | New | Resource Project. The New Resource Project dialog box is displayed. Base your project on the .RC file type.

**2** Choose Resource | New to create a new resource for that project. Resource Workshop displays the New Resource dialog box.

**3** In the Resource Type list, select BITMAP.

**4** Click Options to specify attributes for the bitmap resource.

Resource Workshop opens the Graphics editor where you customize the new bitmap resource.

## Creating a new bitmap in a standalone file

To create a standalone bitmap file with the extension .BMP:

**1** Choose File | New | Resource Project. The New Resource Project dialog box is displayed.

**2** Click Bitmap in the New Project dialog box.

**3** Click Options to display the New Bitmap Project Options dialog box. Choose the colors and size of the bitmap image.

**4** Click OK.

Resource Workshop opens the Graphics editor where you customize the new bitmap resource. To link the standalone bitmap file to a resource project file, you need to save the .BMP file first. Then:

**1** Open a resource project file, or click in a .RC project window.

**2** Choose Add to Project.

**3** Select the .BMP file you created.

## Editing an existing bitmap

To edit an existing bitmap:

**1** Choose File | Open and open an existing project (.RC or .BMP).

**2** If you opened a .RC file, double-click the BITMAP resource you want to edit, or select it and choose Resource | Edit.

After you open the bitmap in the Graphics editor, you can customize it. You may find the bitmap easier to work with if you zoom it first.

In addition to creating and modifying bitmaps directly with the Graphics editor, you can also change the bitmap's resource script. It is unlikely that you'll want to do this because the script is almost entirely a series of hexadecimal values.

You can choose the bitmap's foreground and background colors, and change its attributes. You can also delete bitmap resources.

You cannot, however, add transparent and inverted areas to your bitmap.

# Changing the attributes of a bitmap

You can change a bitmap's attributes with the Bitmap | Size and Attributes command.

This command displays the Set Bitmap Attributes dialog box, where you choose:

- The bitmap image size
- Whether the image will shrink or stretch if you change the overall image size
- The number of colors used in the image
- How the bitmap is stored

# Deleting a bitmap resource

To delete a bitmap resource, select it in the Resource Project window, then:

1 Press the Del key or right-click and choose Remove from Project to completely delete it.

2 Choose Edit | Cut to cut the resource into the Windows Clipboard so you can paste it elsewhere.

# Testing a bitmap

To test your bitmap, you need to compile the bitmap resource and bind it to an executable file. Then you can run the executable file to see what the bitmap looks like.

# Programming a bitmap with OWL

To program a bitmap with OWL, use the *TBitmap*, *TDip*, *TDibDC*, and *TClientDC* classes.

For example, this code displays a bitmap in the center of the main window:

```
TBitmap bitmap1(IDB_BITMAP1);
*GetMode();
TMemoryDC memDC;
memDC.SelectorObject (bitmap1);
TClientDC mainWindowDC *GetMainWindow();
int centerX = GetMainWindow()->GetClientRect(), Width()/2;
int centerY = GetMainWindow()->GetClientRect(), Height()/2;
int bitmapX = bitmap1.Width();
int bitmapY = bitmap1.Height();
mainWindowDC.BitBlt(centerX-bitmapX/2, centerY-bitmapY/2, bitmapX,
    bitmapY, memDC, 0, 0, SRCCOPY);
```

In the code, IDB_BITMAP1 is the identifier for the bitmap.

# Programming a bitmap with the Windows API

To program a bitmap the Windows API, use the *LoadBitmap*, *GetObject*, *GetDC*, *CreateCompatibleDC*, *BitBlt*, *DeleteDC*, and *ReleaseDC* functions.

For example, the following code displays a bitmap in the window represented by the *HWnd* variable:

```
HINSTANCE hInst;
HWND hWnd;
HDC hDC, hDCMemory;
HBITMAP hBitmap, hOldBitmap,
BITMAP bitmap;
// Get the bitmap resource and its handle.
hBitmap = LoadBitmap(hInst, MAKEINTRESOURCE(IDB_BITMAP1);
// Get the bitmap data.
GetObject(hBitmap, sizeof(BITMAP), &bitmap);
// Get the device context of the target window.
hDC = GetDC(hWnd);
// Create a compatible memory device context.
hDCMemory = CreateCompatibleDC(hDC);
// Select the bitmap into the memory DC.
// hOldBitmap = SelectObject (hDCMemory, hBitmap);
// Copy the bitmap onto the windows device context.
BitBlt(hDC, 0, 0, bitmap.bmWidth, bitmap.bmHeight, mDCMemory, 0, 0, SRCCOPY);
// Clean up and exit.
SelectObject(hDCMemory, hOldBitmap);
DeleteDC(hDCMemory);
ReleaseDC(hWnd, hDC);
```

In the code, IDB_BITMAP1 is the identifier for the bitmap.

# Working with cursors

Cursors are bitmapped images 32 x 32 pixels in size that represent the mouse pointer's current location on the screen. A Windows application often has a number of different cursors that represent different program functions.

Windows provides a set of standard cursors you can use in your programs. In addition, you can create your own customized cursors to represent different functions of the program.

To design cursors, you use the Graphics editor.

Working with cursors involves four basic steps:

1  Start the Graphics editor.

2  Create or edit a cursor.

3  Test the cursor.

4  Save the cursor.

# Creating a new cursor

You can add a new cursor to a resource project file, or create the cursor in a standalone file. To add a new cursor to a new or existing .RC file,

1 Open the resource project you want to add the cursor to, or create a new one by choosing File | New | Resource Project. The New Resource Project dialog box is displayed. Base your project on the .RC file type.

2 Choose Resource | New to create a new resource for that project. Resource Workshop displays the New Resource dialog box.

3 In the Resource Type list, select CURSOR.

4 Click Options to specify attributes for the cursor resource.

5 Click OK to create the new cursor.

Resource Workshop opens the Graphics editor where you customize the new cursor resource.

# Creating a new cursor in a standalone file

To create a standalone cursor file with the extension .CUR:

1 Open a resource project or create a new one.

2 Choose Resource | New. Resource Workshop displays the New Resource dialog box.

3 In the Resource Type list box, select CURSOR.

4 Click Options to display the New Cursor Resource Options dialog box.

5 In the Storage Format section, uncheck the Source Form check box.

6 In the Cursor Filename (.CUR) field, enter the path and name of the cursor file. Click OK.

7 Click OK again to create the new cursor.

Resource Workshop opens the Graphics editor where you customize the new cursor resource. The standalone cursor file is linked to the current to a resource project file.

If you choose File | New | Resource Project. and select CURSOR in the New Resource Project dialog box, you automatically create a standalone cursor file. Resource Workshop immediately starts the Graphics editor. You can then link the .CUR file to any resource project with the Add to Project command.

# Editing an existing cursor

To edit an existing cursor:

1 Open an existing resource project.

**2** Double-click the CURSOR resource you want to edit or select it and choose Resource | Edit.

After you have the cursor open in the Graphics editor, you can customize it. Before you begin working on your cursor, you may want to zoom it. You can change the cursor's transparent and inverted areas and the number of colors it uses. You can also delete cursors.

In addition to creating and modifying cursors directly with the Graphics editor, you can also change the cursor's resource script. It's unlikely that you'll want to do this because the script is almost entirely a series of hexadecimal values.

## Design issues

Before you start, you should have an idea of what your cursor is intended to represent. A typical use of a custom cursor is to represent the task the user is performing.

The hot spot is the cursor's active area where the user clicks to activate the task represented by the cursor. You need to make the hot spot obvious.

Do not make the cursor complicated. It should be simple enough to fit into a 32 x 32 pixel area. Think about where the user is most likely to display your cursor. Background colors and patterns can affect the cursor's transparent and inverted areas.

# Setting the hot spot for a cursor

An important consideration when you customize a cursor is where to put the hot spot (the cursor's active area). The hot spot is the single pixel in the cursor that fixes the location when the user places the cursor and clicks to make a selection.

To set a hot spot:

**1** Right-click and choose Zoom In to zoom the cursor image until it is big enough to let you precisely choose the pixel coordinates for the hot spot.

**2** Display a grid on the zoomed image.

**3** Select the Line tool.

**4** Point to the location on the zoomed image where you want the hot spot and look at the coordinates displayed on the status line. Make a note of these coordinates.

**5** Choose Cursor | Set Hot Spot.

**6** Enter the hot spot's pixel coordinates in the Set Hot Spot dialog box. Press OK to accept the values.

# Deleting a cursor

You can delete a cursor resource or a cursor image. Deleting a cursor resource deletes all the images in that resource. Deleting a cursor image removes that single image in the cursor resource.

## Deleting a cursor resource

To delete a cursor resource, select it in the Resource Project window then:

1 Press the Del key or right-click and choose Remove from Project to completely delete it.

2 Choose Edit | Cut to cut the resource into the Windows Clipboard so you can paste it elsewhere.

## Deleting a cursor image

To remove an image from a cursor resource:

1 Open the cursor resource in the Resource Project window by double-clicking it or selecting it and choosing Resource | Edit.

2 In the Cursor Project window select the image entry you want to delete, then:

3 Press the Del key or right-click and choose Remove from Project to completely delete it.

4 Choose Edit | Cut to cut the resource into the Windows Clipboard so you can paste it elsewhere.

# Testing a cursor

Anytime you want, you can test your cursor by choosing Cursor | Test Cursor.

Resource Workshop turns the current cursor into a test version of your cursor. You can move it around to see how it looks on different color backgrounds. When you finish testing, just click the mouse to continue customizing your cursor.

# Adding an image to a cursor resource

You may want to put different color formats of the same cursor in one cursor resource project. These color variations on the same cursor are called images.

The reason the cursor resource supports different color formats is that Windows picks a color format based on the ability of the display hardware to support the format. Windows picks a 16-color format for the standard Windows VGA driver.

Windows 3.x does not fully support the 256-color version of an cursor, even if your display hardware supports it. Your program must supply its own support for 256 colors.

To add a new image with different color formats to an existing cursor resource:

1 Open a resource project.

2 Double-click the CURSOR entry you want to edit or select it and choose Resource | Edit.

**3** Choose Cursor | New Image.

**4** Resource Workshop displays the New Cursor Resource dialog box, where you choose the color format of the new image.

**5** Choose a new color format and click OK.

**6** Double-click the new cursor, or select it and choose Images | Edit Image. You see the Graphics editor where you customize the cursor as needed.

Typically, what you do next is open one of the existing cursor images and copy it into the new (still blank) image. You might also have to customize the image if the colors are translated in a way that changes the form of the cursor.

## Changing the attributes of a cursor

You can change an cursor's attributes—color or size—with the Cursor | Size and Attributes command.

This command displays the Cursor Image Attributes dialog box, where you change an cursor's size and color format.

## Copying a cursor image to a new color format

You might want to have different color formats of the same image for different displays. To create another version, without starting over, you can copy and paste the image.

To copy and paste the image:

**1** Create a new image for your cursor.

**2** Open the image you want to copy in the Graphics editor.

**3** Choose Edit | Select All to select the entire image.

**4** Choose Edit | Copy to copy the cursor image to the Clipboard.

**5** Use File | Close to close the window.

**6** Choose Cursor | New Image to create a new Cursor image. In the New Cursor Image dialog box, choose the color format of the new image.

**7** Double-click the new CURSOR entry in the Cursor Project window.

**8** Choose Edit | Paste to paste the cursor into the new image. It is displayed in the new color format.

## Programming a cursor with OWL

To program a cursor with OWL, use the *TWindow::SetCursor* function.

For example, the following application code assigns a cursor to the main window:

```
GetMainWindow()->SetCursor(this, IDC_CURSOR1);
```

IDC_CURSOR1 is the identifier for the cursor.

# Programming a cursor with the Windows API

To program a cursor with the Windows API, use the *LoadCursor* and *SetCursor* functions.

For example, the following code changes the active cursor:

```
HCURSOR hCursor;
hCursor = LoadCursor(hInst, MAKEINTRESOURCE(IDD_CURSOR1));
SetCursor(hCursor);
```

IDD_CURSOR1 is the identifier for the cursor.

# Working with icons

Icons are small bitmapped images, normally 16 x 16, 32 x 32, 48 x 48, or 64 x 64 pixels in size. Windows programs typically use customized icons to represent minimized windows.

To design icons, use the Resource Workshop Graphics editor.

Working with icons involves four basic steps:

1 Start the Graphics editor.

2 Create or edit an icon.

3 Test the icon.

4 Save the icon.

# Creating a new icon

You can add a new icon to a resource project file, or create the icon in a standalone file. To add a new icon to a new or existing .RC file:

1 Open the resource project you want to add the icon to, or create a new one by choosing File | New | Resource Project. The New Resource Project dialog box is displayed. Base your project on the .RC file type.

2 Choose Resource | New to create a new resource for that project. Resource Workshop displays the New Resource dialog box.

3 In the Resource Type list, select ICON.

4 Click Options to specify attributes for the icon resource.

5 Click OK to create the new icon.

Resource Workshop opens the Graphics editor where you customize the new icon resource.

# Creating a new icon in a standalone file

To create a standalone icon file with the extension .CUR:

1 Open a resource project or create a new one.

2 Choose Resource | New. Resource Workshop displays the New Resource dialog box.

3 In the Resource Type list box, select ICON.

4 Click Options to display the New Icon Resource Options dialog box.

5 In the Storage Format section, uncheck the Source Form checkbox.

6 In the Icon Filename (.CUR) field, enter the path and name of the icon file. Click OK.

7 Click OK again to create the new icon.

Resource Workshop opens the Graphics editor where you customize the new icon resource. The standalone icon file is linked to the current to a resource project file.

If you choose File | New | Resource Project. and select ICON in the New Resource Project dialog box, you automatically create a standalone icon file. Resource Workshop immediately starts the Graphics editor. You can then link the .CUR file to any resource project with the Add to Project command.

# Editing an existing icon

To edit an existing icon:

1 Open an existing resource project.

2 Double-click the icon resource you want to edit, or select it and choose Resource | Edit.

After the icon is opened in the Graphics Editor, you can customize it. Before you begin working on your icon, you may want to zoom it. You can change the icon's transparent and inverted areas and its attributes. You can also delete icon resources and images.

In addition to creating and modifying icons directly with the Graphics editor, you can also change the icon's resource script. It is unlikely that you'll want to do this because the script is almost entirely a series of hexadecimal values.

## Design issues

Before you start, you should have an idea of what the icon represents to the user. The icon should be simple enough to fit into a 64 x 64, 48 x 48, 32 x 32, or 16 x 16 pixel area.

Think about where the user is most likely to display your icon. Background colors and patterns can affect the icon's transparent and inverted areas.

### Drop shading

Drop shading is a technique you can use to make your icon look three dimensional. For example, to make a black box look three dimensional, draw a gray border on the right side and bottom of the box.

# Adding an image to an icon resource

You may want to put different color formats of the same icon in one icon resource project. These color variations on the same icon are called images.

The reason the icon resource supports different color formats is that Windows picks a color format based on the ability of the display hardware to support the format. Windows picks a 16-color format for the standard Windows VGA driver.

Windows 3.x does not fully support the 256-color version of an icon, even if your display hardware supports it. Your program must supply its own support for 256 colors. However, Windows 95 does and typically uses 256 colors for 48 x 48 or large icons.

To add a new image with different color formats to an existing icon resource:

1 Open a resource project.

2 Double-click the ICON entry you want to edit or select it and choose Resource | Edit.

3 Choose Icon | New Image.

4 Resource Workshop displays the New Icon Image dialog box, where you choose the size and color format of the new image.

5 Choose the same size as the existing image and a new color format and click OK.

6 Double-click the new icon, or select it and choose Images | Edit Image. You see the Graphics editor where you customize the icon as needed.

Typically, what you do next is open one of the existing icon images and copy it into the new (still blank) image. You might also have to customize the image if the colors are translated in a way that changes the form of the icon.

# Changing the attributes of an icon

You can change an icon's attributes—color or size—with the Icon | Size and Attributes command.

This command displays the Icon Image Attributes dialog box, where you change an icon's size and color format.

# Copying an icon image to a new color format

You might want to have different color formats of the same image for different displays. To create another version, without starting over, you can copy and paste the image.

To copy and paste the image:

1 Create a new image for your icon.

2 Open the image you want to copy in the Graphics editor.

3 Choose Edit I Select All to select the entire image.

4 Choose Edit I Copy to copy the icon image to the Clipboard.

5 Use File I Close to close the window.

6 Choose Icon I New Image to create a new icon image. In the New Icon Image dialog box, choose the size and color format of the new image.

7 Double-click the new ICON entry in the Icon Project window.

8 Choose Edit I Paste to paste the icon into the new image. It is displayed in the new color format.

# Deleting an icon resource or image

You can delete an icon resource or an icon image. Deleting an icon resource deletes all the images in that resource. Deleting an icon image removes that single image in the icon resource.

## Deleting an icon resource

To delete an icon resource, select it in the Resource Project window then:

1 Press the Del key or right-click and choose Remove from Project to completely delete it.

2 Choose Edit I Cut to cut the resource into the Windows Clipboard so you can paste it elsewhere.

## Deleting an icon image

To remove an image from an icon resource:

1 Open the icon resource in the Resource Project window by double-clicking it or selecting it and choosing Resource I Edit.

2 In the Icon Project window select the image entry you want to delete, then:

3 Press the Del key or right-click and choose Remove from Project to completely delete it.

4 Choose Edit I Cut to cut the resource into the Windows Clipboard so you can paste it elsewhere.

# Testing an icon

The easiest way to test an icon is to use the Icon | Test Icon command. You can also bind the icon resource to an executable file and then run the file to see what the icon looks like.

Two primary reasons for testing an icon are:

1 To see how a color icon looks in black and white when you move it around.

2 To see how transparent and inverted areas look against various backgrounds.

The first test is easy to perform: just move the icon around.

The second test takes a little more work. Here's how:

1 Make sure the icon is visible and is in a spot where the application workspace is its background.

2 Change tasks using Windows NT or Windows 95.

3 Use the Control Panel to change the color of the active window's workspace.

4 Leave the Control Panel Settings window open so you can change the colors again.

5 Change tasks back to Resource Workshop and check the icon against the new background color.

At this point, you should be able to see both Resource Workshop and the Color dialog box (NT) or Display Properties (Windows 95) at the same time. You can select another color for the workspace background and check the icon again.

When you change the color of the application workspace, the operating system changes the color in the application window, where you can check the icon against the new color.

# Programming an icon with ObjectWindows

To program an icon with ObjectWindows, use the *TFrameWindow::SetIcon* function.

For example, the following code assigns an icon to the main window:

```
GetMainWindow()->SetIcon(this, IDC_ICON1);
```

IDC_ICON1 is the identifier for the icon.

# Programming an icon with the Windows API

To program an icon with the Windows API, use the *LoadIcon* function.

For example, this code loads an icon resource into a variable:

```
HICON hIcon;
hIcon = LoadIcon(hInst, MAKEINTRESOURCE(IDD_ICON1));
```

IDD_ICON1 is the identifer for the icon.

# 12

# Using the Graphics editor

You use the Graphics editor to create and edit any bitmapped resource, including bitmaps, cursors, and icons.

Although most of the Graphics editor's features are the same for the bitmapped resource types, there are some features that are unique to each resource type. For example, the name of the Graphics editor menu is the same as the resource type: Icon for an icon resource, Bitmap for a bitmap resource, and Cursor for a cursor resource.

The Graphics editor features whose functionality is generally the same for all types of bitmapped resources are the Color palette, the status line and bar, the Tool palette, and the window panes.

This chapter covers the following topics:

- Using the Color palette
- Selecting a pen style
- Selecting a brush shape
- Selecting a paint pattern
- Drawing and painting
- Adding text
- Selecting an area
- Erasing an area
- Aligning an area
- Moving or resizing an area
- Copying an area
- Removing an area
- Zooming in or out
- Moving a graphic around in the drawing area

# Using the Color palette

Bitmapped images drawn with the Graphics editor are created on a grid of pixels. You create the image by setting each pixel to a foreground or background color. Strictly speaking, there's no difference between the foreground and background color. There is, however, a difference in how you choose foreground and background colors and in how they are created when you edit the bitmapped image.

The Graphics editor's Color palette makes it easy to choose foreground and background colors. You can work with a Color palette even if your image is black and white.

You use the Color palette to choose:

- A foreground color
- A background color
- Transparent and inverted areas (for icons and cursors only)

You can move the palette anywhere you want it. You can also hide it and show it by:

- Right-clicking and choosing the Show | Color Palette command.
- Clicking the palette's Close box.

## Selecting a foreground color

The foreground color is the color you select and draw with the left mouse button. It is typically one of the colors you use to create the features of your resource, such as lines, boxes, shading, and so on. The current foreground color is indicated on the Tool palette.

To select a foreground color:

1 Select the color you want on the Color palette (using the left mouse button).

2 The color is displayed at the bottom of the Tool palette.

3 Select a tool that draws or paints.

4 Click or drag with the left mouse button to draw or paint with the foreground color.

The Eraser tool operates in the opposite fashion from the drawing tools. Dragging it with the left mouse button produces the background color, and dragging it with the right mouse button produces the foreground color.

## Selecting a background color

The background color is the color you select and draw with the right mouse button and is usually the color that appears to underlie your drawing. It is also the color that's left behind when you select an area and delete or move it. The background color is indicated on the Tool pallette.

To select a background color,

**1** Right-click the color you want in the Color palette.

  • The color is displayed on the Tool Palette next to the foreground color

**2** Select a tool that draws or paints.

**3** Click or drag with the right mouse button to draw or paint with the background color.

The Eraser tool operates in the opposite fashion from the drawing tools. Dragging it with the left mouse button produces the background color, and dragging it with the right mouse button produces the foreground color.

# Transparent and inverted areas

Transparent and inverted color areas are unique to icon and cursor resources.

  • A transparent area allows the desktop color behind the icon or cursor to show through.

  • An inverted area reverses the desktop color at run time.

The designated transparent and inverted colors do not appear in your icon or cursor at run time. Instead, they are replaced by the desktop color or its inverse. The colors that you set as Transparent and Inverted should be colors that you will not use in your icon or cursor.

The default transparent color is the current desktop color set in the Windows Control Panel's color palette. If the desktop uses a dithered color, the default transparent color is the nearest solid color that Resource Workshop can provide. (If you have a 256-color device, this restriction does not apply; the default transparent color will always match the desktop color.)

You can change the transparent color to something other than the desktop color, but it will always revert to the desktop color each time you start Resource Workshop. Nevertheless, regions that you designate as transparent—using the default color or a color you assign—remain transparent and take on the current transparent color.

**Note**  You can change colors so that you have transparent and non-transparent regions that use the same color.

To change the colors the Graphics editor displays for transparent and inverted areas,

**1** Double-click the button for Transparent or Inverted in the Color palette.

**2** Select either Transparent or Inverted as the foreground or background color.

  • If you're working with icons, right-click and choose Edit Foreground Color or Edit Background Color.

  • If you're working with cursors, right-click and choose Set Transparent Color.

Resource Workshop displays the Color dialog box, where you can change the color.

# Hiding and showing the Color palette

If you want to hide the Color palette you can close it by clicking the Close button in the upper-right corner of the palette.

You can also right-click and uncheck the Show | Color Palette command. Or you can select Show | Color Palette from the Bitmap, Cursor, or Icon menus.

# Choosing the number of colors for a resource

When you create a bitmap, cursor, or icon, you choose how many colors you want in your resource.

For bitmaps, this dialog box is the New Bitmap Resource Options dialog box.

For cursors, this dialog box is the New Cursor Resource Options dialog box.

For icons, it is the New Icon Resource Options dialog box.

To display these dialog boxes, press the Options button while in the New Resource Project or New Resource dialog boxes.

While you are editing a bitmap, cursor, or icon, you can change the number of colors in the image using the Size and Attributes command. Depending on the type of resource you edit, you find this command on the Bitmap, Cursor, or Icon menu.

You can include up to 256 colors in your bitmap, cursor, or icon. The number of colors you can use (and see in the Color palette) depends on the type of display driver you're using with Windows. The standard Windows VGA driver supports a fixed set of only 16 colors.

# Customizing colors

When you are editing a color image you can modify the Color palette to include any colors supported by your display driver.

It does not make sense to do this if the Color palette already includes all the colors supported by your computer. But if your display driver is capable of displaying 256 colors and you're working with a 16-color image, you can include any of the 256 colors in the 16-color Color palette.

When you're editing a cursor or icon, you can change the color used to display transparent or inverted areas of the image.

## Modifying the Color palette

To edit a color, double-click it.

Resource Workshop displays the Edit Color dialog box, where you can specify a new color.

**Note** You can't change the first or last color in the palette. By default, the first and last entries are always black and white, respectively.

# Selecting a pen style

The pen style affects the width of a line or shape border and whether a line or shape is solid, dashed, or dotted. The pen style applies to the following tools:

- Line
- Ellipse
- Pen
- Rectangle
- Rounded Rectangle

To select a pen style,

1  Choose the Pen Style tool on the Tool Palette. You can also select the Pen Style command from the Bitmap, Cursor, or Icon menu.
   - The Set Pen Style dialog box is displayed.

2  Choose the line style you want.

3  Choose OK. The new pen style displays in the Tool palette.

You can select one of the tools mentioned above and draw with the new pen style.

# Selecting a brush shape

You can select a brush shape for the Paintbrush or Airbrush tool.

To select a brush shape,

1  Select the Paintbrush Shape or Airbrush Shape tool on the Tool palette. You can also select the Paintbrush Shape or Airbrush Shape command from the Bitmap, Cursor, or Icon menu.
   - If you choose the Paintbrush Shape tool, you see the Brush Shape dialog box.
   - If you choose the Airbrush Shape tool, you see the Airbrush Shape dialog box.

2  Select a brush shape.

3  Choose OK. The new shape displays in the Tool palette.

You can select one of the tools mentioned above and draw with the new brush shape style.

# Selecting a paint pattern

The paint pattern affects the interior of a filled shape and the painting styles of the brush tools. The paint pattern applies to the following tools:

- Airbrush
- Filled Ellipse
- Filled Rectangle
- Filled Rounded Rectangle
- Paintbrush

To select a paint pattern,

1 Choose the Pattern tool on the Tool palette. You can also choose Pattern from the Bitmap, Cursor, or Icon menu.

   - The Set Pattern Type dialog box is displayed.

2 Select a paint pattern.

3 Choose OK. The new pattern displays on the Tool palette.

You can select one of the tools mentioned above and draw with the new paint pattern.

# Drawing and painting

You can draw and paint with the Pen, Paintbrush, and Airbrush tools.

The size of the area covered by these tools is proportionate to the size of the drawing area. You can zoom out to paint a larger area, and zoom in to paint a smaller area.

To draw or paint,

1 Choose the Pen, Paintbrush, or Airbrush tool on the Tool palette.

2 In the drawing area, move the cursor to where you want to start drawing, and then click and hold down the left mouse button (for foreground color) or the right mouse button (for background color).

3 Drag the cursor around the drawing area.

4 When you are done, release the mouse button.

# Drawing a line

To draw a line,

1 Choose the Line tool on the Tool palette.

2 In the drawing area, move the cursor to where you want to the line to start, and click and hold down the left mouse button (for foreground color) or the right mouse button (for background color).

**3** Move the cursor to where you want the line to end, and release the mouse button.

**4** To draw a line at a 0-, 45-, or 90-degree angle, hold down the Shift key while you are drawing.

# Drawing a shape

You can draw a filled or unfilled rectangle, rounded rectangle, or ellipse.

To draw a shape,

**1** Choose one of the following tools on the Tool palette:

- Rectangle
- Rounded Rectangle
- Filled Rectangle
- Filled Rounded Rectangle
- Ellipse
- Filled Ellipse

**2** In the drawing area, move the cursor to where you want a corner of the shape to be, and hold down the left button (for the foreground color) or the right mouse button (for the background color).

**3** Move the cursor to the opposite corner of the shape, and release the mouse button.

The interior of a filled shape depends on the current paint pattern, and the shape border depends on the current pen style.

To draw a shape without a border, select Null for the pen style.

# Filling an area with color

You can fill any area that is bounded by one or more different colors.

To fill an area with color,

**1** Choose the Paint Can tool from the Tool Palette.

**2** In the drawing area, move the crosshairs into the area that you want to fill, and hold down the left mouse button (for the foreground color) or the right mouse button (for the background color).

# Adding text

To add text to a graphic,

**1** Choose the Text tool on the Tool palette.

**2** In the drawing area, click where you want to add text.

**3** Type the text.

To change the font and alignment of the text,

**1** Choose Bitmap, Cursor, or Icon | Text Attributes. The Font dialog box is displayed.

**2** Choose the font name, size, style, and text alignment.

**3** Choose OK.

To change the color of text,

- Choose a new color from the Color palette.

After you click to make another selection, you cannot change the attributes of the text you have just typed.

# Erasing an area

To erase an area,

**1** Select the Eraser tool on the Tool palette.

**2** Drag the eraser over the area you want erased.

To erase the entire drawing area, double-click the Eraser tool on the Tool palette.

An erased area is colored the selected background color. This means that you can:

- Erase an area by drawing or painting using the background color.

   For example, you can use the Line tool to erase a line if the selected color for the line is the background color.

- Use the Eraser tool to paint an area with the background color while you hold down the left mouse button, and paint an area with the foreground color while you hold down the right mouse button.

# Selecting an area

You can align, copy, move, and remove any area that you select.

To select a rectangular area,

**1** Choose the Pick Rectangle tool on the Tool palette.

**2** In the drawing area, move the cursor to a corner of the area you want to select and hold down the mouse button.

**3** Move the cursor to the opposite corner of the area you want to select and release the mouse button.

To select a non-rectangular area,

**1** Choose the Scissors tool on the Tool palette.

**2** In the drawing area, move the cursor to a boundary of the area you want to select and hold down the mouse button.

**3** Draw a closed shape around the area you want to select and release the mouse button.

You can now align, copy, move, or delete the selected area.

# Aligning an area

You can align an area with the top, bottom, sides, or center of a graphic.

To align an area,

**1** Choose the area with the Pick Rectangle or Scissors tool.

**2** Choose Bitmap, Cursor, or Icon | Align. The Align Selection dialog box is displayed.

**3** Select a horizontal alignment option.

**4** Select a vertical alignment option.

**5** Choose OK.

Any area that is left open is filled with the current background color.

# Moving or resizing an area

To move an area,

**1** Choose the area with the Pick Rectangle or Scissors tool.

**2** Drag the area to a new location.

To resize an area,

**1** Choose the area with the Pick Rectangle or Scissors tool.

**2** Choose Bitmap, Cursor, or Icon | Size. The Stretch Selection dialog box is displayed.

**3** To move the area, specify new pixel coordinates for the Top and Left sides.

**4** To resize the area, specify a new height and width.

**5** Choose OK.

Any area left open is filled with the current background color.

# Copying an area

To copy an area,

**1** Choose the area with the Pick Rectangle or Scissors tool.

**2** Choose Edit | Copy to place a copy of the area in the Windows Clipboard.

**3** Choose Edit | Paste to insert the area into the image.

**4** A copy of the selected area appears in the upper-left corner of the drawing area. It remains selected.

**5** Drag the selected area to where ever you want to place it.

You can also use this method to copy an area:

**1** Select the area.

**2** Choose Edit | Copy.

**3** Select an area where you want the copied image to appear.

**4** Choose Edit | Paste.

**5** The copied image fits within the selected area as best it can and remains selected. You can move the selected area if you want.

Any area left open is filled with the current background color.

## Removing an area

To remove or delete an area,

**1** Choose the area with the Pick Rectangle or Scissors tool.

**2** Choose Edit | Cut.

**3** You can then paste the removed area somewhere else using the Edit | Paste command.

Any area left open is filled with the current background color.

You can also use Edit | Clear to delete an area. The area is not copied to the Clipboard for pasting.

## Zooming in or out

To zoom in on a graphic,

- Double-click the Zoom tool on the Tool palette. You can also right-click and choose Zoom In, or press Control+Z.

To zoom in on a particular area of a graphic,

**1** Select the Zoom tool.

**2** In the drawing area, move the cursor to a corner of the area and hold down the mouse button.

**3** Drag the cursor to the opposite corner of the area and release the mouse button.

To zoom out from a graphic,

- Hold down the shift key and double-click the Zoom tool on the Tool palette. You can also press Ctrl+O or right-click and choose Zoom Out.

To view the actual size of a graphic,

- Press Ctrl+A or right-click and choose Actual Size.

To help you control images on a pixel-by-pixel basis, you can display a grid on any zoomed image by choosing Bitmap, Cursor, or Icon | Editor Options. Check the Grid on Zoomed Windows check box. Each square of the grid represents a single pixel.

If you zoom an image to a size that is too large to fit in the pane, and the image is displayed at its true size in the other window pane, Resource Workshop places a dotted rectangle over the unzoomed image. This dotted rectangle indicates the portion of the image currently displayed in the zoomed window pane.

## Moving a graphic around in the drawing area

If a graphic is too large to display in the drawing area, you can move it around to see other parts of it.

To move a graphic in the drawing area,

1 Hold down the Ctrl key.

- The cursor becomes the Hand tool.

2 Drag the graphic to a new position.

You can also move a graphic around with the scroll bars on the right and bottom sides of the drawing area.

## Tool palette

When you open a resource in the Graphics editor, the Tool palette is displayed in the edit window. You use the Tool palette to choose the Graphics editor tool you want to work with or to change settings for the various tools.

You can move the Tool palette around, dock it, and you can hide it or show it.

Here are tools on the Tool palette:

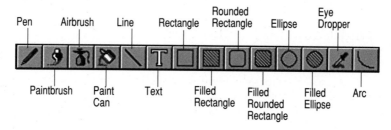

These four buttons, displayed at the bottom of the Tool palette, allow you to customize settings:

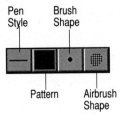

There are also color setting buttons for the foreground color and background color. The current settings are displayed on these buttons.

In addition, there is a Hand tool that you can use to move a zoomed image. It is not displayed in the Tool palette.

# Hiding and showing the Tool palette

To hide or show the Tool palette,

1 Right-click and choose Show | Tool Palette.

2 Toggle the Show | Tool Palette command. This command is located on the menu bar selection that corresponds to the type of resource you are working with (Bitmap, Cursor, or Icon).

The check mark next to the command indicates that it is displayed. No check mark indicates that it is hidden.

# Pick Rectangle tool

You use the Pick Rectangle tool to select a rectangular area of your image for copying, moving, or deleting. To select an area, click the left mouse button and drag the mouse until the flashing outline surrounds the area you want. Release the mouse button. Clicking either mouse button outside the outline turns the area selection off.

When you select an area, you can use the Edit menu commands to cut, copy, clear, duplicate, or paste into the selected area. You can also use the mouse to move (click) or duplicate the area (shift-click). In addition, you can align or resize the selected area.

# Scissors tool

The Scissors tool performs basically the same function as the Pick Rectangle Tool: it selects an area of an image. However, with the scissors you can select and move areas of any shape, not just rectangles. To select an area, click the left mouse button and drag the scissors until the flashing outline surrounds the area you want, then release the mouse button.

When you select an area, you can use the Edit menu commands to cut, copy, clear, duplicate, or paste into the selected area. You can also use the mouse to move (click) or duplicate the area (shift-click). In addition, you can align or resize the selected area.

# Zoom tool

You use the Zoom tool to zoom the entire image, or you can outline an area of an image that you'd like to zoom, and have Resource Workshop zoom that area. Double-click the Zoom tool to zoom in on the entire image. The image is zoomed based on the center of the image.

Images are zoomed one magnification increment per zoom action, until the maximum or minimum magnification is reached.

To zoom out, press Shift and double-click the Zoom tool.

To zoom in on a selected area,

1  Select the Zoom tool.

2  Click and drag to select the area you want to zoom in on.

The magnification depends on the size of the area you select. The smaller the selected area, the greater the magnification.

# Eraser tool

The Eraser tool works like a square paintbrush—you drag the tool over the area you want to erase. To erase an entire image, double-click the Eraser tool.

Use the left mouse button to reveal the current background color. Use the right mouse button to reveal the current foreground color.

Since you use the eraser to reveal colors, the buttons on the mouse are the opposite of other tools you use to paint. For example, when you use the Paintbrush tool, you use the left mouse button to paint the foreground color. But with the eraser, the left mouse button reveals the background color.

Before you use the eraser, you may want to select the foreground and background colors you want to use in the Color palette.

# Pen tool

Use the Pen tool to paint free-form lines and shapes using the current pen style. To sketch with the Pen tool, click a mouse button and drag the pen across your image. Release the mouse button when you finish sketching.

• Use the left mouse button to sketch with the current foreground color.

• Use the right mouse button to sketch with the current background color.

Before you use the Pen tool, you might want to select the pen style and the foreground and background colors.

You can also use the Pen tool to fill individual pixels with a color. Left-click to use the foreground color or right-click to use the background color. You may want to zoom in on the image before making changes to make it easier to color individual pixels.

# Paintbrush tool

Use the Paintbrush tool to paint free-form patterns using the current brush pattern and shape. To paint, click a mouse button and drag the paintbrush across your image. Release the mouse button when you finish painting.

When you choose the Paintbrush tool, you see a cursor that represents the current brush shape. The area painted by the paintbrush is always proportionally the same relative to the size of the image frame.

- Use the left mouse button to paint with the current foreground color.
- Use the right mouse button to paint with the current background color.

Before you use the paintbrush, you might want to select the foreground and background colors and the paintbrush shape and pattern.

# Airbrush tool

The Airbrush tool paints free-form patterns similar to a real airbrush on your image using the current airbrush pattern and shape.

To use the airbrush, you can either click a mouse button once and drag the airbrush, or you can click it repeatedly, as if you were repeatedly pressing the nozzle of a spray can. If you drag it slowly, it paints a thick pattern. If you drag it quickly, it paints a scattered, thinner pattern.

When you choose the Airbrush tool, you see a cursor that represents the Airbrush tool. The area painted by the airbrush is always proportionally the same relative to the size of the image frame.

- Use the left mouse button to paint with the current foreground color.
- Use the right mouse button to paint with the current background color.

Before you use the airbrush, you might want to select the foreground and background colors and specify the airbrush shape and pattern.

# Paint Can tool

Use the Paint Can tool to fill an area of your image with the currently selected color. It fills in any area of your image that is a single color.

- If you use this tool on an area that is not entirely surrounded by other colors, the color leaks out into other parts of the image that are the same color as the original area.

- If you hold down the Shift key when you use the Paint Can, you replace all instances of the color you click on, contiguous or not.

To use the Paint Can tool, point the paint can's cross hairs in the portion of the image you want to fill, then click a mouse button.

- Use the left mouse button to sketch with the current foreground color.

- Use the right mouse button to sketch with the current background color.

Before you use the paint can, you might want to specify the foreground and background colors.

# Line tool

Use the Line tool to paint straight lines. Press the mouse button and drag the Line tool across your image. Release the mouse button when you've finished drawing the line.

If you want the lines you paint to be limited to 45-degree increments, hold down Shift as you draw the line. With Shift down, you can paint only a horizontal or vertical line or a line on a 45-degree angle.

- Use the left mouse button to sketch with the current foreground color.

- Use the right mouse button to sketch with the current background color.

Before you paint a line, you might want to specify the pen style and choose the foreground and background colors.

# Text tool

To add text to your image, choose the Text tool and click where you want the text to begin. A flashing cursor appears and you can begin typing text.

Before you use the Text tool, you might want to specify how and where you want the text displayed: Use the Bitmap, Cursor, or Icon | Text Attributes command to display the Font dialog box, where you specify the typeface, size, style of the text, and how text is aligned.

Text is always displayed in the current foreground color. Before you type text, you might want to specify the foreground color by clicking the left mouse button on the color you want in the Color palette.

# Empty frame tools

You use one of these tools to paint an empty frame in your image:

- Ellipse
- Rectangle
- Rounded Rectangle

To paint an empty frame,

1  Choose the tool you want.

2  Point the tool's cross hair where you want to start a corner of the frame.

3  Click a mouse button and drag the frame tool until the frame outline surrounds the area you want.

4  Release the mouse button.

Use the left mouse button to sketch with the current foreground color. Use the right mouse button to sketch with the current background color.

Before you paint a frame, you might want to specify the pen style, as the frame is affected by the pen style and width. You may also want to choose the foreground and background colors before painting the frame.

## Ellipse tool

Use the Ellipse tool to paint an ellipse-shaped empty frame in your image.

## Rectangle tool

Use the Rectangle tool to paint a rectangular empty frame in your image.

## Rounded Rectangle tool

Use the Rounded Rectangle tool to paint an empty frame shaped like a rounded rectangle in your image.

# Filled-in frame tools

Use one of these tools to paint filled-in frames in your image:

- Filled Ellipse
- Filled Rectangle
- Filled Rounded Rectangle

These tools paint a frame using the current pen style. The frame is filled using the current pattern and color. Specify a null pen style in the Set Pen Style and Width dialog box if you don't want Resource Workshop to put an outline around the filled-in pattern.

To paint a filled-in frame,

1  Choose the tool you want.

2  Point the tool's cross hairs where you want to start a corner of the frame.

3  Click a mouse button and drag the frame tool until the frame outline surrounds the area you want.

4  Release the mouse button.

Use the left mouse button to sketch with the current foreground color. Use the right mouse button to sketch with the current background color.

Before you paint a filled-in frame, you might want to specify the pen style and pattern and choose the foreground and background colors.

## Filled Rectangle tool

Use the Filled Rectangle tool to paint a rectangular filled-in frame in your image.

## Filled Rounded Rectangle tool

Use the Filled Rounded Rectangle tool to paint a filled-in frame, in the shape of a rounded rectangle, in your image.

## Filled Ellipse tool

Use the Filled Ellipse tool to paint an ellipse-shaped filled-in frame in your image.

# Eye Dropper tool

Use the Eye Dropper tool to copy a color from the current image. This is useful when you have a color in an image that isn't displayed in your color palette.

To select a color for use with any tool,

1  Select the Eye Dropper from the Tool palette.

2  Click to copy the color as a foreground color, or right-click to copy the color as a background color.

3  Select the tool you wish to use with the new color.

# Arc tool

Use the Arc tool to create a Bézier arc, curve, or closed loop using the current pen style and color.

To create an arc,

1   Select the Arc tool from the Tool Palette.

2   Click and drag to draw a line of the appropriate length.

3   Click the line you just created and drag it to create the arc you want. The point you select on the line determines the shape of the arc. To create a symmetrical arc, click the center of the line.

4   Without moving the cursor, click again to "set" the arc.

To create a curve,

1   Select the Arc tool from the Tool Palette.

2   Click and drag to draw a line of the appropriate length.

3   Click the line you just created and drag it to create the arc you want. The point you select on the line determines the shape of the arc.

4   Click another part of the line and drag it to create another arc in the line. You can click many points on the line to create the desired curve.

To create a closed loop,

1   Select the Arc tool from the Tool Palette.

2   Click where you want the closed end of the loop to be. This end is stationary and will not move as you create the loop.

3   Click where you want the top of the loop to be. This creates a line. This end may move as you create the loop.

4   Click the line and drag it to adjust the arc. The arc is mirrored, resulting in a closed loop.

To constrain the lines to 45-degree angles, press Shift as you draw the line. You will only be able to draw horizontal, vertical or 45-degree lines.

• Use the left mouse button to draw with the current foreground color.

• Use the right mouse button to draw with the current background color.

# Hand tool

Unlike other tools, the Hand tool isn't included in the Tool palette. But you can change any tool (except the Text tool) into a hand by holding down Ctrl.

The Hand tool is a grabbing tool. You just click the hand on the image and drag it in the direction you want it to move.

The Hand tool is automatically displayed when you select an area using the Pick Rectangle or Scissors tool. Sometimes when you display a zoomed image, not all of it fits in the display. You can use the Hand tool to move the image around to see other parts of it.

# Pattern style tool

The Pattern style tool shows the current pattern style. Some of the tools in the Tool palette use this style when they paint a pattern on your image. These tools are:

- Airbrush
- Filled Ellipse
- Filled Rectangle
- Filled Rounded Rectangle
- Paintbrush

Click the Pattern tool to display the Set Pattern Type dialog box, where you choose the pattern that is painted when you use these tools.

# Pen style tool

The Pen style tool shows the current pen style and width. Some of the tools in the Tool palette use this style when they draw a line on your image. These tools are:

- Line
- Ellipse
- Pen
- Arc
- Rectangle
- Rounded Rectangle

Click the Pen style tool to display the Set Pen Style and Width dialog box, where you choose the pen style and width for these tools. The pen style is drawn relative to the size of the image.

# Airbrush shape tool

The Airbrush shape shows the current shape used for the Airbrush tool. Click the Airbrush shape tool to display the Airbrush Tip Shape dialog box, where you choose the airbrush tip shape.

# Paintbrush shape tool

The Brush shape tool shows the current shape of the Paintbrush tool. Click the Brush shape tool to display the Brush Tip Shape dialog box, where you choose the brush shape.

# 13

# Working with resources

Resources are data that define the visible portions of your Windows program. Resources provide a consistent user interface that makes it easy for users to switch from one Windows program to another.

In general, a Windows application's resources are separate from the program code, letting you make significant changes to the interface without even opening the file that contains your program code. This also lets different applications share the same set of resources, so that you do not have to reinvent all your favorite resources. Instead, you can use them over and over.

When you display resources in the Resource Project window, you see them listed by type, with the names of the resource listed under their type.

To create a new resource, you can do one of the following:

- Double-click the resource type in the Resource Project window. The Options dialog box for that type displays. Click OK to create the new resource. Resource Workshop automatically starts the appropriate editor, if one is available. If an editor is not available (for example, for a user-defined resource), Resource Workshop starts the Text editor.

- Select Resource I New and choose the type of resource you want to create. Resource Workshop automatically starts the appropriate editor, if one is available. If an editor is not available, Resource Workshop starts the Text editor.

To load a resource, you can do one of the following:

- Double-click the resource name in the Resource Project window. Resource Workshop automatically starts the appropriate editor, if one is available. If an editor is not available (for example, for a user-defined resource), Resource Workshop starts the Text editor.

- Select the resource name in the Resource Project window and choose either Resource I Edit or Resource I Edit as Text. Resource I Edit loads a resource editor, if one is available for the selected resource type. Resource I Edit as Text always starts the Text editor.

# Resource file types

A file you create and edit with Resource Workshop can be in either binary or text format. Resource Workshop generates standard Windows file formats, which means you can use Resource Workshop files with programs that generate binary code from resource script files.

Here are the types of resource files you can create with Resource Workshop:

- 16-bit device driver (.DRV)
- Bitmap (.BMP)
- Control Panel applets (.CPL)
- Cursor (.CUR)
- Dialog (.DLG)
- Executable (.EXE)
- Dynamic link library (.DLL)
- Icon (.ICO)
- Resource script (.RC)
- Resource (.RES)
- VBX control libraries (.VBX)

# Executable and dynamic-link library files

An executable (.EXE) or dynamic-link library (.DLL) file is the ultimate destination for all resources you define with Resource Workshop. It is the file that users execute to run your program. In general, you compile the resource script file (.RC file) into the resource file (.RES file), then use your compiler to bind the .RES file to the executable or .DLL file.

If you want to change the resources in a compiled binary file (an executable file, a .DLL file, or a .RES file), Resource Workshop decompiles the file and lets you make the changes, then saves the resources back to the original file.

## Working with binary files

Resource Workshop lets you open executable (.EXE), dynamic-link library (.DLL), and resource (.RES) files as resource projects so you can customize their resources.

When you load one of these files, Resource Workshop decompiles the resources in the file and shows them to you as though they were part of a regular .RC file. When you finish, Resource Workshop compiles the resources again into binary code and stores them in the original file.

Because the resources you work with in this type of resource project are never stored as resource scripts, you cannot assign any identifiers to the resource IDs. However, you can save the resource project as an .RC file. Then the resources can be saved as resource scripts, and you can assign identifiers to them.

**Note** Once you save the resource project as an .RC file, Resource Workshop will not save the resources back to the original file.

## Opening and saving .EXE, .DLL, and .RES files

To open an .EXE, .DLL, or .RES file and save it as a resource script file,

1 Choose File | Open and choose Resource Project in the Viewer field.

2 Select the .EXE, .RES, or .DLL file from the Open a File dialog box. Click OK.

3 Choose File | Save File As. In the Save File As dialog box, select Resource Script (.RC) from the List Files of Type box. In the Filename box, enter the name of the new .RC file.

4 Press OK to save the file.

# Using a resource editor

You can edit any resource in a resource project by double-clicking the resource in the Resource Project window, or by selecting it and choosing Resource | Edit.

Here are the available editors:

• For a dialog resource, Resource Workshop loads the Dialog editor.

• For a menu resource, Resource Workshop loads the Menu editor.

• For an icon, bitmap, or cursor resource, Resource Workshop loads the Graphics editor.

• For all other resources, Resource Workshop loads the Text editor.

## Renaming a resource

To rename a resource in your resource project,

1 Select the resource in the Resource Project window.

2 Choose Resource | Resource Attributes.

Resource Workshop displays the Resource Attributes dialog box, where you rename your resource.

3 Enter the new resource name in the Name box.

If you want to create a new identifier, or change the one you already have, enter the new value in the Identifier Value box.

4 Choose OK.

## Deleting a resource

To delete a resource from a resource project, select it in the Resource Project window, and then do one of the following:

- To delete the resource, press the *Del* key or right-click and choose Remove from Project.

- To reuse the resource, right-click and choose Cut to remove the resource and place it in the Windows Clipboard so you can paste it elsewhere.

## Specifying resource memory options

Resource Workshop makes it easy to specify how each resource in your resource project should be managed in memory. It is better to leave the memory settings at their defaults unless you are an experienced Windows programmer—you might not be able to foresee the implications of changing the way a resource is handled in memory.

To specify memory options,

1 Select the name of the resource in the Resource Project window.

2 Choose Resource | Resource Attributes to open the Resource Attributes dialog box.

3 Check one or more of the Memory Options check boxes.

## Moving a resource

You can move resources from one file in a resource project to another file in the resource project by using the Resource | Resource Attributes command. Both files must be part of the current resource project.

1 Select a resource in the resource project file by either editing it or highlighting it in the Resource Project window.

2 Choose Resource | Resource Attributes to open the Resource Attributes dialog box.

The resource name and the file it currently resides in are displayed in the Resource Attributes dialog box.

3 Click the File drop-down list to choose the file you want to move the resource to. Click OK.

## 16-bit vs. 32-bit resources

By default, new resource projects created with File | New | Resource Project are created as 32-bit resources. This makes two resource types available that are not available for 16-bit resources:

- MENUEX
- DIALOGEX

When resource script files are compiled, they are compiled based on the current IDE project settings. Resource script files originally targeted for 32-bit platforms can easily be recompiled for a 16-bit program without changing the script file as long as they do not contain a MENUEX or DIALOGEX resource type.

Compiled resources (.RES) files are only compatible with the platform they originally targeted. For example, you cannot link a 16-bit compiled resource to a 32-bit compiled executable. If you want to change the target, you have to reload the .RC file with the IDE project and retarget the platform.

## Saving a resource

It is a good idea to save your work often. Resource Workshop provides you with a variety of save commands so you can choose exactly what you want to save and how to save it. You can:

- Rename the current resource file using File | Save As.
- Save the entire resource project and all of the resources it contains.
- Save the resource in a separate file by:
  - Saving the resource in a resource script file.
  - Saving a bitmapped resource as a separate file.

Resource Workshop saves the resource project file and any files it references.

## Saving a resource in a resource script file

To save an individual resource as a resource script file,

1 If the resource is not already open, select the resource name in the Resource Project window.

2 Choose Resource | Save Resource As. This command displays the Save Resource As dialog box.

3 Select Resource Script (.RC) as the resource type.

4 Enter the file name of the new resource script.

If you want to replace the resource in the current project with a reference to this new file, check the Replace Resource With Reference To This File option.

If this box is cleared, the current resource project remains unchanged, and the new file is created. By default, this box is cleared for non-bitmapped resources.

5 Click OK.

Usually, you save a resource with a resource project. You would probably only save it in its own file if you create a separate resource project that contains just related types of resources (such as menus and accelerators). You can then link this resource file to a resource project that uses the same resources.

# Saving a bitmapped resource as a file

You can save a bitmapped resource as a file. You will probably do this step only if you want to put the bitmapped resource in binary format in a separate file for the first time.

To save a bitmapped resource as a file,

1  If the resource is not already open, select the bitmapped resource in the Resource Project window.

2  Choose Resource | Save Resource As. This command displays the Save Resource As dialog box.

3  Select the appropriate resource type.

4  Enter the file name of the resource.

   If you want to replace the bitmapped resource in the current project with a reference to this new file, leave the Replace Resource With Reference To This File option checked.

   To leave the current resource project unchanged, clear this option. By default, this option is checked for bitmapped resources.

5  Click OK.

# Editing a resource as text

In addition to creating and modifying a resource directly with a resource editor, you can work directly with its resource script.

To work with the resource script for a resource, select the resource from the Resource Project window. Then choose Resource | Edit As Text. Resource Workshop brings up the source script for the resource in the Text editor. Here is an example of the resource script for a menu:

```
Edit_Menu MENU
{
  POPUP "&Edit"
  {
    MENUITEM "&Undo\tCtrl+Z", CM_EDITUNDO
    MENUITEM "&Cut\tCtrl+X", CM_EDITCUT
    MENUITEM "&Copy\tCtrl+C", CM_EDITCOPY
    MENUITEM "&Paste\tCtrl+V", CM_EDITPASTE
  }
}
```

The only readily comprehensible parts of a script for a bitmapped resource are the first and second lines (the resource name and BEGIN) and the last line (END).

```
ABitmap BITMAP
BEGIN
'42 4D 66 00 00 00 00 00 00 00 3E 00 00 00 28 00'
'00 00 14 00 00 00 0A 00 00 00 01 00 01 00 00 00'
'00 00 28 00 00 00 00 00 00 00 00 00 00 00 00 00'
```

```
'00 00 02 00 00 00 00 00 00 00 FF FF FF 00 E0 00'
'00 00 EF FF E0 00 EC 08 20 00 EF FF E0 00 EC 41'
'20 00 EF FF E0 00 E1 01 20 00 F5 FF E0 00 F9 FF'
'E0 00 FC 00 00 00'
END
```

Everything between the second line and the last line is hexadecimal code. If you like, you can edit this code to see the effect on the bitmap, but do so at your own risk.

**Note**    Do not spend any time inserting comments in your resource script or formatting the text, because the Resource Workshop incremental compiler does its own formatting and discards all comments.

# 14

# Working with dialog boxes

Dialog boxes give the user a way to interact with your application. A dialog box is usually a pop-up window that lets the user specify information (files to open, colors to display, text to search for, and so on).

When a dialog box is displayed in an application, it is shown as a window. The dialog box usually contains a number of controls, such as buttons, text boxes, and scroll bars. Controls usually let the user specify information, but can also be used to display static text and graphics in a dialog box.

From the perspective of the programmer, the dialog box is the parent window and each control is a child window acting as an input or output device. To create a dialog box, you fill an empty dialog box with the controls you want.

Resource Workshop's Dialog editor makes it easy to create and edit dialog boxes. Working with dialog boxes involves four steps:

* Open an existing resource project or create a new one.

* Create a new dialog box or edit an existing one.

* Test the dialog box.

* Save the dialog box.

## Using DLGINIT resources

A DLGINIT resource is created automatically when a dialog box contains VBX controls. It holds information needed to initialize the controls. Creating or editing a DLGINIT resource explicitly by hand is rarely necessary.

There is no available editor to create an explicit DLGINIT resource.

# Creating a new dialog box

To create a new dialog box:

1 Choose File | New | Resource Project to start a new resource project or File | Open to load an existing resource project.

2 Choose Resource | New. Resource Workshop displays the New Resource dialog box.

3 In the Resource Type list box, select DIALOG or DIALOGEX. Choose DIALOGEX to specify ExStyle information for dialogs whose target is Windows 95 or NT.

4 Choose the Options button to specify the dialog box name and type, and to set other options for the new dialog, including the dialog template.

5 Select OK in the Options dialog to accept the options values. Select OK again in the New Resource dialog to create the new dialog.

You are now in the Dialog editor where you can customize your dialog box.

# Creating a new dialog box in a resource script file

To create a new dialog box as an independent resource script file:

1 In the Resource Project window, right-click to display the SpeedMenu. Choose Add to Project. The Add File to Project dialog box appears.

2 In the List Files of Type box, choose Resource Script (*.dlg).

3 Enter a new name in the File Name box.

4 Choose OK.

5 Choose Yes when Resource Workshop asks you if you want to create the file.

You have created an empty dialog file.

To create a new dialog box and add it to the empty .DLG file:

1 Choose Resource | New to display the New Resource dialog box.

2 For the resource type, choose DIALOG or DIALOGEX. Choose DIALOGEX to specify ExStyle information for dialogs whose target is Windows 95 or NT.

3 Click the Options button.

4 In the New Resource to be Placed In box, choose the name of the dialog script file you just created. Select other options as required.

5 Click OK twice to create the new dialog.

# Editing an existing dialog box

To edit a dialog box that already exists in a project file:

**1** Use File | Open to open the project that contains the dialog box you want to edit.

**2** Double-click the dialog resource name you want to edit, or select it and choose Resource | Edit.

You are now in the Dialog editor.

# Adding a caption to a dialog box

To add a caption to a new dialog box:

**1** Right-click in an empty area of the dialog box and choose Properties to display the Property Inspector.

**2** If not already selected, select the General page.

**3** In the Caption box, type the caption you want to appear at the top of your dialog box.

**4** Choose OK.

# Including a menu in a dialog box

Because it is really a window, a dialog box could include a menu. For example, some applications use a dialog box for the main window, in which case the dialog box would need a menu.

To include a menu in your dialog box:

**1** Define the menu as a separate resource and add it to the project. Remember the menu resource name.

**2** Open the dialog box you want to add the menu to.

**3** Right-click in an empty area of the dialog box and choose Properties to open the Property Inspector.

**4** Click the Window page. Enter the menu resource name in the Menu field.

The Dialog editor will not display the menu until you put the Dialog editor into text mode.

# Choosing a window type, frame style, and dialog box style

You choose a window type, frame style, and dialog box style in the Property Inspector.

To open the Property Inspector, right-click in an empty area of the dialog and choose Properties.

**1** Choose a window type for your dialog box by selecting the Window page. Choose one of the Window Type options.

2  Choose a frame type for your dialog box by selecting the Frame page. Choose one of the Frame Type options. The frame type determines the appearance of the dialog box frame and whether the dialog box displays a title bar at the top.

3  Choose frame styles for your dialog box by selecting the Frame page. Choose one of the Frame Attributes options. The attributes determine what the dialog box looks like and how the user works with it.

For 32-bit applications using DIALOGEX, use the Extended page to determine how the dialog box is positioned, its alignment, reading order, and its behavior.

## Specifying dialog box fonts

To choose how text is displayed in your dialog box:

1  Right-click in an empty area of the dialog box and choose Properties to display the Property Inspector.

2  Choose the Fonts page.

3  Select a typeface, size, and style for text in your dialog box. The characters displayed at the bottom of the Font page show the current typeface, size, and styles you've selected.

4  Choose OK.

**Note**  Changing the font for a dialog box will cause the size and position of the dialog box and any contained controls to change. This is because the coordinate system for dialog boxes (dialog units) is based on the average character width of the font. As the average character width changes, the coordinate system changes.

## Assigning a custom class to a dialog box

If you're an experienced Windows programmer, you might want to assign a custom class to your dialog box. Then you can process dialog box messages with your own Windows procedures instead of using the standard Windows windowing procedure.

Another reason for assigning a custom class is to make the dialog box a Borland-style dialog box.

To assign a custom class to a dialog box:

1  Right-click in an empty area of the dialog box and choose Properties to display the Property Inspector.

2  Click the Window page. Enter the class name in the Class box. If you are creating a Borland-style dialog box, enter bordlg or BorDlg_Gray.

3  Choose OK to save the changes and close the Property Inspector.

# Setting the position of a dialog box

To set the size of the dialog:

1 Right-click in an empty area of the dialog box and choose Properties to display the Property Inspector.

2 Modify the Width and Height values on the General page.

3 Click OK to save the changes.

To set the initial location of a dialog:

1 Right-click in an empty area of the dialog box and choose Properties to display the Property Inspector.

2 Modify the Top and Left values on the General page.

3 Click OK to save the changes.

**Note**  When the dialog box has a title bar (the default), you can drag it with the mouse to position the dialog box. When the dialog box has a resizable border (the default), you can size it with the mouse.

# Testing a dialog box

Choose Dialog | Test Dialog to test your dialog box. To verify that your controls are in the order you want them, press Tab and the arrow. Enter text to see how text is scrolled in an edit text control.

To leave test mode and return to edit mode, do any of the following:

• Click the dialog box's OK or Cancel button.

• Choose Dialog | Test Dialog again.

• Press Enter.

• Press the system close button on the text dialog.

**Note**  Some controls, such as the Tab, ListView, and TreeView common controls, will not display in test mode as they do in design mode or as they will appear in your program. This is because they are dependent on your program to display the correct information.

# Programming a dialog box with OWL

To program a dialog box with OWL, use the *TDialog* class.

For example, this shows how to create and display a modal dialog box:

```
TDialog dialog1(GetApplication()->GetMainWindow(), IDD_DIALOG1);
dialog1.Execute();
```

*dialog1* is the name of the dialog box class, and IDD_IDENTIFIER1 is the identifier for the dialog box resource.

# Programming a dialog box with the Windows API

To program a dialog box with the Windows API, use the *DialogBox* function.

For example, the following code shows how to create and display a dialog box:

```
HINSTANCE hInst;

HWND hwndParent;
DLGPROC dlgProc;
dlgProc = (DLGPROC) MakeProcInstance(ResModeDlgProc, hInst);
DialogBox(hInst, MAKEINTRESOURCE(IDD_RESDEMODIALOG), hwndParent, dlgProc);
FreeProcInstance((FARPROC) dlgProc);
```

where:

| | |
|---|---|
| *ResModeDlgProc* | The dialog procedure function that handles messages from controls |
| *hInst* | The HINSTANCE handler of the Windows module (.EXE or .DLL) which controls the dialog resource |
| *IDD_RESDEMODIALOG* | Replaced with the resource ID of the dialog |
| *hwndParent* | The parent window of the dialog |

# Working with controls

Once you have defined a dialog box, you can create and manipulate its controls. In the Dialog editor, the Dialog menu, Dialog local menu, the Control palette, and the Tool palette make it easy to work with controls.

# Adding controls to a dialog box

To add a new control to a dialog box:

1  Click the page and control you want in the Control palette.

2  Your cursor changes to a cross hair when you move the cursor over the dialog box you are designing.

3  To place the control with the default size, click in the dialog box where you want to place the top left corner of the control.

4  To place the control and size it at the same time, click in the dialog where you want to place the top left corner of the control. Drag the mouse to the lower right until the control is the desired size.

If you select a control from one of the palette pages and change your mind about placing it, choose the Selector tool on any page of the Control palette. Your cursor returns to the arrow shape and you can choose another control or work with existing ones.

You can also use the Dialog menu to add controls to your dialog box:

1 Choose Dialog | Insert New.

2 Choose the control you want, then click OK.

3 Click the spot in the dialog box where you want to add the control.

To add multiple copies of the same control, hold the Shift key down while clicking in the dialog. When you are finished with the control type, click the Selector tool.

# Working with custom controls

In addition to standard controls, common controls, and Borland controls, you can add custom controls to a dialog box. A custom control is any other window class that you want to add to your dialog box, including Visual Basic controls.

Custom controls are stored in .DLL or Visual Basic custom control (.VBX) files. Before you can use custom controls, you must install them.

To install custom controls:

1 Choose Options | Environment | Control Libraries.

2 Click Add.

3 In the File Open dialog box, select the name of the .DLL file you want to open.

4 If you are installing VBX controls, choose the Windows system directory and the name of the .VBX file you want to open. (.VBX files are automatically installed in this directory.)

   • The file name and list of the controls in that file are displayed in the Installed Controls list.

5 Click Add to a.of the Control palette.

For information on adding the control to the dialog box, see Adding controls to a dialog box.

To remove custom controls:

1 Choose Options | Environment | Control Libraries.

2 Choose the name of the control library you want to remove.

3 Click Remove, then OK.

The library and its controls are no longer accessible from Resource Workshop.

**Note**    When you use VBX controls in a dialog box, a DLGINIT resource is produced. In addition, the Property Inspector displayed for a VBX control is always modeless, so the changes take effect immediately. It is always in list format.

# Duplicating a control

To place multiple, identical copies of a control in rows and columns:

1 Select the control you want to duplicate.

2 Right-click the control and choose Duplicate. The Duplicate Control dialog box is displayed.

3 Enter the number of rows and columns into which you want to arrange the duplicated controls. For example, if you are placing push buttons, and want one row of three buttons across, enter 1 in Row and 3 in Column.

4 Enter the spacing you want between rows and columns in the Spacing fields. It is recommended that you enter 6 for row spacing and 8 for column spacing. Units are in dialog units.

5 Click OK.

Your control is now duplicated. The caption is the same as the original, but the ID is automatically incremented.

# Moving and resizing a single control

To move a control with the mouse:

1 Select the control.

2 Hold the left mouse button down and drag the control to a new location.

To resize a control with the mouse:

1 Select the control.

2 Move the mouse cursor to one of the black nibs at the control's edge or corner. When it turns into a double arrow, hold the left mouse button down and drag to the desired size.

To move a control with the keyboard:

1 Press Tab until the control you want is selected.

2 Press the Up arrow key to move the control up; press the Down arrow key to move it down. Press the Right arrow key to move the control to the right; press the Left arrow key to move it to the left.

3 Press Enter when the control is in a satisfactory location.

To size a control with the keyboard:

1 Press Tab until the control you want is selected.

2 Choose Dialog | Size or right-click and choose Size. The Size dialog box is displayed.

3 Choose the Width option and enter the control's width.

**4** Choose the Height option and enter the control's height.

**5** Press OK to change the control's size. Its top left corner stays in the same place.

You can also use arrow keys to size a control:

| Key | Description |
| --- | --- |
| Ctrl + left arrow | Decreases width one dialog unit |
| Ctrl + right arrow | Increases width one dialog unit |
| Ctrl + up arrow | Decreases height one dialog unit |
| Crtl + down arrow | Increases height one unit |

You can also move and resize a control with the General page of the Property Inspector. Select the control, double-click, and change the appropriate Top, Left, Width, and Height values.

If you change your mind about moving or resizing a control, select Edit | Undo.

# Selecting multiple controls

To select multiple controls:

**1** Choose the Selector tool.

**2** Place the cursor where you want the selection frame to start. It must be outside of any controls.

**3** Click the left mouse button and hold it down.

**4** Drag your mouse so that the selection frame surrounds or intersects all the controls you want to select.

**5** Release the mouse button.

**Note** You can also select multiple controls by pressing the Shift key while clicking on controls. The selection becomes cumulative. Clicking a second time while holding the Shift key will unselect the control, while keeping other selections.

Depending on the setting of the Selection Rectangle Must Surround Controls option in Options | Environment | Resource Editors | Dialog, the selection rectangle must either entirely surround the controls, or just intersect them.

You can select all controls in a dialog box by right-clicking and choosing Select All.

# Aligning multiple controls

To display and adjust the alignment grid:

**1** Choose Dialog | Show | Grid to display the alignment grid.

**2** To adjust the grid's granularity, choose Dialog | Grid Spacing. In the Grid Spacing dialog box enter the desired width and height of each grid cell.

**Note**    You may have already set grid spacing defaults with Options | Environment | Resource Editors | Dialog.

3  If you want the controls to "snap to" the grid, select the Snap to Grid option in the Grid Attributes section of Options | Environment | Resource Editors | Dialog. You can also toggle Dialog | Snap to Grid.

To align multiple controls:

1  Select the controls you want to align.

2  Choose Dialog | Align | Controls or right-click one of the selected controls and choose Align. In the Alignment dialog box, choose how you want to align the controls horizontally and vertically. Controls can be aligned to the left, center, or right. They can also be spaced equally or centered in the window.

3  When controls are selected, you can use the arrow keys to fine-tune their positions on the grid. The arrow keys move the selected controls one dialog unit.

To align multiple controls into an array:

1  Select the controls you want to align.

2  Choose Dialog | Align | Array or right-click one of the selected controls and choose Array. In the Array dialog box, choose the format of the array by specifying the number of rows and columns. Order the controls from left to right or top to bottom.

To evenly space multiple controls:

1  Select the controls you want to arrange.

2  To space the selected controls horizontally equidistant from each other in the dialog box, choose Dialog | Space | Horizontally Equal.

3  To space the selected controls vertically equidistant from each other in the dialog box, choose Dialog | Space | Vertically Equal.

You can also use the Tool palette to align and space controls.

To undo alignment options, choose Edit | Undo or press *Alt+Backspace*. You may have to choose Undo more than once.

# Resizing multiple controls

To resize multiple controls:

1  Select the controls you want to resize.

2  Choose Dialog | Size. The Size Controls dialog box is displayed. You use this dialog box to resize controls.

3  Choose the Width option and enter the width for all controls.

4  Choose the Height option and enter the height for all controls.

The size of all selected controls change. Their top left corners stay in the same place.

**Note**  You can undo any sizing options by choosing Edit | Undo or by pressing *Alt+Backspace*. You may have to choose Undo more than once.

You can also move and resize controls with the General page of the Property Inspector. Select the controls, double-click one of them, and change the appropriate Top, Left, Width, and Height values.

# Reordering controls

You can specify the order in which users access the controls in your dialog box. The order is especially important when you have defined groups of related controls.

To specify the order of controls:

1 Choose Dialog | Set Creation Order or Set Creation Order from the SpeedMenu. A special mode is invoked.

2 Each control is numbered to show its current place in the overall order. Initially, this is the order in which you created the controls.

3 Click the items you want to assign new order numbers to, beginning with 1. The Dialog editor displays a blue box around all the controls you have already picked. Once you have clicked a control to assign it an order number, you cannot pick any previously selected controls again.

If you make a mistake and want to go back to the original order, just click on all the controls in the order in which you assigned them. You can also press *Escape* to cancel.

When you finish assigning new order numbers, press Enter to return to design mode. You can also right-click and choose End Mode to exit and save changes, or Cancel Mode to exit without saving changes.

# Grouping controls

You can group controls to let the user move among them using the arrow keys. For example, if you add three radio buttons, you may want them to function as a group.

To group controls:

1 If necessary, move the controls so that they are together.

2 Choose Dialog | Set Group Flags or Set Group Flags from the SpeedMenu.

3 For each group you want to define, click the first member so it is surrounded by a blue box.

You do not have to identify the last member of a group. By clicking the first member of each group, you also identify the last member of the previous group.

To ungroup controls:

1 Choose Dialog | Set Group Flags or Set Group Flags from the SpeedMenu.

2 Click the control that is surrounded by a blue outline. This turns off the group flag.

You mark only the first control in each group with the Group attribute. Controls are included in the group according to the order in which they are added to the dialog box.

For example, if you add seven controls to your dialog box and then turn on the Group property of the first and fifth controls, the first four controls are included in the first group, and the remaining controls are included in the second group.

When you finish grouping controls, press *Enter* to return to design mode. You can also right-click and choose End Mode to exit and save changes, or Cancel Mode to exit without saving changes.

# Specifying which controls are tab stops

When you add a control that can accept user input to a dialog box, it is automatically defined as a tab stop. You can change this so that only some controls are tab stops, and users can use Tab to move only to the controls you want.

To set a tab stop:

1 Choose Dialog | Set Tabstops or Set Tabstops from the SpeedMenu. A special mode is invoked. Any controls currently set as tab stops are outlined with a blue box.

2 To set a tab stop, click any control that is not already outlined in blue.

3 To remove a tab stop, click any control that is already a tab stop (outlined in blue).

4 When you finish changing tab stops, press the *Enter* key.

You can also turn on the Tab Stop property using the General page in the Property Inspector.

When you finish assigning tab stops, press Enter to return to design mode. You can also right-click and choose End Mode to exit and save changes, or Cancel Mode to exit without saving changes.

# Editing control properties

Once you have added a control to your dialog box, you can easily modify it by right-clicking it and choosing Properties. The Property Inspector is displayed, with options that can modify the appearance and behavior of your control. The property settings vary according to the type of control you are working with.

**Note**    You can also double-click a control to display the Property Inspector.

# Using the Dialog editor

You use the Dialog editor to create and edit dialog boxes. The Dialog editor displays:

- The dialog you are designing

- The Control palette that contains pages for standard Windows controls, Windows common controls, BWCC controls, Visual Database controls, and custom controls, including VBX controls

- The Tool palette that contains tools such as alignment tools

- The Property Inspector that lets you set properties for controls and dialog boxes

## Using the Property Inspector

You use the Property Inspector to view and set properties for controls and dialogs. The Property Inspector can be modal or modeless. The Dialog editor uses a WYSIWYG method of displaying properties when it can.

### The modal Property Inspector

The modal Property Inspector only displays property pages. Changes you make in the modal Property Inspector do not take effect until you click the OK or Apply button, or select another property page tab. You can also cancel changes to the current page by clicking Cancel.

The modal Property Inspector lets you set properties for:

- One control

- A group of selected controls with properties in common

- The dialog box

## The modeless Property Inspector

The modeless Property Inspector displays different view of properties:

- Property pages
- The sorted property list box
- The unsorted property list box
- The generic, or summary, property page

Changes you make in the modeless Property Inspector take effect immediately. There are no buttons to click to apply or cancel changes.

The modeless Property Inspector lets you switch between properties for different controls or dialog boxes. To switch between objects, use the drop-down list at the top of the Inspector. The sorted list displays properties in sorted alphabetically; the unsorted list displays properties in the order they are displayed on the Property Page.

To set properties in the sorted or unsorted list,

**1** Click the property you want to change.

**2** Enter a value or choose it from the drop down list.

- If an ellipse is displayed in the right column, click it to display a dialog box where you set multiple properties.

**Note**   If a VBX control is among the selected controls, the Property Inspector is always modeless (changes take effect immediately) and is in list format only.

# Displaying the Property Inspector

To display the modal Property Inspector, do one of the following:

- Right-click the control and choose Properties.
- Right-click in an empty area of the dialog box and choose Properties.
- Double-click the control you want to set properties for.
- Double-click in an empty area of the dialog box.
- Select multiple controls, right-click one of them, and choose Properties.
- Select multiple controls and double-click one of them.

To display the modeless Property Inspector:

- Choose Dialog | Show | Property Inspector. Once the Property Inspector is displayed, right-click the Inspector to choose the view you want.

# About the Control palette

The Control palette consists of the following pages:

- The Standard page contains tools that let you place standard Windows controls.
- The Common page contains tools that let you place common Windows controls.
- The BWCC page contains tools that let you place Borland-style controls.
- The Custom page contains tools that let you place any custom controls you may have installed, including VBX controls.
- The Data Access page contains tools that let you place the Visual Database Tools Data Access controls.
- The Data Aware page contains tools that let you place the Visual Database Tools Data Access controls.

## Moving the Control palette

To move the Control palette, click and drag the title bar of the palette to a new location.

## Hiding and showing the Control palette

To hide and show the Control palette:

- Choose Dialog | Show | Control Palette.
- Right-click outside the dialog box you are designing, and choose Control Palette.

## To place a control

- Click the page of the Control palette you want.
- Select a control tool with your mouse by clicking it.
- To place the control with the default size, click the mouse button on the dialog.
- To place the control and size it at the same time, click and drag the mouse in the dialog to the desired size.

# Standard page of the Control palette

The Standard page of the Control palette contains tools for placing standard Windows controls in your dialog box. Click one of the following tools for more information:

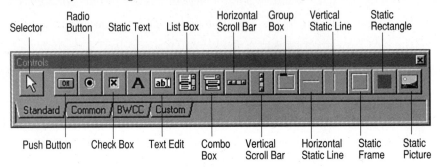

## Selector tool

You use the Selector tool to select one or more controls in your dialog box. To select a single control, click the Selector inside the control. To select more than one control, click and drag your mouse around the controls you want to select.

**Note**  You can also select multiple controls by pressing the Shift key while clicking on controls. The selection becomes cumulative. Clicking a second time while holding the Shift key will unselect the control, while keeping other selections.

When you use the Selector tool, your pointer is the shape of an arrow. Choose the Selector tool to exit another mode and return your pointer to the arrow shape.

The Selector tool is available on all pages of the Control palette.

## Push Button tool

The Push Button tool puts a push button control in your dialog box. A push button control sends a message to its parent when a user selects it. The push button is a rectangle with rounded corners. It can contain text, an icon, or a bitmap.

Windows defines a set of control ID values and names for the standard push buttons used to exit dialog boxes. To use these buttons, you need to enter the predefined value or name in the General page of the Property Inspector.

- Enter the ID name (IDOK, etc.) in the ID box.

- Enter the text you want to display on the button in the Caption box.

The predefined ID values are:

| IDValue | ID Name | Button Type |
|---|---|---|
| 1 | IDOK | OK |
| 2 | IDCANCEL | Cancel |
| 3 | IDABORT | Abort |
| 4 | IDRETRY | Retry |
| 5 | IDIGNORE | Ignore |
| 6 | IDYES | Yes |
| 7 | IDNO | No |

**Note**    The ID name must be entered in uppercase letters.

# Radio Button tool

The Radio Button tool puts a radio button control in your dialog box. A radio button control is a circular button with text, an icon, or a bitmap. The control sends a message to its parent when the user selects it. Radio buttons are used in groups to represent related but mutually exclusive options.

# Check Box tool

The Check Box tool puts a check box control in your dialog box. A check box control is a small button that sends a message to its parent when a user selects it.

When a check box is selected, an X appears on the button. When a check box is not selected, the X disappears. Check boxes are often used to represent Boolean (on/off) states for individual options. Check boxes can also have a third state, represented by a light gray shading. This state is usually interpreted as "indeterminate."

# Static Text tool

The Static Text tool puts a static text control in your dialog box. A static text control is text in a rectangle. The text is displayed as:

- Left-aligned, without word wrap
- Left-aligned, with word wrap
- Centered
- Right-aligned
- Simple

# Text Edit tool

The Text Edit tool puts an edit control in your dialog box. An edit control allows a user to:

- Enter text
- Edit text
- Move the insertion point
- Delete text
- Move text

An edit control receives focus when the user clicks it or presses the Tab key to move to it. Once selected, the edit control displays text and a flashing cursor to indicate the insertion point. The edit control can send a message to its parent when the user selects it.

# List Box tool

The List Box tool puts a list box control in your dialog box. The list box control displays a list of items. The user can browse the list and choose one or more items. List box items can be represented by text strings, bitmaps, or both.

# Combo Box tool

The Combo Box tool puts a combo box control in your dialog box. A combo box control is a combination of a list box control and a static text or edit control.

- The list box control can drop down; it does not have to display all the time.
- The static text control forces an item (if one exists) to be displayed in the list box portion of the combo box control.
- The edit control allows the user to enter a selection. The list box will then higlight the first item that matches the selection. Then, the user can select the highlighted item.

# Horizontal Scroll Bar tool

The Horizontal Scroll Bar tool puts a horizontal scroll bar control in your dialog box. A horizontal scroll bar control consists of a horizontal rectangle with a direction arrow at both ends.

A horizontal scroll bar control lets the user scroll the contents of the window to the left or right. The control sends a message to its parent when a user selects it.

# Vertical Scroll Bar tool

The Vertical Scroll Bar tool puts a vertical scroll bar control in your dialog box. A vertical scroll bar control consists of a vertical rectangle with a direction arrow at both ends.

A vertical scroll bar control lets the user scroll the contents of the window to the up or down. The control sends a message to its parent when a user selects it.

# Group Box tool

The Group Box tool puts a group box control in your dialog box. A group box control is rectangular box around a group of controls. It is used to visually group controls together. You can include a caption in the upper left corner of the group box. An application cannot send messages to a group box.

# Static Frame tool

The Static Frame tool puts a static frame control in your dialog box. A static frame is an empty border that can be black, gray, or white. It can also appear etched.

A Static Frame control is used for visual effect.

# Static Rectangle tool

The Static Rectangle tool puts a static rectangle control in your dialog box. A static rectangle control is a rectangle that can be black, gray, or white.

A static rectangle control is used for visual effect.

# Horizontal Static Line tool

The horizontal static line tool puts a horizontal static line control in your dialog box. A horizontal static line control is used for visual effect.

**Note** Static lines are only displayed when using Windows 95 or Windows NT with the shell.

# Vertical Static Line tool

The vertical static line tool puts a vertical static line control in your dialog box. A vertical static line control is used for visual effect.

**Note** Static lines are only displayed when using the Windows 95 or Windows NT with the shell.

# Static Picture tool

The Static Picture tool puts a static picture control in your dialog box. A static picture control can display an icon, bitmap, or enhanced metafile. A static picture control is used for visual effect.

The Caption property identifies the resource ID of the icon, bitmap, or enhanced metafile. The actual picture can be viewed by putting the Dialog editor into test mode with the Dialog | Test Dialog command.

# Common page of the Control palette

The Common page of the Control palette contains tools for placing Windows common controls in your dialog box. Click one of the following tools for more information:

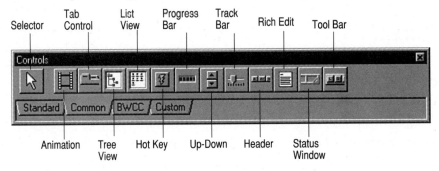

# Animation tool

The Animation tool puts an animation control in your dialog box. An animation control is a window that displays an Audio Video Interleaved (AVI) clip, a series of bitmap frames. The clip is displayed without sound. Set the Caption property to the AVI filename of the clip.

**Note**   You can set up the AVI file to display when the animation control is created. However, you cannot play the clip in design mode. To play the clip, check the Auto Play property on the Animation page and put the Dialog editor into test mode (Dialog | Test Dialog).

# Tab Control tool

The Tab Control tool puts a tab control, like a set of notebook dividers, in your dialog. Tabs contain identifying text. Tabs are used to define multiple pages in a dialog box. A user clicks a tab to switch between dialog box pages.

**Note**   You cannot add the actual tabs using the Dialog editor because the tabs are not encoded in the .RC files. They can only be created through programming. You can use the

Sample Item Count property (one of the properties on the TabControl page) to test what the tabs would look like.

# Tree View tool

The Tree View tool places a tree view control in your dialog. A tree view control displays a group of items in a hierarchy, with icons to expand and collapse the hierarchy. Each item consists of a label and an optional bitmapped image.

# List View tool

The List View tool places a list view control in your dialog. A list view control displays a group of items. You can display the items in the group:

- With their standard icons. Each item is represented by an icon and a text label. Items can be moved.

- With their small icons. Each item is represented by a small icon and a text label to the right of the icon. Items can be moved.

- As a list. Each item is represented by a small icon and a text label. Items are arranged in columns and cannot be moved.

- As a report. Each item is represented by a small icons and text label, and additional information about each item.

A header control is usually associated with a list view control.

# Hot Key tool

The Hot Key tool places a hot key control in a dialog. A hot key control lets the user enter a combination of keystrokes to be used as a shortcut key. The hot key control displays the current choices and makes sure that the key combination selected is valid.

# Progress Bar tool

The Progress Bar tool places a progress bar control in your dialog. A progress bar control, using a range and current position, shows an operation's percentage of completion. It can include text. You usually use a progress bar for an installation program.

# Up-Down tool

The Up-Down tool places an up-down control in your dialog. An up-down control consists of an up and down arrow. The up-down control increments and decrements values in the companion control.

Usually, you use an up-down control in conjunction with a companion control, also referred to as a buddy window.

## Track Bar tool

The Track Bar tool places a track bar control in your dialog box. A track bar control lets the user change a value within a set range. The track bar displays ticks that represent the current value. The user adjusts a slider to change the value.

## Header tool

The Header tool places a header control in a window, usually in a list view window. Headers can contain a string, a bitmapped image, and an application-defined 32-bit value. If a header contains both a string and an image, the image is displayed above the string. If they overlap, the string overwrites the image.

Headers are usually used for column headings. By default, headers appear as text on a gray background. Headers do not have input focus.

## Rich Text Edit tool

The Rich Text Edit tool places a rich text edit control in your dialog box. A user can enter and edit text in this control. The user can assign character and paragraph formatting attributes (font, colors, etc.) to the text, and can include embedded OLE objects.

## Status Window tool

The Status Window tool places a status window control in your dialog box. A status window control is a horizontal window at the bottom of a parent window. The application can display different kinds of status information in the control. The control can be divided into parts to display different kinds of information.

## Tool Bar tool

The Tool Bar tool places a tool bar control in your dialog. A tool bar control contains one or more buttons, that are visual representations of commands. When a button is selected, it sends a command message to the parent window.

# BWCC page of the Control palette

The BWCC page of the Control palette contains tools for placing Borland-style controls in your dialog box. Click one of the following tools for more information:

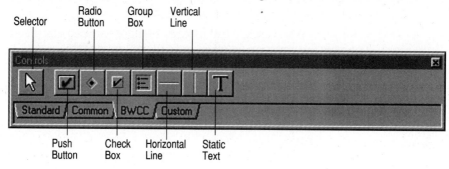

**Note**  When you use one of more BWCC controls, you must link the BWCC library to your program or load it as a DLL.

# BWCC Push Button tool

The BWCC Push Button tool puts a Borland-style push button control in your dialog box. A Borland-style push button control can contain symbols with high visual impact, as well as an owner draw option. A Borland push button is larger than most standard Windows push buttons. Its class is *BorBtn*.

These are the values for the predefined Borland-style bitmap buttons:

| ID Name | ID Value |
|---------|----------|
| IDOK | 1 |
| IDCANCEL | 2 |
| IDABORT | 3 |
| IDRETRY | 4 |
| IDIGNORE | 5 |
| IDYES | 6 |
| IDNO | 7 |
| IDHELP | 998 |

To add your own bitmap to the button, see "Adding a bitmap to a BWCC push button."

## Adding a bitmap to a BWCC push button

To add your own bitmap to a BWCC push button:

1 Use the BWCC Push Button tool to add the generic BWCC button to your dialog box. Note its control ID.

2  Switch to the Graphics editor and create a bitmap image.

3  In the Graphics editor, choose Resource | Resource Attributes to display the Resource Attributes dialog box. Then, do either of the following:

- In the Resource Name box, enter an integer value that equals the control ID of the button plus the appropriate offset from the following table.

- Rename the bitmap and assign it an identifier whose value equals the control ID of the button plus the appropriate offset from the following table.

| Button State | VGA Offset | EGA Offset |
|---|---|---|
| standard | id + 1000 | id + 2000 |
| pressed | id + 3000 | id + 4000 |
| keyboard focus | id + 5000 | id + 6000 |

4  Close the Graphics editor.

5  Return to the Dialog editor. The bitmap displays on the BWCC button.

# BWCC Check Box tool

The BWCC Check Box tool puts a Borland-style check box control in your dialog box. A Borland-style check box control is raised and displays a check mark, rather than an "X." Its class is *BorCheck*.

A BWCC check box can also have a third state, represented by a light gray shading. This state is usually interpreted as "indeterminate."

# BWCC Group Box tool

The BWCC Group Box tool puts a Borland-style group box control in your dialog box. A Borland-style group box control is a shaded rectangular box. The box groups other controls visually. It can appear recessed into the dialog box or raised above its surface. Its class is *BorShade*.

# BWCC Horizontal Line tool

The BWCC Horizontal Line tool puts a Borland-style horizontal line control in your dialog box. The horizontal line control gives the impression of being etched into the surface of the dialog box. Its class is *BorShade*.

You can convert lines to bumps, which appear to be raised above the surface of the dialog box.

# BWCC Radio Button tool

The BWCC Radio Button tool puts a Borland-style radio button control in your dialog box. The radio button control is diamond-shaped and appears raised from the surface of the dialog box.

When the user clicks the button, a black diamond appears in its center and the button shading reverses, giving the impression that it has been pushed down. Its class is *BorRadio*.

# BWCC Vertical Line tool

The BWCC Vertical Line tool puts a Borland-style vertical line control in your dialog box. The vertical line control gives the impression of being etched into the surface of the dialog box. Its class is *BorShade*.

You can convert lines to bumps, which appear to be raised above the surface of the dialog box.

# BWCC Static Text tool

The BWCC Static Text tool places a Borland-style static text control in your dialog box. The static text control is a fixed text string in your dialog box. You use the string principally for labeling parts of the dialog box. Its class is *BorStatic*.

# Custom page of the Control palette

The Custom page of the Control palette contains all installed custom controls, including VBX controls. For information on installing custom controls, see Working with custom controls.

# Data Access page of the Control palette

The Data Access page of the Control palette contains the installed Visual Database Tools Data Access components.

# Data Aware page of the Control palette

The Data Aware page of the Control palette contains the installed Visual Database Tools Data Aware components.

# Tool palette

The Tool palette provides access to some of the most common Dialog editor tools, such as the alignment and spacing tools.

Here are the tools you can choose from:

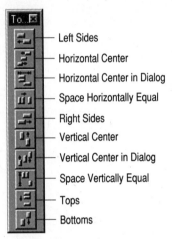

- Left Sides
- Horizontal Center
- Horizontal Center in Dialog
- Space Horizontally Equal
- Right Sides
- Vertical Center
- Vertical Center in Dialog
- Space Vertically Equal
- Tops
- Bottoms

You can also use the Alignment dialog box to align controls and the Dialog I Space command to space controls.

# Left Sides tool

The Left Sides tool aligns selected controls so their left sides are aligned along the left side of the selection frame. The control that is leftmost determines the left edge of the selection frame.

# Horizontal Centers tool

The Horizontal Centers tool aligns controls so their horizontal centers are in the center of the selection frame. The leftmost and rightmost controls determine the size and location of the selection frame.

# Right Sides tool

The Right Sides tool aligns controls so their right sides are aligned along the right side of the selection frame. The control that is rightmost determines the right side of the selection frame.

# Horizontal Center in Dialog tool

The Horizontal Center in Dialog tool moves the selection frame horizontally so it is centered in the dialog box. The relative position of the individual controls within the selection frame is unchanged.

# Tops tool

The Tops tool aligns controls so their tops are aligned along the top of the selection frame. The topmost control determines where the top of the selection frame is located.

# Vertical Centers tool

The Vertical Centers tool aligns controls so their vertical centers are in the center of the selection frame.

# Bottoms tool

The Bottoms tool aligns controls so their bottoms are aligned along the bottom of the selection frame. The bottom most control determines where the bottom of the selection frame is located.

# Vertical Centers in Dialog tool

The Vertical Center in Dialog tool moves the selection frame vertically so it is centered in the dialog box. The relative position of the individual controls within the selection frame is unchanged.

# Space Horizontally Equal tool

The Space Horizontally Equal tool moves the selected controls so that they are horizontally equidistant from one another.

# Space Vertically Equal tool

The Space Vertically Equal tool moves the selected controls so that they are vertically equidistant from one another.

Chapter

# 16

# About menus

Menus are lists of commands the user chooses from. Most Windows applications have a menu bar across the top of the screen that contains the names of the application's menus. Each menu contains a set of commands.

## Terminology

These terms describe the elements of a menu resource: pop-up command, pop-up menu, menu item, and menu separator.

- Pop-up commands cause menus to be displayed. Pop-up commands can appear in the menu bar and can also appear inside pop-up menus, where they cause another menu (called a cascading menu) to be displayed.

- Pop-up menus are the rectangular boxes containing lists of commands from which a user can choose. They come in two forms:
  - Drop-down menus are displayed from the menu bar or from within a menu. They are tied to a pop-up command and are always displayed from that command's name.
  - SpeedMenus (also referred to as floating menus or contextual popup menus) can appear anywhere in the application window.

- Menu items are the commands that appear in the menus, such as Open, Save, or Print.

- Menu separators are the lines that divide the menu items into logical groups. Separators do not do anything other than make the menu easier to read and use.

## Working with menus

The Menu editor makes it easy to create and edit menus. Working with menus involves four basic steps:

1  Create a new menu or edit an existing menu. The Menu Editor opens automatically.

2  Make changes to the menu.

3  Test the menu.

4  Save the menu.

## Using the menu editor

You use the Menu editor to create and edit menus. It provides different views of the menu you are editing:

- The Edit window shows the structure of the menu you are editing. It also has a test mode where you can view the menu as it will appear in your application.

- The Property Inspector is where you customize the currently selected item in the menu.

## Edit window

The Edit window shows you the structure of the menu you are editing. It looks very similar to a real menu. You can modify item text, add or remove items, and move items. To change other properties of the menu, use the Property Inspector. You can also view the menu in Test Mode.
Test Mode allows you to view the menu as it will appear in your applicaiton. You can navigate the menu items as you would in your application.

## Creating a new menu

To create a new menu,

1  Open the resource project you want to add the menu to, or create a new one by choosing File | New | Resource Project. The New Resource Project dialog box is displayed. Base your project on the .RC file type.

2  Choose Resource | New to create a new resource for that project. Resource Workshop displays the New Resource dialog box.

3  In the Resource Type list, select MENU (or MENUEX for 32-bit projects).

4  Click Options to specify a type of menu other than the default.

5  Click OK to place the new menu in the current resource project file.

Resource Workshop displays the Menu editor with a simple application menu you can begin customizing.

## Editing an existing menu

To edit an existing menu, open the resource project in which the menu is stored and do one of the following:

- Double-click the menu resource name in the Resource Project window.

- Highlight the menu resource name and choose Resource | Edit.

  Resource Workshop displays the Menu editor with the menu you have chosen already loaded.

- Once a menu is loaded into the Menu editor, you are ready to add new menu commands, pop-up menus, or separators. You can also move, copy, or delete any part of the menu.

  You can customize your menus by adding accelerators and help messages for menu items using the Menu editor Property Inspector.

# Moving and copying menu statements

You can drag and drop single menu items or entire menus. You can also use Cut, Copy, and Paste on the Menu SpeedMenu to move and copy the items in the menu's Edit window.

To move a item, click and drag it into the desired location. (You can also use Shift+ drag.) If you move a pop-up menu, the entire menu is moved. A blue line with inverted arrows indicates where the top of the box will be placed. If you highlight some or all of the text, cut, copy, and paste actions effect only the highlighted text.

To copy a item, use Control+ left mouse to click and drag it. You can also highlight it, right-click, and choose Copy. A copy is placed in the Windows Clipboard.

To insert the cut or copied item into your menu, select the item immediately after the point at which you want the item to appear, right-click, and Paste.

# Undoing errors

The Menu editor lets you undo and redo changes. Choose Edit | Undo or Edit | Redo.

# Adding menu items and separators

You customize a menu by adding new menu items to it. You can customize your menu by adding new menu items, pop-up menus, and menu separators.

Items are always added before the selected item. To add items to the end, select the empty area at the end and insert the new item.

To add a new menu item, pop-up, or separator to a menu,

1 Decide where you want the new menu item, pop-up, or separator to appear. Click the item in the menu's Edit window above where you want the statement added.

2 Select the new item you want to insert before the selected item.

- To insert a new menu item, right-click and choose New Menuitem or choose Menu | New Menuitem.

- To insert a pop-up menu, right-click and choose New Popup or choose Menu | New Popup

- To insert a new menu separator, right-click and choose New Separator or choose Menu | New Separator.

You can now edit the text string, menu ID, help message, and accelerators, if any.

## Editing a menu item

A newly added menu item has the generic designation "Item." To make it useful, you need to edit it. You can edit the text that displays in the menu directly, or with the Property Inspector. With the Property Inspector, you can also change the menu's numeric ID and put a check mark next to the menu if it is a toggle.

## Deleting a menu item

To delete a menu item, click the item you want to delete, then:

1 Right-click and choose Cut to delete the statement and copy it to the Windows Clipboard.

2 Choose Edit | Clear to remove it completely.

Note that if you delete a POPUP statement, you delete the pop-up command it defines and all the items contained in the pop-up menu.

## Creating a pop-up menu

A pop-up menu is one that can be displayed anywhere in the application's workspace. It is not tied to the menu bar. Pop-up menus display when the right mouse button is clicked. The menu items displayed correspond to the selected object in the application.

Each pop-up menu must be saved as a separate menu resource within the resource project file.

To create a pop-up menu,

1 Choose Resource | New. Resource Workshop displays the New Resource dialog box.

2 In the Resource Type list, select MENU (or MENUEX for 32-bit projects).

When you view the menu in the Test Menu pane, it will still appear tied to the menu bar, but as long as your code uses the **TrackPopupMenu** function correctly, the menu will float at run time.

3 Click the Options button to display the New Resource Options dialog box. Choose a popup menu style.

4 Click OK to create the new pop-up menu. The menu displays as it will appear on the screen at runtime.

5 Add any additional menu items you want.

**6** Edit the menu items using the Property Inspector if needed.

**7** Save your project.

# Adding accelerator text to menus

To let users know what accelerators they can use, you can add accelerator text to your menu items.

For example, if your application includes a Ctrl+X accelerator that duplicates the Cut command on the Edit menu, you can add the text "Ctrl+X" next to that command.

- Use the tab character (\t) to separate the menu title from the accelerator text. For example, Cut\tCtrl+X means that the accelerator Ctrl+X is assigned to the menu command Cut.

- Use the right-align character (\a) to right-align accelerator text.

**Note** Pop-up commands do not have accelerator keys.

When you add accelerator text to menu items, you use the Text and the ID input boxes on the General page of the Menu editor Property Inspector. The items on the General page specify the text that is displayed as part of a menu item.

Use the Accelerator page of the menu editor Property Inspector to create the actual accelerator.

# Adding accelerator resources to menus

The items on the Accelerator page of the Menu editor Property Inspector create an association between a MENU resource and an ACCELERATOR resource.

An ACCELERATOR resource is considered "associated" with a MENU resource if they have the same resource name (either string or numeric value). An individual accelerator is associated with a menuitem if both have the same ID.

# Testing a menu

The Menu editor gives you immediate testing capability. The test menu is updated as you make changes to your menu, so you can test changes whenever you want.

To view the menu in Test Mode, select Menu | Test Menu.

You can navigate the menu structure as you would while running your application.

# Testing for duplicate menu items

The Menu editor also has a built-in debugging tool that you can use to test for duplicate menu item IDs. Choose Menu | Check Duplicates to search for duplicate values. If the Menu editor finds duplicates, it displays a dialog box with the message "Duplicate command value found."

When you close this message box, the Menu editor selects the item with the duplicate value. Determine whether the menu ID is an identifier or a numeric value by looking at the ID input box on the General page of the Menu editor Property Inspector.

- If the menu ID is a number, enter a new number that does not conflict with the other menu IDs.

- If the menu ID is a conflicting identifier, change the identifier text so that it does not conflict, or choose Resource | Identifiers to display the Identifiers dialog box where you can change the identifier.

# Programming menus and accelerators with OWL

To program menus and accelerators with OWL, use the *TMenu* class and the *LoadAccelerators* function.

For example, this code shows how to associate a menu and accelerators with the main window:

```
GetMainWindow()->AssignMenu(IDM_MENU1);
GETMAINWINDOW()->ATTR.ACCELTABLE = IDA_ACCELERATORS1;
```

IDM_MENU1 and IDD_ACCELERATORS1 are the identifiers for the menu and accelerator table, respectively.

# Programming menus and accelerators with the Windows API

To program and menus and accelerators with the Windows API, use the *LoadMenu* and *LoadAccelerators* functions.

For example, this code shows how to associate a menu and accelerators with the main window:

```
HMENU hMenu;
hMenu = LoadMenu(hInst, MAKEINTRESOURCE(IDD_MENU1));
LoadAccelerators(hInst, MAKEINTRESOURCE(IDD(ACCELERATORS1)));
```

IDM_MENU1 and IDD_ACCELERATORS1 are the identifiers for the menu and accelerator table, respectively.

# 17

# Working with identifiers

Windows requires that every resource and user defined resource type be associated with a unique name or a unique integer (called a resource ID). By default, Resource Workshop assigns a name to each new resource.

The default name is not very descriptive, and referring to a resource by name alone decreases the efficiency of the application at run-time. To overcome these shortcomings, you can rename the resource and assign it an identifier (a C *#define*).

## Identifiers

An identifier consists of two parts: a text literal (the identifier name) and a value (typically an integer). Identifiers must be unique within a resource type. Only the first 31 characters are significant; Resource Workshop ignores any characters past the 31st character.

Assigning an integer value to an identifier speeds up calls to the resource at run time, but you will not be able to use the short integer value directly as a parameter. You must either typecast the integer into a long pointer to *char* or use a macro to do the typecasting for you.

- If you write your program in C or C++, use the MAKEINTRESOURCE macro.

- If you are using ObjectWindows, see the class *TResId.*

If you are working with a .RES file, an executable file, or a DLL file, Resource Workshop decompiles all resource IDs in the files into integer values. You cannot add identifiers to this type of file, but you can save the file as an .RC file and assign identifiers to its resources.

# Identifier files

When you create a new project, the first thing you should do is specify a file in which to store your identifiers. Store identifiers in one or more resource header (.RH) files that use *#defines* to assign values to identifier names.

# Creating an identifier file

To add an identifer after you create a new project,

1 Right-click and choose Add to Project. You see the Add to Project dialog box.

2 Click the down-arrow in List Files of Type. Choose:

```
C/C++ header (*.h, *.rh)
```

3 Enter a name for the identifier file in the File Name box.

4 Click OK. Resource Workshop creates the identifier file.

# Adding identifiers

You can add an identifier to your identifier file before you create the resource it will be associated with. To add an identifier,

1 Choose Resource | Identifiers to display the Identifiers dialog box.

2 Right-click and choose Insert. The New/Change Identifiers dialog box is displayed.

3 In the Name box, enter the identifier name.

4 In the Value box, enter the identifier's value.

5 In the File box, enter the name of the file in which the identifier is to be stored.

6 Click the OK button.

**Note**    The new name now appears in the Name list in the Identifers dialog box. The Usage columns says (unused).

# Editing identifiers

To change an identifier name or value,

1 Choose Resource | Identifiers to display the Identifiers dialog box.

2 Double-click the name or value you want to change. The New/Change Identifiers dialog box is displayed.

3 Change the name in the Name box.

4 Change the value in the Value box.

5 Click OK.

The new identifier value will be written to the header file the next time you choose File | Save.

# Moving identifiers from one file to another

To change the file an identifier is placed in,

**1** Choose Resource | Identifiers to display the Identifiers dialog box.

**2** Double-click the name or value of the identifier you want to change. The New/Change Identifiers dialog box is displayed.

**3** Enter a new filename in the File box.

**4** Click OK.

# Deleting identifiers

If an identifier is not used in your project, you should delete it from the header file. There are three reasons you might have an unused identifier:

- You assign an identifier to a resource and then delete the resource.

- You add an identifier to the project and then never use it.

- You rename a resource that already has an integer identifier value.

To delete an identifier:

**1** Choose Resource | Identifiers to display the Identifiers dialog box.

**2** Select the identifier you want to delete. You can delete an identifier that is still in use.

- If the selected identifier is not associated with a resource (either because the resource was deleted or the identifier was never used), the Used By box says (unused).

- If, however, the identifier is still associated with a resource, the Used By box automatically highlights the type and name of the associated resource.

**3** Press the Delete key.

- If the identifier is unused, it is deleted immediately. No warning dialog box is displayed.

- If the identifier is still in use, Resource Workshop displays a warning dialog box that says "define is used. Delete anyway?" To delete the identifier, click the Yes button. If you do not want to delete the identifier, click the No button.

The next time you choose File | Save, Resource Workshop updates the identifier file, removing the deleted identifier.

# Listing identifiers

To list the identifiers in your project,

1 Choose Resource | Identifiers to display the Identifiers dialog box.

2 Choose the name of the file for which you want to view identifiers.

3 The name, value, and usage of all identifiers in that file are displayed.

# Managing identifiers

Resource Workshop can automatically create and delete identifiers for you. To turn on automatic identifier management, choose Options | Environment | Resource Editors. Check the Generate Identifiers Automatically option (one of the Resource Editor SpeedSettings).

**Note** If you are using AppExpert from the Borland C++ IDE, Generate Identifiers Automatically will be checked and unselectable; you will not be able to turn this option off because AppExpert relies on the automatic identifiers syntax.

With automatic identifiers on, every time you create a resource item that uses an identifier (menu items, for example), Resource Workshop creates a unique identifier for that item and places it in the header file for that resource (.RH or .H). Also, if you delete any items, the identifier is deleted.

Resource Workshop uses an identifier prefix, which you can change. The list of default prefixes can be viewed by choosing Options | Environment | Resource Editors | Identifiers. This options page also allows you to change the default prefix.

Chapter

# 18

# Using the Text editor

The text version of a resource is also called source code or script. You can edit the text version of any resource.

To edit the text version of a resource,

1  Click the resource in the Resource Project window.

2  Choose Resource | Edit As Text.

Resource Workshop opens the Text editor and displays the script for the resource.

## Saving your changes

To save your changes to a script,

1  Close the Text editor window.

2  Choose Yes in response to the prompt "Resource has changed. Compile?"

Resource Workshop compiles your resource script and saves the changes. If it encounters a syntax error, you are returned to the Text editor so you can correct the error.

## Compiling a text version of a resource

After editing a text version of a resource, you must compile the resource in order to save it. To compile and save a resource script in the Text editor, right-click and choose Compile.

If you do not compile the resource, Resource Workshop prompts you to compile it when you exit the Text editor.

# Creating resources with the Text editor

Resource Workshop always edits some kinds of resources as scripts. These resources are referred to as scripted resources:

Accelerator
DLGINIT
RCDATA
User-Defined Resources
StringTable
VERSIONINFO

**Note** DLGINIT resources are created whenever dialogs contain VBX controls. This resource type should never be modified.

You can also define bitmapped and dialog template resources with scripts, but you will usually find it easier to use the visual editors in Resource Workshop, especially for creating those resources. You will probably edit bitmap or dialog template scripts only to make changes to existing resources.

# Writing resource scripts

A resource script is a text file that consists of three kinds of items:

• Resource definition statements
• Resource compiler directives
• Comments

The majority of a resource script is made up of resource definition statements. Each resource in the resource script is defined by a definition statement, which has the following general syntax:

```
keyword resource_id [options]
BEGIN
  items
  :
END
```

In this syntax:

*keyword*      is one of the resource keywords.

*resource_id*  is either a numeric constant or an identifier.

*options*      is optional information specific to the type of resource being defined.

*items*        is one or more items within the resource, such as menu items in a menu resource or strings in a string table.

## Comments

A comment can be placed in the script surrounded by a C-style comment string (/* ... */). Do not place a comment within a resource definition block, as the resource compiler will strip it out.

Here as an example of a valid coment:

```
/* This is a valid comment    */
keyword resource_id [options]
BEGIN
  ⋮
END
```

Here is an invalid comment:

```
keyword resource_id [options]
/* Do not put comments here */
BEGIN
/* And don't put them here */
END
```

**Note**   A comment is valid only if it was added before the resource project was opened by Resource Workshop. Comments added to the text of a resource, edited with the Resource | Edit As Text command, will be stripped out by the resource compiler.

# Working with user-defined resources

In addition to defining standard resource types, you can also define your own resource types. After you create a new resource type, you can add any number of user-defined resources of this type to your project.

User-defined resources contain data that do not fit into one of the standard resource types. For example, if you want to create a character string resource that is longer than the STRINGTABLE limit of 255 characters, you can define your own resource type and store your character strings there.

You can also include metafiles in your project as user-defined resources. A metafile is a type of bitmap (in source form, it is a collection of Graphics Device Interface (GDI) calls) that's not only easier to scale and more device-independent than the standard bitmap resource, but also often takes up less storage space than a bitmap resource.

When you define a new resource, you can store data as part of the resource definition in a project file or as a separate file. You can also use the RCDATA resource type to add data to your application.

Working with user-defined resources involves five basic tasks:

- Create a resource type.
- Add a user-defined resource to your project.
- Edit it, if necessary.
- Test it.
- Save it.

## Creating a resource type

Before you can add user-defined resource data to your project, you must first create a type for it. Here's how:

1 Open an existing project or create a new one.

2 Choose Resource | New. You see the New Resource dialog box.

**3** Choose <Custom Resource Type>.

**4** Click the Options button.

**5** In the Resource Type name box, enter a unique name for the resource type you are creating. For example, if you are creating a resource to contain a large block of text, you could name your new resource type TEXT.

**6** If your project is an .RC file, you may want to create an identifier for the new resource type.

**7** Enter a value for the identifier. This value is the ID that Windows and your program will associate with this identifier type. If you use a resource ID, it must be greater than 255, because Windows reserves the values 1 through 255 for standard resources.

**8** Click OK to create the new resource type.

From now on, whenever you create a new resource, you see that resource type listed in the New Resource dialog box with all the standard resource types. To give the resource a name, click the Options button. You can also click OK to use the default name.

# Adding a user-defined resource

After you have created a resource type, you can add a resource of that type to your project. To add a use-defined resource,

**1** Open a resource project or create a new one.

**2** Choose Resource | New. You see the New Resource dialog box.

**3** In the Resource Type list, select your user-defined resource.

**4** Click OK to place the resource in the current project file or click the Options button to add it to another resource project file.

**5** Resource Workshop opens the Text editor with a blank definition for your user-defined resource.

# Using the RCDATA resource type

You can use the predefined RCDATA resource type to add a data resource to your application. It works the same way as a user-defined resource type.

The primary difference between the two is addressability: you might prefer to have many different types of user-defined resources rather than just one type, RCDATA.

To add an RCDATA resource to your project,

**1** Choose Resource | New. You see the New Resource dialog box.

**2** Select RCDATA and click the Options button. You can also change the name in the source script.

**3** Press OK. You see a blank RCDATA definition in the Text editor.

**4** Add resource data.

# Editing a user-defined resource

When you edit a user-defined resource, you work with its resource script.

To edit a user-defined resource,

1 Open a resource project. You can either create a resource type or open an existing one.

2 Select the user-defined resource type to which you want to add a resource.

3 Open the Text editor by:

- Double-clicking the name of the resource you want to edit.

- Selecting the resource name and choosing Resource | Edit or Resource | Edit as Text.

Once you have brought the resource script up in the script editor, you can add or change data. To add data to your resource, do one of the following:

- Use the Text editor to enter data between the BEGIN and END statements.

- Store the data in a separate file and add the file name to the end of the user-defined resource statement. Delete the BEGIN and END statements.

After you make any changes, you must recompile the resource to save your changes. If you exit without recompiling, you lose all your changes.

# Embedding resource data in a project file

You can add data to your resource by storing data in a separate file. The disadvantage to this approach is that if something happens to the file, the data is lost. Another option is to embed the external data into the project file script. Here's how:

1 Right-click and choose Add To Project.

2 Choose User Resource Data in the File Type list.

3 Enter the file name in the File Name input box. (The file must use a non-standard file extension.)

The Custom Resource dialog box is displayed.

4 Double-click the resource type. The resource appears in the Resource Project window.

If you select the new resource and choose Resource | Edit, you see that the resource data is in hexadecimal format. For that reason, you should keep the external data file available in case you want to edit the resource script later.

# Entering data in the resource script

Use the Text editor to change data that is between the BEGIN and END statements. Do not use this editor to do much formatting, since Resource Workshop rearranges the text when it compiles or decompiles the resource.

Here are some guidelines:

- The data can include any mix of numeric values and strings.

- You can use hexadecimal, octal, or decimal notation to represent numeric values. Use either 0x (a zero followed by the letter x) or $ (a dollar sign) as the leading characters for hexadecimal notation. This notation supports only 16-bit values. If you want to use an odd number of hexadecimal values, use a hexstring.

  A hexstring is a string of hexadecimal values enclosed in single quotation marks. The compiler ignores any spaces you insert to make the hex codes more readable.

- If you include text strings in your resource, enclose the strings in quotation marks, like this: `"string"`. Strings are not automatically null-terminated. To terminate a string with a null character, type `\0` `(backslash zero)` at the end of the string.

## Testing a user-defined resource

You cannot test user-defined resources within Resource Workshop. You need to use Resource Workshop to compile the project file that contains the resource and bind it to your executable file. You can then run your program and test the resource.

Part

III

# Borland C++ tools and utilities

Part III covers the additional tools and utilities provided with Borland C++. These tools include compilers, linkers, a resource compiler, a librarian, a project builder (called MAKE), and other utilities. Although most of these tools are documented in this Part, some tools and utilities are documented in the online Help.

While programming, you can use either the IDE or the command-line tools. Although both sets of tools produce the same results, you might choose to use the command-line tools because you prefer to use your own programming editor (such as Brief). Here's

This part is organized into the following chapters:

- **Chapter 20, "Using MAKE,"** describes the Borland C++ *make* utilities MAKE.EXE and MAKER.EXE. These are tools that help you manage projects by building only the files that have changed since the last build.

- **Chapter 21, "Using resource tools,"** describes the Borland C++ resource tools that compile and link application resources.

- **Chapter 22, "Using WinSight,"** explains how to use the WinSight utility to track Windows system messages in your application.

- **Chapter 23, "Using WinSpector,"** explains how to use the WinSpector utility to track fatal system errors.

# Running the command-line tools

The command-line compiler uses DPMI (DOS Protected Mode Interface) to run in protected mode on 386, i486, and Pentium machines with at least 640K conventional RAM and at least 4MB extended memory.

Although the compilers run in protected mode, they generate applications that run in real mode. Protected-mode tools have the advantage that they can access more memory than real-mode tools. This helps to compile large projects at faster speeds, without the cost of extensive disk-swapping.

## Memory and MAKESWAP.EXE

If you get *Out of Memory* errors from DOS when running the 32-bit command-line tools, create a swap file with the MAKESWAP utility. You describe the size of the file to create in kilobytes. MAKESWAP supports the following syntax:

```
MAKESWAP 12M
```

This command creates a 12MB swap file called EDPMI.SWP in the current directory, which the command-line tools use when they need additional memory. To set up a swap file, use the DPMIMEM environment variable at the DOS prompt, or add this line to your AUTOEXEC.BAT file:

```
set DPMI32=SWAPFILE <location of swap file>EDPMI.SWP
```

**Note**     MAKESWAP applies to DOS only, not to DOS text boxes opened under Windows. See the online file INSTALL.TXT for information on running these tools from DOS boxes.

## The run-time manager and tools

The Borland C++ protected-mode applications (such as BCC and BCC32) use the run-time manager tools, RTM.EXE and 32RTM.EXE. The tools that use the run-time manager first load the run-time manager, do their work, and then unload the run-time manager. If you're accessing 32-bit command-line tools that use the run-time manager many times over a short period (perhaps from a makefile), you could speed up the process by loading the run-time manager once, then calling the tools. To load the run-time manager, type `32RTM` at the command line. To unload the run-time manager, type `32RTM -u`.

By default, the run-time manager consumes all available memory when it loads. It then allocates memory to its clients when they request it through the memory manager API routines.

When running in a DOS box under Windows 3.*x*, the amount of memory that RTM reserves is also limited by the XMS Memory KB Limit setting in the corresponding PIF file. Your PIF file setting for the DOS box should set XMS Memory KB Limit to at least 1024. This value sets the limit on the amount of memory that RTM takes for the 16-bit DOS extended-memory application.

# 20

# Using MAKE

MAKE.EXE is a command-line project-manager utility that helps you quickly compile only those files in a project that have changed since the last compilation. (MAKER is a real-mode version of MAKE.) If you work in the IDE, you should use the IDE's Project Manager (see Chapter 2, "Managing projects").

This chapter covers the following topics:

- MAKE basics
- Using explicit and implicit rules
- Using MAKE directives
- Makefile contents
- Using MAKE macros

## MAKE basics

MAKE uses rules from a text file (MAKEFILE or MAKEFILE.MAK by default) to determine which files to build and how to build them. For example, you can get MAKE to compile an .EXE file if the date/time stamps for the .CPP files that contain the code for the .EXE are more recent than the .EXE itself. MAKE is very useful when you build a program from more than one file because MAKE will recompile only the files that you modified since the last compile.

Two types of rules (explicit and implicit) tell MAKE what files depend on each other. MAKE then compares the date/time stamp of the files in a rule and determines if it should execute a command (the commands usually tell MAKE which files to recompile or link, but the commands can be nearly any operating system command).

The general syntax for MAKE is

```
MAKE [options...] [targets[s]]
```

where `options` are MAKE options that control how MAKE works, and `targets` are the names of the files in a makefile that you want MAKE to build. Options are separated from `MAKE` by a single space. Options and targets are also separated by spaces. Targets may contain wildcard characters such as * and ?.

To get command-line help for MAKE, type `MAKE -?` or `MAKE -h`.

If you type `MAKE` at the command prompt, MAKE performs the following default tasks:

MAKE looks in the current directory for a file called BUILTINS.MAK (this file contains rules MAKE always follows unless you use the **–r** option). If it can't find the file in the current directory, it looks in the directory where MAKE.EXE is stored. After loading BUILTINS.MAK, MAKE looks for a file called MAKEFILE or MAKEFILE.MAK. If MAKE can't find any of these files, it gives you an error message.

1　When MAKE finds a makefile, it tries to build *only* the first target file in the makefile (although the first target can force other targets to be built). MAKE checks the time and date of the dependent files for the first target. If the dependent files are more recent than the target file, MAKE executes the target commands, which update the target. See the section called "Using makefiles" for more information on instructions in makefiles.

2　If a dependent file for the first target appears as a target elsewhere in the makefile, MAKE checks its dependencies and builds it before building the first target. This chain reaction is called linked dependency.

3　If the MAKE build process fails, MAKE deletes the target file it was building. To get MAKE to keep a target when a build fails, see the **.precious** directive on page 335.

You can stop MAKE by using *Ctrl+Break* or *Ctrl+C*.

To place MAKE instructions in a file other than MAKEFILE, see the section titled "MAKE options."

## BUILTINS.MAK

BUILTINS.MAK contains standard rules and macros that MAKE uses before it uses a makefile (you can use the **–r** option to tell MAKE to ignore BUILTINS.MAK). Use BUILTINS.MAK for instructions or macros you want executed each time you use MAKE. Here's the default text of BUILTINS.MAK:

```
#
# Borland C++ - (C) Copyright 1993 by Borland International
#

# default is to target 16BIT
# pass -DWIN32 to make to target 32BIT

!if !$d(WIN32)
CC       = bcc
RC       = brcc
AS       = tasm
!else
CC       = bcc32
RC       = brcc32
AS       = tasm32
!endif
.asm.obj:
```

```
    $(AS) $(AFLAGS) $&.asm
.c.exe:
    $(CC) $(CFLAGS) $&.c
.c.obj:
    $(CC) $(CFLAGS) /c $&.c
.cpp.exe:
    $(CC) $(CFLAGS) $&.cpp
.cpp.obj:
    $(CC) $(CPPFLAGS) /c $&.cpp
.rc.res:
    $(RC) $(RFLAGS) /r $&

.SUFFIXES: .exe .obj .asm .c .res .rc

!if !$d(BCEXAMPLEDIR)
BCEXAMPLEDIR = $(MAKEDIR)\..\EXAMPLES
!endif
```

## Using TOUCH.EXE

Sometimes you'll want to force a target file to be recompiled or rebuilt even though you haven't changed it. One way to do this is to use the TOUCH utility. TOUCH changes the date and time of one or more files to the current date and time, making it "newer" than the files that depend on it.

You can force MAKE to rebuild a target file by *touching* one of the files that target depends on. To touch a file (or files), type the following at the command prompt:

```
touch filename [filename...]
```

TOUCH updates the file's creation date and time. It accepts file names that contain the wildcard characters * and ?.

**Note**   Before you use TOUCH, make sure your system's internal clock is set correctly. If it isn't, TOUCH and MAKE won't work properly.

## MAKE options

Command-line options control MAKE behavior. Options are case-sensitive. Type options with either a preceding – or /. For example, to use a file called PROJECTA.MAK as the makefile, type MAKE -fPROJECTA.MAK (a space after **–f** is optional). Many of the command-line options have equivalent directives that are used in the makefile (see page 331 for more information on directives).

**Table 20.1**   MAKE options

| Option | Description |
| --- | --- |
| –a | Checks dependencies of include files and nested include files associated with .OBJ files and updates the .OBJ if the .h file changed. See also **–c**. |
| –B | Builds all targets regardless of file dates. |

**Table 20.1**    MAKE options (continued)

| Option | Description |
|---|---|
| –c | Caches autodependency information, which can improve MAKE's speed. Use with –a; don't use if MAKE changes include files (such as using TOUCH from a makefile or creating header or include files during the MAKE process). |
| –D*macro* | Defines *macro* as a single character, causing an expression **!ifdef** *macro* written in the makefile to return **true**. |
| [–D]*macro=[string]* | Defines *macro* as *string*. If *string* contains any spaces or tabs, enclose *string* in quotation marks. The –D is optional. |
| –d*directory* | Used with –S to specify the drive and directory MAKER uses when it swaps out of memory. MAKE ignores this option. |
| –e | Ignores a macro if its name is the same as an environment variable (MAKE uses the environment variable instead of the macro). |
| –f*filename* | Uses *filename* or *filename*.MAK instead of MAKEFILE (space after –f is optional). |
| –h or –? | Displays MAKE options and shows defaults with a trailing plus sign. |
| –I*directory* | Searches for include files in the current directory first, then in *directory*. |
| –i | Ignores the exit status of all programs run from MAKE and continues the build process. |
| –K | Keeps temporary files that MAKE creates (MAKE usually deletes them). See also KEEP on page 323. |
| –m | Displays the date and time stamp of each file as MAKE processes it. |
| –N | Executes MAKE like Microsoft's NMAKE (see the section following this table for more information). |
| –n | Prints the commands but doesn't actually perform them, which is helpful for debugging a makefile. |
| –p | Displays all macro definitions and implicit rules before executing the makefile. |
| –q | Returns 0 if the target is up-to-date and nonzero if it is not (for use with batch files). |
| –r | Ignores any rules defined in BUILTINS.MAK. |
| –S | Swaps MAKER out of memory while commands are executed, reducing memory overhead and allowing compilation of large modules. MAKE ignores this option. |
| –s | Suppresses onscreen command display. |
| –U*macro* | Undefines previous definitions of *macro*. |
| –W | Writes the current specified non-string options to MAKE.EXE making them defaults. |

## Setting options on as defaults

The **–W** option lets you set some MAKE options on as defaults so that each time you use MAKE, those options are used. To set MAKE options, type

```
make  -option[-]  [-option][-]  . . . -W
```

For example, you could type MAKE -m -W to always view file dates and times. Type MAKE -m- -W to turn off the default option. When MAKE asks you to write changes to MAKE.EXE, type Y.

**Caution!**　The **–W** option doesn't work when the DOS SHARE program is running. The message `Fatal: unable to open file MAKE.EXE` is displayed. The **–W** option doesn't work with the following MAKE options:

| | |
|---|---|
| **–D**_macro_ | **–D**_macro=string_ |
| **–d**_directory_ | **–U**_symbol_ |
| **–f**_filename_ | **–?** or **–h** |
| **–I**_directory_ | |

### Compatibility with Microsoft's NMAKE

Use the **–N** option if you want to use makefiles that were originally created for Microsoft's NMAKE. The following changes occur when you use **–N**:

- MAKE interprets the **<<** operator like the **&&** operator: temporary files are used as response files, then deleted. To keep a file, either use the **–K** command-line option or use KEEP in the makefile.

  MAKE usually deletes temporary files it creates.

  ```
  <<FileName.Ext
  text
  ?
  <<KEEP
  ```

  If you don't want to keep a temporary file, type NOKEEP or type only the temporary (optional) file name. If you don't type a file name, MAKE creates a name for you. If you use NOKEEP with a temporary file, then use the **–K** option with MAKE, MAKE deletes the temporary file.

- The **$d** macro is treated differently. Use **!ifdef** or **!ifndef** instead.

- Macros that return paths won't return the last **\**. For example, if `$(<D)` normally returns `C:\CPP\`, the **–N** option makes it return `C:\CPP`.

- Unless there's a matching **.suffixes** directive, MAKE searches rules from bottom to top of the makefile.

- The **$\*** macro always expands to the target name instead of the dependent in an implicit rule.

# Using makefiles

A makefile is an ASCII file of instructions for MAKE.EXE. MAKE assumes your makefile is called MAKEFILE or MAKEFILE.MAK unless you use the **–f** option (see page 321).

MAKE either builds targets you specify at the MAKE command line or it builds _only_ the first target it finds in the makefile (to build more than one target, see the section "Symbolic targets"). Makefiles can contain

- Comments
- Implicit rules
- Directives
- Explicit rules
- Macros

## Symbolic targets

A symbolic target forces MAKE to build multiple targets in a makefile (you don't need to rely on linked dependencies). The dependency line lists all the targets you want to build. You don't type any commands for a symbolic target.

In the following makefile, the symbolic target *allFiles* builds both FILE1.EXE and FILE2.EXE.

```
allFiles: file1.exe file2.exe      #Note this target has no commands.
file1.exe: file1.obj
   bcc file1.obj
file2.exe: file2.obj
   bcc file2.obj
```

### Rules for symbolic targets

Observe the following rules with symbolic targets:

- Symbolic targets don't need a command line.

- Give your symbolic target a unique name; it can't be the name of a file in your current directory.

- Name symbolic targets according to the operating system rules for naming files.

# Explicit and implicit rules

The explicit and implicit rules that instruct MAKE are generally defined as follows:

- Explicit rules give MAKE instructions for specific files.

- Implicit rules give general instructions that MAKE follows when it can't find an explicit rule.

Rules follow this general format:

```
Dependency line
   Commands
   ?
```

The dependency line is different for explicit and implicit rules, but the commands are the same (for information on linked dependencies see page 320).

MAKE supports multiple rules for one target. You can add dependent files after the first explicit rule, but only one should contain a command line. For example,

```
Target1: dependent1 dep2 dep3 dep4 dep5
Target1: dep6 dep7 dep8
   bcc -c $**
```

### Explicit rule syntax

Explicit rules are instructions to MAKE that specify exact file names. The explicit rule names one or more targets followed by one or two colons. One colon means one rule is written for the target; two colons mean that two or more rules are written for the target.

Explicit rules follow this syntax:

```
target [target...]:[:][{path}] [dependent[s]...]
   [commands]
    ?
```

Braces must be included if you use the *path* parameter.

- `target`   The name and extension of the file to be updated (*target* must be at the start of the line—no spaces or tabs are allowed). One or more targets must be separated by spaces or tabs. Don't use a target's name more than once in the target position of an explicit rule in a makefile.

- `path`   A list of directories, separated by semicolons and enclosed in braces, that points to the dependent files.

- `dependent`   The file (or files) whose date and time MAKE checks to see if it is newer than `target` (dependent *must* be preceded by a space). If a dependent file also appears in the makefile as a target, MAKE updates or creates the target file before using it as a dependent for another target.

- `commands`   Any operating system command. Multiple commands are allowed in a rule. Commands must be indented by at least one space or tab (see the section on commands on page 326).

If the dependency or command continues on to the next line, use the backslash (\) at the end of the line after a target or a dependent file name. For example,

```
MYSOURCE.EXE: FILE1.OBJ'
    FILE3.OBJ
  bcc file1.obj file2.obj file3.obj
```

## Single targets with multiple rules

A single target can have more than one explicit rule. You must use the double colon :: after the target name to tell MAKE to expect multiple explicit rules. The following example shows how one target can have multiple rules and commands.

```
.cpp.obj:
  bcc -c -ncobj $<

.asm.obj:
  tasm  /mx $<, asmobj\

mylib.lib :: f1.obj f2.obj
   echo Adding C files
   tlib mylib -+cobjf1 -+cobjf2

mylib.lib :: f3.obj f4.obj
   echo Adding ASM files
   tlib mylib -+asmobjf3 -+asmobjf4
```

# Implicit rule syntax

An implicit rule starts with either a path or a period and *implies* a target-dependent file relationship. Its main components are file extensions separated by periods. The first extension belongs to the dependent, the second to the target.

If implicit dependents are out-of-date with respect to the target or if they don't exist, MAKE executes the commands associated with the rule. MAKE updates explicit dependents before it updates implicit dependents.

Implicit rules follow this basic syntax:

```
[source_dirs].source_ext[target_dirs].target_ext:
   [commands]
```

- *{source_dirs}*   The directory of the dependent files. Separate multiple directories with a semicolon.
- *.source_ext*   The dependent file-name extension.
- *{target_dirs}*   The directory of the target (executable) files. Separate multiple directories with a semicolon.
- *.target_ext*   The target file-name extension. Macros are allowed here.
- *:*   Marks the end of the dependency line.
- *commands*   Any operating system command. Multiple commands are allowed. Commands must be indented by one space or tab (see the section on commands on page 326).

If two implicit rules match a target extension but no dependent exists, MAKE uses the implicit rule whose dependent's extension appears first in the .SUFFIXES list. See the ".suffixes" section on page 335.

## Explicit rules with implicit commands

A target in an explicit rule can get its command line from an implicit rule. The following example shows an implicit rule and an explicit rule without a command line.

```
.c.obj:
   bcc -c $<    #This command uses a macro $< described later.

myprog.obj:       #This explicit rule uses the command: bcc -c myprog.c
```

The implicit rule command tells MAKE to compile MYPROG.C (the macro $< replaces the name `myprog.obj` with `myprog.c`).

See page 330 for information on default macros.

# Commands syntax

Commands can be any operating system command, but they can also include MAKE macros, directives, and special operators that operating systems can't recognize (note that | can't be used in commands). Here are some sample commands:

```
cd..

bcc -c mysource.c

COPY *.OBJ C:PROJECTA

bcc -c $(SOURCE)      #Macros are explained later in the chapter.
```

Commands follow this general syntax:

```
[prefix...] commands
```

## Command prefixes

Commands in both implicit and explicit rules can have prefixes that modify how MAKE treats the commands. Table 20.2 lists the prefixes you can use in makefiles; each prefix is explained in more detail following the table.

**Table 20.2**    Command prefixes

| Option | Description |
|--------|-------------|
| @ | Don't display *command* while it's being executed. |
| –*num* | Stop processing commands in the makefile when the exit code returned from *command* exceeds *num*. Normally, MAKE aborts if the exit code is nonzero. No white space is allowed between – and *num*. |
| – | Continue processing commands in the makefile, regardless of the exit code returned by them. |
| & | Expand either the macro **$\*\***, which represents all dependent files, or the macro **$?**, which represents all dependent files stamped later than the target. Execute the command once for each dependent file in the expanded macro. |

## Using @

The following command uses the modifier @, which prevents the command from displaying onscreen when MAKE executes it.

```
diff.exe : diff.obj
   @bcc diff.obj
```

## Using –num and –

The **–num** and – modifiers control MAKE processing under error conditions. You can choose to continue with the MAKE process if an error occurs or only if the errors exceed a given number.

In the following example, MAKE continues processing if BCC isn't run successfully:

```
target.exe : target.obj
target.obj : target.cpp
   bcc -c target.cpp
```

## Using &

The & modifier issues a command once for each dependent file. It is especially useful for commands that don't take a list of files as parameters. For example,

```
copyall : file1.cpp file2.cpp
   &copy $** c:\temp
```

results in COPY being invoked twice as follows:

```
copy file1.cpp c:\temp
copy file2.cpp c:\temp
```

Without the **&** modifier, COPY would be called only once.

## Command operators

You can use any operating system command in a MAKE commands section. MAKE uses the normal operators (such as +, –, and so on), but it also has other operators you can use.

**Table 20.3**   Command operators

| Operator | Description |
|---|---|
| < | Take the input for use by *command* from *file* rather than from standard input. |
| > | Send the output from *command* to *file*. |
| >> | Append the output from *command* to *file*. |
| << | Create a temporary, inline file and use its contents as standard input to *command*. |
| && | Create a temporary file and insert its name in the makefile. |
| delimiter | Any character other than # and used with << and && as a starting and ending delimiter for a temporary file. Any characters on the same line and immediately following the starting delimiter are ignored. The closing *delimiter* must be written on a line by itself. |

## Debugging with temporary files

Temporary files can help you debug a command set by placing the actual commands MAKE executes into the temporary file. Temporary file names start at MAKE0000.@@@, where the 0000 increments for each temporary file you keep. You must place delimiters after **&&** and at the end of what you want sent to the temporary file (! is a good delimiter).

The following example shows **&&** instructing MAKE to create a file of the input to TLINK.

```
prog.exe: A.obj B.obj
    TLINK /c &&!
    c0s.obj $**
    prog.exe
    prog.map
    maths.lib cs.lib
    !
```

The response file created by **&&** contains these instructions:

```
c0s.obj a.obj b.obj
prog.exe
prog.map
maths.lib cs.lib
```

# Using MAKE macros

A MAKE macro is a variable that gets expanded into a string whenever the macro is called in a makefile. For example, to define a macro called LIBNAME that represents the string "mylib.lib," type `LIBNAME = mylib.lib`. When MAKE encounters the macro `$(LIBNAME)`, it uses the string `mylib.lib`. Macros let you create template makefiles that you can change to suit different projects.

If MAKE finds an undefined macro in a makefile, it looks for an operating-system environment variable of that name (usually defined with SET) and uses its definition as the expansion text. For example, if you wrote `$(PATH)` in a makefile and never defined *PATH*, MAKE would use the text you defined for PATH in your AUTOEXEC.BAT. (See your operating system manuals for information on defining environment variables.)

## Defining macros

The general syntax for defining a macro in a makefile is `MacroName = expansion_text`.

- *MacroName* is case-sensitive. MACRO1 is different from Macro1.

- *MacroName* is limited to 512 characters.

- *expansion_text* is limited to 4096 characters. Expansion characters may be alphanumeric, punctuation, or whitespace.

Each macro must be on a separate line in a makefile. Macros are usually put at the top of the makefile. If MAKE finds more than one definition for a *macroName*, the new definition replaces the old one.

Macros can also be defined using the command-line option **–D** (see page 322). More than one macro can be defined by separating them with spaces. The following examples show macros defined at the command line:

```
make -Dsourcedir=c:projecta
make command="bcc -c"
make command=bcc option=-c
```

The following differences in syntax exist between macros entered on the command line and macros written in a makefile.

**Table 20.4**   Command line vs. makefile macros

| Syntax | Makefile | Command line |
|---|---|---|
| Spaces allowed before and after = | Yes | No |
| Space allowed before *macroName* | No | Yes |

## Using a macro

To use a macro in a makefile, type `$(MacroName)` where *MacroName* is the name of a defined macro. You can use braces {} and parentheses () to enclose the *MacroName*.

MAKE expands macros at various times depending on where they appear in the makefile:

- Nested macros are expanded when the outer macro is invoked.
- Macros in rules and directives are expanded when MAKE first looks at the makefile.
- Macros in commands are expanded when the command is executed.

## String substitutions in macros

MAKE lets you temporarily substitute characters in a previously defined macro. For example, if you defined a macro called SOURCE as `SOURCE = f1.cpp f2.cpp f3.cpp`, you could substitute the characters .obj for the characters .cpp by using `$(SOURCE:.cpp=.obj)`. The substitution doesn't redefine the macro.

Rules for macro substitution:

- Syntax: `$(MacroName:original_text=new_text)`.

- No whitespace before or after the colon.

- Characters in *original_text* must exactly match the characters in the macro definition; this text is case-sensitive.

MAKE now lets you use macros within substitution macros. For example,

```
MYEXT=.C
SOURCE=f1.cpp f2.cpp f3.cpp
$(SOURCE:.cpp=$(MYEXT))          #Changes f1.cpp to f1.C, etc.
```

## Default MAKE macros

MAKE contains several default macros you can use in your makefiles. Table 20.5 lists the macro definition and what it expands to in explicit and implicit rules.

**Table 20.5**   Default macros

| Macro | Expands in implicit | Expands in explicit | Example |
|-------|--------------------|--------------------|---------|
| $* | path\dependent file | path\target file | C:\PROJECTA\MYTARGET |
| $< | path\dependent file+ext | path\target file+ext | C:\PROJECTA\MYTARGET.OBJ |
| $: | path for dependents | path for target | C:\PROJECTA |
| $. | dependent file+ext | target file + ext | MYSOURCE.C |
| $& | dependent file | target file | MYSOURCE |
| $@ | path\target file+ext | path\target file+ext | C:\PROJECTA\MYSOURCE.C |
| $** | path\dependent file+ext | all dependents file+ext | FILE1.CPP FILE2.CPP FILE3.CPP |
| $? | path\dependent file+ext | old dependents | FILE1.CPP |

**Table 20.6**   Other default macros

| Macro | Expands to | Comment |
|-------|-----------|---------|
| __MSDOS__ | 1 | If running under DOS. |
| __MAKE__ | 0x0370 | MAKE's hex version number. |
| MAKE | make | MAKE's executable file name. |
| MAKEFLAGS | options | The options typed at the command line. |
| MAKEDIR | directory | Directory where MAKE.EXE is located. |

## Modifying default macros

When the default macros listed in Table 20.5 don't give you the exact string you want, macro modifiers let you extract parts of the string to suit your purpose.

To modify a default macro, use this syntax:

```
$(MacroName [modifier])
```

Table 20.7 lists macro modifiers and provides examples of their use.

**Table 20.7** File-name macro modifiers

| Modifier | Part of file name expanded | Example | Result |
|----------|----------------------------|---------|--------|
| D | Drive and directory | $(<D) | C:\PROJECTA\ |
| F | Base and extension | $(<F) | MYSOURCE.C |
| B | Base only | $(<B) | MYSOURCE |
| R | Drive, directory, and base | $(<R) | C:\PROJECTA\MYSOURCE |

# Using MAKE directives

MAKE directives resemble directives in languages such as C and Pascal, and perform various control functions, such as displaying commands onscreen before executing them. MAKE directives begin either with an exclamation point or a period. Table 20.8 lists MAKE directives and their corresponding command-line options (directives override command-line options). Each directive is described in more detail following the table.

**Table 20.8** MAKE directives

| Directive | Option | Description |
|-----------|--------|-------------|
| .autodepend | –a | Turns on autodependency checking. |
| .cacheautodepend | –c | Turns on autodependency caching. |
| !elif | | Acts like a C **else if**. |
| !else | | Acts like a C **else**. |
| !endif | | Ends an **!if**, **!ifdef**, or **!ifndef** statement. |
| !error | | Stops MAKE and prints an error message. |
| !if | | Begins a conditional statement. |
| !ifdef | | Acts like a C **#ifdef**, testing whether a given macro has been defined. |
| !ifndef | | Acts like a C **#ifndef**, testing whether a given macro is undefined. |
| .ignore | –i | MAKE ignores the return value of a command. |
| !include | | Acts like a C #include, specifying a file to include in the makefile. |
| !message | | Prints a message to **stdout** while MAKE runs the makefile. |
| .noautodepend | –a– | Turns off autodependency checking. |
| .nocacheautodepend | –c– | Turns off autodependency caching. |

**Table 20.8**    MAKE directives (continued)

| Directive | Option | Description |
|---|---|---|
| .noIgnore | –i– | Turns off **.Ignore**. |
| .nosilent | –s– | Displays commands before MAKE executes them. |
| .noswap | –S– | Tells MAKE not to swap itself out of memory before executing a command. |
| .path.ext. |  | Tells MAKE to search for files with the extension .ext in *path* directories. |
| .precious |  | Saves the target or targets even if the build fails. |
| .silent | –s | MAKE executes commands without printing them first. |
| .suffixes |  | Determines the implicit rule for ambiguous dependencies. |
| .swap | –S | Tells MAKE to swap itself out of memory before executing a command. |
| !undef |  | Clears the definition of a macro. After this, the macro is undefined. |

## .autodepend

Autodependencies occur in .OBJ files that have corresponding .CPP, .C, or .ASM files. With **.autodepend** on, MAKE compares the dates and times of all the files used to build the .OBJ. If the dates and times of the files used to build the .OBJ are different from the date/time stamp of the .OBJ file, the .OBJ file is recompiled. You can use **.autodepend** or **–a** in place of linked dependencies (see page 320 for information on linked dependencies).

## !error

This is the syntax of the **!error** directive:

```
!error message
```

MAKE stops processing and prints the following string when it encounters this directive:

```
Fatal makefile exit code: Error directive: message
```

Embed **!error** in conditional statements to abort processing and print an error message, as shown in the following example:

```
!if !$d(MYMACRO)
#if MYMACRO isn't defined
!error MYMACRO isn't defined
!endif
```

If MYMACRO in the example isn't defined, MAKE prints the following message:

```
Fatal makefile 4: Error directive: MYMACRO isn't defined
```

### Summing up error-checking controls

Four different controls turn off error checking:

• The **.ignore** directive turns off error checking for a selected portion of the makefile.

- The **–i** command-line option turns off error checking for the entire makefile.

- The **–num** command operator, which is entered as part of a rule, turns off error checking for the related command if the exit code exceeds the specified number.

- The **–** command operator turns off error checking for the related command regardless of the exit code.

## !if and other conditional directives

The **!if** directive works like C **if** statements. As shown here, the syntax of **!if** and the other conditional directives resembles compiler conditionals:

```
!if condition       !if condition       !if condition       !ifdef macro
!endif              !else               !elif condition     !endif
                    !endif              !endif
```

The following expressions are equivalent:

```
!ifdef macro and !if $d(macro)

ifndef macro and !if !$d(macro)
```

These rules apply to conditional directives:

- One **!else** directive is allowed between **!if**, **!ifdef**, or **!ifndef** and **!endif** directives.
- Multiple **!elif** directives are allowed between **!if**, **!ifdef**, or **!ifndef**, **!else** and **!endif**.
- You can't split rules across conditional directives.
- You can nest conditional directives.
- **!if**, **!ifdef**, and **!ifndef** must have matching **!endif** directives within the same file.

The following information can be included between **!if** and **!endif** directives:

- Macro definition
- Explicit rule
- Implicit rule
- **!include** directive
- **!error** directive
- **!undef** directive

*Condition* in **if** statements represents a conditional expression consisting of decimal, octal, or hexadecimal constants and the operators shown in Table 20.9.

**Table 20.9**   Conditional operators

| Operator | Description | Operator | Description |
|----------|-------------|----------|-------------|
| – | Negation | ?: | Conditional expression |
| ~ | Bit complement | ! | Logical NOT |
| + | Addition | >> | Right shift |
| – | Subtraction | << | Left shift |
| * | Multiplication | & | Bitwise AND |
| / | Division | \| | Bitwise OR |
| % | Remainder | ^ | Bitwise XOR |
| && | Logical AND | >= | Greater than or equal* |

**Table 20.9**  Conditional operators (continued)

| Operator | Description | Operator | Description |
|----------|-------------|----------|-------------|
| \|\| | Logical OR | <= | Less than or equal* |
| > | Greater than | == | Equality* |
| < | Less than | != | Inequality* |

*Operator also works with string expressions.

MAKE evaluates a conditional expression as either a simple 32-bit signed integer or as a character string.

# !include

This directive is like the **#include** preprocessor directive for the C or C++ language—it lets you include the text of another file in the makefile:

```
!include filename
```

You can enclose *filename* in quotation marks (" ") or angle brackets (<>) and nest directives to unlimited depth, but writing duplicate **!include** directives in a makefile isn't permitted—you'll get the error message *cycle in the include file*.

Rules, commands, or directives must be complete within a single source file; you can't start a command in an **!include** file, then finish it in the makefile.

MAKE searches for **!include** files in the current directory unless you've specified another directory with the **–I** option.

# !message

The **!message** directive lets you send messages to the screen from a makefile. You can use these messages to help debug a makefile that isn't working the way you'd like it to. For example, if you're having trouble with a macro definition, you could put this line in your makefile:

```
!message The macro is defined here as: $(MacroName)
```

When MAKE interprets this line, it will print onscreen `The macro is defined here as: .CPP`, if the macro expands to .CPP at that line. Using a series of **!message** directives, you can debug your makefiles.

# .path.ext

The **.path.ext** directive tells MAKE where to look for files with a certain extension. The following example tells MAKE to look for files with the .c extension in C:SOURCE or C:CFILES and to look for files with the .obj extension in C:OBJS.

```
.path.c = C:CSOURCE;C:CFILES
.path.obj = C:OBJS
```

## .precious

If a MAKE build fails, MAKE deletes the target file. The **.precious** directive prevents the file deletion, which is desired for certain kinds of targets such as libraries. When a build fails to add a module to a library, you don't want the library to be deleted.

The syntax for **.precious** is

```
.precious: target [target] . . . [target]
```

## .suffixes

The **.suffixes** directive tells MAKE the order (by file extensions) for building implicit rules.

The syntax of the **.suffixes** directive is

```
.suffixes: .ext [.ext]  [.ext] . . . [.ext]
```

**.ext** represents the dependent file extension in implicit rules. For example, you could include the line `.suffixes: .asm .c .cpp` to tell MAKE to interpret implicit rules beginning with the ones dependent on .ASM files, then .C files, then .CPP files, regardless of what order they appear in the makefile.

The following example shows a makefile containing a **.suffixes** directive that tells MAKE to look for a source file (MYPROG.EXE) first with an .ASM extension, next with a .C extension, and finally with a .CPP extension. If MAKE finds MYPROG.ASM, it builds MYPROG.OBJ from the assembler file by calling TASM. MAKE then calls TLINK; otherwise, MAKE searches for MYPROG.C to build the .OBJ file, and so on.

```
.suffixes: .asm .c .cpp

myprog.exe: myprog.obj
tlink myprog.obj

.cpp.obj:
  bcc -P $<
.asm.obj:
  tasm /mx $<
.c.obj:
  bcc -P- $<
```

## !undef

The syntax of the **!undef** directive is

```
!undef MacroName
```

**!undef** (undefine) clears the given macro, causing an **!ifdef** *MacroName* test to fail.

## Using macros in directives

The macro **$d** is used with the **!if** conditional directive to perform some processing if a specific macro is defined. The **$d** is followed by a macro name, enclosed in parentheses or braces, as shown in the following example.

```
!if $d(DEBUG)              #If DEBUG is defined,
bcc -v f1.cpp f2.cpp       #compile with debug information;
!else                      #otherwise (else)
bcc -v- f1.cpp f2.cpp      #don't include debug information.
!endif
```

## Null macros

An undefined macro causes an **!ifdef** *MacroName* test to return false; a null macro returns true. A null macro is a macro defined with either spaces to the right of the equal sign (=) or no characters to the right of the equal sign. For example, the following line defines a null macro in a makefile:

```
NULLMACRO =
```

Either of the following lines can define a null macro on the MAKE command line:

```
NULLMACRO=" "
-DNULLMACRO
```

Chapter

# 21

# Using command-line resource tools

There are several Borland command-line resource tools:

- Resource compiler

  BRCC32.EXE is the Borland resource compiler. It compiles resource script files (.RC files) and produces the binary .RES file.

- Resource linkers

  RLINK.EXE and RLINK32.DLL are the Borland resource linkers that bind re-sources, in .RES file form, to an .EXE file, and mark the resulting .EXE file as a Windows executable. RLINK32.DLL is accessed through TLINK32.EXE. RLINK.EXE is for 16-bit resources only.

- Resource shells

  BRC32.EXE is a shell through which BRCC32 and RLINK or RLINK32 (through TLINK32) can be started in a single step.

**Note**  BRC and BRCC are no longer compliers.These files are shells that call BRC32 or BRCC32 with 16-bit options. All resources are compiled with BRCC32. The command line options are supported for downward compatability.

## Resource compiler (BRCC32)

BRCC32 is the command-line version of the Resource Workshop resource compiler. It accepts a resource script file (.RC) as input and produces a resource object file (.RES) as output. BRCC32 is used for both 16-bit and 32-bit resources.

### Syntax

```
BRCC32 [options] <filename>.RC
```

# Command-line options

BRCC32 accepts these options:

| Option | Description |
| --- | --- |
| @responsefile | Takes instructions from the specified command file. |
| -d<name>[=<string>] | Defines a preprocessor symbol. |
| -fo<filename> | Renames the output .RES file. (By default, BRCC32 creates the output .RES file with the same name as the input .RC file.) |
| -i<path> | Adds one or more directories (separated by semicolons) to the include search path. |
| -r | This switch is ignored. It is included for compatibility with other resource compilers. |
| -v | Prints progress messages (verbose). |
| -x | Deletes the current include path. |
| -? or -h | Displays help. |
| -16 | Builds a 16-bit resource. |
| -32 | Builds a 32-bit resource. |

BRCC32 predefines common resource-related Windows constants such as WS_VISIBLE and BS_PUSHBUTTON. Also, two special compiler-related symbols are defined: RC_INVOKED and WORKSHOP_INVOKED. These symbols can be used in the source text in conjunction with conditional preprocessor statements to control compilation. For example, the following construct can greatly speed up compilation:

```
#ifndef WORKSHOP_INVOKED

#include "windows.h"
#endif
```

# Downward compatability

The following syntax and options are supported for downward compatabliity.

## Syntax

```
BRCC [options] <filename>.RC
```

## Command-line options

BRCC accept these options:

| Option | Description |
| --- | --- |
| -31 | Builds Windows 3.1-compatible .RES files. |
| -w32 | Builds Win32-compatible .RES files. |

## Resource compiler examples

The following example adds two directories to the include path and produces a .RES file with the same name as the input .RC file.

```
brcc32 -i<dir1>;<dir2> <filename>.RC
```

This example produces an output .RES file with a name different from the input .RC file name:

```
brcc32 -fo<filename>.RES <filename>.RC
```

This example builds a 16-bit .RES file:

```
brcc32 -16 -fo<filename>.RES <filename>.RC
```

# Resource linkers (RLINK and RLINK32)

RLINK (and RLINK32) combines a .RES file with an .EXE file to produce a new Windows executable. RLINK accepts as input one or more object files (.RES) and a single Windows executable file. RLINK links the resources by fixing up string tables and message tables and then binding these linked resources to the executable. RLINK32 is called by TLINK32, and is used for 32-bit resources.

## Syntax

```
rlink [options] <filename>.RES <filename>.EXE
```

## Command-line options

RLINK accepts these options:

| Option | Description |
|---|---|
| @<filename> | Takes instructions from the specified command file. |
| -d | Removes resources from the .EXE file (default if no .RES file is specified). |
| -fe<filename> | Renames the output .EXE file. |
| -fi<filename> | Specifies additional input files. |
| -k | Does not reorder segments for fastload. (This option only applies to 16-bit resources.) |
| -v | Prints progress messages (verbose listing). |
| -vx | Lists resources but does not bind to EXE file. |
| -? or -h | Displays help. |
| -Vd.d | Makes the .EXE file with Windows version provided (v3.1 is the default). Version options are listed in the following table. |

| Option | Bit | Resulting look |
|--------|-----|----------------|
| 3.1 | 16 | Gives white background with a non 3-D look for Windows 3.1x, Windows 32s, or WinNT 3.1. |
| 4.0 | 16 | Gives gray 3-D look for Windows 95 and WinNT 3.51. |
| 3.1 | 32 | Gives white background with a non 3-D look for Windows 32s or WinNT 3.1. |
| 4.0 | 32 | Gives gray 3-D look for Windows 95 and WinNT 3.51. |

## Resource linker examples

The following example binds the resources in the .RES file into the .EXE file:

```
rlink <filename>.RES <filename>.EXE
```

This example links the resources in the two .RES files and binds them to the .EXE file:

```
rlink -fi<filename>.RES <filename>.RES <filename>.EXE
```

This example combines the program code in the input .EXE file with the resources in the input .RES file and produces an output .EXE file with a new name:

```
rlink -fe<filename>.EXE <filename>.RES <filename>.EXE
```

This example takes input from an .RLK command file. It then links the resources in three .RES files and binds them to the .EXE file:

```
rlink @<filename>.RLK
```

The command file (<filename>.RLK) contains:

```
-fi<filename>.RES
-fi<filename>.RES
<filename>.RES
<filename>.EXE
```

# Resource shell (BRC32)

The Borland resource compiler (BRC32) is a resource compiler shell. It invokes BRCC32 and RLINK or RLINK32, depending on the command-line syntax.

## Syntax

```
brc32 [options] <filename>.RC [<filename>.EXE]
```

# Command-line options

BRC32 accepts these options:

| Switch | Description |
| --- | --- |
| -d\<name>=string | Defines a symbol you can test with the #IFDEF preprocessor directive. |
| -fo\<filename> | Renames the .RES file. |
| -fe\<filename> | Renames the .EXE file. |
| -i\<path> | Adds one or more directories (separated by semicolons) to the include search path. |
| -r | Creates a .RES file only. The compiled .RES file is not added to the .EXE. |
| -v | Prints progress messages (verbose listing). |
| -x | Directs the compiler to ignore the INCLUDE environment variable when it searches for include or resource files. |
| -16 | Builds 16-bit .RES files. |
| -32 | Builds 32-bit .RES files. |
| -Vd.d | Makes the .EXE file with Windows version provided (v3.1 is the default for 16-bit resources; -v4.0 is the default for 32-bit resources). Version options are listed in the following table. |

| Option | Bit | Resulting look |
| --- | --- | --- |
| 3.1 | 16 | Gives white background with a non 3-D look for Windows 3.1x, Windows 32s, or WinNT 3.1. |
| 4.0 | 16 | Gives gray 3-D look for Windows 95 and WinNT 3.51. |
| 3.1 | 32 | Gives white background with a non 3-D look for Windows 32s or WinNT 3.1. |
| 4.0 | 32 | Gives gray 3-D look for Windows 95 and WinNT 3.51. |

The following switches are invalid when the -r switch is specified:

| | |
| --- | --- |
| -k | Disables the contiguous preload of segments and resources in the .EXE file. Segments are kept in the order in which they appear in the .DEF file. (This option only applies to 16-bit resources.) |
| -t | Creates an application that runs only in protected mode (Windows Standard or 386 Enhanced mode). |

## Downward compatability

The following sytax and options are supported for downward compatability.

### Syntax

```
brc [switches] <filename>.RC [<filename>.EXE]
```

### Command-line options

BRC accept these options:

| Option | Description |
|--------|-------------|
| -31 | Builds Windows 3.1-compatible .RES files. |
| -w32 | Builds Win32-compatible .RES files. |

## Resource shell examples

The following statement compiles the .RC file, creates a .RES file, and adds the .RES file to the executable file:

```
brc32 <filename>.RC [<filename>.EXE]
```

BRC32 automatically seeks an .EXE file with the same name as the .RC file. You need to specify the .EXE file only if its name is different from that of the .RC file.

The following statement creates a .RES file, but not an .EXE file. If you name an .EXE file in the command line, BRC ignores it:

```
brc32 -r <filename>.RC
```

The following statement adds an existing .RES file to an executable file. The .EXE file name is required only if it differs from the .RES file name:

```
brc32 <filename>.RES [<filename>.EXE]
```

This example uses BRC32 to build a 16-bit Windows 3.1 compatible .RES file:

```
brc32 -16 -v3.1 -fo<filename>.RES <filename>.RC
```

# 22

# WinSight

WinSight is a debugging tool that gives you information about windows, window classes, and window messages. You can use it to study a Windows application, to see how windows and window classes are created and used, and to see what messages the windows receive.

You can configure WinSight to trace and display messages by

- Window
- Message type
- Window class
- A combination of these

WinSight is a passive observer: it intercepts and displays information about messages, but it doesn't prevent messages from getting to applications.

To start WinSight, double-click the WinSight icon located in the Borland C++ program group. The WinSight window appears in its default configuration; it displays the Window Tree view that lists all the windows currently active on the desktop. WinSight saves your configuration, so if you open all three views and exit WinSight, the next time you start it, all three views will display.

WinSight has three views: Class List, Window Tree, and Message Trace. You can display these views from left to right or top to bottom by choosing View | Split Horizontal or View | Split Vertical.

You can control the messages traced by WinSight (see page 347) and you can control when messages start and stop tracing as described in the following sections.

## Starting and stopping screen updates

To turn on tracing, choose Start! from the menu (Start! then becomes Stop! on the menu). Normally, all three views are kept current as classes are registered, windows are created and destroyed, and messages are received. However, you can use Messages | Trace Off to suspend tracing of messages only (Class List and Window Tree will continue to update).

Use Stop! and Start! to

- Study a particular situation.
- Control (minimize) the machine time WinSight uses when it updates itself constantly.

### Turning off message tracing

To turn off tracing of message types, choose Messages | Trace Off. The Message Trace view remains visible, and tracing resumes when you choose Messages | Selected Classes, Selected Windows, or All Windows (provided tracing is on).

The following sections describe how to use the three views to get the information you need to debug an application. Choose Spy | Exit to leave WinSight.

# Choosing a view

WinSight has three views that can appear within its main window: Class List, Window Tree, and Message Trace. You can choose to look at any or all of the views. WinSight automatically tiles the views within the main window.

You can hide or display views at any time, using the View menu. Information and selections are not lost when a view is hidden.

- The Class List view shows all the currently registered window classes.

- The Window Tree view displays the hierarchy of all the windows on the desktop. Window Tree displays by default when you start WinSight.

- The Message Trace view displays information about messages received by selected windows or window classes.

To get more detail about an item in Window Tree or Class List,

- Select a window or a class, then choose Spy | Open Detail.
- Double-click the window or class.

The Detail window displays the class name, executable module, and other information about the class or window.

# Class List view

A class is the name with which the window class was registered with Windows. Sometimes, instead of choosing specific windows to trace, you might want to look at messages for entire classes of windows. WinSight lets you do this with the Class List view.

## Using the Class List view

The Class List view shows all the currently registered window classes. To get details about a class, double-click it or select it and press *Enter*.

The diamonds next to the classes turn black momentarily whenever the window receives any messages. This gives you an overview of which windows are currently receiving messages. If a hidden child window receives a message, the diamond for the parent changes color. Use the following format:

```
Class (Module) Function Styles
```

*Class* is the name of the class. Some predefined Windows classes have numeric names. For example, the Popup menu class uses the number 32768 as its name. These predefined classes are shown with both the number and a name, such as #32768:PopupMenu. The actual class name is only the number (using the MAKEINTRESOURCE format, which is also used for resource IDs).

*Module* is the name of the executable module (.EXE or .DLL) that registered the class.

*Function* is the address of the class window function.

*Styles* is a list of the cs_ styles for the class. The names are the same as the cs_ definitions in WinTypes, except the cs_ is removed and the name is in mixed case (uppercase and lowercase).

## Spying on classes

To trace messages for one or more classes, select the classes in Class List (*Shift+Click* or *Ctrl+Click*), then choose Messages I Selected Classes. If the Message Trace view is hidden, it becomes visible when you choose Messages I Selected Classes.

Note that tracing messages to a class lets you see all messages to windows of that class, including creation messages, which would otherwise not be accessible.

To change which classes are traced, change the selection in the Class List. Choose Messages I Trace Off to turn off all message tracing to the Message view.

# Window Tree view

The Window Tree view displays a hierarchical outline of all existing windows on the desktop. This display lets you

- Determine what windows are present on the desktop.
- View the status of windows, including hidden windows.
- See which windows are receiving messages.
- Select windows for message tracing.

The lines on the left of the Window Tree view show the tree structure. Each window is connected to its parent, siblings, and children with these lines. When a window receives a message, the diamond next to it (or its parent window if the tree is collapsed) turns black.

The diamond next to each window shows whether the window has any children. If the diamond is blank, the window has no children. If the diamond contains a **+**, the window has children that are not displayed. To show the next level of children, click the diamond next to the window. To show *all* the levels of child windows (children of children, and so on), right-click the diamond. If the diamond contains a **–**, the children are displayed. To hide *all* of a window's child windows, click the diamond next to the window.

The format of the window details is as follows:

```
Handle {Class} Module (Position) "Title"
```

*Handle* is the window handle as returned by *CreateWindow*.

*Class* is the window class name, as described in the Class List view.

*Module* is the name of the executable module (.EXE or .DLL) that created the window. *Module* is the name of the module owning the data segment passed as the *hInstance* parameter to *CreateWindow*.

*Position* is "hidden" if the window is hidden. If the window is visible, *Position* is indicated by using screen coordinates (for parent windows) or coordinates in the parent's client area (for child windows). *Position* uses the following format:

```
xBegin,yBegin - xEnd,yEnd
```

*Title* is the window title or text, as returned by *GetWindowText* or a *wm_GETTEXT* message. If the title is the null string, the quotation marks are omitted.

## Finding a window

WinSight has a special mode for locating windows. It can work in two ways: either identifying the line in the Window Tree that corresponds to a window you point at with the mouse, or highlighting a window you select in the Window Tree.

**Important**    All other applications are suspended while you're in Find Window mode. Enter Find Window mode by choosing Spy | Find Window. In this mode, whenever the mouse passes into the boundaries of a window, a thick border appears around that window, and the window is selected in the Window Tree view.

Alternatively, once in Find Window mode, you can select windows in the Window Tree with the mouse or cursor keys, and WinSight will put a thick border around the selected window or windows. If you press *Enter*, you will see the Window Detail window for the selected window.

### Leaving Find Window mode

Once you have located the window you want, you can leave Find Window mode by clicking the mouse button or by pressing the *Esc* key. This removes the border from the screen, leaving the current window's description selected in the Window Tree view.

## Spying on windows

To spy on one or more windows, select the windows (using the mouse and the *Shift* or *Ctrl* key), then choose Messages I Selected Windows. To change which windows are traced, change the selected window in Window Tree.

To spy on all windows, regardless of what is selected in the Class List or the Window Tree, choose Messages I All Windows.

Message Trace becomes visible when you choose Messages I Selected Windows or Windows I All Windows.

Choose Messages I Trace Off to disable message tracing without hiding Message Trace.

# Choosing messages to trace

Message Trace displays messages received by selected window classes or windows. Messages received via *SendMessage* are shown twice, once when they are sent and again when they return to show the return value. Dispatched messages are shown once only, since their return value is meaningless. The message display is indented to show how messages are nested within other messages.

## Using the Message Trace view

By default, WinSight traces all messages and displays them in the Message Trace view. WinSight gives you several ways to narrow down the tracing of messages:

- Choose Messages I Selected Classes or Messages I Selected Windows, then select the classes (in the Class List view) or windows (in the Window Tree view) by using the mouse and *Shift* or *Ctrl*.

- Choose Message I All Windows.

- Choose Message I Options, then select any or all of fourteen groups of messages. Check All Messages in the Options dialog box to return to tracing all messages.

### Other tracing options
The Message Trace Options dialog box lets you change the format of the messages in Message Trace. It also lets you trace messages to a file, printer, or an auxiliary monitor or window.

- Normally, the Message Trace view interprets each message's parameters and displays them in a readable format (Interpret Values is checked). Check Hex Values to view message parameters as hex values of *wParam* and *lParam*.

- Information on traced messages usually displays in the Message Trace view. However, you can send messages to a file, printer, or auxiliary monitor by checking Log File in the Message Trace Options dialog box and doing one of the following:
  - Type a file name to trace to a log file. If the file already exists, messages are appended to the file.

- Type the name of the device (for example, type PRN) for the log file to send output to the printer port.

- Type AUX to output trace messages to an auxiliary monitor or window. To do this, you must have WINOX.SYS or OX.SYS installed as a device in your CONFIG.SYS file. To stop logging message traces to a file, printer, or auxiliary monitor, uncheck Log File. Use the following format:

```
Handle ["Title" or {Class}] Message Status
```

*Handle* is the window handle receiving the message.

*Title* is the window's title. If the title is the null string, the class name is displayed instead, in curly braces.

*Message* is the message name as defined by Windows. They are displayed in WinSight in all uppercase letters. Known undocumented Windows messages are shown in lowercase. Unknown message numbers (user-defined) are shown as *wm_User+0xXXXX* if they are greater-than or equal to *wm_User* or as *wm_0xXXXX* if they are less than *wm_User*. Registered message numbers (from *RegisterWindowsMessage*) are shown with their registered name in single quotes.

*Status* is one or more of the following:

- *Dispatched* indicates the message was received via *DispatchMessage*.

- *Sent [from XXXX]* indicates the message was received via *SendMessage*. If it was sent from another window, from xxxx gives that window's handle. If it was sent from the same window receiving it, this is shown with "from self." If it was sent from Windows itself, the "from" phrase is omitted.

- *Returns* indicates the message was received via *SendMessage* and is now returning.

- Additional messages might include a numeric return value or text message such as *wm_GetText*. For sent and dispatched messages, WinSight interprets the parameters and gives a readable display. For messages that have associated data structures (*wm_Create*, for example) it takes those structures and includes them in the display.

**Table 22.1**    Mouse messages

| | | |
|---|---|---|
| WM_HSCROLL | WM_MBUTTONUP | WM_RBUTTONDOWN |
| WM_LBUTTONDBLCLK | WM_MOUSEACTIVATE | WM_RBUTTONUP |
| WM_LBUTTONDOWN | WM_MOUSEFIRST | WM_SETCURSOR |
| WM_LBUTTONUP | WM_MOUSELAST | WM_VSCROLL |
| WM_MBUTTONDBLCLK | WM_MOUSEMOVE | |
| WM_MBUTTONDOWN | WM_RBUTTONDBLCLK | |

**Table 22.2**    Window messages

| | | |
|---|---|---|
| WM_ACTIVATE | WM_GETDLGCODE | WM_QUERYNEWPALETTE |
| WM_ACTIVATEAPP | WM_GETFONT | WM_QUERYOPEN |

**Table 22.2**  Window messages

| | | |
|---|---|---|
| WM_CANCELMODE | WM_GETMINMAXINFO | WM_QUIT |
| WM_CHILDACTIVATE | WM_GETTEXT | WM_SETFOCUS |
| WM_CLOSE | WM_GETTEXTLENGTH | WM_SETFONT |
| WM_CREATE | WM_ICONERASEBKGND | WM_SETREDRAW |
| WM_CTLCOLOR | WM_KILLFOCUS | WM_SETTEXT |
| WM_DDE_FIRST | WM_MOVE | WM_SHOWWINDOW |
| WM_DESTROY | WM_PAINT | WM_SIZE |
| WM_ENABLE | wm_painticon | WM_WINDOWPOSCHANGED |
| WM_ENDSESSION | WM_QUERYDRAGICON | WM_WINDOWPOSCHANGING |
| WM_ERASEBKGND | WM_QUERYENDSESSION | |

**Table 22.3**  Input messages

| | | |
|---|---|---|
| WM_CHAR | WM_KEYUP | WM_SYSKEYDOWN |
| WM_CHARTOITEM | WM_MENUCHAR | WM_SYSKEYUP |
| WM_COMMAND | WM_MENUSELECT | WM_TIMER |
| WM_DEADCHAR | WM_PARENTNOTIFY | WM_VKEYTOITEM |
| WM_KEYDOWN | WM_SYSCHAR | wm_yomichar |
| WM_KEYLAST | WM_SYSDEADCHAR | |

**Table 22.4**  System messages

| | | |
|---|---|---|
| WM_COMPACTING | WM_PALETTECHANGED | WM_SYSCOLORCHANGE |
| WM_DEVMODECHANGE | WM_PALETTEISCHANGING | WM_SYSCOMMAND |
| WM_ENTERIDLE | WM_POWER | WM_TIMECHANGE |
| WM_FONTCHANGE | WM_QUEUESYNCH | WM_WININICHANGE |
| wm_null | WM_SPOOLERSTATUS | |

**Table 22.5**  Pen messages

| | | |
|---|---|---|
| WIN_USER | WM_HOOKRCRESULT | WM_RCRESULT |
| WM_GLOBALRCCHANGE | WM_PENWINFIRST | WM_SKB |
| WM_HEDITCTL | WM_PENWINLAST | |

**Table 22.6**  Initialization messages

| | | |
|---|---|---|
| WM_INITDIALOG | WM_INITMENU | WM_INITMENUPOPUP |

**Table 22.7**    Clipboard messages

| | | |
|---|---|---|
| WM_ASKCBFORMATNAME | WM_DESTROYCLIPBOARD | WM_RENDERALLFORMATS |
| WM_CHANGECBCHAIN | WM_DRAWCLIPBOARD | WM_RENDERFORMAT |
| WM_CLEAR | WM_HSCROLLCLIPBOARD | WM_SIZECLIPBOARD |
| WM_COPY | WM_PAINTCLIPBOARD | WM_UNDO |
| WM_CUT | WM_PASTE | WM_VSCROLLCLIPBOARD |


**Table 22.8**    DDE messages

| | | |
|---|---|---|
| WM_DDE_ACK | WM_DDE_EXECUTE | WM_DDE_REQUEST |
| WM_DDE_ADVISE | WM_DDE_INITIATE | WM_DDE_TERMINATE |
| WM_DDE_DATA | WM_DDE_POKE | WM_DDE_UNADVISE |


**Table 22.9**    Nonclient messages

| | | |
|---|---|---|
| WM_NCACTIVATE | WM_NCLBUTTONDOWN | WM_NCPAINT |
| WM_NCCALCSIZE | WM_NCLBUTTONUP | WM_NCRBUTTONDBLCLK |
| WM_NCCREATE | WM_NCMBUTTONDBLCLK | WM_NCRBUTTONDOWN |
| WM_NCDESTROY | WM_NCMBUTTONDOWN | WM_NCRBUTTONUP |
| WM_NCHITTEST | WM_NCMBUTTONUP | |
| WM_NCLBUTTONDBLCLK | WM_NCMOUSEMOVE | |


**Table 22.10**   Control messages

| | | |
|---|---|---|
| BM_GETCHECK | CBN_SELCHANGE | EN_VSCROLL |
| BM_GETSTATE | CBN_SELENDCANCEL | LB_ADDSTRING |
| BM_SETCHECK | CBN_SETFOCUS | LB_DELETESTRING |
| BM_SETSTATE | DM_GETDEFID | LB_DIR |
| BM_SETSTYLE | DM_SETDEFID | LB_FINDSTRING |
| BN_CLICKED | EM_CANUNDO | LB_FINDSTRINGEXACT |
| BN_DISABLE | EM_EMPTYUNDOBUFFER | LB_GETCARETINDEX |
| BN_DOUBLECLICKED | EM_FMTLINES | LB_GETCOUNT |
| BN_HILITE | EM_GETFIRSTVISIBLELINE | LB_GETCURSEL |
| BN_PAINT | EM_GETHANDLE | LB_GETHORIZONTALEXTENT |
| BN_UNHILITE | EM_GETLINE | LB_GETITEMDATA |
| CB_ADDSTRING | EM_GETLINECOUNT | LB_GETITEMHEIGHT |
| CB_DELETESTRING | EM_GETMODIFY | LB_GETITEMRECT |
| CB_DIR | EM_GETPASSWORDCHAR | LB_GETSEL |
| CB_FINDSTRING | EM_GETRECT | LB_GETSELCOUNT |
| CB_FINDSTRINGEXACT | EM_GETSEL | LB_GETSELITEMS |

**Table 22.10** Control messages

| | | |
|---|---|---|
| CB_GETCOUNT | em_getthumb | LB_GETTEXT |
| CB_GETCURSEL | EM_GETWORDBREAKPROC | LB_GETTEXTLEN |
| CB_GETDROPPEDCONTROLRECT | EM_LIMITTEXT | LB_GETTOPINDEX |
| CB_GETDROPPEDSTATE | EM_LINEFROMCHAR | LB_INSERTSTRING |
| CB_GETEDITSEL | EM_LINEINDEX | LB_MSGMAX |
| CB_GETEXTENDEDUI | EM_LINELENGTH | LB_RESETCONTENT |
| CB_GETITEMDATA | EM_LINESCROLL | LB_SELECTSTRING |
| CB_GETITEMHEIGHT | EM_MSGMAX | LB_SELITEMRANGE |
| CB_GETLBTEXT | EM_REPLACESEL | LB_SETCARETINDEX |
| CB_GETLBTEXTLEN | em_scroll | LB_SETCOLUMNWIDTH |
| CB_INSERTSTRING | EM_SETFONT | LB_SETCURSEL |
| CB_LIMITTEXT | EM_SETHANDLE | LB_SETHORIZONTALEXTENT |
| CB_MSGMAX | EM_SETMODIFY | LB_SETITEMDATA |
| CB_RESETCONTENT | EM_SETPASSWORDCHAR | LB_SETITEMHEIGHT |
| CB_SELECTSTRING | EM_SETRECT | LB_SETSEL |
| CB_SETCURSEL | EM_SETRECTNP | LB_SETTABSTOPS |
| CB_SETEDITSEL | EM_SETSEL | LB_SETTOPINDEX |
| CB_SETITEMDATA | EM_SETTABSTOPS | LBN_DBLCLK |
| CB_SETITEMHEIGHT | EM_SETWORDBREAK | LBN_ERRSPACE |
| CB_SHOWDROPDOWN | EM_UNDO | LBN_KILLFOCUS |
| CBN_CLOSEUP | EN_CHANGE | LBN_SELCANCEL |
| CBN_DBLCLK | EN_ERRSPACE | LBN_SELCHANGE |
| CBN_DROPDOWN | EN_HSCROLL | LBN_SETFOCUS |
| CBN_EDITCHANGE | EN_KILLFOCUS | STM_GETICON |
| CBN_EDITUPDATE | EN_MAXTEXT | STM_SETICON |
| CBN_ERRSPACE | EN_SETFOCUS | |
| CBN_KILLFOCUS | EN_UPDATE | |

**Table 22.11** Multimedia messages

| | | |
|---|---|---|
| MM_ADLIB | MM_MIM_CLOSE | MM_SNDBLST_MIDIIN |
| MM_JOY1BUTTONDOWN | MM_MIM_DATA | MM_SNDBLST_MIDIOUT |
| MM_JOY1BUTTONUP | MM_MIM_ERROR | MM_SNDBLST_SYNTH |
| MM_JOY1MOVE | MM_MIM_LONGDATA | MM_SNDBLST_WAVEIN |
| MM_JOY1ZMOVE | MM_MIM_LONGERROR | MM_SNDBLST_WAVEOUT |
| MM_JOY2BUTTONDOWN | MM_MIM_OPEN | MM_WAVE_MAPPER |
| MM_JOY2BUTTONUP | MM_MOM_CLOSE | MM_WIM_CLOSE |
| MM_JOY2MOVE | MM_MOM_DONE | MM_WIM_DATA |
| MM_JOY2ZMOVE | MM_MOM_OPEN | MM_WIM_OPEN |
| MM_MCINOTIFY | MM_MPU401_MIDIIN | MM_WOM_CLOSE |
| MM_MICROSOFT | MM_MPU401_MIDIOUT | MM_WOM_DONE |
| MM_MIDI_MAPPER | MM_PC_JOYSTICK | MM_WOM_OPEN |

**Table 22.12**    Other messages and messages not documented by Microsoft

| | | |
|---|---|---|
| wm_alttabactive | wm_entersizemove | WM_MDIRESTORE |
| wm_begindrag | wm_exitmenuloop | WM_MDISETMENU |
| WM_COALESCE_FIRST | wm_exitsizemove | WM_MDITILE |
| WM_COALESCE_LAST | wm_filesyschange | WM_MEASUREITEM |
| WM_COMMNOTIFY | wm_gethotkey | WM_NEXTDLGCTL |
| WM_COMPAREITEM | wm_isactiveicon | wm_nextmenu |
| wm_convertrequest | WM_KEYFIRST | wm_querydropobject |
| wm_convertresult | wm_lbtrackpoint | wm_queryparkicon |
| WM_DELETEITEM | WM_MDIACTIVATE | wm_sethotkey |
| wm_dragloop | WM_MDICASCADE | wm_setvisible |
| wm_dragmove | WM_MDICREATE | wm_sizewait |
| wm_dragselect | WM_MDIDESTROY | wm_syncpaint |
| WM_DRAWITEM | WM_MDIGETACTIVE | wm_synctask |
| WM_DROPFILES | WM_MDIICONARRANGE | WM_SYSTEMERROR |
| wm_dropobject | WM_MDIMAXIMIZE | wm_systimer |
| wm_entermenuloop | WM_MDINEXT | wm_testing |

# 23

# WinSpector

WinSpector is a tool that helps you perform *postmortem debugging* (debugging after your program has ungracefully terminated) of Unrecoverable Application Errors (UAEs) and General Protection Faults (GPFs). When a UAE or GPF occurs, WinSpector writes a log file to your disk that shows you helpful information about the cause of the exception, including

- The call stack that was active when an exception occurred
- Function and procedure names in the call stack
- CPU registers
- A disassembly of the machine instructions where the exception occurred
- Windows information about the program environment

Before using WinSpector, be sure that TOOLHELP.DLL (from Windows 3.1 or later) is in your search path (TOOLHELP.DLL ships with Windows). TOOLHELP.DLL is a Windows DLL that lets utilities access low-level system information. WinSpector uses TOOLHELP.DLL to log exceptions and to obtain the system information it writes to the log file. Don't use other exception debugging tools, except for Turbo Debugger, while running with WinSpector.

There are three ways to start WinSpector (it loads minimized):

- Include it in the "load=" section of your WIN.INI file.
- Include it in the Startup folder in Windows.
- Double-click the WinSpector icon to run WinSpector after you load Windows.

When an exception (UAE or GPF) occurs, WinSpector creates a *report* in a file called WINSPCTR.LOG (a text file) with information to help you determine what caused the error. WinSpector also creates a file called WINSPCTR.BIN, a binary file that the DFA utility translates into a text file called DFA.OUT (see page 17 for more information on DFA.EXE).

After the exception, WinSpector displays a dialog box with a brief exception report. Click OK to remove the box and read the log file to find the cause of the exception. You can control the output to WINSPCTR.LOG as described in the following section.

# Configuring WINSPCTR.LOG

There are two ways you can set the WinSpector options that control the output to WINSPCTR.LOG:

- To use the WinSpector Preferences dialog box, start WinSpector, click the WinSpector icon and choose Preferences from the pop-up menu.

- To edit commands in WINSPCTR.INI, load the file into any text editor, edit or add commands, then save the file and restart WinSpector.

The following paragraphs describe each option in the Preferences dialog box. WINSPCTR.INI options are listed in bold.

**LogDir=[directory]:** Directory is the location of WINSPCTR.LOG. Type the path where you want the file (C:WINDOWS is the default).

**LogViewer=[viewername]:** Viewer is the program WinSpector uses to display the log file. Type the path and file name of the viewer you want to use (NOTEPAD.EXE is the default). For example, type C:WIN31WRITE.EXE. If WinSpector can't find the editor, it displays the message Error: Unable to execute: [option], where *option* is the editor file name. Check to make sure the editor you indicated exists in the specified directory.

**CreateNewLog= 0 (append) or 1 (overwrite):** Append New Reports and Overwrite Previous Reports lets you control whether WinSpector appends reports to the existing log file or overwrites the old log file when a new report is generated.

**ShowSystemInfo= 0 (omit) or 1 (show):** Check System Information to add the Task List, the Module List, and information about the USER and GDI heaps to the log file.

**LogToStdAux=0 (on) or 1 (off):** Check AUX Summary to view an abbreviated form of the information sent to the log file on the AUX device. To use this option, you need a terminal connected to AUX or a device driver, such as OX.SYS, that redirects the AUX device to a second monitor.

**PostMortemDump= 1 (show) or 0 (omit):** Check PostMortem Dump to generate a WINSPCTR.BIN file. Use DFA.EXE to translate the BIN file into a text file you can read.

**ShowStackInfo= 1 (show) or 0 (omit):** Check Stack Frame Data to add a verbose stack trace display to the log file. For each stack frame that doesn't exceed 256 bytes, WinSpector performs a hex dump, starting at the SS:BP for that frame. If there are more than 256 bytes between two successive stack frames, the memory display is omitted for that frame. You can use this data to get the values of the parameters that were passed to the function.

It's usually easier to let DFA do the hard work of figuring out what your parameters are. However, for those cases where Turbo Debugger information is not available, you might find that a verbose trace supplies helpful information.

**ShowUserInfo= 1 (show) or 0 (omit):** Check User Comments if you want to add information to the log file about what was happening when the exception occurred. With User Comments checked, WinSpector displays a dialog box immediately after the exception. The comments you type are appended to the log file.

# WINSPCTR.LOG reference

Each report in WINSPCTR.LOG has several sections that help you determine what caused the exception in your program. The first line of a report in WINSPCTR.LOG gives the date and time when the exception occurred; for example,

```
WinSpector failure report - 6/18/1992 11:04:25
```

The second line lists

- What type of exception occurred ( lists frequent exceptions)
- The module name
- The logical address
- The physical address
- The currently active task at the time of the exception.

A second line might look like this:

```
Exception 13 at USER 002A:0429 (079F:0429)  (TASK=BAD)
```

**Table 23.1** Exception types

| Number | Name | Description |
|--------|------|-------------|
| 0 | Division by zero | Occurs during a DIV or an IDIV interaction if the divisor is 0. |
| 12 | Stack fault | Usually occurs when there is not enough room on the stack to proceed. |
| 13 | General protection fault (GPF) | All protection errors that don't cause another exception cause an exception 13. |

Exception 13 errors include, but are not limited to, the following errors:

- Invalid selector loaded into a segment register.

- Segment limit exceeded. Although the selector is valid, the offset value is greater than the segment limit (for example, an array index out of bounds error in DS, ES, or other segments).

- Execution is transferred to a nonexecutable segment, such as a bad function pointer.

- Accessing DS, ES, FS, or GS registers containing a null selector. (This error can cause a 0 to appear in the segment register of the log file.)

A log file lists both the physical and logical addresses where the exception occurred. These two types of addresses are important to Windows programs for the following reasons:

- When a program is loaded, Windows allocates space for each logical segment and assigns each segment a unique selector. The selector and its offset are combined to form a physical address.

- When a Windows .EXE file is linked, each segment is placed in a different section of the file, and a segment table is created.

- A logical address, which is actually a segment's position in the Windows segment table, consists of a module name, a logical segment, and an offset. You can run

TDUMP on the file to find out segment size and other information, or you can generate a .MAP file that contains the same kind of information.

If the stack pointer is too small at the time of exception, TOOLHELP.DLL automatically switches the stack and appends the message `Stack Switched` to the end of the second line of the log.

## Disassembly section

The Disassembly section in WINSPCTR.LOG begins with the assembly language instruction that caused the exception that is followed by the next few instructions in the program, which provide a point of reference for finding the task that caused the exception.

For example, given the following code, where ES is the segment register that contains a selector and BX is the offset into the segment, an exception 13 occurred because the value in BX was greater than the segment limit referenced by ES:

```
079F:0429   CMP     BYTE  PTR  ES:[BX],FF
079F:042D   JNE     043A
079F:042F   CMP     WORD PTR [BP+06],03
079F:0435   MOV     DI, 0001
```

## Stack Trace section

The first line of the Stack Trace section in WINSPCTR.LOG identifies the function or procedure that was executing at the time of the exception. Stack Trace information includes the

- Frame number.

- Module name.

- Name of the closest function before the address of the one that caused the exception, plus a number indicating how far away you were from that function. (This information is present only if a .SYM file is present.)

- Logical and physical address for the stack frame.

- Location where your program returns after the call.

When WinSpector lists function names, it looks in the .SYM file for the closest symbol name that appears before the address in the call stack. Since some .SYM files do not contain information for all functions, the function name in the log file is the closest function in the .SYM file with an address preceding the frame address. If the offset field appears to be too high, function names might not be reliable.

The following stack trace information shows some of the functions that were executing at the time BAD, a sample task, caused an exception:

```
Stack Trace:
0  User  <no info>
   CS:IP 002A:0429   (079F:0429)    SS:BP  10FF:18CA
   C:WIN31SYSTEMUSER.EXE
```

```
3   BAD  function5(unsigned long, unsigned long, unsigned long) + 0014
    CS:IP 0001:0184 (1107:0184)      SS:BP  10FF:1952
    C:BINBAD.EXE
```

## Register section

The Register section in WINSPCTR.LOG lists the values stored in the standard registers when the exception occurred, as the following example shows:

```
Registers:
AX    0037
BX    0000
CX    0008
DX    10EE
SI    0037
DI    0028
```

Limits and access rights are given for the CS, DS, ES, and SS registers.

## Message Queue section

The Message Queue section in WINSPCTR.LOG gives the last message received in the middle of processing. This section also lists any messages that were waiting in the queue at the time of exception. For each message, WinSpector lists the following information:

- The Window handle that identifies the destination window
- The Message ID number that identifies the message
- Two parameters that contain additional message information

**Note**   The Message Queue section might not list the last message the program received: Windows could bypass the message queue by using a *SendMessage* or similar function.

The following Message Queue example shows one message received and one waiting in the queue:

```
Message Queue:
Last message received:
   hWnd: 0000   msg: 0001   wParam: 0002   lParam: 00000003
Waiting in queue:
   hWnd: 0000   msg: 0001   wParam: 0002   lParam: 00000003
```

## Tasks section

The Tasks section in WINSPCTR.LOG lists the programs running when the exception occurred, including the

- Complete path to the executable file
- Module name
- Windows module handle
- Task handle
- Data segment value for the task (the instance handle)

Some of the tasks running when the BAD application caused an exception include

```
C:WIN31SYSTEMNWPOPUP.EXE
    Module: NWPOPUP   hModule: 142F   hTask: 141F   hInstance: 13F6
```

```
C:BINWINSPCTR.EXE
   Module: WINSPCTR    hModule: 1397    hTask: 1387    hInstance: 135E


C:BINBAD.EXE
   Module: BAD    hModule: 1467    hTask: 1127    hInstance: 10FE
```

## Modules section

The Modules section in WINSPCTR.LOG lists the modules that were running at the
time of the exception, including the

- Path to the executable file
- Date stamp of the executable file
- File size
- Module name
- Module handle
- Reference count indicating how many times the module is in use

Three of the modules running when the BAD application caused an exception include

```
C:WIN31SYSTEMKRNL386.EXE    Date: 03/02/1992    Size: 116132
   Module: KERNEL    hModule: 010F    reference count: 21
C:WIN31SYSTEMSYSTEM.DRV    Date: 03/01/1992    Size: 2304
   Module: SYSTEM    hModule: 013F    reference count: 13

C:CBINWINSPCTR.EXE         Date: 06/02/1992    Size: 46256
   Module: WINSPCTR    hModule: 1397 reference count: 1
```

## USER and GDI heap section

The USER and GDI (graphics device interface) heap information section in
WINSPCTR.LOG shows what percentage of the USER and GDI heaps was available at
the time of exception. For example,

```
USER    Free    91%
GDI     Free    83%
```

Because Windows has only 64K of internal heap space for applications to share, it's
often helpful to keep track of how the space is used. If you find that USER and GDI are
taking up a lot of heap space, check to see if you have deallocated resources you are not
using. The Help | About box for Program Manager lists the lower of these values as the
amount of free System Resources.

## System Information section

The System Information section in WINSPCTR.LOG shows the Windows version and
mode you're running, including

- CPU type
- Largest free block of contiguous linear memory in the system
- Total linear address space in pages
- Amount of free memory pages in the linear address space
- Number of pages in the system swap file

The System Information section for a 486 system might look like this:

```
System info: Running in enhanced mode under Windows 3.1 debug version
CPU: 80486
Largest free memory block: 3457024 bytes
Total linear memory space: 19696 K
Free linear memory space : 18212 K
Swap file Pages:           0 (0 K)
```

# Processing WinSpector data

DFA is a utility that takes a WINSPCTR.BIN file and Turbo Debugger information (either in the .EXE, .DLL or .TDS files) and translates the binary data into a useful form by generating a file that contains not only stack trace information similar to the log file but also function names, line numbers, and local and global variables.

DFA post-processes Turbo Debugger information that WinSpector gathered at the time of the exception. If you check the PostMortem dump option (see page 12), WinSpector creates a WINSPCTR.BIN file at the time of the exception. You can use DFA.EXE to translate the binary data in WINSPCTR.BIN into usable information stored in a text file called DFA.OUT.

Because only one WINSPCTR.BIN file is written per Windows session, make sure you run DFA promptly. For example, if you get three UAEs in succession, WinSpector will write three reports to the log file, but binary data will exist for only the first report. It's best to run DFA immediately after receiving the first UAE. You might then want to rename the DFA.OUT file and delete the WINSPCTR.BIN and WINSPCTR.LOG files before continuing.

## DFA output

DFA writes a file only if Turbo Debugger information exists for the file in the stack frame. The DFA output file (DFA.OUT) has a stack trace similar to the one in the WinSpector log file, except that it contains

- Function names
- Line numbers
- Local and global variables
- Data segments and their values (including the stack segment)

## Using DFA with WINSPCTR.LOG

When DFA is used with the WINSPCTR.LOG file alone, it gives minimal stack trace information, such as addresses. If Turbo Debugger information (contained in a .EXE, .DLL, or .TDS file) is present, source file names and line numbers are added to the report.

## Using DFA with WINSPCTR.BIN

When used with the WINSPCTR.BIN file, DFA

- Adds stack-based variables to the log, including local variables, parameters passed to the function, structures, and arrays.

- Lists variable types, values, and addresses by function.

If Turbo Debugger information is present, for each stack frame, DFA reports

- In section one, the
    - Source file
    - Line number
    - Local variables
    - Parameters

- In section two, the
    - Module name for the task with the fault
    - File names
    - Logical segments
    - The segments' selectors
    - Whether the segments are data or code segments

- In section three, the
    - Global variables
    - Static variables
    - The variables' values at the time of the exception

The format is

```
DFA [option] WINSPCTR.LOG [WINSPCTR.BIN]
```

When WINSPCTR.LOG (required) is present, you get source file and line numbers. When WINSPCTR.BIN (optional) is present, you get additional variable information.

**Table 23.2**   DFA options

| Option | What it does |
| --- | --- |
| /O[outputfile] | Renames the output file from the DFA.OUT default |
| /D | Forces DFA to write a hex dump of the saved data segments |

# Other WinSpector tools

WinSpector has three utilities you can use to enhance the information about an exception:

- EXEMAP.EXE creates a .MAP file from a Windows .EXE file. The .MAP file is needed to create a .SYM file, which expands error reporting for the original .EXE.

- TMAPSYM.EXE, used in conjunction with EXEMAP.EXE, creates a .SYM file from a .MAP file.

- BUILDSYM.EXE uses EXEMAP.EXE and TMAPSYM.EXE to create a .SYM file from a Windows .EXE file.

## Using EXEMAP.EXE

EXEMAP creates .MAP files for Windows executables. A .MAP file can be used to create a .SYM file, which can then be used by WinSpector to expand its error reporting. If you are using .DLLs or other programs for which you don't have the source code, this information can be especially useful.

To create a .MAP file from an .EXE, type EXEMAP filename.EXE newname.MAP. If you don't type a new name, EXEMAP creates a .MAP file with the same name as the .EXE.

Although the resulting .MAP file isn't as complete as one generated by the link phase of the compile process, it does include addresses for exported public functions.

## Using TMAPSYM.EXE

TMAPSYM creates .SYM files from existing .MAP files (created either by the compiler or by the EXEMAP utility). The resulting .SYM files make available to WinSpector the public functions, variable names, and functions in the entry table of the executable. Constants and line-number information, however, are not included in a TMAPSYM-generated .SYM file.

To create a .SYM file from a .MAP file, type TMAPSYM filename.MAP (you must type the .MAP extension).

## Using BUILDSYM.EXE

BUILDSYM creates .SYM files from .EXE files. It has the same output as using both EXEMAP and TMAPSYM, since it automatically runs them, but it deletes the .MAP files from your directory. BUILDSYM supports wildcards, so you can create .SYM files for part or all of a directory by entering a single command.

To run BUILDSYM, both EXEMAP and TMAPSYM must be in the same directory as BUILDSYM or in your search path. BUILDSYM places the .SYM files it creates in the current directory. For WinSpector to find a .SYM file, the file must be in the same directory as the executable that caused the exception.

BUILDSYM performs the following tasks:

- Verifies that the files are Windows files, and if not, leaves them alone.

- Calls EXEMAP to create .MAP files.

- Verifies that .MAP files were created.

- Calls TMAPSYM and passes the names of the new .MAP files so TMAPSYM can create .SYM files.

- Deletes the .MAP files because they are no longer needed.

To create a .SYM file from an .EXE, type BUILDSYM filename.EXE.

# IV

# Turbo Profiler user's guide

Borland's Turbo Profiler is the missing link in your software development cycle. Once you have your code doing what you want, Turbo Profiler helps you do it faster and more efficiently. It is a performance analyzer and a resource monitor.

Turbo Profiler is a performance analyzer, a software tool that measures your program's performance by finding

- Where your program spends its time
- How many times a line executes
- What lines have been executed
- How many times a routine is called, and by which routines
- What files your program accesses most and for how long

Turbo Profiler also monitors critical computer resources, such as
- Processor time
- Disk access
- Keyboard input
- Printer output
- Interrupt activity

By monitoring vital activities and providing detailed statistical reports on every part of your program's performance, Turbo Profiler enables you to fine-tune your programs. By opening up the inside of your program and exposing its most intricate operations—from execution times to statement counts, from interrupt calls to file access activities—Turbo Profiler helps you polish your code and speed up your programs.

Turbo Profiler surpasses other profilers on the market both in power and ease of use by providing the following features:

- Interactive profiling quickly reveals inefficient code in a program.

- Lets you read and edit any text file during profiling sessions.

- Profiles any size program that runs under DOS or Windows.

- Handles programs written using Borland's C++ compilers and Turbo Assembler.

- Provides an easy-to-use interface with multiple overlapping windows, mouse support, and context-sensitive help.

- Reports execution time and execution count for routines and program lines.

- Tracks which blocks of code have and haven't been executed.

- Tracks complete call path history for all routines. Analyzes frequency of calls with complete call stack tracing.

- Monitors DOS file activities from the Files window by file handle and time of open, close, read, or write. Uses an event list to log the number of bytes read or written.

- Supports complete tracking of overlays.

- Allows remote serial and network profiling.

By picking up where code optimizers leave off, Turbo Profiler directs you immediately to slow code, pointing out where to open up bottlenecks and when to rework algorithms.

# The difference between optimizing and profiling

An optimizer makes your program run a little faster by replacing time-consuming instructions with less-expensive ones. But optimizing can't fix inefficient code.

Turbo Profiler helps you detect the least efficient part of your code and helps point to algorithms that can be modified or rewritten. Studies show that the largest performance improvements in programs come from changing algorithms and data structures, rather than from optimizing small segments of compiled code. Trying to find program bottlenecks without a profiler is like trying to find bugs without a debugger; Turbo Profiler reduces both the time and effort it takes to improve your program's performance.

# How this part is organized

Part IV is divided into the following chapters:

**Chapter 24, "A sample profiling session,"** is a tutorial that takes you through a simple profiling session. The tutorial starts with a "let's see what's going on" profile, then takes you through interpreting the profile data collected, modifying and refining the program based on insight gained from the profile, and running additional profiles to gauge the effect of each successive modification.

**Chapter 25, "The Turbo Profiler environment,"** explains in detail each menu item and dialog box option in the Turbo Profiler environment.

**Chapter 26, "Profiling strategies,"** provides general guidelines and tips for conducting a fruitful profiling session.

**Chapter 27, "Inside the profiler,"** uses analogy to explain how Turbo Profiler gathers execution-time and execution-count data while your program runs.

**Chapter 28, "Turbo Profiler's command-line options,"** lists each Turbo Profiler command-line option and explains what the option accomplishes.

**Chapter 29, "Customizing Turbo Profiler,"** explains how to use TFINST to change the configuration defaults of TPROF and TPROFW.

**Chapter 30, "Remote profiling,"** describes how to profile with two systems; you run your program on one and Turbo Profiler on the other.

**Chapter 31, "Turbo Profiler for Windows,"** describes how to run Turbo Profiler for Windows and how to use its special features.

**Chapter 32, "Prompts and error messages,"** lists all prompts and error messages that can occur, with suggestions on how to respond to them.

Chapter

# 24

# A sample profiling session

Profiling is one of the least-understood yet most useful and vital areas of good software development. Surveys indicate that only a small fraction of professional programmers actually use profilers to improve their code. Other studies show that, most of the time, even the best programmers guess wrong about where the bottlenecks are in their programs.

What is the advantage to using this widely overlooked tool? For one, profiling your program can increase its overall performance. Second, profiling can augment your ability to produce efficient code. The bottom line is that profiling, like debugging, can be a cog in the wheel of the program development cycle.

We've based the examples in this chapter on John Bentley's "Programming Pearls" column (July 1987) in *Communications of the ACM*.

In this chapter we show you an example of profiling put to good use, and how—in the long run—profiling can save you hours of hunting for that expensive line of code. You use Turbo Profiler to:

- See where your program spends its time.
- Create an annotated source listing and a profile statistics report.
- Save profile statistics, then start up again with saved statistics.
- Analyze profile statistics and source code in side-by-side windows.

All the tutorial examples were run on a 486 machine with an SVGA video adapter.

The examples in this chapter are based on finding and printing all prime numbers between 1 and 1,000. Recall that a number is prime if it is an integer and is divisible by only the integer 1 and itself; it must also be odd, since any even number is divisible by 2 and therefore is not prime (actually, 2 is the only even prime number). You can tell whether a particular number is prime by checking to see if it is divisible by other, smaller primes, or by any integer larger than the first two primes, 2 and 3.

The object of profiling the example programs is to speed up the process of finding and printing the prime numbers. As you work through the examples, you'll learn how to use Turbo Profiler to test the efficiency of each example's structure.

The first program you'll look at is PRIME0. Once you've profiled it and seen where to modify the code, all you need to do is load and profile PRIME1. With the exception of PRIME1, each of the programs covered in this chapter (PRIME2, PRIME3, PRIME4, and PRIME5) is a variation on its predecessor.

## About the sample programs

The Turbo Profiler package comes complete with the sample programs used in this chapter. Both the source code and the executable code are provided; Turbo Profiler requires both to analyze a program. Each of the sample programs was compiled with full symbolic information, since the profiler also requires this information.

To ensure that your own programs contain full symbolic information, you must compile them with the appropriate compiler options turned on, as shown in the following list:

- **Borland's line of C++ compilers:** If you are compiling in the IDE,

  1 Choose Options | Project.

  2 Choose the Compiler | Debugging topic, then check Include Debug Information.

  3 Choose the Linker | General topic, then check Include Debug Information.

  If you are compiling from the command line, use the –v command-line option.

- **Turbo Assembler:** Use the /zi command-line option, then link the program with TLINK, using the /v option.

# Profiling a program (PRIME0)

You profile and improve a program in four steps:

1 Set up the program before profiling it.

2 Collect data while the program runs.

3 Analyze the collected data.

4 Modify the program and recompile it.

After modifying your program, repeat steps 1 through 3 to see if the modifications have improved your program's performance.

PRIME0 uses Euclid's method of testing for prime numbers, a straightforward integer test for a remainder after division. As each prime number is found, it is stored in the array *primes*, and each successive number is tested for "primeness" by being divided by each of the numbers already stored in *primes*.

Leaving Turbo Profiler at any time is a simple, one-step procedure: just choose **File | Quit** or press *Alt+X*.

Load PRIME0 into Turbo Profiler by typing

    TPROF PRIME0

and pressing *Enter.*

The profiler comes up with two windows open: the Module window (which displays PRIME0's source code) and the Execution Profile window (which will display profile statistics after you run PRIME0).

**Figure 24.1**  Turbo Profiler with PRIME0 loaded

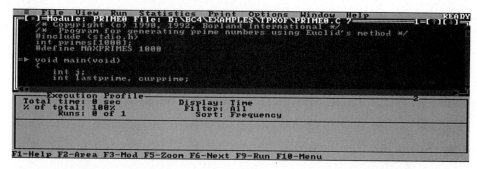

For a more detailed description of the profiler's environment, see Chapter 25, "The Turbo Profiler environment."

The Module and Execution Profile windows are concerned with steps 1 and 3 in the profiling process. You use the Module window to determine what parts of the program to profile. Once you run a program, the Execution Profile window displays the information you need to analyze your program's behavior.

## Setting up the profile options

Before you begin to profile your program, you might want to specify the areas you want to profile. An *area* is a location in your program where you want to collect statistics: an area can be a single line, a construct such as a loop, or an entire routine.

To analyze a small number of short routines (like **prime** and **main** in this program), you have to know how often each line executes and how much time each line takes. To get this information, every line in the program must be marked as an area.

By default, Turbo Profiler marks every line in a small program. To verify that this is true, you can check the Module window to see that all executable lines are tagged with a marker symbol (=➤).

1   Press *Alt+F10* to open the Module window SpeedMenu.

2   Choose Add Areas from the SpeedMenu. This menu lists area boundaries for you to choose from.

3   Choose Every Line in Module. This sets area markers for all lines in the module, then returns the cursor to the Module window.

## Collecting data

Now you're ready for the second step in the profiling process. Press *F9* to run PRIME0 under Turbo Profiler. The program prints the prime numbers between 1 and 1,000 on your screen. When the program finishes, look at the information in the Execution Profile window. These are your *program statistics*.

Zoom the Execution Profile window: Press *F5* or choose Zoom from the Window menu. The Execution Profile window should now look similar to this:

**Figure 24.2**   Program statistics, PRIME0

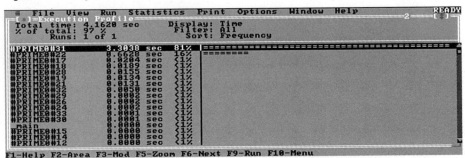

The upper pane of the Execution Profile window displays the program's total execution time, along with information about the data in the lower pane. The lower pane has four fields for each line:

- An area name
- The number of seconds spent in that area
- The percentage of total execution time spent in that area
- A *magnitude bar* displaying a proportional graph of the execution time spent in that area

The line

```
#PRIME0#31   3.3038 sec   81%   |=======================================
```

tells you that the thirty-first line of code in module PRIME0 executed for about 3.3 seconds—which was 81 percent of the total execution time for all marked areas. The magnitude bar automatically shows line 31's time full-scale because line 31 is the most time-consuming of the marked areas.

Actual time and percentage statistics will vary from system to system.

## Displaying statistics

You can also display this program's collected data as *execution counts*.

**1** Press *Alt+F10* to bring up the SpeedMenu for the Execution Profile window.

**Figure 24.3**    The SpeedMenu

```
Display...
Filter      All ▶

Module
Remove
```

**2** Choose Display on the SpeedMenu.

**3** The Display Options dialog box lists six possible ways to display data in the Execution Profile window.

**Figure 24.4**    The Display Options dialog box

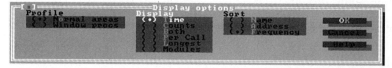

- Time (the default setting) shows the total time spent in each marked area.
- Counts displays the number of times program control entered each area.
- Both shows time and counts data on the same screen.
- Per Call displays the average amount of time per call.
- Longest shows the longest time spent in each area.
- Modules (used with passive analysis) displays the time spent in each program module.

**4** Choose Counts under Display in this dialog box. (Click Counts with the mouse, or use the arrow keys to move to it and press *Enter*, or press *C*, the hot key for this option.)

**5** Choose OK (or press *Enter*).

The Execution Profile window now displays PRIME0's statistics as execution counts instead of execution times, as shown in this figure:

**Figure 24.5**    Counts display in the Execution Profile window

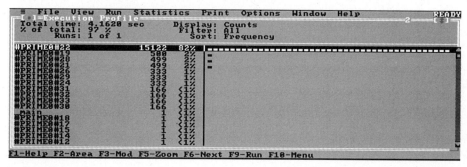

This display of PRIME0's statistics shows that line 22 is the most frequently called line in PRIME0.

You can also see counts and times together. Bring up the Display Options dialog box again (either press *Alt+F10* and choose Display, or press *Ctrl+D*).

Choose Both under Display, then choose OK or press *Enter*. (To choose Both, either click it, or press *Down* to get to it, then press *Enter*, or press *B*, the hot key for this option.)

When the Execution Profile window displays time and counts together, the first entry for each area is execution counts, and the second is execution time.

# Printing modules and statistics

In this section, you print two things:

**1** A profile source listing of the code that's in the Module window, with time and counts data attached to each marked area.

**2** The profile statistics displayed in the Execution Profile window.

## Time and counts profile listing

Before you print the time-and-counts statistics to a file, you must first set the appropriate printing options:

**1** Choose Print | Options.

**2** In the Printing Options dialog box, choose the File radio button (press *Tab* until the radio buttons become active, then press *Down* to turn the setting to File).

**3** Tab to the Destination File input box and type

```
PRIME0SC.LST
```

**4** Choose ASCII to use the standard ASCII character set (rather than the IBM extended character set).

**5** Choose OK (or press *Enter*).

The cursor returns to the active Execution Profile window.

Now, to print the listing file, choose Print | Module. In the Pick a Module dialog box, press *Down* to highlight the module name PRIME0, then press *Enter* (or choose OK).

To inspect the file PRIME0SC.LST, choose View | Text File, and at the File Name prompt, type

```
PRIME0SC.LST
```

This is what you see if you're profiling the C program PRIME0.C. The times in your file will probably vary from the ones shown here because of the differences in computer systems.

```
Turbo Profiler  Version 4.5  Tue Aug 20 15:16:47 1995

Program: D:TPROFPRIME0.EXE  File prime0.c

Time  Counts
```

```
                /* Copyright (c) 1990, Borland International */
                /*  Program for generating prime numbers using
                     Euclid's method */
                int primes[1000];
                #define MAXPRIMES 1000

0.0000 1        main()
                {
                    int j;
                    int lastprime, curprime;

0.0000 1            primes[0] = 2;
0.0000 1            primes[1] = 3;
0.0000 1            lastprime = 1;
0.0000 1            curprime  = 3;

0.0359 1            printf("prime %d = %d \n", 0, primes[0]);
0.0354 1            printf("prime %d = %d \n", 1, primes[1]);
0.0059 500          while(curprime < MAXPRIMES)
                    {
0.0071 499             for(j = 0; j <= lastprime; j++)
0.3069 15122              if((curprime % primes[j]) == 0)
                          {
0.0038 333                   curprime += 2;

0.0034 333                   break;
                          }
0.0060 499             if(j <= lastprime)
0.0037 333                continue;
0.0017 166             lastprime++;
6.2655 166             printf("prime %d = %d \n", last prime, curprime);
0.0019 166             primes[lastprime] = curprime;
0.0018 166             curprime += 2;
                    }
0.0000 1        }
```

This profile source listing is useful because it's a permanent record that shows, for each area in your program, the execution time and execution counts.

When you have finished examining the listing, press *Alt+F3*, or click the close box, to close the File window.

## Profile statistics report

You can also print a replica of the open Execution Profile window's contents to your printer or to a disk file.

1 Choose Print | Options again.

2 Choose the Printer radio button.

**3** Choose Graphics to include extended ASCII characters in the printed report. (If your printer does not support extended ASCII characters such as É and Ê, skip this step and proceed to step 4.)

**4** Press *Enter* (or choose OK).

**5** Choose Print | Statistics.

The resulting printout, like the profile source listing, is a permanent record of your progress as you go through the steps of profiling, modifying, recompiling, and reprofiling in your quest for the sleekest and most efficient code possible (and practical) for your program.

## Saving and restoring statistics

Before you go on, here's how to save PRIME0's profile statistics to a file, so you can quit Turbo Profiler at any time without losing the data. We also show you how to restore those statistics the next time you start Turbo Profiler.

Choose Statistics | Save to save your program's profile statistics to a .TFS (Turbo Profiler Statistics) file. Because PRIME0 is in the Module window, the File Name input box lists PRIME0.TFS as the default. Choose OK to create this file. All the statistical data from the current profile run of PRIME0 is now saved in the file PRIME0.TFS in the current directory, so you can quit the profiler at any time without losing any of that information.

To restore the statistics you saved for PRIME0, open PRIME0 in Turbo Profiler and choose Statistics | Restore. The File Name input box lists *.TFS as the default. Press *Enter* to go to the Files list box, then highlight PRIME0.TFS and choose OK to recover the data from this file.

The File Name input box lists *.TFS as the default. Press Enter to go to the Files list box, then highlight PRIME0.TFS and choose OK to recover the data from this file.

## Analyzing the statistics

In this section you will learn how to analyze the statistics in the Execution Profile window so you can use what they reveal to streamline your program.

First, though, take another look at the time and count statistics in the Execution Profile window. Unzoom the Execution Profile window (choose Zoom from the Window menu or press *F5*) and look at the statistics for lines 22 and 31 (the **if** and **printf** statements).

We cover modifications to the **printf** statement in program PRIME5.

A time and count profile like this tells a lot about a program. For instance, you can see that line 22 in PRIME0 executes far more frequently than any other statement. It makes sense that line 22 executes 15,122 times, since it tests every number between 4 and 1,000 against every number in the array *primes*, until there is even division or the array is exhausted. That means a lot of numbers to be tested. You can also see that line 31, the **printf** statement, accounts for most of the program's total execution time.

# Viewing both source code and statistics

The data in the Execution Profile window shows that the test in line 22 is doing more work than it should. But you can't really get the entire picture until you look at execution time and count data and source code together.

What you need to do is compare time and count data in the Execution Profile window and the corresponding source code in the Module window.

Here's one way to display source code and profile statistics simultaneously:

1  Resize and move the Execution Profile window so it occupies the right half of your screen: Choose Window | Size | Move, or press *Ctrl+F5*.

2  Follow the directions on the status line to:

   1  Resize the window to full-screen height and half-screen width.

   2  Move the resized window to the right.

   When you've done steps 1 and 2, press *Enter*.

3  Activate the Module window by pressing *F6*, then resize and move it so it occupies the left half of the screen.

4  Go back to the Execution Profile window (press *F6* again).

To resize a window with the mouse, drag the Resize box in the lower right corner; to move the window, drag the title bar or any double-line left or top border character (‖ or =).

There is an automatic link between the Execution Profile window and the Module window, so that when you move through the source code, the execution profile display tracks the cursor's current line position. To see this tracking feature in action,

1  Activate the Execution Profile window (press *F6*), and move the highlight bar to the first line.

2  Open the SpeedMenu (press *Alt+F10*) and choose Module (or just press *Ctrl+M*).

   The profiler positions the cursor on line 31 in the Module window.

3  Use the arrow keys to move through the source code to line 22.

   This line is the second-largest time consumer in PRIME0. The top two statistics lines in the Execution Profile window now display the profile data for this **if** statement.

4  Move the cursor in the Module window to line 21 and note how the display in the Execution Profile window tracks with it. The top lines in the Execution Profile window are now the profile statistics for line 21.

5  Move the cursor to line 30 and note the display in the Execution Profile window.

Having the two windows synchronized this way makes it easy to find the greatest resource hogs in your program. Once you get a better feel for interpreting the data onscreen, you won't need to rely as much on profile listings like the one on page 372.

## Saving the window configuration

This is a good time to save your customized version of Turbo Profiler. If you don't save your customized window arrangement, the windows will revert to their default size and placement the next time you load a program into Turbo Profiler.

1 Choose Options | Save Options. This brings up the Save Configuration dialog box.

2 By default, the Options check box is already checked. This records settings (such as the Execution Profile window's display options) in the configuration file.

3 In the Save Configuration dialog box, tab to Layout and press *Spacebar*. This causes your side-by-side window layout to be saved in the configuration file.

4 By default, the configuration file to be saved is TFCONFIG.TF, listed in the Save To input box. Choose OK, or press *Enter*, to save your options to this file in the current directory.

Wherever you start up Turbo Profiler, it looks for TFCONFIG.TF, the default configuration file. When the profiler finds that file, the options and layout you've set will come up automatically.

## Measuring an area's efficiency

The ratio of execution time to execution counts is a good measure of a line's or routine's overall efficiency. To see this ratio for the areas in PRIME0, change the display option in the Execution Profile window. Here's how:

1 From the Execution Profile window's SpeedMenu (press *Alt+F10*), choose Display.

2 Under Display in the dialog box, choose Per Call.

3 Choose OK (or press *Enter*).

Now you can see that line 22 is much more efficient than line 31. It uses up a lot of execution time because it executes so many times, but each individual call averages much less than a millisecond. Line 31, on the other hand, averages nearly 20 milliseconds per call.

**Note**  The output from the profiler points the way to improving the execution time of PRIME0 and making it structurally simple. The task of improving the program can be divided into two strategies:

1 Reduce the amount of time spent in input/output.

2 Rewrite the looping structure to be more streamlined and efficient.

The input/output problem can be partially resolved by reducing the **printf** statement from its present form

```
printf("prime %d = %d \n", last prime, curprime);
```

to simply

```
printf("%d\n", curprime);
```

Just this simple modification results in a considerable savings in the execution time. However, you can't reduce the number of times you call the output statement; for the given problem, there will always be 168 primes to print out. And apart from this minor improvement, there is not a great deal you can do to speed up the execution of PRIME0. Its algorithm, which requires saving all the previous results in an array and then using them to divide, is thorough but virtually impossible to streamline. (It's also not very memory-efficient, because the array requires an allocation of memory equal to the number of primes being tested. Eventually this imposes a limit on the number of primes that could be tested without running out of memory.)

Fortunately, there is a better way to test for prime numbers: You can change the algorithm itself. That's what happens in the next example program, PRIME1.

# A modularized primes test (PRIME1)

You're finished with PRIME0 now, so load PRIME1 (the next version of the prime number program) into the Module window and look at the code:

1 Choose File | Open.

2 By default, the File Name input box is activated and contains the file-name mask *.EXE. Press *Enter*.

3 In the Files list box, use the *Up* and *Down* keys to highlight PRIME1.EXE.

4 Press *Enter*. Turbo Profiler loads PRIME1 into the Module window.

5 Zoom the Module window (press *F5*). Note the added **prime** (*Prime*) routine on line 4.

You can see right away that two major changes have occurred:

• The array *primes* is gone. This program does not test by dividing each number by all smaller primes; it simply uses a loop to divide by all the odd numbers up to but not including the suspected prime. Initially this algorithm results in more iterations, but we will see that it eventually can be refined into a more streamlined and readable program.

• The prime number test itself has been placed in a separate routine that is called from the main program.

Run PRIME1 in Turbo Profiler (press *F9*) and look at the statistics. Then choose Display from the Execution Profile window SpeedMenu to open the Display Options dialog box and turn on the Both radio button. Press *Enter*, then zoom the Execution Profile window (*F5*).

The execution time has improved somewhat (this is due in part to the fact that PRIME1 prints out less information than PRIME0). The main bottleneck is still the **printf** statement (now line 21).

Notice in particular that the test for prime numbers (line 9 in PRIME0) now executes 78,022 times instead of 15,122. This may be surprising at first, but notice that it only increases execution time for this line by about 1 second; we have already seen that this statement is time-efficient.

One obvious way to improve efficiency, now that we have isolated the test loop in a separate routine, is to cut down on the number of calls to the routine. There are ways of limiting the number of integers that have to be passed to the routine for testing; the more you can eliminate at the main program level, the fewer calls you have to make and the faster your program executes. That is the strategy we employ in the next sample programs.

# Modifying the program and reprofiling

Earlier, we pointed out that instead of testing for all factors between 1 and *n* in the modulus statement, you can set the upper limit of the test to the square root of the number you're testing. That's what we've done in program PRIME2 (PRIME2PA).

## Loading another program (PRIME2)

Go ahead and load PRIME2, the next version of the sample program, into the Module window. In program PRIME2, we've added a **root** (*Root*) routine that calls a square root library routine and returns an integer result.

You need to set areas for all lines in the module, so bring up the SpeedMenu in the Module window, choose Add Areas I Every Line, then press *Enter*.

Press *F9* to start profiling. Once again, you'll see the primes between 1 and 1,000 print to the user screen.

When the program finishes running, open the Display Options dialog box (choose Display from the Execution Profile SpeedMenu) and set Display to *Both*. Choose OK. Despite decreasing the number of calls to line 15 (from 78,022 to 5,288) and reducing the time spent in the same statement, there's still a substantial increase in overall execution time.

The problem with PRIME2 is the expense of the new root routine. Line 7 inside the routine executes 5,456 times, consuming the most time of any routine.

When the Execution Profile window shows both time and count information, certain patterns are worth looking for. In inefficient routines, the second line (time data) is much longer than the first line (count data), which means the ratio of time to counts is high. This is the case for line 27, the **printf** statement.

When a routine's time:count ratio is high, the best thing to do is substitute another routine.

However, the **return** statement in the **root** routine (line 7) presents a different problem. It accounts for the largest number of calls and the largest amount of time. Two other lines (line 5 and line 8) have 5,456 calls, but the magnitude bar for each of these cases shows small execution times. This is good: It means the statements are fast. So the biggest problem right now is the number of calls made to the **root** routine.

## Reducing calls to a routine (PRIME3)

The problem now is to reduce the number of calls to the **root** routine. Load PRIME3 into the Module window, then zoom the Module window and take a look at the source code.

In PRIME3, the only routine modified is **prime**. We've added a new integer variable, *limit*, and set *limit* equal to **root**(*n*) before entering the **for** loop. The test in the **for** loop is based on *limit*.

In the Module window SpeedMenu, set areas to Every Line in Module. When you profile the program this time (choose Run | Run or press *F9*), the program runs quite a bit faster. PRIME3 shows an almost 25 percent decrease in total execution time.

The **printf** routine is now the major resource consumer, eating up over half the execution time. By reducing the number of calls to the square root routine in **root** (from 5,456 to 999), we've decreased computational time substantially.

## Still more efficiency (PRIME4)

There are still more ways to increase the efficiency of the **prime** routine. Load PRIME4 into the Module window now, then examine lines 8 through 17 of the source code.

```
/****** PRIME4.C ******/

if (n % 2 == 0)
   return (n==2);

if (n % 3 == 0)
   return (n==3);

if (n % 5 == 0)
   return (n==5);

for (i=7; i*i <= n; i+=2)
   if (n % i == 0)
      return 0;

return 1;
```

There are a number of improvements here.

- The three **if** statements in the **prime** routine weed out factors that are multiples of 2, 3, and 5, respectively. If you can't throw out a number *n* based on one of these tests, you must test the remaining numbers, up to the root of *n*. You can start at the value 7—the **if** statements have eliminated all possibilities below this number.

- The **for** loop now increments by two on each iteration, because there's no point in testing even numbers.

- The test `i * i <= n` has replaced the more expensive test involving the **root** routine.

The net result is that we've shaved nearly half a second off the execution time.

## Eliminating CR/LF pairs (PRIME5)

Here's one last change. Instead of printing a carriage return/linefeed pair after each prime number, try printing just a space. This is the only change made in program PRIME5.

Load PRIME5, set areas for every line, then run it.

Surprise! Eliminating the carriage return/linefeed pair cuts execution time by a factor of almost 7. Apparently, printing newline characters is expensive. The distribution of profiles is fairly even for execution times and counts. We'd be hard-pressed to squeeze more out of this program without substantially changing the algorithm.

## Where to now?

We've taken you through the basics of profiling in this tutorial. By now, you should be familiar with using Turbo Profiler: loading and profiling programs, printing the contents of various windows, saving and restoring profile statistics, and rearranging the windows so you can analyze the statistics.

Go ahead and quit Turbo Profiler now (choose File I Quit, or press *Alt+X*).

For more information about Turbo Profiler's environment, as well as details about parts of the profiler not mentioned here, refer to Chapter 25.

If you want more challenges than we've given in this tutorial, try these:

- Profile for primes less than
  - 2,500
  - 5,000
  - 7,500
  - 10,000

- Set the profile mode (choose Statistics I Profiling Options to bring up the Profiling Options dialog box) to Passive analysis. What does this do to profiler overhead? What kinds of information do you lose in passive analysis? (See Chapter 26, "Profiling strategies," for information on passive profiling.)

- Find out what kind of performance improvement you get by implementing the Sieve of Eratosthenes to compute primes up to 10,000.

- Compare the cost of printing newline characters with calls to position the cursor.

Note    There are a number of articles on the subject of profiling, but not many books. John Bentley's book, *Writing Efficient Programs*, provides a summary of rules for designing efficient code, suggests a comprehensive methodology for profiling, and contains an extensive bibliography.

Chapter

# 25

# The Turbo Profiler environment

Turbo Profiler makes it as easy and efficient as possible for you to profile your programs. When you start Turbo Profiler, everything you need is literally at your fingertips. That's what an *environment* is all about.

The Turbo Profiler environment also boasts these extras to make program profiling smooth:

- Multiple, movable, resizable windows

- Mouse support for any mouse compatible with the Microsoft mouse version 6.1 or later

- Dialog boxes to replace multilevel menus

## Part 1: The environment components

There are three visible components to the integrated environment: the *menu bar* at the top, the *window area* in the middle, and the *status line* at the bottom. Many menu items also offer dialog boxes. Before we discuss each menu item in the environment, we'll describe these more generic components.

### The menu bar and menus

Turbo Profiler has both global and SpeedMenus. *Global menus* are ones you access via the menu bar, and *SpeedMenus* are ones you access from within a window.

The menu bar is your primary access to all the global menu commands. In addition, it displays a program activity indicator on the right side that tells, for example, whether the profiler is READY for you to do something, RUNNING your program, or WAITing while it processes a processor-intensive task. The only time the menu bar is not visible is when you're viewing your program's output in the user screen.

## Choosing menu commands from the keyboard

Here's how to execute global menu commands using just the keyboard:

**1** Press *F10*. This makes the menu bar *active*, which means the next thing you type pertains to it, and not to any other component of the environment.

You see a highlighted menu title when the menu bar is active. The menu title that's highlighted is the currently *selected* menu.

**2** Once the global menu is active, use the arrow keys to select the menu you want to display. Then press *Enter*.

**Note**    To cancel an action, press *Esc*.

As a shortcut for this step, just press the initial letter of the menu title. (For example, press *F* to display the Files menu.)

If an ellipsis (...) follows a menu command, the command displays a dialog box when you choose it. If an arrow (▶) follows the command, the command leads to another menu.

**3** If the command opens another menu, use the arrow keys again to select the command you want. Then press *Enter*.

Again, as a shortcut, you can just press the highlighted letter of a command to choose it, once the menu is displayed.

At this point, Turbo Profiler either carries out the command, displays a dialog box, or displays another menu.

### SpeedMenus

In addition to the global menus that you access through the menu bar, each of Turbo Profiler's windows has its own unique SpeedMenu. When you're in a window, press *Alt+F10* to bring up the SpeedMenu. For more information on accessing SpeedMenus, refer to the discussion on page 389.

## Choosing menu commands with the mouse

To use the mouse to choose commands from global menus, click the desired title on the menu bar to display the menu, then click the desired menu command. You can also drag straight from the menu title down to the menu command. Release the mouse button on the command you want. (If you change your mind, just drag off the menu; no command will be chosen.)

## Shortcuts

Turbo Profiler offers many quick ways to choose menu commands. For example, with a mouse you can combine the two-step process into one: Drag from the menu title down to the menu commands, then release the mouse button when the command you want is selected.

From the keyboard, you can use keyboard shortcuts (or *hot keys*) to access the menu bar and choose commands.

**Table 25.1**    Menu hot keys

| Press this shortcut... | To accomplish this... |
| --- | --- |
| *Ctrl* and the highlighted letter of the SpeedMenu command | Carry out the SpeedMenu command |
| *Alt* plus the highlighted letter of the menu command | Display a menu from the menu bar |
| The highlighted letter of the dialog box component | Execute that menu command or select that dialog box component |
| The hot key combination listed next to a menu command | Carry out the menu command |

# Turbo Profiler windows

Most of what you see and do in the Turbo Profiler environment happens in a *window*. A window is an area of the screen that you can move, resize, zoom, layer, close, and open.

You can have many windows open in Turbo Profiler (memory allowing), but only one window can be *active* at any time. Any command you choose or text you type applies only to the active window.

**Note**    The active window is the one that you're currently working in.

Turbo Profiler makes it easy to spot the active window by placing a double-lined border around it. The active window always has a *close box*. If your windows are overlapping, the active window is the one on top of all the others (the frontmost one).

There are several types of windows. Most of them have these things: a title bar, a close box, two scroll bars, a resize corner, a zoom box, an iconize box, and a window number (1 to 9).

## Window management

Some windows are divided into two or more panes for displaying different kinds of information. Individual panes often have their own SpeedMenu.

The following table provides a quick rundown of how to handle windows in Turbo Profiler. You can perform these actions with a mouse or the keyboard.

**Table 25.2**    Manipulating windows

| To accomplish this... | Use one of these methods... |
| --- | --- |
| Open a window | Choose View to open a profiler window that's not already open. |
| Close a window | Choose Close from the Window menu or press *Alt+F3* or, if active, click the window's close box. |

**Table 25.2**    Manipulating windows (continued)

| To accomplish this... | Use one of these methods... |
| --- | --- |
| Activate a window | Click anywhere in the window, or |
| | Press *Alt* plus the window number (1 to 9, in the upper right border of the window), or |
| | Choose Window and select the window from the list at the bottom of the menu, or |
| | Choose Next from the Window menu (or press *F6*) to make the next window active (next in the order you first opened them). |
| View the window's contents | Use cursor keys to scroll the window up and down or left and right, or |
| | Use the mouse to operate the scroll bars: |
| | • Click the direction arrows at the ends of the bar to move one line or one character in the indicated direction. |
| | • Click the area in the middle of the bar to move one window size in the indicated direction. |
| | • Drag the scroll box to move as much as you want in the direction you want. |
| Move the active window | Drag its title bar or any left border character that isn't a scroll bar, close box, or zoom or iconize box, or |
| | Choose Size/Move from the Window menu (or press *Ctrl+F5*), use the arrow keys to place the window where you want it, then press *Enter*. |
| Resize the active window | Drag the resize corner, or |
| | Choose Size/Move from the Window menu (or press *Ctrl+F5*), press *Shift+Arrow* to change the size of the window, then press *Enter*, or |
| | Drag any part of the right or bottom border that isn't a scroll bar to resize the window. |
| Zoom the active window | Click the zoom box, or |
| | Double-click the window's title bar, or |
| | Choose Zoom from the Window menu, or press *F5*. |
| Iconize the active window | Click the iconize box, or |
| | Choose Iconize/Restore from the Window menu. |
| | When a window is fully zoomed, it has only an unzoom box.([↕]) When it is iconized, it has only a zoom box (↑). In its restored state, it has both an up and a down arrow. |
| Move from pane to pane | Press *Tab*, *Shift+Tab*, or *Shift+Arrow*, or |
| | Choose Window \| Next Pane. |

# The status line

The status line at the bottom of the Turbo Profiler screen provides the following information:

- It reminds you of basic keystrokes and shortcuts applicable at that moment in the active window. (You will see that the status bar changes if you hold down *Alt* or *Ctrl*.)

- It provides onscreen shortcuts you can click to carry out the action (instead of choosing the command from the menu or pressing the hot key on the keyboard).

- It offers one-line information on any selected menu command or dialog box item.

The status line changes as you switch windows or activities. You can click any of the shortcuts to carry out the command.

The only time the status line is unavailable is when a dialog box or menu is open. You must close the dialog box or menu before doing anything else.

When you've selected a menu command, the status line changes to display a one-line summary of the routine of the selected item. For example, if the Options menu title is selected (highlighted), the status line displays the currently selected item in the Options menu.

## Dialog boxes

If a menu command has an ellipsis after it (...), the command opens a *dialog box*. A dialog box is a convenient way to view and set multiple options.

When you're making settings in dialog boxes, you work with six basic types of controls: radio buttons, check boxes, action buttons, text boxes, list boxes, and standard buttons.

If you have a color monitor, Turbo Profiler uses different colors for various elements of the dialog box.

# Part 2: The menu reference

This section gives you an item-by-item description of each menu command and dialog box option in the Turbo Profiler environment.

## ≡ menu (System)

The ≡ menu (called the *System menu*) appears on the far left of the menu bar. To activate the ≡ menu, either press *Alt+Spacebar*, or press *F10*, then use *Right* or *Left* to go to the ≡ symbol and press *Enter*.

With the commands in the ≡ menu, you can

• Repaint the screen
• Restore your original window configuration
• Activate the Turbo Profiler information box

### Repaint Desktop
Choose Repaint Desktop when you want Turbo Profiler to redraw the screen. You might need to do this, for example, if a memory-resident program has left stray characters on the screen, or possibly if you have display swapping turned off.

### Restore Standard
When you start up Turbo Profiler, it sets the environment windows' size, window status (open or closed), and placement according to information stored in the configuration file TFCONFIG.TF. Once Turbo Profiler is onscreen, you can move and resize the windows, close some and open others, and generally make a real mess of your screen. The Restore Standard command provides a quick way to rectify such a situation.

When you choose Restore Standard, Turbo Profiler puts all the windows back the way they were when you first started the profiler.

## About

When you choose About from the ≡ menu, the About box pops up. This box lists the Turbo Profiler version number. Press *Enter* or choose OK to close the box.

# File menu

The File menu contains commands for

- Opening and loading a program to be profiled
- Changing the current directory
- Obtaining information about your program and system memory allocation
- Opening up a DOS shell
- Quitting the profiler

## Open

The File | Open command, used to load an explicit file into the Module window, opens a two-tiered set of dialog boxes. The first is the Load a New Program to Profile dialog box.

**Figure 25.1**    The Load A New Program to Profile dialog box

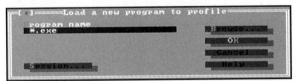

TRPOF.EXE's Load a New Program to Debug dialog box contains an additional button, Session, to support its remote profiling feature. For more information on remote profiling, and the Session button, see Chapter 30, "Remote profiling."

If you know the name of the program you want to load, enter the executable name into the Program Name input box and press *Enter*.

To search through directories for your program, click the Browse button to open the second dialog box (the Enter Program Name to Load dialog box):

**Figure 25.2**    The Enter Program Name to Load dialog box

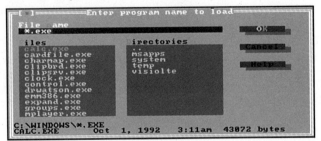

The Files list box displays the files in the currently selected directory. By entering a file mask into the File Name input box (such as *.*EXE*), you can specify which files should be listed. You can also use the File Name input box to change disk drives.

To "walk" through disk directories, double-click the entries listed in the Directories list box (the .. entry steps you back one directory level). Once you've selected a directory, choose a file to load from the Files list box. To quickly search for a file, type a file name into the Files list box. Turbo Profiler's incremental matching feature moves the highlight bar to the file that begins with the letters you type. Once you've selected a file, press OK. This action returns you to the Load a New Program to Profile dialog box.

To support remote debugging, TPROF.EXE contains buttons in the Load a New Program to Profile dialog box. The Session radio buttons specify whether or not the program you're debugging is on a local or remote system. If it's located on a remote system, select the Remote Windows radio button; if it's not on a remote system, select Local. See Chapter 29, "Customizing the Turbo Profiler," for complete instructions on remote debugging.

**Note**    Before loading a program into the profiler, be sure to compile your source code into an executable file (.EXE or .DLL) with full debugging information. Although you can load programs that don't have debug information, you will not be able to use the Module window to view the program's source code. (The profiler cannot reference the source code of executable modules that lack debug information. If you load a module that doesn't contain debug information, Turbo Profiler opens the Disassembly window to show the disassembled machine instructions of that module.)

When you run a program under the control of Turbo Profiler, the program's executable files (including all .DLL files) and original source files must be available. In addition, all .EXE and .DLL files for the application must be located in the same directory.

## Session Saving

When you exit Turbo Profiler, it saves to the current directory a *session-state file* that contains information about the profiling session you're leaving. When you reload your program from that directory, Turbo Profiler restores the history lists from the last profiling session.

By default, all history lists are saved to the session-state file. Session-state files are named *XXXX*.TP and *XXXX*.TPW by TPROF.EXE and TPROFW.EXE, respectively, where *XXXX* is the name of the program you're profiling. If no program is loaded when you exit Turbo Profiler, then *XXXX* is named either TPROF or TPROFW.

The Options | Set Restart Options command opens the Restart Options dialog box, from where you can set how Turbo Profiler handles the session-state files. In this dialog box, the Restore at Restart check box specifies whether you want to save the profiler's history lists. The Use Restart Info radio buttons specify how you want to handle the file:

**Table 25.3**    Turbo Profile session-state saving options

| Option | Description |
| --- | --- |
| Always | Always use the session-state file. |
| Ignore if old | Don't use the session-state file if you've recompiled your program. |

**Table 25.3**  Turbo Profile session-state saving options  (continued)

| Option | Description |
|---|---|
| Prompt if old | Prompts if you want to use the session-state file if you've recompiled your program. |
| Never | Do not use the session-state file. |

## Get Info

The File | Get Info command displays a text box with information about the program being profiled and your system's current memory configuration.

Information in the Get Info box is for display only; you can't change any settings from this box. Here's what the categories in this information box represent:

- Program is the program being profiled; you determine which file to profile with the File | Open command.

- Status describes how Turbo Profiler gained control: it can be any one of the following messages:

  ```
  Loaded
  Control-Break
  Terminated, exit code XX
  Stopped by area
  NMI Interrupt
  Exception XX
  Divide by zero
  No program loaded
  ```

- Mode is the profiling mode (active, passive, or coverage); you specify the profiling mode with the Profile Mode radio button in the Profiling Options dialog box (accessed by choosing Statistics | Profiling Options).

- Collection tells whether automatic data collection is enabled or disabled; you specify the data-collection setting with the Statistics | Accumulation command.

- Memory shows the use of memory:
  - DOS: Memory occupied by DOS and/or various device drivers
  - Profiler: Total memory used by the profiler
  - Symbols: Memory allocated for the program's symbol table
  - Program: Memory allocated to the current program being profiled
  - Available: Amount of remaining available memory

- DOS version shows the current DOS version on your system.

- Current date and time is taken from the system clock.

After reviewing the information in the Get Info box, click OK or press *Enter* to return to the current window.

## DOS Shell

The File | DOS Shell command steps you out of Turbo Profiler and into a DOS shell. To return to Turbo Profiler, type EXIT at the DOS prompt.

**Note**    In remote profiling mode, the DOS command line appears on the Turbo Profiler screen rather than on the user screen; this allows you to switch to DOS without disturbing your program's output. Because your program's output is always available on one screen in the system, Window | User Screen and *Alt+F5* are disabled during remote profiling. (See Chapter 30 for details about remote profiling.)

## Quit

$\boxed{\text{Alt}}\boxed{\text{X}}$    The File | Quit command exits Turbo Profiler, removes it from memory, and returns to the DOS command line.

If you have any profile data or setup parameters that you want to keep (such as the profile statistics, profiling and display options, and screen layout options), save them with the Statistics | Save and Options | Save commands before exiting. If you don't, you'll lose the options you've set.

**Note**    Each time you exit Turbo Profiler, it remembers the areas you set up for the current program by saving the settings in a .TFA file. Then, the next time the program is loaded, the area settings are automatically put into effect.

# View menu

The View menu lets you open several kinds of windows in which you can examine information about your program's performance.

**Table 25.4**    Summary of Turbo Profiler windows

| Window name | What this window displays |
| --- | --- |
| Module | Source code for the program being profiled |
| Execution Profile | Statistical information about a program after the program has run |
| Callers | Information about how often a routine is called and which routines call it |
| Overlays | Information about overlays for Borland's line of Pascal compilers, Borland's C and C++ compilers, and Turbo Assembler |
| Interrupts | Information about interrupt calls made by the program |
| Files | Information about file activity |
| Areas | Detailed information about data-collection activities at the places marked in your source code |
| Routines | All routines that can be used as profile area markers |
| Disassembly | The current profile area in the Module window, as disassembled source code |
| Text File | Contents of any text file you specify |
| Coverage | In its default setting, lists the code blocks which haven't yet been executed |

## SpeedMenus

Each Profiler window has its own *SpeedMenu* (actually, some windows have more than one SpeedMenu, depending on the number of panes in the window). A SpeedMenu contains commands and settings specific to the window pane.

To activate a SpeedMenu, press *Alt+F10* (if there is more than one window pane, press *Tab* to alternate between the panes). When the SpeedMenu pops up, use the arrow keys to select the command you want and press *Enter*, or press the highlighted letter. Once you choose a SpeedMenu command, Turbo Profiler either carries it out, displays a dialog box, or displays another menu.

To activate a SpeedMenu item directly from the window (without bringing up the SpeedMenu), press the *Ctrl+(letter)* hot key, where *letter* is the menu item's highlighted letter.

To pop up the active menu's SpeedMenu using a mouse, click the mouse's right button. Then, select the command you want by clicking on the menu item.

## Module

The Module window displays source code for the program being profiled. In the Module window, you can examine code and set areas to be profiled. Special hot keys and window links connect the code in this window to data and statistics in other windows.

When you choose View I Module, a list box appears that lists all the source modules linked with the program currently loaded into the Module window. Highlight the new module you want to display, and press OK to load it into the Module window.

If the Modified appears in the title bar of the Module window, it indicates that the source code to the file you're viewing has changes since the program was last compiled.

**Figure 25.3**   The Module window (zoomed)

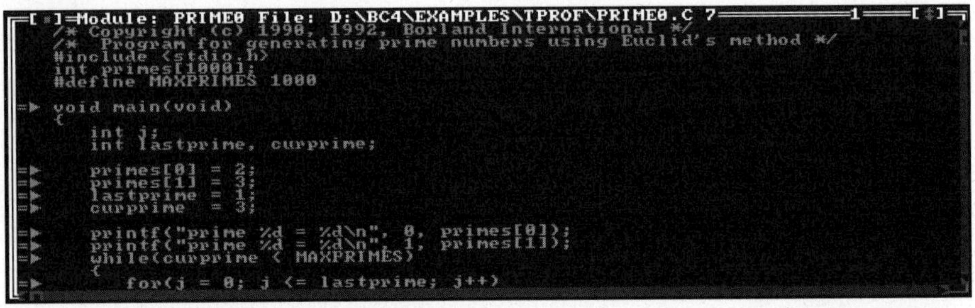

When you run the profiler, both the .EXE file and the original source file must be available. Turbo Profiler looks for your program's source code in these places, in this order:

1   In the directory where the program was originally compiled. The name of the directory where the program was originally compiled is contained in .EXE and .OBJ files if you compiled your program with symbolic debugging information.

2   In the directories (if any) you've listed under Options I Path for Source (or stated in the command-line option using the **–sd** switch).

3   In the current directory.

4   In the directory that contains the .EXE file of the program you're profiling.

Press *Alt+F10* or click the right mouse button to bring up the Module window's SpeedMenu. With the SpeedMenu commands, you can perform these actions:

- Move the cursor to a specific line or code label.

- Search for text in the source code.

- Add and remove profile areas.

- Set the profiling action that will occur for a given area.

- Specify the level of call-path recording for a given routine.

- Load another module or another source file of the current module into the Module window.

- Invoke the editor specified when you run TFINST.

### Line

Ctrl L    To move swiftly to a particular line of code in the Module window, choose Line from the SpeedMenu. The dialog box that pops up requests the line number you seek; type in the new line number, then choose OK (or press *Enter*). If you enter a line number after the last line in the file, you will be positioned at the last line in the file.

### Search

Ctrl S    To search for a character string in the current module, choose Search. The prompt box that pops up requests the string to search for; type in the string, then choose OK (or press *Enter*).

If the cursor is positioned over text that looks like a variable name, the prompt box comes up initialized to that name. If you mark a block in the file, the profiler uses that block to initialize the search prompt. This saves you from extraneous typing if the text you want to search for is a string already in the Module window.

You can use the standard DOS wildcards (? and *): The ? indicates a match on any single character, and the * matches 0 or more characters.

The search begins from the current cursor position and does not wrap around from the end of the file to the beginning. To search the entire file, start at the first line.

### Next

Ctrl N    Once you've defined a search string with the Module window's local Search command, you can search for successive occurrences of that string with the Next command. Choose Next from the SpeedMenu, or press the shortcut, *Ctrl+N*. You can use Next only after issuing a Search command.

### Goto

Ctrl G    To position the Module window's cursor on a particular routine or other code label in your program's source code, choose Goto. The prompt box that pops up requests the address you want to examine. Type in a line number, a routine name, or a hex address, then choose OK (or press *Enter*).

Note    Use the hex format of your program language.

### Add Areas

Ctrl A Add Areas on the Module window's SpeedMenu leads to another menu.

- All Routines adds area markers for all routines in the program being profiled, including routines for which source code is unavailable (such as library routines linked in as object modules).

- Modules with Source adds area markers for all routines in modules whose source code is available.

- Routines in Module adds area markers for all routines in the current module (the one in the Module window).

- Every Line in Module adds area markers for all lines in the current module.

- Lines in Routine adds area markers for all lines in the current routine (whichever routine the cursor is on in the Module window).

- Current Routine adds an area marker for whichever routine the cursor is on in the Module window.

- This Line adds an area marker for the line the cursor is on in the Module window.

### Remove Areas

Ctrl R Choosing Remove Areas on the Module window's SpeedMenu displays another menu. This menu is almost identical to the Add Areas menu just described. Except for the All Areas command, which removes all markers, each command on the Remove Areas menu erases area markers the same way as the respective Add Areas command adds area markers.

### Operation

Ctrl O The Operation command opens the Area Options dialog box, which contains settings for the area marker on the current line in the Module window.

**Figure 25.4** The Area Options dialog box

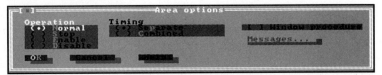

You can specify two options with the radio buttons in this dialog box: Operation and Timing. In addition, the Window Procedure check box enables message tracking for Windows programs.

- *Operation* specifies what profiling action will occur for the current area. *Window Procedure*, when checked, specifies that the current area marks a procedure specific to Windows.

  When you mark an area, a marker symbol signifying the chosen operation appears to the left of that area in the Module window. A different symbol is used to refer to each type of area marker: A Normal area is marked with =➤, a Stop area is marked with s➤, an Enable area is marked with e➤, and a Disable area is marked with d➤.

- *Normal* collects profile statistics for this area as specified in the Statistics menu (callers, file activity, interrupts, overlays, and so on) and Area Options dialog box, which you reach through the SpeedMenus of the Module and Areas windows.

- *Stop* stops program execution at this marker.

- *Enable* turns on the collection of statistics at this point in the program.

- *Disable* temporarily turns off the collection of statistics at this point in the program. Data collection resumes once program control passes an Enable marker.

**Note**    Coverage mode provides only one type of area marker, denoted by a single ➤ character. The marker indicates that the block has not been executed.

- *Messages* becomes active when the Window Procedure check box is checked. Choosing Messages displays the Window Procedure Messages dialog box.

- *Timing* specifies whether the profiler will add the current area's execution time to a higher-level area or keep it separate.

  - *Separate* adds any timer ticks in the current routine to that routine's statistics.

  - *Combined* sums the timer ticks of the marked routine with the timer ticks of *all* the children of that routine. You can specify combined time for an area only if that area's Callers setting is *Immediate* or *All*.

    When you set a routine's Timing to Combined, Turbo Profiler does not display timing statistics for the children of that routine—their times are reported as part of the routine whose timing is set to Combined.

The following illustration shows how Combined timing works:

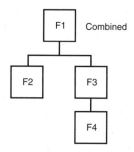

In this illustration, the routine *F1* has its Timing set to Combined. Turbo Profiler collects the timing information for all the routines (*F1*, *F2*, *F3*, and *F4*), and sums them into the timing information collected for the routine *F1*.

## Callers

Ctrl C    The Callers command on the SpeedMenu leads to the Stack Trace dialog box.

**Figure 25.5**    The Stack Trace dialog box

You specify how callers are handled with two sets of radio buttons, Areas and Stack.

- Areas specifies which areas you want call paths recorded for.
  - This Routine sets only the current routine (the one the cursor is on in the Module window) to the setting specified in Stack.
  - This Module sets all routines in the current module to the setting specified in Stack.
  - All Routines sets all routines in all program modules to the option specified in Stack.
- Stack specifies how extensive ("deep") the recorded call stack should be.
  - All Callers records all available call stack information for the routine(s) you've specified with the Areas option.
  - Immediate Caller records only "parent" information for the routine(s) you've specified with the Areas option.
  - None turns off call stack information for the routine(s) you've specified with the Areas option.

When OK is selected from the Stack Trace dialog box, the areas specified by the Areas options are set according to the selected Stack option. Changes made in this dialog box are reflected in the Areas window.

### Module

Ctrl M    The Module command on the SpeedMenu leads to the Pick a Module dialog box that lists all your program's modules for which source code is available.

Most modules have only a single source code file; other files included in a module (such as C header files) usually define only constants and data structures. Use this command to open a different module in the Module window.

This option displays only the file names for the source code modules that are associated with the program being profiled. It allows you to move rapidly from one module to another without having to search your source directory explicitly.

The Module command searches for the source code in the following places, in the order listed:

1  In the directory where the program was originally compiled.

2  In the directories (if any) you've listed under Options | Path for Source (or stated in the command-line option using the –sd switch).

3  In the current directory.

4  In the directory that contains the .EXE file of the program you're profiling.

### File

Ctrl F    The File command on the Module SpeedMenu leads to a dialog box that lists all the source files used to compile the current module. Use this command if your module has source code in more than one file and the file you want is not displayed in the module window.

The File command searches for the source code in the same order as the Module command in the previous section.

### Edit command

Ctrl E   Although Turbo Profiler does not have a built-in editor, you can specify your own favorite editor as an option when you customize the profiler with the Turbo Profiler installation program, TFINST. See Chapter 29 for information about TFINST.

Once you've installed an editor using TFINST, whenever you choose Edit from the Module window's SpeedMenu, Turbo Profiler automatically shells out to DOS and invokes your editor. To return to the profiler from your editor, simply quit the editor.

## Execution Profile

The Execution Profile window is where Turbo Profiler displays your program's profile statistics (after you've set areas and run the program under control of the profiler).

The Execution Profile window consists of one pane, divided into two display areas (top and bottom). The top display area lists

- Total Time: your program's total execution time.

- % of Total: how much of that total (a percentage) is represented by the statistics for the areas you've chosen.

- Runs: the current profile run (if you're collecting and averaging statistics from more than one run).

- The options you've chosen from the SpeedMenu (display format, filter status, and sort order).

- Total Ticks: the total number of timer ticks which occurred during the program run. Timer Ticks displays only during passive mode profiling.

The bottom display area lists one or two lines of profile data for each area you've marked. The information shown in this display area can include each area's name or line number, the execution counts for each marked area, the time spent in each marked area, the average time per pass for each marked area, and the most time spent in a marked area on a single pass.

If you have a Module window and an Execution Profile window onscreen at the same time, the Execution Profile window is positioned automatically to show the statistics for the area the cursor is on in the Module window.

To specify how the Execution Profile window displays your program's statistics, activate the SpeedMenu (press *Alt+F10*). Through this SpeedMenu, you can

- Select what type of modules will be profiled: Window procedures or normal areas.

- Choose any one of six different ways to display profile statistics in the Execution Profile window.

- Sort the displayed statistics.

- Temporarily remove one or more areas' statistics from the display.

- Examine the source code for an area.

- Delete an area's statistics from memory and erase the associated area marker.

### Display

Ctrl D When you choose Display from the Execution Profile window's SpeedMenu, the Display Options dialog box comes up.

**Figure 25.6** The Display Options dialog box

You can specify three options with the radio buttons in this dialog box: Profile, Display, and Sort.

- Profile specifies which areas are displayed in the Execution Profile window.
  - Normal Areas displays all marked areas, including any Window procedures that are marked.
  - Window Procs filters the displayed areas to show only the classes and Windows messages that are specified in the Windows Procedure Messages dialog box.

    See Chapter 31 for a complete description of the Windows Procedure Messages dialog box.

- Display specifies what form the data will be displayed in.
  - Time displays the profile statistics for each area as the time (in milliseconds) program control was in that area.
  - Counts displays profile statistics for each area as pass counts: how many times program control entered that area.
  - Both displays the statistics for each area as both time (the top line) and counts. This provides a graphic measure of a routine's efficiency.
  - Per Call displays each area's statistics as the *Time:Counts* ratio. This provides the average time spent in each call to the routine.
  - Longest displays, for each area, the longest single time program control was in that area.
  - Module displays, for each module in the program, the time program control was in that module. This setting is useful only if Turbo Profiler is in passive mode, which means it's recording with every clock tick which module the program is in. This option is helpful as a first cut at profiling a large program.

- Sort specifies what order the data will be sorted in.
  - Name sorts the profile statistics by area name, in alphanumeric order.
  - Address sorts profile statistics by memory location, starting with the lowest address.
  - Frequency sorts the statistics numerically, with the highest frequency at the top.

The top display area of the Execution Profile window lists the current display and sort options.

## Filter

Ctrl F   The Filter command on the SpeedMenu leads to the three-item menu shown here.

- All restores all collected statistics for the current program to the Execution Profile window.

  After you've filtered out certain statistics from the Execution Profile window (with Filter | Module or Filter | Current), choose Filter | All to restore all profile statistics to the window.

- Module filters out all but one module's statistics.

  This command leads to the Pick a Module dialog box, which lists all modules for the current program. Use the *Up* and *Down* arrow keys to highlight one module in the list, then press *Enter*. Only the areas in the chosen module show up in the Execution Profile window.

- Current temporarily removes the highlighted area's statistics from the Execution Profile window.

  Choose Filter | Current if you want to throw out one area's statistics and see what happens to the remaining percentages. The Current command is a temporary filter that hides report information from sight without deleting any information; it does the following:

  1  Removes the current area's statistics from the Execution Profile window.

  2  Calculates original total execution time minus the time of the removed area.

  3  Recalculates the remaining areas' percentages as fractions of the newly calculated total execution time.

When you filter one or more areas' statistics from the Execution Profile window, the profiler calculates a new total execution time based on the statistics displayed in the window, but the Total Time value shown in the top of the window does not change.

When you use Filter | Current, the original total execution time for the entire program remains displayed in the Execution Profile window's top display area.

Filter | Current is a temporary filter that hides report information from sight; Remove actually affects area marker settings by removing them in both the Module and Areas windows.

**Note**   Don't confuse Filter | Current with the Remove command on the Execution Profile window's SpeedMenu.

## Module

Ctrl M   The Module command on the SpeedMenu takes you to the line of source code in the Module window for which the statistics are highlighted in the Execution Profile Window. Note that in addition to the *Ctrl+M* hot key, you can press *Enter* from the Execution Profile window to execute the same command.

Suppose you highlight the statistics for routine **frank** in the Execution Profile window, then choose Module from the SpeedMenu to activate the link. Turbo Profiler activates the Module window and places the cursor on the first line of **frank** in the source code. After that, you move the cursor to line 25 in the Module window (line 25 has an area marker). Automatically, the Execution Profile window's contents scroll so that the statistics for line 25 show at the top of the statistics display area.

The link is unidirectional: If you go back to the Execution Profile window (after going to the Module window) and move the highlight bar, the source code in the Module window does not scroll or track the highlight bar's position. (If it did, you could get very frustrated.)

If, when you choose the Module command, source code for the highlighted line is unavailable, the link goes to the corresponding line of code in the Disassembly (CPU) window. This happens, for example, if you've marked areas for All Routines and the highlighted line is a library routine. (See page 409 for details about the Disassembly window.)

## Position

Ctrl P   The Position command is identical to the Module command, with the exception that the Position command does not activate the Module window; the Execution Profile window remains active. Another shortcut for this command is the *Spacebar*.

## Remove

Ctrl R   The Remove command removes area marker settings from the currently highlighted line in the Execution Profile window.

**Warning**   The Remove command *erases* statistical data. Use it with discretion.

Once you remove the line's area markers with the Remove command, the statistics you had gathered for that line are erased and no more statistics are gathered for that line of code. To undo a Remove action, you must

1  Activate the Module window and bring up its SpeedMenu.

2  Place the cursor on the line whose marker you removed.

3  Choose Add Areas | This Line.

4  Run the program again (collecting a new set of statistics).

## Callers

The Callers window is where Turbo Profiler displays the *call paths* for each marked routine in your program. A call path is a list of all the routines that were called to execute the currently selected routine. The call path starts with the original calling routine. You must set the Statistics | Callers menu item to *Enabled* before the profiler will record any call-path information.

**Figure 25.7**  The Callers window, showing calls in CALLTEST

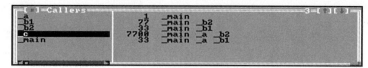

The left pane in the Callers window lists each marked routine by name. When you highlight a routine name in the left pane, the right pane displays each unique call path for that routine. If a call path is wider than the right pane, you can zoom the window or switch to the right pane and scroll left and right through the path.

**Note**   An underscore precedes the identifier names in this Callers window because Borland's C and C++ compilers add the underscore to all symbol names appearing in .OBJ files and symbolic debugging information.

Although the Callers window displays the call-path information, you must specify what type of call path recording you want. This is done through either the Module window or the Areas window.

In the Module window, you can set callers options for whole groups of routines.

**1**   With the cursor on a marked routine in the Module window, press *Alt+F10* to bring up the SpeedMenu.

**2**   Choose Callers to see the Stack Trace dialog box.

**3**   Set the Areas option. You can choose to record call paths for the current routine, all routines in the current module, or all routines in the program (including library routines).

**4**   Set the Stack option. You can choose to record all callers for the chosen routine(s), immediate callers (the routines' parents only), or no callers at all.

**5**   Press *Enter* or choose OK to go back to the Module window.

In the Areas window, you can set callers options for individual marked routines. (See page 405 for more information about the Areas window.)

**1**   In the Areas window, place the highlight bar on the routine you want to set call-path options for, then press *Alt+F10* to bring up the SpeedMenu.

**2**   Choose Options to see the Area Options dialog box.

**3**   Set the Callers option. You can choose to record all callers for the chosen routine(s), immediate callers (the routines' parents only), or no callers at all.

**4**   Press *Enter* or choose OK to go back to the Areas window.

Figure 25.7 shows routine **c** highlighted in the left pane of the Callers window, after a profile run of this program, CALLTEST:

```
/* Program CALLTEST */
/* Copyright (c) 1990, Borland International */
#include <stdio.h>

main()
```

```
{
    c();
    b2();
    b1();
    a();
}

a()
{
    int i;

    for (i = 0; i < 100; i++)
        b2();
    b1();
}

b1()
{
    int i;

    for (i = 0; i < 33; i++)
        c();
}

b2()
{
    int i;

    for (i = 0; i < 77; i++)
        c();
}

c()
{
    int i;

    for (i = 0; i < 3; i++)
        ;
}
```

The Callers window's right pane lists each unique call path for routine **c**:

- 1 call from **main** to **c**
- 77 calls from **main** to **b2** to **c**
- 33 calls from **main** to **b1** to **c**
- 7,700 calls from **main** to **a** to **b2** to **c**
- 33 calls from **main** to **a** to **b1** to **c**

You'll find the Callers window useful when you must make decisions about restructuring code, especially when it's possible to reach a routine through several different call paths.

Both panes of the Callers window have SpeedMenus. In the Callers window's right pane, the Inspect SpeedMenu item brings up a subsequent menu containing the commands areas, module, and profile.

### Inspect (left pane)

Ctrl+I
When the highlight bar is on a routine name in the left pane, choose Inspect (or press its shortcut, *Ctrl+I*) to view the source code for that routine in the Module window.

### Inspect (right pane)

Ctrl+I
When the highlight bar is on a call path in the right pane of the Callers window, you can "inspect" (view information about) elements in that call path in one of three other windows.

1 Choose Inspect to bring up a list of those other windows.

2 Choose the window you're interested in (Areas, Module, or Profile) from the list. This brings up the Pick a Caller dialog box, which lists all callers on the current call path.

3 In the dialog box, highlight the caller in question (use the arrow keys or a mouse click), then choose OK or press *Enter*. If the window you choose to inspect isn't already open, the profiler opens it automatically, then goes to the caller's location in that window.

### Sort (right pane)

Ctrl+S
With the local Sort command in the Callers window's right pane, you can sort the list of call paths in two ways:

• Called sorts the call paths in the same order that program control traversed them at run time.

• Frequency sorts the call paths by how often program control traversed each path, with the most-used path at the top of the list.

## Overlays

The Overlays window is where Turbo Profiler displays information about overlay activity for Borland's Pascal compilers, Borland's C and C++ compilers, and Turbo Assembler programs. You must set the Statistics I Overlays menu item to Enabled before the profiler will record any overlay information (if your program has overlays, Turbo Profiler automatically enables the Overlay option).

**Figure 25.8**  The Overlays window

The information listed in this window can include:

• How many times your program loads each overlay into memory.
• When each overlay was loaded.

- The sequence in which your program loads the overlays.
- The size of the overlay

Like the Execution Profile window, the Overlays window is divided into two display areas, top and bottom. The top display area lists total execution time for your program and the current display option for overlay statistics. The bottom display area lists the overlay statistics as either a histogram or a list of events.

**Note**  Press any key to halt the execution of the program OVRDEMO.

If you have one of Borland's Pascal compilers, there's a program, OVRDEMO, that gives a live demonstration of how the Overlays window works. Load this program into the profiler. Then set area markers for every line in the module OVRDEMO, enable Statistics | Overlays, and run the program. (You'll need the files OVRDEMO.PAS, OVRDEMO1.PAS, OVRDEMO2.PAS, and OVRDEMO.EXE to profile this program.)

The Overlays window's SpeedMenu provides two commands, shown here.

### Display
Ctrl D  Display specifies how the data will appear; you toggle between Count and History by pressing *Enter*.

Count produces a histogram that shows, for each overlay, how much memory that overlay consumes and how many times your program loaded the overlay into memory.

History lists your program's overlay activity as a sequence of events; each line names the overlay and specifies when, in the course of program events, that overlay was loaded.

### Inspect
Ctrl I  Inspect goes automatically to the Module window (opening it, if necessary) and places the cursor on the source code for the highlighted overlay.

## Interrupts
The Interrupts window is where Turbo Profiler displays information about the video, disk, keyboard, DOS, and mouse interrupt events in your program. The Statistics | Interrupts menu item must be *Enabled* before the profiler will record any interrupt-call information.

**Figure 25.9**  The Interrupts window

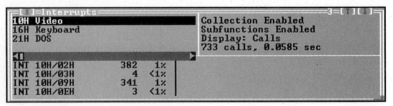

The Interrupts window is divided into three panes: top left, top right, and bottom.

- The top left pane displays the list of specific interrupts to be profiled (by INT number and name).

- The top right pane lists information about the display mode and the current interrupt (the one highlighted in the top left pane), number of calls, and execution time. You cannot tab to the top right pane; it only displays information.

- In the bottom pane, you see a profile of data for each interrupt, shown as a histogram or as start time and duration.

Each entry in the bottom pane of the Interrupt window can list

- The interrupt by name or INT number (or both)

- The number of calls to that interrupt (as an absolute number and as a percentage)

- The total amount of execution time spent in that interrupt (as an absolute number and as a percentage)

Both active panes of the Interrupts window have SpeedMenus.

### Collection (top pane)

Ctrl C  The Collection command enables or disables collection of statistics for the current interrupt (the one highlighted in the left display area of the top pane).

### Subfunctions (top pane)

Ctrl S  The Subfunctions command enables or disables collection of statistics for subfunctions of the current interrupt (this is particularly useful for DOS INT 21H calls). Subfunction numbers are determined from the value in the AH register when the interrupt is called.

### Add (top pane)

Ctrl A  The Add command adds an interrupt, by number, to the list in the pane's left display area. Type the interrupt number in hexadecimal notation. For example, type 21 for INT 21H (if you type 33, Turbo Profiler adds INT 33H to the list).

### Pick (top pane)

Ctrl P  The Pick command displays a predetermined list of interrupts, so you can pick one to add to the list in the left display area.

### Remove (top pane)

Ctrl R  The Remove command removes the current highlighted interrupt from the list in the pane's left display area.

### Delete All (top pane)

Ctrl D  The Delete All command removes all the listed interrupts in the pane's left display area.

### Display (bottom pane)

Ctrl D  The Interrupt window's bottom pane has a one-item SpeedMenu; its command, Display, leads to a subsequent menu. From this second menu, you can choose to display interrupt statistics in one of four different formats, as shown in Table 25.5:

**Table 25.5**   Summary of interrupt statistic formats

| Format | Function |
|---|---|
| Time | Displays the amount of time spent in each interrupt and its subfunctions. |
| Calls | Displays the number of times each interrupt and its subfunctions were called. |
| Both Time and Calls | Displays both the amount of time and the number of times that each interrupt and its subfunctions were called. |
| Events | Displays a time-ordered list of interrupt calls. |

## Files

The Files window is where Turbo Profiler displays information about file activity that occurred during your program's run. For Turbo Profiler to record any file-activity information (such as read, write, open, or close), Statistics | Files must be set to *Enabled*.

**Figure 25.10**   The Files window

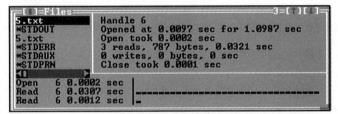

The Files window is divided into three panes: top left, top right, and bottom.

The top left pane lists files by name, including STDIN and STDOUT. As you move the highlight bar over the file name you're interested in, the top right pane shows, for that file,

- The handle number
- The time the file was opened
- How long the file was open
- The time required to open the file
- The number of reads and writes from and to the file
- The total number of bytes read and written
- The time for all reads from and writes to the file
- The time required to close the file

The top right pane only displays information. You can't tab to it, and it does not have a SpeedMenu.

The lower pane displays file activity statistics (reads, writes, opens, and closes) as individual entries, rather than as statistical totals associated with a single file-name entry. Each entry provides information about a given file activity.

Both active panes of the Files window have SpeedMenus.

### Collection (top pane)

Ctrl C  The Collection command enables or disables the collection of file activity statistics for the current file (the one highlighted in the left display area of the top pane).

Each entry in the bottom pane of the Files window provides information about a given file activity.

### Detail (top pane)

Ctrl D  The Detail command enables or disables the collection of a detailed listing of file-activity statistics. A detailed listing logs each file read and write separately, the time it occurred (calculated from the from the program start), and the number of bytes transferred. When Detail is disabled, only file open and close activities are logged; reads and writes are summarized.

### When Full (top pane)

Ctrl W  The When Full command specifies what happens when the memory set aside for file-activity statistics fills up.

*Wrap* means that the newest file-activity statistics will overwrite the oldest ones when the memory area fills up.

*Stop* means that file-activity statistics gathering will stop when the memory area fills up.

### Display (bottom pane)

Ctrl D  In the Files window's bottom pane, you can choose one menu item, Display, which leads to the Display Options dialog box.

You can specify two options with the radio buttons in this dialog box: Display and Sort.

- Display specifies how you want file-activity statistics to appear in the bottom pane.
  - Graph displays each activity's total time as a bar graph.
  - Detail displays each activity's exact time in seconds.

  Both options display the execution time in seconds; however, Graph also graphs the display and Details tells when, in the course of program execution, the file activity took place.

- Sort specifies the order in which Turbo Profiler sorts the displayed statistics.
  - Start Time sorts the files' statistics by sequential order of occurrence.
  - Duration sorts the files' statistics by how long the open, read, write, or close operation took.

## Areas

The Areas window is where Turbo Profiler displays detailed information about your program's marked profile areas. The Areas window is used to inspect areas that have been set and to adjust the behavior of individual areas.

**Figure 25.11**    The Areas window

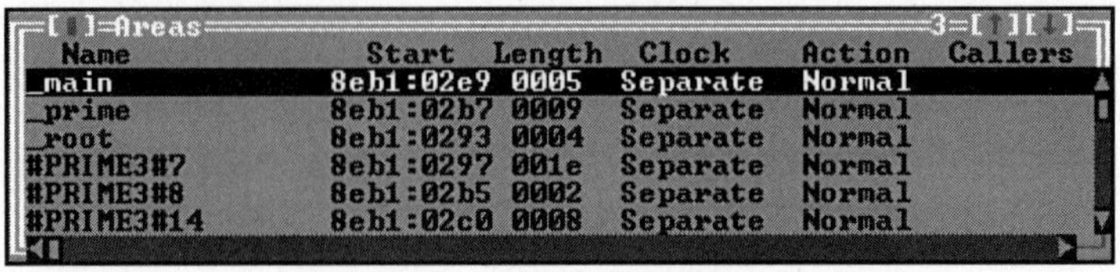

By default, the Areas window lists each area in alphabetical order. For typical programs, these areas are designated by the names of the routines to which they correspond. However, if you mark each line in a routine, the area name is (generically)

```
ModName#FileName#NN
```

where *ModName* is the module name, *FileName* is the file name, and *NN* is the line number. If you mark a line associated with a label (for example, a routine name), the profiler uses the label as the area name.

**Note**    The file name appears only if the module is made up of more than one file.

The Areas window shows the following information associated with each marked area:

- Start: starting address in hexadecimal.

- Length: length in bytes, as a hexadecimal number.

- Clock: whether the area uses a separate or combined clock in timing descendent areas.

- Action: the area operation (what Turbo Profiler should do when it passes the marker).

- Callers: whether the profiler tracks the area's immediate caller only, all callers, or no callers.

- Winproc: "Yes" if the area is a Windows procedure, otherwise it is blank. This column is pertinent only if a Windows program is being profiled with TPROFW, or with TPROF acting as a remote Windows profiler.

The Areas window is more than a source window for static display of information. With the SpeedMenu, you can

- Add or remove areas
- Inspect areas
- Change options for individual areas
- Sort the displayed information

## Add Areas

Ctrl A    Choose Add Areas to add area markers. When selected, this command leads to another menu that contains the commands All Routines, Module, and Routine.

- All Routines places markers at each routine in the current module.

- Module leads to the Pick a Module dialog box. This command lets you place markers in a program module other than the one present in the Module window.

For more information on the Pick a Module dialog box, refer to the "Module" section on page 394.

- Routine, when selected, leads to the Enter Routine Name to Add text box. Type the name of the routine that you want to select, and choose OK.

### Remove Areas

Ctrl R  Remove Areas is used to erase markers that have been set.

- All Areas removes the markers from all areas in the program, including the modules not currently displayed in the Module window.

- Module leads to the Pick a Module dialog box. From this dialog box, choose a module whose area markers you want to delete.

- This Area removes the area marker currently highlighted in the Areas window.

### Inspect

Ctrl I  When you choose Inspect, the profiler switches to the Module window and places the cursor on the first line of source code corresponding to the current area highlighted in the Areas window. If the area highlighted does not correspond to a program source line, the CPU window is opened instead.

### Options

Ctrl O  When you choose Options from the Areas window's SpeedMenu, the Area Options dialog box comes up.

**Figure 25.12**    The Area Options dialog box

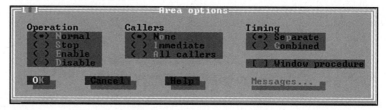

You can specify three options with the radio buttons in this dialog box: Operation, Callers, and Timing.

- Operation specifies what profiling action will occur for the current area.

  See page 392 for a complete discussion on the Operation option.

- Callers specifies the depth of call-path information.
  - All Callers records all available call-path information for the current routine.
  - Immediate Callers records only "parent" information for the current routine.
  - None turns off call-path information for the current routine.

- Timing specifies whether the profiler will add the execution time of the current area's child routines to a higher-level area or keep it separate.

  The timing option is described in detail on page 393.

- Window Procedure, when checked, specifies that the current area marks a procedure used by Windows.

- The Messages box becomes active when the Window Procedure check box is checked. When Messages is chosen, the Window Procedure Messages dialog box is displayed.

For a complete discussion of the Window Procedure Messages dialog box, refer to Chapter 31.

### Sort

Ctrl S  The Sort command rearranges the information displayed in the Areas window. You can sort alphabetically (by Name) or numerically (by Address). Sorting by Address lists the areas in an order more consistent with the order in which they appear in your source code.

## Routines

The Routines window is where Turbo Profiler displays a list of all routines that you can use as area markers. Use it when you can't remember the name of a routine, or when you want to see which routines have markers set on them. You can use the Inspect command on the Areas SpeedMenu to go to other modules by "inspecting" a routine in a particular module.

The information displayed is basically a list of all global symbols available from debug information included in the executable file. These symbols include all routine and procedure names in standard libraries for Borland's line of C++ or Pascal compilers, as well as the names of routines in any third-party libraries you might be using (provided you link to those libraries with symbolic debug information turned on).

**Note**  The Routines menu gives you easy access to information related to symbols.

**Figure 25.13**   The Routines window

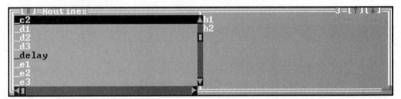

The Routines window is divided into two panes. The left pane lists routines global to your whole profiled program, and the right pane lists routines that are local to the current module of the program you're profiling.

Local routines include nested routines and procedures in Pascal, and static routines in C. Global routines with area markers appear highlighted in the right pane. (By default, an underscore ( _ ) precedes all global variables in Borland C and C++ programs.)

Both panes of the Routines window have SpeedMenus.

### Local Module (right pane)

Ctrl L   When you choose Local Module in the Local Routines pane, the Pick a Module dialog box pops up, listing all modules in your program.

After you highlight a module and choose OK, the profiler displays that module's local symbols in the right pane of the Routines window.

### Areas (both panes)

Ctrl A   The Areas command opens an Areas window and positions that window's highlight bar on the current routine (the one that's highlighted in the Routines window).

### Callers (both panes)

Ctrl C   The Callers command opens a Callers window and shows the current routine's callers.

### Module (both panes)

Ctrl M   The Module command opens a Module window and positions the cursor on the source code for the current routine.

### Profile (both panes)

Ctrl S   The Profile command opens the Execution Profile window and shows the profile statistics for the current routine.

## Disassembly (CPU)

The Disassembly window (labeled "CPU" when it's on the screen) displays the current area in the Module window as disassembled source code. The title bar of the Disassembly window indicates your system processor type and the word Protected appears if your program is a protected-mode program. You use the Disassembly (CPU) window to help determine if you want to rewrite parts of your program in assembly language.

**Figure 25.14**   The Disassembly (CPU) window

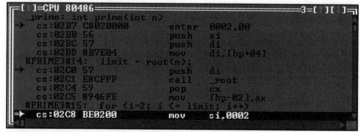

The left part of each disassembled line shows the instruction's address, either as a hexadecimal *Segment:Offset* value or, if the segment value is the same as the current CS register, as a CS:*Offset* value. If the window is wide enough (zoomed or resized), it also displays the bytes that make up the instruction. The disassembled instruction appears to the right of each line.

In the Disassembly (CPU) window, global symbols appear simply as the symbol name. Static symbols appear (generically) as

```
THAT#ModName#SymbolName       /* Borland C++ */

ModName.SymbolName       { Borland Pascal }
```

where *ModName* is the module name and *SymbolName* is the static symbol name. Line numbers appear (also generically) as

```
#ModName#LineNumber      /* Borland C++ */

ModName.LineNumber       { Borland Pascal }
```

where *ModName* is the module name and *LineNumber* is the decimal line number.

In the Disassembly (CPU) window, you can use the *F2* function key to set area markers for each machine instruction you want to monitor. Any marked instructions that have no symbol name appear in the Areas window as hex addresses in *Segment:Offset* form. (Note that *F2* can also be used to remove a marker from an area.)

With the Disassembly (CPU) window's SpeedMenu commands, you can go immediately to any of these locations:

- A specified address
- The current program location (CS:IP)
- The destination address of the current instruction
- The previous instruction pointer address
- The address in the source code

You can also choose a SpeedMenu item to activate the Module window and move its cursor to the source for the current instruction, or to display disassembled instructions and source code three different ways.

## Goto

Ctrl G

When you choose Goto, a dialog box pops up and requests the address you want to go to. Enter a hexadecimal address, using the hex format for your programming language.

You can enter addresses outside of your program to examine code in the BIOS ROM, inside DOS, and in resident utilities.

The Previous command restores the Disassembly (CPU) window to the position it had before you chose Goto.

## Origin

Ctrl O

You choose Origin to position the window's highlight bar at the current program location as indicated by the CS:IP register pair. This command is useful when you have been looking at your code and want to get back to the address of the current instruction pointer (CS:IP), where your program is stopped.

The Previous command restores the Disassembly (CPU) window to the position it had before you chose Origin.

### Follow

Ctrl F    The Follow command positions the Disassembly (CPU) window's highlight bar at the destination address of the currently highlighted instruction. The window scrolls to display the code at the address where the currently highlighted instruction will transfer control. For conditional jumps, the window shows the address as if the jump occurred.

You can use this command with CALL, JMP, and conditional jump (JZ, JNE, LOOP, JCXZ, and so on) instructions.

The Previous command restores the Disassembly (CPU) window to the position it had before you chose Follow.

### Previous

Ctrl P    When you issue a command that changes the instruction pointer address (such as Goto, Origin, or Follow), the Previous command goes back to the address displayed before you issued that address-changing command. If you move around with the arrow keys and the *PgUp* and *PgDn* keys, the profiler does not remember the window's position, but you can always return to the origin, which is the current CS:IP.

Repeated use of the Previous command switches the Disassembly (CPU) window back and forth between two addresses.

### View Source

Ctrl V    The View Source command opens a Module window and shows the source code for the current routine.

### Mixed

Ctrl M    There are three ways to display disassembled instructions and source code in the Disassembly (CPU) window. You choose the window's display format with the SpeedMenu's Mixed command, which toggles between three choices: No, Yes, and Both.

- *No* means that no source code is displayed, only disassembled instructions.

  In No mode, global label names are still used in place of addresses for calls, jumps, and references to data items.

- *Yes* means that source code lines appear before the first disassembled instruction for that source line.

  The profiler automatically sets the window to Yes if your current module is a high-level language source module.

- *Both* means that source code lines replace disassembled lines for those lines that have corresponding source code; otherwise, the disassembled instruction appears.

  The profiler sets the window to Both if your current module is an assembler source module.

  Use Both if you're profiling an assembler module and want to see the original source code line, instead of the corresponding disassembled instruction.

## Text File

You can examine or modify any file on your system by using a Text File window. You can view the file only as ASCII text, so files containing binary data may display characters from the extended ASCII character set.

Before you can open a File window, you must choose the View | Text File command from the menu bar. This command brings up a dialog box in which you can use DOS-style wildcards to get a list of file choices, or you can type a specific file name to load.

Once you've chosen your file, Turbo Profiler displays it in the File window.

The File window shows the contents of the file you've selected. The name of the file you're viewing is displayed at the top of the window, along with the line number the cursor is on.

The File window SpeedMenu has a number of commands for moving around in a disk file, changing the way the contents of the file are displayed, and making changes to the file.

### Goto

Ctrl G   Positions you at a new line number in the file when you enter the new line number to go to. If you enter a line number after the last line in the file, you will be positioned at the end of the file.

### Search

Ctrl S   Searches for a character string, starting at the current cursor position. You are prompted to enter the string to search for. If you have marked a block in the file using the *Ins* key, that block will be used to initialize the Search dialog box. This saves you from typing if you want to search for a string that is already in the file you are viewing. The search string can include simple wildcards, with ? indicating a match on any single character, and * matching 0 or more characters.

The search begins from the current cursor position and does not wrap around from the end of the file to the beginning. To search the entire file, start at the first line (press *Ctrl+PgUp* to move to the top of the file).

You can also invoke this command by simply starting to type the string you want to search for. This brings up a dialog box exactly as if you had specified the Search command.

### Next

Ctrl N   Searches for the next instance of the character string you specified with the Search command; you can use this command only after first issuing a Search command.

This command is useful when your Search command didn't find the instance of the string you wanted. You can keep issuing this command until you find what you want.

### File

Ctrl F Displays the same Program Load dialog box as the View I Text File command, enabling you to load a different file.

### Edit

Ctrl E Lets you make changes to the file you're viewing by invoking the editor you specified with the TFINST installation program. This is done through the Editor Program Name field (located under the Options I Directories dialog box in TFINST). This option is not available when profiling Windows applications with TPROFW.

## Coverage

The Coverage window has two panes: the left pane displays a list of selected modules, and the right pane shows the blocks contained in those modules. A *block* is a section of code that has only one entry point and one exit point; there are no jumps into or out of a block.

**Figure 25.15**     The Coverage window

Selecting coverage mode (Statistics I Profiling Options) opens the Coverage window, replacing the Execution Profile window. By default, Turbo Profiler selects as many program modules as possible in the left pane and all blocks within those modules are listed in the right pane.

**Note**   The Coverage window and the Execution Profile window are mutually exclusive; only one can be open at any given time.

In its default setting, the Coverage window lists only unexecuted blocks in the right pane. Blocks that have been executed (*hit*) during a program run will be deleted from the listing.

Before a program run, all program blocks are marked in the Module window with a ▶ character. In the default Coverage mode, Turbo Profiler removes the ▶ character from each block as it is hit. Successive program runs continue to remove block markers, allowing you to attempt different actions in order to hit the remaining marked blocks.

**Note**   Turbo Profiler automatically marks all program blocks with a single marker.

To restore all program blocks to an unhit status, choose Delete All from the Statistics menu.

Each pane of the Coverage window has its own SpeedMenu.

The left pane's SpeedMenu provides commands for selecting which modules are to be included in the profiling session. The right pane's SpeedMenu provides commands pertaining to how blocks are displayed.

### Add All Modules (left pane)

Ctrl A  When you choose Add All Modules, the blocks from all program modules contained in the executable program are marked for the profile session. The keyword *All* indicates this selection.

### Remove All Modules (left pane)

Ctrl R  Remove All Modules removes all modules from the module list, leaving both panes in the Coverage window empty.

### Add Module (left pane)

Ctrl M  The Add Module command opens the Pick a Module dialog box, allowing you to select from the list of modules in the current program.

For more information on the Pick a Module dialog box and its use, refer to page 394.

### Remove Module (left pane)

Ctrl V  Choosing Remove Module opens the Pick a Module dialog box. Using this dialog box, you can remove a module from subsequent profile runs.

### Delete This Item (left pane)

Ctrl D  The Delete This Item command either deletes or adds the currently highlighted item for the remaining profile runs. If the item has no dash (—) in front of it, the item is deleted. If the item does have a dash in front of it, it's added.

### Display (right pane)

Ctrl D  When you choose Display from the right pane's SpeedMenu, the Coverage Display dialog box appears.

**Figure 25.16**    The Coverage Display dialog box

- The Display buttons define what gets displayed in the right pane of the Coverage window.
  - When you choose All, all blocks (both hit and unhit) are displayed in the right pane. Blocks that have been hit show how many times they've been hit, and blocks that haven't been hit display a zero (0) next to their entries. You can set the number of hit counts that the Profiler tracks from the Profiling Options dialog box's Maximum Coverage Count option.

    See Figure 25.18 on page 418 for more information on setting Turbo Profiler's coverage hit count.

- Not Hit (the default setting) means that only blocks that haven't been hit are displayed.

- The Sort buttons define the order of block display. This menu item is available only if All is selected from the Display option and Max Coverage Count in the Profiling Options dialog box is greater than 1.

  - A sort by Address lists blocks in alphabetical order.

  - A sort by Count lists the blocks in order of number of hits, starting with those blocks that have not been hit.

- The Group radio buttons allow you to group blocks individually, or by routine or module.

**Note**     The Group buttons are available only if Display is set to All.

  - Selecting Block (the default setting) causes all blocks to be listed in the window pane.

  - Selecting Routine causes blocks to be grouped together by routine. With this selection, only routine names from the modules displayed in the left pane are listed in the right pane. However, in addition to each routine name, a count of blocks contained in the routine and the total number of blocks that have been hit is displayed.

**Figure 25.17** The Coverage window, listing blocks by routine

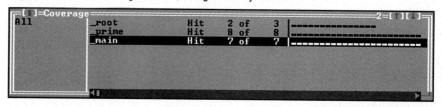

- The Module radio button applies only to programs with multiple modules. It works similarly to the Routine button, except that it groups blocks by module instead of by routine name.

## Position (right pane)

**Ctrl P**     Use the Position command to inspect source code for a particular block of code. When in the right pane, select a block by moving the highlight bar with the arrow keys. After you select a block, choose Position to bring the source code into view in the Module window or the CPU window while keeping the Coverage window active.

Pressing *Spacebar* also executes the Position command.

## Module (right pane)

**Ctrl M**     The Module command is much like Position, except that Module activates the Module or CPU window and positions the cursor at the top of the block selected.

Pressing *Enter* also executes the Module command.

**Note**     When Coverage mode is in effect, certain Turbo Profiler functions are no longer pertinent, and respective menu items will be dimmed. Specifically, the following windows are unavailable from the View menu: Execution Profile, Callers, Files, Areas, and Routines. The Statistics menu dims both the Callers and Files functions. Also, the Accumulation toggle switch in the Statistics menu is automatically set to Enabled. Lastly, the SpeedMenu of the Module window dims the functions Add areas, Remove Areas, Operation, and Callers.

## Run menu

The Run menu provides three commands for running your program: Run, Program Reset, and Arguments. Control returns to the profiler when one of the following events occurs:

- Your program finishes running
- Your program encounters an area marker whose operation is Stop
- You interrupt execution with the interrupt key
- Your program causes an exception

(Usually, the interrupt key is the *Ctrl+Break* key combination; you can change this to another key with TFINST, the profiler installation program. When profiling a Windows application using TPROFW, use the keystroke sequence *Ctrl+Alt+SysRq* to interrupt the program. See Chapter 31 for details.)

You can run your program even if the Module window is closed (as long as there's a program loaded into Turbo Profiler).

**Note**    When you choose Run | Run or Run | Program Reset after reaching the run count limit, any statistics collected for a previous execution are reset. If you want to save a set of statistics, use Statistics | Save before you select Run or Program Reset, or use Statistics | Profiling Options to set the run count greater than 1.

### Run

The Run command runs your program and collects performance statistics.

If you set the Display Swapping option in the Display Options dialog box to Always, your program's output replaces the Turbo Profiler environment screen until the program finishes or you interrupt it.

### Program Reset

The Run | Program Reset command reloads your program from disk. Use this command if you've run your program too far during a profiling session and need to restart execution at the start of the program.

If you select Run | Program Reset when the Module or Disassembly (CPU) window is active, the display in that window won't return to the start of the program. Instead, the cursor stays exactly where it was when you chose Program Reset.

### Arguments

The program you're profiling might expect command-line arguments. With Run | Arguments, you can store your program's command-line arguments within Turbo Profiler. Then, when you choose Run | Run or Run | Program Reset, the profiler passes the arguments to your program just as if you had typed them in at the command line. You can change these arguments from within Turbo Profiler and rerun your program.

Enter the arguments exactly as you would at the DOS command line. (Do not enter the program name.)

## Statistics menu

The Statistics menu contains commands to

- Specify the type of data the profiler will collect (callers, files, interrupts, overlays)
- Set the profile mode to active, passive, or coverage
- Determine the number of program runs and areas
- Turn automatic data collection on and off
- Erase profile statistics
- Save profile statistics to a file
- Restore previously saved statistics

The default extension is .TFS, but you can use any extension you want.

You can save all statistical information from the current profile to a .TFS file. Then, whenever you want to study the profile results, you can load that .TFS file—recovering all the saved statistics without having to rerun the profile.

This feature is most useful if your programs take a long time to run or profile. You can save multiple versions of profiles under different conditions, then restore each of the resulting profiles for quick comparison at a later date. To automate this process, you can create a macro or DOS batch file to automatically run several profiles with different options or area markers, saving the results to individual .TFS files. Then, using the macro or batch file, you can run the profiles and view your results later.

**Note** The first four items on the Statistics menu are toggle switches. When selected, the Callers, Files, Interrupts, and Overlay options will toggle between the *Enabled* and *Disabled* modes.

### Callers

When you set the Callers option to Enabled, the profiler gathers statistics about which routines call other routines. To specify which routines you want call histories for, you choose the Callers command on the Module window's SpeedMenu or the Options command on the Areas window's SpeedMenu, then select the appropriate radio buttons under Callers and Areas.

**Note** You must run your program and accumulate some statistics before these windows show any information.

After running your program and gathering the profile information, use the Callers window to look at the call-history statistics.

Gathering caller information consumes memory and slows down your program's run speed. If you don't need caller information, set Callers to Disabled.

## Files

When you enable the Files option, the profiler gathers statistics about which files your program opens, and which read and write operations take place.

After running your program and gathering the profile information, use the Files window to look at your program's file activity.

Gathering file-activity information consumes memory and slows down your program's run speed. If you don't need file-activity information, set Files to Disabled.

## Interrupts

When the Interrupts option is set to Enabled, the profiler collects statistics about which interrupts your program calls. The profiler keeps separate statistics for DOS, video, disk BIOS, mouse, and keyboard interrupts.

After running your program and gathering the profile information, use the Interrupts window to look at which interrupts your program called.

Gathering interrupt information consumes memory and slows down your program's run speed. If you don't need interrupt information, set Interrupts to Disabled.

## Overlays

The Overlays option toggles whether statistics are collected for the overlays your program loads. If your program does not contain overlays, an error message is displayed if you try to enable this menu item, and the option remains disabled.

Gathering overlay information consumes memory and slows down the speed at which your program runs. If you don't need overlay information, set this option to Disabled.

## Profiling Options

The Statistics | Profiling Options command opens the Profiling Options dialog box, shown here:

**Figure 25.18**    The Profiling Options dialog box

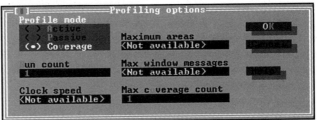

With the Profiling Options dialog box, you can set any of the following options:

- Profile Mode specifies the analysis mode. The default mode is Active.
  - *Active analysis* means full statistical information is collected for each marked area. This includes basic clock timing information, and for routines, how many times the routine was called and where it was called from.

- *Passive analysis* means only basic clock timing information for each marked area is collected. Passive mode is not available in TPROFW when running Windows in 386 enhanced mode.

- *Coverage analysis*, in its default setting, means that Turbo Profiler tracks the blocks of code that haven't been hit during a succession of program runs.

**Note**   If you change analysis mode from Active or Passive to Coverage (or vice versa), you'll be prompted with `Reload program and change profiling mode?` If you select the YES button in answer to this prompt, the current set of statistics is deleted, and the new analysis mode becomes effective. Be sure to save any vital profile statistics before changing analysis modes, or they'll be lost.

- Run Count sets how many times your program will run while the profiler collects statistics. The default is 1.

**Note**   If Run Count is set to a number higher than 1, Turbo Profiler will reset statistics only after the specified number of runs.

- Clock Speed defines the speed of the timing clock, in ticks per second. The default is 100 ticks per second. Clock speed is available only in passive mode.

- Maximum Areas specifies the maximum number of areas you can divide the current program into. Turbo Profiler sets default areas based on the density of the symbols it finds appended to the executable file. Increasing this setting will decrease the amount of memory left for the profiled program.

- Maximum Windows Messages sets the maximum number of Windows messages that can be marked. The default setting is 20. Increasing this setting will decrease the amount of memory left for the profiled program.

- Maximum Coverage Count sets the maximum number of hit counts that the Profiler will keep track of while in coverage mode. The default for this setting is 1 (a block has either been hit, or it has not). Increasing this setting will decrease the amount of memory left for the profiled program and will increase the time it takes to run.

With the options in this dialog box, you can tailor the profiling session to meet your unique programming needs.

Active analysis mode provides the most detailed analysis of your program at the cost of slowing program execution speed. On the other hand, passive mode allows your program to run at almost full speed, but does not provide any information about how many times a routine was called or which routines called it.

If there are not many clock ticks during the time your profiled program runs, the data collected might not accurately reflect the time spent in various parts of the program. Running the program several times helps improve the accuracy by increasing the total number of data points collected. Speeding up the clock is another way to increase the total number of data points; this increases the accuracy of the timing statistics for each region at the expense of slowing down program execution speed.

**Note**   The profiler doesn't actually time each area, but uses the interrupt timer to increment a timer count. When the program terminates, the profiler converts the values in the timer counts to execution times, based on the current setting of the Clock Speed option in the Profiling Options dialog box.

## Accumulation

The Statistics | Accumulation option turns automatic data collection on and off. This means you can collect data for a subset of all marked areas without removing any area markers, and manually turn data collection on after your program begins running.

To collect data for a subset of all marked areas, do this:

1  In the Areas window's SpeedMenu, choose Options to open the Area Options dialog box.

2  For those areas whose statistics you want, change the area marker from Normal to Enable (to start data collection) or to Disable (to stop data collection).

3  Set Statistics | Accumulation to *Disabled*.

4  Run your program. The profiler will not start collecting data until it trips an area marker that's set to Enable.

To turn on data collection manually after your program has started running, do this:

1  Set area markers.

2  Set Statistics | Accumulation to *Disabled*.

3  Run your program from the profiler (press *F9*).

4  When the program is in the appropriate run-time state, interrupt it.

5  Enable the collection of profile data (set Statistics | Accumulation to *Enabled*).

6  Resume program execution (press *F9* again).

Turbo Profiler starts accumulating statistics immediately for the marked areas.

### Disabling accumulation

Sometimes when many different places in your program call a routine or family of routines, you want to know only

- The time spent in the routine
- When a specific part of your code calls the routine
- The time spent in the routine after a specific event

To monitor only certain calls to a routine, use Statistics | Accumulation to disable data collection at the start. Mark an area that enables collection just before the call to the routine that you want to collect statistics for (set the area marker to Enabled). Mark another area that disables collection after the routine returns. You can also enable and disable areas in unrelated parts of the code; do this when you want to collect statistics only after a certain event.

**Example #1: Collecting only for a specific call to a routine**
Suppose you're interested in calls to **abc** only when it is called from **xyz**, but not at any other time.

```
=>     main()              /* normal area marker at routine */
       {
         ⋮
```

```
        abc();                  /* don't want to collect stats for this call */
        ⋮
        xyz();
      }


  =>    xyz()                   /* normal area marker at routine */
      {
        ⋮
  e>      abc();                /* want to collect statistics for this call */
  d>      ⋮
      }


  =>    abc()                   /* normal area marker at routine */
      {
        ⋮
      }
```

Notice the e▶ that enables collection and the d▶ that disables collection. You must disable Statistics | Accumulation before running your program, or the profiler will erroneously collect statistics for the first call to **abc** in **main**.

### Example #2: Collecting after a certain event has occurred

Suppose that routine **xyz** behaves differently depending on some global state information controlled by the two routines **bufferon** and **bufferoff**. You are interested only in the time spent in **xyz** when bufferflag equals 1.

```
  =>    main()              /* normal area marker at routine */
      {
        ⋮
        xyz();              /* no statistics collected here */
        ⋮
        bufferon();
        ⋮
        xyz();              /* will collect statistics for this call */
        ⋮
        bufferoff();
        ⋮
        xyz();              /* no statistics collected here */
      }


  =>    bufferon()          /* normal area marker at routine */
      {
        ⋮
        bufferflag = 1;
  e>    }


  d>    bufferoff()         /* normal area marker at routine */
      {
        ⋮
        bufferflag = 0;
      }
```

```
=>     xyz()                    /* normal area marker at routine */
       {
         ⋮
       }
```

Notice that the use of e► to enable collection and the d► to disable collection are not near the calls to **xyz**. Once again, you must disable data collection at the start (by setting Statistics | Accumulation to *Disabled*), or the first call to **xyz** will erroneously contribute to the collected statistics.

## Delete All

The Statistics | Delete All command erases all statistics collected for the current profiling session—essentially wiping the data slate clean so you can start afresh. Delete All removes all profile data from the open profile report windows (Execution Profile, Callers, Interrupts, Files, Overlays, and Coverage), but it does not delete the profiling options you've set.

## Save

The Statistics | Save command saves the following data, settings, and options:

- All statistics for which collection was enabled when you ran the current profile (execution times and counts, callers, file activity, interrupts, overlays, coverage counts).

- All area information (area names, operations, callers, separate versus combined timing) displayed in the Execution Profile window.

Once you've saved statistics to a file, you can recover them at any time with the Statistics | Restore command.

When you choose Statistics | Save, the Enter File Name to Save dialog box appears.

The Name input box lists a default .TFS file name (*progname*.TFS, where *progname* is the current program's name).

### Saving Files

To save the current profile statistics to the default file, choose OK.

To save them to a different file,

1  Activate the File | Name input box.

2  Type in the desired file name (including disk drive and path, if you so choose).

3  Choose OK (or press *Enter*).

If the statistics file already exists, a message box asks if it's all right to overwrite the file.

## Restore

When you choose Statistics | Restore, the Enter File Name to Restore dialog box appears.

The Restore dialog box works just like the profiler's other file-loading dialog boxes. You can

- Enter a file name or a specification (with DOS wildcards) in the File Name input box.

- Choose a different disk drive or directory from the directory tree.

- Choose a file name from the Files list box.

- Choose OK to complete the transaction (or choose Cancel to leave the dialog box without loading a file).

- Choose Help to open a window of information about how to use the dialog box.

After you load a statistics file, Turbo Profiler restores all the saved options, settings, and resulting statistical information to the environment screen.

# Print menu

Turbo Profiler's Print menu enables you to print the contents of any open profiler window to a new or existing disk file, or directly to the printer.

## Statistics

The Print | Statistics command prints the contents of all open profiler windows (*except* for the Module, Routines, Text File, and Disassembly windows) to the printer, or to the destination file named in the Printing Options dialog box.

Before you choose Print | Statistics, open the Printing Options dialog box (choose Print | Options) and verify that the current printing options (dimensions, output location, character set used, and—if you're printing to a file—destination file name) are what you want.

If you choose to print statistics to an existing disk file, a menu pops up so you can choose whether to append the existing file, overwrite it, or cancel the printing operation.

## Module

From the Pick a Module dialog box accessed by choosing Print | Module, you specify which of your program's modules you want printed to the printer or to the disk file named in the Printing Options dialog box.

You can choose a specific module by name, or choose All Modules to print all your program's available source code. When the profiler prints a module, it produces an *annotated source listing* that lists execution time and counts data next to each source line or routine you've marked as an area, as shown in the following listing:

```
Program: C:TPROFILEPRIME1.EXE   File PRIME1.C

Time    Counts
                #include <stdio.h>

0.0090 999      prime(int n)
                {
                        int i;

0.0117 999              for (i=2; i<n; i++)
1.1456 78022                    if (n % i == 0)
0.0080 831                              return 0;
0.0017 168              return 1;
0.0101 999      }

0.0000 1        main()
                {
                        int i, n;

0.0000 1                n = 1000;
0.0000 1                for (i=2; i<=n; i++)
0.0255 999                      if (prime(i))
4.1670 168                              printf("%d
0.0000 1        }
```

## Options

When you choose Options from the Print menu, the Printing Options dialog box appears.

- Width is the number of characters printed per line (default = 80).

- Height is the total number of lines per page (default = 66).

- The Printer/File radio buttons let you choose between sending the printed statistics to the current printer or to a file. The default is Printer.

- The Graphics/ASCII radio buttons let you toggle between printing characters from the IBM extended character set (including semigraphic characters) and printing only ASCII characters. The default is ASCII.

- Destination File is the disk drive (optional), path name (optional), and file name (required) of the printed disk file.

## Options menu

With the Options menu, you can

- Record a keystroke macro.

- Remove one or all macros.

- Set display options that control Turbo Profiler's overall appearance and operation.

- Specify directories (other than the current one) where Turbo Profiler will search for source code.

- Save your window layout, macros, options set in other menus, and some other miscellaneous options to a configuration file.

- Restore the settings and options previously saved in a configuration file.

## Macros

The Options | Macro command leads to a menu that lets you define new keystroke macros or delete ones that have already been assigned.

The profiler's macro facility gives you the ability to record frequently used keystroke sequences and place the recording into a single *macro* keystroke. For example, during profiling, you may often repeat the same sequence of commands. With macros, you can define a single keystroke that "plays" this sequence of keystrokes. Once defined, you can simply press the macro key to perform the tedious task.

(Alt)(=)  ### Create

When issued, the Create command starts recording keystrokes into an assigned macro key. As an alternative, press the *Alt=* hot key for Create.

When you choose Create to start recording, a prompt asks for a key to assign the macro to. Respond by typing in a keystroke or combination of keys (for example, *Alt+M*). The message RECORDING will be displayed in the upper right corner of the screen while you record the macro.

(Alt)(-)  ### Stop Recording

The Stop Recording command terminates the macro recording session. Use the *Alt+-* (*Alt+Hyphen*) hot key to issue this command, or press the macro keystroke that you are defining to stop recording.

**Important**   Do *not* use the Options | Macro | Stop Recording menu selection to stop recording your macro, because these keystrokes will then be added to your macro! (The menu item is added to remind you of the hot key.)

### Remove

The Remove command removes a macro assigned to a keystroke. When you choose this menu item, a list box pops up, displaying a list of the currently defined macros. Select the macro that you want to delete, and press *Enter*.

### Delete All

The Delete All command removes all macro keystroke definitions and restores all keys to their original (default) meanings.

### Recording macros

To record a macro,

1  Choose Options | Macros | Create (or press *Alt=*) to begin the macro definition. A prompt appears, asking which key you want the macro assigned to.

2  Enter a key that isn't already assigned, for example, *Shift+F10*.

**3** Once you begin recording the macro, all keystrokes entered become part of the macro definition. However, keystrokes entered as program input and mouse actions will *not* be included in the macro definition.

**4** Stop recording the macro: Press *Alt-* or press the keystroke of the macro you are defining (*Shift+F10* in this example).

**5** Save the macro to a configuration file: Choose Macros from the Save Configuration dialog box (Options | Save Options). Type the name of the configuration file you want (or use one listed in the dialog box), and press OK.

**6** Continue profiling.

## Display Options

The Options | Display Options command opens the Display Options dialog box, shown here.

**Figure 25.19** The Display Options dialog box

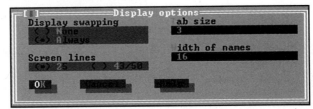

With the Display Options dialog box, you can do any of the following:

- Specify whether Turbo Profiler will swap screens while your program runs
- Set how many columns each tab stop occupies in the Module window
- Set the Turbo Profiler screen to 25-line or 43/50-line mode
- Specify how wide your program's routine names display in the Execution Profile and Areas windows

### Display Swapping

The Display Swapping radio buttons None and Always specify whether Turbo Profiler swaps the user screen back and forth with the Turbo Profiler environment.

- *None* means don't swap between the two screens.

  Use this option if you're profiling a program that does not send any output to the user screen.

- *Always* means swap to the user screen every time your program runs.

  Use this option if your program does writing to the screen.

  When profiling a Windows application, display swapping is automatically set to *Always*, and it cannot be changed.

### Screen Lines

You use Screen Lines to specify whether Turbo Profiler's screen uses the normal 25-line display or the 43-line or 50-line display available on EGA and VGA display adapters.

One or both of these buttons will be available, depending on the type of video adapter in your PC. The 25-line mode is the only screen size available to systems with a monochrome display or Color Graphics Adapter (CGA).

### Tab Size

With the Tab Size input box, you set how many columns each tab stop occupies, from 1 to 32 columns. You can reduce the tab column width to see more text in source files with a lot of tab-indented code.

### Width of Names

The Width of Names input box is where you specify how wide routine names display in the Execution Profile, Callers, and Areas windows.

## Path for Source

By default, Turbo Profiler looks for your program's source code in these places, in this order:

1 In the directory where the program was originally compiled

2 In the directories (if any) you've listed under Options | Path for Source (or stated in the command-line option using the **–sd** switch)

3 In the current directory

4 In the directory that contains the .EXE file of the program you're profiling

With the Options | Path for Source command, you can add a list of directories that Turbo Profiler searches before it searches in the current directory.

Enter the new to-be-searched directories in this format:

```
Directory; Directory; Directory
```

For example,

```
C:BorlandTC; C:Borland'TASM
```

## Save Options

With Options | Save Options, you can save all your current profiler options to a configuration file on disk. Then, whenever you want to reset the profiler options to those saved settings, you can load that configuration file with Options | Restore Options.

When you choose Options | Save Options, the Save Configuration dialog box appears:

**Figure 25.20**   The Save Configuration dialog box

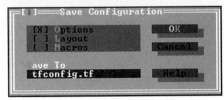

With this dialog box, you can save your current profiler setup's options, layout, and macros. Options, Layout, and Macros are check boxes; you can save one, two, or all three types of information to a configuration file.

- Options are menu options not saved in a .TFA or .TFS file (such as Options | Path for Source, command-line options, and settings in the Display Options dialog box).

- Layout includes which windows are currently open, plus their order, position, and size.

- Macros are all keystroke macros currently defined.

- Save To lists the default configuration file. To save your options there, choose OK (or press *Enter*).

    To save your options to a different file, type in the different file's name (including disk drive and path, if you want), then choose OK (or press *Enter*).

Once you've saved options to a configuration file, you can recover them at any time with Options | Restore Options.

## Restore Options

Options | Restore Options restores your profiling options from a disk file. You can have multiple configuration files, containing different macros, window layouts, and so on.

When you choose Options | Restore Options, the Restore Options dialog box appears.

The Restore Options dialog box works just like the profiler's other file-loading dialog boxes. You can

- Enter a file name or a specification (with DOS wildcards) in the File name input box

- Choose a different disk drive or directory from the directory tree

- Choose a file name from the Files list box

- Choose OK to complete the transaction (or choose Cancel to leave the dialog box without loading a file)

- Choose Help to open a window of information about how to use the dialog box

After you type in or choose a configuration file name and load that file, Turbo Profiler restores all the saved options, settings, layout, and macros to the current Turbo Profiler environment. (You can restore only a configuration file that was created by the Options | Save Options command.)

# Window menu

The Window menu contains commands to

- Manipulate Turbo Profiler's windows
- Navigate within and through the windows
- Toggle windows to icons, and vice versa
- Close and reopen windows
- Go to your program's output screen
- Make an open window active

The commands in the top portion of the Window menu are for moving about within the profiler's windowed environment and for rearranging the windows to your satisfaction. Most Turbo Profiler windows have all the standard window elements (scroll bars, a close box, zoom icons, and so on). Refer to the section "Turbo Profiler windows" earlier in this chapter for information on these elements and how to use them.

## Zoom

The Zoom command zooms the active window (the one with a double-line border) to full-screen, or returns the active window to the pre-zoomed size.

## Next

The Next command activates the window whose number succeeds the number of the current window.

## Next Pane

In windows with multiple panes, the Next Pane command moves the cursor to the next pane.

## Size/Move

The Size/Move command activates Turbo Profiler's window-arranging mode. You move the current window with the *Left, Right, Up* and *Down* keys. Shifted arrow keys expand or contract the window. The legend in the status line explains which key combinations do which action. The hot key for this command is *Ctrl+F5*.

## Iconize/Restore

The Iconize/Restore command shrinks the active window to an icon or restores the active icon to a window.

Turbo Profiler's iconize feature is a handy tool for keeping several windows open without cluttering up the screen. A window icon is a small representation of an open window.

To make a window into its icon, choose Iconize/Restore from the Window menu, or click the iconize box in the window's top frame. To restore an icon to its previous size, choose Iconize/Restore again, or click in the icon's zoom box.

## Close

The Close command temporarily removes the current window from the Turbo Profiler screen. To redisplay the window just as it was, choose Undo Close.

## Undo Close

The Undo Close command reopens the most recently closed window and makes it the active window.

## User Screen

Choose Window | User Screen (or press *Alt+F5*) to view your program's full-screen output. Press any key to return to the windowed environment.

## The open window list

At the bottom of the Window menu is a numbered list of open windows. Press the number corresponding to one of these windows to make it the active window. For a full explanation of how to manage windows, see page 383.

# Help menu

The Help menu gives you access to online help in a special window. There is help information on virtually all aspects of the environment and Turbo Profiler. (Also, one-line menu and dialog hints appear on the status line whenever you select a command.)

To open the Help window, you can either

- Press *F1* or *Alt+F1* at any time (including from any dialog box or when any menu command is selected), or

- Click Help whenever it appears on the status line or in a dialog box.

To close the Help window, press *Esc,* click the close box, or choose Window | Close.

Help screens often contain *keywords* (highlighted text) you can choose to get more information. Press the arrow keys to move to any keyword; then press *Enter* to get more detailed help on the chosen keyword. You can press *Home* and *End* to go to the first and last keywords on the screen, respectively. With a mouse, you can click any keyword to open the help text for it.

## Index

The Help | Index command opens a dialog box displaying a full list of help keywords (the special highlighted text in help screens that let you quickly move to a related screen).

You can page down through the list. When you find a keyword that interests you, choose it by using the arrow keys to move to it and pressing *Enter.* (You can also use the mouse to click it.)

## Previous Topic

The Help | Previous Topic command opens the Help window and redisplays the text you last viewed.

Turbo Profiler lets you back up through 20 previous help screens. You can also click the *PgUp* command in the status line to view the last help screen displayed.

## Help on Help

The Help | Help on Help command opens up a text screen that explains how to use the Turbo Profiler help system.

# 26

# Profiling strategies

Improving your program's performance through profiling is not a simple linear process; you don't just profile the program, modify the source code, and call it a day. Profiling for improved performance with Turbo Profiler is dynamic and interactive. You collect statistics, analyze the results in a variety of windows, perhaps change the profiling parameters so you'll get different statistics, profile again, analyze again, modify the source code and recompile, profile again, analyze again, and so on.

If you're not sure at first where the bottlenecks in your program are, go ahead and profile using Turbo Profiler's default settings. When you look at the results in the Execution Profile window, you get an idea of which routines in your program consume the most overall time. By looking at time and count data together, you find out which parts of the program are most expensive in terms of time per call. Armed with that knowledge, you can start zeroing in on your program's problem areas.

Turbo Profiler provides several different report windows for analyzing the collected data; you can also print report window contents to paper or your screen for a running account of performance improvements. In the report windows, you can look at your program's execution times and counts, file-access activity, DOS interrupts, and overlay activity, along with call histories for routines.

What do you do with all this power and flexibility? How do you use Turbo Profiler for efficient and effective profiling? And what are the tricks of the profiling trade? Obviously, we can't answer all these questions in this chapter. We do, however, provide some general guidelines, techniques, and strategies to get you moving.

The first time you load a program into Turbo Profiler, it

- Sets the profile mode to Active.
- Automatically scans through your .EXE file to find the main program module.
- Loads the main source module into the Module window.
- Sets area markers for the program.
- Positions the cursor at the main module's starting point.

The main module is the one that contains the first source line to be executed in your program. *Area markers* are "trip points" that mark the locations where you want to gather statistics; the number of markers set depends on the number of lines in the .EXE file that have debug information associated with them.

**Note**   Whenever you exit Turbo Profiler, it saves information about the areas you set up for the currently loaded program in an *area file* named *filename*.TFA, where *filename* is the name of your program. Each time you load a program to profile, Turbo Profiler looks for a corresponding .TFA file. If it finds one, it automatically uses the area settings in that file.

It's a good idea to save the results of a profile that takes a long time to run, in case you want to study the results later.

You can also save the results of a profile to a .TFS file with the Statistics | Save command. By default, the file name assigned to a statistics file is *filename*.TFS. You can use the default or change the name (in case you want to save more than one set of statistics for a single program).

# Preparing to profile

The examples in Chapter 24, "A sample profiling session," are small and simple; we designed them to show the general process of profiling. The problem presented in that chapter was to optimize the routine **prime**, rather than to identify specific program bottlenecks.

However, you actually need a profiler more when you're writing very large programs, rather than small ones, because you must identify which program fragments are bottlenecks before you can figure out how to optimize any given fragment. In many ways, it's easier to find the bottlenecks than it is to figure out what to do about them.

## Adjusting your program

The first adjustment to your program is to set it up so you can find out what you need to know from the profile. For example, if you're writing an interactive program that gets a lot of input from the keyboard, you don't need to find out that most of your time is spent waiting for the user to press a key.

Carefully think through how you would like to gather profile statistics, and adjust your source code so the statistics gathered are useful and sufficient. Once the source code is modified (if it needs to be), compile the program with debug information turned on. Then, set area markers that tell the profiler where to collect statistics and what kind of statistics to collect.

Here are some basic techniques for finding bottlenecks in large programs:

- Select data sets large enough to give you a useful profile.

   Selecting pertinent input data is important. A string search program evoked on a three-line file won't tell you very much. Likewise, searching for a short string found in nearly every line of a 10,000-line file will give a different kind of profile than searching for a long string found only once in 10,000 lines.

- If you know your program runs quickly, set the profiler to collect statistics over several runs. (The Run Count setting in the Profiling Options dialog box allows statistics to be accumulated for the number of runs specified.)

- Modify the program to work independently of keyboard input, or disable accumulation of statistics in any areas that require keyboard input.

  If your program requires keyboard input, read data from a file or use a random number generator to stuff numbers into an array. The main idea is to select data that's typical of the real-world data the module operates on.

- Isolate the modules of the program that you know need improvement.

## Compiling your program

After you've adjusted your program so that the profiling session won't become a wild goose chase, compile it again with debug information turned on. Files that you've compiled for debugging with Turbo Debugger can be handled by Turbo Profiler without recompilation.

Turbo Profiler works with 16-bit Turbo C++, Borland C++, and Turbo Assembler programs. You must compile your source code with full symbolic debugging information turned on, as follows:

- **Borland C++:** In the Project Options dialog box, check the following two options:
  - Compiler | Debugging | Debug Information in OBJs.
  - Linker | General | Include Debug Information.

- **Turbo Assembler:** Source code must be assembled with the **/zi** command-line option and linked with TLINK, using the **/v** option.

To run Turbo Profiler, you need *both* the .EXE file and the original source files. Turbo Profiler searches for the source files in these directories, in this order:

1 In the directory in which they were found at compile time (this information is included in the executable file).

2 In the directories specified with the Options | Path for Source command (or in the directories specified with the **–sd** command-line option).

3 In the current directory.

4 In the directory containing the executable program being profiled.

## Setting profile areas

Once you've adjusted your program so you can concentrate on the troublesome areas and have compiled it with debug information turned on, you're ready to run it through the profiler and collect statistics for individual areas. You can start out by profiling your whole program in general, then focus in on more and more detail as you find the trouble spots. Start by accepting the default area settings—Turbo Profiler sets default areas based on the density of the symbols it finds appended to the executable file.

An *area* is a location in your program where you want to collect statistics: It can be a single line, a construct such as a loop, or an entire routine. An *area marker* sets an internal breakpoint. Whenever the profiler encounters one of these breakpoints, it executes a certain set of code—depending on the options you've set for the area in question. This profiling code could be a bookkeeping routine or a simple command to stop program execution.

These are the actions the profiler can perform when execution encounters an area marker:

| Operation | What it does |
|---|---|
| *Normal* | Activates the default counting behavior (collects execution time and counts for all marked areas). |
| *Enable* | Turns on the collection of statistics (if they've been previously disabled). |
| *Disable* | Turns off the collection of statistics, but lets your program keep running. When your program enters an area where the action is set to *Enable*, the profiler resumes data collection. |
| *Stop* | Stops the program, and returns control to the Turbo Profiler environment (or to DOS, if you are using batch mode execution). At that point, you can examine the collected statistics, then resume execution. |

By default, Turbo Profiler counts the number of times execution enters an area and how long it stays there. You can change what the profiler does when an area executes by setting the Operation option in the Area Options dialog box—accessed through the Module or Areas window SpeedMenus.

When you're setting areas in your program before running a profile, you should consider these questions:

- How many areas should statistics be collected for?
- Which parts of the program should be profiled?
- What should happen at each marked area?

## What level of detail do you need?

You must first decide how much information you want. Keep in mind how large your program is and how long it takes to run.

- For a small program, you probably want statistics for every executable line—the maximum level of detail.

- For large programs, you need less detail; just profiling the amount of time spent in each routine is probably enough.

"Large" is a bit vague. You need to take into account the number of modules of source code, the number of routines, and the number of lines.

If your source consists of 10,000 lines in ten modules, you should probably analyze only one module at a time in active analysis. (Your program is factored into discrete functional modules, right?)

On the other hand, if your program is less than 100 lines and you need detailed analysis, you probably want to collect statistics for all the lines.

If your program runs in less than five seconds, you'll get more accurate profile results if you set up multiple runs with averaged results. (Set the number of runs with the Statistics | Profiling command.) If the program takes an hour to run (not counting profiler overhead), be careful not to set so many areas that you slow down execution to an unacceptable crawl.

## Adding areas

Divide your program into a number of areas by selecting Add Areas from the Module window's SpeedMenu. After this, run your program to accumulate statistics for each area.

If you don't tell Turbo Profiler how to divide your program, it uses a default scheme to intelligently select appropriate areas in your program. Based on information it finds in a program's symbol tables, Turbo Profiler selects one of several default options for setting areas in a program.

- If there are few symbols in the table, and there is a single module, Turbo Profiler selects Every Line in Module as the default area setting.

- If there are many symbols and several modules, Turbo Profiler selects All Routines as the default area setting.

**Note**     If your program is very large, profile it first in passive mode to get the big picture, then select areas for more detailed analysis.

## What type of data do you need?

For each area in your program, Turbo Profiler accumulates the following default information for Active and Passive modes:

- The number of calls to the area
- How much time was spent in the area (active mode)
- How many clock ticks occurred while the area executed (passive mode)

You can also collect more extensive information during the profiling session.

- By enabling Statistics | Callers and setting Call Stack options in the Area Options dialog box, you can track which routines call a marked routine—how often and through what pathway.

- With the Statistics | Files option enabled, you can monitor your program's file-access activity.

- The Statistics | Interrupts option, when it is enabled, records your program's interrupts.

- You can monitor your program's overlay file activity by enabling the Statistics | Overlays option.

Once you've enabled the appropriate Statistics menu options, you can open the corresponding profile report windows (through the View menu), then call up each window's SpeedMenu to specify details about how you want the data collected.

Remember, to get the Turbo Profiler reports you want, set all options before you run the program.

## When should data collection start?

Often, you want to collect timing information only when a certain portion of a program is running. To do this, start the program executing without collecting any information; set the Statistics | Accumulation option to *Disabled*. You can determine the Accumulation option's setting at any time by bringing up the File | Get Info box and checking the status of Collection.

With Accumulation disabled, you must set an area marker to *Enable* for the area where you want data collection to start, then set another marker to *Disable* for the area where you want data collection to stop. The actual number of start and stop points you set is determined by the amount of available memory; generally, you can set as many as you need.

## How do you want time data grouped?

The profiler can keep each routine's execution-time statistics separate from others, or it can combine each routine's times with those of the routines calling them.

By default, as soon as an active routine calls a routine that has an area marker, the profiler puts the calling routine on the call stack and makes it inactive. The profiler associates any timer counts made while program control is in the routine with that routine only, not with the caller.

However, if you specify that the caller should use a combined clock (rather than a separate clock), the profiler associates timer ticks that occur while control is in the routine with the caller.

Turbo Profiler's default analysis mode uses a separate timer for each marked routine. So normally, the time spent in a routine is measured exclusive of calls to other routines. If you want a routine's time data to include time spent in child routines, choose Combined under Timing from the Areas window local Option command.

## Which data do you want to view?

It's important to know how to control the amount of information Turbo Profiler collects and subsequently displays, particularly if you want detailed information about just part of a large program. Turbo Profiler provides two ways to control how much information you view about your program:

- Before you profile, you can limit the collection to specific areas and types of data by setting options and parameters.

- After the profile, you can filter the collected statistics (without erasing any) and display only the data you're currently interested in.

In the Module, Areas, and Interrupt windows, you can specify which parts of your program you want Turbo Profiler to collect information about, and how much information to collect. You can choose to make data collection as coarse as all routines in a module or as fine as a single statement. You can choose to collect time-related data only (by setting the analysis mode to Passive), or you can choose to collect the full gamut of data, including complete call-stack histories, all file-access and overlay activities, and all DOS interrupt calls. You can slow down or speed up the profiler's timer, thus decreasing or increasing the resolution of data collected (passive mode only).

**Note**   There's a basic tradeoff in how much data you choose to collect: The more information Turbo Profiler collects, the slower your program runs and the more memory it needs to store the collected statistics.

See page 447 for more information about filtering displayed statistics.

Once you've collected the data, you can use commands in the profile report windows to temporarily exclude the data you don't want to look at from the displayed statistics.

# Profiling your program

Once you've selected appropriate areas to monitor, run the profile. You can save the resulting profile with the Statistics | Save command. This command saves the statistics to a .TFS (Turbo Profiler Statistics) file. If you plan to save several different profile results, use a file-naming convention that uniquely identifies each of the runs (for example, RUN1.TFS, RUN2.TFS, and so on). This simplifies your task of comparing them later.

You might not know if a profile is worth saving until you look at several sets of statistics.

After you save the .TFS file, you can study the profile's results in the profile report windows, sorting and filtering the displayed data as you explore their meanings. You won't lose any area markers or statistical reports, because all this information can be reproduced (simply restore the profile from the .TFS file). In general, if a profile took a long time to create, save it unless you're absolutely sure you won't need it.

## Focusing the profile session

Normally, programmers use a profiler to get answers to one or more of these questions:

- How efficient is this algorithm? (*Algorithm testing*)

- Is this program doing what I think it is? Is all of it running? (*Program testing and verification*)

- How long does each routine run? How much time does the program spend using various resources? (*Execution timing and resource monitoring*)

- What's the structure of this code? (*Program structure analysis*)

The following table relates your profiling session to the type of information you'd like to gather:

**Table 26.1**   Ways of using a profiler

| Purpose of profile | Type of information needed |
| --- | --- |
| Algorithm testing | Line-count information<br>Dynamic call history |
| Program testing and verification | Coverage analysis<br>Dynamic call history |

**Table 26.1**   Ways of using a profiler (continued)

| Purpose of profile | Type of information needed |
|---|---|
| Execution timing and resource monitoring | Execution time<br>Execution counts<br>Interrupt activity File-access activity<br>Overlay activity |
| Program structure analysis | Dynamic call history<br>File-access activity<br>Execution profile (time and counts)<br>Interrupt activity<br>Overlay activity |

## Testing algorithms

If you're analyzing an algorithm, you'll probably concentrate on a small number of routines, so it's more important to gather information about line count than execution times. You need to do the following:

1  Isolate the algorithm and its supporting routines by marking them as areas.

2  Make sure you've set area markers for all lines in all routines that implement the algorithm in question.

The examples in Chapter 24 demonstrate algorithm analysis, especially as it relates to execution time statistics.

## Verifying and testing programs

In program verification and testing, block execution information is more pertinent than execution times. Since the verification and testing process looks at the program as a whole, you want to see how everything works together in an integrated system. Profiling a program while you run it through standard tests can point out areas of the program that execute very little or not at all. Coverage analysis mode is most useful for this type of verification testing.

If you deal with large pieces of code when you test and verify programs, you won't need as much detail as you would for algorithm analysis. However, it's still useful to know how many times a routine has been called. Organize a program test into groups of routines that create a call hierarchy. With this type of test, coverage analysis can help prove that every path in a switch statement or conditional branch has executed at least once.

By studying *call paths* in the Callers window and printing out a source code listing (annotated with execution counts) from the Module window, you can verify that routines are called at the right time. And, if a block of code does not get hit at the appropriate time, you can investigate why the piece of code does not get executed.

## Timing execution and monitoring performance

When timing a large program to see where it's slow, you rarely need information at the line-count level. In execution timing, you need to know two things:

1  How much time is spent in individual routines.

2  What times propagate from low-level routines to higher-level routines.

Before timing a program's execution, you need to set areas for all routines with source code. In very large programs, limit your selection of area markers to a single module per profile run.

Once you've set the area markers in a single module, profiling becomes a matter of successive grouping and refinement. These are the techniques you use to refine the profiling process:

- Use filters to temporarily mask out unwanted information (with the Execution Profile window's local Filter command).

- Unmark routines whose statistics you don't want (with the local Remove command in the Module, Execution Profile, and Areas windows).

- Combine the timer counts for specified routines (with the Timer option, which you set from either the Statistics | Profiling Options command or the Areas window's local Options command).

If you're not completely familiar with the program you're profiling, you can use execution timing and performance monitoring in conjunction with studying the unfamiliar code.

## Studying unfamiliar code

One of the best ways to study code you don't know is to analyze the dynamic call history that Turbo Profiler generates in the Callers window. This history shows the program's structural hierarchy. Although you can see only one routine's call paths at a time, you can print all recorded call paths by choosing Print | Statistics with the Callers window open.

By noting a program's called routines, their callers, and the number of times the program traverses each call path, you can see which routines are most important. You can also predict which higher-level routines will be affected by changes you make to lower-level routines.

Execution times and counts give you a sense of the program's important routines. File and overlay monitoring reveal any temporary files opened and closed during program execution as well as any overlays swapped into memory. This information is harder to find through lexical program analysis.

The profiler's link between the Execution Profile, Module, and Areas windows enables you to move back and forth quickly to specified symbols, thus revealing the connections between functionally related but physically separated pieces of source code.

# Which analysis mode to use

One important consideration when you're profiling is whether to use active, passive, or coverage analysis. You set the profiling mode from the Profiling Options dialog box (choose Statistics | Profiling Options).

Once you know your program works correctly, active and passive analysis are important tools for helping to improve the overall performance of your program. Coverage analysis, on the other hand, is a useful tool to use while developing your code.

Does the program call all routines at the appropriate time? Are there any sections of code that do not get executed? These are important questions that can be answered by profiling in coverage mode.

## Active analysis

Turbo Profiler's default mode is active analysis; it collects execution times and execution counts automatically, as well as any other data (such as call histories or DOS interrupts) that you've enabled in the Statistics menu.

When you profile in active mode, keep in mind how frequently the program execution trips area markers. For instance, you can mark every line in a program except a loop statement, but if the program spends 95 percent of its time inside that loop, the number of marked areas won't slow the profile much.

See the section "Speeding up profiling" for other ways to make your profiling sessions go faster.

The profiler slows down program execution if it must perform a lot of bookkeeping every time it executes a source statement. If that happens, you can always switch to passive analysis, which turns off all automatic calls to the expensive bookkeeping routines that the profiler performs under active analysis mode.

## Passive analysis

If your program runs very slowly and you can do without execution counts and call histories, use passive analysis; in passive mode, the profiler collects only time-related statistics for marked areas (such as execution times, interrupt calls, and file activity). Your profile runs will go much faster in passive analysis mode.

In passive analysis, Turbo Profiler interrupts your program's execution at regular intervals to sample the value of the program counter, CS:IP. If the sampled value points to an address inside an area that you're monitoring (a marked area), the profiler increments the ticks in that area's timer compartment. If the value in the CS:IP does not point to an address inside a marked area (for example, it points to an address within a DOS interrupt or BIOS call), the profiler throws out that timer tick.

It's hard to interpret the results of passive analysis unless your program runs a long time, or unless you accumulate timing statistics over many runs. Some areas of your code might never show up even though they execute, because they're never being executed at the time the profiler interrupts the program's execution. To obtain greater statistical accuracy, collect statistics over several program runs (be sure to set the Run Count in the Profiling Options dialog box to coincide with the number of runs you plan to monitor).

Passive analysis doesn't add noticeable overhead to program run time, but it does sacrifice some detail in the resulting reports. When you set passive analysis, there is no noticeable slowdown in program execution. However, you might not be able to get all the information you require. You can't get count information or callers information, but you can monitor interrupt calls and file activity.

### Passive versus active analysis

Some of the data you collect under passive analysis might be misleading if you don't take these points into consideration when you analyze the results:

- If your program does disk I/O, the profiler gives file-access time to the calling routine under active mode, but not under passive mode.

- If your program calls an interrupt that's not marked as an area, the profiler gives the interrupt's time to the calling routine in active mode, but excludes the interrupt's time in passive mode.

## Coverage analysis

Coverage analysis lets you verify program structure and execution sequence. Because coverage analysis doesn't slow down program execution (unless Max Coverage count is set to a high number), you can perform two tasks with one profiling pass. Coverage allows you to count how many times a block has been executed (set the Maximum Coverage Count using Statistics | Profiling Options). With this, you can verify that a block of code does get called and, at the same time, determine if it is getting called too many or too few times.

# Speeding up profiling

Each time your program enters a routine that you have defined as a data-collection area, Turbo Profiler must perform certain processing ("bookkeeping" code). The execution speed of a program under the control of Turbo Profiler depends on how frequently area markers are tripped and on the kind of information being collected for the most frequently tripped areas. The greater the level of information being collected (particularly call-stack history), the longer it takes to execute bookkeeping code associated with an area. Even if your program runs slower, Turbo Profiler still keeps track of timing information properly.

Sometimes your program speed might be unacceptably slow under Turbo Profiler. That might be because your program is frequently calling a deeply nested routine with call-stack tracing set to *All Callers* for *All Areas*. If you've defined this deeply nested routine as an area, Turbo Profiler will spend a lot of time keeping track of the calls to it.

To determine if your program is frequently calling a low-level routine, switch to the Execution Profile window and display the areas by execution counts. (Set the SpeedMenu Display option to Counts.) This displays an execution-count histogram sorted by the number of times each area is executed.

If the program calls one or more routines much more frequently than the rest, you can exclude them from the list of displayed areas with the Execution Profile window's local Filter | Current command. You can also unmark areas with the local Remove command in the Module, Areas, and Execution Profile windows.

# Improving statistical accuracy

If you don't collect enough data (because your program runs too fast for the profiler to gather a statistically significant number of data points) or if you collect a skewed data set (because of resonance), you won't be able to make informed decisions about the changes needed in your source code. Here's what to do if either of these problems should occur.

## Insufficient data

To improve the accuracy of timing statistics and to get a statistically significant average, run your program more than once. Be sure to set the Run Count option in the Profiling Options dialog box. When your program terminates and you run it again, the profiler adds the times for the new run to times accumulated for previous runs. This continues until you've executed your program the number of times specified in the Run Count option.

**Caution!** Running your program after the specified number of runs will reset all statistical information in preparation for a new set of runs. Be sure to save (or analyze) the statistics before embarking on a new set of runs.

## Resonance

Resonance occurs, for example, if a loop cycles at the same frequency as the timer tick. If resonance is causing the profiler to return inaccurate data, use the Clock Speed setting in the Profiling Options dialog box to set the profiler's clock to anywhere between 18 and 1,000 ticks per second. Choose a speed that is not an integral multiple or fraction of the speed that is causing the resonance. For example, if your program exhibits resonance at 100 ticks per second, try 70 or 130 ticks per second.

If you suspect that resonance is causing biased statistics, try different clock speeds that are not integral multiples, and compare the collected statistics. If resonance is the problem, the various sets of statistics will vary considerably.

Changing the clock speed can be done only in passive mode; active mode doesn't use clock ticks.

The faster the clock speed, the more accurately Turbo Profiler can determine where your program spends its time. So, will setting the clock speed to 1000 ticks per second produce incredibly accurate timing information? Not necessarily. The faster you set the clock speed, the slower your program will run (because Turbo Profiler must perform certain lookup operations each time a clock tick occurs). So if you want greater accuracy than the default 100 ticks per second, increase the clock speed until you reach an acceptable compromise between accuracy and execution speed.

Also note that if a section of your program disables interrupts, only the first clock tick during execution of that section will be counted, and your system's internal clock will run slower. Avoid setting the clock speed so fast that it causes multiple ticks while interrupts are disabled.

## Some tips for profiling overlays

Overlays allow large programs to run in limited memory by storing portions of the code on disk and loading that code only as needed. If you use overlays, the program's modules share the same memory—thereby reducing total RAM requirements.

Unfortunately, swapping code in and out of memory can lead to slow program execution because it wastes time accessing disk drives. Because even a fast disk drive is still the slowest storage device in most PCs, improper overlay management can dramatically reduce performance. To make a difficult situation worse, the overlay manager code in the compiled program is normally hidden. Turbo Profiler brings overlay management code out in the open so you can adjust your program's overlay behavior.

To fine-tune overlay performance, you need to choose the right overlay buffer size, select algorithms for managing overlays in the buffer, and set other parameters that can help keep the most frequently used overlay modules in memory for longer periods of time. You can reduce "thrashing," which results from too many disk accesses as the program reads overlay, by keeping frequently used overlays in memory longer.

Statistics displayed in the profiler's Overlay window include

- The number of times your program loads each overlay from disk.
- The time-ordered event sequence in which your program loads overlays.

The load-count and execution-time information is useful for determining which overlays should stay in RAM longer. By comparing this data with a profile of non-overlay routines, you can decide which modules should be overlays and which shouldn't.

With the overlay event history, you can choose optimal algorithms for overlay buffer management. By examining a list of overlays and seeing when and how often each was loaded, you can decide which main program modules might work better as overlays, and which overlays might benefit from being made part of your main program.

## Profiling object-oriented programs

In general, profiling object-oriented programs is not much different from conventional profiling; treat object-oriented programs just like ordinary programs and consider each method to be just like a call to a routine.

# Interpreting and applying the profile results

OK, so you've decided what profile statistics you want to collect, adjusted your program accordingly, and run it enough times to gather a statistically significant (if not downright daunting) set of data. Now what?

Now comes the fun part. First you analyze the data to figure out what the profiler is telling you, then you apply that newfound knowledge to your source code to make your program faster and more efficient than ever.

## Analyzing profile data

The Turbo Profiler windows you'll use to study the collected statistics fall into two categories: *program source* windows and *profile report* windows.

Turbo Profiler's program source windows are the Module, Areas, Routines, and Disassembly (CPU) windows. Before running the profile, you mainly use source windows to set areas and to specify profiling actions at the marked areas. After you examine the profile statistics (in one or more report windows), you use source windows again to analyze your program's source code.

Turbo Profiler's report windows are the Execution Profile, Callers, Overlays, Interrupts, Files, and Coverage windows. You use report windows to display profile statistics gathered from your running program, so you can evaluate the collected data and determine where changes in the source code might improve your program's performance.

## Execution Profile window

This window is your primary focus for improving the performance of your program. In general you will want to examine those lines of source code that account for most of the program execution time. Next, look for lines (or routines) with a high ratio of execution time to execution count. And finally, it is always good form to check on the routines that account for the most "per call" execution time.

## Callers window

Once you have isolated a routine you want to improve, use the Callers window to locate all of the areas in your program that call the selected routine. The Callers window displays the number of times the routine was called, and the source of those calls (the caller).

## Overlays window

The Overlays window lets you detect excessive overlay calls, which will then become candidates for placement in a non-overlaid module (unit).

## Interrupts window

The Interrupts window reveals all the (selected) interrupts made by your program. This revelation may prompt you to combine video output for some lines of code, or for file-intensive programs, suggest that disk I/O be buffered.

## Files window

The Files window quickly discloses the number of reads and writes performed to the files manipulated by your program. In I/O-intensive applications, this window will point out which files deserve your attention.

## Coverage window

The Coverage window, in its default setting, displays blocks of code that have not been hit during the profiling session runs. This window helps to isolate sections of code that do not get called (dead code) and areas that need to be called. In addition, the Coverage window can be adjusted so that it displays the number of times each block of code has been hit during the program runs.

# Filtering collected data

Turbo Profiler's windows provide SpeedMenu commands for temporarily or permanently filtering data out of the current display. Here's a table summarizing the profiler's filtering options:

**Table 26.2**    SpeedMenu commands for filtering collected statistics

| Window | SpeedMenu command | What it does for you |
|---|---|---|
| Execution profile | Filter | Temporarily removes the current area's statistics, or shows only the current module's statistics, or restores all collected statistics to the window. (You choose Current, Module, or All from the Filter menu.) |
| | Remove | Permanently erases the current area's statistics from the collected data. *Use with caution!* |
| Files | Collection (top pane) | When disabled, no file statistics are collected. |
| | Detail (top pane) | When disabled, displays only file open and close activities. When enabled, also displays file read and write activities. |
| | Display (bottom pane) | Displays each event either as a bar graph element, or as text showing the exact time and duration of the event. |
| Interrupts | Remove (top pane) | Removes the currently selected interrupt from the top pane. |
| | Display (bottom pane) | Displays an interrupt's statistics as either (1) summary histograms of time, calls, or both, or (2) a detailed sequence of events. |
| Overlays | Display | Displays each overlay's profile statistics as either (1) Count, a summary of memory consumed and times loaded, or (2) History, a detailed sequence of events, with a line of data for every time the overlay loaded. |
| Coverage | Display | Specifies blocks to display: (1) display all blocks or (2) display only blocks not hit. |
| | Sort | Determines the order of display for the blocks (either by address or by number of times hit). |
| | Group | Sets the method of block display as either (1) display all blocks, (2) group blocks by routine, or (3) group blocks by module. |

When you choose Remove from the Execution Profile's SpeedMenu to permanently filter out an area's statistics, the profiler

- adjusts the report by discounting time spent in that area.

- adjusts the percentages of remaining areas by calculating them as percentages of the revised total time:

    (*revised total time = total profile time – time for the removed area*)

- unmarks that area in the Module window.

- removes the area from the areas list in the Areas window.

**Note**    When you remove an area from the Execution Profile window, the remaining area's statistics will be recalculated for the current run only. A subsequent run of the program will most likely show the time for the removed area shifted into one or more other areas.

To permanently remove an area (and the time spent in that area) from the statistics, you must set the area to *Disable*. Be sure you don't forget to set a following area to *Enable*.

## Revising your program

Here's a general plan of attack for finding routines where simple changes can improve your program's performance.

1  Look for large routines with a disproportionate share of execution time, or for routines with a large number of calls. Working from the highest level of your program, follow flow of control through successive levels of calls, looking for places to optimize by reducing or eliminating excessive calls and operations.

2  Look for statements and routines that have a high ratio of time to count. From the Execution Profile window's SpeedMenu, set Display to Both or Per Call. Then look for those areas that show a long time magnitude bar and a short count magnitude bar. Statements and routines of this sort usually represent an inefficient segment of code. Recode them to produce the same result in a more efficient way.

3  As a last resort, you can optimize the program's innermost loops; here are some techniques:

   • Unroll loops
   • Cache temporary results calculated on each iteration
   • Put calculations for which results don't change outside loops
   • Code routines in assembly language

Usually you'll see less improvement with inner-loop optimization than you'll see if you modify control constructs, algorithms, or data structures.

Besides the general guidelines just listed, here are some specific things you can do to improve your program's performance:

   • Modify data structures and algorithms
   • Store precomputed results
   • Cache frequently accessed data
   • Evaluate data only as needed
   • Optimize loops, procedures, and expressions

### Modifying data structures

Try using more sophisticated data structures or algorithms. For example, a QuickSort routine will generally operate faster than a bubble sort for a random distribution of key values. Consult a book on data structures and algorithms for other examples.

Switch from real numbers to integers for fast calculations, such as window and string management for screen I/O and graphics routines. Use long integers for data manipulation or any other value that does not require floating-point precision.

Instead of sorting an array of lines of text, add an array of pointers into the text array. All text access occurs via the pointers. To sort or insert a new line of text, you need to reorder only the pointers, rather than entire lines of text.

## Storing precomputed results

If a set of computed numbers is referenced more than once in a program, it is best to do the computations once, and store the results in a table that can then be accessed. For example, build a sine table, then look up sine as a function of degrees based on an integer index.

## Caching frequently accessed data

C buffers low-level character input from files. The **getc** routine reads a whole sector of bytes from the disk into a buffer, but returns only the first character read. The next call to **getc** returns the next character in the buffer, and so on, until the buffer is empty, in which case **getc** reads another sector in from disk.

In an interactive editor or file-dump utility, you can keep a number of buffers that are updated while the program waits for user input. You might have two buffers that always contain screenfuls of information read from the beginning and the end of the file. Another two buffers can keep the previous and next screenful of bytes in the disk file relative to the position currently onscreen. This way, for those file-navigation commands the user is most likely to select, your interactive program can update the screen without disk access.

## Evaluating data as needed

Structure the order of conditional tests and switches so that those most likely to yield results are evaluated first. This will reduce the number of times that low-incident switches will be tested.

For a large table of lookup information, evaluate entries only as you need them, and use a supplemental array to track entries that have already been computed.

You might need to calculate the length of a line only when you need to reformat output—not each time a new line is read from a file.

## Optimizing existing code

Loops, procedures, and expressions all offer potential for improvement.

**For loops:**

- Whenever possible, move calculations outside of loops. Repeatedly calculating the same value inside a loop is both time-consuming and unnecessary.

  Store the results of expensive calculations.

  For example, an insertion sort routine doesn't need to swap every pair of numbers as it works up an array. If you save the value of the starting element, the inner loop needs to move the successive element down only as long as that element is less than the starting one. When this test fails, you insert the stored value at the current position. This process replaces the expensive swap operation for each element called for in the traditional insertion sort algorithm.

- If two loops perform similar operations over the same set of data, combine them into a single loop.

- Reduce two or more conditional tests in a loop to a single test, if possible.

For example, add an extra element to an array and initialize it to some sentinel value that will cause the loop test to fail. (This is how C handles text strings.)

- Unroll loops.

  For example, replace this

  ```
  for (x = 0; x < 4; x++)
          y += items[x];
  ```

  with this

  ```
  y += items[0] + items[1] + items[2] + items[3];
  ```

**For routines:**

- Rewrite frequently called routines as inline routines, or replace their definitions with inline macros.

- Use co-routines for multipass algorithms that operate on large data files. (See the **setjmp** and **longjmp** routines in C.)

- Recode recursive routines to use an explicitly managed data stack.

**For expressions:**

- Use compile-time initialization.

- Combine returned results in a single call.

  For example, write routines that return sine/cosine, quotient and remainder, or x-y screen coordinates as a pair.

- Replace indexed array access with pointer indirection.

# Wrapping it up

In this chapter, we've covered most of the things you need to consider before, during, and after a profiling session. We've explained how to prepare your program, and yourself, for the profile; we've given you some hints and caveats about the process of profiling; and we've given you some ideas about how to apply the results after you've run the profile.

In the next chapter, we show the details of how Turbo Profiler accumulates statistics; how area markers affect data collection, where time and count information gets calculated, and how Turbo Profiler keeps track of routine calls.

Chapter

# 27

# Inside the profiler

If you want to use Turbo Profiler to your best advantage, you need to understand its inner workings. Knowing what the profiler does when it encounters an area marker or what happens each time the profiler interrupts program execution allows you to fine-tune your techniques both for specifying the type of information to collect and for interpreting the resulting reports.

Consider the source code in PTOLL.C:

```
#include <stdio.h>
#include <dos.h>

void main()
{
   printf("Entering main\n");
   route66()
   printf("Back in main\n");
   delay(1000);
   highway80();
   printf("Back in main\n");
   delay(1000);
   printf("Leaving main\n\n");
}

route66()
{
   printf("Entering Route 66\n");
   delay(2000);
   printf("Leaving Route 66\n");
}

highway80()
{
   printf("Entering Highway 80\n");
   delay(2000);
   printf("Leaving Highway 80\n");
}
```

In the previous program, setting areas to Routines in Module effectively sets up four time-collection compartments and four count-collection compartments. Turbo Profiler keeps execution times and counts for *main*, *route66*, and *highway80*. In addition, Turbo Profiler keeps a total for both execution times and for counts.

# Area boundaries

In this section, you follow program execution and see what the profiler does as each area marker is passed. It's best to think of this process as going through a series of tollbooths. After you pass a tollbooth, you're on a section of road associated with that tollbooth until you come to another tollbooth.

You're in no tollbooth's territory before you reach the first tollbooth. When you pass the first tollbooth, time spent on each section of roadway is tracked by the tollbooth in charge of that section of the road. Note that you can only go one direction down the road: Loops and jumps are like airlifts that take you back to some previous position on the road.

## Time and count collection

Before you enter the main program block, C startup code is executed, which is equivalent to no tollbooth's territory. Any timer ticks encountered here are thrown away, unless you have explicitly set an area in the startup code.

As soon as you pass the area marker (tollbooth) at *main*, the count associated with *main* increments by 1. Any timer tick that occurs between the time you enter *main* and the time when *route66* is called goes into *main*'s timer compartment.

Next, *main* calls *route66* and you enter a new stretch of highway. The moment execution passes through the area marker (the tollbooth) at *route66*, several things happen:

- The current area is set to *route66*.
- The compartment for the caller (*main*, in this case) goes on a stack.
- The count-collection compartment associated with *route66* increments by 1.

Any timer tick that occurs between now and the time you return from *route66* automatically increments *route66*'s time-collection compartment. The global program time-collector also continues to increment with each timer tick.

As soon as execution passes through a return point for *route66*, the profiler pops the caller's compartment from a stack. The caller's count compartment is not incremented on a return. However, any timer ticks that occur between now and the call to *highway80* are added to the time-collection compartment for *main* as well as to the program's global compartment.

To verify this, turn off *route66*'s area marker (position the cursor on *route66*'s area marker and press *F2*) and compare the result with a profile for which that area marker was set. You should see essentially the same total execution time. However, *main*'s execution time should increase by the amount of time it took to execute *route66*.

## Showing routine call overhead

You might want to measure the time consumed by calling a routine (for example, **route66**) and ignore the time spent inside the routine. You can also get this kind of information using *passive analysis*, discussed in Chapter 26, "Profiling strategies." The easiest way to get this information is to disable collection at the entry point for *route66*, and then to reenable collection upon return from *route66*.

To disable **route66**, position the cursor on the function header. Next, choose Operation from the Module window's SpeedMenu to open the Area Options dialog box, and set Operation to Disable.

When you disable collection on entry to *route66*, returning from it doesn't automatically reenable collection. You must set an area marker at the closing brace for *route66*, and set the operation for that area marker to Enable (using the Area Operations dialog box).

## Who pays for loops?

The tollbooth analogy helps explain why passing through an area marker and jumping back to a program statement that precedes that marker (using a loop or goto statement) doesn't change the current area. Even though you're lexically outside the scope of the marker, you haven't passed through any new markers. Any timer ticks that occur will still be associated with the most recently tripped marker.

Knowing this, take a look at the next program:

```
     #include <stdio.h>
     #include <dos.h>
     lost_in_town();

=> void main()
   {
       printf("Entering main\n")
       lost_in_town();
       delay(1000);
       printf("Leaving main \n\n");
       delay(1000);
   }

=> lost_in_town()
   {
       int i;
       printf("Looking for highway...\n");
       delay(100);
       for (i=0; i<10; i++)
       {
           printf("Ask for directions \n");
=>          printf("Wrong turn \n\n");
           delay(1000);
       }
       printf("On the road again \n");
   }
```

In program *plost*, we've complicated the routine *lost_in_town* by using a compound statement inside a loop. Assume that three area markers have been set: one for *main*, one for *lost_in_town*, and one for the line that prints Wrong turn.

Things get tricky when you get into *lost_in_town*. When you first enter the routine, *lost_in_town* becomes the current area. The time associated with printing Looking for highway is associated with this marker.

Time for executing the loop statement is still associated with the routine marker, and the first time you Ask for directions, timing information is associated with the routine marker. However, once you trip the line marker for Wrong turn, the remainder of the time spent in the routine is associated with that line marker.

Just because you pass into an area that was previously associated with another marker doesn't mean the current area changes. The current area changes only when you trip an area marker. This can produce unexpected results.

For instance, if you set the three markers for program *plost* as already described (one each for the *main* function, the *lost_in_town* function, and the Wrong Turn statement), approximately 84 percent of program time will be associated with printing "Wrong turn," while only 1 percent of execution time will be associated with *lost_in_town*. This is because nine out of ten calls to Ask for directions, plus all calls to the subsequent delay statement, occur after the Wrong Turn marker was tripped.

If you toggle off the area marker for Wrong turn, 84 percent of the remaining execution time will be logged to the routine *lost_in_town*.

Now, consider the following code:

```
main
{
   while(!kbhit() )
   {
      func1();
      statement1;
      statement2;
      func2();
   }
}
func1()
{
}
func2()
{
}
```

Assume that areas are set for All Routines in the module so that routines *main*, *func1*, and *func2* each mark the beginning of an area. You enter *main*, which trips *main*'s area marker. When this happens, Turbo Profiler internally encounters a breakpoint. This encounter sets a variable indicating that, until you trip another breakpoint, *main* is the current area. This encounter also increments a variable associated with execution counts for *main* by 1.

The scope of these areas is dynamic rather than lexical. That is, *main* is the current area until *func1* is called. As soon as you enter *func1*, you're in a new area until you encounter another function call or until you return from *func1*. This means that the profiler puts the caller (*main*, in this case) on a stack.

When you exit *func1*, you trip a return marker that the profiler set up when it entered *func1*. The routine *main* becomes the current area again. Any timer ticks that occur while the program is executing `statement1` or `statement2` will update the timer for the area associated with *main*.

Two things are going on here:

1 Every time you encounter an area, the profiler calls an internal routine that adjusts variables and updates a routine call stack. Two variables are associated with each area: execution counts and execution time. Each time you enter an area, the execution count associated with that area increments.

2 Every time a timer tick occurs, the profiler calls another internal routine that checks to see what area is current, then increments the timer variable associated with that area by the appropriate amount of time.

When the program terminates, Turbo Profiler converts the *counts* variable for each area to an actual time (based on the total number of timer ticks that occurred for the entire program).

## Multiple return statements

What do you do about multiple `return` statements? The answer is related to the implicit return points at the end of routines.

**Note**    Even though you might have several explicit return points in your function, Borland's C and C++ compilers actually turn all returns into jumps to a single exit point at the end of the routine. The line that receives the area marking for a return statement is the line associated with the closing brace for the routine. This is the actual assembly language return statement to which all other return statements in the routine are vectored.

## Disabling often-called functions

The easiest way to disable collection for a function is to set a Disable marker at the function header and an Enable marker on the line after the call to the function. However, if a function is called from more than one place, it may be difficult to set Enable markers after each function call. In this case, set the Enable marker at the closing brace of the function, or (better yet) at the actual return statement in the function code.

For example, if you want to overlook the time spent in *func1*, set a Disable marker at the header for *func1*. Then, enable collection again at the return statement for *func1*:

1 Go to the Disassembly window (View I Disassembly).

2 Set an area marker at the `ret` statement of the function.

3 Go to the View I Areas window.

**4** Set options to Enable (*Ctrl+O, E*).

Now, whenever *func1* is called, collection will be disabled upon entry to the function, and enabled at the exact point that the function returns.

A simpler yet less accurate way to reenable collection is to set the Enable marker at the closing curly brace of the function in question. The drawback of this method, however, is that timing information will be collected for the time it takes to return from the function.

# Logging callers

An active routine is a routine currently on the profiler's routine call stack. In active analysis, Turbo Profiler maintains its own routine call stack. This stack is similar to the stack found in any DOS program. However, the profiler's stack is separate from the user's program stack and is used strictly to retain information about routine calls for which a return statement has not yet been executed.

In order to maintain an active routine stack, Turbo Profiler recognizes two types of area markers:

- Routine-entry area markers (routine markers)
- Normal area markers (label markers)

When the profiler encounters a routine-entry area marker, it pushes the currently active routine (the *last* encountered routine-entry marker) onto its active routine stack. The newly encountered routine marker then becomes the active routine marker.

Now, if a normal area marker trips, this encounter will have no effect on the current routine or on the active routine stack. When a normal area marker trips, it simply becomes the active *area*, which means that the profiler forgets the previously active area. The currently active *routine*, however, remains on the stack until the profiler encounters a return statement.

When a return is issued within an active routine, the area marker associated with that routine becomes inactive. The routine on top of the profiler's active routine stack pops off the stack and becomes the active routine until a return statement executes within that routine, or until another routine-entry area marker is tripped.

Thus the profiler can maintain a complete call history for every marked routine. If you have enabled Statistics | Callers for all marked routines, then each time a routine-entry area marker is tripped, the profiler saves the entire profiler call stack in a buffer linked directly to the routine-entry marker.

If that call stack is identical to a call stack that was saved for a prior entry to this routine, the profiler increments a counter, rather than saving the call stack again. If, however, the call stack is different, the profiler allocates a new buffer and logs the profiler call stack to that new buffer. This makes it possible to maintain a record of every call path to a routine and the number of times each call path is traversed.

The profiler's active routine stack is related to three menu settings:

- Statistics | Callers (set to either Enabled or Disabled)

- The Callers option, set from the Areas' local window Option selection
- The Stack option, set from the Module's local window Callers selection

While all selections relate to callers, you gain finer control over logging call paths by using the SpeedMenu of the Module window. From this menu, you can set the Areas option to log callers for a single routine, for all the routines in a single module, or for all the routines in the program. As well, the Stack command allows you to specify callers as All Callers, Immediate Caller, or None.

- All Callers means log the entire routine call stack each time the entry point is tripped.

- Immediate Caller means log only the top entry on the routine call stack when the entry point is tripped.

- None means don't log any routine stack information when this routine-entry marker is tripped.

By default, when you first profile a program, the Callers option for all routine-entry area marks is set to None.

Enabling Statistics | Callers from the main menu is the same as setting the Callers option to All Callers for each area marker listed in the Areas window. However, once you've hand-set any of the Callers options in the Areas window, setting Statistics | Callers to Enable won't change the value of the Callers options for any of the areas.

Disabling the Statistics | Callers option at this point tells the profiler not to log any stack information, but doesn't change the Caller settings in the Areas window. (Neither does setting Statistics | Caller.)

# Sampling vs. counting

This section relates only to passive mode.

The profiler doesn't actually measure time: It comes up with a very accurate estimate of time based on information from timer tick counts. This is a form of *statistical sampling*. By taking regular periodic samples of the current area, and by keeping a count for each area (which increments each time that area is active when the timer interrupts), the profiler can estimate the time spent in a given area.

The profiler knows the total time taken to run the program. It also knows the total number of times the timer interrupted the program. The time spent in a given area can be calculated as

$$time_{area} = timer_{total} * counts_{area} / counts_{total}$$

This is *not* the true time spent in an area. If your program iterates over some routine at a frequency that is a multiple of the timer frequency (for example, a routine that generates a steady sound tone), the execution of a particular line (or area) might exactly coincide with most of the timer interrupts. This resonance could occur even though that line is not where the program is spending most of its time. This is rare, but possible.

If you suspect this sort of frequency collision, change the value of the clock speed (Statistics | Profiling Options | Clock Speed) and compare the resulting profile to the previous one.

## Profiler memory use

The profiler allocates memory for area information on the far heap. If you add areas while the program is running, the far heap will expand into the user program area to make room for new area variables and buffers. This is why, if you modify areas during a run, you should always reset the program with Run | Program Reset. If you don't, the results of a profile might be unpredictable; you could hang your computer.

# 28

# Turbo Profiler's command-line options

This is the generic command-line format for running Turbo Profiler:

```
TPROF [tprof_options] [progname [program_args]]
```

where *tprof_options* is a list of one or more command-line options for the profiler (see Table 28.1), *progname* is the name of the program you want to profile, and *program_args* is a list of one or more command-line arguments for the profiled program.

You can type TPROF without a program name or any arguments; if you do, you must then load the program you want to profile with Turbo Profiler's environment.

Here are some example Turbo Profiler command lines:

tprof –sc prog1 a b      Starts the profiler with the **–sc** option and loads program PROG1 with two command-line arguments, *a* and *b*.

tprof prog2 –x      Starts the profiler with default options and loads program PROG2 with one argument, *–x*.

## The command-line options

All of Turbo Profiler's command-line options start with a hyphen (–). At least one space or tab separates each option from the TPROF command and any other command-line components.

To turn an option off at the command line, type a hyphen *after* the option. For example, **–vg–** explicitly turns the *graphics save* option off. Normally you'll turn an option off only if it's permanently enabled in the profiler's configuration file, TFCONFIG.TF. (You can modify the configuration file with the TFINST installation program described in Chapter 29, "Customizing Turbo Profiler.")

Table 28.1 summarizes Turbo Profiler's command-line options; we cover these options in greater detail in the following pages.

**Table 28.1** Turbo Profiler command-line options

| Option | What it does |
|--------|--------------|
| –b | Loads Turbo Profiler in batch mode. |
| –b*count* | Run in batch mode with run count of *count*. |
| –c*file* | Reads in configuration file *file*. |
| –do | Runs the profiler on a secondary display. |
| –dp | Shows the profiler on one display page, the output of the profiled program on another. |
| –ds | Maintains separate screen images for the profiler and the program being profiled. |
| –h | Displays a help screen. |
| –? | Also displays a help screen. |
| –ji | Session-state saving: Don't use session-state file if you've recompiled your program. |
| –jn | Session-state saving: Don't use session-state file. |
| –jn | Session-state saving: Prompt for session-state file use if you've recompiled your program. |
| –jn | Session-state saving: Use session-state file, even if you've recompiled your program. |
| –p | Enables mouse support. |
| –r | Enables profiling on a remote system. |
| –rn*L;R* | Remote network profiling, where *L* is the local machine and *R* is the remote machine. |
| –rp*N* | Sets the remote link port to port *N*. |
| –rs*N* | Sets the remote link speed. |
| –sc | Ignores case when you enter symbol names. |
| –sd*DIR* | Sets one or more source directories to scan for source files. |
| –Sn | Don't load symbols. |
| –vg | Saves complete graphics image on program screen. |
| –vn | Disables 43/50 line display. |
| –vp | Enables EGA palette save for program output screen. |

## Batch mode (–b)

The **–b** command-line argument instructs Turbo Profiler to run in *batch mode*. Turbo Profiler's environment isn't activated in batch mode; instead, the profiler runs the program and saves all statistics to a *filename.TFS* file, where *filename* is the name of the executable file.

The **–b** argument lets you create a DOS batch file of one or more TPROF commands. If the program you're profiling doesn't require any keyboard input, you can run the batch process while you're doing something else.

**Note**    Before profiling in batch mode, an area file must be set up to instruct the profiler what areas to inspect and what profiling mode to use.

To set up the area file, load your program and choose the profiling mode you want to use (Statistics | Profiling Options). Next, mark areas that you want inspected, setting up all Enable and Disable markers as needed. Then, exit Turbo Profiler. This creates a .TFA file that records the selected areas and profiling mode.

Once the area file is set, create a DOS batch file with the desired Turbo Profiler commands. Here's an example:

```
TPROF -b MYPROG arg1 arg2
rename MYPROG.TFS MYPROG1.TFS
TPROF -b MYPROG arg1 arg3
rename MYPROG.TFS MYPROG2.TFS
TPROF -b MYPROG arg2 arg2
rename MYPROG.TFS MYPROG3.TFS
TPROF -b MYPROG arg2 arg3
```

Alternately, you can set run count >1 to accumulate all statistics into the same file.

Notice that you must rename the .TFS file after each TPROF command. If you fail to do so, successive runs of the same program will overwrite the statistics file already created. Once you've written your batch file, run it from the DOS command line.

## Configuration file (–c)

This option tells Turbo Profiler to use the indicated configuration file. The default is TFCONFIG.TF; if you want to load a different one, you must use –c, followed immediately (no space) by the name of the configuration file you want to use.

## Display update (–d)

All –d options affect the way Turbo Profiler updates the display.

**–do**    Runs the profiler on a secondary display. You can view the program's screen on the primary display while Turbo Profiler runs on the secondary display.

**–dp**    This is the default option for color displays. It shows the profiler on one display page, and the output of the program being profiled on another.

Using two display pages minimizes the time it takes to swap between two screens. You can use this option only on a color display, because only color displays have multiple display pages. You can't use this option if the profiled program itself uses multiple display pages.

**–ds**    This is the default option for monochrome displays. It maintains separate screen images for the profiler and the program being profiled.

Each time you run the program or reenter the profiler, Turbo Profiler loads an entire screen from memory. This is the most time-consuming method of displaying the two screen images, but it works on any display and with programs that do unusual things to the display.

## Help (–h and –?)

Both of these options display Turbo Profiler's command-line syntax and options.

## Session-state saving (–j*n*)

The session-state options specify how you want Turbo Profiler to handle the session-state files. See "Session Saving" on page 25 for more information.

## Mouse support (–p)

This option enables mouse support (on by default).

## Remote profiling (–r)

All –r options affect Turbo Profiler's remote profiling link.

**–r**
Enables profiling on a remote system. If no other –r command-line options are specified, –r uses the default serial port (COM1) and speed (115K baud), unless these have been changed using TFINST.

**–rn*L*;*R***
Enables profiling on a remote system over a local area network link. *L* and *R* are optional arguments, specifying the local and remote system names respectively.

**–rp*N***
Sets the remote serial link port to port *N*. Set *N* = 1 for COM1; *N* = 2 for COM2, *N*=3 for COM3, and *N*=4 for COM4.

**–rs*N***
Sets the remote serial link speed to the value associated with *N*. Set *N*=1 for 9,600 baud, *N*=2 for 19,200 baud, *N*=3 for 38,400 baud, and *N*=4 for 115,000 baud.

## Source code and symbols (–s)

All –s options affect the way Turbo Profiler handles source code and program symbols.

**–sc**
Ignores case when you enter symbol names, even if your program has been linked with case-sensitivity enabled.

Without the –sc option, Turbo Profiler ignores case only if you've linked your program with the "case ignore" option enabled.

**–sd*DIR***
Sets one or more source directories to scan for source files; the syntax is:
**Note:** There shouldn't be a space between –sd and the directory name.

```
-sddirname
```

*dirname* can be a relative or absolute path and can include a disk letter. To set multiple directories, use the –sd option for each separate directory, or list them together like this:

```
sddir1;dir2;dir3
```

Turbo Profiler searches directories in the order specified.

If the configuration file specifies a directory list, the profiler appends the ones specified by the –sd option to that list.

# Video hardware (–v)

All **–v** options affect how Turbo Profiler handles the video hardware.

**–vg**      Saves the program screen's complete graphics image. This option requires extra memory but lets you profile programs that use special graphics display modes. Try this option if your program's graphics screen becomes corrupted when running under Turbo Profiler.

**–vn**      Disables the 43/50 line display mode. Specify this option to save some memory. Use **–vn** if you're running on an EGA or VGA and know you won't switch into 43- or 50-line mode once Turbo Profiler is running.

**–vp**      Enables you to save the EGA/VGA palette for the program output screen. Use this option for programs that output to special EGA/VGA graphics modes.

# Customizing Turbo Profiler

Turbo Profiler is ready to run as soon as you make working copies of the files on the distribution disk. However, you can change many of the default settings by running the customization program called TFINST. You also can change settings using command-line options when you load Turbo Profiler. If you find yourself frequently specifying the same command-line options over and over, you can make those options permanent by running the customization program.

The customization program lets you set the following items:

- Window and screen colors and patterns

- Display parameters: screen-swapping mode, screen lines, tab column width, fast screen update, 43/50-line mode, full graphics saving, and user-screen updating

- Your editor startup command and directories to search for source files and the Turbo Profiler help and configuration files

- User input and prompting parameters: history list length, beep on error, interrupt key, mouse, and control-key shortcuts

- NMI intercept and remote profiling

- Display mode

## Running TFINST

To run the customization program, enter TFINST at the DOS prompt. As soon as TFINST comes up, it displays its main menu. You can either press the highlighted first letter of a menu option or use the *Up* and *Down arrow* keys to move to the item you want and then press *Enter*. For instance, press *D* to change the display settings. Use this same technique for choosing from the other menus in the installation utility. To return to a previous menu, press *Esc*. You may have to press *Esc* several times to get back to the main menu.

Choose Quit (or *Alt+X*) from the menu to exit TFINST.

# Setting the screen colors

Choose Colors from the main menu to bring up the Colors menu. It offers you two choices: Customize and Default Color Set.

## Customizing screen colors

If you choose Customize, a third menu appears, with options for customizing Windows, Dialogs, Menus, and Screens.

### Windows

To customize windows, choose the Windows command. This command opens a fourth menu, from which you can choose the kind of window you want to customize: Text, Statistics, or Disassembly (the CPU window). Choosing one of these options brings up yet another menu listing the window elements, together with a pair of sample windows (one active, one inactive) in which you can test various color combinations. The screen looks like this:

**Figure 29.1**  Customizing colors for windows

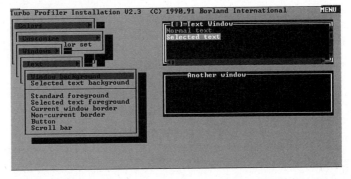

When you select an item you want to change, a palette box pops up over the menu. Use the arrow keys to move around in the palette box. As you move the selection box through the various color choices, the window element whose color you are changing is updated to show the current selection. When you find the color you like, press *Enter* to accept it.

**Note**     Turbo Profiler maintains three color tables: one for color, one for black and white, and one for monochrome. You can change only one set of colors at a time, based on your current video mode and display hardware. So, if you are running on a color display and want to adjust the black-and-white table, first set your video mode to black and white by typing MODE BW80 at the DOS prompt, and then run TFINST.

### Dialog boxes and menus

If you choose Dialogs or Menus from the Customize menu, a screen appears with a menu listing dialog box or menu elements, and a sample dialog box or menu for you to experiment with.

As with the Windows menu, choosing an item from the current menu opens a palette from which you can choose the color for that item.

### Screen

Choosing Screen from the Customize menu opens a menu from which you can access another menu with screen patterns and palettes for screen elements, as well as a sample screen background on which to test them.

## The default colors

If you choose Default Color Set from the Colors menu, facsimiles of an active text window and an inactive window appear onscreen. The facsimiles show you the default colors for their elements. A dialog box lets you select text, statistics, or low-level windows to view.

# Setting Turbo Profiler display parameters

Choose Display from the main menu to bring up the Display Options dialog box.

**Figure 29.2**   The Display Options dialog box

**Note**   These display options include some you can set from the DOS command line when you start up Turbo Profiler, as well as some you can set only with TFINST. See page 474 for a table of Turbo Profiler command-line options and corresponding TFINST settings.

## Display Swapping

You use the Display Swapping radio buttons to control whether Turbo Profiler switches between its own display and the output of the program you're profiling. You can toggle between the following settings:

**None**   Don't swap between the two screens. Use this option if you're profiling a program that does not output to the user screen.

**Always**   Swap to the user screen every time the user program runs. Use this option if your program writes to the user screen.
This is the default option.

## Screen Lines

Use these radio buttons to toggle whether Turbo Profiler should start up with a display screen of 25 lines or a display screen of 43 or 50 lines.

**Note** Only EGA and VGA monitors can display more than 25 lines.

## Fast Screen Update

The Fast Screen Update check box lets you toggle whether your displays will be updated quickly. Toggle this option off if you get "snow" on your display with fast updating enabled. You need to disable this option only if the "snow" annoys you. (Some people prefer the snowy screen because it gets updated more quickly.)

## Permit 43/50 Lines

Turning this check box on allows big (43/50-line) display modes. If you turn it off, you save approximately 8K, since the large screen modes need more window buffer space in Turbo Profiler. This may be helpful if you are profiling a very large program that needs as much memory as possible to execute in. When the option is disabled, you will not be able to switch the display into 43/50-line mode even if your system is capable of handling it.

## Full Graphics Saving

Turning this check box on causes the entire graphics display buffer to be saved whenever there is a switch between the Turbo Profiler screen and the user screen. If you turn it off, you can save approximately 12K of memory, which is helpful if you are profiling a very large program that needs as much memory as possible to execute. Generally the only drawback to disabling this option is that the user screen might show a small number of corrupted locations that usually don't interfere with profiling.

## Tab Size

In this input box, you can set the number of columns between tab stops in a text or source file display. You are prompted for the number of columns (a number from 1 to 32); the default is 8.

## User Screen Updating

The User Screen Updating radio buttons set how the user screen is updated when Turbo Profiler switches between its screen and your program's user screen. There are three settings:

| | |
|---|---|
| Other Display | Runs Turbo Profiler on the other display in your system. If you have both a color and monochrome display adapter, this option lets you view your program's screen on one display and Turbo Profiler's on the other. |
| Flip Pages | Puts Turbo Profiler's screen on a separate display page. This option works only if your display adapter has multiple display pages, like a CGA, EGA, or VGA. You can't use this option on a monochrome display. This option works for the majority of profiling situations; it's fast and disturbs only the operation of programs that use multiple display pages—which are few and far between. |
| Swap | Uses a single display adapter and display page, and swaps the contents of the user and Turbo Profiler screens in software. This is the slowest method of display swapping, but it is the most protective and least disruptive. If you are profiling a program that uses multiple display pages, use this option. Also use the Swap option if you shell to DOS and run other utilities or if you are using a TSR (such as SideKick) and want to keep the current Turbo Profiler screen as well. |

# Turbo Profiler options

The Options command in the main menu opens a menu of options, which in turn open dialog boxes for you.

## The Directories dialog box

This dialog box contains input boxes in which you can enter:

| | |
|---|---|
| Editor program name | Specifies the DOS command that starts your editor. This lets Turbo Profiler start up your favorite editor when you are profiling and want to change something in a file. Turbo Profiler adds to the end of this command the name of the file that it wants to edit, separated by a space. |
| Source directories | Sets the list of directories Turbo Profiler searches for source files. |
| Turbo directory | Sets the directory that Turbo Profiler searches for its help and configuration files. |

## The User Input and Prompting dialog box

This dialog box lets you set options that control how you input information to Turbo Profiler, and how Turbo Profiler prompts you for information:

**Figure 29.3**  The User Input and Prompting dialog box

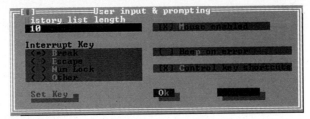

## History List Length
This input box lets you specify how many earlier entries are to be saved in the history list of an input box.

## Interrupt Key
The Interrupt Key radio buttons let you change the Turbo Profiler interrupt key from its default of *Break* to *Escape, NumLock,* or another key or key combination. Pushing the Other radio button displays a prompt asking you to press the key or key combination you want to use as the interrupt key.

## Mouse Enabled
This check box controls whether Turbo Profiler defaults to mouse support.

## Beep on Error
Turbo Profiler can give a warning beep when you press an invalid key or do something that generates an error message. Checking the Beep on Error check box enables the warning beep.

## Control Key Shortcuts
This check box enables or disables the control-key shortcuts. When control-key shortcuts are enabled, you can invoke any SpeedMenu command directly by pressing the *Ctrl* key in combination with the first letter of the menu item. However, in that case, you can't use those control keys as WordStar-style cursor-movement commands.

# The Miscellaneous Options dialog box

The Miscellaneous Options dialog box contains options controlling interrupts, EMS memory, DOS shell swapping, and remote profiling.

**Figure 29.4**   The Miscellaneous Options dialog box

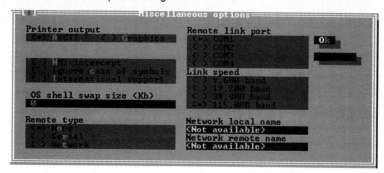

## Printer Output

This option lets you toggle whether to print both extended and standard ASCII characters, or just the straight ASCII character set.

## NMI Intercept

The nonmaskable interrupt (NMI) is a hardware interrupt that the processor must deal with immediately. It is typically used to halt processing when there is a memory parity error: an error message like "Memory Parity Error" is displayed and the system hangs.

Another use for this interrupt is to enable a debugger board to perform a breakout when you press the breakout button. Because the NMI defaults to OFF with Turbo Profiler, you will probably want to turn this interrupt on if you use a debugger board.

If your computer is not a Tandy 1000, IBM PC compatible, ACER 1100, or NEC MultiSpeed, you can run TFINST and try turning on the NMI Intercept check box. Some computers use the NMI in ways that conflict with Turbo Profiler, so if you have problems loading in applications under Turbo Profiler after turning this option on, run TFINST again and disable Turbo Profiler's use of this interrupt.

## Ignore Case of Symbols

If this check box is turned on, Turbo Profiler will ignore the difference between uppercase and lowercase. If it is not checked, case sensitivity will be in effect.

## International support

If this check box is checked, Turbo Profiler will sort all items in list boxes according to the *country* setting in your CONFIG.SYS file (when using DOS), or according to the country checked in the Windows Control Panel (when using Windows). For more information on setting the country code, refer to your DOS or Windows User's Guide.

If the box is not checked, Turbo Profiler will sort entries in list boxes according to the ASCII values of the items in the box (when using DOS), or according to the ANSI values of the items in the box (when using Windows).

### DOS Shell Swap Size (Kb)

In this input box you can set the number of kilobytes of memory to be swapped out for the DOS shell. Memory swapping allows you to use the File | DOS Shell command even when a large program is loaded.

DOS Shell Swap Size is not available in TPROFW.

### Remote type

The Remote Type radio buttons let you specify the type of remote profile link. None, the default mode, specifies that profiling is local; there is no remote link. The Serial button enables remote serial profiling. The communication port and link speed are defined by Remote Link Port and Link Speed options. The Network button specifies remote LAN profiling.

**Warning!**  Usually you won't want to save a configuration file that specifies remote profiling, since Turbo Profiler will then look for the remote link each time it's loaded.

### Remote Link Port

The Remote Link Port radio buttons let you choose either the COM1, COM2, COM3, and COM4 serial ports for the remote serial link.

### Link Speed

The Link Speed radio buttons let you choose one of the four speeds that are available for the remote serial link: 9,600 baud, 19,200 baud, 38,400 baud, or 115,000 baud.

### Network local name

This text box lets you define the default name of the local system when using remote LAN profiling. By default, the name *LOCAL* is given to the local system. This name should be changed if more than one person is using the network for remote profiling.

### Network remote name

This text box lets you define the default name of the remote system when using remote LAN profiling. By default, the name *REMOTE* is given to the local system. This name should be changed if more than one person is using the network for remote profiling.

## Setting the mode for display

Choosing Mode for Display from the main menu opens a menu from which you can select the display mode for your system.

### Default

Turbo Profiler automatically detects the kind of graphics adapter on your system and selects the display mode appropriate for it.

### Color

If you have an EGA, VGA, CGA, MCGA, or 8514 graphics adapter and choose this as your default, the display will be in color.

### Black and White

If you have an EGA, VGA, CGA, MCGA, or 8514 graphics adapter and choose this as your default, the display will be in black and white.

### Monochrome

Choose this only if you are using a color monitor with a Hercules or monochrome text display adapter.

### LCD

Choosing this instead of Black and White if you have an LCD monitor makes your display much easier to read.

# When you're through...

After configuring and customizing the way Turbo Profiler looks and behaves, you'll want to save the settings out to disk. You can either modify the Turbo Profiler executable program directly (TPROF.EXE), or you can create a configuration file that gets loaded as you load Turbo Profiler.

## Saving changes

When you have all your Turbo Profiler options set the way you want, choose Save from the main menu to determine how you want them saved.

### Save Configuration File

If you choose Save Configuration File, a dialog box opens, initialized to the default configuration file TFCONFIG.TF. You can accept this name by pressing *Enter*, or you can type a new configuration file name. If you specify a different file name, you can load that configuration by using the –c command-line option when you start Turbo Profiler. For example,

```
tprof -cmycfg myprog
```

You can also use the Turbo Profiler Options | Restore Configuration command to load a configuration once you have started Turbo Profiler.

### Modify TPROF.EXE

If you choose Modify TPROF.EXE, any changes you've made to the configuration are saved directly into the Turbo Profiler executable program file TPROF.EXE. The next time you enter Turbo Profiler, those settings will be your defaults.

**Note**  If at any time you want to return to the default configuration that Turbo Profiler is shipped with, copy TPROF.EXE from your master disk onto your working system disk, overwriting the TPROF.EXE file that you modified.

## Exiting TFINST

To get out of TFINST at any time, choose Quit from the main menu.

# Command-line options and TFINST equivalents

Some of the options described above can be overridden when you start Turbo Profiler from DOS. The following table shows the correspondence between Turbo Profiler command-line options and the TFINST program command that permanently sets that option.

Table 29.1  Command-line options and TFINST equivalents

| Option | TFINST menu path and dialog box |
|--------|---------------------------------|
|        | Display \| Display Options |
| –do | (•)   Other Display |
| –dp | (•)   Flip Pages |
| –ds | (•)   Swap |
|     | Options \| Input and Prompting \| User Input and Prompting |
| –p | [X]   Mouse Enabled |
| –p– | [ ]   Mouse Enabled |
|      | Options \| Miscellaneous \| Miscellaneous Options |
| –r– | (•)   None |
| –r | (•)   Serial |
| –rn | (•)   Network |
|      | Options \| Miscellaneous \| Miscellaneous Options |
| –rp1 | (•)   COM1 |
| –rp2 | (•)   COM2 |
|      | Options \| Miscellaneous \| Miscellaneous Options |
| –rs1 | (•)   9,600 baud |
| –rs2 | (•)   19,200 baud |
| –rs3 | (•)   38,400 baud |
| –rs4 | (•)   115,000 baud |
|      | Options \| Miscellaneous \| Miscellaneous Options |
| –sc | [X]   Ignore Case of Symbol |
| –sc– | [ ]   Ignore Case of Symbol |
|      | Options \| Directories \| Directories |
| –sd | Source Directories |

**Table 29.1**     Command-line options and TFINST equivalents (continued)

| Option | TFINST menu path and dialog box |
|--------|----------------------------------|
| | Display I Display Options |
| **–vn** | [ ]      Permit 43/50 Lines |
| **–vn–** | [X]      Permit 43/50 Lines |

TFINST.EXE uses the following syntax:

```
TFINST [options] [exefile]
```

Items enclosed in brackets are optional. For a list of options, see the following table.

**Table 29.2**     TFINST.EXE options

| Option | Description |
|--------|-------------|
| *–cfile* | Use configuration file *file*. |
| –h, –? | Display help screen. |
| –p | Enable mouse support. |
| –w | Configure TPROFW.EXE. |

# 30

# Remote profiling

Remote profiling is just what it sounds like: You run Turbo Profiler on one computer and run the program you're profiling on another. The systems can be connected by either the serial ports of the systems or through a NETBIOS-compatible local area network (LAN).

Remote profiling is useful in several situations:

- When your program needs a lot of memory, and you can't run both the program and Turbo Profiler on the same computer. When this happens, you'll get Not enough memory error messages.

- When your program loads under Turbo Profiler, but there's not enough memory left for it to operate properly. Here, you'll get memory allocation errors during the profiling session.

- When you are profiling a Windows program.

If you're profiling a Windows application, you have the choice of running Turbo Profiler for Windows (TPROFW) and the application on a single machine, or of running Windows, WREMOTE, and the application on one machine and running Turbo Profiler (TPROF) on another.

Although there are many reasons why you'll want to profile a program using two systems, the advantages become even greater when you are developing a Windows application:

- If you have a single monitor, running Turbo Profiler and the application on the same machine means that you must switch between Turbo Profiler's character mode screens and the application's graphics mode screens.

  If you use remote profiling, you can see the application's screens and Turbo Profiler's screens at the same time. (This same result can be achieved if you have two monitors attached to the same system.)

- TFREMOTE and WREMOTE use far less memory than Turbo Profiler, so the program you're profiling will behave more like it does when running normally, without the profiler in the background.

# Hardware and software requirements

You choose between a serial or a LAN connection for the remote session. The two setups do use different hardware; however, both share the following requirements:

- A development system with enough memory to load TPROF (this is the *local* system).

- Another PC with enough memory and disk space to hold either TFREMOTE and the DOS program you want to profile or WREMOTE, Windows, and the Windows program you want to profile (this is the *remote* system).

  If you're going to profile a Windows application, the remote machine must be able to run in protected mode, which means that the CPU must be at least an 80286. The amount of memory required depends on the mode in which you're running Windows, but must be at least 1MB.

For a serial connection, you'll need a null modem cable to connect the serial ports of the two systems. Make sure the cable connecting the two systems is set up properly: You can't use a straight-through extension-type cable. At the very least, the cable must swap the transmit and receive data lines (lines 2 and 3 on a 25-pin cable).

For a LAN connection, you'll need a LAN running Novell Netware-compatible software (IPX and NETBIOS version 3.0 or later).

**Note**  NETBIOS must be loaded onto *both* the local and remote systems before TPROF, TFREMOTE, TFREMOTE, or WREMOTE can be loaded. This is true for both DOS and Windows profiling.

# Profiling remote DOS applications

To profile a remote DOS application, you must run TFREMOTE and the application on one machine and Turbo Profiler on another. In this discussion, the machine running TFREMOTE and the application is called the *remote* machine, and the machine running Turbo Profiler is called the *local* machine.

## Setting up the remote system

Copy the remote profiling driver TFREMOTE.EXE onto the remote system, as well as any files required by the program you're profiling. These files can be data input files, configuration files, help files, and so on. If you want, you can also copy your application program onto the remote system. However, Turbo Profiler automatically sends it over the remote link if necessary.

To put files on the remote system, you can use floppy disks or the TDRF remote file transfer utility.

# Configuring TFREMOTE

When starting TFREMOTE, you must configure it so it can communicate over the remote link. You do this by starting the driver with specific command-line options. Start an option with either a hyphen (–) or a slash (/).

**Table 30.1**  TFREMOTE command-line options

| Option | What it does |
| --- | --- |
| –? or –**h** | Displays a help screen |
| –**rn**<*remotename*> | Remote LAN profiling |
| –**rp1** | Port 1, (COM1); default |
| –**rp2** | Port 2, (COM2) |
| –**rp3** | Port 3, (COM3) |
| –**rp4** | Port 4, (COM4) |
| –**rs1** | Slowest speed (9,600 baud) |
| –**rs2** | Slow speed (19,200 baud) |
| –**rs3** | Medium speed (38,400 baud) |
| –**rs4** | High speed (115,000 baud); default |
| –**w** | Writes options to the executable program file |

**Note**  For a list of all available TFREMOTE command-line options, type the following at the remote DOS prompt:

```
TFREMOTE -h
```

## Customizing TFREMOTE

If TFREMOTE is started without command-line options, it assumes remote serial profiling at the default port and speed built into TFREMOTE.EXE (COM1 and 115,000 baud respectively, unless you've changed them with the –**w** option).

You can make TFREMOTE's command-line options permanent by writing them back to disk. To do this, specify –**w** on the command-line along with the other options you want to make permanent. TFREMOTE then prompts for the name of the executable file to write to; if you enter a nonexistent executable file name, TFREMOTE creates the file. If you press *Enter*, the currently running program (usually TFREMOTE.EXE) is overwritten.

If you are running DOS version 3.0 or later, the prompt indicates the path and file name from which you executed TFREMOTE. You can accept this name (press *Enter*), or enter a new executable file name. (If you're running DOS 2.xx, you must supply the full path and file name of the executable program.)

For example, on the remote system, type the following command line at the DOS prompt:

```
TFREMOTE -w -rs3 -rp2
```

When prompted, enter the name of the program to modify, for instance, *tfremot2.exe*. With this, TFREMOTE creates a new remote driver named TFREMOT2.EXE, where the default speed is 38,400 baud (–**rs3**) and the default port is COM2 (–**rp2**).

# The remote DOS driver

To begin a remote profiling session, you must first start the driver on the remote system and then load TPROF on the local system.

Before starting TFREMOTE, be sure the directory on the remote system is set to the one that contains the program files. This is essential because TFREMOTE puts the program to be profiled into the directory that is current when you start TPROF. You don't give the program name on the TFREMOTE command line, since TPROF controls the loading of the program.

When loaded, TFREMOTE signs on with a copyright message, then indicates that it's waiting for you to start Turbo Profiler at the other end of the link. To stop and return to DOS, press *Ctrl+Break*.

## Starting the remote serial driver

If you're using a null modem cable to connect the two systems, you must use the command-line options **–rs** and **–rp** to indicate the speed and port of the data communications.

If the remote system's serial port is set up as COM1, type

```
TFREMOTE -rp1 -rs4
```

Note that this is the default setting of TFREMOTE, and is the same as issuing the command

```
TFREMOTE
```

if the default settings haven't been changed. If the remote system's serial port is set up as COM2, type

```
TFREMOTE -rp2 -rs4
```

to start TFREMOTE.

If you're using a PS/2, use the command-line option **–rs1**.

All three of these commands start the link at its maximum speed (115,000 baud). This speed works with most PCs and cable setups. However, if you experience communication difficulties, see Table 30.1 on page 479 for how to start the link at a slower speed.

Note
It's possible that the local and remote systems use different serial ports for the null modem cable connection. In this case, the two systems' serial port settings will not match. However, the communication speed of the two systems must always be the same for the connection to work.

## Starting the remote LAN driver

If you're using a LAN to connect the two systems, you must use the **–rn** command-line option to start TFREMOTE. For example, issuing the following command at the DOS prompt will start TFREMOTE over a LAN connection, naming the remote system *remotelink*:

```
TFREMOTE -rnremotelink
```

If a remote name is left out of the command, the default name *REMOTE* is used.

For more on naming remote systems, see the "LAN connection" section that follows.

## Establishing the remote DOS link

Once TFREMOTE has been loaded on the remote system, start Turbo Profiler on the local system using command-line options that correspond to the established data link (serial or LAN).

### Serial connection

TPROF and TFREMOTE use the same syntax for specifying the speed and port settings for remote serial communications. For the link to work properly, you must set both systems to the same speed (with the **–rs** option).

After loading TFREMOTE on the remote system, run TPROF on the local system to complete the remote link. The following DOS command will load Turbo Profiler, establishing a connection through serial port 2, at the default speed of 115,000 baud:

```
TPROF -rp2 filename
```

When the link is successful, the message Link established appears on the remote system, and the activity indicator on the local system displays READY. Turbo Profiler's display then appears on the local system.

If the program *filename* is not on the remote system, then Turbo Profiler will send the program over the remote link. For more about loading programs over the link, refer to "Loading programs onto the remote system" on page 485.

Instead of using **–rs** and **–rp**, you can use the **–r** command-line option, which starts the remote serial link using the default speed and serial port. Unless you've changed the defaults using TFINST, **–r** specifies COM1 at 115,000 baud.

### LAN connection

TPROF uses the **–rn** command-line option to initiate a remote LAN link. However, the syntax used with Turbo Profiler is slightly different from that used with TFREMOTE. Following is the Turbo Profiler remote LAN syntax:

```
TPROF -rn [Local][;Remote] filename
```

The **–rn** command-line option takes two optional parameters: the local system name and the remote system name, separated by a semicolon. Since both parameters are optional, there are four ways to use the **–rn** command-line option with TPROF. These DOS commands all load Turbo Profiler, specify a remote LAN connection, and load the program **filename** for profiling.

```
TPROF -rn filename
```

Uses the default names *Local* and *Remote* for both the local and remote systems.

```
TPROF -rnLOCAL1 filename
```

Specifies LOCAL1 as the local system name, but uses the default (*Remote*) for the remote system name.

```
TPROF -rn;REMOTE1 filename
```

Uses the default (*LOCAL*) for the local system name, but specifies *REMOTE1* for the remote system.

```
TPROF -rnLOCAL1;REMOTE1 filename
```

Specifies both system names.The handshake should take less than 15 seconds after you enter the TPROF command.

Local and remote system names can be up to 16 characters long.

**Note**   If only one person on a network is using remote profiling, then it isn't necessary to define special local and remote system names. However, if more than one person uses remote profiling on a given network, unique names must be given to all systems.

# Profiling remote Windows applications

To profile a remote Windows application, you must run Windows, WREMOTE, and the application on one machine and Turbo Profiler on another. In this discussion, the machine running Windows, WREMOTE, and the application is called the *remote* system, and the machine running Turbo Profiler is called the *local* system.

## Setting up the remote system

Copy to the remote system the remote profiling driver WREMOTE.EXE, the configuration program WRSETUP.EXE, and any files required by the program you're profiling. These files include data input files, configuration files, help files, Windows DLL files, and so on. If you want, you can also copy your application program onto the remote system. However, Turbo Profiler automatically sends it over the remote link if necessary.

To put files on the remote system, you can use floppy disks or the TDRF remote file transfer utility. TDRF is described in the online Help.

## Configuring WREMOTE

Before running WREMOTE for the first time, you should run the WRSETUP program to establish the communication settings.

Set up WREMOTE with WRSETUP. When you run WRSETUP, you see a window displaying the commands File, Settings, and Help. Choosing Settings displays the following screen:

**Figure 30.1**   WRSETUP main window and Settings dialog box

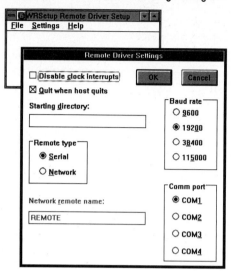

## Serial configuration

If you're using serial communications, select the Serial radio button, and set a baud rate and communications port that works for your hardware setup. The defaults are 19,200 baud and COM1.

## LAN configuration

If you're using LAN communications, select the Network radio button, and specify the desired remote system name in the Network Remote Name text box. By default, the remote system name is *REMOTE*. For more on remote system names, refer to "LAN connection" on page 481.

In the Starting Directory text entry box, enter the directory path where Turbo Profiler should look for the program you're profiling. If you want WREMOTE to return control to Windows when you terminate Turbo Profiler on the local machine, select Quit When Host Quits. If you are using the higher transmission speeds (38,400 or 115,000 baud) check the Disable Clock Interrupts box. This will help WREMOTE and Turbo Profiler establish a connection in the Windows environment.

As with any *.INI* file, you can edit the file directly using any word processor that produces ASCII text.

Once you've set your options and closed the WRSETUP window, WRSETUP will save your settings to the file TDW.INI in your Windows directory. The following TDW.INI file sets WREMOTE at 19,200 baud on COM2 with clock interrupts disabled and the program returning control to Windows when Turbo Profiler terminates:

```
[WRemote]
BaudRate=2
Port=2
```

```
Quit=1
Clock=1
```

## WREMOTE command-line options

You can use WREMOTE command-line options to override the default settings or the settings listed in the WREMOTE.INI file. Start an option with either a hyphen (–) or a slash (/).

**Table 30.2** WREMOTE command-line options

| Option | What it does |
| --- | --- |
| –c*<filename>* | Use *<filename>* as the configuration (.INI) file |
| –d*<dir>* | Use *<dir>* as the startup directory |
| –rc0 | Clock interrupts enabled |
| –rc1 | Clock interrupts disabled |
| –rn*<remotename>* | Remote LAN profiling |
| –rp1 | Port 1 (COM1); default |
| –rp2 | Port 2 (COM2) |
| –rp3 | Port 3 (COM3) |
| –rp4 | Port 4 (COM4) |
| –rq0 | Don't quit when Turbo Profiler quits |
| –rq1 | Quit when Turbo Profiler quits |
| –rs1 | Slowest speed (9,600 baud) |
| –rs2 | Slow speed (19,200 baud) |
| –rs3 | Medium speed (38,400 baud) |
| –rs4 | Fast speed (115,000 baud); default |

## Starting the remote Windows driver

After you start WREMOTE from Windows, the program displays an hourglass at the mouse cursor location, indicating that it's ready for you to start Turbo Profiler at the other end of the link.

To terminate WREMOTE while it is waiting to establish a connection with TPROF, press *Ctrl+Break* on the remote machine.

## Establishing the remote Windows link

If you're using a null modem cable to connect the two systems, you may use the command-line options –**rs** and –**rp** to indicate the speed and port of the data communications.

For more on command-line options, see "Serial connection" on page 481.

Both Turbo Profiler and WREMOTE must be set to the same speed to work properly. You can use the –**rs** parameter to set the baud rate for Turbo Profiler, or you can use the –**r** command-line option, which starts the remote serial link using the default speed and serial port. Unless you've changed the defaults using TFINST, –**r** specifies COM1 at 115,000 baud.

### LAN connection

TPROF uses the **-rn** command-line option to initiate a remote LAN link. For more on **-rn**, see "LAN connection" on page 481.

Here's a typical Turbo Profiler command to start the remote Windows link:

```
TPROF -rs2 myprog
```

This command begins the link on the default serial port (usually COM1) at the link speed (19,200 baud), and loads the program *myprog* into the remote system if it's not already there.

When Turbo Profiler starts on the local machine, it displays copyright and version information and the following message:

```
Waiting for handshake from remote driver (Ctrl+Break to quit)
```

While waiting for a connection, an hourglass is displayed on the remote system. Turbo Profiler's normal window display comes up on the local machine. Press *Ctrl+Break* to exit WREMOTE if the link is not successful.

# Loading programs onto the remote system

If a file name is included as a TPROF command-line argument, or if you load a new file into the profiler using the File | Open command, Turbo Profiler will automatically check to see if the program needs to be sent to the remote system.

Windows DLL files are not automatically transferred to the remote system.

Turbo Profiler is smart about loading programs onto the remote system. First, a check is made to see if the program exists on the remote system. If the program doesn't exist on the remote system, it's sent over the link right away. If the program does exist on the remote system, Turbo Profiler looks at the date and time of the program on the local system and compares this with the copy on the remote system. If the program on the local system is later (newer) than the remote copy, Turbo Profiler assumes you've recompiled or relinked the program, and sends it over the link.

At the highest link speed, file transfers move at a rate of about 10K per second. A typical 60K program takes roughly six seconds to transfer. On DOS systems, Turbo Profiler indicates that the system is working by displaying the number of bytes transferred on the remote system.

# Remote profiling sessions

Once you start TPROF in remote mode (using either TFREMOTE or WREMOTE), the Turbo Profiler commands work exactly the same as they do on a single system; there is nothing new to learn.

Because the program you're profiling is actually running on the remote system, any screen output or keyboard input to that program happens on the remote system. The Window | User Screen command has no effect when you're running on the remote link.

The remote system's CPU type appears as part of the CPU window title, with the word REMOTE before it.

To send files over to the remote system while running Turbo Profiler, go to DOS (choose File | DOS Shell) and then use TDRF to perform file-maintenance activities on the remote system. To return to Turbo Profiler, type EXIT at the DOS prompt and continue profiling your program.

## Troubleshooting

Here's a list of troubleshooting techniques you can try if you experience problems with the remote setup:

- Check your cable hookups.

- Check that you're using the correct serial port settings or that you're properly connected to the network.

- Try running the link at a slower speed (using the **-rs** command-line option) until you find a speed that works.

- Some hardware and cable combinations don't always work properly at the highest speed, so if you can get the link to work only at a lower speed, you might want to try a different cable or different computers.

- If you're profiling a Windows program and can't get the connection to work at any speed, use WRSETUP to *Disable clock interrupts* and try running the link at 9,600 baud. If that works, try successively higher speeds.

## TFREMOTE messages

### nn bytes downloaded
TFREMOTE is receiving a file from the local system. This message shows the progress of the file transfer. At the highest link speed (115,000 baud), transfer speed is about 10K per second.

### Can't create file
TFREMOTE can't create a file on the remote system. This can happen if there isn't enough room on the remote disk to transfer the executable program across the link.

### Can't modify .exe file
You specified a file name to modify that is not a valid copy of the TFREMOTE utility. You can modify a copy of the TFREMOTE utility only with the -w option.

### Can't open .exe file to modify
TFREMOTE can't open the file name you specified. You've probably entered an invalid file name.

### Download complete
Your file has been successfully sent to TFREMOTE.

### Download failed, write error on disk

TFREMOTE can't write part of a received file to disk. This usually happens when the disk fills up. You must delete some files before TFREMOTE can successfully download the file.

### Enter program file name to modify

If you are running on DOS version 3.0 or later, the prompt indicates the path and file name from which you executed TFREMOTE. You can accept this name (press *Enter*), or enter a new executable file name.

If you're running DOS version 2.xx, you must supply the full path and file name of the executable program.

### Interrupted

You pressed *Ctrl+Break* while waiting for communications to be established with the other system.

### Invalid command-line option

You gave an invalid command-line option when you started TDRF from the DOS command line.

### Link broken

The program communicating with TFREMOTE has stopped and returned to DOS.

### Link established

A program on the other system has just started to communicate with TFREMOTE.

### Loading program *name* from disk

Turbo Profiler has told TFREMOTE to load a program from disk into memory in preparation for profiling.

### No network present

TFREMOTE is unable to detect a NETBIOS compatible network. Make sure you have loaded NETBIOS (version 3.0 or greater) and are connected to the network.

### Program load failed, EXEC failure

DOS could not load the program into memory. This can happen if the program has become corrupted or truncated. Delete the program file from the remote system's disk to force Turbo Profiler to send a new copy over the link. If this message appears again after deleting the file, you should relink your program using TLINK on the local system and try again.

### Program load failed; not enough memory

The remote system doesn't have enough free memory to load the program you want to profile.

### Program load failed; program not found

TFREMOTE could not find the program on its disk.

### Program load successful

TFREMOTE has finished loading the program Turbo Profiler wants to profile.

### Reading file *name* from Turbo Profiler

This appears on your remote screen so that you know when a remote file is being sent to Turbo Profiler.

### Unknown request: *message*

TFREMOTE has received an invalid request from the local system (where you're running Turbo Profiler). If you get this message, check that the link cable is in good working order. If you keep getting this error, try reducing the link speed (use the –rs command-line option).

### Waiting for handshake (press *Ctrl+Break* to quit)

TFREMOTE has started and is waiting for a program on the local system to start talking to it. To return to DOS before the other system initiates communication, press *Ctrl+Break*.

## WREMOTE messages

### Can't find configuration file

You used the –c command-line option to specify a file that doesn't exist.

### Can't load WINDEBUG.DLL

The dynamic link library WINDEBUG.DLL isn't in the current directory. WREMOTE requires this DLL in order to run.

### Can't open COMx serial port

WREMOTE is trying to use a COM port that is either in use or doesn't exist.

### Invalid switch

You specified an unknown option on the WREMOTE command line.

### No network present

WREMOTE is unable to detect a NETBIOS compatible network. Make sure you've loaded NETBIOS (version 3.0 or greater) and are connected to the network.

# 31

# Turbo Profiler for Windows

Turbo Profiler for Windows (TPROFW) lets you profile applications you've written for Microsoft Windows, version 3.0 and higher. It runs under Windows on the same machine as the program you are profiling and switches between its own screens and your application's screens, just as Turbo Profiler does.

You profile in Windows much as you would in DOS, except that you can also access information particular to Windows applications, such as

- Messages received and sent by your application's windows
- The complete list of modules loaded by Windows (including dynamic-link libraries)
- Dynamic-link library (DLL) profiling

TPROFW runs in Windows standard mode or 386 enhanced mode, which means that your computer must have an 80286 processor or higher and at least 1MB of memory.

TPROFW.EXE supports several different video adapters through the use of several DLLs. After you've installed TPROFW, run TDWINI.EXE to help you select or modify the driver that's used with your setup.

By default, TPROFW uses the SVGA.DLL video driver, which supports most video adapters and monitors. For more information on the available video DLLs, refer to the entries for DUAL8514.DLL, STB.DLL, SVGA.DLL, and TDWGUI.DLL in the online Help system of TDWINI.EXE.

Like Turbo Profiler, TPROFW can also take advantage of a second monitor attached to your computer, allowing you to view TPROFW screens on one monitor and your application's screens on another. You select this display option by starting TPROFW with the **–do** command-line switch or by running the TFINST utility and setting User Screen Updating to *Other display*.

# Installing TPROFW

When you install Turbo Profiler on your system, the installation program puts the following two Windows-related files in the same directory as your Turbo Profiler files:

- TPROFW.EXE, the TPROFW program
- TFWHELP.TFH, the TPROFW help files

The installation process creates an icon for TPROFW and installs it in the Windows Program Manager group for your Borland language. You can run TPROFW by choosing the icon, just as you can with any other Windows application.

## Installing TDDEBUG.386

The TDDEBUG.386 file on your installation disks provides the same functionality as the Windows SDK file WINDEBUG.386. In addition, it provides better support than WINDEBUG.386 for the *Ctrl+Alt+SysRq* key combination (used to break out of a Windows application and return to TPROFW).

The installation program should copy this file to your hard disk and alter your Windows SYSTEM.INI file so that Windows loads TDDEBUG.386 instead of WINDEBUG.386. If, for some reason, the installation program can't complete this task, you'll have to do it by hand as follows:

1 The installation program will have copied TDDEBUG.386 from the installation disks to your hard disk. The standard directory for this file is C:\WINDOWS. If you move the file to another directory, substitute that directory in the instructions.

2 With an editor, open the Windows SYSTEM.INI file, search for *[386enh]*, and add the following line to the 386enh section:

```
device=c:\windows\ddebug.386
```

3 If there's a line in the 386enh section that loads WINDEBUG.386, either comment the line out with a semicolon or delete it altogether. (You can't have both TDDEBUG.386 and WINDEBUG.386 loaded at the same time.)

For example, if you load WINDEBUG.386 from the C:\WINDOWS directory, the commented-out line would be

```
;device=c:\windows\windebug.386
```

# Configuring TPROFW

Just as with Turbo Profiler, you can configure TPROFW two ways: by entering command-line options or by using the TFINST utility.

# Using TPROFW command-line options

You can set the configuration of TPROFW by using various command-line options followed by an optional program name with its own command-line options. The program name can be preceded by a path name.

Because TPROFW is a Windows program, you will probably enter any command-line options either by using the Program Manager's File | Run command or by using the Program Manager's File | Properties command to change the command-line property of the TPROFW icon. You can also start Windows and TPROFW from the DOS command line. Follow the Windows command with the TPROFW command, optionally followed by switches or a program name (with or without switches).

The command-line syntax for TPROFW is

```
TPROFW [options] [program-name [program-args]]
```

Table 31.1 provides a summary of the command-line options for TPROFW:

**Table 31.1**   TPROFW command-line options

| Option | What it does |
| --- | --- |
| −?,−h | Displays help on TPROFW command-line options. |
| −b | Uses batch-mode profiling. |
| −b*count* | Use batch-mode profiling, and run the progrm *count* number of times. |
| −c*filename* | Uses configuration file *filename*. |
| −do | Runs TPROFW on the secondary display. |
| −ds | Updates screens by swapping pages. |
| −p | Uses a mouse. If the mouse driver is disabled for Windows, it will be disabled for TPROFW as well, and the −p command-line option will have no effect. |
| −sc | Ignores case for symbol names. |
| −sd*dir*[;*dir*...] | Sets one or more source file directories. |
| −t*dir* | Sets the starting directory. |

See Chapter 28, "Turbo Profiler's command-line options," for a complete description of the command-line options.

**Note**   The command-line option −t is available only with TPROFW. This option changes TPROFW's starting directory, which is where TPROFW looks for the configuration file and for .EXE files not specified with a full path. The syntax is

```
-tdirname
```

You can set only one starting directory with this option. If you enter this command more than once on the same command line, TPROFW uses only the last entry.

# Using TFINST with TPROFW

To use TFINST with TPROFW, start TFINST using the −w command-line option. TFINST for TPROFW works just like TFINST for Turbo Profiler, except that the default configuration file is TFCONFIG.TFW and fewer options are available. (See the list of TPROFW command-line options in the previous section.)

For a description of how to use TFINST, see Chapter 29, "Customizing Turbo Profiler."

# Using TPROFW

When you load TPROFW, it comes up in full-screen DOS character mode, not in a DLL (unless you're using the TDWGUI.DLL video driver). Unlike other applications that run under Windows, you can't use the Windows shortcut keys (like *Alt+Esc* or *Ctrl+Esc*) to switch out of TPROFW and run another application. However, if the application you are profiling is active (the cursor is active in one of its windows), you can use these keys or the mouse to switch to other programs.

**Note**    If you do use *Ctrl+Esc* to switch out of an application running under TPROFW, you see the application name on the list of tasks. You will never see TPROFW on the task list because TPROFW is not a normal Windows task that you can switch into or out of.

Profiling using TPROFW is pretty much the same as profiling using Turbo Profiler. However, there are some differences:

- Switching from your application to TPROFW is accomplished by using the *Ctrl+Alt+SysRq* key combination. This operation is similar to using *Ctrl+Break* to switch out of a DOS application and back to Turbo Profiler, except that the DOS application terminates, while the Windows application is only suspended.

- If possible, run your application to completion or use the System command to exit it before exiting TPROFW or loading in another program to be profiled. Failing to exit a Windows application properly can leave resources allocated that would otherwise have been deallocated, potentially causing problems with TPROFW or other applications.

- The DOS Shell command from the File menu is not available.

- The Edit command on the Module and Text File SpeedMenus are not available.

- Interrupts, File I/O, and Overlay windows are not available.

- Display Swapping settings are not available in the Display Options dialog box.

## Profiling window procedures

TPROFW keeps track of routines inside window procedures by tracking the *message classes* called by the routine and *window messages* sent to the procedures. Before message classes and window messages can be tracked, you must first specify that an area marker represents a window procedure. Specifying a window procedure area marker is done from either the Module window's SpeedMenu | Operation command, or the Areas window SpeedMenu | Option command.

## The Window Procedure Messages dialog box

After an area marker is specified as a window procedure marker, you must then select which messages and classes you want to track for that particular procedure. When *Messages* is selected from either the Module window's SpeedMenu | Operation command or the Areas window SpeedMenu | Option command, the Window Procedure Messages dialog box is displayed.

With the Window Procedure Messages dialog box, you can select the window messages and message classes that are tracked for the current area marker. TPROFW, by default, tracks all message classes.

The Window Procedure Messages dialog box uses check boxes and text boxes for the following:

- The Window Messages list box displays specially selected window messages.

- Message Name is a text box that accepts a window message name or window message number. Use the Add command to append the specified message to the Window Messages list.

  Turbo Profiler will recognize only window message names that begin with *WM_*. If you wish to track a message other than a *WM_* message, you must provide the window message number (window message numbers are acquired from either your program source files or from the windows header include files).

  Window message names are case sensitive.

- Delete removes the currently highlighted message from the Window Messages list box.

- Remove All deletes all specially selected messages from the Window Messages list box. When this command is selected, the Window Messages list box will be cleared of all entries.

- Add All selects all *WM_* messages from all classes. Each message is listed in the Window Messages list box after this command is chosen. Because so many messages come through, you'll probably want to narrow the focus by selecting only the classes of interest from the list of message names.

**Note**    Before selecting Add All, ensure the Max Windows Messages setting (Statistics | Profiling Options) has been adjusted to accommodate the number of messages you want to track.

  Including all message classes, there are over 140 *WM_* messages.

- Add appends the message name specified in the Message Name text box to the Window Messages list.

- The Message Classes check boxes allow you to choose specific classes of messages to watch. When a specific Windows message class is selected, all *WM_* messages from that class will be tracked.

Table 31.2 describes the window message classes:

**Table 31.2**  Window's message classes

| Message class | Description |
| --- | --- |
| All Messages | All messages starting with WM_. |
| Mouse | Messages generated by a mouse event (for example, WM_LBUTTONDOWN and WM_MOUSEMOVE). |
| Window | Messages from the window manager (for example, WM_PAINT and WM_CREATE). |
| Input | Messages generated by a keyboard event or by the user's accessing a System menu, scroll bar, or size box (for example, WM_KEYDOWN). |
| System | Messages generated by a system-wide change (for example, WM_FONTCHANGE and WM_SPOOLERSTATUS). |
| Initialization | Messages generated when an application creates a dialog box or a window (for example, WM_INITDIALOG and WM_INITMENU). |
| Clipboard | Messages generated when one application tries to access the Clipboard of a window in another application (for example, WM_DRAWCLIPBOARD and WM_SIZECLIPBOARD). |
| DDE | Dynamic Data Exchange messages, generated by applications communicating with one another's windows (for example, WM_DDE_INITIATE and WM_DDE_ACK). |
| Non-client | Messages generated by Windows to maintain the non-client area of an application window (for example, WM_NCHITTEST and WM_NCCREATE). |
| Other | Any messages starting with WM_ that don't fall into any of the other categories, such as owner draw control messages and multiple document interface messages. |

For a complete list of all WM_ messages, refer to your Borland compiler's online Help.

**Note**  When you've selected the appropriate window messages, profile your program as usual. To view window message statistics, choose Window Procedures from the Display Options dialog box, accessed through the Execution Profile SpeedMenu.

## Profiling dynamic-link libraries (DLLs)

A *DLL* (dynamic-link library) is a Windows library of routines and resources that is linked to your application at run time instead of at compile time. This run-time linking allows multiple applications to share a single copy of routines, data, or device drivers, thus saving on memory usage. When an application that uses a DLL starts up, Windows loads it in memory so the application can access the DLL's entry points (if the DLL isn't already loaded into memory).

TPROFW can load a DLL that doesn't have a symbol table, but only into a CPU window.

When you load an application with DLLs linked to it, TPROFW determines which of these DLLs, if any, have symbol tables (were compiled with the debugging option turned on) and tracks them for you.

TPROFW automatically loads in the symbol table and source of every DLL that's linked to your application, but only if the DLL has a compatible symbol table. A DLL has a symbol table compatible with TPROFW if it was compiled with debugging information turned on and the compiler was one of Borland's C++ Windows compilers, or Turbo Assembler.

**Note**  DLLs that are loaded via the LoadLibrary call will not be automatically tracked by Turbo Profiler. To track these DLLs, you must set a Stop area marker after the LoadLibrary call. When the profiler encounters this area marker, you'll be able to access the DLL through the Module command on the Module window's SpeedMenu, or through View | Module. You'll need to set up a stop area on the last line of the DLL function in order to view the DLL's statistics. If you don't set the stop area, you will not be able to view or analyze the statistics.

Because the symbol table for the DLL is not associated with the symbol table for the executable program, Turbo Profiler will produce a separate statistics file (.TFS) and a separate areas file (.TFA) for *each* DLL profiled.

# TPROFW error messages

There is only one error message returned solely by TPROFW. In addition to this error message, Turbo Profiler error messages can also be returned.

### Ctrl+Alt+SysRq interrupt. System crash possible. Continue?

You attempted either to exit TPROFW or to reload your application program while the program was suspended as a result of your having pressed *Ctrl+Alt+SysRq*. Because Windows kernel code was executing at the time you suspended the application, exiting TPROFW or reloading the application will have unpredictable results (most likely hanging the system and forcing a reboot).

# 32

# Prompts and error messages

Turbo Profiler displays messages and prompts at the current cursor location. This chapter describes the prompts and error and information messages Turbo Profiler generates.

We tell you how to respond to both prompts and error messages. All the prompts and error messages are listed in alphabetical order, with a description provided for each one.

## Turbo Profiler prompts

Turbo Profiler displays a prompt in a dialog box when you must supply additional information to complete a command. The prompt describes the information that's needed. The contents may show a history list of previous responses that you have given.

You can respond to a prompt in one of two ways:

• Enter a response and accept it by pressing *Enter*.
• Press *Esc* to cancel the dialog box and return to the menu command that opened it.

Some prompts only present a choice between two items (like Yes/No). You can use *Tab* to select the choice you want and then press *Enter*, or press *Y* or *N* directly. Cancel the command by pressing *Esc*.

For a more complete discussion of the keystroke commands to use when a dialog box is active, refer to Chapter 25, "The Turbo Profiler environment."

Here's an alphabetical list of all the prompts and messages generated by dialog boxes:

### Enter code label to position to

Enter the address you wish to examine in the Disassembly pane. The Disassembly pane shows the disassembled instructions at the specified address.

### Enter command line arguments

Enter the command-line arguments for the program you're profiling. You can modify the current command-line arguments or enter a new set.

You will then be prompted whether you want to reload your program from disk. Some languages or programs, such as programs written in C, require you to reload the program before the arguments take effect.

**Enter file name to restore from**

Enter the name of the file to restore the statistics from. If you specify an extension to the file name, it will be used. Otherwise the extension .TFS will be used.

**Enter file name to save areas to**

Enter the name of the file to save the current areas to. If you specify an extension to the file name, it will be used. Otherwise the extension .TFS will be used.

**Enter file name to save to**

Enter the name of the file to save the current statistics to. If you specify an extension to the file name, it will be used. Otherwise the extension .TFS will be used.

**Enter interrupt number**

Enter the number of the interrupt that you wish to track.

**Enter name of file to view**

Enter the name of a text file that you want to inspect. The file specified will be brought into the File window.

**Enter new directory**

Enter the new drive and/or directory name that you want to become the current drive and directory.

**Enter new line number**

Enter a new line number to position the text file to. The first line in the file is line 1. If you specify a line number that is greater than the last line in the file, the file is positioned to the last line.

**Enter program name to load**

Enter the name of the program to load. If the program has the .EXE extension, you don't have to specify it; if the program has any other extension, you must supply it.

If you supply a wildcard specification or accept the default *.EXE, a list of matching files is displayed for you to select from.

**Enter routine name to add**

Enter the name of the function you wish to include, exclude, or set.

**Enter search string**

Enter a character string to search for. You can use a simple wildcard matching facility to specify an inexact search string; for example, use * to match zero or more of any characters, and ? to match any single character.

**Enter source directory list**

Enter the directory or directories to search for source files.

If you want to enter more than one directory, separate the different directory paths with a space or a semicolon (;). These directories will be searched, in the order that they appear in this list, for your source files.

### Pick a caller

Pick a routine from the list of callers. You will then be positioned to that routine in the window that you picked from the previous menu.

### Pick a method name

You have specified a routine name that can refer to more than one method in an object. Pick the correct one from the list presented, with the arguments you want.

### Pick a module

Select a module name to view in the Module window. You are presented with a list of all the modules in your program. Either use the cursor keys to move to the desired module, or start typing the name of the module. As you type the module name, the highlight bar will move to the first module that matches the letters you typed. When the highlight bar is on the desired module, press *Enter*.

### Pick a source file

Pick a new source file to display in the Module window. The list shows all the source files that make up the module.

### Pick interrupt

Pick an interrupt from the list of interrupts built into Turbo Profiler.

### Pick macro to delete

Pick a macro to erase from the list of defined macros.

### Reload program and change profiling mode?

When you change the profiling mode from active or passive to coverage, or from coverage to active or passive, all current profile statistics will be erased. If you wish to save the statistics before changing modes, answer NO to this prompt and save the statistics to a .TFS file. Otherwise, answer YES to the prompt.

# Turbo Profiler error messages

Turbo Profiler uses error messages to tell you about things you haven't quite expected. Sometimes the command you have issued cannot be processed. At other times the message warns that things didn't go exactly as you wanted.

Error messages can be accompanied by a beep. You can turn the beep on or off in the customization program, TFINST.

### Already recording, do you want to abort?

You are already recording a keystroke macro. You can't start recording another keystroke macro until you finish the current one. Press *Y* to stop recording the macro, *N* to continue recording the macro.

### Ambiguous symbol *symbol name*

You have entered a member function or data item name and Turbo Profiler can't tell which of the multiple instances of this member you mean.

This can happen when a member name is duplicated in two multiply inherited classes. Use the *classname::* override to name explicitly the member you want.

### Bad or missing configuration file name

You have specified a nonexistent file name with the –c command-line option when you started Turbo Profiler. The built-in default configuration values are used instead.

### Bad interrupt number entered

You have entered an invalid interrupt number. Valid interrupt numbers are 9 to FF.

### Bad module name *module name*

The module name that you have entered does not exist.

### Can't execute DOS command processor

Either there was not enough memory to execute the DOS command processor, or the command processor could not be found (the COMSPEC environment variable is either absent or incorrect). Make sure that the COMSPEC environment variable correctly specifies where to find the DOS command processor.

### Can't find *filename.DLL*

You attempted to load a program that requires one or more DLLs, but TPROFW can't find one of them. Make sure your executable file and the DLLs it requires are in the same directory, then load the program again.

### Can't swap user program to disk

The program being profiled could not be swapped to disk. There is probably not enough room on the disk to swap the program. You will not be able to edit any files or execute DOS commands until some more room is made available.

### Edit program not specified

You tried to use the Edit SpeedMenu command from a Module or Disk File window, but you cannot edit the file because Turbo Profiler does not know how to start your editor.

Use the configuration program TFINST to specify an editor.

### Error loading program

Your program could not be loaded. The format of the .EXE does not match the operating system.

### Error printing statistics

There was an error sending to the printer. Check that the printer is online and not out of paper.

### Error reading statistics file

An error occurred while you were restoring the collected statistics. Make sure that the disk is ready.

### Error saving configuration

Your configuration could not be saved to disk. The disk might be full, or there might be no more free directory entries in the root directory.

You can use the File | DOS Shell command to go to DOS and delete a file or two to make room for the configuration file.

### Error swapping in user program, program reloaded

An error occurred while you were reloading your program that was swapped to disk. This usually means that the swap file was accidentally deleted.

You will have to reload your program using the Run | Program Reset command before you can continue profiling.

**Error writing statistics file**

An error occurred while you were writing to the statistics file that stores your program statistics. Your disk is probably full.

Make sure that the disk is ready and that there is enough room on the disk.

**Exception *N*, error code *N***

Turbo Profiler encountered either an invalid memory reference or an invalid instruction in your program. You must correct the error before continuing profiling.

**Help file TFHELP.TFH not found**

You asked for help, but the disk file that contains the help screens could not be found. Make sure that the help file is in the same directory as Turbo Profiler.

**Invalid number entered**

The line number you specified is either a negative number, or contains an alphabetic character. Make sure you specify a positive integer as a line number.

**Invalid statistics file**

The file you specified to restore statistics from has an invalid format. Make sure the file name you specified was created using the Statistics | Save command.

**Invalid switch**

An invalid command-line option was encountered during program loading.

**Invalid window message number**

The window message that you have specified is not a valid name or number. Make sure that the message name is correctly spelled (window message names are case sensitive).

**Maximum number of areas has been reached**

There is no more room to add areas. Use the Options | Number of Areas command to increase the amount of memory set aside for areas.

**Maximum number of interrupts being monitored**

You can't watch any more interrupts; you have already told Turbo Profiler to watch as many interrupts as it is capable of doing. You will have to use the SpeedMenu Remove command to remove an existing interrupt before you can add any more.

**Maximum number of windows messages has been reached**

By default, Turbo Profiler sets the maximum number of window messages. If you attempt to track more than the number of messages specified in the Max Windows Messages text box (found through the Statistics | Profiling Options command), you'll receive this error message.

When cited with this error message, no window messages will be added to the list by Turbo Profiler. Make sure to reset the Max Windows Messages count to reflect the number of messages that you want to watch, and then add the appropriate messages through the Window Procedure Messages dialog box.

**NMI interrupt**

The program you're profiling has generated an NMI (non-maskable interrupt).

### No help for this context

You pressed *F1* to get help, but Turbo Profiler could not find a relevant help screen. Please report this to Borland Technical Support.

### No file name was given

You have indicated that you wish to output a file, but you have not specified a file name. You must either specify a file name or switch to another output location before you can leave the dialog box.

### No modules with statistics

There are no modules with any statistics collected, so there is nothing to print.

### No network present

You must load NETBIOS (version 3.0 or above) before running TPROF or TFREMOTE with the –rn option.

### No previous search expression

You have used the Next command from the SpeedMenu of a text pane, without previously issuing a Search command. First use Search to specify what to search for, then use Next to look for subsequent instances.

### No program loaded

You tried to issue a command that requires a program to be loaded. There are many commands that can be issued only when a program is loaded, for example, the commands in the Run menu. Use the File I Open command to load a program before issuing these commands.

### No source file for module *module name*

The source file cannot be found for the module that you wish to view. The source file is searched for first in the current directory, and then in any directories specified in the configuration file and then in any directories specified by the command line –sd option.

### Not a code address

You have entered an address that is not a code address in your program. You can set profiling areas only on code addresses.

### Not available when in coverage mode

This error message appears when you attempt to use a function that can't be used in coverage mode. Most likely, you're trying to set (or remove) an area marker. Since Turbo Profiler automatically sets coverage mode markers, you can't set or remove them manually.

### Not enough memory for selected operation

You issued a command that has to create a window, but there is not enough memory left for the new window. You must first remove or reduce the size of some of your windows before you can reissue the command. Also see the –m option in Chapter 28, "Turbo Profiler's command-line options."

### Not enough memory to load program

Your program's symbol table has been successfully loaded into memory, but there is not enough memory left to load your program. You can hook two systems together and run Turbo Profiler on one system and the program you're analyzing on the other. See Chapter 30, "Remote profiling," for more information on how to do this.

### Not enough memory to load symbol table

There is not enough room to load your program's symbol table into memory. The symbol table contains the information that Turbo Profiler uses to show you your source code and program variables. If you have any resident utilities consuming memory, you may want to remove them and then restart Turbo Profiler. You can also try making the symbol table smaller by having the compiler generate debug symbol information only for those modules you are interested in analyzing.

When this message is issued, your program itself has not yet been loaded. This means you must free enough memory for both the symbol table and your program.

### Out of heap space

Turbo Profiler ran out of memory to collect the information you requested. You'll need to reduce the amount of data that you want to gather in a single run.

### Overlay not loaded

You have attempted to examine code in an overlay that is not loaded into memory. You can examine code only for overlays that are already in memory.

However, you can still look at the source code for a module in a Module window. Setting an area's operation to stop will let you view the disassembled overlay.

### Overwrite existing macro on selected key

You have pressed a key to record a macro, and that key already has a macro assigned to it. If you want to overwrite the existing macro, press *Y*; otherwise, press *N* to cancel the command.

### Overwrite file name?

You have specified a file name to write to that already exists. You can choose by entering *Y* to overwrite the file, replacing its previous contents, or you can cancel the command by entering *N* and leave the previous file unchanged.

### Path not found

You entered a drive and directory combination that does not exist. Check that you have specified the correct drive and that the directory path is spelled correctly.

The current drive and directory are left as they were before you issued the command.

### Premature end of string in *symbol name*

The symbol name that you have entered is incomplete. If you specify a module name, it must be followed by either a line number or local symbol name.

### Press key to assign macro to

Press the key that you want to assign the macro to. Then press the keys to do the command sequence that you want to assign to the macro key. The command sequence will actually be performed as you type it. To end the macro recording sequence, press the key you assigned the macro to. This macro will be recorded on disk along with any other keystroke macros.

### Procedure stack overflow

Your program has too many nested procedure or function calls. You must remove some of the areas that are set on routines in the deepest calling path. Use the Callers window to find this area.

### Program does not have overlays

The program you are profiling does not have any overlays, so you can't open an Overlay window.

### Program has invalid symbol table

The program that you wish to load has a symbol table with an invalid format. Re-create your .EXE file and reload it.

### Program has no symbol table

The program you want to analyze has been successfully loaded, but it does not contain any debug symbol information. Relink the program so that it has a symbol table.

### Program linked with wrong linker version

The program you tried to load was linked with a linker whose version is incompatible with that of Turbo Profiler. Either the linker was an old one or you're using an old version of Turbo Profiler.

### Program not found

The program you wish to load does not exist. Check that the name you supplied to the File | Open command is correct and that you supplied a file-name extension if it is different from .EXE.

### Program out of date or missing on remote, send over link?

You have specified a program to analyze on the remote system, but it either does not exist on the remote, or the file is newer on the local system than on the remote system.

If you press *Y*, the program is sent across the link. If you press *N*, the program is not sent, and the File | Open command is aborted.

You'll usually respond with *Y*. If you are running the link at the slowest speed (using the **–rs**1 command-line option), you might want to abort the command with *N* and transfer the file to the remote system using a floppy disk.

### Reload program so arguments take effect?

With most programs, you must reload after changing their arguments.

When you press *Y*, a Run | Program Reset command is automatically performed for you.

### Reload program so new area count takes effect?

In order for Turbo Profiler to reallocate the memory used for statistics areas, your program must be unloaded from memory and then reloaded and executed from the beginning again.

Press *Y* to make this happen, or press *N* if you can wait for the next manual program load for the new area size to take effect.

### Run out of space for keystroke macros

There is not enough memory to record all your keystroke macro.

### Search expression not found

The specified text string or byte list is not present in the file. Since the search proceeds forward from the current cursor position, you should return to the top of the file via the *Ctrl+PgUp* hot key, then repeat the search.

### Stopped by area

Turbo Profiler encountered an area whose operation you set to "stop." You can continue profiling by using the Run | Run command.

### Symbol not a routine name

The symbol name that you supplied is not a valid name of a routine.

### Symbol not found

You have entered an expression containing an invalid symbol name. A valid symbol name consists of one of the following:

- A global symbol name
- A module name, followed by #, followed by a local symbol name
- A module name, followed by a #, followed by a decimal line number

### Syntax error in symbol *SymbolName*

You have entered an invalid symbol name. A valid symbol name consists of one of the following:

- A global symbol name
- A module name, followed by #, followed by a local symbol name
- A module name, followed by a #, followed by a decimal line number

### Too many areas for a Windows program

You've attempted to profile a program with more areas than the 511 supported by Windows. Some of the areas you set will not be profiled. You'll have to reduce the number of areas in order to control which areas are not included.

### Too many files match wildcard mask

You specified a wildcard file mask that included more than 100 files. Only the first 100 file names are displayed.

### Unknown control point

Turbo Profiler has encountered an INT 3 instruction in your program that it doesn't recognize. Because Turbo Profiler uses INT 3 instructions to indicate control points, if you've put any in your program yourself, there will be a conflict. It's also possible that Turbo Profiler inserted a control point and then lost track of it.

If you inserted the INT 3 in your program, you'll have to remove it to run Turbo Profiler on your program.

If you didn't put the INT 3 in, then it's one of Turbo Profiler's. Removing the area containing the INT 3 will allow you to continue profiling the program.

### Unable to determine procedure type

Turbo Profiler can't determine whether the current area is a near or far procedure. You'll have to remove it from the list of areas for Turbo Profiler to proceed.

### Value must be between *nn* and *nn*

You have entered an invalid numeric value for an editor setting (such as the tab width) or printer setting (such as the number of lines per page). The error message will tell you the allowed range of numbers.

### Video mode switched while flipping pages

You've started Turbo Profiler with a display updating mode that does not allow display pages to be saved, and the program that you are profiling has switched into a graphics mode.

Turbo Profiler has changed the display mode back to text display, so the screen contents of the program you are profiling have been lost.

To avoid this situation, start Turbo Profiler with display-swapping enabled (**–ds** command-line option).

### Waiting for remote driver. Press Esc to stop waiting

You've started a remote profiling session, and Turbo Profiler is waiting to connect to the remote driver. Press *Esc* to about the remote session.

# Error messages and warnings

This appendix describes the error messages that can be generated by Borland C++. It begins by describing the four types of messages you can receive: fatal errors, errors, warnings, and informational messages.

Next, it covers the different components that can generate messages: the compiler, the MAKE utility, the linker (TLINK), the librarian (TLIB), the integrated debugger, and the Windows Help compiler. This appendix also lists the errors that you can receive when you run your program (run-time errors).

The remainder of the appendix lists messages ASCII alphabetic order and provides a description of each message that includes where the message was generated.

## Message categories

Messages fall into four categories: fatal errors, errors, warnings, and informational messages.

### Fatal errors

Fatal errors can be generated by the compiler, the linker, and the MAKE utility. Fatal errors cause the compilation to stop immediately; you must take appropriate action to fix the error before you can resume compiling.

If the compiler or MAKE utility issues a fatal error, no .EXE file is created. If the linker issues a fatal error, any .EXE file that might have been created by the linker is deleted before the linker returns.

### Errors

Errors can be generated by the compiler, the linker, the MAKE utility, and the librarian. In addition, errors can be generated by your program at run time.

Errors generated by the compiler indicate program syntax errors, command-line errors, and disk or memory access errors. Compiler errors don't cause the compilation to stop—the compiler completes the current phase of the compilation and then stops and reports the errors encountered. The compiler attempts to find as many real errors in the source program as possible during each phase (preprocessing, parsing, optimizing, and code-generating).

Errors generated by the linker don't cause the linker to delete the .EXE or .MAP files. However, you shouldn't execute any .EXE file that was linked with errors. Linker errors are treated like fatal errors if you're compiling from the Integrated Development Environment (IDE).

The MAKE utility generates errors when there is a syntax or semantic error in the source makefile. You must edit the makefile to fix these types of errors.

Run-time errors are usually caused by logic errors in your program code. If you receive a run-time error, you must fix the error in your source code and recompile the program for the fix to take effect.

## Warnings

Warnings can be issued by the compiler, the linker, and the librarian. Warnings do not prevent the compilation from finishing. However, they do indicate conditions that are suspicious, even if the condition that caused the warning is legitimate within the language. The compiler also produces warnings if you use machine-dependent constructs in your source files.

## Informational messages

Informational messages inform you about the progress of tasks such as the status of a build.

# Message generators

The messages in this appendix include messages that can be generated by the compiler, the MAKE utility, the linker (TLINK), the librarian (TLIB), the integrated debugger (IDE), and the Windows Help compiler. Run-time errors (errors you can receive when you run your program) are also included.

## Compiler errors and warnings

Compile-time error messages indicate errors in program syntax, command-line errors, or errors in accessing a disk or memory. When most compile-time errors occurs, the compiler completes the current phase (preprocessing, parsing, optimizing, and code-generating) of the compilation and stops. But when fatal compile-time errors happen, compilation stops completely. If a fatal error occurs, fix the error and recompile.

**Note**   Be aware that the compiler generates messages as they are detected. Because C and C++ don't force any restrictions on placing statements on a line of text, the true cause of the error might be one or more lines before or after the line number mentioned in the error message.

Warnings indicate that conditions which are suspicious but legitimate exist or that machine-dependent constructs exist in your source files. Warnings do not stop compilation.

Warnings are issued as a result of a variety of conditions, such as:

| | |
|---|---|
| ANSI violations | Warn you of code that is acceptable to Borland C++ (because of C++ code or Borland C++ extensions), but is not in the ANSI definition of C. |
| Frequent warnings | Alert you to common programming mistakes. These warning messages point out conditions that are not in violation of the Borland C++ language but can yield the wrong result. |
| Less frequent warnings | Alert you to less common programming mistakes. These warning messages point out conditions that are not in violation of the Borland C++ language but can yield the wrong result. |
| Portability warnings | Alert you to possible problems with porting your code to other compilers. These usually apply to Borland C++ extensions. |
| C++ warnings | Warn you of errors you've made in your C++ code. They might be due to obsolete items or incorrect syntax. |

## Run-time errors and warnings

Run-time errors occur after the program has successfully compiled and is running. These errors are usually caused by logic errors in your program code. If you receive a run-time error, you must fix the error in your source code and recompile the program for the fix to take effect.

## Linker errors and warnings

As a rule, linker errors do not stop the linker or cause .EXE or .MAP files to be deleted. When such errors happens, don't try to execute the .EXE file. Fix the error and relink.

A fatal link error, however, stops the linker immediately. In such a case, the .EXE file is deleted. All Linker errors are treated as fatal errors if you are compiling from the Integrated Development Environment (IDE).

Linker warnings point out conditions that you should fix. When warnings occur, .EXE and .MAP files are still created.

## Librarian errors and warnings

Librarian errors and warnings occur when there is a problem with files or extended dictionaries, when memory runs low, or when there are problems as libraries are accessed.

## IDE debugger messages

IDE debugger messages are generated by the integrated debugger and appear under the Runtime tab of the Message window. Many of these messages relate to options not set properly in the IDE integrated debugger screens.

## ObjectScripting error messages

ObjectScripting error messages are messages that result from running scripts in the IDE. They appear under the Script tab in the Message window.

## Help compiler messages

The Help compiler displays messages when it encounters errors or warnings while building the Help resource file. Messages generated during the processing of the project file begin with the letter **P** and are followed by an error number. Messages that occur during the processing of the RTF topic file(s) begin with the letter **R** and are followed by an error number.

Whenever possible, the Help compiler displays the topic number and/or the file name that contains the error. If you've numbered your topics, the topic number is given with an error message that refers to that topic's sequential position in your RTF file (first, second, and so on). These numbers might be identical to the page number shown by your word processor. In your Help source files, topics are separated by hard page breaks even though there are no "pages" in the Help system.

Messages beginning with the word "Error" are fatal errors. Errors are always reported, and no usable Help resource file will result from the build. Messages beginning with the word "Warning" are less serious in nature. A build with warnings produces a valid Help resource file that loads under Windows, but the file might contain operational errors.

# Message formats

Messages are displayed with the message class first, followed by the source file name and line number where the error was detected, and finally with the text of the message itself.

Many of the messages appear in the Message view. For those messages, context-sensitive help is available. Point to the message and press F1 to display the message description.

If you are working from the command line or want to look up information on an error message, refer to the alphabetical list of error and warning messages in "Alphabetical list of messages" later in this chapter. Find the message you're interested in and click on it to display its description.

## Symbols in messages

Some messages include a symbol (such as a variable, file name, or module) that is taken from your program. In the following example, 'filename' will be replaced by the name of the file causing the problem:

**Error opening 'filename' for output**

Table A.1 describes what the symbols in error and warning messages stand for.

**Table A.1**    Symbols that appear in error messages and warnings

| Symbol | Meaning |
| --- | --- |
| address | A hexadecimal number indicating the address where the error occurred |
| argument | An argument |
| base | The name of a base element such as a base class |
| class | A class name |
| constructor | The name of a constructor such as a class constructor |
| filename | A file name (with or without extension) |
| function | A function name |
| group | A group name |
| identifier | An identifier (variable name or other) |
| language | The name of a programming language |
| macroname | The name of a macro |
| member | The name of a data member or member function |
| message | A message string |
| module | A module name |
| name | Any type of name |
| number | An actual number |
| operator | The symbol for an operator such as ++ |
| option | An option |
| parameter | A parameter name |
| path | A path name |
| reason | Reason given in message |
| segment | A segment name |
| size | An actual number |
| specifier | A type specifier |
| symbol | A symbol name |
| type | A type name |
| variable | A program variable |

# Alphabetical list of messages

Messages are listed in ASCII alphabetic order. Messages beginning with symbols come first, then messages beginning with numbers, and then messages beginning with letters of the alphabet. Messages that begin with symbols are alphabetized by the type of the symbols. For example, you might receive the following error message if you incorrectly declared your function *my_func*:

**my_func must be declared with no parameters**

To find this error message, look under the alphabetized listing of "function."

**')' missing in macro invocation**                                              *MAKE error*

A left parenthesis is required to invoke a macro.

**( expected**                                                                   *Compiler message*

A left parenthesis was expected before a parameter list.

**) expected**                                                                   *Compiler message*

A right parenthesis was expected at the end of a parameter list.

**, expected**                                                                   *Compiler message*

A comma was expected in a list of declarations, initializations, or parameters.

This problem is often caused by a missing syntax element earlier in the file or one of its included headers.

**: expected after private/protected/private**                                   *Compiler message*

When used to begin a private, protected, or public section of a C++ class, the reserved words "private," "protected," and "public" must be followed by a colon.

**< expected**                                                                   *Compiler message*

The keyword template was not followed by <.

Every template declaration must include the template formal parameters enclosed within < >, immediately following the template keyword.

**> expected**                                                                   *Compiler message*

A new-style cast (for example, dynamic_cast) was found with a missing closing ">".

**@ seen, expected a response-files name**                                       *Librarian message*

The response file name is not given immediately after @.

**{ expected**                                                                   *Compiler message*

A left brace was expected at the start of a block or initialization.

**} expected**                                                                   *Compiler message*

A right brace was expected at the end of a block or initialization.

**16-bit segments not supported in module 'module'**                             *Linker message*

16-bit segments are not supported for Win32 applications. Check to make sure that you have not compiled the application with the 16-bit compiler.

### 286/287 instructions not enabled
*Compiler message*

Use the 2 command-line compiler option or the 80286 option in the Options | Project | 16-bit Compiler | Processor settings to enable 286/287 opcodes. Be aware that the resulting code cannot be run on 8086- and 8088-based machines.

### 32-bit format in resource file. Please recompile.
*Resource Linker message*

The compiled resource (.RES) file you are trying to use with your application contains 32-bit resources, but the target type of your application is for 16-bit Windows.

Recompile the resource file for Windows 3.1 or change the target type for your application to Win32.

### 32-bit processing not supported in overlays
*Linker message*

An invalid combination of /o (overlays) and /3 (32-bit processing) was specified in the link command line.

### 32-bit record encountered
*Linker message*

An object file that contains 80386 32-bit records was encountered, and the /3 option was not used.

### Abnormal program termination
*Run-time message*

The program called abort because there wasn't enough memory to execute. This message can be caused by memory overwrites.

### Access can only be changed to public or protected
*Compiler message*

A C++ derived class can modify the access rights of a base class member, but only to public or protected. A base class member can't be made private.

### Added file 'filename' does not begin correctly, ignored
*Librarian message*

The librarian has decided that the file being added is not an object module. It will not try to add it to the library. The library is created anyway.

### Address of overloaded function 'function' doesn't match 'type'
*Compiler message*

A variable or parameter is assigned (or initialized with) the address of an overloaded function.

However, the type of the variable or parameter doesn't match any of the overloaded functions with the specified name.

### Alias 'alias' defined in module 'module' is redefined in module module name
*Linker message*

A second definition to the alias was encountered, so the second alias is being used.

### Ambiguity between 'function1' and 'function2'
*Compiler message*

Both of the named overloaded functions could be used with the supplied parameters. This ambiguity is not allowed.

### Ambiguous member name 'name'
*Compiler message*

Whenever a structure member name is used in inline assembly, such a name must be unique. (If it is defined in more than one structure, all of the definitions must agree as to its type and offset within the structures). In this case, an ambiguous member name has been used.

For example:

```
struct A
{
    int a;
    int b;
};
...
asm ax,.a;
```

### Ambiguous operators need parentheses
*Compiler message*

(Command-line equivalent for displaying this warning = -wamb)

This warning is displayed whenever two shift, relational, or bitwise-Boolean operators are used together without parentheses. Also, an addition or subtraction operator that appears without parentheses with a shift operator will produce this warning.

Default = not displayed

### Ambiguous override of virtual base member 'base_function': 'derived_function'
*Compiler message*

A virtual function in a virtual base class was overridden with two or more different functions along different paths in the inheritance hierarchy. For example,

```
struct VB
{
    virtual f();
};

struct A:virtual VB
{
    virtual f();
};

struct B:virtual VB
    virtual f();
}
```

### Application is running
*Run-time message*

The application you tried to run is already running.

For Windows, make sure the message loop of the program has properly terminated.

```
PostQuitMessage(0);
```

### Array allocated using 'new' may not have an initializer
*Compiler message*

When initializing a vector (array) of classes, you must use the constructor that has no arguments.

This is called the default constructor, which means that you can't supply constructor arguments when initializing such a vector.

### Array must have at least one element
*Compiler message*

ANSI C and C++ require that an array be defined to have at least one element (objects of zero size are not allowed).

An old programming trick declares an array element of a structure to have zero size, then allocates the space actually needed with malloc. You can still use this trick, but you must declare the array element to have (at least) one element if you are compiling in strict ANSI mode.

Declarations (as opposed to definitions) of arrays of unknown size are still allowed.

Example:

```
char ray[];        /* definition of unknown size -- ILLEGAL */
char ray[0];       /* definition of 0 size -- ILLEGAL */
extern char ray[]; /* declaration of unknown size -- OK */
```

### Array of references is not allowed
*Compiler message*

It is illegal to have an array of references, because pointers to references are not allowed and array names are coerced into pointers.

### Array size for 'delete' ignored
*Compiler message*

(Command-line equivalent for displaying this warning = -wdsz)

The C++ IDE issues this warning when you've specified the array size when deleting an array.

With the new C++ specification, you don't need to make this specification. the compiler ignores this construct.

This warning lets older code compile.

Default = displayed

### Array size too large
*Compiler message*

The declared array is larger than 64K and the 'huge' keyword was not used.

If you need an array of this size, either use the 'huge' modifier, like this:

```
int huge array[70000L];  /* Allocate 140000 bytes */
```

or dynamically allocate it with farmalloc( ) or farcalloc( ), like this:

```
int huge *array = (int huge *) farmalloc (sizeof (int) * 70000); ?? Allocate 140,000 bytes
```

### Array variable 'identifier' is near
*Compiler message*

(Command-line equivalent for displaying this warning = -wias)

When you use set the Far Data Threshold option, the compiler automatically makes any global variables that are larger than the threshold size be far.

When the variable is an initialized array with an unspecified size, its total size is not known when the compiler must decide whether to make it near or far, so the compiler makes it near.

The compiler issues this warning if the number of initializers given for the array causes the total variable size to exceed the data size threshold.

If the fact that the compiler made the variable be near causes problems, make the offending variable explicitly far. To do this, insert the keyword 'far' immediately to the left of the variable name in its definition.

Default = displayed

### Assembler stack overflow
*Compiler message*

The assembler ran out of memory during compilation. Review the portion of code flagged by the error message to ensure that it uses memory correctly.

### Assembler statement too long
*Compiler message*

Inline assembly statements can't be longer than 480 bytes.

### Assigning 'type' to 'enumeration'
*Compiler message*

(Command-line equivalent for displaying this warning = -weas)

Assigning an integer value to an enum type.

This is an error in C++, but is reduced to a warning to give existing programs a chance to work.

Default = displayed

### Assignment to 'this' not allowed, use X::operator new instead
*Compiler message*

In early versions of C++, the only way to control allocation of class of objects was by assigning to the 'this' parameter inside a constructor.

This practice is no longer allowed, because a better, safer, and more general technique is to define a member function operator new instead.

For example:

```
this = malloc(n);
```

### Attempt to export non-public symbol 'symbol'
*Linker message*

A symbol name was listed in the EXPORTS section of the module definition file, but no symbol of this name was found as public in the modules linked.

If compiling in C++ mode, this is usually caused by the name mangling that occurs as a result of C++'s type safe linkage. Inserting the _export keyword in the function prototype and function definition is required for all C++ Windows callback functions.

Language-independent causes result from a mistake in spelling or case, case-sensitive exports, or a procedure with this name that was not defined.

If you are using case sensitive exports, the Pascal calling convention used by Windows requires these symbols to be all upper-case characters.

### Attempt to export non-public symbol 'symbol'
*Linker message*

The EXPORTS section in the .DEF file specified the name of a symbol which has no public definition.

### Attempt to grant or reduce access to 'identifier'
*Compiler message*

A C++ derived class can modify the access rights of a base class member, but only by restoring it to the rights in the base class. It can't add or reduce access rights.

### Attempting to return a reference to a local object
*Compiler message*

You attempted to return a reference to a temporary object in a function that returns a reference type. This may be the result of a constructor or a function call. This object will disappear when the function returns, making the reference illegal.

### Attempting to return a reference to local variable 'identifier'

*Compiler message*

This C++ function returns a reference type, and you are trying to return a reference to a local (auto) variable. This is illegal, because the variable referred to disappears when the function exits.

You can return a reference to any static or global variable, or you can change the function to return a value instead.

### Automatic data segment exceeds 64K

*Linker message*

The sum of the DGROUP physical segment, local heap, and stack exceeded 64K. You need to either specify smaller values for the HEAPSIZE and STACKSIZE statements in the module definition file, or decrease the size of your near data in DGROUP.

The map file will show the sizes of the component segments in DGROUP.

### Bad character in parameters -> 'char'

*Linker message*

One of the following characters was encountered in the command line or in a response file:

```
"    *    <    =    >    ?    [    ]    |
```

or any control character other than horizontal tab, line feed, carriage return, or Ctrl+Z.

### Bad 'directive' directive syntax

*Compiler message*

A macro definition starts or ends with the ## operator, or contains the # operator that is not followed by a macro argument name.

An example of this might be:

```
Bad ifdef directive syntax
```

Note that an **#ifdef** directive must contain a single identifier (and nothing else) as the body of the directive.

Another example is:

```
Bad undef directive syntax
```

An **#undef** directive must also contain only one identifier as the body of the directive.

### Bad call of intrinsic function

*Compiler message*

You have used an intrinsic function without supplying a prototype. You may have supplied a prototype for an intrinsic function that was not what the compiler expected.

### Bad EXE header format in file.

### Executable format not recognized in file.

*Resource Linker message*

The executable file contained invalid information in its header. The file might not be a valid executable or might contain corrupted data.

### Bad EXE segment table in file.

*Resource Linker message*

The executable file contained invalid information in its segment table. The file might not be a valid executable or might contain corrupted data.

### Bad field list in debug information in module 'module'

*Linker message*

This is typically caused by bad debug information in the OBJ file. Borland Technical Support should be informed.

### Bad file name 'filename'

*Linker message*

An invalid file name was passed to the linker.

**Bad file name format in include directive**

**Bad file name format in line directive**                           *Compiler message*

Include and line directive file names must be surrounded by quotes (`"filename.h"`) or angle brackets (`<filename.h>`).

The file name was missing the opening quote or angle bracket.

If a macro was used, the resulting expansion text is not surrounded by quote marks.

**Bad filename format in include statement**                         *MAKE message*

Include file names must be surrounded by quotes or angle brackets. The file name was missing the opening quote or angle bracket.

**Bad GRPDEF type encountered, extended dictionary aborted**          *Librarian message*

The librarian has encountered an invalid entry in a group definition (GRPDEF) record in an object module while creating an extended dictionary.

The only type of GRPDEF record that the librarian and the linker support is segment index type. If any other type of GRPDEF is encountered, the librarian can't create an extended dictionary. It is possible that an object module created by products other than Borland tools can create GRPDEF records of other types. A corrupt object module can also generate this warning.

**Bad header in input LIB**                                           *Librarian message*

When adding object modules to an existing library, the librarian found a bad library header. Rebuild the library.

**Bad LF_POINTER in module 'module'**                                 *Linker message*

This is typically caused by bad debug information in the OBJ file. Borland Technical Support should be informed.

**Bad line number 'linenumber'**                                      *IDE Debugger message*

You tried to add a source breakpoint at a specific line number but you typed an invalid line number. Use the IDE Debugger and correct the line number in the Add Breakpoint dialog box. Breakpoints must be set on executable lines of code.

**Bad loc for fixup in module 'module' near file offset 'offset'**     *Linker message*

The linker encountered an object file with an incompatible .OBJ file format.

This error generally occurs due to an incompatible .OBJ file format. If you're linking .OBJ files compiled using another compiler, these files may be incompatible with TLINK32. You'll need to recompile all modules using one of the Borland C++ compilers.

This can also occur if the machine was rebooted during a compile, or if a compiler did not delete its output object file when Ctrl+Break was pressed. Recompile.

If the error persists, call Borland Technical Support.

**Bad macro output translator**                                       *MAKE message*

Invalid syntax for substitution within macros.

**Bad object file 'filename' near file offset 'offset'**              *Linker message*

The linker has found a bad OBJ file. This is usually caused by a translator error.

**Bad object file record**

**Bad object file record in library file 'filename' near module file offset '0xxxxxxxxx'**

**Bad object file record in library file 'filename' in module 'module' near module file offset '0xxxxxxxxx'**
*Linker messages*

An ill-formed object file was encountered.

This is most commonly caused by specifying a source file, by naming an object file that was not completely built, or by corrupting the response file so that a non-OBJ file is included in the .OBJ file list or library file list.

This can occur if the machine was rebooted during a compile, or if a compiler did not delete its output object file when Ctrl+Break was pressed.

Recompile. If the error persists, call Borland Technical Support.

**Bad OMF record type 'type' encountered in module 'module'**
*Librarian message*

The librarian encountered a bad Object Module Format (OMF) record while reading through the object module.

Because the librarian has already read and verified the header records in 'module', the object module is probably corrupt. Recreate it.

**Bad secondary target for fixup in module 'module'**
*Linker message*

The linker encountered an object file with an incompatible .OBJ file format.

This error generally occurs due to an incompatible .OBJ file format. If you're linking .OBJ files compiled using another compiler, these files may be incompatible with TLINK32. You'll need to recompile all modules using one of the Borland C++ compilers.

This can also occur if the machine was rebooted during a compile, or if a compiler did not delete its output object file when Ctrl+Break was pressed. Recompile.

If the error persists, call Borland Technical Support.

**Bad syntax for pure function definition**
*Compiler message*

Pure virtual functions are specified by appending "= 0" to the declaration, like this:

```
class A { virtual void f () = 0;}
class B : public A { void f () {}; }
```

You wrote something similar, but not quite the same.

**Bad 'type' debug info in module 'module'**
*Linker message*

The linker encountered an object file with an incompatible .OBJ file format.

This error generally occurs due to an incompatible .OBJ file format. If you're linking .OBJ files compiled using another compiler, these files may be incompatible with TLINK32. You'll need to recompile all modules using one of the Borland C++ compilers.

This can also occur if the machine was rebooted during a compile, or if a compiler did not delete its output object file when Ctrl+Break was pressed. Recompile.

If the error persists, call Borland Technical Support.

**Bad undef statement syntax**
*MAKE message*

An **!undef** statement must contain a single identifier and nothing else as the body of the statement.

**Base class 'class' contains dynamically dispatchable functions** *Compiler message*

This error occurs when a class containing a DDVT function attempts to inherit DDVT functions from multiple parent classes. Currently, dynamically dispatched virtual tables do not support the use of multiple inheritance.

**Base class 'class' is included more than once** *Compiler message*

A C++ class can be derived from any number of base classes, but can be directly derived from a given class only once.

**Base class 'class' is initialized more than once** *Compiler message*

In a C++ class constructor, the list of initializations following the constructor header includes base class 'class' more than once.

**Base class 'class1' is also a base class of 'class2'** *Compiler message*

(Command-line equivalent for displaying this warning = -wibc)

A class inherits from the same base class both directly and indirectly. It is best to avoid this non-portable construct in your program code.

Default = displayed

**Base initialization without a class name is now obsolete** *Compiler message*

(Command-line equivalent for displaying this warning = -wobi)

Early versions of C++ provided for initialization of a base class by following the constructor header with just the base class constructor parameter list. It is now recommended to include the base class name.

This makes the code much clearer, and is required when you have multiple base classes.

Old way:

```
derived::derived(int i) : (i, 10) { ... }
```

New way:

```
derived::derived(int i) : base(i, 10) { ... }
```

Default = displayed

**'base' is an indirect virtual base class of 'class'** *Compiler message*

You can't create a pointer to a C++ member of a virtual base class.

You have attempted to create such a pointer (either directly, or through a cast) and access an inaccessible member of one of your base classes.

**Bit field cannot be static** *Compiler message*

Only ordinary C++ class data members can be declared static, not bit fields.

**Bit field too large** *Compiler message*

This error occurs when you supply a bit field with more than 16 bits.

**Bit fields must be signed or unsigned int** *Compiler message*

In ANSI C, bit fields may only be signed or unsigned int (not char or long, for example).

**Bit fields must be signed or unsigned int** *Compiler message*

(Command-line equivalent for displaying this warning = -wbbf)

In ANSI C, bit fields may not be of type signed char or unsigned char. When you're not compiling in strict ANSI mode, the compiler allows these constructs, but flags them with this warning.

Default = not displayed

### Bit fields must contain at least one bit

*Compiler message*

You can't declare a named bit field to have 0 (or less than 0) bits. You can declare an unnamed bit field to have 0 bits.

This is a convention used to force alignment of the following bit field to a byte boundary (or to a word boundary, if you choose the or turn on the Word Alignment option in the Code Generation dialog box.

### Bit fields must have integral type

*Compiler message*

In C++, bit fields must have an integral type. This includes enumerations.

### Block overflow for block 'block'

*Linker message*

This message results from one of the linker's internal tables overflowing.

The internal linker tables contain information such as linker or debugging data. The tables are set to a default size which was not sufficient for the data in your application.

When this error occurs, the linker emits an INI file called TLINK32.INI and includes the name of the block that overflowed along with its size. Edit the INI file and increase the size.

The .DEF file is ill formed. You typed an illegal import sequence in the .DEF file.

### Body has already been defined for function 'function'

*Compiler message*

A function with this name and type was previously supplied a function body. A function body can only be supplied once.

One cause of this error is not declaring a default constructor which you implement. For example:

```
class A {
public:
   virtual myex();
};
A::A() {} // error
```

Having not seen you declare the default constructor in the class declaration, the compiler has had to generate one, thus giving the error message when it sees one. this is a correct example:

```
class A {
public:
   A();
   virtual myex();
};
A::A() {}
```

### Both return and return of a value used

*Compiler message*

(Command-line equivalent for displaying this warning = -wret)

The current function has return statements with and without values. This is legal C, but almost always an error. Possibly a return statement was omitted from the end of the function.

Default = displayed

### Call of nonfunction

The name being called is not declared as a function. This is commonly caused by incorrectly declaring the function or misspelling the function name.

### Call to function 'function' with no prototype

This message is given if the "Prototypes required" warning is enabled and you call function 'function' without first giving a prototype for that function.

### Call to function with no prototype

(Command-line equivalent for displaying this warning = -wpro)

This message is given if the "Prototypes required" warning is enabled and you call a function without first giving a prototype for that function.

Default = displayed

### Call to undefined function 'function'

Your source file declared the current function to return some type other than *void* in C++ (or *int* in C), but the compiler encountered a return with no value. All *int* functions are exempt in C because in old versions of C, there was no *void* type to indicate functions that return nothing.

### Can't convert 'string' [which evaluates to 'result'] to an address

The debugger dialog was expecting a memory address as input and it couldn't interpret the user input as a valid address.

### Can't debug during asynchronous compile

While compiling code with the Environment | Process Control | Asynchronous option set, you tried to issue a debugger command. Because the compiler is not re-entrant and the debugger and browser use the compiler code, you cannot debug or browse while an asynchronous (background) compile is taking place.

### Can't evaluate 'expression:' 'reason'

The expression you tried to evaluate did not return a valid value. This error will be given any time invalid input is entered in a debugger dialog and there is no more information about the error. Every debugger dialog uses the debugger's evaluator to validate and interpret user input.

### Can't grow LE/LIDATA record buffer

Command-line error.

The librarian is attempting to read a record of data from the object module, but it cannot get a large enough block of memory.

If the module being added has a large data segment or segments, try adding this module before other modules.

**Can't inherit non-RTTI class from RTTI base**

**Can't inherit RTTI class from non-RTTI base**                                        *Compiler messages*

When virtual functions are present, the RTTI attribute of all base classes must match that of the derived class.

**Can't inspect 'itemname'**                                                            *IDE Debugger message*

You specified an invalid item for inspection.

**Can't navigate to address 0**                                                         *IDE Debugger message*

You are trying to bring up a source view on an address that evaluates to 0.

**Can't run to 'filename', line 'linenumber'**                                          *IDE Debugger message*

You tried to run the specified line of the specified file. Either the file does not exist or there is no executable code associated with the line.'

**Cannot access an inactive scope**                                                     *Compiler message*

You have tried to evaluate or inspect a variable local to a function that is currently not active. (This is an integrated debugger expression evaluation message.)

**Cannot add or subtract relocatable symbols**                                          *Compiler message*

The only arithmetic operation that can be performed on a relocatable symbol in an assembler operand is addition or subtraction of a constant.

Variables, procedures, functions, and labels are relocatable symbols.

**Cannot allocate a reference**                                                         *Compiler message*

You have attempted to create a reference using the new operator. This is illegal, because references are not objects and can't be created through new.

**Cannot call 'main' from within the program**                                          *Compiler message*

C++ does not allow recursive calls of *main( )*.

**Cannot call near class member function with a pointer of type 'type'**                *Compiler message*

Member functions of near classes can't be called via a member pointer. This also applies to calls using pointers to members. (Remember, classes are near by default in the tiny, small, and medium memory models.)

Either change the pointer to be near, or declare the class as far.

**Cannot cast from 'type1' to 'type2'**                                                 *Compiler message*

A cast from type 'ident1' to type 'ident2' is not allowed. In C++, you cannot cast a member function pointer to a normal function pointer.

For example:

```
class A {
public:
    int myex();
};
typedef int (*fp)();
test()
{
    fp myfp - (fp) &A::myex; //error
```

The reason being that a class member function takes a hidden parameter, the this pointer, thus it behaves very differently than a normal function pointer.

A static member function behaves as normal function pointer and can be cast.

For example:
```
class A {
public:
   static int myex();
};
typedef int (*fp)();
test()
{
   fp myfp - (fp) &A::myex; //ok
```
However, static member functions can only access static data members of the class.

In C:

- A pointer can be cast to an integral type or to another pointer.
- An integral type can be cast to any integral, floating, or pointer type.
- A floating type can be cast to an integral or floating type.

Structures and arrays can't be cast to or from.

You usually can't cast from a void type.

In C++:

- User-defined conversions and constructors are checked for. If one can't be found, the preceding rules apply (except for pointers to class members).
- Among integral types, only a constant zero can be cast to a member pointer.
- A member pointer can be cast to an integral type or to a similar member pointer.

A similar member pointer points to a data member (or to a function) if the original does.

The qualifying class of the type being cast to must be the same as (or a base class of) the original.

**Cannot convert 'type1' to 'type2'** *Compiler message*

An assignment, initialization, or expression requires the specified type conversion to be performed, but the conversion is not legal.

In C++, the compiler will convert one function pointer to another only if the signature for the functions are the same. Signature refers to the arguments and return type of the function. For example:
```
myex( int );
typedef int ( *ffp )( float );
test()
{
   ffp fp = myex; //error
}
```
Seeing that *myex* takes an *int* for its argument, and *fp* is a pointer to a function which takes a float as argument, the compiler will not convert it for you.

In cases where this is what is intended, performing a typecast is necessary:
```
myex( int );
typedef int ( *ffp )( float );
test()
```

```
    {
        ffp fp = (ffp)myex;    //ok
    }
```

## Cannot create instance of abstract class 'class'

*Compiler message*

Abstract classes (those with pure virtual functions) can't be used directly, only derived from.

When you derive an abstract base class, with the intention to instantiate instances of this derived class, you must override each of the pure virtual functions of the base class exactly as they are declared.

For example:

```
class A {
public:
    virtual myex( int ) = 0;
    virtual twoex( const int ) const = 0;
};
class B : public A {
public:
    myex( int );
    twoex( const int );
};
B b;    // error
```

The error occurs because we have not overridden the virtual function which twoex can act on const objects of the class. We have created a new one which acts on non-const objects. This would compile:

```
class A {
public:
    virtual myex( int ) = 0;
    virtual twoex( const int ) const = 0;
};
class B : public A {
public:
    myex( int );
    twoex( const int ) const;
};
B b;    // ok
```

## Cannot create pre-compiled header: 'reason'

*Compiler message*

This warning is issued when pre-compiled headers are enabled but the compiler could not generate one, for one of the following reasons:

| Reason | Explanation |
|---|---|
| write failed | The compiler could not write to the pre-compiled header file. This is usually because the disk is full. |
| code in header | One of the headers contained a non-inline function body. |

| Reason | Explanation |
|---|---|
| initialized data in header | One of the headers contained a global variable definition (in C, a global variable with an initializer; in C++ any variable not declared as 'extern'). |
| header incomplete | The pre-compiled header ended in the middle of a declaration, for example, inside a class definition (this often happens when there is a missing "}" in a header file). |

### Cannot declare or define 'identifier' here
*Compiler message*

You tried to declare a template in an illegal place or a namespace member outside of its namespace.

### Cannot define 'identifier' using a namespace alias
*Compiler message*

You cannot use a namespace alias to define a namespace member outside of its namespace.

### Cannot define a pointer or reference to a reference
*Compiler message*

It is illegal to have a pointer to a reference or a reference to a reference.

### Cannot evaluate function call
*Compiler message*

The error message is issued if someone tries to explicitly construct an object or call a virtual function.

In integrated debugger expression evaluation, calls to certain functions (including implicit conversion functions, constructors, destructors, overloaded operators, and inline functions) are not supported.

### Cannot find 'class::class' ('class'&) to copy a vector
### Cannot find 'class'::operator=('class'&) to copy a vector
### Cannot find class::class ...
*Compiler messages*

When a C++ class 'class1' contains a vector (array) of class 'class2', and you want to construct an object of type 'class1' from another object of type 'class 1', you must use this constructor:

```
class2::class2(class2&)
```

so that the elements of the vector can be constructed.

The constructor, called a copy constructor, takes just one parameter (which is a reference to its class). Usually, the compiler supplies a copy constructor automatically. However, if you have defined a constructor for class 'class2' that has a parameter of type 'class2&' and has additional parameters with default values, the copy constructor can't exist and can't be created by the compiler.

This is because these two can't be distinguished:

```
class2::class2(class2&)
class2::class2(class2&, int = 1)
```

You must redefine this constructor so that not all parameters have default values. You can then define a reference constructor or let the compiler create one.

### Cannot find class::operator= ...
*Compiler message*

When a C++ class 'class1' contains a vector (array) of class 'class2', and you want to copy a class of type 'class1', you must use this assignment operator so that the elements of the vector can be copied:

```
class2::class2(class2&)
```

Usually, the compiler automatically supplies this operator. However, if you have defined an operator= for class 'class2' that does not take a parameter of type 'class2&,' the compiler will not supply it automatically--you must supply one.

### Cannot find default constructor to initialize array element of type 'class' *Compiler message*

When declaring an array of a class that has constructors, you must either explicitly initialize every element of the array, or the class must have a default constructor.

The compiler will define a default constructor for a class unless you have defined any constructors for the class.

### Cannot find default constructor to initialize base class 'class' *Compiler message*

Whenever a C++ derived class 'class2' is constructed, each base class 'class1' must first be constructed.

If the constructor for 'class2' does not specify a constructor for 'class1' (as part of 'class2's' header), there must be a constructor `class1::class1()` for the base class.

This constructor without parameters is called the default constructor. The compiler will supply a default constructor automatically unless you have defined any constructor for class 'class1'. In that case, the compiler will not supply the default constructor automatically—you must supply one.

```
class Base {
public:
   Base(int) {}
};
class Derived = public Base {
   Derived():Base(1) {}
}

// must explicitly call the Base constructor, or provide a
// default constructor in Base.
```

Class members with constructors must be initialized in the class' initializer list, for example:

```
class A {
public
   A( int );
};
class B {
public:
   A a;
   B() : a( 3 ) {}; //ok
};
```

### Cannot find default constructor to initialize member 'identifier' *Compiler message*

This error is displayed when the following occurs:

- A C++ class 'class1' contains a member of class 'class2.'
- You want to construct an object of type 'class1' (but not from another object of type 'class1'). There must be a constructor class2::class2() so that the member can be constructed.

This constructor without parameters is called the default constructor. The compiler will supply a default constructor automatically unless you have defined any constructor for class 'class2'. In that case, the compiler will not supply the default constructor automatically—you must supply one.

**Cannot find MAKE.EXE**                                                                    *MAKE message*

The MAKE command-line tool cannot be found. Be sure that MAKE.EXE is in either the current directory or in a directory contained in your directory path.

**Cannot generate 'function' from template function 'template'**                            *Compiler message*

A call to a template function was found, but a matching template function cannot be generated from the function template.

**Cannot generate COM file: data below initial CS:IP defined**                              *Linker message*

This error results from trying to generate data or code below the starting address (usually 100) of a .COM file. Be sure that the starting address is set to 100 by using the (ORG 100H) instruction. This error message should not occur for programs written in a high-level language. If it does, ensure that the correct startup (COx) object module is being linked in.

**Cannot generate COM file: invalid initial entry point address**                          *Linker message*

You used the **/Tdc** or **/t** option, but the program starting address is not equal to 100H, which is required with .COM files.

**Cannot generate COM file: program exceeds 64K**                                           *Linker message*

You used the **/Tdc** or **/t** option, but the total program size exceeds the .COM file limit.

**Cannot generate COM file: segment-relocatable items present**                             *Linker message*

You used the **/Tdc** or **/t** option, but the program contains segment-relative fixups, which are not allowed with .COM files.

**Cannot generate COM file: stack segment present**                                         *Linker message*

You used the **/Tdc** or **/t** option, but the program declares a stack segment, which is not allowed with .COM files.

**Cannot have a non-inline function/static data in a local class**                          *Compiler message*

All members of classes declared local to a function must be entirely defined in the class definition.

This means that local classes cannot contain any static data members, and all of their member functions must have bodies defined within the class definition.

**Cannot have multiple paths for implicit rule**                                            *MAKE message*

You can have only one path for each of the extensions in an implicit rule; for example, `{path}.c.obj`. Multiple path lists are allowed only for dependents in an explicit rule.

**Cannot have path list for target**                                                        *MAKE message*

You can only specify a path list for dependents of an explicit rule. For example, an invalid and a valid path list are shown here:

```
{path1;path2}prog.exe: prog.obj # Invalid
prog.exe: {path1;path2}prog.obj # Valid
```

**Cannot initialize 'type1' with 'type2'** *Compiler message*

You are attempting to initialize an object of type 'type1' with a value of type 'type2' which is not allowed. The rules for initialization are essentially the same as for assignment.

**Cannot initialize a class member here** *Compiler message*

Individual members of structs, unions, and C++ classes can't have initializers. A struct or union can be initialized as a whole using initializers inside braces. A C++ class can only be initialized by the use of a constructor.

**Cannot modify a const object** *Compiler message*

This indicates an illegal operation on an object declared to be const, such as an assignment to the object.

**Cannot overload 'main'** *Compiler message*

*main* is the only function that can't be overloaded.

**Cannot take address of 'main'** *Compiler message*

In C++, it is illegal to take the address of the *main* function.

**Cannot take address of member function 'function'** *Compiler message*

An expression takes the address of a class member function, but this member function was not found in the program being debugged. The evaluator issues this message.

**Cannot throw 'type'—ambiguous base class 'base'** *Compiler message*

It is not legal to throw a class that contains more than one copy of a (non-virtual) base class.

**Cannot use local type 'identifier' as template argument** *Compiler message*

A local type was used in an actual template type argument, which is illegal.

**Cannot use tiny or huge memory model with Windows** *Compiler message*

This message is self-explanatory. Use small, medium, compact, or large instead.

**Cannot write a string option** *MAKE message*

The –W MAKE option writes a character option to MAKE.EXE. If there's any string option, this error message is generated. For example, the following string option generates this message:

```
-Dxxxx="My_foo" or -Uxxxxx
```

**Cannot write GRPDEF list, extended dictionary aborted** *Librarian message*

The librarian cannot write the extended dictionary to the end of the library file. There may not be enough space on the disk.

**Case bypasses initialization of a local variable** *Compiler message*

In C++ it is illegal to bypass the initialization of a local variable.

This error indicates a case label that can transfer control past this local variable.

**Case outside of switch** *Compiler message*

The compiler encountered a case statement outside a switch statement.

This is often caused by mismatched braces.

**Case statement missing :**  *Compiler message*

A case statement must have a constant expression followed by a colon.

The expression in the case statement either was missing a colon or had an extra symbol before the colon.

**'catch' expected**  *Compiler message*

In a C++ program, a 'try' block must be followed by at least one 'catch' block.

**Character constant must be one or two characters long**  *Compiler message*

Character constants can only be one or two characters long.

**Character constant too long**  *MAKE message*

A char constant in an expression is too long.

**Circular dependency exists in makefile**  *MAKE message*

The makefile indicates that a file needs to be up-to-date before it can be built. Take, for example, the explicit rules

```
filea:  fileb
fileb:  filec
filec:  filea
```

This implies that filea depends on fileb, which depends on filec, and filec depends on filea. This is illegal because a file cannot depend on itself, indirectly or directly.

**Class 'class' may not contain pure functions**  *Compiler message*

The class being declared cannot be abstract, and therefore it cannot contain any pure functions.

**Class 'classname' is abstract because of 'member = 0'**  *Compiler message*

This message is issued immediately after the "Cannot create instance of abstract class 'classname' error message and is intended to make it easier to figure out why a particular class is considered abstract by the compiler.

For example, consider the following example of an illegal attempt to instantiate an abstract class:

```
struct VB
{
   virtualvoid  f() = 0;
   virtualvoid  g() = 0;
   virtualvoid  h() = 0;
};
struct D1 : virtual VB
{
     void   f();
};
struct D2 : virtual VB
{
     void   h();
};
struct DD : D1, D2
{
}
  v;   // error 'DD' is an abstract class
```

The above code will cause the following two error messages:

```
Error TEST.CPP 21: Cannot create instance of abstract class 'DD'
Error TEST.CPP 21: Class 'DD' is abstract because of 'VB::g() = 0'
```

### Class member 'member' declared outside its class
*Compiler message*

C++ class member functions can be declared only inside the class declaration. Unlike nonmember functions, they can't be declared multiple times or at other locations.

### Code has no effect
*Compiler message*

(Command-line equivalent for displaying this warning = -weff)

This warning is issued when the compiler encounters a statement with some operators that have no effect.

For example, the statement
```
a + b;
```
has no effect on either variable.

The operation is unnecessary and probably indicates a bug.

Default = displayed

### CodeGuarded programs must use the large memory

#### model and be targeted for Windows
*Compiler message*

Only issued by the 16-bit compiler. Programs that have CodeGuard enabled must use the large memory model and be targeted for Windows.

### Colon expected
*MAKE message*

Your implicit rule is missing a colon at the end.

```
.c.obj:     # Correct
.c.obj      # Incorrect
```

### Command arguments too long
*MAKE message*

The arguments to a command exceeded the 511-character limit imposed by DOS.

### Command syntax error
*MAKE message*

This message occurs if

- The first rule line of the makefile contains any leading whitespace.
- An implicit rule does not consist of .ext.ext:.
- An explicit rule does not contain a name before the : character.

A macro definition does not contain a name before the = character.

### Common segment exceeds 64K
*Linker message*

The program has more than 64K of near uninitialized data. Try declaring some uninitialized data as far.

### Compiler could not generate copy constructor for class 'class'
### Compiler could not generate default constructor for class 'class'
### Compiler could not generate operator = for class 'class'
*Compiler messages*

Sometimes the compiler is required to generate a member function for the user.

Whenever such a member function can't be generated due to applicable language rules, the compiler issues one of these error messages.

### Compiler stack overflow
*Compiler message*

The compiler's stack has overflowed. This can be caused by a number of things, among them deeply nested statements in a function body (for example, if/else) or expressions with a large number of operands. You must simplify your code if this message occurs.

Adding more memory to your system will not help.

### Compiler table limit exceeded
*Compiler message*

One of the compiler's internal tables overflowed. This usually means that the module being compiled contains too many function bodies. This limitation will not be solved by making more memory available to the compiler. You need to simplify the file being compiled.

### Compound statement missing }
*Compiler message*

The compiler reached the end of the source file and found no closing brace. This is most commonly caused by mismatched braces.

### Condition is always true OR Condition is always false
*Compiler message*

(Command-line equivalent for displaying this warning = -wccc)

Whenever the compiler encounters a constant comparison that (due to the nature of the value being compared) is always true or false, it issues this warning and evaluates the condition at compile time.

For example:

```
void proc(unsigned x){
  if (x >= 0)        /* always 'true' */
  {
    ...
  }
}
```

Default = displayed

### Conflicting type modifiers
*Compiler message*

This occurs when a declaration is given that includes more than one addressing modifier on a pointer or more than one language modifier for a function.

Only one language modifier (cdecl, and pascal) can be given for a function.

One cannot multiply derive from a class declared to use the fast this pointer optimization, and one that was not.

For example:

```
class __fastthis A { // one way to declare a class as using the
  myex();            // fast this optimization, note that
};                   // #pragma option -po- turns it off.
class B {
  twoex();
};
class c : A , B {}; // error
// note that __fastthis is only recognized in BC 4.0 or later
```

### Constant expression required
*Compiler message*

Arrays must be declared with constant size. This error is commonly caused by misspelling a **#define** constant.

### Constant is long
*Compiler message*

(Command-line equivalent for displaying this warning = -wcln)

The compiler encountered one of the following:

- A decimal constant greater than 32,767 or
- An octal, hexadecimal, or decimal constant greater than 65,535 without a letter l or L following it

The constant is treated as a long.

Default = not displayed

### Constant out of range in comparison
*Compiler message*

(Command-line equivalent for displaying this warning = -wrng)

Your source file includes a comparison involving a constant sub-expression that was outside the range allowed by the other sub-expression's type.

For example, comparing an unsigned quantity to -1 makes no sense.

To get an unsigned constant greater than 32,767 (in decimal), you should either

- Cast the constant to unsigned—for example, (unsigned) 65535, or
- Append a letter u or U to the constant—for example, 65535u.

Whenever this message is issued, the compiler still generates code to do the comparison.

If this code ends up always giving the same result (such as comparing a char expression to 4000), the code will still perform the test.

Default = displayed

### Constant/Reference member 'member' in class without constructors
*Compiler message*

A class that contains constant or reference members (or both) must have at least one user-defined constructor. Otherwise, there would be no way to ever initialize such members.

### Constant/Reference variable 'variable' must be initialized
*Compiler message*

This C++ object is declared constant or as a reference, but is not initialized. It must be initialized at the point of declaration.

### Constructor cannot have a return type specification
*Compiler message*

C++ constructors have an implicit return type used by the compiler, but you can't declare a return type or return a value.

### Constructor initializer list ignored
*Compiler message*

An error has occurred while using the command-line utility H2ASH. See the online file "tsm_util.txt" for further information about this utility.

### Constructor/Destructor cannot be declared 'const' or 'volatile'
*Compiler message*

A constructor or destructor has been declared as const or volatile. This is not allowed.

**'constructor' is not an unambiguous base class of 'class'**                    *Compiler message*

A C++ class constructor is trying to call a base class constructor 'constructor.' This error can also occur if you try to change the access rights of 'class::constructor.'

Check your declarations.

**Continuation character \ found in // comment**                    *Compiler message*

This warning message is issued when a C++ // comment is continued onto the next line with backslash line continuation. The intention is to warn about cases where lines containing source code unintentionally become part of a comment because that comment happened to end in a backslash.

If you get this warning, check carefully whether you intend the line after the // comment to be part of the comment. If you don't, either remove the backslash or put some other character after it. If you do, it's probably better coding style to start the next comment line with // also.

The warning can be disabled altogether by #pragma warn -com.

**Conversion may lose significant digits**                    *Compiler message*

(Command-line equivalent for displaying this warning = -wsig)

For an assignment operator or some other circumstance, your source file requires a conversion from long or unsigned long to int or unsigned int type. Because int type and long type variables don't have the same size, this kind of conversion might alter the behavior of a program.

Default = not displayed

**Conversion of near pointer not allowed**                    *Compiler message*

A near pointer cannot be converted to a far pointer in the expression evaluation box when a program is not currently running. This is because the conversion needs the current value of DS in the user program, which doesn't exist.

**Conversion operator cannot have a return type specification**                    *Compiler message*

This C++ type conversion member function specifies a return type different from the type itself. A declaration for conversion function operator can't specify any return type.

**Conversion to 'type' will fail for members of virtual base 'class'**                    *Compiler message*

This warning is issued only if the -Vv option or Options | Project | C++ Options | C++ Compatibility | Deep Virtual Bases option is in use.

The warning may be issued when a member pointer to one type is cast to a member pointer of another type and the class of the converted member pointer has virtual bases.

Encountering this warning means that at run time, if the member pointer conversion cannot be completed, the result of the cast will be a NULL member pointer.

**Conversions of class to itself or base class not allowed**                    *Compiler message*

You tried to define a conversion operator to the same class or a base class.

**Could not allocate memory for per module data**                    *Librarian message*

The librarian has run out of memory.

**Could not create list file 'filename'**                                         *Librarian message*

The librarian could not create a list file for the library. This could be due to lack of disk space.

**Could not create swapfile**                                                      *Linker message*

This error message refers to an UNDOCUMENTED optimization feature.

**Could not find a match for argument(s)**                                         *Compiler message*

No C++ function could be found with parameters matching the supplied arguments.

Check parameters passed to function or overload function for parameters that are being passed.

**Could not find file 'filename'**                                                 *Compiler message*

The compiler is unable to find the file supplied on the command line.

**Could not write output**                                                         *Librarian message*

The librarian could not write the output file.

**Couldn't build command line to RLINK.EXE**                                       *Linker message*

The command line that was generated by the command-line linker was linger than 128 bytes. RLINK.EXE was not run on the EXE. Shorten the file names passed in the .RES file list, put in fewer .RES files, or run RLINK separately.

**Couldn't exec RLINK.EXE**                                                        *Linker message*

The command-line linker could not spawn RLINK.EXE to bind resources. Check to make sure that RLINK.EXE is on your path.

**Couldn't get LE/LIDATA record buffer**                                           *Librarian message*

Command-line error.

The librarian is attempting to read a record of data from the object module, but it cannot get a large enough block of memory.

If the module being added has a large data segment or segments, try adding this module before other modules.

**Couldn't get procedure address from DLL 'dll'**                                  *Linker message*

The linker was not able to get a procedure from the specified DLL. Check to make sure that you have the correct version of the DLL.

**Couldn't load DLL 'dll'**                                                        *Linker message*

The linker was not able to load the specified DLL. Check to make sure that the DLL is on your path.

**Cycle in include files: 'filename'**                                             *MAKE message*

This error message is issued if a makefile includes itself in the make script.

**Debug info switch ignored for COM files**                                        *Linker message*

Borland C++ does not include debug information for .COM files. See the description of the **/v** option.

**Debug information enabled, but no debug information found in OBJs**               *Linker message*

No part of the application was compiled with debug information, but you requested that debug information be turned on in the link.

### Debug information in module 'module' will be ignored

Object files compiled with debug information now have a version record. The version of this record is inconsistent with what the linker currently supports.

The linker did not generate debug information for the module in question. Recompile with the current compiler to generate correct debug information.

### Debugging information overflow; try fewer modules with debug info
*Linker message*

Too many modules containing debugging information are included in the link.

This message is generated when you have more than 64K of types or symbols in a single .OBJ file, or if you get more than 64K modules, source files (including .h files), scopes, logical debug segments, classes, or optimized variables in the link.

Recompile your program with fewer modules marked for debug information.

### Declaration does not specify a tag or an identifier
*Compiler message*

This declaration doesn't declare anything. This may be a struct or union without a tag or a variable in the declaration. C++ requires that something be declared.

For example:

```
struct
{
int a
};
//no tag or identifier
```

### Declaration ignored
*Compiler message*

An error has occurred while using the command-line utility H2ASH. See the online file "tsm_util.txt" for further information about this utility.

### Declaration is not allowed here
*Compiler message*

Declarations can't be used as the control statement for while, for, do, if, or switch statements.

### Declaration missing ;
*Compiler message*

Your source file contained a struct or union field declaration that was not followed by a semicolon.

Check previous lines for a missing semicolon.

### Declaration of static function '(...)' ignored
*Compiler message*

An error has occurred while using the command-line utility H2ASH. See the online file "tsm_util.txt" for further information about this utility.

### Declaration syntax error
*Compiler message*

Your source file contained a declaration that was missing a symbol or had an extra symbol added to it.

Check for a missing semicolon or parenthesis on that line or on previous lines.

### Declaration terminated incorrectly
*Compiler message*

A declaration has an extra or incorrect termination symbol, such as a semicolon, placed after a function body.

A C++ member function declared in a class with a semicolon between the header and the opening left brace also generates this error.

### Declaration was expected
*Compiler message*

A declaration was expected here but not found. This is usually caused by a missing delimiter such as a comma, semicolon, right parenthesis, or right brace.

### Declare operator delete (void*) or (void*, size_t)

### Declare operator delete[] (void*) or (void*, size_t)
*Compiler messages*

Declare the operator delete with one of the following:

- A single void* parameter, or
- A second parameter of type size_t

If you use the second version, it will be used in preference to the first version. The global operator delete can only be declared using the single-parameter form.

### Declare type 'type' prior to use in prototype
*Compiler message*

(Command-line equivalent for displaying this warning = -wdpu)

When a function prototype refers to a structure type that has not previously been declared, the declaration inside the prototype is not the same as a declaration outside the prototype.

For example,

```
int func(struct s *ps);   struct s  /* ... */ ;
```

Because there is no "struct s" in scope at the prototype for func, the type of parameter ps is pointer to undefined struct s, and is not the same as the "struct s" that is later declared.

This will result in later warning and error messages about incompatible types, which would be very mysterious without this warning message.

To fix the problem, you can move the declaration for "struct s" ahead of any prototype that references it, or add the incomplete type declaration "struct s;" ahead of any prototype that references "structs".

If the function parameter is a struct, rather than a pointer to struct, the incomplete declaration is not sufficient.

You must then place the struct declaration ahead of the prototype.

Default = displayed

### .DEF file stack/heap reserve size < 64K; 1MB default will be used
*Linker message*

The reserve size for either the STACK or the HEAP specified in the .DEF file is less than 64K. The linker emits this warning to inform you that it will use the default of 1MB instead of the value specified.

### Default argument value redeclared
*Compiler message*

When a parameter of a C++ function is declared to have a default value, this value can't be changed, redeclared, or omitted in any other declaration for the same function.

**Default argument value redeclared for parameter 'parameter'** *Compiler message*

When a parameter of a C++ function is declared to have a default value, this value can't be changed, redeclared, or omitted in any other declaration for the same function.

**Default expression may not use local variables** *Compiler message*

A default argument expression is not allowed to use any local variables or other parameters.

**Default outside of switch** *Compiler message*

The compiler encountered a default statement outside a switch statement. This is most commonly caused by mismatched braces.

**Default value missing** *Compiler message*

When a C++ function declares a parameter with a default value, all of the following parameters must also have default values. In this declaration, a parameter with a default value was followed by a parameter without a default value.

**Default value missing following parameter 'parameter'** *Compiler message*

All parameters following the first parameter with a default value must also have defaults specified.

**Define directive needs an identifier** *Compiler message*

The first non-whitespace character after a **#define** must be an identifier. The compiler found some other character.

**Destructor cannot have a return type specification** *Compiler message*

C++ destructors never return a value, and you can't declare a return type or return a value.

**Destructor for 'class' required in conditional expression** *Compiler message*

If the compiler must create a temporary local variable in a conditional expression, it has no good place to call the destructor because the variable might or might not have been initialized.

The temporary can be explicitly created, as with classname(val, val), or implicitly created by some other code. You should recast your code to eliminate this temporary value.

**Destructor for class is not accessible** *Compiler message*

The destructor for this C++ class is protected or private, and can't be accessed here to destroy the class. If a class destructor is private, the class can't be destroyed, and thus can never be used. This is probably an error. A protected destructor can be accessed only from derived classes. This is a useful way to ensure that no instance of a base class is ever created, but only classes derived from it.

**Destructor name must match the class name** *Compiler message*

In a C++ class, the tilde (~) introduces a declaration for the class destructor. The name of the destructor must be same as the class name. In your source file, the ~ preceded some other name.

**Disable Group checked but no value entered** *IDE Debugger message*

You checked the Disable Group check box, but forgot to specify a group name.

**Divide error** *Run-time message*

You tried to divide an integer by zero, which is illegal.

**Division by zero** *Compiler message*

Your source file contains a divide or remainder in a constant expression with a zero divisor.

**Division by zero** *Compiler message*

(Command-line equivalent for displaying this warning = -wzdi)

A divide or remainder expression had a literal zero as a divisor.

Default = displayed

**Division by zero** *MAKE message*

A division or remainder operator in an **!if** statement has a zero divisor.

**do statement must have while** *Compiler message*

Your source file contained a do statement that was missing the closing while keyword.

**do-while statement missing OR For statement missing ;** *Compiler message*

In a do or for statement, the compiler found no semicolon after the right parenthesis.

**DOS error, ax = 'decimal number'** *Linker message*

This occurs if a DOS call returned an unexpected error. The ax value printed is the resulting error code. This could indicate a linker internal error or a DOS error. The only DOS calls the linker makes where this error could occur are read, write, seek, and close.

Make sure that there are no zero length .OBJ files included in the link.

**DOSSEG directive ignored** *Linker message*

This warning indicates that the linker no longer supports the DOSSEG directive.

**DPMI programs must use the large memory model** *Compiler message*

DPMI programs can only use large memory model. Tiny, Small, Medium, Compact, and Huge memory models are not allowed.

**Duplicate case** *Compiler message*

Each case of a switch statement must have a unique constant expression value.

**Duplicate file 'filename' in list, not added!** *Librarian message*

When building a library module, you specified an object file more than once.

**Duplicate handler for 'type1', already had 'type2'** *Compiler message*

It is not legal to specify two handlers for the same type.

**Duplicate ordinal 'number' in exports** *Linker message*

The linker encountered two exports with the same ordinal value.

Check the module definition file to ensure that there are no duplicate ordinal values specified in the EXPORTS section.

If not, you are linking with modules that specify exports by ordinals and one of two things happened:

- Two export records specify the same ordinal, or
- The exports section in the module definition file duplicates an ordinal in an export record.

**Duplicate ordinal for exports: 'string' ('ordval1') and 'string' ('ordval2')**  *Linker message*

Two exports share the same ordinal. The linker cannot resolve which export should get which ordinal.

**Earlier declaration of 'identifier'**  *Compiler message*

This error message only shows up after the messages "Multiple declaration for 'identifier'" and "Type mismatch in redeclaration of 'identifier'". It tells you where the previous definition of the identifier in question was found by the compiler, so you don't have to search for it.

**Empty LEDATA record in module 'module'**  *Linker message*

This warning can happen if the translator emits a data record containing data. If this should happen, report the occurrence to the translator vendor. There should be no bad side effects from the record.

**Enable Group checked but no value entered**  *IDE Debugger message*

You checked the Enable Group check box, but forgot to specify a group name.

**End of system input buffer encountered**  *Linker message*

The input line you typed is too long. Instead of typing all you're object and library files on the command line, put them into a response file.

**Ensuring executable is up to date**  *IDE Debugger message*

The IDE Debugger is checking to be sure that the executable file is up to date, recompiling, if necessary.

**Enum syntax error**  *Compiler message*

An enum declaration did not contain a properly formed list of identifiers.

**Error changing file buffer size**  *Librarian message*

The librarian is attempting to adjust the size of a buffer used while reading or writing a file, but there is not enough memory. You'll need to free up a lot of system memory to resolve this error.

**Error creating file.**  *Resource Linker message*

An error occurred when the resource linker tried to create a file. This error occurs if the work disk is full or write-protected. It can also occur if the output directory does not exist.

Solutions:

- If the disk is full, try deleting unneeded files and restarting the resource link.
- If the disk is write-protected, direct the output to a writeable disk and restart the resource link.

**Error creating temporary file in directory.**  *Resource Linker message*

An error occurred when the resource linker tried to create a temporary file. This error occurs if the work disk is full or write-protected. It can also occur if the output directory does not exist.

Solutions:

- If the disk is full, try deleting unneeded files and restarting the resource link.
- If the disk is write-protected, direct the output to a writeable disk and restart the resource link.

**Error deleting file.** *Resource Linker message*

An error occurred when the resource linker tried to delete a file. This error occurs if the file is marked as read-only or does not exist.

If the disk is read-only, change its attributes so that it can be deleted.

**Error directive: 'message'** *Compiler message*

This message is issued when an **#error** directive is processed in the source file. 'message' is the text of the **#error** directive.

**Error directive: 'message'** *MAKE message*

MAKE has processed an **#error** directive in the source file, and the text of the directive is displayed in the message.

**Error in CURSDIR. Cannot find CURS.** *Resource Linker message*

An entry was found in the cursor directory that had no corresponding cursor resource.

The resource file is probably corrupted.

**Error in EXE's resource table format.** *Resource Linker message*

There is invalid information in the executable files resource table. The executable file might contain invalid resource information or be corrupt.

**Error in FONTDIR. Cannot find FONT.** *Resource Linker message*

An entry was found in the font directory that had no corresponding font resource. The resource file is probably corrupted.

**Error in ICONDIR. Cannot find ICON.** *Resource Linker message*

An entry was found in the icon directory that had no corresponding icon resource. The resource file is probably corrupted.

**Error in RES format.** *Resource Linker message*

There is invalid information in the binary resource file. The resource file might contain invalid resource information or be corrupt. Try recompiling the resources and restart the resource link.

**Error in RES format. Cannot find NAMEDIR resource.** *Resource Linker message*

An entry was found in the name-table that had no corresponding resource. Verify that you have included the appropriate resource in your resource script. Name-tables are not used for Windows version 3.1 or greater.

**Error in resource binary length (bad format?).** *Resource Linker message*

There is an error in the size of a binary resource. The format of the resource might be invalid or the resource has been corrupted.

**Error in packing preload area. Turn off preload packing.** *Resource Linker message*

An error occurred while the resource linker was trying to optimize how resources and segments are arranged in the executable file. (This error only occurs for 16-bit resources.)

To correct this error, turn off the Pack Fastload Area option in the Resources Options.

**Error opening file.** *Resource Linker message*

An error occurred when the resource linker tried to open a file. This error occurs if the file does not exist, another process has denied access to the file, the path or filename is incorrect, or there are no more available file handles.

**Error opening 'filename'**                                              *Librarian message*

The librarian cannot open the specified file.

**Error opening 'filename' for output**                                   *Librarian message*

The librarian cannot open the specified file for output.

**Error positioning file.**                                          *Resource Linker message*

An error occurred trying to seek to a location in a file. This file could be truncated or corrupted. Try verifying the disk integrity using CHKDSK or recompile the resource files and restart the resource link.

**Error reading file.**                                              *Resource Linker message*

An error occurred when the resource linker tried to read a file. This error typically occurs when there is a disk error while the file is being read.

**Error renaming file.**                                             *Resource Linker message*

An error occurred when the resource linker tried to rename a file. This error occurs if the file is marked as read-only or does not exist or a file already exists having the name that the resource linker is trying to use.

Solutions:

- If the disk is read-only, change its attributes so that it can be deleted.
- If a file having the name already exists you can either delete that file or choose another name.

**Error renaming 'filename' to 'filename'**                               *Librarian message*

This error occurs when the librarian is building a temporary library file and renaming the temporary file to the target library file name. The error indicates that the target file is read only.

**Error seeking point in file.**                                     *Resource Linker message*

An error occurred trying to seek to a location in a file. This file could be truncated or corrupted. Try compiling the resource files and restart the resource link.

**Error sizing file.**

**Error getting size of file.**                                     *Resource Linker messages*

A disk error occurred when trying to determine the file size.

**Error trying to change value**                                       *IDE Debugger message*

You tried to change a value of an object being inspected, but the debugger was unable to change the value.

**Error writing file.**                                              *Resource Linker message*

An error occurred when the resource linker tried to write to a file. This error occurs if the work disk is full or write-protected.

Solutions:

- If the disk is full, try deleting unneeded files and restarting the resource link.
- If the disk is write-protected, direct the output to a writeable disk and restart the resource link.

**Error writing output file**                                            *Compiler message*

A DOS error that prevents the C++ IDE from writing an .OBJ, .EXE, or temporary file.

Solutions:

- Make sure that the Output directory in the Directories dialog box is a valid directory.
- Check that there is enough free disk space.

**Error. EXE alignment too small for packing resources too.**  *Resource Linker message*

You have pre-packing turned on and the resources will not fit with the current image alignment. Try increasing the alignment, re-link, and restart the resource link.

**Error. Expecting RES file, not EXE. File: <filename>**  *Resource Linker message*

The resource linker was expecting a compiled resource (.RES) file, but found an executable (.EXE) instead. Verify that you have the correct node and file types specified.

**Error: File not specified**  *IDE Debugger message*

You forgot to specify a filename in the Run To dialog.

**Error: Line not specified**  *IDE Debugger message*

You forgot to specify a line number in the Run To dialog.

**Error. Missing NAME resource. RES not for Windows 3.**  *Resource Linker message*

The binary resource file is missing the NAME resource. The resource file is probably not a Windows 3 resource file.

**Eval Expr checked but no value entered**  *IDE Debugger message*

You checked the Eval Expr check box, but forgot to specify an expression.

**Example for "Temporary used ..." error messages**  *Compiler message*

In this example, function f requires a reference to an int, and c is a char:

```
f(int&);
char c;
f(c);
```

Instead of calling f with the address of c, the compiler generates code equivalent to the C++ source code:

```
int X = c, f(X);
```

**'__except' or '__finally' expected following '__try'**  *Compiler message*

In C, a '__try block' must be followed by a '__except' or '__finally' handler block.

**Exception handling not enabled**  *Compiler message*

A 'try' block was found with the exception handling disabled.

**Exception handling variable may not be used here**  *Compiler message*

An attempt has been made to use one of the exception handling values that are restricted to particular exception handling constructs, such as *GetExceptionCode()*.

**Exception specification not allowed here**  *Compiler message*

Function pointer type declarations are not allowed to contain exception specifications.

**Explicit stacks are ignored for PE images**  *Linker message*

Win32 apps are PE format applications, which do not have explicit stacks. The stack segment will be linked into the image, but it will not be used as the application stack. Instead, the stack size parameter will be used to set the stack size, and the operating system will allocate a stack for the application.

### Export 'symbol' has multiple ordinal values: 'value1' and 'value2'
*Linker message*

The linker encountered one symbol with multiple ordinal values. The linker cannot resolve which value to export, and will use the first value.

Check the EXPORTS section of the module definition file and make sure that the export name applies only once.

### Export 'symbol' is duplicated
*Linker message*

This warning will occur if two different functions with the same name are exported by the use of _export. The linker cannot resolve which definition to export, and will use the first symbol.

### Expr True check but no value entered
*IDE Debugger message*

You checked the Expr True check box, but forgot to provide an expression.

### Expression expected
*Compiler message*

An expression was expected here, but the current symbol can't begin an expression.

This message might occur where the controlling expression of an if or while clause is expected or where a variable is being initialized.

This message is often due to a symbol that is missing or has been added.

### Expression of scalar type expected
*Compiler message*

The !, ++, and -- operators require an expression of scalar type.

Only these types are allowed:

- char
- short
- int
- long
- enum
- float
- double
- long double
- pointer

### Expression syntax
*Compiler message*

This is a catch-all error message when the compiler parses an expression and encounters a serious error.

Possible Causes:

This is most commonly caused by one of the following:

- Two consecutive operators
- Mismatched or missing parentheses
- A missing semicolon on the previous statement.

Solutions:

- If the line where the error occurred looks syntactically correct, look at the line directly above for errors.
- Try moving the line with the error to a different location in the file and recompiling.

- If the error still occurs at the moved statement, the syntax error is occurring somewhere in that statement.
- If the error occurred in another statement, the syntax error is probably in the surrounding code.

### Expression syntax error in !if statement
*MAKE message*

The expression in an **!if** statement is badly formed—it contains a mismatched parenthesis, an extra or missing operator, or a missing or extra constant.

### Extended dictionary not found in library 'library': extended dictionaries ignored
*Linker message*

When you specify that extended dictionaries be used, all libraries must have extended dictionaries. In this case, a library was encountered that did not have an extended dictionary, thus aborting the link. Use the TLIB /E option to generate an extended dictionary for the library in question.

### 'reason' - extended dictionary not created
*Librarian message*

Library contains COMDEF records - extended dictionary not created

If the Library contains COMDEF records message is displayed, an object record being added to a library contains a COMDEF record. This is not compatible with the extended dictionary option.

### Extern 'symbol' was not qualified with __import in module 'module'
*Linker message*

Win32 applications which make reference to imported symbols need to make indirections to get to the data. For calls, this is handled automatically by the linker. For references to imported DATA, the compiler must generate an indirection, or the application will function incorrectly. The compiler knows to generate the indirection when the symbol is qualified with __import. If the linker sees a segment relative reference to a symbol which is imported, and if the symbol was not qualified with __import, you will get this message.

You can suppress this warning from the Linker | Warnings page of the Project options dialog box or with the **/w-inq** command-line option.

### Extern variable cannot be initialized
*Compiler message*

The storage class extern applied to a variable means that the variable is being declared but not defined here--no storage is being allocated for it.

Therefore, you can't initialize the variable as part of the declaration.

### Extra argument in template class name 'template'
*Compiler message*

A template class name specified too many actual values for its formal parameters.

### Extra parameter in call
*Compiler message*

A call to a function, via a pointer defined with a prototype, had too many arguments.

### Extra parameter in call to function
*Compiler message*

A call to the named function (which was defined with a prototype) had too many arguments given in the call.

### Failed read from 'filename'
*Linker message*

The linker was unable to read from the file.

**Failed write to 'filename'**                                          *Linker message*

The linker was unable to write to the file.

**Far COMDEFs are not supported**                                       *Linker message*

The linker encountered an object file with an incompatible .OBJ file format.

This error generally occurs due to an incompatible .OBJ file format. If you're linking .OBJ files compiled using another compiler, these files may be incompatible with TLINK32. You'll need to recompile all modules using one of the Borland C++ compilers.

This can also occur if the machine was rebooted during a compile, or if a compiler did not delete its output object file when Ctrl+Break was pressed. Recompile.
If the error persists, call Borland Technical Support.

**FATAL ERROR: GP FAULT**                                               *MAKE message*

Your program caused a general protection fault and exited fatally. This type of error is caused by various reasons such as attempting to access or write to out of bound memory. For best results, use CodeGuard to locate the error.

**File 'filename' does not exist**                                      *IDE Debugger message*

You tried to bring up a source view on an address, and the associated file does not exist. This problem can usually be fixed by setting the appropriate source path on the debugger option page.

**File 'filename' does not exist (trying to load it anyway...)**        *IDE Debugger message*

The debugger tried to load an executable that does not exist. Check to make sure that the executable exists and that the path to the executable was correctly specified.

**File must contain at least one external declaration**                 *Compiler message*

This compilation unit was logically empty, containing no external declarations. ANSI C and C++ require that something be declared in the compilation unit.

**'filename' ('linenum'): Duplicate external name in exports**          *Linker message*

Two export functions listed in the EXPORTS section of a module definition file defined the same external name.

For example:

```
EXPORTS   AnyProc=MyProc1   AnyProc=MyProc2
```

**'filename' ('linenum'): Duplicate internal name in exports**          *Linker message*

Two export functions listed in the EXPORTS section of the module definition file defined the same internal name.

**'filename' ('linenum'): Duplicate internal name in imports**          *Linker message*

Two import functions listed in the IMPORTS section of the module definition file defined the same internal name.

**'filename' ('linenum'): File read error**                             *Linker message*

A DOS error occurred while attempting to read the specified file.

This usually means that a premature end of file occurred. Check for 0 length files.

**'filename' ('linenum'): Incompatible attribute**                      *Linker message*

The linker encountered incompatible segment attributes in a CODE or DATA statement. For instance, both PRELOAD and LOADONCALL can't be attributes for the same segment.

**'filename' ('linenum'): Missing internal name**                                    *Linker message*

In the IMPORTS section of the module definition file, there was a reference to an entry specified via module name and ordinal number.

When an entry is specified by ordinal number, an internal name must be assigned to this import definition.

It is this internal name that your program uses to refer to the imported definition.

The syntax in the module definition file should be:

```
<internalname>=<modulename>.<ordinal>
```

**'filename' ('linenum'): Syntax error**                                             *Linker message*

The linker found a syntax error in the module definition file.

The file name and line number tell you where the syntax error occurred.

**'filename' couldn't be created, original won't be changed**                      *Librarian message*

You tried to extract an object, but the librarian cannot create the object file into which to extract the module.

Either the object already exists and is read only, or the disk is full.

**'filename' does not exist: don't know how to make it**                             *MAKE message*

The build sequence includes a nonexistent file name, and no rule exists that would allow the file name to be built.

**'filename' file not found**                                                        *Librarian message*

Command-line error.

The command-line librarian attempted to add a nonexisting object but created the library anyway.

**'filename' file not found**                                                        *Librarian message*

The IDE creates the library by removing the existing library and rebuilding it. If any of the specified objects do not exist, the library is incomplete and this error is generated. If the IDE reports that an object does not exist, either the source module has not been compiled or there were errors during compilation. Using either the Project I Make All or Project I Build All commands should resolve the problem or indicate where the errors occurred.

**'filename' is not a valid library**                                                *Linker message*

This error happens when the first record in a library file is not the LIBSTART record.

This can happen when something that is not a library is passed as a library file to the linker, or if the library file was corrupted.

**'filename' not a MAKE**                                                            *MAKE message*

The file you specified with the –f option is not a makefile.

**File name not specified**                                                          *IDE Debugger message*

You tried to add a source breakpoint using the IDE Debugger but you omitted a file name. Enter the name of the file into which you want to insert the breakpoint in the Add Breakpoint dialog box.

**File name too long** *Compiler message*

The file name given in an **#include** directive was too long for the compiler to process. File names in DOS must be no more than 79 characters long.

**Filename too long** *MAKE message*

The path name in an **!include** directive overflowed MAKE's internal buffer (512 bytes).

**Fixup overflow at 'address,' target = 'address'**

**Fixup overflow at 'address,' target = 'symbol' in module 'module'** *Linker messages*

Either of these messages indicates an incorrect data or code reference in an object file that the linker must fix up at link time.

These messages are most often caused by a mismatch of memory models. A near call to a function in a different code segment is the most likely cause. These errors can also occur if you generate a near call to a data variable or a data reference to a function. In either case, the symbol named as the target in the error message is the referenced variable or function.

The reference is in the named module, so look in the source file of that module for the offending reference.

Rebuild the entire program to ensure that all modules have been compiled with in the same memory model. Checked that linked libraries were also compiled in the same memory module.

If this technique does not identify the cause of the failure, or if you are programming in assembly language or a high-level language besides C or C++, there might be other possible causes for this message.

Even in C++, this message could be generated if you are using different segment or group names than the default values for a given memory model.

**Fixup to zero length segment in module 'module'** *Linker message*

A reference has been made past the end of an image segment. This reference would end up accessing an invalid address, and has been flagged as an error.

**Fixups found for an LIDATA record** *Linker message*

The linker encountered an object file with an incompatible .OBJ file format.

This error generally occurs due to an incompatible .OBJ file format. If you're linking .OBJ files compiled using another compiler, these files may be incompatible with TLINK32. You'll need to recompile all modules using one of the Borland C++ compilers.

This can also occur if the machine was rebooted during a compile, or if a compiler did not delete its output object file when Ctrl+Break was pressed. Recompile.

If the error persists, call Borland Technical Support.

**Floating point error: Divide by 0**

**Floating point error: Domain**

**Floating point error: Overflow** *Run-time messages*

These fatal errors result from a floating-point operation for which the result is not finite:

- Divide by 0 means the result is +INF or -INF exactly, such as $1.0/0.0$.
- Domain means the result is NAN (not a number), like $0.0/0.0$.

Overflow means the result is +INF (infinity) or -INF with complete loss of precision, such as assigning 1e200*1e200 to a double.

**Floating point error: Partial loss of precision**

**Floating point error: Underflow** *Run-time messages*

These exceptions are masked by default, because underflows are converted to zero and losses of precision are ignored.

**Floating point error: Stack fault** *Run-time message*

The floating-point stack has been overrun. This error may be due to assembly code using too many registers or due to a misdeclaration of a floating-point function.

The program prints the error message and calls abort and _exit.

These floating-point errors can be avoided by masking the exception so that it doesn't occur, or by catching the exception with signal.

**FONTDIR resource too big to link.**

**FONTDIR too large to handle.** *Resource Linker messages*

The directory of fonts table size has been exceeded. Try splitting your fonts into multiple FON files.

**Friends must be functions or classes** *Compiler message*

A friend of a C++ class must be a function or another class.

**Function 'function' cannot be static** *Compiler message*

Only ordinary member functions and the operators new and delete can be declared static. Constructors, destructors and other operators must not be static.

**Function body ignored** *Compiler message*

An error has occurred while using the command-line utility H2ASH. See the online file "tsm_util.txt" for further information about this utility.

**Function call missing )** *Compiler message*

The function call argument list had some sort of syntax error, such as a missing or mismatched right parenthesis.

**Function call terminated by unhandled exception** *IDE Debugger message*

This message is emitted when an expression you are evaluating while debugging includes a function call that terminates with an unhandled exception. For example, if in the debugger's evaluate dialog, you request an evaluation of the expression foo()+1 and the execution of the function foo() causes a GP fault, this evaluation produces the above error message.

You may also see this message in the watches window because it also displays the results of evaluating an expression.

**Function defined inline after use as extern** *Compiler message*

Functions can't become inline after they have already been used.

Either move the inline definition forward in the file or delete it entirely.

The compiler encountered something like:

```
myex();
twoex() { myex(); }
inline myex() { return 2; } // error
```

and already used the function as an extern before it saw that it was specified as inline.

This would be correct:

```
myex();
inline myex() { return 2; }

twoex() { myex(); }
```

or better:

```
inline myex();
inline myex() { return 2; }

twoex() { myex(); }
```

**Function definition cannot be a typedef'ed declaration** *Compiler message*

In ANSI C, a function body cannot be defined using a typedef with a function Type.

Redefine the function body.

**'function' must be declared with no parameters** *Compiler message*

This C++ operator function was incorrectly declared with parameters.

**'function' must be declared with one parameter** *Compiler message*

This C++ operator function was incorrectly declared with more than one parameter.

**'function' must be declared with two parameters** *Compiler message*

This C++ operator function was incorrectly declared with other than two parameters.

**Function should return a value** *Compiler message*

(Command-line equivalent for displaying this warning = -wrvl)

Your source file declared the current function to return some type other than int or void, but the compiler encountered a return with no value. The compiler found a return statement without a return value, or it reached the end of the function without finding a return statement.

Either return a value or change the function declaration to return void.

Default = displayed

**'function' was previously declared with the language 'language'** *Compiler message*

Only one language modifier (cdecl pascal) can be given for a function.

This function has been declared with different language modifiers in two locations.

**Functions are not expanded inline** *Compiler message*

Exception specifications are not expanded inline: Check your inline code for lines containing exception specification.

Functions taking class-by-value argument(s) are not expanded inline: When exception handling is enabled, functions that take class arguments by value cannot be expanded inline.

**Note:** Functions taking class parameters by reference are not subject to this restriction.

**Functions cannot return arrays or functions**                                            *Compiler message*

A function was defined to return an array or a function. Check to see if either the intended return was a pointer to an array or function (and perhaps the * is missing) or if the function definition contained a request for an incorrect data type.

**Functions containing reserved words are not expanded inline**

**Functions containing local destructors are not expanded inline**

**in function 'function'**                                                                  *Compiler messages*

(Command-line equivalent for displaying this warning = -winl)

### Reserved words

Functions containing any of these reserved words can't be expanded inline, even when specified as inline:

- break
- case
- continue
- do
- for
- goto
- switch
- while

The function is still perfectly legal, but will be treated as an ordinary static (not global) function.

A copy of the function will appear in each compilation unit where it is called.

### Local destructors

You've created an inline function for which the compiler turns off inlining. You can ignore this warning; the function will be generated out of line.

Default = displayed

**Functions 'function1' and 'function2' both use the same dispatch number**                *Compiler message*

This error indicates a dynamically dispatched virtual table (DDVT) problem.

**Functions may not be part of a struct or union**                                          *Compiler message*

This C struct or union field was declared to be of type function rather than pointer to function.

Functions as fields are allowed only in C++.

**'function1' cannot be distinguished from 'function2'**                                    *Compiler message*

The parameter type lists in the declarations of these two functions do not differ enough to tell them apart.

Try changing the order of parameters or the type of a parameter in one declaration.

**'function1' hides virtual function 'function2'**                          *Compiler message*

(Command-line equivalent for displaying this warning = -whid)

A virtual function in a base class is usually overridden by a declaration in a derived class.

In this case, a declaration with the same name but different argument types makes the virtual functions inaccessible to further derived classes.

Default = displayed

**General error**

**General error in library file 'filename' in module 'module' near module file offset '0xyyyyyyyy'**

**General error in module 'module' near module file offset '0xyyyyyyyy'**                *Linker messages*

The linker gives as much information as possible about what processing was happening at the time of the unhandled exception. Call Borland Technical Support with information about the .OBJ or .LIB files.

**General error in module 'module'**                                        *Linker message*

TLink32 emits a General Error and crashes if the user specifies a map file that cannot be opened. This usually occurs when the directory (or drive) for the command-line specified map file doesn't exist. This linker is trying to emit the following message to the map file:

```
Fatal: cannot open mapfile...
```

Make sure that the map file destination drive and directory is correct.

**Global anonymous union not static**                                       *Compiler message*

In C++, a global anonymous union at the file level must be static.

**Goto bypasses initialization of a local variable**                        *Compiler message*

In C++ it is illegal to bypass the initialization of a local variable.

This error indicates a goto statement that can transfer control past this local variable.

**Goto into an exception handler is not allowed**                           *Compiler message*

It is not legal to jump into a try block, or an exception handler that is attached to a try block.

**Goto statement missing label**                                            *Compiler message*

The goto keyword must be followed by an identifier.

**Group 'group' exceeds 64K**                                               *Linker message*

This message occurs when there was too much data to fit in the available data segments.

To resolve the problem, you can try the following:

1   Switch to a memory model with multiple data segments (small, compact, or huge).

2   Put large global variables in far data. This is called Automatic Far Data & Far Data Threshold in the IDE (Options | Compiler | Advanced CG) and Far Global Variables (-Ff=size) on the command line.

3   Use the far keyword to force data objects into far data.

**4** Allocate variables dynamically (off the heap) instead of statically.

**5** If using C++ virtual tables, enable Far Virtual Tables (Options | Compiler | C++ Options in the IDE; -Vf on the command line).

### Group 'group1' overlaps group 'group2'

*Linker message*

The linker encountered nested groups. This warning occurs only when overlays are used.

### Group overflowed maximum size: 'name'

*Compiler message*

The total size of the segments in a group (for example, DGROUP) exceeded 64K.

### Handler for 'type1' hidden by previous handler for 'type2'

*Compiler message*

This warning is issued when a handler for a type 'D' that is derived from type 'B' is specified after a handler for B', since the handler for 'D' will never be invoked.

### Heap size is less than 1000h. It has been reset to 1000h

*Linker message*

The minimum allowable heap size is 1000h. When the linker detects that the heap size is less than this value, the linker automatically resets the size to 1000h and issues this message.

To eliminate this message, you need to change the HEAPSIZE specification in the DEF file to 1000h or greater.

### Hexadecimal value contains more than three digits

*Compiler message*

(Command-line equivalent for displaying this warning = -wbig)

Under older versions of C, a hexadecimal escape sequence could contain no more than three digits.

The ANSI standard allows any number of digits to appear as long as the value fits in a byte.

This warning results when you have a long hexadecimal escape sequence with many leading zero digits (such as \x00045).

Older versions of C would interpret such a string differently.

Default = displayed

### Identifier expected

*Compiler message*

An identifier was expected here, but not found.

In C, an identifier is expected in the following situations:

- In a list of parameters in an old-style function header
- After the reserved words struct or union when the braces are not present, and
- As the name of a member in a structure or union (except for bit fields of width 0).

In C++, an identifier is also expected in these situations:

- In a list of base classes from which another class is derived, following a double colon (::).
- After the reserved word "operator" when no operator symbol is present.

**'identifier' cannot be declared in an anonymous union**                    *Compiler message*

The compiler found a declaration for a member function or static member in an anonymous union. Such unions can only contain data members.

**'identifier' cannot start a parameter declaration**                    *Compiler message*

An undefined 'identifier' was found at the start of an argument in a function declarator.

Often the type name is misspelled or the type declaration is missing. This is usually caused by not including the appropriate header file.

**Identifier 'identifier' cannot have a type qualifier**                    *Compiler message*

A C++ qualifier class::identifier can't be applied here.

A qualifier is not allowed on the following:

- typedef names
- function declarations (except definitions at the file level)
- on local variables or parameters of functions
- on a class member--except to use its own class as a qualifier (redundant but legal).

**'identifier' is assigned a value that is never used**                    *Compiler message*

(Command-line equivalent for displaying this warning = -waus)

The variable appears in an assignment, but is never used anywhere else in the function just ending.

The warning is indicated only when the compiler encounters the closing brace.

Default = displayed

**'identifier' is declared as both external and static**                    *Compiler message*

(Command-line equivalent for displaying this warning = -wext)

This identifier appeared in a declaration that implicitly or explicitly marked it as global or external, and also in a static declaration. The identifier is taken as static.

You should review all declarations for this identifier.

Default = displayed

**'identifier' is declared but never used**                    *Compiler message*

(Command-line equivalent for displaying this warning = -wuse)

This message can occur in the case of either local or static variables. It occurs when the source file declares the named local or static variable as part of the block just ending, but the variable was never used.

In the case of local variables, this warning occurs when the compiler encounters the closing brace of the compound statement or function.

In the case of static variables, this warning occurs when the compiler encounters the end of the source file.

Default = not displayed

**'identifier' is not a member of 'struct'**                    *Compiler message*

You are trying to reference 'identifier' as a member of 'struct', but it is not a member.

Check your declarations.

**'identifier' is not a non-static member and can't be initialized here** *Compiler message*

Only data members can be initialized in the initializers of a constructor.

This message means that the list includes a static member or function member.

Static members must be initialized outside of the class, for example:

```
class A { static int i; };
int A::i = -1;
```

**'identifier' is not a parameter** *Compiler message*

In the parameter declaration section of an old-style function definition, 'identifier' is declared t not listed as a parameter. Either remove the declaration or add 'identifier' as a parameter.

**'identifier' is not a public base class of 'classtype'** *Compiler message*

The right operand of a .*, ->*, or ::operator was not a pointer to a member of a class that is either identical to (or an unambiguous accessible base class of) the left operand's class type.

**'identifier' is obsolete** *Compiler message*

Issues a warning upon usage for any "C" linkage function that has been specified. This will warn about functions that are "obsolete".

Here's an example of its usage:

```
#ifdef __cplusplus
extern "C" {
#endif
void my_func(void);
#ifdef __cplusplus
}
#endif

#pragma obsolete my_func

main()
{
    my_func();   // Generates warning about obsolete function
```

**'identifier' must be a member function** *Compiler message*

Most C++ operator functions can be members of classes or ordinary non-member functions, but these are required to be members of classes:

- operator =
- operator ->
- operator ( )
- type conversions

This operator function is not a member function but should be.

**'identifier' must be a member function or have a parameter of class type** *Compiler message*

Most C++ operator functions must have an implicit or explicit parameter of class type.

This operator function was declared outside a class and does not have an explicit parameter of class type.

**'identifier' must be a previously defined class or struct**                       *Compiler message*

You are attempting to declare 'identifier' to be a base class, but either it is not a class or it has not yet been fully defined. Correct the name or rearrange the declarations.

**'identifier' must be a previously defined enumeration tag**                       *Compiler message*

This declaration is attempting to reference 'ident' as the tag of an enum type, but it has not been so declared.

Correct the name, or rearrange the declarations.

**'identifier' specifies multiple or duplicate access**                       *Compiler message*

A base class can be declared public or private, but not both.

This access specifier can appear no more than once for a base class.

**If statement too long**                       *MAKE message*

An If statement has exceeded 4,096 characters.

**Ifdef statement too long**                       *MAKE message*

An Ifdef statement has exceeded 4,096 characters.

**Ifndef statement too long**                       *MAKE message*

An Ifndef statement has exceeded 4,096 characters.

**Ignored 'module', path is too long**                       *Librarian message*

The path to a specified .OBJ or .LIB file is greater than 64 characters. The maximum path to a file for the librarian is 64 characters.

**Ill-formed pragma**                       *Compiler message*

(Command-line equivalent for displaying this warning = -will)

A pragma does not match one of the pragmas expected by the compiler.

Default = displayed

**Illegal ACBP byte in SEGDEF in module 'module'**                       *Linker message*

This error generally occurs due to an incompatible .OBJ file format. If you're linking .OBJ files compiled using another compiler, these files may be incompatible with TLINK32. You'll need to recompile all modules using one of the Borland C++ compilers.

This can also occur if the machine was rebooted during a compile, or if a compiler did not delete its output object file when Ctrl+Break was pressed. Recompile.

If the error persists, call Borland Technical Support.

**Illegal character 'character' (0x'value')**                       *Compiler message*

The compiler encountered some invalid character in the input file. The hexadecimal value of the offending character is printed. This can also be caused by extra parameters passed to a function macro.

**Illegal character in constant expression 'expression'**                       *MAKE message*

MAKE encountered a character not allowed in a constant expression. If the character is a letter, this probably indicates a misspelled identifier.

**Illegal component to GRPDEF in module 'module'**                    *Linker message*

This error generally occurs due to an incompatible .OBJ file format. If you're linking .OBJ files compiled using another compiler, these files may be incompatible with TLINK32. You'll need to recompile all modules using one of the Borland C++ compilers.

This can also occur if the machine was rebooted during a compile, or if a compiler did not delete its output object file when Ctrl+Break was pressed. Recompile.

If the error persists, call Borland Technical Support.

**Illegal group definition: 'group' in module 'module'**                    *Linker message*

This error results from an invalid GRPDEF record in an .OBJ file.

This could also result from custom-built .OBJ files or a bug in the translator used to generate the .OBJ file.

If this occurs in a file created by a Borland compiler, recompile the file. If the error persists, contact Borland Technical Support.

**Illegal initialization**                    *Compiler message*

Initializations must be one of the following:

- Constant expressions
- Address of a global extern or static variable plus or minus a constant

**Illegal local public in 'module'**                    *Linker message*

This message occurs when the linker sees an LPUBDEF record with an offset of zero for a VIRDEF that resides in an overlay segment. This can happen if you are trying to use structured exception support in an application that uses overlays.

**Illegal octal digit**                    *Compiler message*

The compiler found an octal constant containing a non-octal digit (8 or 9).

**Illegal octal digit**                    *MAKE message*

An octal constant containing a digit of 8 or 9 was found.

**Illegal parameter to _ _emit_ _**                    *Compiler message*

There are some restrictions on inserting literal values directly into your code with the __emit__ function.

For example, you cannot give a local variable as a parameter to __emit__.

**Illegal pointer subtraction**                    *Compiler message*

This is caused by attempting to subtract a pointer from a non-pointer.

**Illegal structure operation**                    *Compiler message*

Structures can only be used with dot (.), address-of (&) or assignment (=) operators, or be passed to or from a function as parameters.

The compiler encountered a structure being used with some other operator.

**Illegal to take address of bit field**                    *Compiler message*

It is not legal to take the address of a bit field, although you can take the address of other kinds of fields.

**Illegal type of entry point**                                          *Linker message*

The linker encountered an object file with an incompatible .OBJ file format.

This error generally occurs due to an incompatible .OBJ file format. If you're linking .OBJ files compiled using another compiler, these files may be incompatible with TLINK32. You'll need to recompile all modules using one of the Borland C++ compilers.

This can also occur if the machine was rebooted during a compile, or if a compiler did not delete its output object file when Ctrl+Break was pressed. Recompile.

If the error persists, call Borland Technical Support.

**Illegal use of floating point**                                        *Compiler message*

Floating-point operands are not allowed in these operators

- Shift (SHL, SHR)
- Bitwise Boolean (AND, OR, XOR, NOT)
- Conditional (? :)
- Indirection (*)
- Certain others

The compiler found a floating-point operand with one of these prohibited operators.

**Illegal use of member pointer**                                        *Compiler message*

Pointers to class members can only be passed as arguments to functions, or used with the following operators:

- assignment
- comparison
- .*
- ->*
- ?:
- &&
- ||
- The compiler has encountered a member pointer being used with a different operator.

To call a member function pointer, one must supply an instance of the class for it to call upon.

For example:

```
class A {
public:
    myex();
};
typedef int (A::*Amfptr)();
myex()
{
    Amfptr mmyex = &A::myex;
    (*mmyex)():  //error
}
```

This will compile:

```
class A {
public:
   myex();
};
typedef int (A::*Amfptr)();
foo()
{
   A a;
   Amfptr mmyex - &A::myex;
   (a.*mmyex)90;
}
```

### Illegal use of pointer

*Compiler message*

Pointers can only be used with these operators:

- addition (+)
- subtraction (-)
- assignment (=)
- comparison (==)
- indirection (*)
- arrow (->)

Your source file used a pointer with some other operator.

Example:

```
int main (void)
{
   char *p;
   p /= 7;     /* ERROR: Illegal Use of Pointer */
   return 0;
}
```

### Illegal/invalid option in CMDSWITCHES directive 'option'

*MAKE message*

The **!CMDSWITCHES** preprocessing directive turns on or off one or more command-line options. Specify an operator, either a plus sign (+) to turn options on, or a minus sign (-) to turn options off, followed by one or more letters specifying options. An invalid or illegal option is specified in the **!CMDSWITCHES** directive.

### Image base address must be a multiple of 0x10000

*Linker message*

Based images must be aligned on 64K boundaries.

### Image linked as EXE, but with DLL extension

*Linker message*

The linker generates this warning when an executable file has been generated and stored in a file with a .DLL extension.

This usually occurs when you intended to build a .DLL but forgot to specify a .DLL target with the /T linker option (or you forgot the /T option altogether) on the command line. If you want to generate a DLL as a target, use the appropriate /T option.

**Images fixed at specific addresses typically will not run under Win32s** *Linker message*

Windows 32s loads all applications in a single address space. It's possible to predict where your application is going to be loaded, because other 32-bit applications might have been loaded before yours.

**Implicit conversion of 'type1' to 'type2' not allowed** *Compiler message*

When a member function of a class is called using a pointer to a derived class, the pointer value must be implicitly converted to point to the appropriate base class.

In this case, such an implicit conversion is illegal.

**Import library 'library' encountered in obj list** *Linker message*

Import libraries (import.lib) cannot be listed in a response file as OBJ files. They must always appear in the LIB file list.

**Import record does not match previous definition** *Linker message*

This warning usually occurs if an IMPDEF record appears in an import library when the import in question is also imported from a .DEF file. If the description of the imports differ in internal name or ordinal, this warning appears, and the first definition is used.

You can suppress this warning from the Linker | Warnings page of the Project options dialog box or with the **/w-imt** command-line option.

**Import 'symbol' in module 'module' clashes with prior module** *Librarian message*

An import symbol can appear only once in a library file. A module that is being added to the library contains an import that is already in a module of the library and it cannot be added again.

**Improper use of typedef 'identifier'** *Compiler message*

Your source file used a typedef symbol where a variable should appear in an expression.

Check for the declaration of the symbol and possible misspellings.

**Include files nested too deep** *Compiler message*

This message flags (directly or indirectly) recursive **#include** directives.

**Incompatible type conversion** *Compiler message*

The cast requested can't be done.

**Incorrect command line argument: 'argument'** *MAKE message*

You've used incorrect command-line arguments. Reenter the command and arguments.

**Incorrect number format** *Compiler message*

The compiler encountered a decimal point in a hexadecimal number.

**Incorrect option:** *Compiler message*

An error has occurred in either the configuration file or a command-line option. The compiler may not have recognized the configuration file parameter as legal; check for a preceding hyphen (-), or the compiler may not have recognized the command-line parameter as legal.

This error can also occur if you use a **#pragma** option in your code with an invalid option.

### Incorrect use of default
*Compiler message*

The compiler found no colon after the default keyword.

### Incorrect version of RLINK32.DLL
*Linker message*

You don't have a the right version of RLINK32.DLL. Check to make sure that you have the correct version of the DLL. If not, delete that DLL and reinstall Borland C++.

### Initialization is only partially bracketed
*Compiler message*

(Command-line equivalent for displaying this warning = -wpin)

When structures are initialized, braces can be used to mark the initialization of each member of the structure. If a member itself is an array or structure, nested pairs of braces can be used. This ensures that the compiler's idea and your idea of what value goes with which member are the same. When some of the optional braces are omitted, the compiler issues this warning.

Default = not displayed

### Initializer for object 'x' ignored
*Compiler message*

An error has occurred while using the command-line utility H2ASH. See the online file "tsm_util.txt" for further information about this utility.

### Initializing 'identifier' with 'identifier'
*Compiler message*

(Command-line equivalent for displaying this warning = -wbei)

You're trying to initialize an enum variable to a different type.

For example, the following initialization will result in this warning, because 2 is of type int, not type enum count:

```
enum count zero, one, two x = 2;
```

It is better programming practice to use an enum identifier instead of a literal integer when assigning to or initializing enum types.

This is an error, but is reduced to a warning to give existing programs a chance to work.

### Initializing enumeration with type
*Compiler message*

You're trying to initialize an enum variable to a different type. For example,

```
enum count { zero, one, two } x = 2;
```

will result in this warning, because 2 is of type int, not type enum count. It is better programming practice to use an enum identifier instead of a literal integer when assigning to or initializing enum types.

This is an error, but is reduced to a warning to give existing programs a chance to work.

### Inline assembly not allowed
*Compiler message*

Your source file contains inline assembly language statements and you are compiling it from within the integrated environment.

You must use the BCC command to compile this source file from the DOS command line.

### Inline assembly not allowed in inline and template functions
*Compiler message*

The compiler can't handle inline assembly statements in a C++ inline or template function.

You could eliminate the inline assembly code or, in the case of an inline function, make this a macro, and remove the inline storage class.

### Int and string types compared
*MAKE message*

You tried to compare an integer operand with a string operand in an **!if** or **!elif** expression.

### Internal code generator error
*Compiler message*

An error has occurred in the internal logic of the code generator. Contact Borland Technical Support.

### Internal compiler error
*Compiler message*

An error occurred in the internal logic of the compiler. This error shouldn't occur in practice, but it could be generated if a more specific error message is not available.

### Internal linker error 'errorcode'
*Linker message*

An error occurred in the internal logic of the linker. This error shouldn't occur, but it could be generated if a more specific error message is not available.

If this error persists, write down the errorcode number and contact Borland Technical Support.

### Internal software error!
*Resource Linker message*

The resource linker encountered unexpected data. Restart the resource link. If the error persists, contact Borland Technical Support.

### Invalid 'expression' in scope override
*Compiler message*

The evaluator issues this message when there is an error in a scope override in an expression you are watching or inspecting. You can specify a symbol table, a compilation unit, a source file name, etc. as the scope of the expression, and the message will appear whenever the compiler cannot access the symbol table, compilation unit, or whatever.

### Invalid combination of opcode and operands
*Compiler message*

The built-in assembler does not accept this combination of operands.

Possible Causes:

- There are too many or too few operands for this assembler opcode.
- The number of operands is correct, but their types or order do not match the opcode.

### Invalid entry at 'segment:xxxxh'
*Linker message*

This error indicates that a necessary entry was missing from the entry table of a Windows executable file.

The application may not work in real mode unless you fix the code and the data.

### Invalid entry point offset
*Linker message*

This message occurs when modules with 32-bit records are linked. It usually means that the initial program entry point offset exceeds the DOS limit of 64K.

Sample code that could produce this is:

```
_TEXT  segment public 'CODE'
main:
```

```
_TEXT   ends
    end main
```

In this case, the linker is trying to apply the fixup contained in the record for main, but there is no code.

**Invalid exe filename: 'filename'** *Linker message*

The .EXE file name has an incorrect extension such as .OBJ, .MAP, .LIB, .DEF, or .RES.

**Invalid extended dictionary in library 'library': extended dictionaries ignored** *Linker message*

An extended dictionary in the library in question was generated with an outdated version of TLIB. Rebuild the library with a current version of TLIB, specifying that an extended dictionary be created.

**Invalid file/object alignment value 'value'** *Linker message*

You specified an incorrect value for file or object alignment in the 32-bit linker options.

The value must be a number (either decimal or hex) that is a power of 2. The smallest allowable file alignment value is 16. The smallest allowable object alignment value is 4096.

**Invalid function call** *Compiler message*

A requested function call failed because the function is not available in the program, a parameter cannot be evaluated, and so on. The evaluator issues this message.

**Invalid indirection** *Compiler message*

The indirection operator (*) requires a non-void pointer as the operand.

Example

```
int main (void)
{
 void *p;
 *p = 10;      /* ERROR: Invalid Indirection */
 return 0;
}
```

**Invalid initial stack offset** *Linker message*

This message occurs only when modules with 32-bit records are linked. It means that the initial stack pointer value exceeds the DOS limit of 64K.

**Invalid macro argument separator** *Compiler message*

In a macro definition, arguments must be separated by commas. The compiler encountered some other character after an argument name.

This is correct:

```
#define tri_add(a, b, c)   ((a) + (b) + (c))
```

This is incorrect:

```
#define tri_add(a  b. c)   ((a) + (b) + (c))
```

**Invalid map filename: 'filename'** *Linker message*

The map file name had an incorrect extension, such as .OBJ, .EXE, .DLL, .LIB, .DEF, or .RES.

**Invalid overlay switch specification**                                       *Linker message*

  ▸  You specified an overlay option but omitted the file name or names. Delete the switches
     or add the names of the files containing the overlays.

**Invalid page size value ignored**                                           *Librarian message*

  The librarian encountered an invalid page size. The page size must be an integer that is a
  power of 2.

**Invalid Pass Count value entered**                                      *IDE Debugger message*

  The Pass Count value you gave was invalid. Valid values for Pass Count are from 0 to
  4294967295.

**Invalid pathname for executable**                                       *IDE Debugger message*

  The debugger was unable to find the executable you tried to load.

**Invalid pointer addition**                                                  *Compiler message*

  Your source file attempted to add two pointers together.

**Invalid process id**                                                    *IDE Debugger message*

  You specified a process ID that does not match the ID of any active process.

**Invalid register combination (e.g., [BP+BX])**                              *Compiler message*

  The built-in assembler detected an illegal combination of registers in an instruction.

  These are valid index register combinations:

  - [BX]
  - [BP]
  - [SI]
  - [DI]
  - [BX+SI]
  - [BX+DI]
  - [BP+SI]
  - [BP+DI]

  Other index register combinations are not allowed.

**Invalid segment definition in module 'module'**                             *Linker message*

  This error results from an invalid GRPDEF record in an .OBJ file.

  This could result from custom-built .OBJ files or a bug in the translator used to generate
  the .OBJ file.

  If this occurs in a file created by a Borland compiler, recompile the file. If the error
  persists, contact Borland Technical Support.

**Invalid size specified for segment alignment**                              *Linker message*

  This error occurs if an invalid value is specified for the Segment Alignment setting. The
  value specified must be an integral multiple of 2 and less than 64K. Common values are
  16 and 512. This error only occurs when linking Windows applications.

**Invalid size specified for segment packing**                                *Linker message*

  A non-decimal number was provided on the command line for the segment packing
  size limit.

### Invalid stack reserve/commit size 'size' *Linker message*

The heap or stack commit size specified is not valid. The default and minimum values for reserve and commit sizes are shown here.

| Reserve | Default | Minimum |
|---------|---------|---------|
| Stack   | 1Mb     | 4K      |
| Heap    | 1Mb     | 0K      |
| Commit  | Default | Minimum |
| Stack   | 8K      | 4K      |
| Heap    | 4K      | 0K      |

Change the stack and heap reserve or commit sizes by changing the 32-bit linker values in the IDE or by changing HEAPSIZE and STACKSIZE in the module definition file.

### Invalid target /T 'target' *Linker message*

The command-line linker found an invalid target. Valid targets are 'w' and 'd.'

### Invalid template argument list *Compiler message*

This error indicates that an illegal template argument list was found.

In a template declaration, the keyword template must be followed by a list of formal arguments enclosed within < and > delimiters.

### Invalid template member definition *Compiler message*

After the declarator of a template member, either a semicolon, an initialization, or a body was expected, but some other, illegal token was found. This message appears when a template member is declared outside of the template, but the syntax was wrong.

### Invalid template qualified name 'template::name' *Compiler message*

When defining a template class member, the actual arguments in the template class name used as the left operand for the :: operator must match the formal arguments of the template class.

### Invalid Thread Id entered *IDE Debugger message*

The Thread ID value you gave was invalid. Valid values for Thread Id are from 0 to 4294967295.

### Invalid use of dot *Compiler message*

An identifier must immediately follow a period operator (.).

Example

```
struct foo {
  int x;
  int y;
}p = 0,0;
int main (void)
{
  p.x++;         /* Correct */
  p. y++;        /* Error: Invalid use of dot */
  return 0;
}
```

### Invalid use of namespace 'identifier'
*Compiler message*

A namespace identifier was used in an illegal way, for example, in an expression.

### Invalid use of template 'template'
*Compiler message*

You can only use a template class name without specifying its actual arguments inside a template definition.

Using a template class name without specifying its actual arguments outside a template definition is illegal.

### Irreducible expression tree
*Compiler message*

This is a sign of some form of compiler error. An expression on the indicated line of the source file caused the code generator to be unable to generate code.

The expression should be avoided. Notify Borland if an expression can consistently reproduce this error.

### Last parameter of 'operator' must have type 'int'
*Compiler message*

When a postfix operator ++ or operator––is overloaded, the last parameter must be declared with the type int.

### Library too large, restart with library page size 'size'
*Librarian message*

The library being created could not be built with the current library page size.

You can set the library page size with the Library Page Size option.

### Limit of 254 segments for new executable file exceeded
*Linker message*

You have reached the limit of segments that can be specified by the executable file format. Only 254 segments can be represented in Windows EXEs and DLLs.

Usually one of two things causes this problem. If the application is a large model, the code segment packing size could be so small that there are too many code segments. To reduce the total number of segments to below 254, turn on the Pack Code Segments option.

The other possibility is that you have a lot of far data segments with only a few bytes of data in them. Examine the map file. It should tell you if this is happening. In this case, reduce the number of far data segments.

### Linkage specification not allowed
*Compiler message*

Linkage specifications such as extern "C" are only allowed at the file level. Move this function declaration out to the file level.

### Linker stack overflow
*Linker message*

The linker uses a recursive procedure for marking modules to be included in an executable image from libraries. This procedure can cause stack overflows in extreme circumstances.

If you get this error message, remove some modules from libraries, include them with the object files in the link, and try again.

### Loading: 'programname'
*IDE Debugger message*

The debugger is loading the specified program.

**Local data exceeds segment size limit** *Compiler message*

The local variables in the current function take up more than 64K. Due to limitations of the processor, this is illegal in 16-bit programs.

**Log Expr checked but no value entered** *IDE Debugger message*

You checked the Log Expr check box, but forgot to specify an expression.

**Log Msg checked but no value entered** *IDE Debugger message*

You checked the Log Msg check box, but forgot to specify a message.

**Lvalue required** *Compiler message*

The left side of an assignment operator must be an addressable expression.

Addressable expressions include the following:

- Numeric or pointer variables
- Structure field references or indirection through a pointer
- Subscripted array element

**Macro argument syntax error** *Compiler message*

An argument in a macro definition must be an identifier.

The compiler encountered some non-identifier character where an argument was expected.

**Macro definition ignored** *Compiler message*

An error has occurred while using the command-line utility H2ASH. See the online file "tsm_util.txt" for further information about this utility.

**Macro expansion too long** *Compiler message*

A macro can't expand to more than 4,096 characters.

**Macro expansion too long** *MAKE message*

A macro cannot expand to more than 4,096 characters. This error often occurs if a macro recursively expands itself. A macro cannot legally expand to itself.

**Macro replace text 'string' is too long** *MAKE message*

The macro replacement text string overflowed MAKE's internal buffer of 512 bytes.

**Macro substitute text 'string' is too long** *MAKE message*

The macro substitution text string overflowed MAKE's internal buffer of 512 bytes.

**'macroname' - ')' missing in macro invocation** *MAKE message*

The macro you entered is missing a right parenthesis.

**Main must have a return type of int** *Compiler message*

In C++, function *main* has special requirements, one of which is that it cannot be declared with any return type other than int.

**Make failed** *IDE Debugger message*

The make spawned by the debugger to try to bring the current target up to date failed. Check the Build Time tab in the Message view to see the reason for the failure.

### Make the modified code? *IDE Debugger message*

You had a process loaded in the integrated debugger and then you modified the source code for the process. You should probably build the new code instead of continuing to debug the old executable.

### Malformed command-line *Linker message*

You specified an invalid entry on the command line. Check the command you entered.

### Matching base class function 'function' has different dispatch number *Compiler message*

If a DDVT function is declared in a derived class, the matching base class function must have the same dispatch number as the derived function.

### Matching base class function 'function' is not dynamic *Compiler message*

If a DDVT function is declared in a derived class, the matching base class function must also be dynamic.

### Maximum precision used for member pointer type 'type' *Compiler message*

When a member pointer type is declared, its class has not been fully defined, and the -Vmd option has been used, the compiler has to use the most general (and the least efficient) representation for that member pointer type. This can cause less efficient code to be generated (and make the member pointer type unnecessarily large), and can also cause problems with separate compilation; see the -Vm compiler switch for details.

### Member 'member' cannot be used without an object *Compiler message*

This means that you have written class::member, where 'member' is an ordinary (non-static) member, and there is no class to associate with that member.

For example, it is legal to write this:

```
obj.class::member
```

but not to write this:

```
class::member
```

### Member 'member' has the same name as its class *Compiler message*

A static data member, enumerator, member of an anonymous union, or nested type cannot have the same name as its class. Only a member function or a non-static member can have a name that is identical to its class.

### Member 'member' is initialized more than once *Compiler message*

In a C++ class constructor, the list of initializations following the constructor header includes the same member name more than once.

### Member function must be called or its address taken *Compiler message*

A reference to a member function must be called, or its address must be taken with & operator. In this case, a member function has been used in an illegal context.

For example:

```
class A
{
    void (A::* infptr)(void);
public;
    A();
```

```
        void myex(void);
    };
    A::A()
    {
        infptr = myex;     //illegal - call myex or take address?
        infptr = A::& myex;    //correct
    }
```

## Member identifier expected

*Compiler message*

The name of a structure or C++ class member was expected here, but not found. The right side a dot (.) or arrow (->) operator must be the name of a member in the structure or class on the left of the operator.

## Member is ambiguous: 'member1' and 'member2'

*Compiler message*

You must qualify the member reference with the appropriate base class name.

In C++ class 'class', member 'member' can be found in more than one base class, and it was not qualified to indicate which one you meant.

This applies only in multiple inheritance, where the member name in each base class is not hidden by the same member name in a derived class on the same path.

The C++ language rules require that this test for ambiguity be made before checking for access rights (private, protected, public).

It is possible to get this message even though only one (or none) of the members can be accessed.

## 'member' is not a valid template type member

*Compiler message*

A member of a template with some actual arguments that depend on the formal arguments of an enclosing template was found not to be a member of the specified template in a particular instance.

## 'member' is not accessible

*Compiler message*

You are trying to reference C++ class member 'member,' but it is private or protected and can't be referenced from this function.

This sometimes happens when you attempt to call one accessible overloaded member function (or constructor), but the arguments match an inaccessible function.

The check for overload resolution is always made before checking for accessibility.

If this is the problem, try an explicit cast of one or more parameters to select the desired accessible function.

Virtual base class constructors must be accessible within the scope of the most derived class. This is because C++ always constructs virtual base classes first, no matter how far down the hierarchy they are. For example:

```
class A {
public:
    A();
};
class B : private virtual A {};
```

```
class C : private B {
public:
C();
};

C::C() {} // error, A::A() is not accessible
```

Since A is private to B, which is private to C, it makes A's constructor not accessible to C. However, the constructor for C must be able to call the constructors for its virtual base class, A. If B inherits A publicly, the above example would compile.

### Member pointer required on right side of .* or ->*
*Compiler message*

The right side of a C++ dot-star (.*) or an arrow star (->*) operator must be declared as a pointer to a member of the class specified by the left side of the operator.

In this case, the right side is not a member pointer.

### Memory full listing truncated!
*Librarian message*

The librarian ran out of memory while creating a library listing file. An incomplete list file will be created.

### Memory reference expected
*Compiler message*

The built-in assembler requires a memory reference.

You probably forgot to put square brackets around an index register operand.

### Misplaced break
*Compiler message*

The compiler encountered a break statement outside a switch or looping construct.

You can only use break statements inside of switch statements or loops.

### Misplaced continue
*Compiler message*

The compiler encountered a continue statement outside a looping construct.

### Misplaced decimal point
*Compiler message*

The compiler encountered a decimal point in a floating-point constant as part of the exponent.

### Misplaced elif directive
*Compiler message*

The compiler encountered an **#elif** directive without any matching **#if**, **#ifdef**, or **#ifndef** directive.

### Misplaced elif statement
*MAKE message*

An **!elif** directive is missing a matching **!if** directive.

### Misplaced else
*Compiler message*

The compiler encountered an **else** statement without a matching **if** statement.

Possible Causes:

- An extra "**else**" statement
- An extra semicolon
- Missing braces
- Some syntax error in a previous "**if**" statement

**Misplaced else directive**                                                      *Compiler message*

The compiler encountered an **#else** directive without any matching **#if**, **#ifdef**, or **#ifndef** directive.

**Misplaced else statement**                                                      *MAKE message*

An **!else** directive is missing a matching **!if** directive.

**Misplaced endif directive**                                                     *Compiler message*

The compiler encountered an **#endif** directive without any matching **#if**, **#ifdef**, or **#ifndef** directive.

**Misplaced endif statement**                                                     *MAKE message*

An **!endif** directive is missing a matching **!if** directive.

**Missing 'identifier' in scope override**                                        *Compiler message*

The syntax of a scope override is somehow incomplete. The evaluator issues this message.

**missing ]**                                                                     *Compiler message*

This error is generated if any of the following occur:

- Your source file declared an array in which the array bounds were not terminated by a right bracket.
- The array specifier in an operator is missing a right bracket.
- The operator [ ] was declared as operator [.
- A right bracket is missing from a subscripting expression.

Add the bracket or fix the declaration.

Check for a missing or extra operator or mismatched parentheses.

**Mixed common types in module 'module'. Cannot mix COMDEFs and VIRDEFs.**        *Linker message*

You cannot mix both COMDEFs and VIRDEFs. Turn off the -Fc switch to stop generating COMDEFs, or turn on the -Vs switch to stop generating VIRDEFs.

**Mixing pointers to different 'char' types**                                     *Compiler message*

(Command-line equivalent for displaying this warning = -wucp)

You converted a signed char pointer to an unsigned char pointer, or vice versa, without using an explicit cast. (Strictly speaking, this is incorrect, but it is often harmless.)

Default = not displayed

**'module' already in LIB, not changed!**                                         *Librarian message*

This warning indicates that you attempted to use the + action on the library, but an object with the same name already exists in the library. To update the module, the action should be +–. The library was not modified.

**'module' not found in library**                                                 *Librarian message*

An attempt to perform either a remove (–) or an extract (*) on a library has occurred and the indicated object does not exist in the library.

**Multiple base classes not supported**                                           *Compiler message*

An error has occurred while using the command-line utility H2ASH. See the online file "tsm_util.txt" for further information about this utility.

**Multiple base classes require explicit class names**                    *Compiler message*

In a C++ class constructor, if there is more than one immediate base class, each base class constructor call in the constructor header must include the base class name.

**Multiple declaration for 'identifier'**                                  *Compiler message*

This identifier was improperly declared more than once.

This might be caused by conflicting declarations such as:

- int a; double a;
- a function declared two different ways, or
- a label repeated in the same function, or
- some declaration repeated other than an extern function or a simple variable

This can also happen by inadvertently including the same header file twice. For example, given:

```
//a.h
struct A { int a; };

//b.h
#include "a.h"

//myprog.cpp
#include "a.h"
#include "b.h"
```

myprog.cpp will get two declarations for the struct A. To protect against this, one would write the a.h header file as:

```
//a.h
#ifndef __A_H
#define __A_H

struct A { int a; };

#endif
```

This will allow one to safely include a.h several times in the same source code file.

**Multiple entry points defined**                                          *Linker message*

Multiple entry points were defined for the application. This can happen if you have specified the startup code twice, or if you are making use of assembler code which defines a starting address for the application.

**Multiple public definitions for symbol 'symbol' in module 'module;' link case sensitively**    *Linker message*

The specified symbol was encountered twice in the same module. This is usually caused by the use of case-sensitive symbols. Try linking case sensitively.

**Multiple stack segments found. The most recent one will be used.**       *Linker message*

This warning occurs when two stack segments of different names are defined in the object modules. The startup code defines a stack segment for the application.

You can suppress this warning with the **/w-msk** command-line option.

**Must take address of a memory location**                                      *Compiler message*

Your source file used the address-of operator (&) with an expression that can't be used that way; for example, a register variable.

**NAMEDIR resource too big to link.**                                    *Resource Linker message*

The name-table maximum size has been exceeded. Name-table entries are not used in Windows 3.1 or later.

**Namespace member 'identifier' declared outside its namespace**                 *Compiler message*

Namespace members must be declared inside their namespace. You can only use explicit qualification to define a namespace member (for example, to give a body for a function declared in a namespace). The declaration itself must be inside the namespace.

**Namespace name expected**                                                      *Compiler message*

The name of a namespace symbol was expected.

**Need an identifier to declare**                                                *Compiler message*

In this context, an identifier was expected to complete the declaration. This might be a typedef with no name, or an extra semicolon at file level.

In C++, it might be a class name improperly used as another kind of identifier.

**'new' and 'delete' not supported**                                             *Compiler message*

The integrated debugger does not support the evaluation of the new and delete operators.

**New executable header overflowed 64K**                                          *Linker message*

Industry standards require that headers be no larger than 64K in size. If you encounter this message, check to see if the resident name table is increasing the size of the header so that it exceeds this limit.

**No : following the ?**                                                         *Compiler message*

The question mark (?) and colon (:) operators do not match in this expression. The colon might have been omitted, or parentheses might be improperly nested or missing.

**No automatic data segment**                                                     *Linker message*

No group named DGROUP was found.

Because the Borland initialization files define DGROUP, you will only see this error if you don't link with an initialization file and your program doesn't define DGROUP.

Windows uses DGROUP to find the local data segment. The DGROUP is required for Windows applications (but not DLLs) unless DATA NONE is specified in the module definition file.

**No base class to initialize**                                                  *Compiler message*

This C++ class constructor is trying to implicitly call a base class constructor, but this class was declared with no base classes. Check your declarations.

**No closing quote**                                                                 *MAKE message*

A string expression is missing a closing quote in an **!if** or **!elif** expression.

**No declaration for function 'function'**                                       *Compiler message*

(Command-line equivalent for displaying this warning = -wnod)

This message is given if you call a function without first declaring that function.

In C, you can declare a function without presenting a prototype, as in

```
int func();
```

In C++, every function declaration is also a prototype; this example is equivalent to

```
int func(void);
```

The declaration can be either classic or modern (prototype) style.

Default = not displayed

**No expression specified**                                                  *IDE Debugger message*

You forgot to specify an expression in the Add Watch dialog.

**No file corresponds to this item**                                         *IDE Debugger message*

You tried to bring up a source view on an address, and there is no source file for the address.

**No file line specified**                                                   *IDE Debugger message*

You tried to add a Source breakpoint using the IDE Debugger but did not include the line number. Specify the line in the file where you want the breakpoint to occur in the Add Breakpoint dialog box.

**No file name ending**                                                      *Compiler message*

The file name in an #include statement was missing the correct closing quote or angle bracket.

**No file names given**                                                      *Compiler message*

The command line of the Borland C++ command-line compiler (BCC) contained no file names. You must specify a source file name.

**No filename ending**                                                       *MAKE message*

The file name in an **!include** statement is missing the correct closing quote or angle bracket.

**No internal name for IMPORT in .DEF file**                                 *Linker message*

The .DEF file has a semantic error. You typed an illegal import sequence or forgot to put the internal name for an import before the module name. For example:

```
IMPORTS
  _foo.1
```

Here, _foo was to be the function to be imported, but the proper syntax is:

```
IMPORTS
  _foo=mydll.1
```

**No line corresponds to this item**                                         *IDE Debugger message*

You tried to bring up a source view on an address, and there is no line number for the address.

**No macro before =**                                                        *MAKE message*

You must name a macro before you can assign it a value.

**No match found for wildcard 'expression'** *MAKE message*

No files match the wildcard expression that you want MAKE to expand. For example, the following causes MAKE to send this error message if there are no files with the extension .OBJ in the current directory:

**No module definition file specified: using defaults** *Linker message*

This warning occurs when you do not specify a .DEF file for the link.

The following defaults are assumed:

| Statement | Default value |
| --- | --- |
| CODE | PRELOAD MOVEABLE DISCARDABLE |
| DATA | PRELOAD MOVEABLE MULTIPLE (if an .EXE) |
| DATA | PRELOAD MOVEABLE SINGLE (if a .DLL) |
| HEAPSIZE | 1048576 |
| STACKSIZE | 1048576 |

You can suppress this warning from the Linker | Warnings page of the Project options dialog box or with the **/w-def** command-line option.

**No module name specified** *IDE Debugger message*

You tried to add a module breakpoint using the IDE Debugger but you omitted the module name. Specify the module name where you want to insert the breakpoint in the Add Breakpoint dialog box.

**No module specified** *IDE Debugger message*

You tried to add an Address breakpoint using the IDE Debugger but you omitted the module. Specify the module where you want to insert the breakpoint in the Add Breakpoint dialog box.

**No object specified** *IDE Debugger message*

You tried to add an Address breakpoint using the IDE Debugger but you omitted the object. Specify the name of the object into which you want to insert the breakpoint in the Add Breakpoint dialog box.

**No offset specified** *IDE Debugger message*

You tried to add an Address breakpoint using the IDE Debugger but you omitted the offset that indicates where you want to insert the breakpoint. Specify the offset in the Add Breakpoint dialog box.

**No output file specified** *Linker message*

You did not specify an output file.

**No process selected** *IDE Debugger message*

You pressed the Attach button on the debugger's Attach dialog when there was no process selected in the process list.

**No process to load** *IDE Debugger message*

You left the Program Name field blank on the Load Program dialog.

**No process to reset** *IDE Debugger message*

You tried to reset a process but there was no process running.

**No process to stop**                                                     *IDE Debugger message*

You tried to pause a process but there was no process running.

**No process to terminate**                                                *IDE Debugger message*

You tried to terminate processes but there was no process running at the time.

**No program entry point**                                                 *Linker message*

This message appears if no starting execution point was defined in the application. This usually happens if you forget to link in the startup code.

You can suppress this warning from the Linker | Warnings page of the Project options dialog box or with the **/w-ent** command-line option.

**No program starting address defined**                                    *Linker message*

This warning means that no module defined the initial starting address of the program.

You probably forgot to link in the initialization module C0x.OBJ.

This warning should not occur when linking a Windows DLL.

**No resources.**                                                          *Resource Linker message*

This warning message occurs if the resource linker is given a resource file that contains no resources.

**No stack**                                                               *Linker message*

This warning is issued if no stack segment is defined in any of the object files or in any of the libraries included in the link. Except for DLLs, this indicates an error.

If a Borland C++ program produces this message, make sure you are using the correct C0x startup object files.

You can suppress this warning from the Linker | Warnings page of the Project options dialog box or with the **/k** (16-bit) or **/w-srf** (32-bit) command-line option.

**No stub for fixup at 'address' in module 'module'**                      *Linker message*

This error occurs when the target for a fixup is in an overlay segment, but no stub is found for a target external. This is usually the result of not making public a symbol in an overlay that is referenced from the same module.

**No terminator specified for in-line file operator**                      *MAKE message*

The makefile contains either the && or << command-line operators to start an inline file, but the file is not terminated.

**No thread ID specified**                                                 *IDE Debugger message*

You tried to add a thread breakpoint using the IDE Debugger but you omitted the thread ID. Type the ID number of the thread you want to monitor in the Add Breakpoint dialog box.

**No type information**                                                     *Compiler message*

The integrated debugger has no type information for this variable. Ensure that you've compiled the module with debug information. If it has, the module may have been compiled by another compiler or assembler.

**No type specified** *IDE Debugger message*

You tried to add a C++ exception breakpoint using the IDE Debugger. You must specify a type in the Add Breakpoint dialog box to set this type of breakpoint.

**No watch address specified** *IDE Debugger message*

You specified a data watch breakpoint using the IDE Debugger but you omitted the watch address. You need to specify both a memory address and the number of bytes to watch.

**No watch length specified** *IDE Debugger message*

You specified a data watch breakpoint using the IDE Debugger but you omitted the watch length. You need to specify both a memory address and the number of bytes to watch.

**Non-ANSI keyword used: 'keyword'** *Compiler message*

A non-ANSI keyword (such as '__fastcall') was used when strict ANSI conformance was requested via the -A option.

**Non-const function 'function' called for const object** *Compiler message*

(Command-line equivalent for displaying this warning = -wncf)

A non-const member function was called for a const object. (This is an error, but was reduced to a warning to give existing programs a chance to work.)

Default = displayed

**Non-existent segment 'segment' in SEGMENTS section of .DEF file** *Linker message*

You specified a segment name in the SEGMENTS section of the .DEF file which doesn't exist in any of the object files or library files included in the link.

**Non-portable pointer comparison** *Compiler message*

(Command-line equivalent for displaying this warning = -wcpt)

Your source file compared a pointer to a non-pointer other than the constant 0. You should use a cast to suppress this warning if the comparison is proper.

Default = displayed

**Non-portable pointer conversion** *Compiler message*

(Command-line equivalent for controlling display = -wrpt)

An implicit conversion between a pointer and an integral type is required, but the types are not the same size. This can't be done without an explicit cast. This conversion might not make any sense, so be sure this is what you want to do.

**Non-virtual function 'function' declared pure** *Compiler message*

Only virtual functions can be declared pure, because derived classes must be able to override them.

**Non-volatile function 'function' called for volatile object** *Compiler message*

In C++, a class member function was called for a volatile object of the class type, but the function was not declared with volatile following the function header. Only a volatile member function can be called for a volatile object.

For example, if you have

```
class c
{
public:
    f() volatile;
    g();
};
volatile c vcvar;
```

it is legal to call `vcvar.f()`, but not to call `vcvar.g()`.

### Nonportable pointer conversion

*Compiler message*

(Command-line equivalent for displaying this warning = -wrpt)

A nonzero integral value is used in a context where a pointer is needed or where an integral value is needed; the sizes of the integral type and pointer are the same. Use an explicit cast if this is what you really meant to do.

Default = displayed

### Nonresident Name Table is greater than 64K

*Linker message*

Industry standards require that nonresident name tables be no larger than 64K in size. If you encounter this message and do not require the nonresident name table to remain intact, you can discard it by linking with the **/Gn** linker option.

If you do require that the nonresident name table remain intact, you must restructure your program, so that names are shorter or explicitly use the resident name table for a portion of the defines.

### Nontype template argument must be of scalar type

*Compiler message*

A nontype formal template argument must have scalar type; it can have an integral, enumeration, or pointer type.

### Not a valid expression format type

*Compiler message*

Invalid format specifier following expression in the debug evaluate or watch window. A valid format specifier is an optional repeat value followed by a format character (c, d, f[n], h, x, m, p, r, or s).

### Not a Windows format EXE file.

*Resource Linker message*

The executable file you tried to bind resources to is not a valid Windows or Win32 executable file.

### Not all breakpoints were valid

*IDE Debugger message*

You set breakpoints in your program but they were not all valid. Check the breakpoint view to see which breakpoints were invalid.

### Not an allowed type

*Compiler message*

Your source file declared some sort of forbidden type; for example, a function returning a function or array.

### Not enough memory

*MAKE message*

All of your working storage has been exhausted.

### Not enough memory for command-line buffer

*Librarian message*

This error occurs when the librarian runs out of memory.

**Not enough memory to run application**                            *Linker message*

There is not enough memory to run the linker. Try closing one or more applications, then run the linker again.

**Null pointer assignment**                                         *Run-time message*

When a small or medium memory model program exits, a check is made to determine if the contents of the first few bytes within the program's data segment have changed.

These bytes would never be altered by a working program. If they have been changed, this message is displayed to inform you that (most likely) a value was stored to an uninitialized pointer.

The program might appear to work properly in all other respects; however, this is a serious bug which should be attended to immediately. Failure to correct an uninitialized pointer can lead to unpredictable behavior (including locking the computer up in the large, compact, and huge memory models).

You can use the integrated debugger to track down null pointers.

**Numeric constant too large**                                      *Compiler message*

String and character escape sequences larger than hexadecimal or octal 77 can't be generated. Two-byte character constants can be specified by using a second backslash.

For example,

```
\\
```

represents a two-byte constant.

A numeric literal following an escape sequence should be broken up like this:

```
printf("" "12345");
```

This prints a carriage return followed by 12345.

**Object module 'filename' is invalid**                             *Librarian message*

The librarian could not understand the header record of the object module being added to the library.

The librarian assumes that it is an invalid module.

**Objects of type 'type' cannot be initialized with {}**            *Compiler message*

Ordinary C structures can be initialized with a set of values inside braces.

C++ classes can only be initialized with constructors if the class has constructors, private members, functions, or base classes that are virtual.

**Old debug information in module 'module' will be ignored**        *Linker message*

Debug information in the OBJ is incompatible with this linker, and will be ignored.

**Only <<KEEP or <<NOKEEP**                                         *MAKE message*

You specified something besides KEEP or NOKEEP when closing a temporary inline file.

**Only member functions may be 'const' or 'volatile'**              *Compiler message*

Something other than a class member function has been declared const or volatile.

**Only one of a set of overloaded functions can be "C"**

C++ functions are by default overloaded, and the compiler assigns a new name to each function.

If you wish to override the compiler's assigning a new name by declaring the function extern "C", you can do this for only one of a set of functions with the same name. (Otherwise the linker would find more than one global function with the same name.)

**Operand of 'delete' must be non-const pointer** *Compiler message*

It is illegal to delete a variable that is not a pointer. It is also illegal to delete a pointer to a constant.

For example:

```
const int x=10;
  const int * a = &x;
  int * const b = new int;
  int &c = *b;
  delete a;    //illegal - deleting pointer to constant
  delete b;    //legal
  delete c;    //illegal - operand not of pointer type
                  //should use 'delete&c' instead
```

**operator -> must return a pointer or a class** *Compiler message*

The C++ operator -> function must be declared to either return a class or a pointer to a class (or struct or union). In either case, it must be something to which the -> operator can be applied.

**operator delete must return void** *Compiler messages*

This C++ overloaded operator delete was declared in some other way.

Declare the operator delete with one of the following:

**1** A single void* parameter, or

**2** A second parameter of type size_t

If you use the second version, it will be used in preference to the first version.

The global operator delete can only be declared using the single-parameter form.

**Operator must be declared as function** *Compiler message*

An overloaded operator was declared with something other than function type.

For example:

```
class A
{
   A& operator +;    ..note missing parenthesis
};
```

In the example, the function operator '()' is missing, so the operator does not have function type and generates this error.

**'operator' must be declared with one or no parameters** *Compiler message*

When operator ++ or operator—-is declared as a member function, it must be declared to take either:

- No parameters (for the prefix version of the operator), or
- One parameter of type int (for the postfix version)

**'operator' must be declared with one or two parameters**                                          *Compiler message*

When operator ++ or operator––is declared as a non-member function, it must be declared to take either:

- one parameter (for the prefix version of the operator), or
- two parameters (for the postfix version)

**operator new must have an initial parameter of type size_t**                                      *Compiler messages*

Operator new can be declared with an arbitrary number of parameters. It must always have at least one, the amount of space to allocate.

**Operator new must return an object of type void \***

**Operator new[] must return an object of type void \***                                             *Compiler messages*

This C++ overloaded operator new was declared in some other way.

**Operators may not have default argument values**                                                  *Compiler message*

It is illegal for overloaded operators to have default argument values.

**Optimizer: Error Reading Input File**                                                             *Linker message*

The hardware error "read failed" occurred.

**Optimizer: Error Writing Output File**                                                            *Linker message*

The disk is either full, or the hardware error "write failed" occurred.

**Optimizer: File is not new exe (NE format), optimization request ignored**                        *Linker message*

The 16-bit /O*x* linker switches are valid for only 16-bit Windows and DPMI executables.

**Optimizer: Out of Memory**                                                                        *Linker message*

Not enough memory available to perform optimizations.

**OS exception number not specified**                                                               *IDE Debugger message*

You tried to add an OS exception breakpoint using the IDE Debugger. You must include an OS exception number if you want to add a breakpoint when a particular OS exception occurs. Select one of the exceptions in the list box next to the Exception # field or enter a user-defined exception number.

**Out of memory**                                                                                   *Librarian message*

For any number of reasons, the librarian or the C++ IDE ran out of memory while building the library. For many specific cases, a more detailed message is reported. Close one or more applications.

**Out of memory**                                                                                   *Compiler message*

The total working storage is exhausted.

This error can occur under the following circumstances:

Not enough virtual memory is available for compiling a particular file. In this case, shut down any other concurrent applications. You may also try to reconfigure your machine for more available virtual memory, or break up the source file being compiled into smaller separate components. You can also compile the file on a system with more available RAM.

The compiler has encountered an exceedingly complex or long expression at the line indicated and has insufficient reserves to parse it. Break the expression down into separate statements.

**Out of memory**                                                                    *Linker message*

The linker has run out of dynamically allocated memory needed during the link process. The total working storage is exhausted.

This error is a catchall for running into a limit on memory usage. This usually means that too many modules, externals, groups, or segments have been defined by the object files being linked together.

Solutions:

- You can try reducing size of active RAM disks and/or disk caches.
- Close one or more applications to free memory.

**Out of memory!**                                                          *Resource Linker message*

Not enough memory is available for compiling a particular file. In this case, shut down any other concurrent applications. You may also try to re-configure your machine for more available memory, or break up the source file being compiled into smaller separate components. You can also compile the file on a system with more available RAM.

**Out of memory at library 'library': extended dictionaries ignored**              *Linker message*

The linker has run out of dynamically allocated memory needed during the link process. The total working storage is exhausted. This error is a catchall for running into a limit on memory usage.

Solutions:

- You can try reducing size of active RAM disks and/or disk caches.
- Close one or more applications to free up memory.

**Out of memory creating extended dictionary**                                 *Librarian message*

The librarian ran out of memory while creating an extended dictionary for a library. The library is created but will not have an extended dictionary.

**Out of memory for block 'block'**                                                *Linker message*

The linker ran out of memory. Try reducing the size of disk caches and/or RAM drives.

**Out of memory reading LE/LIDATA record from object module**                  *Librarian message*

The librarian is attempting to read a record of data from the object module, but it cannot get a large enough block of memory. If the module being added has a large data segment or segments, try adding this module before other modules.

**Out of space allocating per module debug struct**                            *Librarian message*

The librarian ran out of memory while allocating space for the debug information associated with a particular object module. Try removing debugging information from the modules being added to the library to resolve the problem.

**Output device is full**                                                      *Librarian message*

The output device is full. This error usually means that there is no space left on the disk.

**Overlays generated and no overlay manager included**                     *Linker message*

This warning is issued if overlays are created but the symbol _ _OVRTRAP_ _ is not defined in any of the object modules or libraries linked in. The standard overlay library (OVERLAY.LIB) defines this symbol.

**Overlays ignored in new executable image**                     *Linker message*

This error occurs if you attempt to link a Windows program with the **/o** option on.

Windows executables can't be overlaid, although, with discardable code segments, you should be able to achieve a similar effect.

**Overlays only supported in medium, large, and huge memory models**                     *Compiler message*

Only programs using the medium, large, or huge memory models can be overlaid.

**Overload is now unnecessary and obsolete**                     *Compiler message*

(Command-line equivalent for displaying this warning = -wovl)

Early versions of C++ required the reserved word "overload" to mark overloaded function names.

C++ now uses a "type-safe linkage" scheme, whereby all functions are assumed overloaded unless marked otherwise.

The use of "overload" should be discontinued.

Default = displayed

**Overloadable operator expected**                     *Compiler message*

Almost all C++ operators can be overloaded. These are the only ones that can't be overloaded:

- the field-selection dot (**.**)
- dot-star (**.** *****)
- double colon (**: :**)
- conditional expression (**?** **:**)

The preprocessor operators (# and ##) are not C or C++ language operators and thus can't be overloaded.

Other non-operator punctuation, such as semicolon (;), can't be overloaded.

**Overloaded 'function name' ambiguous in this context**                     *Compiler message*

The only time an overloaded function name can be used or assigned without actually calling the function is when a variable or parameter of the correct function pointer type is initialized or assigned the address of the overload function.

In this case, an overloaded function name has been used in some other context, for example, the following code will generate this error:

```
class A{
   A(){myex;}          //calling the function
   void myex(int) {}   //or taking its address?
   void myex(float){}
};
```

### Overloaded function resolution not supported
*Compiler message*

In integrated debugger expression evaluation, resolution of overloaded functions or operators is not supported, not even to take an address.

### Overloaded prefix operator 'operator' used as a postfix operator
*Compiler message*

(Command-line equivalent for displaying this warning = -wpre)

With the latest C++ specification, it is now possible to overload both the prefix and postfix versions of the ++ and -- operators.

Whenever the prefix operator is overloaded, but is used in a postfix context, the compiler uses the prefix operator and issues this warning. This allows older code to compile.

Default = not displayed

### Parameter 'number' missing name
*Compiler message*

In a function definition header, this parameter consisted only of a type specifier 'number' with no parameter name.

This is not legal in C. (It is allowed in C++, but there's no way to refer to the parameter in the function.)

### Parameter 'parameter' is never used
*Compiler message*

(Command-line equivalent for displaying this warning = -wpar)

The named parameter, declared in the function, was never used in the body of the function. This might or might not be an error and is often caused by misspelling the parameter. This warning can also occur if the identifier is redeclared as an automatic (local) variable in the body of the function.

The parameter is masked by the automatic variable and remains unused.

Default = displayed

### Parameter names are used only with a function body
*Compiler message*

When declaring a function (not defining it with a function body), you must use either empty parentheses or a function prototype.

A list of parameter names only is not allowed.

Example declarations

```
int func();              /* declaration without prototype -- OK */
int func(int, int);      /* declaration with prototype -- OK */
int func(int i, int j);  /* parameter names in prototype -- OK */
int func(i, j);          /* parameter names only -- ILLEGAL */
```

### Pass Count checked but no value entered
*IDE Debugger message*

You checked the Pass Count check box, but forgot to provide a pass count. You need to specify a valid pass count.

### 'path' - path is too long
*Librarian message*

This error occurs when the length of any of the library file or module file's 'path' is greater then 64.

**Pointer to structure required on left side of -> or ->\***  *Compiler message*

Nothing but a pointer is allowed on the left side of the arrow (->) in C or C++.

In C++ a -> operator is allowed.

**Possible reference to undefined extern xxxx::i**  *Linker message*

Static data member has been declared but not defined in application.

This warning occurs by itself (i.e., without an accompanying 'undefined symbol' error) whenever code declares a static data member that is not defined anywhere, and then that symbol is not actually referenced (it is then 'idle' code).

**Possible unresolved external 'symbol' referenced from module 'module'**  *Linker message*

This warning appears only for static data members of classes that have been declared but not defined.

**Possible use of 'identifier' before definition**  *Compiler message*

(Command-line equivalent for displaying this warning = -wdef)

Your source file used the variable 'identifier' in an expression before it was assigned a value. The compiler uses a simple scan of the program to determine this condition.

If the use of a variable occurs physically before any assignment, this warning will be generated. Of course, the actual flow of the program can assign the value before the program uses it.

Default = not displayed

**Possibly incorrect assignment**  *Compiler message*

(Command-line equivalent for displaying this warning = -wpia)

This warning is generated when the compiler encounters an assignment operator as the main operator of a conditional expression (part of an **if**, **while**, or **do-while** statement).

This is usually a typographical error for the equality operator.

If you want to suppress this warning, enclose the assignment in parentheses and compare the whole thing to zero explicitly.

For example, this code

```
if (a = b) ...
```

should be rewritten as

```
if ((a = b) != 0) ...
```

Default = displayed

**Printf/Scanf floating-point formats not linked**  *Run-time message*

Floating-point formats contain formatting information that is used to manipulate floating-point numbers in certain run-time library functions, such as *scanf()* and *atof()*.

Typically, you should avoid linking the floating-point formats (which take up about 1K) unless they are required by your application. However, you must explicitly link the floating-point formats for programs that manipulate fields in a limited and specific way.

Refer to the following list of potential causes (listed from most common to least common) to determine how to resolve this error:

**Cause**: Floating point set to None. You set the floating-point option to None when it should be set to either Fast or Normal.

**Fix**: Set Floating Point to Fast or Normal.

**Cause**: Either the compiler is over-optimizing or the floating-point formats really do need to be linked. You need the floating-point formats if your program manipulates floats in a limited and specific way. Under certain conditions, the compiler will ignore floating-point usage in *scanf()*. For example, this may occur when trying to read data into a float variable that is part of an array contained in a structure.

**Fix**: Add the following code to one source module:

```
extern _floatconvert;
#pragma extref _floatconvert
```

**Cause**: You forgot to put the address operator & on the scanf variable expression. For example:

```
float foo;
scanf("%f", foo);
```

**Fix**: Change the code so the & operator is used where needed. For example, change the above code to the following:

```
float foo;
scanf("%f", &foo);
```

### Process Created: 'processname'                                    *IDE Debugger message*

The process specified in the message has been created.

### Process 'processname' (0x%X) is already being debugged          *IDE Debugger message*

You tried to attach to a process that is already being debugged.

### Process 'processname' (0x%X) is the IDE                          *IDE Debugger message*

You tried to attach to the IDE. This is not allowed. Specify another process.

### Process Stopped: 'processname'                                    *IDE Debugger message*

The process specified in the message was stopped.

### Process terminated: 'programname'                                 *IDE Debugger message*

The specified process has been terminated.

### Program entry point may not reside in an overlay                       *Linker message*

Although almost all of an application can be overlaid, the initial starting address cannot reside in an overlay. This error usually means that an attempt was made to overlay the initialization module C0x.OBJ, for instance, by specifying the **/o** option before the startup module.

### Public 'symbol' in module 'module1' clashes with prior module 'module2'     *Librarian message*

A public symbol can only appear once in a library file. A module, which is being added to the library, contains a public 'symbol' that is already in a module of the library and cannot be added.

The command-line message reports the module2 name.

**Public symbol 'symbol' defined in both module 'module1' and 'module2'** *Linker message*

There is a conflict between two public symbols. This usually means that a symbol is defined in two modules.

- An error occurs if both are encountered in the .OBJ file(s), because TLINK doesn't know which is valid.
- A warning results if TLINK finds one of the duplicated symbols in a library and finds the other in an .OBJ file; in this case, TLINK uses the one in the .OBJ file.

**Pure virtual function called** *Run-time message*

This is a run-time error. It is generated if the body of a pure virtual function was never generated and somehow the compiler tried to call it.

**Qualifier 'identifier' is not a class or namespace name** *Compiler message*

The C++ qualifier in the construction qual::identifier is not the name of a struct or class.

**Record kind 'num' found, expected theadr or lheadr in module 'filename'** *Librarian message*

The librarian could not understand the header record of the object module being added to the library and has assumed that it is an invalid module.

**Record length 'len' exceeds available buffer in module 'module'** *Librarian message*

This error occurs when the record length 'len' exceeds the available buffer to load the buffer in module 'module'.

This occurs when the librarian runs out of dynamic memory.

**Record type 'type' found, expected theadr or lheadr in 'module'** *Librarian message*

The librarian encountered an unexpected type instead of the expected THEADR or LHEADER record in the specified module.

**Recursive template function: "' instantiated "** *Compiler message*

The compiler has detected a recursive template function instance. For example:

```
template<class T> void f(T x)
{
    f((T*)0);   // recursive template function!
}


void main()
{
    f(0);
}
```

The compiler will issue one message per each nesting of the recursive instantiation, so it is usually quite obvious where the recursion has occurred. To fix a recursive template, either change the dependencies, or provide a specialized version that will stop the recursion. For example, adding the following function definition to the above program will remove the endless recursion:

```
void f(int **)
{
}
```

**Redefinition of 'macro' is not identical** *Compiler message*

(Command-line equivalent for displaying this warning = -wdup)

Your source file redefined the macro 'ident' using text that was not exactly the same as the first definition of the macro. The new text replaces the old.

Default = displayed

### Redefinition of target 'filename'

The named file occurs on the left side of more than one explicit rule.

### Reference initialized with 'type1', needs lvalue of type 'type2'
*Compiler message*

A reference variable that is not declared constant must be initialized with an lvalue of the appropriate type. In this case, the initializer either wasn't an lvalue, or its type didn't match the reference being initialized.

### Reference member 'member' initialized with a non-reference parameter
*Compiler message*

An attempt has been made to bind a reference member to a constructor parameter. Since the parameter will cease to exist the moment the constructor returns to its caller, this will not work correctly.

### Reference member 'member' is not initialized
*Compiler message*

References must always be initialized, in the constructor for the class. A class member of reference type must have an initializer provided in all constructors for that class.

This means you can't depend on the compiler to generate constructors for such a class, because it has no way of knowing how to initialize the references.

### Reference member 'member' needs a temporary for initialization
*Compiler message*

You provided an initial value for a reference type that was not an lvalue of the referenced type.

This requires the compiler to create a temporary for the initialization. Because there is no obvious place to store this temporary, the initialization is illegal.

### Register allocation failure
*Compiler message*

This is a compiler error. An expression on the indicated line of the source file was so complicated that the code generator could not generate code for it.

Simplify the expression. If this does not solve the problem, avoid the expression. Notify Borland if an expression can consistently reproduce this error.

### Relocation item exceeds 1 Meg DOS limit
*Linker message*

The DOS executable file format doesn't support relocation items for locations exceeding 1 MB. Although DOS could never load an image this big, DOS extenders can, and thus TLINK supports generating images greater than DOS could load. Even if the image is loaded with a DOS extender, the DOS executable file format is limited to describing relocation items in the first 1MB of the image.

### Relocation offset overflow
*Linker message*

This error only occurs for 32-bit object modules and indicates a relocation (segment fixup) offset greater than the DOS limit of 64K.

### Relocation table overflow
*Linker message*

This error only occurs for 32-bit object modules. The file being linked contains more base fixups than the standard DOS relocation table can hold (base fixups are created mostly by calls to far functions).

**Repeat count needs an lvalue** *Compiler message*

The expression before the comma (,) in the Watch or Evaluate window must be an accessible region of storage. For example, expressions like this one are not valid:

```
i++,10d
x = y, 10m
```

**Reporting error.** *Resource Linker message*

The resource linker encountered a problem while trying to report an error.

**Resetting** *IDE Debugger message*

The process is being reset to its initial condition.

**Resident Name Table is greater than 64K** *Linker message*

Exports too great for 64K limit. When this error is encountered, break exports up or make some exported by name and some by ordinal number. Another possible fix is to have the linker transfer the resident name table to the nonresident name table and discard the nonresident name table. (TLINK options **/Gr /Gn**, IDE options on 16-bit linker page.)

**Resource binding failed** *Linker message*

While you were linking from the command line, RLINK.EXE reported an error when binding resources to your image.

**Resource format not recognized in file.** *Resource Linker message*

The format of a .RES file that you are attempting to use contains a resource with an unknown format. This is normally due to a corrupt resource file. Make sure that you are binding a legitimate resource file, and rebuild the .RES file, if necessary.

**Restarting compile using assembly** *Compiler message*

The compiler encountered an asm with no accompanying or #pragma inline statement. The compile restarts using assembly language capabilities.

**Results are safe in file 'filename'** *Librarian message*

The librarian has successfully built the library into a temporary file, but it cannot rename the file to the desired library name. The temporary file will not be removed (so that the library can be preserved).

**RTTI not available for expression evaluation** *Compiler message*

Expressions requiring RTTI are not supported by the expression evaluator in the integrated debugger. This error message is only issued by the expression evaluator (if you try to Inspect, Watch, or Evaluate), not by the compiler.

**Rule line too long** *MAKE message*

An implicit or explicit rule was longer than 4,096 characters.

**Running** *IDE Debugger message*

The process is running.

**Segment 'segment' exceeds 64K** *Linker message*

Industry standards require that segments be no larger than 64K in size. If you encounter this message, the segment in question has exceeded this limit.

### Segment 'segment' is in two groups: 'group1' and 'group2'
*Linker message*

The linker found conflicting claims by the two named groups. Usually, this happens only in assembly language programs. It means that two modules assigned the segment to two different groups.

### Segment 'segment' relocation data exceeds 64K
*Linker message*

16-bit Windows programs have a limit of 64K of relocation data per segment. It is unlikely that this limit will ever be exceeded, but can be if a particular module contains extremely large jump tables or virtual tables in the code segment itself. If you get this message, try breaking the associated code module into two pieces, as this may reduce the total number of relocations per segment to below 64K.

### Segment alignment factor too small
*Linker message*

Segment alignment factor is too small to allow access to segments. If you encounter this error, use the /A linker option and try a larger alignment factor, like 1024. The /A option defaults to 512.

### Segment too large for segment table
*Linker message*

Industry standards require that segments be no larger than 64K in size. If you encounter this message, the segment in question has exceeded this limit.

### Self relative fixup overflowed in module 'module'
*Linker message*

This message appears if a self-relative reference (a call or a jump) is made from one physical segment to another. This often happens when employing assembler code, but can occur if you use the segment-naming options in the compiler. If the reference is from one code segment to another, you are safe. If, however, the reference is from a code segment to a data segment, you have probably made a mistake in some assembler code.

You can suppress this warning from the Linker | Warnings page of the Project options dialog box or with the /w-srf command-line option.

### Side effects are not allowed
*Compiler message*

Side effects such as assignments, ++, or -- are not allowed in the debugger watch window. A common error is to use x = y (not allowed) instead of x == y to test the equality of x and y.

### Size of 'identifier' is unknown or zero
*Compiler message*

This identifier was used in a context where its size was needed.

A struct tag might only be declared (the struct not defined yet), or an extern array might be declared without a size. It's illegal then to have some references to such an item (like sizeof) or to dereference a pointer to this type. Rearrange your declaration so that the size of 'identifier' is available.

### Size of the type 'identifier' is unknown or zero
*Compiler message*

This type was used in a context where its size was needed. For example, a struct tag might only be declared (the struct not defined yet).

It's illegal then to have some references to such an item (like sizeof) or to dereference a pointer to this type. Rearrange your declarations so that the size of this type is available.

### Size of the type is unknown or zero
*Compiler message*

This error message indicates that an array of unspecified dimension nested within another structure is initialized and the -A (ANSI) switch is on. For example:

```
        struct
        {
                char a[];            //Size of 'a' is unknown or zero
        }
                b = { "hello" }; //Size of the type is
                                     //unknown or zero
```

### sizeof may not be applied to a bit field
*Compiler message*

sizeof returns the size of a data object in bytes, which does not apply to a bit field.

### sizeof may not be applied to a function
*Compiler message*

sizeof can be applied only to data objects, not functions.

You can request the size of a pointer to a function.

### Specialization after first use of template
*Compiler message*

A new ANSI C++ rule requires that a specialization for a function template be declared before its first use. This error message is only issued when the ANSI conformance option (-A) is active.

### 'specifier' has already been included
*Compiler message*

This type specifier occurs more than once in this declaration.

Delete or change one of the occurrences.

### Stack overflow
*Run-time message*

This error is reported when you compile a function with the Test Stack Overflow option on, but there is not enough stack space to allocate the function's local variables.

This error can also be caused by the following:

* Infinite recursion
* An assembly language procedure that does not maintain the stack project
* A large array in a function

### Stack size is less than 1400h. It has been reset to 1400h
*Linker message*

The minimum allowable stack size is 1400h. When the linker detects that the stack size is less than this value, the linker automatically resets the size to 1400h and issues this message.

To eliminate this message, you need to change the STACKSIZE specification in the .DEF file to 1400h or greater.

The size of the stack added to the size of the Automatic Data Segment (ADS) must not exceed 64K. If it does, you won't get any linker errors regarding stack size or the message "Automatic data segment exceeds 64K." However, the Windows loader will not be able to load the .EXE at run time.

### STACK/HEAP commit 'size' greater than reserve 'size'
*Linker message*

The heap or stack commit size has to be less than or equal to the stack or heap reserve size. Change the stack and heap reserve or commit sizes by changing the 32-bit linker values in the IDE or by changing HEAPSIZE and STACKSIZE in the module definition file.

### statement missing (
*Compiler message*

In a do, for, if, switch, or while statement, the compiler found no left parenthesis after the while keyword or test expression.

**statement missing )**  *Compiler message*

In a do, for, if, switch, or while statement, the compiler found no right parenthesis after the while keyword or test expression.

**Statement missing ;**  *Compiler message*

The compiler encountered an expression statement without a semicolon following it.

**Stopping**  *IDE Debugger message*

The process is stopping.

**Storage class 'storage class' is not allowed here**  *Compiler message*

The given storage class is not allowed here.

Probably two storage classes were specified, and only one can be given.

**String literal not allowed in this context**  *Compiler message*

This error message is issued by the evaluator when a string literal appears in a context other than a function call.

**String type not allowed with this operand**  *MAKE message*

You tried to use an operand that is not allowed for comparing string types. Valid operands are ==, !=, <, >, <=, and >=.

**Structure packing size has changed**  *Compiler message*

This warning message is issued when the structure alignment is different after including a file than it was before including that file. The intention is to warn you about cases where an include file changes structure packing, but by mistake doesn't restore the original setting at the end. If this is intentional, you can give a #pragma nopackwarning directive at the end of an include file to disable the warning for this file.

The warning can be disabled altogether by #pragma warn -pck.

**Structure passed by value**  *Compiler message*

(Command-line equivalent for displaying this warning = -wstv)

This warning is generated any time a structure is passed by value as an argument. It is a frequent programming mistake to leave an address-of operator (&) off a structure when passing it as an argument. Because structures can be passed by value, this omission is acceptable. This warning provides a way for the compiler to warn you of this mistake.

Default = not displayed

**Structure required on left side of . or .***  *Compiler message*

The left side of a dot (.) operator (or C++ dot-star operator, .*) must evaluate to a structure type. In this case it did not.

This error can occur when you create an instance of a class using empty parentheses, and then try to access a member of that 'object'.

**Structure size too large**  *Compiler message*

Your source file declared a structure larger than 64K.

**Stub program exceeds 64K**  *Linker message*

This errors occurs if a DOS stub program written for a Windows application exceeds 64K.

Stub programs are specified via the STUB module definition file statement.

The linker only supports stub programs of 64K or smaller.

### Style of function definition is now obsolete

*Compiler message*

(Command-line equivalent for displaying this warning = -wofp)

In C++, this old C style of function definition is illegal:

```
int func(p1, p2) int p1, p2; { /* ... */ }
```

This practice might not be allowed by other C++ compilers.

Default = displayed

### Superfluous & with function

*Compiler message*

(Command-line equivalent for displaying this warning = -wamp)

An address-of operator (&) is not needed with function name; any such operators are discarded.

Default = not displayed

### Suspicious pointer conversion

*Compiler message*

(Command-line equivalent for displaying this warning = -wsus)

The compiler encountered some conversion of a pointer that caused the pointer to point to a different type.

You should use a cast to suppress this warning if the conversion is proper.

A common cause of this warning is when the C compiler converts a function pointer of one type to another (the C++ compiler generates an error when asked to do that). It can be suppressed by doing a typecast. Here is a common occurrence of it for Window programmers:

```
#define STRICT
#include <windows.h>

LPARAM _export WndProc( HWND , UINT , WPARAM , LPARAM );

test() {
    WNDCLASS wc;
    wc.lpfnWndProc = WndProc;   //warning
}
```

It is suppressed by making the assignment to lpfnWndProc as follows:

```
wc.lpfnWndProc = ( WNDPROC ) WndProc;
```

Default = displayed

### Switch selection expression must be of integral type

*Compiler message*

The selection expression in parentheses in a switch statement must evaluate to an integral type (char, short, int, long, enum). You might be able to use an explicit cast to satisfy this requirement.

**'symbol' conflicts with module 'module'**                                          *Linker message*

> This indicates an inconsistency in the definition of 'symbol.' It means that either the linker found one virtual function and one common definition with the same name.

**'symbol' defined in module 'module' is duplicated in module 'module'**               *Linker message*

> This message results from a conflict between two symbols (either public or communal).

> It usually means that a symbol is defined in two modules. An error occurs if both are encountered in the .OBJ file(s), because the linker doesn't know which is valid.

> You can suppress this warning from the Linker | Warnings page of the Project options dialog box or with the **/w-dup** command-line option.

**'symbol' defined in module 'module1' is duplicated in module 'module2'**             *Linker message*

> There is a conflict between two symbols (either public or communal). This usually means that a symbol is defined in more than one object or library file.

> The linker issues a warning because the symbol exists in more than one object file. The linker will use the first instance of the symbol that is encountered.

> You can suppress this warning from the Linker | Warnings page of the Project options dialog box or with the **/d** (16-bit) or **/w-dpl** (32-bit) command-line option.

**T3 and T7 fixups not allowed (module 'module')**                                     *Linker message*

> The linker encountered an object file with an incompatible .OBJ file format.

> This error generally occurs due to an incompatible .OBJ file format. If you're linking .OBJ files compiled using another compiler, these files may be incompatible with TLINK32. You'll need to recompile all modules using one of the Borland C++ compilers.

> This can also occur if the machine was rebooted during a compile, or if a compiler did not delete its output object file when Ctrl+Break was pressed. Recompile.

> If the error persists, call Borland Technical Support.

**Table limit exceeded**                                                                *Linker message*

> This message results from one of the linker's internal tables overflowing. This usually means that the programs being linked have exceeded the linker's capacity for public symbols, external symbols, or logical segment definitions.

> Each instance of a distinct segment name in an object file counts as a logical segment; if two object files define this segment, then this results in two logical segments.

> When the table limit is exceeded, try linking with extended dictionaries.

**Target index of FIXUP is 0 in Module 'module'**                                       *Linker message*

> This is a translator error.

**Template argument must be a constant expression**                                     *Compiler message*

> A non-type template class argument must be a constant expression of the appropriate type.

> This includes constant integral expressions and addresses of objects or functions with external linkage or members.

**Template class nesting too deep: 'class'** *Compiler message*

The compiler imposes a certain limit on the level of template class nesting. This limit is usually only exceeded through a recursive template class dependency.

When this nesting limit is exceeded, the compiler issues this error message for all of the nested template classes. This usually makes it easy to spot the recursion.

This error message is always followed by the fatal error "Out of memory".

**Template function argument 'argument' not used in argument types** *Compiler message*

The given argument was not used in the argument list of the function.

The argument list of a template function must use all of the template formal arguments; otherwise, there is no way to generate a template function instance based on actual argument types.

**Template functions may only have 'type-arguments'** *Compiler message*

A function template was declared with a non-type argument. This is not allowed with a template function, as there is no way to specify the value when calling it.

**Templates and overloaded operators cannot have C linkage** *Compiler message*

You tried to use a linkage specification with a template or overloaded operator. The most common cause for this error message is having the declaration wrapped in an extern "C" { linkage specification.

**Templates can only be declared at file level** *Compiler message*

Templates cannot be declared inside classes or functions. They are only allowed in the global scope, or file level.

For example:

```
template <class T, class U>
void foo(Ta,Tb)
{
   ⋮
}
           // error U is not used
```

**Templates must be classes or functions** *Compiler message*

The declaration in a template declaration must specify either a class type or a function.

**Templates not supported** *Compiler message*

An error has occurred while using the command-line utility H2ASH. See the online file "tsm_util.txt" for further information about this utility.

**Temporary used for parameter '???'** *Compiler message*

In C++, a variable or parameter of reference type must be assigned a reference to an object of the same type. If the types do not match, the actual value is assigned to a temporary of the correct type, and the address of the temporary is assigned to the reference variable or parameter.

The warning means that the reference variable or parameter does not refer to what you expect, but to a temporary variable, otherwise unused.

In the following example, function *f* requires a reference to an int, and *c* is a char:

```
f(int &amp);
char c;
f(c);
```

Instead of calling *f* with the address of *c*, the compiler generates code equivalent to the C++ source code:

```
int X = c, f(X);
```

**Temporary used for parameter 'parameter'**

**Temporary used for parameter 'parameter' in call to 'function'**

**Temporary used for parameter 'number'**

**Temporary used for parameter 'number' in call to 'function'**                    *Compiler messages*

Command-line equivalent for displaying this warning = -wlvc)

In C++, a variable or parameter of reference type must be assigned a reference to an object of the same type.

If the types do not match, the actual value is assigned to a temporary of the correct type, and the address of the temporary is assigned to the reference variable or parameter.

The warning means that the reference variable or parameter does not refer to what you expect, but to a temporary variable, otherwise unused.

Default = displayed

**Temporary used for parameter 2 in call to '???'**                    *Compiler message*

In C++, a variable or parameter of reference type must be assigned a reference to an object of the same type. If the types do not match, the actual value is assigned to a temporary of the correct type, and the address of the temporary is assigned to the reference variable or parameter.

The warning means that the reference variable or parameter does not refer to what you expect, but to a temporary variable, otherwise unused.

In the following example, function *f* requires a reference to an int, and *c* is a char:

```
f(int &amp);
char c;
f(c);
```

Instead of calling f with the address of c, the compiler generates code equivalent to the C++ source code:

```
int X = c, f(X);
```

**Temporary used to initialize 'identifier'**                    *Compiler message*

(Command-line equivalent for displaying this warning = -wlin)

In C++, a variable or parameter of reference type must be assigned a reference to an object of the same type.

If the types do not match, the actual value is assigned to a temporary of the correct type, and the address of the temporary is assigned to the reference variable or parameter.

The warning means that the reference variable or parameter does not refer to what you expect, but to a temporary variable, otherwise unused.

Default = displayed

**Terminated by user** *Linker message*

You cancelled the link (that is, a Ctrl+Break was detected).

**Terminating** *IDE Debugger message*

The process is terminating.

**The '...' handler must be last** *Compiler message*

In a list of catch handlers, if the '...' handler is present, it must be the last handler in the list (i.e., it can not be followed by any more catch handlers).

**The combinations '+"' or '"+' are not allowed** *Librarian message*

It is not legal to add and extract an object module from a library in one action.

**The constant member 'identifier' is not initialized** *Compiler message*

(Command-line equivalent for displaying this warning = -wnci)

This C++ class contains a constant member 'member' that doesn't have an initialization.

Note that constant members can be initialized only; they can't be assigned to.

Default = displayed

**The constructor 'constructor' is not allowed** *Compiler message*

Constructors of the form

```
X::(X)
```

are not allowed.

This is the correct way to write a copy constructor:

```
X::(const X&).
```

**The expression cannot be modified.** *IDE Debugger message*

This is an integrated debugger error. You entered an expression in the Evaluator dialog box and clicked on Modify but the expression cannot be modified.

**The expression you entered could not be evaluated.** *IDE Debugger message*

This is an integrated debugger error. The integrated debugger could not interpret the expression you entered in the Evaluator dialog box.

**The function 'function' is not available** *Compiler message*

You tried to call a function that is known to the evaluator, but which was not present in the program being debugged-for example, an inline function.

**The value for 'identifier' is not within the range of an int** *Compiler message*

All enumerators must have values that can be represented as an integer.

You have attempted to assign a value that is out of the range of an integer.

If you need a constant of this value, use a const integer.

**There is no code for 'file', line 'linenumber'** *IDE Debugger message*

You tried to view the disassembly for the given line of source code. The specified line of the file has no code associated with it.

**There is no expression to evaluate** *IDE Debugger message*

This is an integrated debugger error. You forgot to enter an expression in the Evaluator dialog box and no program is loaded.

**There is no expression to evaluate and no process is loaded** *IDE Debugger message*

This is an integrated debugger error. You forgot to enter an expression in the Evaluator dialog box and no program is loaded.

**'this' can only be used within a member function** *Compiler message*

In C++, "this" is a reserved word that can be used only within class member functions.

**This operation not supported for 16 bit executables** *IDE Debugger message*

You tried to use a command (such as Reset or Pause) in the integrated debugger while the project was set to produce a 16-bit executable. The integrated debugger does not support 16-bit executables except to run or terminate them.

**THREAD fixup found in module 'module'** *Linker message*

The linker encountered an object file with an incompatible .OBJ file format.

This error generally occurs due to an incompatible .OBJ file format. If you're linking .OBJ files compiled using another compiler, these files may be incompatible with TLINK32. You'll need to recompile all modules using one of the Borland C++ compilers.

This can also occur if the machine was rebooted during a compile, or if a compiler did not delete its output object file when Ctrl+Break was pressed. Recompile.

If the error persists, call Borland Technical Support.

**Thread stopped 'programname' 'reason'** *IDE Debugger message*

A thread in the specified program has stopped running for the reason listed.

**Too few arguments in template class name 'template'** *Compiler message*

A template class name was missing actual values for some of its formal parameters.

**Too few parameters in call** *Compiler message*

This error message occurs when a call to a function with a prototype (via a function pointer) had too few arguments. Prototypes require that all parameters be given. Make certain that your call to a function has the same parameters as the function prototype.

**Too few parameters in call to 'function'** *Compiler message*

A call to the named function (declared using a prototype) has too few arguments.

Make certain that the parameters in the call to the function match the parameters of the function prototype.

**Too many commas on command-line** *Linker message*

You specified an invalid entry on the command line. Check the command you entered.

**Too many decimal points** *Compiler message*

The compiler encountered a floating-point constant with more than one decimal point.

**Too many default cases** *Compiler message*

The compiler encountered more than one default statement in a single switch.

**Too many default libraries** *Linker message*

The linker can handle a maximum of 128 default libraries.

**Too many error or warning messages** *Compiler message*

There were more errors or warnings than set in the Options | Settings | Compiler Messages.

**Too many error or warning messages** *Linker message*

The limit on the number of error messages or warnings to be displayed has been reached.

**Too many errors** *Linker message*

The linker got more errors than the maximum number of errors specified by the user.

**Too many exponents** *Compiler message*

The compiler encountered more than one exponent in a floating-point constant.

**Too many file names** *Linker message*

This error occurs if the linker encounters more than 64K characters in the response file.

The linker only handles response files up to 64K.

You'll need to shorten the response file, shorten the pathnames, or chunk the .OBJs into a library.

**Too many files to open.** *Resource Linker message*

You have exceeded the resource linkers limit on files. Try combining some of your individual resource files into a single resource.

**Too many initializers** *Compiler message*

The compiler encountered more initializers than were allowed by the declaration being initialized.

**Too many LNAMEs** *Linker message*

TLINK32 supports up to 255 LNAMEs appearing in an OBJ file.

**Too many resources to handle.** *Resource Linker message*

You have too many resources for the resource linker to handle. Try reducing the total number of resources you are trying to link.

**Too many rules for target 'target'** *MAKE message*

MAKE can't determine which rules to follow when building a target because you've created too many rules for the target. For example, the following makefile generates this error message:

```
abc.exe : a.obj
bcc -c a.c
abc.exe : b.obj

abc.exe : c.obj
bcc -c b.c c.c
```

**Too many storage classes in declaration** *Compiler message*

A declaration can never have more than one storage class, either Auto, Register, Static, or Extern.

**Too many STRINGTABLEs to link.** *Resource Linker message*

The resource linker (RLINK) should not generate this message.

You have too many string tables for the resource linker to handle. Try reducing the total number of string tables in your resource.

**Too many suffixes in .SUFFIXES list** *MAKE message*

The suffixes list can include up to 255 suffixes.

**Too many types in declaration** *Compiler message*

A declaration can never have more than one of these basic types:

- char
- class
- int
- float
- double
- struct
- union
- enum
- typedef name

**Too much global data defined in file** *Compiler message*

The sum of the global data declarations exceeds 64K bytes. This includes any data stored in the DGROUP (all global variables, literal strings, and static locals).

Solutions:

Check the declarations for any array that might be too large. You can also remove variables from the DGROUP.

Here's how:

- Declare the variables as automatic. This uses stack space.
- Dynamically allocate memory from the heap using calloc, malloc, or farmalloc for the variables. This requires the use of pointers.

Literal strings are also put in the DGROUP. Get the file farstr.zip from our BBS to extract literal strings into their own segment.

**Trying to derive a far class from the huge base 'base'** *Compiler message*

If a class is declared (or defaults to) huge, all derived classes must also be huge.

**Trying to derive a far class from the near base 'base'** *Compiler message*

If a class is declared (or defaults to) near, all derived classes must also be near.

**Trying to derive a huge class from the far base 'base'** *Compiler message*

If a class is declared (or defaults to) far, all derived classes must also be far.

**Trying to derive a huge class from the near base 'base'** *Compiler message*

If a class is declared (or defaults to) near, all derived classes must also be near.

**Trying to derive a near class from the far base 'base'** *Compiler message*

If a class is declared (or defaults to) far, all derived classes must also be far.

**Trying to derive a near class from the huge base 'base'**  *Compiler message*

If a class is declared (or defaults to) far, all derived classes must also be far.

**Two consecutive dots**  *Compiler message*

Because an ellipsis contains three dots (...), and a decimal point or member selection operator uses one dot (.), two consecutive dots cannot legally occur in a C program.

**Two operands must evaluate to the same type**  *Compiler message*

The types of the expressions on both sides of the colon in the conditional expression operator (? :) must be the same, except for the usual conversions.

Following are some examples of usual conversions:

```
char to int
float to double
void* to a particular pointer
```

In this expression, the two sides evaluate to different types that are not automatically converted. This might be an error or you might merely need to cast one side to the type of the other.

When compiling C++ programs, this message is always preceded by another message that explains the exact reason for the type mismatch. The other message is usually "Cannot convert 'type1' to 'type2'" but the mismatch might be due to many other reasons.

**'type' is not a polymorphic class type**  *Compiler message*

This error is generated if the -RT compiler option (for run-time type information) is disabled and either

- dynamic_cast was used with a pointer to a class, or
- you tried to delete a pointer to an object of a class that has a virtual destructor

**Type mismatch in default argument value**  *Compiler message*

The default parameter value given could not be converted to the type of the parameter.

The message "Type mismatch in default argument value" is used when the parameter was not given a name.

When compiling C++ programs, this message is always preceded by another message that explains the exact reason for the type mismatch. The other message is most often "Cannot convert 'type1' to 'type2'" but the mismatch could be due to another reason.

**Type mismatch in default value for parameter 'parameter'**  *Compiler message*

The default parameter value given could not be converted to the type of the parameter.

The message "Type mismatch in default argument value" is used when the parameter was not given a name.

When compiling C++ programs, this message is always preceded by another message that explains the exact reason for the type mismatch.

That other message is usually "Cannot convert 'type1' to 'type2'" but the mismatch might be due to many other reasons.

**Type mismatch in parameter 'number'** *Compiler message*

The function called, via a function pointer, was declared with a prototype.

However, the given parameter number (counting left to right from 1) could not be converted to the declared parameter type.

When compiling C++ programs, this message is always preceded by another message that explains the exact reason for the type mismatch. The other message is usually "Cannot convert 'type1' to 'type2'" but the mismatch might be due to many other reasons.

**Type mismatch in parameter 'number' in call to 'function'** *Compiler message*

Your source file declared the named function with a prototype, and the given parameter number (counting left to right from 1) could not be converted to the declared parameter type.

When compiling C++ programs, this message is always preceded by another message that explains the exact reason for the type mismatch.

That other message is usually "Cannot convert 'type1' to 'type2'", but the mismatch might be due to many other reasons.

**Type mismatch in parameter 'number' in template class name 'template'** *Compiler message*

The actual template argument value supplied for the given parameter did not exactly match the formal template parameter type.

When compiling C++ programs, this message is always preceded by another message that explains the exact reason for the type mismatch. That other message is usually "Cannot convert 'type1' to 'type2'" but the mismatch might be due to many other reasons.

**Type mismatch in parameter 'parameter'** *Compiler message*

Your source file declared the function called via a function pointer with a prototype.

However, the named parameter could not be converted to the declared parameter type.

When compiling C++ programs, this message is always preceded by another message that explains the exact reason for the type mismatch. That other message is usually "Cannot convert 'type1' to 'type2'" but the mismatch might be due to many other reasons.

**Type mismatch in parameter 'parameter' in call to 'function'** *Compiler message*

Your source file declared the named function with a prototype, and the named parameter could not be converted to the declared parameter type.

When compiling C++ programs, this message is always preceded by another message that explains the exact reason for the type mismatch.

That other message is usually "Cannot convert 'type1' to 'type2'" but the mismatch might be due to many other reasons.

**Type mismatch in parameter 'parameter' in template class name 'template'** *Compiler message*

The actual template argument value supplied for the given parameter did not exactly match the formal template parameter type.

When compiling C++ programs, this message is always preceded by another message that explains the exact reason for the type mismatch.

That other message is usually "Cannot convert 'type1' to 'type2'" but the mismatch might be due to many other reasons.

### Type mismatch in redeclaration of 'identifier' *Compiler message*

Your source file redeclared a variable with a different type than was originally declared for the variable.

This can occur if a function is called and subsequently declared to return something other than an integer.

Solution: If this happens, you must declare the function before the first call to it.

### Type name expected *Compiler message*

One of these errors has occurred:

- In declaring a file-level variable or a struct field, neither a type name nor a storage class was given.
- In declaring a typedef, no type for the name was supplied.
- In declaring a destructor for a C++ class, the destructor name was not a type name (it must be the same name as its class).

In supplying a C++ base class name, the name was not the name of a class.

### Type 'type' is not a defined class with virtual functions *Compiler message*

A dynamic_cast was used with a pointer to a class type that is either undefined, or doesn't have any virtual member functions.

### Type 'typename' may not be defined here *Compiler message*

Class and enumeration types may not be defined in a function return type, a function argument type, a conversion operator type, or the type specified in a cast. You must define the given type before using it in one of these contexts.

**Note**   This error message is often the result of a missing semicolon ( **;** ) for a class declaration.

You might want to verify that all the class declarations preceding the line on which the error occurred end with a semicolon.

### Unable to create output file 'filename' *Compiler message*

This error occurs if the work disk is full or write protected. It also occurs if the output directory does not exist.

Solutions:

- If the disk is full, try deleting unneeded files and restarting the compilation.
- If the disk is write-protected, move the source files to a writeable disk and restart the compilation.

### Unable to create turboc.$ln *Compiler message*

The compiler cannot create the temporary file TURBOC.$LN because it cannot access the disk or the disk is full.

### Unable to execute command 'command' *Compiler message*

TLINK or TASM cannot be found, or possibly the disk is bad.

**Unable to execute command: 'command'** MAKE message

A command failed to execute. This might be because the command file could not be found or was misspelled, there was no disk space left in the specified swap directory, the swap directory does not exist, or (less likely) the command itself exists but has been corrupted.

**Unable to load 16 bit compiler**

**Unable to load 16 bit linker**

**Unable to load 32 bit compiler**

**Unable to load 32 bit linker** Compiler messages

For the 16-bit linker and compiler, the file BCWS16.DLL must be either in the directory where BCW.EXE resides or somewhere in your path. If the DLL is in the correct location and still will not load, you may not have enough memory for the DLL to load. BCW operates optimally when you have at least 12 MB of memory in any combination of physical RAM and virtual memory.

For the 32-bit linker and compiler, the same rules apply for BCWS32.EXE. In addition, you must have a system running that supplies the Win32 API. Check to make sure that you have properly installed either NT or Win32s on your Windows system by running another 32-bit application such as the FreeCell game which accompanies the operating system.

**Unable to open 'filename'** Compiler message

This error occurs if the specified file can't be opened.

Make sure the file is on the specified disk or directory. Check Options | Settings | Directories and verify the proper paths are listed. If multiple paths are required, use a semicolon to separate them, like this:

```
C:\bc\include;c:\bc\include\owl
```

**Unable to open 'filename' for output** Librarian message

The librarian cannot open the specified output file. This is usually due to lack of disk space for the target library, or a listing file.

**Unable to open file 'filename'** Linker message

The named file can't be found, possibly because it does not exist or is misspelled, or it resides in a different directory than those being searched.

If you are using the IDE, make sure you have set the appropriate directory paths in the Options | Directories dialog box.

**Unable to open file 'filename'** MAKE message

This error occurs if the named file does not exist or is misspelled.

**Unable to open include file 'filename'** Compiler message

The compiler could not find the named file.

Possible Causes:

- The named file does not exist.
- An **#include** file included itself.
- You do not have FILES set in CONFIG.SYS on your root directory.

Solutions:

- Verify that the named file exists.
- Set FILES = 20 in CONFIG.SYS.

### Unable to open include file 'filename' *MAKE message*

The compiler could not find the named file. This error can also be caused if an **!include** file included itself, or if you do not have FILES set in CONFIG.SYS on your root directory (try `FILES=20`). Check whether the named file exists.

### Unable to open input file 'filename' *Compiler message*

This error occurs if the source file can't be found. Check the spelling of the name. Make sure the file is on the specified disk or directory.

Check under Options | Settings | Directories and verify that the proper directory paths are listed. If multiple paths are required, use a semicolon to separate them, like this:

```
C:\bc\lib;C:\bc\owl\lib
```

### Unable to open makefile *MAKE message*

The current directory does not contain a file named MAKEFILE or MAKEFILE.MAK, or it does not contain the file you specified with –f.

### Unable to process debug info, disable TASM /zi option *Linker message*

Debug information is too complex. Disable the TASM **/zi** option.

If C debug information is required, it should be obtained at the C source level.

### Unable to redirect input or output *MAKE message*

MAKE was unable to open the temporary files necessary to redirect input or output. If you are on a network, make sure you have access rights to the current directory.

### Unable to rename 'filename1' to 'filename2' *Librarian message*

The librarian builds a library into a temporary file (filename1) and then renames the temporary file to the target library file name (filename2). This message appears if an error occurs during the renaming process, such as insufficient disk space.

### #undef directive ignored *Compiler message*

An error has occurred while using the command-line utility H2ASH. See the online file "tsm_util.txt" for further information about this utility.

### Undefined alias symbol 'symbol' *Linker message*

The symbol being aliased was undefined. This occurred either because of an invalid function name or the function itself was not included in the link.

### Undefined label 'identifier' *Compiler message*

The named label has a goto in the function, but no label definition.

### Undefined structure 'structure' *Compiler message*

(Command-line equivalent for displaying this warning = -wstu)

The named structure was used in the source file, probably on a pointer to a structure, but had no definition in the source file. This is probably caused by a misspelled structure name or a missing declaration.

Default = displayed

**Undefined structure 'structure'** *Compiler message*

Your source file used the named structure on some line before where the error is indicated (probably on a pointer to a structure) but had no definition for the structure. This is probably caused by a misspelled structure name or a missing declaration.

**Undefined symbol 'identifier'** *Compiler message*

The named identifier has no declaration.

Possible Causes:

- actual declaration of identifier has been commented out.
- misspelling, either at this point or at the declaration.
- there was an error in the declaration of the identifier.

Tools to help track down the problem:

- CPP
- GREP

**Undefined symbol 'symbol' in module 'module'** *Linker message*

The named symbol is referenced in the given module but is not defined anywhere in the set of object files and libraries included in the link.

Check to make sure the symbol is spelled correctly.

You will usually see this error from the linker for C or C++ symbols if any of the following occur:

- You did not properly match a symbol's declarations of pascal and cdecl type in different source files.
- You have omitted the name of an .OBJ file your program needs.
- You did not link in the emulation library.

If you are linking C++ code with C modules, you might have forgotten to wrap C external declarations in extern "C".

You could also have a case mismatch between two symbols.

**Unexpected }** *Compiler message*

An extra right brace was encountered where none was expected. Check for a missing {.

**Useful Tip:** The IDE has a mechanism for finding a matching curly brace. If you put the cursor on the '{' or '}' character, hold down control, hit 'Q' and then '{' or '}', it will position the cursor on the matching brace.

**Unexpected char X in command line** *Librarian message*

The librarian encountered a syntactical error while parsing the command line.

**Unexpected end of file** *MAKE message*

The end of the makefile was reached before closing a temporary inline file.

**Unexpected end of file in comment started on 'line number'** *Compiler message*

The source file ended in the middle of a comment. This is normally caused by a missing close of comment (*/).

**Unreachable code**                                                          *Compiler message*

(Command-line equivalent for displaying this warning = -wrch)

A break, continue, goto, or return statement was not followed by a label or the end of a loop or function.

The compiler checks while, do,, and for loops with a constant test condition, and attempts to recognize loops that can't fall through.

Default = not displayed

**Unresolved external 'symbol' referenced from module 'module'**              *Linker message*

The named symbol is referenced in the given module but is not defined anywhere in the set of object files and libraries included in the link.

Check to make sure the symbol is spelled correctly.

You will usually see this error from the linker for C or C++ symbols if any of the following occur:

- You did not properly match a symbol's declarations of pascal and cdecl type in different source files.
- You omitted the name of an .OBJ file your program needs.
- You did not link in the emulation library.

If you are linking C++ code with C modules, you might have forgotten to wrap C external declarations in `extern "C" {...}`.

You could also have a case mismatch between two symbols.

**Unsupported COMENT OMF extension 'extension'**                              *Linker message*

The linker encountered an object file with an incompatible .OBJ file format.

This error generally occurs due to an incompatible .OBJ file format. If you're linking .OBJ files compiled using another compiler, these files may be incompatible with TLINK32. You'll need to recompile all modules using one of the Borland C++ compilers.

This can also occur if the machine was rebooted during a compile, or if a compiler did not delete its output object file when Ctrl+Break was pressed. Recompile.

If the error persists, call Borland Technical Support.

**Unsupported EXE RC version.**                                      *Resource Linker message*

The executable you are attempting to link the resources to already has resources attached. The version number of these resources is not recognized by this resource linker. Try removing the resources or relinking.

**Unsupported option 'string'**                                               *Linker message*

You specified an unknown option on the command line.

**Unterminated string or character constant**                                *Compiler message*

The compiler found no terminating quote after the beginning of a string or character constant.

### Use '> >' for nested templates instead of '>>'

Whitespace is required to separate the closing ">" in a nested template name, but since it is an extremely common mistake to leave out the space, the compiler accepts a ">>" with this warning.

### Use . or -> to call 'member', or & to take its address
*Compiler message*

A reference to a non-static class member without an object was encountered.

Such a member can't be used without an object, or its address must be taken with the & operator.

### Use . or -> to call function
*Compiler message*

You attempted to call a member function without providing an object. This is required to call a member function.

```
class X {
    member func() {}
};
X x;
X*xp = new X;
X.memberfunc();
Xp-> memberfunc();
```

### Use /e with TLINK to obtain debug information from library
*Librarian message*

The library was built with an extended dictionary and also includes debugging information. TLINK cannot extract debugging information if it links using an extended dictionary.

To obtain debugging information in an executable from this library, use the **/e** switch to cause the linker to ignore the extended dictionary.

**Note:** The IDE linker does not support extended dictionaries; therefore, no settings need to be altered in the IDE.

### Use :: to take the address of a member function
*Compiler message*

If f is a member function of class c, you take its address with the syntax

```
&c::f
```

Note the use of the class type name (not the name of an object) and the :: separating the class name from the function name.

(Member function pointers are not true pointer types, and do not refer to any particular instance of a class.)

### Use of : and :: dependents for target 'target'
*MAKE message*

You tried to use the target in both single and multiple description blocks (using both the : and :: operators).

Examples:

```
filea: fileb
filea:: filec
```

### Use qualified name to access member type 'identifier'
*Compiler message*

(Command-line equivalent for displaying this warning = -wnst)

In previous versions of the C++ specification, **typedef** and tag names declared inside classes were directly visible in the global scope. In the latest specification of C++, these names must be prefixed with `class::qualifier` if they are to be used outside of their class scope.

The compiler issues this warning whenever a name is uniquely defined in a single class.

The compiler permits this usage without `class::`. This allows older versions of code to compile.

Default = displayed

**User break**                                                                     *Compiler message*

You typed a Ctrl+Break while compiling in the IDE. (This is not an error, just a confirmation.)

**User break, library aborted**                                                    *Librarian message*

You pressed Cancel while compiling in the IDE. The library was not created. (This is not an error, just a confirmation.)

**User-defined message**                                                           *Compiler message*

The error message on which you have requested Help, is a user-defined warning.

In Borland C++ code, user-defined messages are introduced by using the #pragma message compiler syntax.

**Note:** In addition to messages that you introduce with the **#pragma** message compiler syntax, user-defined warnings can be introduced by third party libraries. Should you require Help about a third party warning, please contact the vendor of the header file that issued the warning.

**Using based linking for DLLs may cause the DLL to malfunction**                  *Linker message*

This warning occurs if you use the **/B** switch when linking a DLL. In almost every case, this is an error that will prevent the application from running. You can suppress this warning from the Linker | Warnings page of the Project options dialog box or with the **/w-bdl** command-line option.

**Value of type void is not allowed**                                              *Compiler message*

A value of type void is really not a value at all, so it can't appear in any context where an actual value is required.

Such contexts include the following:

- the right side of an assignment
- an argument of a function
- the controlling expression of an if, for, or while statement.

**Variable 'identifier' is once**                                                  *Compiler message*

This variable has more than one initialization. It is legal to declare a file level variable more than once, but it can have only one initialization (even if two are the same).

**'variable' requires run-time initialization/finalization**                       *Compiler message*

This message is issued when a global variable that is declared as __thread (a Win32-only feature) or a static data member of a template class is initialized with a non-constant initial value.

This message is also issued when a global variable that is declared as __thread (a Win32-only feature) or a static data member of a template class has the type class with constructor or destructor.

### Variable 'variable' has been optimized and is not available                    *Compiler message*

You have tried to inspect, watch, or otherwise access a variable which the optimizer removed.

This variable is never assigned a value and has no stack location.

### VIRDEF name conflict for 'function'                    *Compiler message*

The compiler must truncate mangled names to a certain length because of a name length limit that is imposed by the linker. This truncation may (in very rare cases) cause two names to mangle to the same linker name. If these names happen to both be VIRDEF names, the compiler issues this error message. The simplest workaround for this problem is to change the name of 'function' so that the conflict is avoided.

### Virtual base classes not supported                    *Compiler message*

An error has occurred while using the command-line utility H2ASH. See the online file "tsm_util.txt" for further information about this utility.

### 'virtual' can only be used with member functions                    *Compiler message*

A data member has been declared with the virtual specifier.

Only member functions can be declared virtual.

For example:

```
class myclass
{
public:
   virtual int a;    //error
};
```

### Virtual function 'function1' conflicts with base class 'base'                    *Compiler message*

A virtual function has the same argument types as one in a base class, but a different return type. This is illegal.

### virtual specified more than once                    *Compiler message*

The C++ reserved word "virtual" can appear only once in one member function declaration.

### void & is not a valid type                    *Compiler message*

A reference always refers to an object, but an object cannot have the type void.

Thus, the type void is not allowed.

### Void 'function' cannot return a value                    *Compiler message*

A function with a return type void contains a return statement that returns a value; for example, an int.

Default = displayed

**Void functions may not return a value**                    *Compiler message*

Your source file declared the current function as returning void, but the compiler encountered a return statement with a value. The value of the return statement will be ignored.

**Warning. Duplicate resources.**                    *Resource Linker message*

If multiple resource files are linked in to the image, the user could have duplicate resources in the resource files. For example, you might have the same ICON in two different RES files. The resource linker flags this and the second resource is removed.

**Note:**The resources must have the same type and identifier to be declared duplicates.

**Windows version is set to Win32, but target type is Win16.**                    *Resource Linker message*

The version for your resources is set to Win32, but the target type for your project is for a 16-bit Windows application. 16-bit Windows applications cannot use 32-bit resources.

Either change the version for your resources to Windows 3.1 or change the target type for your application to Win32.

**Write error on file 'filename'**                    *MAKE message*

MAKE couldn't open or write to the file specified in the makefile. Check to ensure that there's enough space left on your disk, and that you have write access to the disk.

**Write failed, disk full?**                    *Linker message*

Writing to the specified disk failed. Check to see if the disk is full.

**Wrong number of arguments in call of macro 'macro'**                    *Compiler message*

Your source file called the named macro with an incorrect number of arguments.

# Index

## Symbols

! operator (MAKE) 333
!= operator (MAKE) 334
$& macro 330
$* macro 323, 330
$** macro 330
$: macro 330
$< macro 330
$? macro 330
$@ macro 330
% operator (MAKE) 333
& operator (MAKE) 327, 333
&& operator (MAKE) 328, 333
* (search wildcard) 391
* operator (MAKE) 333
+ (plus sign)
    Environment Options dialog
      box 13
    Project Manager 22
    operator (MAKE) 333
.APX Database file 152
.TFA files 389, 434
/ (slash)
    command-line options 199
    MAKE options 321
    operator (MAKE) 333
: (colon), makefiles 324
:: operator (MAKE) 325
< operator (MAKE) 328, 334
<< operator (MAKE) 328, 333
<= operator (MAKE) 334
== operator (MAKE) 334
> operator (MAKE) 328, 334
>= operator (MAKE) 333
>> operator (MAKE) 328, 333
? (search wildcard) 391
-? MAKE option 320, 322, 461
?: operator (MAKE) 333
@ prefix (MAKE) 327
\ (backslash), makefiles 325
^ operator (MAKE) 333
| operator (MAKE) 333
| | operator (MAKE) 334
~ operator (MAKE) 333
– (hyphen)
    command-line options 199
    Environment Options dialog
      box 13
    makefiles 321, 327
    Project Manager 22
    operator (MAKE) 333

## Numerics

16-bit
    command-line switches 113, 115
    compiler options 45, 102
    linker options 84
    optimizations 86
    resource options 110
    resources, 110, 266
32-bit
    command-line switches 113, 117
    compiler options 57, 102
    linker options 87
    processing option 84
    resources 112, 266
80186 option, 16-bit compilers 52
80286 option, 16-bit compilers 53
80386 option, 16-bit compilers 53
8086 option, 16-bit compilers 53
8514 graphics adapter 473

## A

-a MAKE option 321
video adapters
    *See* Enhanced Graphics Adapter;
      Video Graphics Array
      Adapter
About Turbo Profiler command 386
accelerators 303-304
Accumulation option 438
Acer 1100 and NMI 471
active analysis
    *See also* passive analysis
    *See also* profiling, analysis modes
    area markers 442
    disk I/O and 443
    passive analysis, compared 442
    setting 441
active windows *See* windows, active
adapters, video, *See* video adapters
Add Areas command 406
Add command 403
Add Node option 27
Address option 396
addresses
    exceptions 355
    jumping to
      Disassembly (CPU)
        window 410
      Module window 391
Advanced Options dialog box
    adding tools 34
    specifying source nodes 27
Airbrush tool
    Graphics editor 261
    Graphics tool 256

## [algorithms]

algorithms
    analyzing 439
    multipass 450
All Callers option 394, 407
All command 397
All Routines 392-394
All Windows command (Messages
    menu) 347
alternative translators 34
Always Build option 60
Always option, 16-bit compilers 49
Animation tool, Dialog editor 290
ANSI Violations options 97
AppExpert 151
applications 21
    creating 33
    testing 33, 162
Arc tool, Graphics editor 260
area files, automatic saving 389
area markers
    *See also* areas
    active analysis and 442
    defined 436
    function entry 392
    lines 392
    modules 392
    normal 456
    operation 393
    program execution speed 443
    routine-entry 456
    routines
      add all 392
      add current 392
      available for profiling 389
    single lines, removing 398
    symbols 392
Area Options dialog box 407
areas 436, 451
    *See also* area markers
    adding 406
    current
      changing 454
      disassembled source code
        as 389
      settings for 392
      specifying profiling action 392
      statistics 447
    default 435
    defined 436
    execution counts and times 455
    function-entry markers 392
    inspecting 407
    maximum 419
    measuring efficiency 376
    names 406
    normal markers 456

node attributes 28-30
resources as text 268
user-defined resources 315
editors 8, 197
installing 395
reconfiguring IDE 13
efficiency, measuring 376
!elif directive 333
Ellipse tool, Graphics editor 258
ellipsis mark (...) 385
embedding resources
project files 315
resource projects 225
empty frame tools, Graphics
editor 258
enabling statistics collection 393
Enhanced Graphics Adapter (EGA)
468
Enter Program Name to Load dialog
box 386
environment, saving IDE
settings 16
Environment command (Options
menu) 12, 157
Environment Options dialog
box 12–13
expanding/contracting lists 13
Project View options 31
environment variables, MAKE
macros 322, 329
Eraser tool, Graphics editor 255
erasing areas, Graphics editor 250
error handling, MAKE 327,
332–333
error messages 507, 512-607
beeps, enabling 470
compilers 508
fatal 507-510
Help compiler 510
logical 160
MAKE 332
makefiles 508
memory 477
run-time 159-160, 508
TFREMOTE 487
TLINK 508
TPROFW 495
Turbo Profiler 506
Euclid's method, prime numbers,
testing 368
Evaluate/Modify command 186
Events command 404
Events pane, ClassExpert 145
Every Line in Module command
(Add Areas menu) 392
Exception handling/RTTI
options 64
exceptions
addresses 355
logging 355–359

reports, WinSpector 355
Exclude from Parent option, Build
Attributes 60
excutable files, system files
creating 161, 264, 361
execution counts and times
areas 455
default behavior 436
passive analysis and 443
program structure analysis 440
program testing and
verification 439
resource monitoring and 440
Execution Profile window 398, 446
description 370
local menu 395
Module window 395, 398
execution timing, statistics for 440
EXEMAP.EXE 360-361
EXETYPE statement 207
Exit command (Spy menu) 344
exit status, MAKE, ignoring 322
exiting
TFINST 474
Turbo Profiler 368, 389
WinSight 344
expanding lists
dialog boxes 13
Project Manager 22
EXPORTS statement 208
Expression Evaluator dialog
box 185–186
expressions
changing 185
conditional 333
current value, viewing 182
debugging 181–188
entering problems with 505
evaluating 186–188
inspecting 188
optimizing 450
external programs, debugging 166
Eye Dropper tool, Graphics
editor 259

**F**

-f MAKE option 322
Far 50
Far data class option 56
Far data group option 56
Far Data option 56
Far data segment option 56
Far Data Threshold option, 16-bit
compilers 50
Far Virtual Tables option, 16-bit
compilers 50
Far virtual tables option 57
Fast huge pointers option, 16-bit
compilers 50

Fast Screen Update check box
(TFINST) 468
fatal errors 507-510
features 364
File command 6, 394-395
File Manager (Windows), adding
source nodes 28
File menu commands, Open 222,
230
file names 8, 24
file search algorithms 81
files
access
monitoring 437
profiling purposes 440
text files 389
tracking 389
activities, displaying 447
adding to projects 27
batch 322
disks, problems with 500-501
information 388
keyboard mapping 13
loading 377
log 354–359
needed for profiling 390
opening 386, 412, 504-506
Project Description Language
(.PDL) files 40
searching 412
sources
current routine 409
directories 394
inspecting 401
list of 394
loading 499, 502
options 462
searching for 435
setting directory path 469
statistics 375
viewing 396
swap 501
symbol tables 161
TDDEBUG.386 490
temporary, MAKE 322-323, 328
text 389, 412
TFWHELP.TFH 490
TPROF.EXE 473
TPROFW program 490
tutorial, copying 217, 317
viewing in IDE 22
WREMOTE.EXE 482
Files option 437
Files window 405, 446
Filled Rectangle tool, Graphics
editor 259
Filled Rounded Ellipse tool,
Graphics editor 259
Filled Rounded Rectangle tool,
Graphics editor 259
filled-in frame tools, Graphics
editor 258

stack
 calls, size of 394
 IDE options 25
 tracing into 354
Stack radio buttons 394
Stack trace dialog box 394
Stack Trace section,
 WINSPCTR.LOG 356
STACKSIZE statement 212
standalone bitmap files,
 creating 230
standalone cursor files, creating 233
Standard Libraries options (IDE) 25
Start Time option 405
Start! command (WinSight) 344
starting
 Browsers 154
 ClassExpert 143
 MAKE 319
 Resource Workshop 222
 TOUCH 321
 WinSight 343
 WinSpector 353
statements
 checking 160
 debugging 162
 execution, verifying 440
Static Frame tool, Dialog editor 289
Static Picture tool, Dialog editor 290
Static Rectangle tool, Dialog
 editor 289
Static Text tool, Dialog editor 287
statistics
 accumulation, disabling 420
 accuracy 443-444
 areas 406
 collection 436-437, 447
  automatic 388
  disabling 393, 436
  enabling 393
  normal 393
  options 407
  program speed 439
  type to collect 439
 current
  area 447
  removing 397
  routine 409
 default 436
 displaying 370-371, 396, 439
 erasing 398
 file activity 404-405
 files, writing to problems 501
 filtering 397, 438, 441, 447
 limiting 438
 module 396
 overlays 401-402
 partial 438
 printing 373
 problems 501
 program execution speed 443
 removing 395-396

sorting 395-396
start and stop points,
 maximum 438
time 396-397
types of 437
viewing 395
 choices 395
 number of passes 396
 source code with 375
 time 396
status bars, IDE 7
status line 384
Status Window tool, Dialog
 editor 292
Step Over button 166
Step Over command 166
stepping through programs
 164-166
Stop option 405
Stop! command (WinSight) 344
stopping program execution 166
strings
 MAKE macros 322
 searching for 412, 498
 substitutions 330
structure analysis, statistics 440
structures 187-188
STUB statement 213
Style Sheets
 managing 38
 nodes, attaching 39
 project options 38-40
Subfunctions command 403
SUBSYSTEM statement 213
suffixes directive 335
swapping memory, MAKER 322
SYM files 356, 361
Symbol Declaration window,
 Browser 155
symbol names, problems 500
symbol tables 161, 504
 adding to files 161
 dynamic-link libraries 494
 invalid 504
symbolic debug information 161
symbols
 code, browsing 155
 disassembled 410
 messages 511
 problems 505
syntax
 command-line compilers 198
 format specifiers, watches 183
 MAKE 319, 321
  commands 326–328
  explicit rules 324-326
  implicit rules 326
  macros 329-331
 TOUCH 321
Syntax Highlighting option 14

System Information section,
 WINSPCTR.LOG 358

# T

-t option (starting directory)
 491-492
Tab Control tool, Dialog editor 290
Tab Size input box, TFINST 468
tabs, setting 468, 506
Tandy 1000 and NMI 471
target files 21
Target Model options (IDE) 25
target nodes (IDE) 22
 adding 29
 attributes 30
 deleting 30
 multiple 32
 types, defined 29
 updating 32
 viewing 31
target platforms, setting 24
TargetExpert 25, 30
TargetExpert dialog box 30
Tasks section, WINSPCTR.LOG 357
TDDEBUG.386 file 490
TDRF (remote file transfer
 utility) 478, 486
templates, makefiles 329
Templates options 67
temporary files, MAKE 322-323, 328
Terminate Program command 167
terminating programs 167
testing
 applications 33, 162
 bitmaps 231
 cursors 235
 dialog boxes 275
 icons 241
 menus 303
 program setup 8
 programs 160, 187
 user-defined resources 316
text
 adding to graphics, Graphics
  editor 249
 editors 469, 500
 files
  searching 412
  viewing 389
 makefiles 334
 resources, editing as 268
 searching for 391, 505
Text Edit command (View
 menu) 23
Text Edit tool, Dialog editor 288
Text editor 8, 197, 309-310
Text File window 413
text files, MAKE 323
Text tool, Graphics editor 257

TFCONFIG.TF 376
TFINST 474
  command-line options 475
  exiting 474
  main menu 465
  options, saving 473
  TPROFW, using with 491
TFREMOTE (remote profiling
    utility)
  configuring 479
  customizing 479
  error messages 487
  installing 478
  LAN link 480
  loading 480
  problems with 504
  serial link 480
This Line command (Add Areas
    menu) 392
This Module option 394
This Routine option 394
time and counts profile listing 372
Time option
  Execution Profile window 396
  Interrupt window 404
time stamps (MAKE) 320-322
timer
  combined clock 438
  data grouping 438
  inaccurate results 457
  separate, combined clock,
    compared 393
  setting 419
  sound routines 457
Timer radio buttons 393, 407
Tiny option, 16-bit compilers 52
title bars 383
TLINK 201
  command-line syntax 201
  configuration files 203
  errors 508
  file-name extensions 202
  libraries 204
  options, overriding 203
TLINK.CFG 200
TLINK32 201, 203
TLINK32.CFG 200
TMAPSYM.EXE utility 360-361
Tool Bar tool, Dialog editor 292
Tool command (IDE) 6
Tool menu
  adding files 34
  customizing 16
  ol palette, Graphics editor
    3-254, 296
  LHELP.DLL 353
  33–35
  ommand (Options) 34
  lialog box 34
  ol, Dialog editor 297

TOUCH utility 321
TPROF
  error messages 506
  modifying with TFINST 473
TPROFW
  command-line options 491
  configuring 490
  dynamic-link libraries,
    profiling 494
  error messages 495
  installation 489-490
  list of files 490
  message classes 494
  profiling Windows,
    programs 489
  running 492
  switching applications 492
Trace Into command 165
Trace Off command (Messages
    menu) 343
tracing messages
  WinSight 343-345
  WinSign 347
tracing into code 165, 195
tracing messages (WinSight) 347
Track Bar tool, Dialog editor 292
transfer macros 34
translating 359
translating project nodes 28, 33
translators 29, 33
transparent color area, Graphics
    editor 245
Tree View tool, Dialog editor 291
TSR programs, display
    swapping 469
Turbo Assembler 368
Turbo Debugger 159, 359
Turbo language products 435
Turbo Profiler 368
turning off
  command-line options 199
  syntax highlighting 14
tutorial 3, 217, 317, 380
typographic conventions
    (documentation) 1

## U

-U MAKE option 322
UAEs (Unrecoverable Application
    Errors) 353
unconditional breakpoints,
    setting 168
undefining MAKE macros 322, 329,
    335-336
Undo command (Edit menu) 8, 222
undocumented Windows
    messages 348
Uninitialized data (BSS class)
    option 56

Uninitialized data (BSS group)
    option 56
Uninitialized data (BSS segment)
    option 56
Uninitialized data option 55
unions, watching 187
updating targets 32
Up-Down tool, Dialog editor 291
Use Borland optimizing compiler
    option 57
Use Intel optimizing compiler
    option 57
USER and GDI heap section,
    WINSPCTR.LOG 358
user interfaces, testing 160
user screen
  display buffer 468
  remote profiling 485
  updating 469
User Screen Updating radio buttons
    (TFINST) 469
user-defined resources 313-316

## V

-v option (video hardware) 463
values
  changing 185-188
  checking 160-161, 181
  decimal watches 183, 186
  expressions, viewing 182
  floating-point, watches 183, 186
  hexadecimal, watches 183, 186
variables
  debugging 185
  values
    changing 185, 187
    checking 160-161, 181
verbose stack trace 354
version number information 386
Vertical Center in Dialog tool,
    Dialog editor 297
Vertical Centers tool, Dialog
    editor 297
Vertical Scroll Bar tool, Dialog
    editor 289
Vertical Static Line tool, Dialog
    editor 289
video adapters 472
  display pages 469
  options 463
Video Graphics Array Adapter
    (VGA), line display 468
View command (IDE) 6
View menu 159, 389
View Source command 195, 411
viewers 33
viewing
  arguments 195
  compile-time errors 45